MOON HANDBOOKS®
COASTAL MAINE

SECOND EDITION

HILARY NANGLE

© TOM NANGLE

AVALON TRAVEL

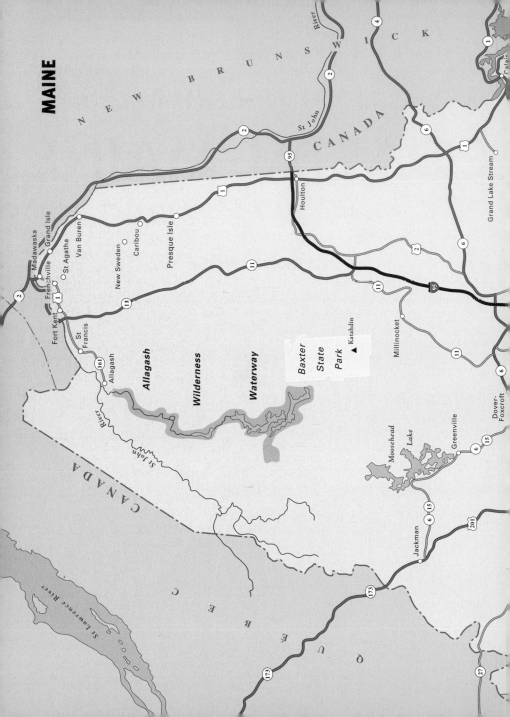

Acadia National Park

© AVALON TRAVEL PUBLISHING, INC.

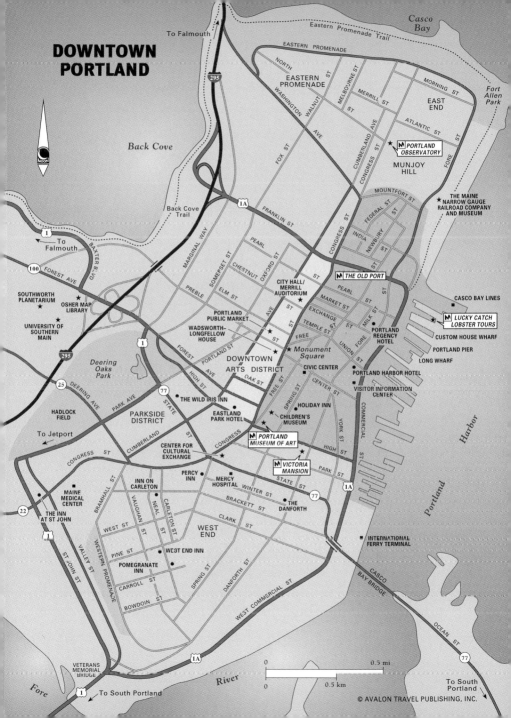

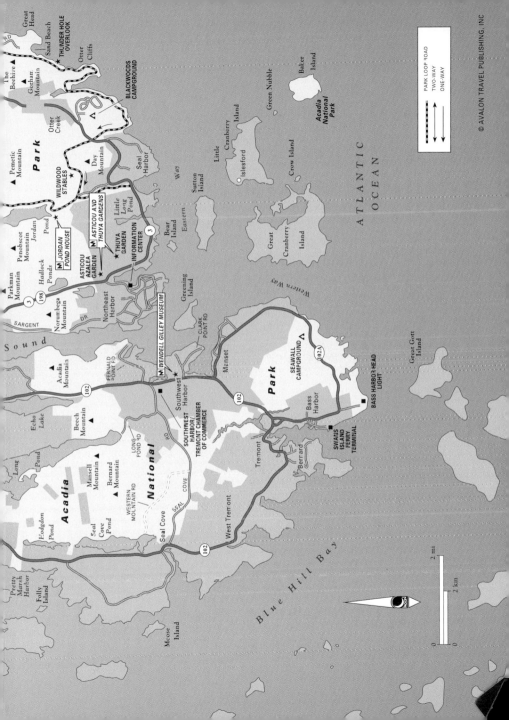

CONTENTS

Discover Coastal Maine

Explore Coastal Maine

Penobscot Bay

Blue Hill Peninsula

Know Coastal Maine

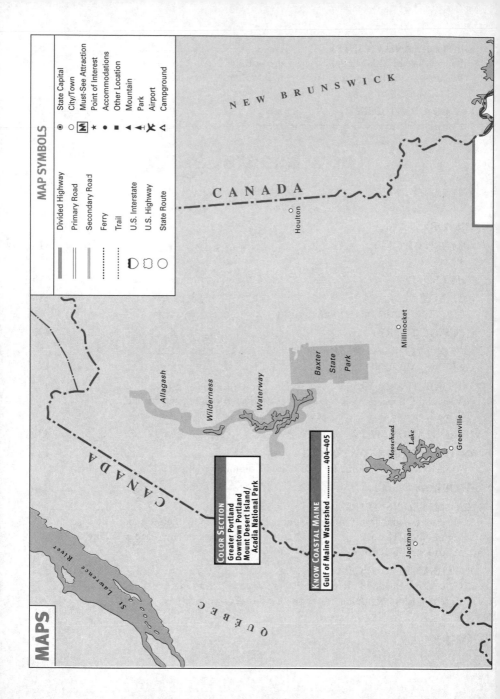

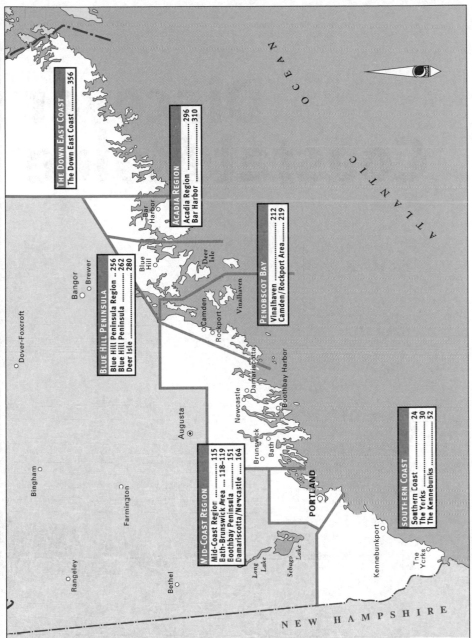

THE DOWN EAST COAST
The Down East Coast 356

ACADIA REGION
Acadia Region 296
Bar Harbor 310

PENOBSCOT BAY
Vinalhaven 212
Camden/Rockport Area 219

BLUE HILL PENINSULA
Blue Hill Peninsula Region .. 256
Blue Hill Peninsula 262
Deer Isle 280

MID-COAST REGION
Mid-Coast Region 115
Bath-Brunswick Area 118–119
Boothbay Peninsula 151
Damariscotta/Newcastle 164

SOUTHERN COAST
Southern Coast 24
The Yorks 30
The Kennebunks 52

ATLANTIC OCEAN

NEW HAMPSHIRE

Dover-Foxcroft
Bangor
Brewer
Blue Hill
Deer Isle
Bar Harbor
Vinalhaven
Camden
Rockport
Bingham
Farmington
Augusta
Newcastle
Damariscotta
Boothbay Harbor
Rangeley
Bethel
Long Lake
Sebago Lake
Brunswick
Bath
PORTLAND
Kennebunkport
The Yorks

© AVALON TRAVEL PUBLISHING, INC.

Discover
Coastal Maine

From the glacier-scoured beaches of the Southern Coast to the massively rugged boulders of the Down East Coast, Maine's coastline follows a wildly zigzagging route that would measure about 5,500 miles if you stretched it taut. But taut it isn't—it's a wrinkled landscape whose countless bony fingers jut into the sea. Eons ago, glaciers came crushing down from the north—inch by massive inch—and squeezed Maine's coastline into these splayed fingers. Each of these peninsulas now has its own character—as does each island offshore. To appreciate it all, you'll need to meander down this or that peninsula, up and around to another one, and then out to one island after another.

Lots of states have ocean shorelines—at least a third of them. But most of them look out onto azure seas, which can be mesmerizing, lonely, scary, and—let's face it—just a little boring after a while. But, thanks to its geography, Maine coastal vistas are much more intimate, full of spruce-clad islands and gray granite and sometimes-forbidding headlands.

Along this coast are 64 lighthouses, 90 percent of the *nation's* lobsters, and the eastern seaboard's highest peak. And then there are the coastal Mainers who lend this place its specialness. No individuals are more rugged than the umpteenth-generation fishermen who make their honest living from these bone-chilling waters. And even the summerfolk tend to be different here—many have come back year after year to the same place and the same neighbors and the same pursuits. Some came as kids and now return to share this special place with their grandchildren.

Coastal Maine is a national natural treasure—a fact observed enthusiastically by 19th-century author Harriet Beecher Stowe from her home in Brunswick. It seems as though she could never quite say enough about her temporarily adopted state:

The sea, living, beautiful and life-giving, seems . . . to be everywhere about you . . . behind, before, around. Now it rises like a lake, gemmed with islands and embosomed by rich swells of woodland. Now you catch a peep of it . . . among tufts of oak and maple, and anon it spreads . . . to a majestic sheet of silver, among rocky shores hung with dark pines, hemlocks, and spruces. . . . It seems to us quite wonderful that in all the ecstasies that have been lavished on American scenery, this beautiful state of Maine should have been so much neglected [by visitors]; for nothing is or can be so wildly and peculiarly beautiful.

WHEN TO GO

If you truly want to see *everything,* you'll need three weeks to a month, minimally, especially if you're someone who would rather do than just see. If your plans don't permit getting away for that long, the best strategy is to focus on a region or two, or three, and immerse yourself.

SPRING

You might have to rethink your definition of spring. Melting winter snows combined with spring rains have earned March and April the well-deserved title Mud Season. Spring doesn't really begin to arrive until late April. By May, flowers begin to bloom and trees begin to leaf. While it seems like a beautiful time to visit, the scourge of Maine, the black fly, is at its worst from mid-May through mid-June, making outdoor activities pretty miserable. Most businesses in coastal towns and cities remain open year-round, but smaller towns and villages don't even begin to wake up until mid-May, and sometimes not even until mid-June.

SUMMER

July and August are the peak months for visiting Maine, and with good reason. These are the warmest months of the year and also the easiest times for families to travel. It's also when you'll have the greatest choice of recreation options. Of course, that means peak-season rates, congested roads, and difficulty getting reservations at the best restaurants and accommodations, so plan well ahead.

AUTUMN

Ahhh, September. Maine heaves a collective sigh of relief after Labor Day. It is arguably the best time of the year to travel in the state. Days are warm and mostly dry, nights are cool, fog is rare, bugs are gone, and crowds are few. Foliage begins to change color by early October, usually reaching its peak by the middle of the month. At many accommodations, rates are lower in autumn, offering even more incentive to visit during this appealing season.

WINTER

The Maine coast slumbers in winter. While choices in lodging, dining, and activities are far fewer than in other months, the rates are at their lowest (except for special events). Instead of sunbathing on the sand, bundle up and take an invigorating walk or cross-country ski across a beach. In Camden, you can glide down alpine trails overlooking Penobscot Bay, then warm yourself with a bowl of lobster stew. In areas with solid year-round populations, life goes on full tilt, with an impressive array of cultural activities in cities such as Portland and college towns like Brunswick.

The adage "If you don't like the weather, wait a minute," certainly applies to Maine. I've seen June days that begin in the 70s and finish in the 30s. Similarly, it can be 80 degrees and sunny a mile or so inland and damp and foggy on the coast. A coastal breeze can make it feel much cooler than the temperature indicates. Layering clothing is the best option.

Do bring a fleece jacket or pullover, a windbreaker, a lightweight sweater, and rain gear. In spring and autumn, add a wool sweater and a micro-fleece top for cool, damp days. In the peak of summer, temperatures can range from the 60s to the 80s, usually with a handful of hot, muggy days that might reach into the 90s. Bring pants and shorts—I've found that pants that convert to shorts take me through a long day of touring, from foggy morning through hot afternoon to cool evening.

Unless you're dining at the White Barn Inn or Arrows, you won't need fancy clothing. Resort casual is the dress code in most good restaurants and in downtown Portland, with nice T-shirts and shorts being acceptable almost everywhere in beach communities.

Good walking shoes are a must. If you're planning on getting afloat in a canoe or kayak, bring backup footwear. Little is worse than spending a day in wet, squishy sneakers.

A bathing suit, quick-drying shorts, a brimmed hat, and sunglasses are all useful. Either take or plan to purchase on arrival sunscreen and, in late spring and early summer especially, bug dope. You can find Buzz Off, a Maine-made bug repellent based on a Native American herbal recipe, in many shops. Unless you're heading into deep woods, it works well and has a pleasant scent.

If you're planning on going out on a windjammer sail, whale-watching cruise, puffin excursion, or kayak tour, check with the outfitter about appropriate gear for the outing. Many of these boats venture well off shore, where it can be significantly colder. Extra fleece, wool sweaters, gloves, and a hat can be worth their weight in gold, even in summer. If you're prone to motion sickness, pack appropriate precautions.

In winter and spring, add warm, waterproof boots, gloves, hat, and winter-weight clothing to your list.

No matter when you come, bring a camera and plenty of film or memory cards (you can purchase both here, and many photo shops in larger communities will download images onto a CD for a small fee). Don't forget prescription glasses, prescription medicines, binoculars, perhaps a journal or sketchpad, and any financial cards you plan on using, such as debit, credit, and ATM. If you're planning to venture into Canada, make sure you have appropriate identification and paperwork.

Other handy items are a small backpack for day trips or light hiking and a small or collapsible cooler for picnics or storing food. You can greatly reduce the cost of eating by purchasing food at grocery stores or supermarkets instead of dining out.

SOUTHERN COAST

Sand and sun are the two biggest draws to this region of Maine, thanks to miles of beaches, but they're not the only reasons to visit. Maine's Southern Coast delights history buffs with homes dating from the 17th century, such as those at Old York. Architecture buffs will treasure scads of sea captains' and shipbuilders' homes in towns like Kennebunkport. Art connoisseurs can peruse plentiful galleries and the Ogunquit Museum of American Art. Numerous preserves for walking, hiking, and canoeing, such as the Wells National Estuarine Research Reserve at Laudholm Farm, appeal to outdoors-oriented folks. Sights drawing maritime heritage aficionados include lighthouses (The Nubble), forts (Foster and McClary), and fishing villages (Cape Porpoise). Shoppers have antique shops (Wells) and outlets (Kittery) galore. Families will enjoy the state's best concentration of amusement parks (Funtown/Splashtown USA, York's Wild Kingdom, Palace Playland) and amusing places, such as the Seashore Trolley Museum.

GREATER PORTLAND

Like most cities, Portland offers a wealth of cultural and entertainment options. What surprises many visitors is the wide range of outdoor-oriented activities available both in the city itself and in its suburbs. As far as cities go, Maine's largest is not overwhelming, and most of its must-see sights, including the Portland Museum of Art, Victoria Mansion, Portland Observatory, and Old Port, are within walking distance of one another on the downtown peninsula. A Casco Bay tour will introduce you to the nearby islands, while a biking or driving tour to Cape Elizabeth will encompass Portland Head Light. Go on a lobstering cruise, and you might actually catch your dinner. Venture north to Freeport, and you'll find L.L. Bean and nearly 180 outlets to browse. But if what you really want to do is to go hiking, birding, deep-sea fishing, sea kayaking, or bicycling, all that's at your fingertips, too, thanks to plentiful preserves, a vibrant working waterfront, and miles of well-marked trails.

MID-COAST REGION

Although technically the Mid-Coast stretches from Brunswick to Bucksport, here we're referring to the region between Brunswick and Waldoboro. This region is a bit less touristy than other parts, and that's a surprise, because there is much here to see and do. Long granite-tipped fingers of land are dotted with small fishing villages, sea captains' homes, lobster wharves, nature preserves, antique and artisans' shops, and occasionally beautiful stretches of sand, such as Popham Beach. You'll need to get off Route 1 and explore these peninsulas and the towns that anchor them to begin to get a sense of what makes each tick. Brunswick is home to Bowdoin College and the Joshua L. Chamberlain Museum, which honors the Civil War hero. Bath's proud shipbuilding heritage is brought to life in the Maine Maritime Museum. Wiscasset is famed for its antique shops, while Boothbay is the departure point for many excursion boats, including one that takes in a living-history lighthouse tour of Burnt Island. The adjacent Pemaquid Peninsula is tipped by Pemaquid Point Lighthouse, a beacon that's appeared on countless calendars. Nearby Colonial Pemaquid/Fort William Henry is a good place to learn about one of the earliest English settlements in North America. And no place along the Maine coast has as many places for enjoying alfresco lobster-in-the-rough.

PENOBSCOT BAY

Island-studded Penobscot Bay is a sailor's dream. The rugged coastline hides protected harbors and links fishing villages with rather cosmopolitan towns. The jagged coastlineis punctuated by beacons, such as Owls Head Light and Rockland Breakwater Light. Islands, including Monhegan, which is south of Penobscot Bay, frame the seaward background, while the Camden Hills are the inland backdrop. Lighthouses and lobster are two of the region's calling cards, but they're complemented by museums, such as The Farnsworth Art

Museum, Owls Head TransportationMuseum, and Penobscot Marine Museum. Throughout the region are antique shops, art galleries, and artisans' studios. Places such as BlueJacket Shipcrafters, where museum-quality ship models are handcrafted, tie the seemingly diverse elements tidily together.

BLUE HILL PENINSULA

From many points along the Penobscot Bay coastline, you can look across and see the Blue Hill Peninsula, which extends far into the bay before giving way to Deer Isle and Stonington. Yet this region has a far different character than those across the bay. It's much more artsy and rich with galleries. It also is home to pockets of back-to-the-landers, thanks to movement pioneers Helen and Scott Nearing, whose home here, The Good Life Center, continues to espouse their values. History, too, is palpable, especially in Castine, where signs throughout the beautifully preserved town explain its turbulent past. Another sign of that past is Fort Knox, which protected the all-important Penobscot River from invaders. And there's the blissfully peaceful home of Parson Fisher, a true Renaissance man if there ever was one. Venture farther down the peninsula and cross the bridge over Eggemoggin Reach to Deer Isle, and the character changes again, from communities dominated by active retirees to ones presided over by fisherfolk. From Stonington, it's a short boat ride to Isle au Haut, where a remote and rugged piece of Acadia National Park awaits those wishing to explore it.

ACADIA REGION

Ahhh, yes, Acadia. Acadia National Park is a place of raw beauty, where you can immerse yourself as much as you desire. You can get a taste of the park with a drive along the Park Loop; venture in a bit with a walk or ride on the famed carriage roads; or go all out and hike rugged trails, kayak along undeveloped coastline, scale soaring cliffs, or canoe quiet ponds. And yet, for all its wildness, the park is very civilized. Case in point: Tea and popovers at the Jordan Pond House is a long-standing tradition. While the park is what attracts most people to Mount Desert Island and its environs, there is so much more here. Somes Sound is a rare fjord; the Abbe Museum traces Maine's Native American history; the Wendell Gilley Museum is a testament to one man's craftsmanship; Asticou and Thuya gardens show that the wilds of Acadia can be tamed. It's also easy to get off-island and see the region by boat, perhaps on a whale-watching excursion or with Diver Ed, who exposes the mysteries of the deep. And while it's tempting to think that if you've been to Mount Desert, you've experienced Acadia, you haven't. Even more of the park awaits at the tip of the Schoodic Peninsula. While you can get there by passenger ferry from Bar Harbor, driving rewards those who prize artisans' studios.

THE DOWN EAST COAST

Everything changes when you decide to continue north on Route 1 from Ellsworth. Traffic subsides, fast-food joints, shopping plazas, and chain motels all but disappear; towns are smaller, and the stretches of roads between towns get longer. This is a region where independence reigns. Artisans are plentiful. Fishing and lobstering are big business. Even the coastal geography changes, with blueberry barrens a frequent sight and huge tides ruling daily life. While you won't find a big choice in restaurants here, you will find some of the best fried fish you've ever tasted. And although hotels are few, pleasant B&Bs and homey small motels and tourist courts abound. But the biggest reason to come is for the wild expanse of coastline, something that is shrinking as developers carve it up and sell it off. Hiking and birding are renowned here and easy, thanks to a multitude of refuges, parks, and preserves, places such as Petit Manan National Wildlife Refuge, Great Wass Island Preserve, West Quoddy Head State Park, and Shackford Head State Park, to name just a few. And then there's Machias Seal Island, a nesting ground for puffins, those clowns of the sea. Putting the region's history, heritage, and natural resources in perspective is the Downeast Heritage Center. Make it a two-nation vacation with a trip over the international bridge in Lubec to Campobello Island, where President Roosevelt's summer home is now an international heritage site.

It's a tough job to single out Maine's sightseeing icons. There are just so many. But, unless you have years to spend, such a big, meandering chunk of real estate needs some whittling to be made explorable. This itinerary exposes you to a good chunk of Maine, while taking in most of the state's icons in 10 days. The downside: You'll be doing a fair bit of driving on Route 1, the major thoroughfare that strings these sights together. It's primarily a two-lane road, where speeds through towns are often 25 mph or below. Not exactly ideal for a speed trip through Maine. While this itinerary is planned as 10 days, if your schedule permits, you'll be rewarded if you spend longer in any of the locations, but especially on Mount Desert.

If you're arriving by airplane, your best bet is to arrive at Portland International Jetport and depart from Bangor International, but if you can't swing that, use Portland only (but add an extra last night in Portland). Book your first two nights' lodging in Portland, nights three and four in Rockland or vicinity, nights five and six on Mount Desert Island, nights seven and eight in either the Jonesport or Cutler area, to coincide with taking a puffin-sighting trip from either location (make reservations). Book your ninth night in the Calais area or Eastport.

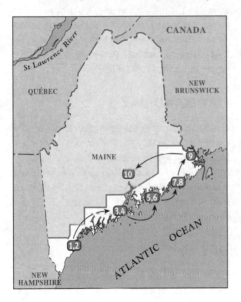

of sand along Maine's fabled rockbound coast. Afterward, head to Kennebunkport and indulge your passions: shopping in the boutiques and galleries that crowd Dock Square, taking a walking tour to view the historic homes, or a leisurely drive along the waterfront.

DAY 2

Begin the day with a visit to Portland Head Light, a Cape Elizabeth landmark and Maine's oldest lighthouse (1791), at the edge of 94-acre Fort Williams Park. Spend the afternoon in the Portland Museum of Art, Maine's premier art museum, smack in the heart of the state's largest city. End the day with a sunset cruise on Casco Bay.

DAY 1

Stretch your legs after your journey to Maine with a refreshing walk on Ogunquit Beach, one of Maine's prettiest, and proof that there's plenty

DAY 3

Make a pilgrimage to gigunda sports retailer and outfitter L.L. Bean, hub of the hubbub in Freeport — Maine's outlet bonanza. Spend the morning either shopping or taking a Walk-On Adventure class. In the afternoon, visit the Maine Maritime Museum

Monhegan Island's lobsterboat-filled harbor is protected by barren Manana Island, once home to a famous hermit.

in Bath, 10 acres of indoor and outdoor exhibits celebrating the state's nautical heritage.

DAY 4

Take a day trip to Monhegan Island from Port Clyde. This car-free, carefree gem, about a dozen miles off the coast, is laced with hiking trails and has earned a place in art history books as the Artists' Island.

DAY 5

Drive or hike to the top of Mount Battie, in Camden Hills State Park, on the northern fringe of Camden. The vistas are magnificent, with the broad sweep of Penobscot Bay for a backdrop. Then continue up the coast to Mount Desert Island and begin your explorations of Acadia National Park. If you've

arrived on the island before noon, pick up a picnic lunch, then drive the Park Loop, a perfect introduction to Acadia that covers many of the highlights. Otherwise, take a whale-watching trip from Bar Harbor (advance reservations are wise).

DAY 6

Welcome the day by watching the sunrise from the summit of Cadillac Mountain. Afterward, if you haven't either driven or bicycled the Park Loop, do so. If you have, then explore the park in more depth: go hiking, bicycling, or sea kayaking, take a carriage ride, or book an excursion boat to Islesford or a whale-watching trip.

DAY 7

Depart Mount Desert Island and continue north on Route 1, dipping down the Gouldsboro Peninsula and looping through the Schoodic section of Acadia National Park. Continue on to either the Jonesport or Cutler area (wherever your lodging reservations are for that night).

DAY 8 AND DAY 9

These two days are interchangeable. Book a puffin sighting trip on Day 8, with Day 9 as a weather backup. You will need advance reservations. Afterward, drive to Lubec and visit West Quoddy Head State Park. On Day 9, drive north to Calais, visiting Eastport, home of the highest tides in the country, if time permits.

DAY 10

Travel day. Return to Bangor via Route 9 (allow three hours), then connect to I-95 if you're heading to Portland (allow three hours) or points south or west.

This six-day tour concentrates on the Southern Coast, Greater Portland, Mid-Coast, and Penobscot Bay regions. Book your first two nights' lodging in Portland, the second two in Damariscotta/Newcastle, the final two in the Thomaston/Rockland area. If you simply must stay in a lighthouse, real or close-enough-to-fool-most-folks, add two nights on the Blue Hill Peninsula, either at the First Light B&B, in East Blue Hill, or The Keeper's House, on Isle au Haut.

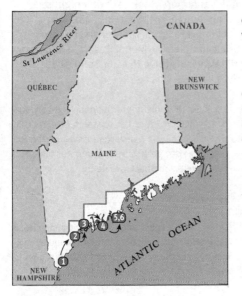

cruise with Lucky Catch Lobster Tours; perhaps you'll catch your dinner.

DAY 3

Get an early start and begin at L.L. Bean, in Freeport. In the afternoon, visit the Maine Maritime Museum in Bath, and, if time permits, take a lighthouse cruise on the Kennebec River.

DAY 4

Take a morning Burnt Island tour out of Boothbay Harbor. In the afternoon, visit Pemaquid Light and the Fisherman's Museum at the tip of the Pemaquid Peninsula. Afterward, head to Round Pond for lobster-in-the-rough.

DAY 5

Visit Marshall Point Lighthouse, in Port Clyde, then take the mail boat to Monhegan Island. Alternatively, take a lighthouse-themed cruise or sea kayak tour out of Rockport or Rockland. Either way, end with lobster-in-the rough at Waterman's Beach Lobster in Spruce Head.

DAY 1

Begin in York and view The Nubble, then head north to the Lighthouse Depot, in Wells, allowing plenty of time to shop and visit the adjacent museum. If time permits, veer down to East Point Sanctuary for distant views of Wood Island Light (bring binoculars).

DAY 2

Begin at the Portland Harbor Museum and nearby Spring Point Ledge Lighthouse. Have lunch at The Lobster Shack at Two Lights, overlooking Cape Elizabeth Light. Next, visit Portland Head Light and its museum. Allow time for a late afternoon

DAY 6

Begin your day with a sunrise walk out the breakwater to Rockland Breakwater Light. Tour the Maine Lighthouse Museum and, if time permits, take a short jaunt out to Owls Head Light, in Owls Head, before returning to Portland for the flight home.

For many folks, the Blue Hill Peninsula, Acadia, and Down East regions represent the *real* Maine. Spend 12 days here, and you can visit Acadia National Park, browse the studios of mega-talented artisans, go whale-watching or puffin-sighting, hike magnificent trails, kayak along undeveloped coastline, and view working lobstering villages and lighthouses. This tour circles you clockwise through the region, beginning in Calais and ending with the Blue Hill Peninsula.

Best air access is via Bangor International Airport. Book your first night's lodging in the Calais area, the second night in Eastport, the third night in or around Jonesport (Addison, Jonesboro, Columbia Falls), nights four and five on the Gouldsboro Peninsula, nights six, seven, and eight on Mount Desert Island, and your last three nights on the Blue Hill Peninsula (Blue Hill and Brooksville lodgings will be most central to all activities).

excellent introduction to the region. Afterward, head south on Route 1 to **Eastport**, the first U.S. city to see the sun rise each morning. Spend the rest of the day poking around, perhaps taking an easy hike out to **Shackford Head.**

DAY 3

Drive south to **Lubec** and visit **West Quoddy Head State Park,** allowing time to visit the museum at the base of the candy-striped lighthouse and to walk the trail edging the seaside cliffs.

DAY 4

Take a puffin-watching trip from Jonesport to **Machias Seal Island** or spend the morning hiking and birdwatching on **Great Wass Island.** In the afternoon, either visit the **Maine Central Model Railroad**, in Jonesport, and the **Ruggles House,** in Columbia Falls, or go hiking in **Petit Manan National Wildlife Refuge.**

DAY 1

A travel day. From Bangor, drive Route 9 (The Airline) to Calais (allow 2–3 hours).

DAY 2

Begin your explorations with a tour of the **Downeast Heritage Center,** which provides an

DAY 5

Begin with a drive or bicycle loop around the **Schoodic section of Acadia National Park.** Depending on your interests, spend the rest of the day hiking in the park, sea kayaking, or browsing the numerous artisans' galleries tucked in all corners of the region.

DAY 6

Head for **Mount Desert Island**. Begin on the outskirts, visiting **Northeast Harbor** and **Southwest Harbor**, with stops to see the **Asticou** and **Thuya** gardens, **Somes Sound**, and the **Wendell Gilley Museum**. Enjoy a lobster dinner at Thurston's Lobster Pound.

DAY 7

Spend the day in **Acadia National Park**. Begin by driving or bicycling the **Park Loop** to take in the park's highlights, then indulge your passions: hiking, sea kayaking, bicycling, a carriage tour. Be sure to stop for tea and popovers at the **Jordan Pond House**.

DAY 8

Visit the **Abbe Museum** and go whale-watching. In between poke around **Bar Harbor**.

DAY 9

Depart Mount Desert for the **Blue Hill Peninsula**. En route, visit **Birdsacre**, a peaceful preserve and bird refuge. In **Blue Hill**, begin with a tour of the **Parson Fisher House**. Afterward, visit some of the many galleries in town. Do ask locally to see if the **Flash in the Pans** are performing during your days on the peninsula, and make it a point to hear them.

DAY 10

Mosey over to **Castine** and pick up a brochure for a self-guided walking tour. Spend the afternoon on a guided sea kayaking tour.

© TOM NANGLE

Candy-striped Quoddy Head Lighthouse is an icon on the Down East Coast. A visitors center and museum are located at its base, and hiking trails edge the cliffs.

DAY 11

Explore **Deer Isle** and **Stonington**, allowing plenty of time to browse the galleries along the way or hike on one of the island's preserves. If time permits, take a cruise to **Isle au Haut**.

DAY 12

Visit **Fort Knox** in the morning, before heading home. If you're flying out of Bangor, you can either mosey up Route 15 or connect via Route 174 to Route 1A north.

In recent years, Maine's restaurant scene has gained increasing national attention, with top awards and mentions in foodie magazines such as *Bon Appétit, Food and Wine, Gourmet,* and *Saveur.* If you want to dine your way through Maine, here's where to go to hit the biggies. You definitely want to plan well in advance for a summer visit, and even then, you might have to be flexible in your seating time.

SOUTHERN COAST

ARROWS
A quiet, country farmhouse is the understated setting for this restaurant, named by *Gourmet* as one of America's Top 50 Restaurants. Chefs Clark Frasier and Mark Gaier were nominated for a James Beard award in 2004 and have received accolades from magazines such as *Gourmet, Bon Appétit,* and even *Time.* They're renowned for their fresh flavorful cuisine, with many ingredients sourced from the restaurant's gardens. Jackets preferred for men.

WHITE BARN INN
Maine's only five-diamond restaurant regularly gets kudos from publications such as *Food and Wine, Travel + Leisure,* and *Condé Nast Traveler.* The dining room is an elegantly restored barn, where chef Jonathan Cartwright's fixed-price, four-course menu, offering contemporary New England cuisine with European accents, is served by formally dressed waiters. Jackets are required for gentlemen.

AND WHILE YOU'RE HERE . . .
Don't miss Provence, a fabulous country-French Ogunquit restaurant, owned by chef Pierre Gignac, that always wins top marks from local critics.

GREATER PORTLAND

For any of these three, you'll feel most comfortable in resort casual wear. No need for jackets, although you wouldn't feel out of place in one, either.

FORE STREET
Ask any Maine foodie who the dean of Maine foods is, and likely the answer will be Sam Hayward. Here, Hayward has teamed with another highly regarded restaurateur, Dana Street, of Street and Co. The result won Hayward the "Best Chef in the Northeast" award from the James Beard Foundation in 2004.

HUGO'S
In 2004, *Food and Wine* named chef Rob Evans one of America's Ten Best New Chefs. You'll learn why when you step into this fine restaurant, decorated in soothing shades, where Evans prepares New American cuisine presented in 3- and 10-course fixed-price menus.

AND WHILE YOU'RE HERE . . .
This one won't be a secret for long. At Bandol, in the Old Port, chef Erik Desjarlais prepares to-die-for, classic French, five- and nine-course fixed-price menus. Also gaining attention well beyond Portland is Cinque Terre Ristorante, an authentic Northern Italian restaurant in the Old Port.

PENOBSCOT BAY

PRIMO
James Beard award–winning chef Melissa Kelly and her partner, Price Kushner, keep earning kudos for their farmhouse restaurant on the Rockland/Owls Head border. Resort casual is the preferred dress.

WATERMAN'S BEACH LOBSTER
What's a lobster-in-the-rough spot doing on this

© WHITE BARN INN

crème brûlée at the White Barn Inn

list? Well, the folks at the James Beard House thought it deserved an award, and we think you deserve a night where you can dress down and drink in the view (if you want anything more potent to drink, be sure to bring it with you). You'll be eating lobster on a picnic table; jeans, shorts, and T-shirts are the dress code.

AND WHILE YOU'RE HERE . . .

Don't miss Francine Bistro, chefs/owners Lindsey Schechter's and Brian Hill's lovely little bistro in a residential section of downtown Camden.

ACADIA REGION

LE DOMAIN

It doesn't look like much from the road, but step inside. Chef/owner Nicole Purslow has created a touch of France on the coast of Maine, right down to the wine list. Before dinner, stroll the lovely grounds, laced with trails. When you make dining reservations, book a room for the night, too. Then all you'll have to do after wining and dining is head upstairs. Any local folks celebrating special occasions will likely be dressed to the nines, but resort casual is fine.

AND WHILE YOU'RE HERE . . .

Pay a visit for either lunch or dinner to La Matta Cena, a casual Tuscan-inspired bistro, with most seating outdoors in Northeast Harbor. Outdoor heaters keep things comfortable. You're in yacht land, so dress the part, keeping in mind the outdoor seating, especially in the evening: A lightweight colorful sweater or jacket over a polo shirt paired with khakis will do just fine.

Searching for treasures? Whether you have a practiced eye or just enjoy the thrill of the hunt, you'll find these the best places for finding genuine antiques and collectibles or can't-resist treasures. This six-day tour stretches from Wells, in the Southern Coast region, to Searsport, in the Penobscot Bay region. Book your first two nights in Wells or a nearby town, your third night in Bath, fourth night in Wiscasset or one of the towns north of it, your last two nights in Belfast or Searsport. If you're arriving by air, fly in and out of Portland.

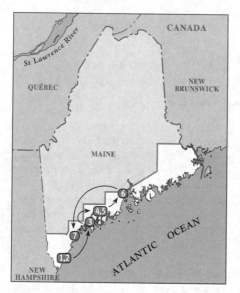

Day's Antiques downtown, on Park Row. Then continue northeast to Bath. The lower end of Bath's Front Street has side-by-side antique shops, some with good-sized collections of antiquarian books. Don't miss the **Maine Maritime Museum**, with its emphasis on nautical and boat-building antiquities.

DAY 4

Woolwich and Wiscasset: Get an early start for the best pickings at the famous **Montsweag Flea Market.** Afterward, continue north on Route 1, stopping at the large, multidealer shops along the way. Spend the afternoon in downtown Wiscasset, which boasts about two dozen antique shops. If time permits, visit two antiques-filled treasure houses in Wiscasset, **Castle Tucker** and the **Nickels-Sortwell House**, and the **Musical Wonder House**, brimming with antique music boxes.

DAYS 1 AND 2

Wells and vicinity: Antiquarian bookstores, huge barns and old houses filled with genuine antiques or overflowing with "good stuff," and flea-market-style shops line both sides of Route 1 in Wells and overflow into nearby towns.

DAY 3

Brunswick and Bath: Begin in Brunswick. For variety, visit **Cabot Mill Antiques,** where more than 140 dealers show their wares in a restored 1820s riverside mill. For a smaller selection, visit

DAY 5

More than two dozen antiques dealers have shops on the **Pemaquid Peninsula.** Begin in the twin towns of **Damariscotta** and **Newcastle**, at **Antiques with Attitude**, then mosey along Route 130 south. Return to Route 1 and continue northeast, stopping at the many antique shops and auction houses along the way. You'll find clusters in **Nobleboro, Thomaston,** and **Lincolnville.** Do stop at **Nobleboro Antique Exchange**, a huge multidealer antique mall that's much, much larger than it first appears.

DAY 6

Hard to believe there could be a town that rivals Wiscasset for the title Antiques Capital, but **Searsport** does. Sea captains' homes, big barns, and newish buildings house individual shops, such as **Antiques at the Hillman's** and **Primrose Farm Antiques,** as well as multidealer shops such as **Pumpkin Patch** and the **Searsport Antique Mall.** Flea-market stands, with tables and small buildings, line a stretch of Route 1 northeast of town. Learn more about how all these treasures arrived here by visiting the **Penobscot Marine Museum.**

DAY 7

Return to Belfast, then take Route 17 west, stopping in **Liberty** to visit **Liberty Tool Company,** three floors of antiques, mostly tools. Then continue west to I-95 and head south to Portland for an afternoon flight home.

rare book finds in Wells

© TOM NANGLE

After years of fielding requests from visitors for lists of cultural-heritage sites and special-interest activities, the Maine Office of Tourism has teamed up with the state's arts and culture organizations to create a whole range of "trails" that cover maritime history, art museums, outstanding gardens, outdoor sculpture, and Wabanaki (Native American) sites. With state support, several counties and groups have produced their own regional cultural maps. Request copies of any of the first five publications at any of the state Visitor Information Centers or call 800/782-6497. The Wabanaki guide is available for a fee.

MAINE ARCHITECTURAL TRAIL

Travelers in Maine pass through many small towns and villages, and it's not uncommon for them to stop and marvel at the wondrous architectural details. Presented in this brochure are six specific routes, three emphasizing coastal sights, each explaining the connection between the landscape, the people, and the architecture by focusing on specific sights and putting it all in historical context.

MAINE ART MUSEUM TRAIL

An attractive brochure focuses on the state's seven significant art museums, containing more than 50,000 works of art—ancient to contemporary, painting and sculpture, furniture and textiles. Four of the seven are in coastal Maine. From south to north: Ogunquit Museum of American Art (Ogunquit); Portland Museum of Art (Portland); Bowdoin College Museum of Art (Brunswick); and The Farnsworth Art Museum (Rockland). (The museums inland are Bates College Museum of Art in Lewiston, the Colby Museum of Art in Waterville, and the University of Maine Museum of Art in Orono.) The trail website is www.maineart museums.org.

MAINE ARCHIVES AND MUSEUMS DIRECTORY

More than 125 institutions are listed by region in this 72-page directory of museums, historical societies, historic sites, and archives. Four of the regions fall within coastal Maine. (The directory includes some of the highlights of the maritime heritage and art museum trails.) The website is www.mainemuseums.org.

MAINE GARDEN AND LANDSCAPE TRAIL

A handy foldout map lists and locates more than 50 gardens—a huge variety from pocket parks to city parks; formal, English, and experimental gardens; even a monastery and a cemetery. Although the trail covers the entire state, two-thirds of the sites are in coastal Maine. You'll find the finest displays in June and July, when garden tours are also on the agenda. The best of these tours are in Camden, Damariscotta, the Kennebunks, and Mount Desert Island. The "trail" map also lists several dozen garden and plant centers with wonderful display gardens where you can indulge your horticultural habit.

MAINE MARITIME HERITAGE TRAIL

Any state that claims more than 5,000 miles of in-and-out coastline can logically also claim a rich maritime heritage. The Maritime Heritage Trail focuses on the sites that represent coastal Maine's rich history—maritime museums, boatbuilding schools, lighthouses, and sea captains' mansions. Also part of the story are maritime celebrations—windjammer and lobsterboat races, lighthouse tours, and clam and lobster festivals. The special large-format, two-sided map serves as a handy reference as you travel the trail. The website www.maritimemaine.org has even more sights and information.

MAINE OUTDOOR SCULPTURE GUIDE

Three tours are highlighted in this handy and fun-to-read 64-page guidebook. The Seacoast Tour visits outdoor sculptures from Kittery to Machias, detailing each sculpture and explaining its history. The Sculpture Garden Tour highlights classic and whimsical coastal sculpture gardens in Ogunquit, Bath, Islesboro, and Mount Desert. The Civil War Tour explains coastal Civil War–related monuments in York and Calais. Noncoastal outdoor sculptures are also featured in the guide, which also includes walking tours of outdoor sculpture in Portland and Bangor. Call 207/287-2724 to request a copy.

WABANAKI GUIDE TO MAINE: A VISITOR'S GUIDE TO NATIVE AMERICAN CULTURE IN MAINE

This splendid 86-page spiral-bound booklet, published in 2001, is an excellent guide. The Wabanaki Trail is a go-at-your-own-pace route that leads you to museums, workshops, festivals, shops, significant landmarks, and even ancient canoe routes. Two trail sections are in the Acadia and Down East regions of coastal Maine, where two of Maine's four tribes live. The guide is available for $10 (check or money order) from the Maine Indian Basketmakers Alliance (P.O. Box 3253, Old Town 04468, 207/827-0391).

Explore Coastal Maine

Southern Coast

Drive over the I-95 bridge from New Hampshire into Maine's Southern Coast region on a bright summer day and you'll swear the air is cleaner, the sky bluer, the trees greener, the roadside signs more upbeat. "Welcome to Maine: The Way Life Should Be."

Most visitors come to this region for the spectacular attractions of the justly world-famous Maine coast—the inlets, islands, and especially the beaches. But it's rich in history, too. Southernmost York County, part of the Province of Maine, was incorporated in 1636 (only 16 years after the Mayflower pilgrims reached Plymouth,

Massachusetts) and reeks of history: ancient cemeteries, musty archives, and architecturally stunning homes and public buildings. Probably the best places to dive into that history are in the sites of the Old York Historical Society in York Harbor.

Geological fortune smiled on this 50-mile ribbon, endowing it with a string of sandy beaches—nirvana for sun worshipers, but less enchanting to swimmers, who need to steel themselves to spend much time in the ocean (especially in early summer, before the water temperature has reached a tolerable level). Complementing those beaches are

Must-Sees

Look for **M** to find the sights and activities you can't miss and **M** for the best dining and lodging.

M Nubble Light/Sohier Park: You'll likely recognize this often-photographed Maine coast icon, which is the easiest lighthouse to see in the region (page 29).

M York Village: York dates from the 1640s, and on this campus of historic buildings, you can peek into early life here (page 31).

Nubble Light

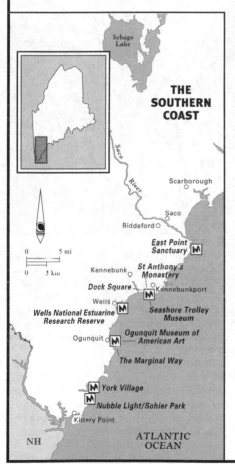

THE SOUTHERN COAST

M Ogunquit Museum of American Art: Hard to say which is more jaw-dropping, the art or the view (page 39).

M The Marginal Way: Escape the hustle and bustle of Ogunquit with a stroll on this paved, shorefront path (page 40).

M Wells National Estuarine Research Reserve: Orient yourself at the visitor center, where you can learn about the history, flora, and fauna, then take a leisurely walk to the seashore, passing through a variety of habitats (page 40).

M Seashore Trolley Museum: Ring-ring-ring goes the trolley . . . zing-zing-zing go your heartstrings, especially if you're a trolley fan (page 51).

M Dock Square: Busy, busy, busy is this heart of Kennebunkport, and with good reason. Brave the crowds and explore (page 55).

M St. Anthony's Monastery: Hard to believe this oasis of calm is just a short stroll from busy-busy-busy Dock Square (page 55).

M East Point Sanctuary: A must for birders, this coastal preserve provides dramatic views (page 68).

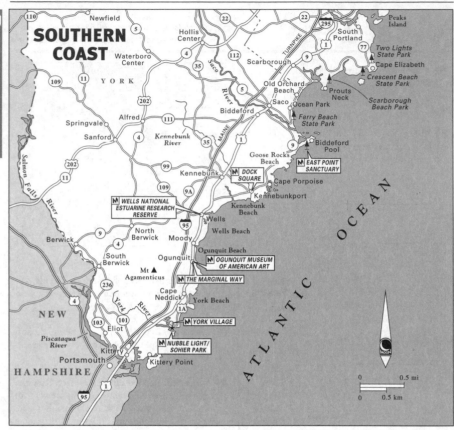

amusement parks and arcades, fishing shacks turned chic boutiques, a surprising number of good restaurants (given the region's seasonality), and some of the state's prettiest parks and preserves.

PLANNING YOUR TIME

The good news is that Maine's Southern Coast is a rather compact region. The bad news is that it's heavily congested, especially in summer. Still, with a minimum of four days, you should be able to take in most of the key sights, from beaches to museums, as long as you don't want to spend hours basking in the sun.

If dining out is a priority, consider joining the **Seacoast Fine Dining Club** (P.O. Box 228, New-

market, NH 03857, 603/292-5093, www.seacoast finedining.com). More than two dozen restaurants on Maine's Southern Coast participate in it, and a membership of $29.95 entitles you to buy one entrée and get a second one of equal or lesser value free. It also provides discounts on some area attractions, such as the Seashore Trolley Museum, Ogunquit Playhouse, etc.

Instead of zipping into the state on I-95, take the more leisurely Route 1, then noodle along scenic Route 103 to York, where you can immerse yourself in the region's deep history touring at least one, if not more, of the buildings of the **Old York Historical Society.** From there, follow the coastline along Route 1A, detouring to the **Nubble Lighthouse,** all the prettier during the holiday season. Spend the rest of the afternoon on the beach, soaking in the rays, braving a dip, or just walking Long Sands Beach.

Day two, follow Shore Road into Ogunquit, stopping at the **Ogunquit Museum of American Art** to admire the art and the views before shopping for a parking space in Ogunquit. Walk the **Marginal Way** to Perkins Cove, then return either by trolley or by sidewalk along Shore Road. Spend the afternoon in Wells, either at **Wells National Estuarine Research Reserve** at Laudholm Farm or on the beach. Finish off the day with a fine meal at one of Ogunquit's restaurants or perhaps a show at the Ogunquit Playhouse.

On day three, continue north to the Kennebunks, allowing time to browse the shops in **Dock Square** or take a historical walking tour. Seek respite from the crowds by visiting the riverfront **St. Anthony's Franciscan Monastery,** where you can meander along trails and view a sculpture from the 1964 World's Fair. Finish the afternoon at the **Seashore Trolley Museum,** then head to Cape Porpoise for a lobster dinner.

Begin your last day with a morning stroll at the **East Point Sanctuary.** Afterward, meander through Saco, Camp Ellis, Ocean Park, and Old Orchard, taking time to do what interests you— a last swim or beach walk, a game at an arcade, or a thrilling ride—before heading home.

Getting There

Amtrak's **Downeaster** (800/872-7245, www.the downeaster.com) connects Boston's North Station with Portland, Maine, with stops in Wells, Saco, and Old Orchard Beach (seasonal).

Vermont Transit (800/552-8737, www .vermonttransit.com), a division of Greyhound bus lines, stops at the Wells Regional Transportation Center daily on the Boston–Portland–Bangor route. The trolley connects with the bus in season.

Getting Around

The Maine Turnpike, a toll road, is generally the fastest route, if you're trying to get between two towns. Route 1 parallels the turnpike, on the ocean side. It's mostly two lanes and is lined with shops, restaurants, motels, and other tourist-oriented sites, which means stop-and-go traffic that often slows to a crawl. If you're traveling locally, it's best to walk or use the local trolley systems, which have the bonus of saving you the agony of finding a parking spot.

Kittery

Besides being a natural point of entry into the state, Kittery also competes with Freeport, farther up the coast, as an outlet-shopping mecca. Kittery boasts more than 120 factory outlets lining both sides of Route 1. But before or after you overdose on shoes, china, tools, toys, candles, and underwear, take time to explore the back roads of Maine's oldest town—settled in 1623 and chartered in 1647. Maine is home to a lot of well-kept secrets, Kittery being one of them. Parks, a small nautical museum, historic architecture, and lobster restaurants are only a few of the attractions in Kittery and its "suburb," Kittery Point. It was on Kittery's Badger Island where the sloop *Ranger* was launched in 1777. The shipbuilding continues at Portsmouth Naval Shipyard, on Kittery's Dennet's Island, the first government shipyard in America.

To reach Kittery's shops and services, and Eliot's lodgings, from I-95 northbound take the Exit 3 cloverleaf, designated Kittery, Coastal Route 1 North, and continue to Route 1. From I-95 southbound, take the Yorks/Berwicks exit; then take Coastal Route 1 South. Follow signs; the twists and turns can be confusing.

SIGHTS

Kittery Historical and Naval Museum

Maritime history buffs shouldn't miss the small but well-stocked Kittery Historical and Naval Museum (Rogers Road Extension, near the junction of Routes 1 and 236, Kittery, 207/439-3080, 10 A.M.–4 P.M. Tues.–Sat. June–mid-Oct., $3 adults, $1.50 kids 7–15, family max. $6). A large exhibit hall and a small back room contain ship models, fishing gear, old photos and paintings, and an astonishing collection of scrimshaw (carved whale ivory).

Lady Pepperrell House

The 1760 Georgian Lady Pepperrell House (Pepperrell Rd., Rte. 103, shortly before the Fort McClary turnoff) is now privately owned and no longer open to the public, but it's worth admiring from afar. Nearby, across from the First Congregational Church, is the area's most-visited burying ground. Old-cemetery buffs should bring rubbing gear here for some interesting grave markers. The tomb of Levi Thaxter (husband of poet Celia Thaxter) bears an epitaph written for him by Robert Browning.

Fort McClary Historic Site

Since the early 18th century, fortifications have stood on this 27-acre headland, protecting Portsmouth Harbor from seaborne foes. Contemporary remnants at Fort McClary (Rte. 103, Kittery Point, 207/439-2845, $2 adults, $1

kids 5–11) include several outbuildings, an 1846 blockhouse, granite walls, and earthworks—all with a view of Portsmouth Harbor. Opposite are the sprawling buildings of the Portsmouth Naval Shipyard. Bring a picnic (covered tables and a lily pond are across the street) and turn the kids loose to run and play. It's officially open May 30–October 1, but the site is accessible in the off-season. The fort is 2.5 miles east of Route 1.

Brave Boat Harbor

One of the Rachel Carson National Wildlife Refuge's 10 Maine coastal segments is Brave Boat Harbor (207/646-9226), a beautifully unspoiled, 560-acre wetlands preserve in Kittery Point with a four-mile (round-trip) trail. Carry binoculars, wear rubberized boots to maneuver the squishy areas, and slather on the insect repellent. The habitat is particularly sensitive here, so be kind to the environment. Take Route 103 to Chauncey Creek Road and continue past the Gerrish Island bridge to Cutts Island Lane. Just beyond it and across a small bridge is a pullout on the left. You have a

Fort McClary's 1846 blockhouse still guards Portsmouth Harbor.

couple of options for hikes: a 1.8-mile loop trail, including a spur, or a half-mile loop. Bring binoculars to spot waterfowl in the marshlands.

Route 103

Avoid the outlet sprawl and see the prettiest part of the area by driving along squiggly Route 103 from the Route 1 rotary in Kittery through Kittery Point (administratively part of Kittery) and on to Route 1A in York. You can even make a day of it, stopping at all the sites mentioned above. Be very careful and watch for cyclists and pedestrians, as there are no shoulders but lots of blind corners and hills.

RECREATION

River Tours

Take a spin around the Piscataqua River Basin with **Captain & Patty's Piscataqua River Tours** (Town Dock, Pepperrell Rd., Kittery Point, 207/439-8976 home or 207/451-8156 boat, $12 adults, $10 kids under 10). The one-hour historical tour departs seven times daily, including once in the evening for a two-hour twilight cruise for adults only. Along the way, Captain Neil Odams points out historic forts, lighthouses, and the naval shipyard.

Fort Foster

The only problem with Fort Foster is that it's no secret, so parking can be scarce (and expensive) at this 90-acre municipal park at the entrance to Portsmouth Harbor (Pocahontas Rd., off Rte. 103, Gerrish Island, Kittery Point, 207/439-3800, 10 A.M.–8 P.M. daily Memorial Day to Labor Day, weekends in May and Sept., $10 vehicle pass, $5 adult walk-in, $1 child walk-in). On a hot day, arrive early. Then you can swim, hike the nature trails, fish off the pier (no license needed), picnic, and investigate the tidepools. Bring your sailboard and a kite—there's almost always a breeze. From nearby **Seapoint Beach** (park in the small roadside lot and walk down to the beach; the lower lot is for residents only) on a clear day, there's a wide-open view of the offshore Isles

of Shoals, owned jointly by Maine and New Hampshire. No facilities.

SHOPPING

No question, you'll find bargains at Kittery's 120-plus factory outlets (www.thekitteryoutlets .com)—actually a bunch of minimalls clustered along both sides of Route 1. All the household names are here: Bass, Calvin Klein, Eddie Bauer, J Crew, Mikasa, Esprit, Lenox, Timberland, Tommy Hilfiger, Gap, Villeroy & Boch, and a hundred more. All shops are open daily; hours tend to vary. You'll even find the local version of famous Freeport outfitter L.L. Bean: the three-story **Kittery Trading Post** (301 Rte. 1, 207/439-2700 or 888/587-6246, www.kittery tradingpost.com), a humongous sporting-goods and clothing emporium. Try to avoid the outlets on weekends, when you might need to take a number for the try-on rooms. Most of the minimalls have telephones; several have ATM machines; all have restrooms.

ACCOMMODATIONS

Put a little oooh and aaaah into your touring with a visit to the **Portsmouth Harbor Inn and Spa** (6 Water St., Kittery 03904, 207/439-4040, www.innatportsmouth.com, $145–210). The handsome brick inn, built in 1889, looks out over the Piscataqua River, Portsmouth, and the Portsmouth Naval Shipyard. Five attractive Victorian-style rooms (most with water views) are furnished with antiques and have air-conditioning, TV, and phones. There's an outdoor hot tub, and beach chairs and bicycles are available. Breakfasts are multicourse feasts. Request a back room if you're noise-sensitive, although the air-conditioning camouflages traffic noise in summer. Rooms on the third floor have the best views, but these also have hand-held showers. Now for the aaaah part. The inn also has a full-service spa. Ease the kinks out with a hot stone massage. The inn has lots of intriguing special packages and fair prices. It's an easy walk across the bridge to Portsmouth for plentiful dining options.

FOOD

Lobster and Clams

Fancy dining isn't a Kittery specialty—there's plenty of that within walking distance in Portsmouth (New Hampshire) or driving distance in York. If you came to Maine to eat lobster, though, Kittery has two good spots for a quick fix. Expect to pay market rates at each. **Chauncey Creek Lobster Pier** (16 Chauncey Creek Rd., off Rte. 103, Kittery Point, 207/439-1030, 11 A.M.–8 P.M. mid-May–Columbus Day—closing at 7 P.M. after Labor Day), has the least pretense and the most character. Step up to the window, place your order, take a number, and grab a table (you may need to share) overlooking tidal Chauncey Creek and the woods on the close-in opposite shore. It's a particularly picturesque—and extremely popular—place. Parking is a nightmare. BYOL. Also in Kittery Point is **Cap'n Simeon's Galley** (90 Pepperrell Rd., Rte. 103, Kittery Point, 207/439-3655, 11:30 A.M.–9 P.M. and Sunday brunch 10 A.M.–2 P.M.). Fresh seafood (mostly fried, albeit in vegetable oil) and a spectacular view are the draws here. Nothing particularly unusual—just decent cooking at reasonable prices and a casual atmosphere conducive to bringing the kids. There's entertainment in the lounge Thursday through Sunday nights. The building was the original Frisbee's Store, and some of the beams date back to 1680.

If clams are high on your must-have list, you can't do much better than **Bob's Clam Hut** (315 Rte. 1, Kittery, 207/439-4233, 11 A.M.–8 P.M. Sun.–Thurs., to 9 P.M. Fri. and Sat.), next to the Kittery Trading Post. Using vegetable oil for frying, Bob's turns out everything from scallops to shrimp to calamari to, of course, clams. A clamburger sandwich runs $3.20 with fries; a lobster roll is $10.95. And the tartar sauce is the secret weapon. Unlike most lobster pounds and clam shacks, Bob's is open all year.

Picnic Goodies

What Kittery does have is an abundance of excellent specialty food stores that are perfect for stocking up for a picnic lunch or dinner. Most are along the section of Route 1 between the Portsmouth bridge and the traffic circle.

Three are within steps of each other. At **Beach Pea Baking Co.** (53 Rte. 1, 207/439-3555, 7:30 A.M.–6 P.M. Tues.–Sat.) you can purchase fabulous breads and pastries. Sandwiches are made to order daily 11 A.M.–3 P.M. There's pleasant seating indoors and on a patio. Next door is **Golden Harvest** (7 A.M.–6:30 P.M. Mon.–Sat. and 9 A.M.–6 P.M. Sun.), where you can load up on luscious produce. Across the street is **Terracotta Pasta Co.** (207/475-3025, 10 A.M.–6 P.M. Mon., 9 A.M.–6:30 P.M. Tues.–Sat., and noon–5 P.M. Sun.), where in addition to handmade pastas you'll find salads, soups, sandwiches, and lots of other goodies. Finally, about a half mile or less north is **Enoteca Italiana** (207/439-7216, 10 A.M.–7 P.M. Mon. and Wed.–Sat. and noon–4 P.M. Sun.), which is filled with wine, an extensive selection of cured meats, cheeses, and other gourmet goods.

What's a meal without chocolate? At **Cacao** (64 Government St., just off the town green, 207/438-9001, noon–6 P.M. Tues.–Fri. and 10 A.M.–4 P.M. Sat.), Susan Tuveson handcrafts outrageously decadent chocolates.

In Kittery Point, **Frisbee's Supermarket** (207/439-0014, Mon.–Sat. 7 A.M.–8 P.M., Sun. 8 A.M.–8 P.M.) is an experience in itself. Established in 1828, the store has marginally modernized but still earns its label as North America's oldest family store—run by the fifth generation of Frisbees.

INFORMATION AND SERVICES

Information

The Maine Tourism Association operates a **Maine State Visitor Information Center** (207/439-1319) in Kittery, between Route 1 and I-95, with access from either road. It's chock-full of brochures, has restrooms and a picnic area, and the staff is extremely helpful.

Hospitals

Hospitals serving the region are: **York Hospital** (15 Hospital Dr., York 03909, emergency room 207/351-2157), **Southern Maine Medical**

Center (1 Medical Center Dr., Biddeford 04005, emergency room 207/283-7100), Goodall Hospital (25 June St., Sanford 04073, 207/324-4310).

For minor medical problems, York Hospital's Tel-a-Nurse service (800/283-7234) provides free over-the-phone advice for minor medical problems.

The Yorks

Four villages with distinct personalities—upscale York Harbor, historic York Village, casual York Beach, and semirural Cape Neddick—make up the Town of York. First inhabited by Native Americans, who named it Agamenticus, the area was settled as early as 1624—so history is serious business here. Town high points were its founding, by Sir Ferdinando Gorges, and the arrival of well-to-do vacationers in the 19th century. In between were Indian massacres, economic woes, and population shuffles. The town's winter population explodes in summer (pretty obvious in July and August, when you're searching for a free patch of York Beach sand or a parking place).

History and genealogy buffs can study the headstones in the Old Burying Ground or comb the archives of the Old York Historical Society.

For lighthouse fans, there's Cape Neddick Light Station (Nubble Light) and, six miles offshore, Boon Island. You can rent horses or mountain bikes on Mount Agamenticus, or spend an hour hiking the Cliff Path in York Harbor. For the kids, there's a zoo, a taffymaker, or, of course, the beach.

SIGHTS

🅜 Nubble Light/Sohier Park

The best-known photo op in York is the distinctive 1879 lighthouse known formally as Cape Neddick Light Station and familiarly as "The Nubble." Although there's no access to the lighthouse's island, Sohier Park Welcome Center (Nubble Rd., off Rte. 1A, between Long and Short Sands Beaches,

© TOM NANGLE

Nubble Light, built in 1879, is a York icon.

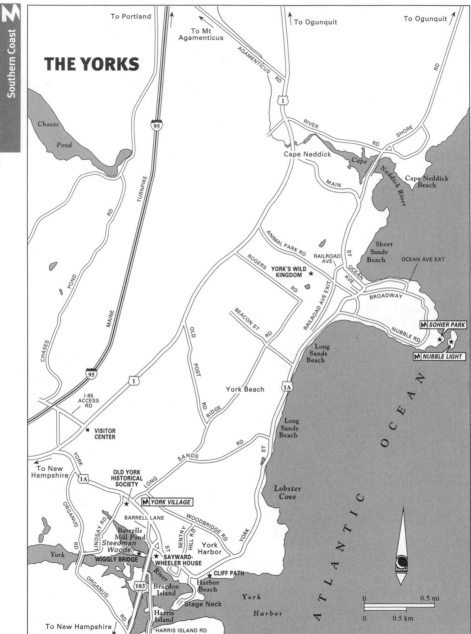

THE YORKS

© TOM NANGLE

York's Sayward-Wheeler House is filled with period furnishings in pristine condition.

York Beach, 207/363-7608, 10 A.M.–8 P.M. daily June–mid-Sept. and weekends in May and to early Oct.) provides the perfect viewpoint (and has restrooms). Parking is limited, but the turnover is fairly good. It's not a bad idea, however, to walk from the Long Sands parking area or come by bike, even though the road has inadequate shoulders. Weekdays, this is also a popular spot for scuba divers.

York Village

The Old York Historical Society (207 York St., P.O. Box 312, York 03909, 207/363-4974, www.oldyork.org) is the driving force behind this collection of eight colonial and post-colonial buildings (plus a research library) open throughout the summer (10 A.M.–5 P.M. Mon.–Sat. early June–early Oct., $10 adults or $5 one building, $8 seniors or $4 one building, $5 children 4–16 or $3 one building). Start at the Jefferds' Tavern Visitor Center (5 Lindsay Rd., York), where you'll need to pick up tickets for visiting. Don't miss the Old Burying Ground, dating from 1735, across the street (rubbings are a no-no). Nearby are the Old Gaol and the School House (both fun for kids), Ramsdell

House, and the Emerson-Wilcox House. About one-half mile down Lindsay Road, on the York River, are the John Hancock Warehouse and the George Marshall Store Gallery (140 Lindsay Rd.; operated in the summer as a respected contemporary-art gallery); across the river is the Elizabeth Perkins House. Antiques buffs shouldn't miss the Wilcox and Perkins Houses. These two are open by guided tour, while other buildings are self-guided. Visit some or all of the buildings, at your own pace—no one leads you from one to another. In July and August, an architectural walking tour of York Village begins at 10 A.M. every Wednesday ($2 pp; meet at Jefferds' Tavern). Across from the jail is the well-stocked Museum Shop (196 York St.). Note: Some sites you can walk to from the tavern, others you'll need a car to reach, and parking may be limited.

Sayward-Wheeler House

Owned by the Boston-based Society for the Preservation of New England Antiquities (SPNEA), the 1718 Sayward-Wheeler House (9 Barrell Lane Extension, York Harbor, 207/384-2454, www.historicnewengland.org, $5) occupies a prime site at the edge of York Harbor. Open the first Saturday of the month, from June through October, with tours on the hour 11 A.M.–4 P.M. In the house are lots of period furnishings—all in pristine condition. Take Route 1A to Lilac Lane (Route 103) to Barrell Lane, then to Barrell Lane Extension.

Talk to the Animals

More than 250 creatures—including tigers, zebras, llamas, deer, lions, elephants, and monkeys—find a home at **York's Wild Kingdom** (102 Railroad Ave., off Rte. 1, York Beach, 207/363-4911 or 800/456-4911, www.yorkzoo.com, 10 A.M.–5 P.M., to 6 P.M. in July and Aug., with the amusement park open until 9:30 P.M. Memorial Day to Labor Day). It's not what you'd call a state-of-the-art zoo, but it keeps the kids entertained. Elephant shows and other animal "events" occur three times daily in July and August—usually at noon, 2 P.M., and 4 P.M., but the schedule is posted, or you can call ahead. Between the zoo and the amusement-park rides, it's easy to spend a day here—and there are snack bars on the grounds. Admission (covering the zoo and some of the rides) is $16.25 adults, $12.75 children 4–10, $3.50 for ages 3 and younger. Zoo-only admission is $12.50 adults, $8.25 or $1 kids.

Spooky Sightseeing

Flickering candles and a black-hooded guide get you right in the spirit of things during imaginative evening candlelight walking tours of historic York village. **Ghostly Tours** (250 York St., Rte. 1A, York 03909, 207/363-0000, www.ghostlytours.com) specializes in ghost stories and 18th-century folklore during its 45-minute meanders through burial grounds in the oldest part of town. (Even the phone number is kinda weird.) Cost is $10 pp. To continue the theme, **Gravestone Artwear** (at the same address, 207/351-1434 or 800/564-4310) carries wizard capes, gravestone rubbing kits (but don't try them out in the Old Burying Ground), notecards, T-shirts, and lots of other cemetery-centered items.

Wild About Wildlife

Although not really geared for visitors, about a

half dozen times during summer, **The Center for Wildlife** (P.O. Box 620, Cape Neddick, 207/361-1400, www.yorkcenterforwildlife.org) opens its doors for one-hour public tours, and in early September, it holds an annual open house. The center provides care and shelter for sick and injured animals, then releases those able to survive back into the wild. More than 1,500 animals are brought to the center each year for rehabilitative care. Call or check the website to see if a tour or open house fits with your visit. If not, consider the center's popular Adopt a Raptor program, which helps support the care of seven non-releasable raptors residing at the center. Prices range from $25 for a kestrel to $75 for a saw-whet owl.

RECREATION

Walk the Walks

Next to Harbor Beach, near the Stage Neck Inn, a sign marks the beginning of the **Cliff Path,** an ill-maintained walkway worth taking for its dramatic harbor views in the shadow of elegant summer cottages.

A less strenuous route is known variously as the **Shore Path, Harbor Walk,** or **Fisherman's Walk,** running west along the harbor and river from Stage Neck Road (next to Edwards' Harborside Inn) and passing the Sayward-Wheeler House before crossing the tiny, green-painted Wiggly Bridge leading into the **Steedman Woods** preserve. Carry binoculars for good boat-watching and birding in the 16-acre preserve, owned by the Old York Historical Society. A one-mile double-loop trail takes less than an hour of easy strolling.

Mount Agamenticus

Drive to the summit of Mount Agamenticus ("The Big A") and you're at York County's highest point. It's only 692 feet, but on a clear day you'll have panoramic views of ocean, lakes, woods, and sometimes the White Mountains. A billboard map of the hiking-trail network and a curious memorial to St. Aspinquid, a 17th-century Algonquian Indian leader, are at the top. Also here are riding stables, offering trail rides Memorial Day to mid-September. Mountain

© TOM NANGLE

The Wiggly Bridge leads to York's Steedman Woods preserve, a fine place for an easy walk or for bird watching.

biking is also hugely popular on Agamenticus. Take a picnic, a kite, and binoculars. In the fall, if the wind's from the northwest, watch for migrating hawks; in winter, bring a sled for the best downhill run in southern Maine. Contact the **York Parks and Recreation Department** (207/363-1040) for info about the trail rides and other activities at the mountain park. From Route 1 in Cape Neddick, take Mountain Road (also called Agamenticus Road) 4.2 miles west to the access road.

Golf
The **Ledges Golf Club** (1 Ledges Dr., off Rte. 91, York, 207/351-9999, www.ledgesgolf.com) is an 18-hole course with daily public tee times.

Swimming
Sunbathing and swimming are big draws in York, with four beaches of varying sizes and accessibility. Bear in mind that traffic can be gridlocked along the beachfront (Route 1A) in midsummer, so it may take longer than you expect to get anywhere. **Lifeguards** are on duty mid-June to Labor Day 9:30 A.M.–4 P.M. at Short Sands Beach, Long Sands Beach, and Harbor Beach. Bathhouses at Long Sands and Short Sands are open daily 9 A.M.–7 P.M. in midsummer. The biggest parking space (metered) is at Long Sands, but that 1.5-mile beach also draws the most customers. Scarcest parking is at Harbor Beach, near the Stage Neck Inn, and at Cape Neddick (Passaconaway) Beach, near the Ogunquit town line.

Bikes and Scooters
Rent a bike from **Berger's Bike Shop** (241 York St., York, 207/363-4070) and you'll probably get around faster in July and August than you would by car.

Another choice is **Beached Wheels** (52 Main St., Rte. 1A, York, 207/363-8021, www.beachedwheels.com), which rents scooters and bikes. Scooters are $25 single or $45 double for the first hour. Bikes are $5 per hour or $25 per day single, $10 per hour or $50 per day tandem. The shop has another outlet in Ogunquit (207/646-4166).

Sea Kayaking
Kayak rentals are available for $30 a day single, $45

double, from **Excursions: Coastal Maine Outfitting Company** (1399 Rte. 1, Cape Neddick, 207/363-0181, www.excursionsinmaine.com), owned by Mike Sullivan and Scott Leighton. Or sign up for one of their half-day tours: $55 (afternoon) or $60 (morning, with lunch). An overnight camping excursion, with meals, is $225.

Harbor Adventures (York Harbor, 207/363-8466, www.harboradventures.com) offers guided sea kayaking trips from Kittery through Kennebunkport. A two-hour harbor tour is $39. A half-day tour is $53. A sunset tour is $32, and a full moon paddle is $40.

Scuba and Surfing

York Beach Scuba (19 Railroad Ave., P.O. Box 850, York Beach 03910, 207/363-3330), a source for rentals, air, and trips, is conveniently situated not far from Sohier Park, a popular dive site. For surfing information, lessons, or rentals, call **Liquid Dreams Surf Shop** (171 Long Beach Ave., York, 207/351-2545).

Fishing

The local expert on fly-fishing, spin fishing, and conventional tackle is **Eldredge Bros. Guide Service** (1480 Rte. 1, Cape Neddick, 207/373-9269, www.eldredgeflyshop.com). Guided trips for one or two anglers begin at $200 for four hours.

SHOPPING

York Village Marketplace (211 York St., Rte. 1A, York Village, 207/363-4830) is a three-level emporium based in a restored 1834 church. There's lots of tasteful stuff, with an emphasis on antiques; bet you won't leave empty-handed.

For quilts or quilting supplies, head to **Knight's Quilt Shop** (1901 Rte. 1, Cape Neddick, 207/361-2500). You'll find an extensive and well-chosen selection of quilts and other handcrafted items as well as quilting supplies.

Tony Sienicki and Jerry Rippetoe have turned their four-acre gardens into **TJ's at the Sign of the Goose** (1287 Rte 1, Cape Neddick, 207/363-5673), a gallery of designer gardenware, such as urns, birdhouses, sculptures, and other delights.

ENTERTAINMENT

Live Music

Inn on the Blues (7 Ocean Ave., York Beach, 207/351-3221, www.inontheblues.com) has live music (acoustic, blues, reggae) every night but Monday during the summer. If you want to be close to both the music and the beach, consider booking one of the suites upstairs ($155–390).

Free concerts are often held at the **Ellis Park Gazebo,** from early July to early September, usually 7–9 P.M.

FESTIVALS AND EVENTS

Each year, the Old York Historical Society invites decorators to transform a local house for the **Decorator Show House,** culminating in an open house from mid-July to mid-August.

From late July into early August, the **York Days** festivities enliven the town for 10 days with concerts, dances, walking tours, a road race, sandcastle contests, antique and art shows, a dog show, fireworks, a parade, and public suppers.

York Village's **Annual Harvestfest** takes place 10 A.M.–4 P.M. the weekend after Columbus Day in October and combines colonial crafts and cooking demonstrations, hayrides, museum tours, entertainment for adults and kids, and an ox roast with beanhole beans. This is one of the town's most popular events; most activities are free.

The annual **Lighting of the Nubble,** in late November, includes cookies, hot chocolate, music, and an appearance by Santa Claus. The best part, though, is seeing the lighthouse glowing for the holidays.

ACCOMMODATIONS
York Harbor

All of the York Harbor lodgings described are within easy walking distance of Harbor Beach.

B&Bs: Tanglewood Hall (611 York St., P.O. Box 490, York Harbor 03911, 207/351-1075, www.tanglewoodhall.com) has a gracious country-inn feel in an in-town setting. Relax on the broad veranda (or enjoy your Big Breakfast there) and you'll understand. Built in 1889, it served as the summer home of Jimmy and Tommy Dorsey. In the spring of 2000, Bill and Bonnie Alstrom bought this former 15-room "designer show house," retaining some of the decorators' intriguing features (wonderful painted floors) and adding their own unique touches (a tranquil meditation corner). Five rooms and a suite have lots of antiques, featherbeds, robes, air-conditioning, and journals for comments; some have gas fireplaces. Rates are $150–225 d. Open May–October.

Since 1984, hospitable Sue Antal has operated the **Inn at Harmon Park** (415 York St., P.O. Box 495, York Harbor 03911, 207/363-2031, www.yorkme.org/inns/harmonpark.html), a 14-room "cottage" just a block from the water. Having run the chamber of commerce and devoted many hours to community organizations, Sue's a great touring resource. (She's also a justice of the peace, with a price that's right and a long string of weddings under her belt.) In 2000, she turned the tables at her B&B: it's open September through mid-June rather than during the summer. Four comfortable guest rooms and a suite have private baths. Rates are $79–99 d ($129 d for the suite). Breakfast is a creative treat, sometimes served on the porch. No credit cards.

Hosts Donna and Paul Archibald have turned Fannie Chapman's 1889 summer cottage into the elegant and romantic **M Chapman Cottage** (370 York St., P.O. Box 575, York Harbor 03911, 207/363-2059 or 877/363-2059, www.chapmancottagebandb.com, $150–250), a truly special retreat. Rooms are huge and plush, with air-conditioning and spacious baths; most have Jacuzzis and fireplaces (some in the bathrooms), a few have private decks and harbor views. The pampering includes a welcome fruit basket, fresh flowers, chocolate truffles, bathrobes, hors d'oeuvres, and evening aperitifs.

Inviting Adirondack-style chairs accent the green lawn rolling down to the harbor at **Edwards' Harborside Inn** (Stage Neck Rd., P.O. Box 866, York Harbor 03911, 207/363-3037, www.edwardsharborside.com, $120–180 rooms, $270 and higher suites). Many of the 10 rooms

can be combined into suites, and most have water views. All have TV, phone, air-conditioning, and private and semiprivate baths. Watch the sunset from the inn's pier or stroll the adjacent shorefront paths or just settle into one of those shorefront chairs and watch the world go by. A buffet breakfast is served in the water-view sun porch.

Full-Service Inns: M York Harbor Inn (Rte. 1A, P.O. Box 573, York Harbor 03911, 207/363-5119 or 800/343-3869, www.yorkharborinn.com) is an accommodating in-town spot with a country-inn flavor and a wide variety of room and package-plan options throughout the year. Accommodations are in four buildings. The oldest section dates from the 17th century. The 34 rooms in the Main Inn and Yorkshire building are the most moderate. All have phones and air-conditioning; some have four-poster beds, fireplaces, and whirlpools; many have water views ($139–209 d, including generous continental breakfast). Two adjacent properties have resident innkeepers. **Harbor Cliffs Inn**, a lovely old home with the flavor and service of a B&B, has seven desirable rooms (five with ocean views, several with fireplaces); rate range is $229–299 d. **Harbor Hill Inn** is the most luxurious. Its seven rooms have king-size beds, gas stoves, whirlpool tubs, ocean views, and heated tile bathrooms ($289–329). Be forewarned that Harbor Cliffs is across from a social club, where weekends might include loud wedding parties and bands. The premises also hold an excellent dining room and casual pub.

You can't miss the **Stage Neck Inn** (100 Stage Neck Rd., P.O. Box 70, York Harbor 03911, 207/363-3850 or 800/340-9901, www.stageneck.com), occupying its own private peninsula overlooking York Harbor. Modern, resort-style facilities include two pools (one indoors), tennis courts, golf privileges, fitness center, and spectacular views from balconies and terraces. The formal Harbor Porches restaurant (no jeans; entrées $21–30) and the casual Sandpiper Bar & Grille are open to the public. Peak season rates are $235–345 d mid-May through Labor Day (special packages and meal plans are available). Open all year.

York Beach

Hotel and Motel: For more than 150 years, **The Union Bluff** (8 Beach St., P.O. Box 1860, York Beach, 207/363-1333 or 800/833-0721, www.unionbluff.com, $129–279) has stood sentry, like a fortress, overlooking Short Sands Beach. Many of the 63 rooms have ocean views. All have TV, air-conditioning, and phones; some have fireplaces, Jacuzzis, or ocean-view decks. Furnishings are modern motel style. The Beach Street Grill dining room and a pub serving lighter fare are also on the premises. Best deals are the packages, which include breakfast and dinner, with rates beginning at $195 d for one night. The hotel and pub are open year-round; the restaurant is seasonal.

B&Bs: Everything's casual and flowers are everywhere at the brightly painted **Katahdin Inn** (11 Ocean Ave. Extension, P.O. Box 193, York Beach 03910, 207/363-1824 or 207/363-9625 off-season), overlooking the breakers of Short Sands Beach. Eleven first-, second-, and third-floor rooms (eight with water views) have lots of four-poster beds and shared baths. Breakfast is not included, but coffee is always available, the rooms have refrigerators, and several eateries are nearby. Rooms cost $85–105 d. Open mid-May through October.

Just up the street and similar in style is the **Sand and Surf** (58 Ocean Ave. Extension, York Beach 03910, 207/363-2554 in season, 860/872-2200 off season, www.sandandsurf.islovely.com, $76–118), another 19th-century guesthouse. Most rooms have shared baths and a decidedly old-fashioned decor. A full breakfast is served buffet-style.

Not oceanfront, but offering ocean views from many rooms and just a short walk from Short Sands Beach, is Barbara and Michael Sheff's **Candleshop Inn** (44 Freeman St., P.O. Box 1216, York Beach 03910, 207/363-4087 or 888/363-4087, www.candleshopinn.com, $90–145). The 10 guest rooms (private and shared baths) are decorated in a country cottage style, with area rugs, painted furniture, and florals; many are set up for families. The day begins with a vegetarian breakfast and a stretch-and-relaxation class. Spa services, including massage and Reiki, are available on-site by appointment.

Condominium Suites: Fabulously sited on the oceanfront and overlooking The Nubble, the high-end **ViewPoint** (229 Nubble Rd., York Beach 03910, 207/363-2661, www.viewpointhotel.com, $325–695 for 1–3 bedrooms per night, $2,000–3,600 per week) comprises luxuriously appointed one-, two-, and three-bedroom suites. All have gas fireplaces, fully equipped kitchens, washer/dryer units, TV/VCRs, phones, private patios, porches, or decks, and daily maid service is included. Amenities include an outdoor heated pool, grilling area, gardens, and playground.

Seasonal Rentals

Several companies manage week- or month-long rental properties, usually houses or condos. Weekly rentals begin and end on Saturday. Best is **Seaside Vacation Rentals** (Meadowbrook Plaza, 647 Rte. 1, P.O. Box 2000, York 03909, 207/363-1825, fax 207/351-1091, www.seasiderentals.com), a longtime family-operated firm with more than 500 properties in York, Ogunquit, Wells, Kennebunk, and Kittery.

CAMPING

Dixon's Coastal Maine Campground (1740 Rte. 1, Cape Neddick 03902, 207/363-3626, www.dixonscampground.com, $26–32) has more than 100 well-spaced sites on 40 wooded and open acres. It can accommodate tents and small RVs. Electric and water hookups are available. Facilities include a playground and a good-sized outdoor-heated pool.

The waterfront **Cape Neddick Oceanside Campground** (Shore Rd., Cape Neddick, 207/363-4366) has 80 tight sites under towering pines at the water's edge. It's across the street from the Cape Neddick Lobster House and a pleasant stroll into York Beach. Trailers and tents only, no RVs. Sites are $35.

FOOD

Breakfast, Lunch, and Miscellany

Breakfast and lunch, with an emphasis on fresh pastries and homemade sandwiches, are served at **Carla's Bakery and Café** (241 York St., York Village, 207/3633-4637, 7 A.M.–4 P.M. Mon.–Fri., to 1 P.M. Sat.). Lunch, served 11 A.M.–2 P.M., includes sandwiches, wraps, a protein salad, and special entrées such as blue cheese meatloaf and Mexican pie. Nothing is fancy, but everything's good.

Both *Gourmet* and *Saveur* know where to get dogs. Sometimes the line runs right out the door of the low-ceilinged, reddish-brown roadside shack that houses local institution **Flo's Steamed Dogs** (Rte. 1, opposite the Mountain Road turnoff, Cape Neddick 03902). Founder Flo Stacy died at age 92 in June 2000, but her legend and her family live on. No menu here—just steamed Schultz wieners, buns, chips, beverages, and an attitude. The secret? The spicy, sweet-sour hot-dog sauce (allegedly once sought by the H. J. Heinz corporation, but the proprietary Stacy family isn't telling or selling). The cognoscenti know to order their dogs only with mayonnaise and the special sauce—nothing heretical like ketchup or mustard. Open all year Thursday–Tuesday 11 A.M.–3 P.M., and not a minute later.

See those people with their faces pressed to the glass? They're all watching the taffymakers inside **The Goldenrod** (2 Railroad Ave., York Beach 03910, 207/363-2621), where machines spew out 180 Goldenrod Kisses a minute, 65 tons a year—and have been at it since 1896. (The shop also accepts mail orders.) The Goldenrod is an old-fashioned place, with a tearoom, gift shop, old-fashioned soda fountain (135 ice cream flavors), and casual dining room, with equally old-fashioned prices. Open for breakfast (8 A.M.), lunch, and dinner late May to Columbus Day.

It's hard to know whether Food or Shopping is the right category for **Stonewall Kitchen** (Stonewall Ln., York 03909, 207/351-2712 or 800/207-5267, www.stonewallkitchen.com). This phenomenally successful company has mushroomed from a tiny farmers'-market gig to an award-winning year-round operation creating more than 120 ultimately imaginative condiments and other food products. The packages are as outstanding as the tastes. The headquarters building—including a handsome shop with tasting areas and a "viewing gallery" where you can watch it all happen—is next to the Yorks Chamber of Commerce building, on Route 1. Go hungry: there's also an excellent café on the premises, open 8 A.M.–6 P.M. Monday–Saturday (and for dinner Thurs.–Sat.) and 9 A.M.–6 P.M. Sunday for breakfast, lunch, and dinner ($11–15). Dine in or on the patio or pick up something to go.

Much simpler is the **Gateway Farmers Market** (Yorks Chamber of Commerce Visitor Center, Rte. 1, York, 9 A.M.–noon Sat., mid-June–mid-Oct.). Stop in and stock up for a picnic. If you still need more, head next door to Stonewall Kitchen.

Burgers, Pizza, and Pub Fare

The York Harbor Inn's **Ship's Cellar Pub** (11:30 A.M.–12:30 A.M. Mon.–Sat. and 4 P.M.–midnight Sun.) is a popular alternative to the fine dining upstairs. On the menu are soups, sandwiches, and salads as well as heftier entrées ($14–20) such as chicken marsala and pan-roasted swordfish. The food's good; the service is so-so. The pub doubles as a favorite local watering hole, with live music Wednesday–Sunday. Happy hour, with free munchies, is 4–6 P.M. and draws a raucous local crowd.

Ruby's Genuine Wood Grill (433 Rte. 1, a mile south of the I-95 exit, York 03909, 207/363-7980, 11:30 A.M.–10 P.M., to 11 P.M. Fri. and Sat.) is a popular place with a huge menu. The wood-fired grill does a great job with some intriguing pizza combos (pulled pork and barbecue sauce, for instance, $9.95) and entrées ranging from St. Louis ribs ($13.95) to fajitas ($11.95) to mahimahi ($12.95). Pastas, sandwiches, salads, and burgers fill out the menu. Lots of variety and flair here. In nice weather, opt for the enclosed deck, where there's often live music Saturday nights. In summer, Ruby's is open daily for dinner.

Wild Willy's (765 Rte. 1, York, 207/3363-9924, 11 A.M.–7 P.M. Mon.–Thurs., to 8 P.M. Fri. and Sat.) has turned burgers into an art form. More than a dozen burgers, all made from certified Angus beef, are available, from the classic Willy burger ($4.85) to the Rio Grande, with roasted green chiles from New Mexico and cheddar cheese ($4.95). Chicken sandwiches, steak chili, fries, and frappes are also served, as are beer and wine.

Casual to Fine Dining

Don't let the strip mall location deter you from sampling **M J. Ellen's Café and Wine Bar** (647 Rte. 1, in Meadowbrook Plaza, York, 207/363-3571, 11:30 A.M.–2:30 P.M. and 5–10 P.M. Tues.–Sat.). Inside it's another world altogether. More than 75 wines, most less than $30, are listed, with many available by the glass. Dinner begins with a delicious house-made tapenade that sets the stage for the excellent Mediterranean fare (entrées $15–28). There's often light entertainment in the bar.

The **Clay Hill Farm** (on the York-Ogunquit town line, 220 Clay Hill Rd., Cape Neddick 03902, 207/361-2272) is an attractive country-inn type of restaurant two miles west of Route 1. It's convenient from both Ogunquit and York. Predictably good regional American entrées are in the $17–26 range; daily specials tend to be more imaginative. Service is not in keeping with the setting. Allow time to wander the beautifully landscaped grounds, popular for weddings. Open all year: daily 5:30–9 P.M. in summer; closed Monday–Wednesday in winter. Reservations are essential in July and August.

Serving "food that loves you back," **Frankie & Johnny's Natural Foods** (1594 Rte. 1 North, Cape Neddick 03902, 207/363-1909) has an eclectic menu ranging from bean-curd satay, vegan delight, and Cajun crab cakes to toasted peppercorn-seared sushi-grade tuna and smoked mozzarella ravioli. Best vegetarian menu in York—in a funky, roadside place where you'll need a dinner reservation on summer weekends. No credit cards ("plastic is not natural"). BYOL. Open for dinner 5 P.M.–close Wednesday–Sunday in July and August, Thursday–Sunday in spring and fall.

Just follow your nose to **Mimmo's Ristorante** (243 Long Sands Rd., York Beach 03910, 207/363-3807)—the scent of garlic'll meet you halfway down the beach. The well-prepared Italian menu is moderately priced (entrées $16–20). BYOL. It's wildly popular, so reservations are essential in midsummer (try for the patio). Open 5–10 P.M., and for breakfast (7 A.M.–noon) in summer.

The glass-walled dining room at the **York Harbor Inn** (11:30 A.M.–2:30 P.M. and 5:30–9:30 P.M.

and Sun. brunch, 8:30 A.M.–2:30 P.M.) gets high marks for creative cuisine (the head chef has been here since 1982), so reservations are essential. Entrées run $21–35, but if you're seated before 6 P.M. you can order the early bird special: a three-course meal with choice of six entrées plus salad and dessert for $18.

Surf and Turf

Steaks are the specialty at **Talpey's Tavern** (Rte. 1, Cape Neddick, 207/351-1145, 4–9:30 P.M., bar to 11:30 P.M.), but you also can get seafood, chicken, and, of course, lobster, all served in a pleasant dining room by an efficient staff.

Since 1972, **The Lobster Barn** (Rte. 1, York 03909, 207/363-4721 or 800/341-4849, 4–9 P.M. Mon.–Fri., noon–9 P.M. Sat. and Sun.) has been drawing a devoted local clientele to its roadside site. All the usual suspects are here—fried clams, baked haddock, etc.—plus good steaks. BYOL. Open daily mid-May–October for lunch and dinner; open weekends off-season. From Memorial Day weekend to Labor Day, its super-casual outdoor area, **Lobster in the Rough,** is a good option, and there's a playground for the kids.

Before heading for the **Cape Neddick Lobster Pound/Harborside Restaurant** (Shore Road, Cape Neddick 03902, 207/363-5471), check the tide calendar. The rustic shingled building dripping with lobster-pot buoys has a spectacular harbor view (especially from the deck) at high tide, a rather drab one at low tide, so plan accordingly. Bouillabaisse with half a lobster goes for $23; other entrées are $15–24. Open daily at noon. Entertainment Friday and Saturday in summer, beginning at 10 P.M.

INFORMATION AND SERVICES

Information

For York area information, head for the Shingle-style palace of the **Yorks Chamber of Commerce** (1 Stonewall Ln., off Rte. 1, York 03909, 207/363-4422, www.gatewaytomaine.org), at I-95's York exit. Inside the elegant hillside building, you'll find racks of brochures, restrooms, and a cheerful staff. Open daily in summer.

Hospitals

Hospitals serving the region are: **York Hospital** (15 Hospital Dr., York 03909, emergency room 207/351-2157), **Southern Maine Medical Center** (1 Medical Center Dr., Biddeford 04005, emergency room 207/283-7100), **Goodall Hospital** (25 June St., Sanford 04073, 207/324-4310).

For minor medical problems, York Hospital's **Tel-a-Nurse** service, 800/283-7234, provides free over-the-phone advice for minor medical problems.

Getting Around

The **York Trolley** (207/748-3030, www.yorktrolley.com) provides a number of options for getting around the Yorks. A York tour, available Monday and Friday, departs hourly 10 A.M.–4 P.M. with stops at Short Sands, York Village, York Harbor, and Nubble Lighthouse. A day pass is $7 adult, $4 kids 3–10. On Tuesdays and Thursdays, the trolley travels to Ogunquit and Perkins Cove hourly 10 A.M.–9 P.M. A day pass is $5 adults, $3 kids. On Wednesdays and rainy days, the trolley heads to the Kittery Outlet Malls 10 A.M.–7 P.M. for $5 adult, $3 kids. All trolleys begin at the Ellis Park Beach Loop, Short Sands, and operate late June through Labor Day. In the fall, three scenic tours are offered, each lasting about 2.5 hours and departing from the Short Sands beach parking lot twice daily for $10 pp.

Ogunquit and Wells

Ogunquit has been a holiday destination since the indigenous residents named it "beautiful place by the sea." What's the appeal? An unparalleled, unspoiled beach, several top-flight (albeit pricey) restaurants, a dozen art galleries, and a respected art museum with a view second to none. The town has been home to an art colony attracting the glitterati of the painting world starting with Charles Woodbury in the late 1880s. The summertime crowds continue, multiplying the minuscule year-round population of just under 1,400. Besides the beach, the most powerful magnet is Perkins Cove, a working fishing enclave that looks more like a movie set. Best way to approach the cove is via trolley-bus or on foot, along the shoreline Marginal Way from downtown Ogunquit—midsummer parking in the cove ($3 per hour) is madness.

Wells, once the parent of Ogunquit and since 1980 its immediate neighbor to the north, was settled in 1640. Nowadays, it's best known as a long, skinny, family-oriented community with about 10,300 year-round residents, seven miles of splendid beachfront, and heavy-duty commercial activity: lots of antiques and used-book shops, and a handful of factory outlets. It also claims two spectacular nature preserves worth a drive from anywhere. At the southern end of Wells, abutting Ogunquit, is Moody, an enclave named after 18th-century settler Samuel Moody and even rating its own post office.

If swimming isn't your top priority, plan to visit Ogunquit and Wells after Labor Day, when crowds let up, lodging rates drop dramatically, weather is still good, and you can find restaurant seats and parking spots.

SIGHTS

M Ogunquit Museum of American Art

Not many museums can boast a view as stunning as the one at the Ogunquit Museum of American Art (OMAA, 543 Shore Rd., P.O. Box 815, Ogunquit 03907, 207/646-4909), nor can many communities boast such renown as a summer art colony. Overlooking Narrow Cove, 1 4 miles south of downtown Ogunquit, the museum prides itself on its distinguished permanent collection—works of Marsden Hartley, Rockwell Kent, Walt Kuhn, Henry Strater, and Thomas Hart Benton, among others. Newest feature (since July 1996) is the 1,400-square-foot Barn Gallery Associates Wing. Special exhibits are mounted each summer, when there is an extensive series of lectures (Wednesday evenings at 6 P.M.), concerts, and other programs. OMAA has a well-stocked gift shop, wheelchair access, and landscaped grounds

© TOM NANGLE

Lobsterboats and excursion boats fill Ogunquit's Perkins Cove.

with sculptures, a pond, and manicured lawns. Admission is $5 adults, $4 seniors, $3 students, and free for kids under 12. Open 10:30 A.M.–5 P.M. Monday–Saturday, 2–5 P.M. Sunday July–mid-October. Closed Labor Day and for four days in mid-August for rehanging.

The Marginal Way

No visit to Ogunquit is complete without a leisurely stroll along the Marginal Way, the mile-long footpath edging the ocean from Shore Road (by the Sparhawk Resort) to Perkins Cove. It's been a must-walk since Josiah Chase gifted the right-of-way to the town in the 1920s. The best times to appreciate this mile-long, shrub-lined, shorefront walkway in Ogunquit are early morning or when everyone's at the beach. En route you'll find tidepools, intriguing rock formations, crashing surf, pocket beaches, benches (though the walking's a cinch, even partially wheelchair-accessible), and a marker listing the day's high and low tides. When the surf's up, keep a close eye on the kids—the sea has no mercy. A midpoint access is at Israel's Head (behind a sewage plant masquerading as a tiny

lighthouse), but getting a parking space is pure luck. Best advice is to stroll the Marginal Way to Perkins Cove for lunch, shopping, and maybe a boat trip, then return to downtown Ogunquit via trolley-bus.

Perkins Cove

Turn-of-the-20th-century photos show Ogunquit's Perkins Cove lined with gray-shingled shacks used by a hardy colony of local fishermen—fellows who headed offshore to make a tough living in little boats. They'd hardly recognize it today. Though the cove remains a working lobster-fishing harbor, several old shacks have been reincarnated as boutiques and restaurants, and photographers go crazy shooting the quaint inlet spanned by a little pedestrian drawbridge. In midsummer, you'll waste precious time looking for one of the three or four dozen parking places ($3 an hour), so take advantage of the trolley-bus service.

Wells National Estuarine Research Reserve

Known locally as Laudholm Farm (the name of the restored 19th-century visitor center), Wells

National Estuarine Research Reserve (342 Laudholm Farm Rd., Wells 04090, 207/646-1555, fax 207/646-2930, www.wellsreserve.org) occupies 1,690 acres of woods, beach, and coastal salt marsh on the southern boundary of the Rachel Carson National Wildlife Refuge, just one-half mile east of Route 1. Seven miles of trails wind through the property. The Salt Marsh Loop is the best trail, with a boardwalk section leading to an overlook with panoramic views of the marsh and Little River inlet. Another winner is the Barrier Beach Walk, a 1.3-mile round-trip that goes through multiple habitats all the way to beautiful Laudholm Beach. Allow 1.5 hours for either; you could also combine the two. Lyme disease ticks have been found here, so tuck pant legs into socks and stick to the trails (some of which are wheelchair-accessible). The informative exhibits in the visitor center (open 10 A.M.–4 P.M. Mon.–Sat. and noon–4 P.M. Sun. May–Oct., weekdays Oct.–March) make a valuable prelude to enjoying the reserve. An extensive program schedule, April–November, includes lectures, nature walks, and children's programs. Reservations are required for some programs. Trails are accessible 7 A.M.–dusk. In July and August, and May, June, September, and October weekends, there's a $2 adult, $1 ages 6–16.

Rachel Carson National Wildlife Refuge

Ten chunks of coastal Maine real estate—now more than 4,700 acres, eventually 7,600 acres, between Kittery Point and Cape Elizabeth—make up this refuge (Rte. 9, 321 Port Rd., Wells 04090, 207/646-9226, http://rachelcarson.fws .gov/), headquartered at the northern edge of Wells, near the Kennebunkport town line. Pick up a *Carson Trail Guide* at the refuge office (parking space is very limited) and follow the mile-long walkway (wheelchair-accessible) past tidal creeks, salt pans, and salt marshes. It's a birder's paradise during migration seasons. As with the Laudholm Farm reserve, the Lyme disease tick has been found here, so tuck pant legs into socks and stick to the trail. Office hours are weekdays

Laudholm Farm is home to the Wells National Estuarine Research Reserve, with exhibits, programs, and trails.

8 A.M.–4:30 P.M., year-round; trail access: sunrise to sunset, year-round. Leashed pets are allowed.

Ogunquit Arts Collaborative Gallery

Closer to downtown Ogunquit is the Ogunquit Arts Collaborative Gallery, also known as the Barn Gallery (Shore Rd. and Bourne Ln., P.O. Box 529, Ogunquit 03907, 207/646-8400), featuring the works of member artists—an impressive group. The OAC is the showcase for the Ogunquit Art Association, established by Charles Woodbury, who was inspired to open an art school in Perkins Cove in the late 19th century. Special programs throughout the season include concerts, workshops, gallery talks, and an art auction. The gallery is open 11 A.M.–5 P.M. Monday–Saturday and 1–5 P.M. Sunday late May–October 1. Admission is free.

Wells Auto Museum

More than 80 vintage vehicles, plus a collection of old-fashioned nickelodeons (bring nickels and dimes; they work), are jam-packed into the Wells

Auto Museum (Rte. 1, Wells 04090, 207/646-9064). From the outside, it just looks like a big warehouse, right on the highway. Admission is $5 adults, $2 children 6–12. Open 10 A.M.–5 P.M. daily Memorial Day to Columbus Day.

Local History Museums

Ogunquit's history is preserved in the **Ogunquit Heritage Museum** (86 Obeds Ln., Dorthea Grant Common, Ogunquit, 207/646-0296, 1–4 P.M. Tues.–Sat.). The museum opened in 2002 in the restored Captain James Winn House, a 1785 cape listed on the National Register. Plans call for the construction of a fishing shack and boat shop to display appropriate exhibits, including an Ogunquit dory.

Right on the historic Post Road that once linked Boston with points north stands the **Historic Meetinghouse Museum** (938 Post Road, Rte. 1, opposite Wells Plaza, P.O. Box 801, Wells 04090, 207/646-4775), a handsome steepled structure on the site of the town's first church (1643). Preserved and maintained by the Historical Society of Wells and Ogunquit, its displays include old photos, ship models, needlecraft, and local memorabilia. On the second floor is a genealogical library where volunteers will help you research your roots (photocopier available). Enter in the rear. Open 10 A.M.–4 P.M. Tuesday–Thursday and 10 A.M.–1 P.M. Saturday June to Columbus Day. Winter hours are 10 A.M.–4 P.M. Wednesday and Thursday.

RECREATION

Beaches

One of Maine's most scenic and unspoiled sandy beachfronts, Ogunquit's 3.5-mile stretch of sand fringed with seagrass is a major magnet for hordes of sunbathers, spectators, swimmers, surfers, and sandcastle-builders. Getting there means crossing the Ogunquit River via one of three access points. For the **Main Beach**—with a spanking new bathhouse and high crowd content—take Beach Street. To reach **Footbridge Beach,** marginally less crowded, either take Ocean Street and the footbridge or take Bourne Avenue to Ocean

Avenue in adjacent Wells and walk back toward Ogunquit. **Moody Beach,** at Wells's southern end, technically is private property—a subject of considerable legal dispute. Lifeguards are on duty all summer at the public beaches, and there are restrooms in all three areas. The beach is free, but parking is not; parking lots charge by the hour ($4 an hour at Main Beach) or the day ($12 a day at Main Beach, Footbridge Beach, and Moody Beach), and they fill up early on warm midsummer days. After 3 P.M., some are free. It's far more sensible to opt for the frequent trolley-buses.

Wells beaches continue where Ogunquit's leave off. **Crescent Beach** (Webhannet Dr. between Eldredge Rd. and Mile Rd.) is the tiniest, with tidepools, no facilities, and limited parking. **Wells Beach** (Mile Rd. to Atlantic Ave.) is the major (and most crowded) beach, with lifeguards, restrooms, and parking. Around the other side of Wells Harbor is **Drakes Island Beach** (take Drakes Island Rd., at the blinking light), a less crowded spot with restrooms and lifeguards. Walk northeast from Drakes Island Beach and you'll eventually reach **Laudholm Beach** (see Wells National Estuarine Research Reserve), with great birding along the way. Summer beach-parking fees in Wells are $7 a day for nonresidents ($17 for an RV); if you're staying longer, a $35 10-visit pass is a better bargain.

Municipal Recreation Areas

On Route 9A, west of I-95 (take Burnt Mill Road), the 70-acre **Wells Recreation Area** (Rte. 9A, 207/646-5826) has four tennis courts, a fitness trail, basketball courts, baseball field, picnic tables, a jogging track, a large playground, and restrooms. Three-acre **Wells Harbor Community Park** (Lower Landing Rd.—turn off Rte. 1 at the fire station) has a playground, restrooms, and a bandstand (Hope Fenderson Hobbs Memorial Gazebo) where frequent concerts are held during the summer. **Ogunquit Recreational Area** (Agamenticus Rd., west of I-95, Ogunquit, 207/646-3032) has three tennis courts.

Bike and Surfboard Rentals

At **Wheels & Waves** (579 Post Rd., Rte. 1, Wells 04090, 207/646-5774, www.wheelsnwaves.com), mountain-bike rentals begin at $25 a day; tandems are $40. Surfboards are $20–40.

Boating Excursions

Depending on your interest, you can go deep-sea fishing or whale-watching or just gawking out of Perkins Cove, Ogunquit. Between April and early November, Captain Tim Tower runs half-day (departing 4 P.M.; $40 pp) and full-day (departing 7 A.M.; $65 pp) **deep-sea-fishing trips** aboard the 40-foot *Bunny Clark* (P.O. Box 837, Ogunquit 03907, 207/646-2214, www.bunny clark.com). Reservations are necessary. Tim has a science degree, so he offers a wealth of marine-biology information. All gear is provided, and the crew'll fillet your catch for you; dress warmly and wear sunblock.

Perkins Cove (Barnacle Billy's Dock) is also home port for the Hubbard family's **Finestkind Cruises** (207/646-5227, www.finestkindcruises .com), offering 1.5-hour, 14-mile Nubble Lighthouse cruises (10 A.M., noon, 2 and 4 P.M. daily; $16 adults, $10 kids) and one-hour cocktail cruises (5:45 P.M. daily; two extra trips in July and Aug.; $11 adults, $7 kids; cash bar) in a sheltered powerboat. A 75-minute breakfast cruise, complete with coffee, juice, and muffin, departs at 9 A.M. daily ($14 adults, $9 kids). The family also does 50-minute lobsterboat trips, 4–6 cruises Monday–Saturday; look and listen—no helping; $11 adults, $7 kids) in a real lobsterboat (no toilets). Also available are 1.75-hour sails aboard *The Cricket*, a locally built wooden sailboat. It departs three times daily and costs $25 pp. High season runs July–Labor Day; limited schedule May, June, September, October. Reservations are advisable but usually unnecessary midweek. No credit cards.

Whale-watching is the specialty of the 40-foot *Deborah Ann* (207/361-9501, www.deborah annwhalewatching.com), departing 8 A.M. and 1:30 P.M. daily from Perkins Cove, afternoon trip only off-season. Trips last 4.5 hours, going 20 or 30 miles offshore; reservations are essential. Dress warmly and don't forget binoculars. If you're especially motion-sensitive, plan ahead with appropriate medication. Cost (no credit cards) is $40 adults, $35 seniors 70 and older, $25 children 12 and under.

Golf

The 18-hole, Donald Ross–designed **Cape Neddick Country Club** (650 Shore Rd., 207/361-2011) is a semiprivate course.

Sea Kayaking

World Within Sea Kayaking (746 Ocean Ave., Wells, 207/646-0455, www.worldwithin.com) has both tours and rentals. Rentals are available to experienced kayakers for $35 half day or $50 full day single, $45 half day or $60 full day tandem. Guided tours begin with one hour of land instruction followed by two hours on the water for $65 pp; advanced tours are $75 pp.

SHOPPING

Antiques and Antiquarian Books

Antiques are a Wells specialty. You'll find more than 50 shops, with a huge range of prices. The majority are on Route 1. **R. Jorgensen Antiques** (502 Post Rd., Rte. 1, R.R. 1, Box 1125, Wells 04090, 207/646-9444) is a phenomenon in itself, filling 11 showrooms in two buildings with European and American 18th- and 19th-century furniture and accessories. **MacDougall-Gionet Antiques and Associates** (2104 Post Rd., Rte. 1, Wells 04090, 207/646-3531) has been here since the mid-1960s, and its reputation is stellar. The 65-dealer shop—in an 18th-century barn—carries American and European country and formal furniture and accessories.

If you've been scouring antiquarian bookshops for a long-wanted title, chances are you'll find it at **Douglas N. Harding Rare Books** (2152 Post Rd., Rte. 1, P.O. Box 184, Wells 04090, 207/646-8785 or 800/228-1398, fax 207/646-8862). Well-cataloged and organized, the sprawling bookshop at any given time stocks upward of 100,000 books, prints, and maps. Hefty selection of Maine and New England histories. Other Wells antiquarian bookshops are **The Arringtons** (1908 Post Rd., Rte. 1, P.O. Box 160, Wells 04090, 207/646-4124), specializing in military books, and **East Coast Books and Art** (Depot Rd., P.O. Box 849, Wells 04090, 207/646-3584, fax 207/646-0416). Depot Road is off Route 109 (Sanford Road), west of Route 1.

© TOM NANGLE

Need a good read? You'll undoubtedly find one at Douglas N. Harding Rare Books, in Wells.

Art Galleries

There's no scarcity of the spectacular scenery that drew artists to Ogunquit in the early 20th century, but it's not the artistic magnet it once was. Yet galleries have popped up here and there. After you've been to the art museum, do your art browsing along Shore Road and in Perkins Cove.

Lighthouse Extravaganza

Several mini-lighthouses stand watch over the **Lighthouse Depot** (Post Rd., Rte. 1, P.O. Box 1690, Wells 04090, 207/646-0608 or 800/758-1444, fax 207/646-0516, www.lighthousedepot.com)—a truly amazing mecca for lighthouse aficionados. Imagine this: two floors of lighthouse books, sculptures, videos, banners, Christmas ornaments, lawn ornaments, paintings, and replicas running the gamut from pure kitsch to attractive collectibles. Its *Maine Lighthouse Map and Guide* ($5.95) is particularly helpful for tracking down the state's sentinels. Next door is a small lighthouse museum containing memorabilia from the United States Lighthouse Service. Depot owners Tim Harrison and Kathy Finnegan also publish the *Lighthouse Digest,* a monthly

magazine focusing on North American lighthouses (annual subscription $28), and produce a large mail-order catalog. The shop is about 1.5 miles north of the junction of Routes 1 and 109.

ENTERTAINMENT

Theater

Having showcased top-notch professional theater since the 1930s, the 750-seat **Ogunquit Playhouse** (Rte. 1, P.O. Box 915, Ogunquit 03907, 207/646-5511, www.ogunquitplayhouse.org) knows how to do it right: presenting comedies and musicals each summer, with big-name stars. The air-conditioned building is wheelchair-accessible. The box office is open daily in season, beginning in early May. Performances are at 8 P.M. Monday–Friday, 8:30 P.M. Saturday, with matinees at 2:30 P.M. Wednesday and Thursday mid-June–Labor Day. Prices range $29–45. The playhouse also presents a children's series and a handful of Sunday night concerts. Parking can be a hassle; consider walking the short distance from the Bourne Lane trolley-bus stop.

An even older local institution is the 640-seat

Leavitt Fine Arts Theatre (410 Main St., Ogunquit 03907, 207/646-3123), a handsome landmark since 1923. Nightly first-run films in summer, with matinees on rainy days. Down the road in Wells, the seven-screen **Cinema Center** multiplex (Wells Plaza, Rte. 1, Wells 04090, 207/646-0500) shows kids' flicks beginning around noon and first-run films at night.

Live Music

Ogunquit has several nightspots with good reputations for food and live entertainment. Best known is **Jonathan's** (2 Bourne Lane, P.O. Box 1879, Ogunquit 03907, 207/646-4777 or 800/464-9934), where national headliners often are on the schedule upstairs. Advance tickets are cheaper than at the door, and dinner guests get preference for seats. Reservations are essential at this popular spot. The well-respected downstairs restaurant has creative entrées for $18–30 and ethnic flavors at the oyster bar. Open 5–9:30 P.M., to 10 P.M. Friday and Saturday.

Ogunquit Performing Arts (207/646-6170) presents a full slate of programs, including classical concerts, ballet, and theater.

The **Wells Summer Concert Series** runs from early July through early September, at the Hope Hobbs Gazebo in Wells Harbor Park. A wide variety of music is represented, from sing-alongs to swing.

FESTIVALS AND EVENTS

The **Fourth of July** celebration on Ogunquit Beach includes fireworks and live music. **Harbor Fest,** with a concert, craft fair, parade, chicken barbecue, and children's activities, takes place the second weekend of July in Harbor Park in Wells.

In mid-August, Ogunquit Beach hosts a **Sandcastle-Building Contest,** and in late August is the annual **Sidewalk Art Show and Sale.**

Capriccio is a performing-arts festival, with daytime and evening events held throughout Ogunquit the first week of September. Then, the second weekend that month, Wells National Estuarine Research Reserve (Laudholm Farm) hosts the **Laudholm Nature Crafts Festival,** a two-day juried crafts fair with children's activities

and guided nature walks. This is an especially fine event. And the *third* weekend of September, the **Annual Ogunquit Antiques Show** benefits the Historical Society of Wells and Ogunquit (at the Dunaway Center, School St., Ogunquit).

Christmas by the Sea, the second weekend of December, features caroling, tree lighting, shopping specials, Santa Claus, a chowderfest, and a beach bonfire in Ogunquit.

ACCOMMODATIONS

Ogunquit

Motel-style accommodations are everywhere in Ogunquit, most along Route 1, yet finding last-minute rooms in July and August can be a challenge, so book well ahead if you'll be here then.

Hotels and Motels: The Seafarer Motel (Rte. 1, P.O. Box 2099, Ogunquit 03907, 207/646-4040 or 800/646-1233, fax 207/646-7142, www.seafarermotel.com) is a great place to take kids: there are indoor and outdoor pools, a coin-operated laundry, air-conditioning, cable TV, phones, and no charge for children under seven. Half of the 78 rooms and suites have kitchenettes, and most have two double beds. The Ogunquit Playhouse is across the street; motel staff can arrange for tickets. The clean, well-managed motel is set back a bit from the highway, but if you're noise-sensitive or prefer a woodsy view, ask for a back-facing room. Prices run $129–229 peak season. Open May to late October.

You're almost literally within spitting distance of Perkins Cove at the 37-room **Riverside Motel** (159 Shore Rd., P.O. Box 2244, Ogunquit 03907, 207/646-2741, fax 207/646-0216, www.riversidemotel.com), where you can perch on your balcony and watch the action—or, for that matter, join it. Rooms with phones, air-conditioning, refrigerators, cable TV, and fabulous views are $135–175, with continental breakfast. Open May to mid-October.

Juniper Hill Inn (336 Main St., Rte. 1, P.O. Box 2190, Ogunquit 03907, 207/646-4501 or 800/646-4544, fax 207/646-4595, www.ogunquit.com) is a particularly well-run motel-style lodging on five acres close to downtown Ogunquit and the beach. Amenities include refrigerators, cable TV, coin-operated laundry, fitness center, indoor and outdoor pools, and golf privileges. Rooms are $149–219. Open all year.

Eclectic Properties: It's not easy to describe the **Sparhawk Oceanfront Resort** (41 Shore Rd., P.O. Box 936, Ogunquit 03907, 207/646-5562), a sprawling, one-of-a-kind place popular with honeymooners, sedate families, and seniors. Lots of tradition in this thriving, six-acre complex—it's had various incarnations since the turn of the 20th century—and the Happily Filled sign regularly hangs out front. Out back is the Atlantic, with forever views, and the Marginal Way starts right here. Tennis courts, gardens, heated freshwater pool. No restaurant, but Ogunquit has plenty of options, and breakfast is included with your room. The 87 rooms vary in the different buildings—from motel-type rooms (best views) and suites to inn-type suites; rates run $170–300 (seven-night minimum July 4 to mid-Aug.). Open mid-April through October.

Nor is it easy to describe **The Beachmere Inn** (62 Beachmere Pl., Ogunquit 03907, 207/646-2021 or 800/336-3983, www.beachmereinn.com, $140–240), a private, oceanfront property comprising a Victorian-style inn, a vintage motel, and other buildings as well as its own beaches. All rooms have air-conditioning, TV, and phone; many rooms have kitchenettes; most have balconies, decks, or terraces; some have fireplaces. One-week minimum July and August; closed January–late March.

You can't get much closer to the water than the **Above Tide Inn** (66 Beach St., P.O. Box 2188, Ogunquit 03907, 207/646-7454, www.abovetideinn.com, $165–225), which is built on a wharf over the tidal Ogunquit River and has views to the open Atlantic. It's just steps from the beach and downtown Ogunquit. Each of the nine rooms has air-conditioning, TV, and mini-fridge, and a light breakfast is provided. Open mid-May–Columbus Day.

B&Bs: Within walking distance to many Ogunquit attractions, Jane and Fred Garland have created a very warm and welcoming ambience at **The Morning Dove** (13 Bourne Ln., P.O. Box 1940, Ogunquit 03907, 207/646-3891, www.themorningdove.com), a restored 1860s farmhouse with lovely gardens. Seven

first-, second-, and third-floor rooms have family quilts, mini-fridges, and air-conditioning; two have gas fireplaces. A hearty breakfast is served in the huge living/dining room (with a fireplace in winter) or on the porch. Rates run $145–175. Open all year.

Conveniently close to the center of town and an easy walk to the beach, **The Nellie Littlefield House** (9 Shore Rd., Ogunquit 03907, 207/646-1692, fax 207/361-1206) is a handsomely restored 1889 Victorian. The once-decrepit building was gutted to become a B&B in the 1990s, but some original fixtures were saved. Antiques and replicas fill the eight rooms, all named after members of the distinguished 19th-century Littlefield family; the third-floor Grace Littlefield even has a turret. The air-conditioning muffles street noise, but request a back- or side-facing room if you're extremely noise-sensitive. One room is wheelchair-accessible. Rates are $165–220, including an excellent breakfast buffet. Open April through October.

Built in 1899 for a prominent Maine lumbering family, **M Rockmere Lodge** (40 Stearns Rd., P.O. Box 278, Ogunquit 03907, 207/646-2985, www.rockmere.com) underwent a meticulous six-month restoration, thanks to preservationists Andy Antoniuk and Bob Brown. Near the Marginal Way on a peaceful street, the handsome home has eight very comfortable Victorian guest rooms, all with private baths and cable TV and most with ocean views. Rooms go for $150–200, including a generous continental breakfast. A wraparound veranda and "The Lookout," a third-floor windowed nook with wicker chairs, are both available for guests. The woodwork throughout is gorgeous. Beach towels, chairs, and umbrellas are provided for guests. Open April–late November.

Floors glisten, brass gleams, and breakfast is served on the glass-walled porch at the **Hartwell House** (118 Shore Rd., P.O. Box 393, Ogunquit 03907, 207/646-7210 or 800/235-8883, fax 207/646-6032, www.hartwellhouseinn.com), where the 11 rooms and three good-sized suites, all with air-conditioning, are divided between two buildings straddling Shore Road. Rooms are beautifully decorated with antiques and reproductions;

try for a garden-view room in the main house. Prices run $150–265, including a full breakfast and afternoon tea.

Amidst the Victorian homes and farmhouses that dominate the coastline, the **M Beauport Inn** (339 Agamenticus/Clay Hill Road, P.O. Box 941, Ogunquit 03907, 207/361-2400 or 800/646-8681, www.beauportinn.com, $175–185), a newly constructed stone English manor, stands out, as does the hospitality of experienced innkeepers and world travelers Cathy and George Wilson. The three rooms and one suite are meticulously decorated with antiques and collectibles from around the globe, and all have gas stoves, air-conditioning, TV/VCR, and refrigerators. Two have screened porches that open to the 40-foot granite lap pool and Jacuzzi. There's also a steam room and a great room with piano and fireplace. The architectural artifacts include stained-glass front doors from an old London hotel, oak floor-to-ceiling wainscoting from an old English schoolhouse, and rosewood doors built for a palace in Saudi Arabia. As you might expect, breakfast is a treat. Also available is a fully equipped apartment; weekly rental is $1,350.

Resorts: Founded in 1872, **The Cliff House Resort and Spa** (Shore Road, P.O. Box 2274, Ogunquit 03907, 207/361-1000, fax 207/361-2122), a self-contained Victorian-era complex, sprawls over 70 acres at the edge of Bald Head Cliff, midway between the centers of York and Ogunquit. Third-generation innkeeper Kathryn Weare keeps updating and modernizing the facilities. Among the most recent additions is a spa building with oversized rooms with king-size beds, gas fireplaces, and balconies, as well as a full-service spa, indoor pool, and glass-walled fitness center overlooking the Atlantic. A new central check-in building with indoor amphitheater connects the main building to the spa building. A hotel trolley shuttles guests to Perkins Cove and elsewhere; don't expect to walk anywhere from here. The 150 room and suite styles and prices vary widely in decor, from old-fashioned to contemporary; all have cable TV and phones, some have gas fireplaces, and most have a spectacular ocean view ($230–310). Packages are the way to go here. The dining room, with fantastic ocean

views, serves breakfast, lunch, dinner (no jeans, T-shirts, or sneakers; reservations required), and Sunday brunch. Facilities include a fitness center, indoor and outdoor pools, and tennis courts. Open late March to early December.

Wells

Like Ogunquit, Wells has a long list of motel-type lodgings, mostly on Route 1, and everything fills up in late July and early August. If you're arriving then, don't count on finding last-minute space.

Once part of a giant 19th-century dairy farm, the **Beach Farm Inn** (97 Eldredge Rd., Wells 04090, 207/646-8493, fax 207/646-5738, www.beachfarminn.com) is a 2.5-acre oasis in a rather congested area .2 mile off Route 1. Guests can borrow bikes, swim in the pool, relax in the library, or walk one-quarter mile down the road to the beach. Eight rooms (five with private baths, two detached) are $100–135 d; two cottages go for $650 and $950 a week. Third-floor rooms have air-conditioning. Open all year.

Even closer to the beach is **M Haven by the Sea** (59 Church St., Wells Beach 04090, 207/646-4194, www.havenbythesea.com, $129–300), a lovely and modern B&B in a former church. Innkeepers John and Susan Jarvis have kept the original floor plan. Inside are hardwood floors, cathedral ceilings, and stained-glass windows. The altar has been converted to a dining area that opens to a marsh-view terrace.

FOOD

Ogunquit

Breakfast, Lunch, and Miscellany: The Egg and I (501 Main St., Rte. 1, Ogunquit 03907, 207/646-8777, 6 A.M.–2 P.M.) earns high marks for its omelets and waffles. You can't miss it—there's always a crowd. No credit cards.

Another excellent choice is **Amore Breakfast** (178 Shore Rd., Ogunquit, 207/646-6661, 7 A.M.–1 P.M. Fri.–Tues.). Choose from a baker's dozen omelets, seven versions of eggs Benedict (including lobster), as well as various French toast, waffles, and all the regulars and irregulars.

Eat in or take out from **Village Food Market** (Main St., Ogunquit Center, 207/646-2122,

7 A.M.–11 P.M.). A breakfast sandwich is less than $3; subs and sandwiches are available in three sizes, and there's even a children's menu.

Scrumptious baked goods and panini sandwiches are available to go at **M Bread & Roses** (28A Main St., Ogunquit, 207/646-4227), a small bakery right downtown with a few tables outside. **Harbor Candy Shop** (26 Main St., Ogunquit 03907, 207/646-8078 or 800/331-5856, open all year) is packed with the most outrageous chocolate imaginable. Fudge, truffles, and turtles are all made here in the shop. Fortunately (or maybe unfortunately), it also accepts mail orders.

Lobster: In Ogunquit's Perkins Cove is the landmark **Lobster Shack** (207/646-2941, 11 A.M.–9 P.M. summer only), a converted fishing shanty where they've been turning out first-rate lobster rolls (and chowder) since the 1950s. Beer, wine, and a few picnic tables.

Creative marketing, a knockout view, and efficient service help explain why more than a thousand pounds of lobster bite the dust every summer day at **Barnacle Billy's** (Perkins Cove, Ogunquit, 207/646-5575 or 800/866-5575, 11 A.M.–9 P.M. mid-Apr.–mid-Oct.). For ambience, stick with the original operation; Barnacle Billy's Etc., next door (formerly the Whistling Oyster), is an upmarket version of the same thing. Full liquor license. Try for the deck, with a front-row seat on Perkins Cove.

Second-generation Hancocks now operate the **Ogunquit Lobster Pound** (Rte. 1, one-quarter mile north of downtown, Ogunquit 03907, 207/646-2516), the town's oldest lobster place (since 1944). Choose your own lobster from the tank outside; it's cooked in a numbered mesh bag, in sea water, so what you see is what you get. Steak, pasta, and chicken are also available. Eat indoors (in a rustic log cabin) or outdoors (shaded by pines); beer and wine only. No reservations, so be prepared to wait on midsummer weekends. Open May to mid-October, 5–9:30 P.M. daily in midsummer.

Ethnic: The closest thing to an upscale-rustic French country inn is the dining room at **M Provence,** also referred to as 98 Provence (262 Shore Rd., Ogunquit 03907, 207/646-9898, fax 207/641-8786). Chef/owner Pierre Gignac produces the cuisine, turning out appetizers such as stewed pheasant in baked tomato and chevre gratin and superb entrées in the $26–33 range; there's always a daily three-course fixed menu (around $45). Duck, venison, seafood, veal, and lamb are all represented. Service is attentive and well paced. Don't miss it, and be sure to reserve ahead. Open for the season in mid-April, Wednesday–Monday at 5:30 P.M.

Cross the street from Provence and you're in Italy—sort of. Vegetarians and pasta fanatics gravitate to **The Impastable Dream** (261 Shore Rd., Ogunquit 03907, 207/646-3011). Entrée range is $10–19; choices are predictable (ravioli, gnocchi, lasagna, Mediterranean tomato-based sauces over pasta, etc.) in this comfortable, casual spot. No reservations, so you may have to wait. Open 5–9 P.M., with a restricted schedule off-season.

Julie's Ristorante (369 Main St., Rte. 1, Ogunquit, 207/641-2522) regularly earns top marks from food critics, despite its so-so decor. The classic Italian menu is augmented with Maine seafood. How about lobster ravioli? Everything's prepared to order, so this is not the place to dine if you're in a rush. Entrées run $10–26. Patio dining in summer.

Eclectic: Brunch is the specialty at **Bintliff's Ogunquit** (335 Main St., Ogunquit, 207/646-3111, 8 A.M.–2 P.M. and 5 P.M. to close), but it's equally good for dinner. The brunch menu is huge, with 500 possible combinations for frittatas and omelets alone, or how about Ghirardelli chocolate chip macadamia pancakes or a spicy Korean garlic chili scramble? The dinner menu reflects a classic Continental/French cuisine with a few surprises (entrées $18–24). The restaurant is classy, but you don't need to dress up to dine here.

Like several other Ogunquit restaurants, **Poor Richard's Tavern** (125 Shore Rd., P.O. Box 894, Ogunquit 03907, 207/646-4722, 5:30–9:30 P.M. Apr.–Dec.) occupies downstairs rooms of a former residence. Veteran local restaurateur Richard Perkins has found a marketable mix: sensible prices ($12–26 for entrées), a "comfortable" menu (the Yankee pot roast and meatloaf Florentine are big favorites), some creativity (chicken Normande), and a reasonable wine list ($16–35 a bottle). All this means it's jammed in summer, so be sure to reserve.

Also downtown, **Gypsy Sweethearts** (10 Shore Rd., P.O. Box 593, Ogunquit 03907, 207/646-7021, 5:30–9 P.M. Tues.–Sun. mid-Apr.–mid-Nov.) occupies four rooms on the ground floor of a restored house. The creative menu is infused with ethnic accents and includes vegetarian choices (entrées $17–27). Reservations advised in midsummer.

Just south of it is **Five-O** (50 Shore Rd., Ogunquit, 207/646-6365, 5–10 P.M.), where executive chef Jonathan MacAlpine turns out classics with flare. Entrées such as gingered salmon fillet or a half-roasted chicken with pancetta and fresh tomatoes are $20–29. Lighter fare is available in the lounge to 11 P.M., where martinis are a specialty. In the off-season, multicourse regional dinners are held about once a month ($65).

Diners (and lodgers) have been stopping at **The Old Village Inn** (30 Main St., Ogunquit 03907, 207/646-7088) since 1833; the food, service, and warmth continue to draw crowds. One of the dining rooms in the historic house has only a single table and a fireplace. Entrées are $16–22. Off-season "winter warmer specials" and summertime early-bird specials (5:30–6:15 P.M.) are bargains. Midsummer reservations are essential. Open 5:30–9 P.M. Mon.–Thurs., to 9:30 P.M. Friday and Saturday, early Feb.–mid-June and early Sept.–Dec. 31, to 9:30 P.M. daily mid-June–early September.

Gourmet store by day, wine bistro by night. **Perkins & Perkins** (478 Main St., P.O. Box 2027, Ogunquit 03907, 207/646-0288) serves a light menu ($10–16) daily in summer beginning at 5 P.M. on its outside patio. Nearly two dozen wines are available by the glass, more by the bottle.

The View's the Thing: There's not much between you and Spain when you get a window seat at **Hurricane** (Oarweed Lane, Perkins Cove, Ogunquit 03907, 207/646-6348 or 800/649-6348). Although still considered one of Ogunquit's top restaurants, it can be hit or miss (common complaints are rushed and poor service, uneven quality), but when it's on, it's on. Dinner entrées are in the $16–33 range. Reservations are essential in July and August, for Sunday jazz brunch (1:30–4:30 P.M.), and on weekends all year. Open daily at 11:30 A.M. for lunch (entrées

$7–15) and dinner—until 9:30 P.M. to 10:30 P.M. Friday, Saturday, and late May–mid-October.

A self-contained Victorian-era resort complex, **The Cliff House** (Shore Road, P.O. Box 2274, Ogunquit 03907, 207/361-1000, fax 207/361-2122) sprawls over 70 acres at the edge of Bald Head Cliff, midway between the centers of York and Ogunquit. The dining room, with fantastic ocean views, is open to the public for breakfast (7:30–10:30 A.M.), lunch (noon–3 P.M. July and Aug.), and dinner (5:30–8:30 P.M., to 9 P.M. Fri. and Sat.). Try for the Sunday brunch buffet (7:30 A.M.–1 P.M.). Service can be so-so. Reservations are required for dinner (no jeans, T-shirts, or sneakers); entrée range is $23–33. Before or after dining, wander the grounds. Open late March to early December.

Destination Dining: Restrain yourself for a couple of days and then splurge on an elegant dinner at **⛰ Arrows** (Berwick Road, about 1.5 miles west of Rte. 1, Ogunquit 03907, 207/361-1100), definitely one of Maine's finest restaurants. In a beautifully restored 18th-century farmhouse overlooking well-tended gardens (including a one-acre kitchen garden), co-owners/chefs Mark Gaier and Clark Frasier do everything right here, starting with the artistic presentation. Prices are stratospheric by Maine standards—with wine and all, count on paying at least $200 a couple—but well worth it. "Innovative" is too tame to describe the menu; entrées range $40–44, so the best deal is the six-course tasting menu ($95). A credit card is required for reservations—essential in midsummer and on weekends. Jackets are preferred for men; no shorts. Open for dinner at 6 P.M. late April to early December (Tues.–Sun. in July and Aug., Wed.–Sun. in June and Sept.–Columbus Day, mostly weekends other months).

Wells

Breakfasts and Miscellany Best homemade doughnuts in Wells (and beyond), hands down, are at **Congdon's Doughnuts** (Rte. 1, Wells 04090, 207/646-4219, 6 A.M.–3 P.M. year-round, closed Tues.). Also try the strata.

Bean Suppers are held 5–7 P.M. on the first Saturday of the month, May–October, at the Masonic Hall on Sanford Road, and on the second

Saturday at the Wells Congregational Church, on Route 1.

Pick up all sorts of fresh goodies at the **Wells Farmer's Market** in the Town Hall parking lot, 3–6 P.M. Wednesdays.

Family Favorites: No eatery in this category qualifies as heart-healthy, so don't say you weren't forewarned.

Longtime favorite **Billy's Chowder House** (216 Mile Rd., just off Rte. 1, 207/646-7558) has a prime marsh-view location—with wall-to-wall cars in the parking lot. Seafood is the specialty here, but you can get just about anything. Open 11:30 A.M.–10 P.M. July and August, to 9 P.M. other months, mid-January through early December. **The Hayloft** (124 Post Rd., Rte. 1, Moody 04054, 207/646-4400) gets gold stars for hearty seafood chowder (clams, shrimp, and chunks of lobster) and good burgers. It's a casual, popular place, great for families, so go early. Open all year 8 A.M.–9:30 P.M. (to 9 P.M. in winter). Fried-clam aficionados swear by **Jake's Seafood** (Rte. 1 and Bourne Ave., Moody 04054, 207/646-6771), but you'll also like the clam chowder and onion rings. Open all year for breakfast, lunch, and dinner, 5 A.M.–8 P.M.

Your basic family-oriented place, the **Maine Diner** (2265 Post Rd., Rte. 1, Wells 04090, 207/646-4441) has a reputation built on lobster pie and award-winning seafood chowder. Beer and wine only. Open 7 A.M.–9:30 P.M. (8 P.M. in winter) for breakfast, lunch, and dinner (breakfast available anytime). Prices run from less than $10 for diner food to $15.95 for surf and turf.

Turf and Surf: A good steak in the land of lobster? You betcha. **The Steakhouse** (1205 Post Rd., Rte. 1, 207/646-4200, 4–9:30 P.M. Tues.–Sun.) is a great big barn of place where steaks are hand cut from U.S.D.A. prime and choice, corn-fed western beef that's never been frozen. Chicken, seafood, lobster (great stew), and even a vegetarian stir-fry are also on the menu (entrées $12–24); children's menu available. Service is efficient. No reservations, so be prepared for a wait. This place is *very* popular.

Seals and surf are just beyond the windows at **The Grey Gull Inn** (475 Webhannet Dr., a mile west of Rte. 1, Wells 04090, 207/646-7501), the best restaurant in town. Seafood is a specialty (lobster's always on the menu), but so are Yankee pot roast, creative chicken dishes, pasta entrées, and diet-conscious items; prices range $16–28. Service is superb, wine list is selective, and there's a kids' menu. Reservations are essential in July and August (request a window table). Open for dinner at 5:30 P.M. Upstairs, the Grey Gull Inn has five reasonably priced rooms with private baths.

INFORMATION AND SERVICES

Information

At the southern edge of Ogunquit, right next to the Ogunquit Playhouse, the Ogunquit Chamber of Commerce's **Welcome Center** (Rte. 1, Box 2289, Ogunquit 03907, 207/646-2939, www.ogunquit.org) provides all the usual visitor information, including restaurant menus. Ask for the *Touring and Trolley Route Map,* showing the Marginal Way, beach locations, and public restrooms. The chamber of commerce's annual visitor booklet thoughtfully carries a high-tide calendar for the summer months. The Welcome Center also has public restrooms.

Just over the Ogunquit border in Wells (actually in Moody) is the **Wells Information Center** (Rte. 1 at Bourne Ave., P.O. Box 356, Wells 04090, 207/646-2451, www.wellschamber.org). A touchpad kiosk takes over when the office is closed.

Hospitals

Hospitals serving the region are: **York Hospital** (15 Hospital Dr., York 03909, emergency room 207/351-2157), **Southern Maine Medical Center** (1 Medical Center Dr., Biddeford 04005, emergency room 207/283-7100), **Goodall Hospital** (25 June St., Sanford 04073, 207/324-4310).

For minor medical problems, **Wells Regional Medical Community,** operated by York Hospital (114 Sanford Rd., Rte. 109, Wells, 207/646-5211), provides daily walk-in urgent care and other services 9 A.M.–8 P.M. York Hospital's **Tel-a-Nurse** service (800/283-7234) provides free over-the-phone advice for minor medical problems.

Local Libraries

The handsome fieldstone **Ogunquit Memorial Library** (74 Shore Rd., Ogunquit 03907, 207/

646-9024) is the downtown's only National Historic Register building. Open 9 A.M.–noon and 2 P.M.–5 P.M. Monday–Saturday June–October; same hours other months, but closed Monday in addition to Sunday.

The **Wells Public Library** (1434 Post Rd., Rte. 1, 207/646-8181) is open 10 A.M.–6 P.M. Monday, 1–8 P.M. Tuesday, 10 A.M.–8 P.M. Wednesday, 1–6 P.M. Thursday, and 10 A.M.–5 P.M. Friday and Saturday.

GETTING AROUND

Ogunquit

From mid-May through Columbus Day, **trolley-buses** weave through Ogunquit; the 39 stops are signposted. Each time you board, it'll cost you $1.50 (kids 10 and younger free with adult), but for the same price you can go the whole route—a great way to get your bearings—in about 40 minutes. Hours are 9 A.M.–5 P.M. early to mid-May, to 9 P.M. mid-May–late June, to 11 P.M. late June–Labor Day, and to 9 P.M. Labor Day–Columbus Day.

Wells

Wells, too, has a seasonal **trolley-bus service** on Route 1, operating daily 9 A.M.–10 P.M. late June to Labor Day, then 9 A.M.–9 P.M. Saturday and 9 A.M.–5 P.M. Sunday until Columbus Day. Fare is $1 per trip or $3 for a day pass; family day passes are also available.

The Kennebunks

The world may have first learned of Kennebunkport when George Herbert Walker Bush was president, but Walkers and Bushes have owned their summer estate here for three generations. Visitors continue to come to the Kennebunks (the collective name for Kennebunk, Kennebunkport, Cape Porpoise, and Goose Rocks Beach—combined population about 15,200) hoping to catch a glimpse of the former first family, but they also come for the terrific ambience, the B&Bs, boutiques, boats, biking, and beaches.

The Kennebunks' earliest European settlers arrived in the mid-1600s. By the mid-1700s, shipbuilding had become big business in the area. Two ancient local cemeteries—North Street and Evergreen—provide glimpses of the area's heritage. Its historic district reveals Kennebunk's moneyed past—the homes where wealthy ship owners and shipbuilders once lived, sending their vessels to the Caribbean and around the globe. Today, unusual shrubs and a dozen varieties of rare maples still line Summer Street—the legacy of ship captains in the global trade. Another legacy is the shiplap construction in many houses—throwbacks to a time when labor was cheap and lumber plentiful. Closer to the beach, in Lower Village, stood the workshops of sailmakers, carpenters, and mastmakers whose output drove the booming trade to success.

While Kennebunkport draws most of the sightseers and summer traffic, Kennebunk feels more like a year-round community. It boasts an interesting, old-fashioned downtown and a mix of shops, restaurants, and attractions. Yes, its beaches, too, are well known, but many visitors drive right through the middle of Kennebunk without stopping to enjoy its assets.

The Kennebunks are communities with conscience—loaded with conservationists working to preserve hikable, bikable green space for residents and visitors. Be sure not to miss these trails, bikeways, and offshore islets. Gravestone rubbers will want to check out Evergreen Cemetery, and history buffs should pick up a copy of *Walking in the Port*, the Kennebunkport Historical Society's well-researched booklet of three self-guided historic walking tours. To appreciate the area another way, climb aboard the Intown Trolley, with regular summertime service and lots of entertaining tidbits from the driver.

SIGHTS

Seashore Trolley Museum

There's nothing quite like an antique electric trolley to dredge up nostalgia for bygone days. With a collection of more than 250 transit vehicles

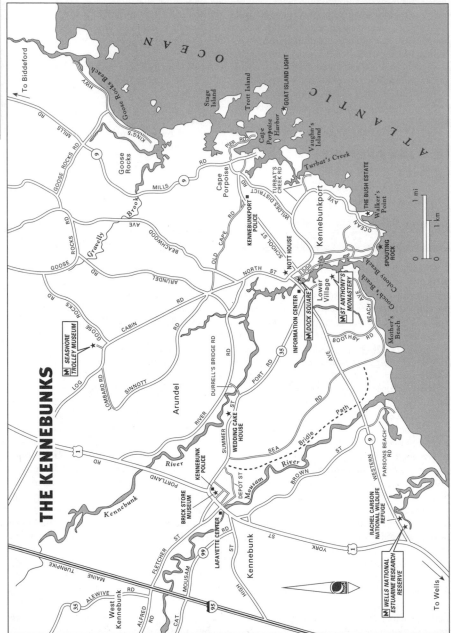

THE KENNEBUNKS

SOUTHERN COAST LIGHTHOUSE TOUR

The lure of lighthouses is understandable. Legends tell of heroic keepers, prank-playing ghosts, and death-defying storms. Lighthouse lovers will find five in southern Maine, all viewable (binoculars will help) from land. Most of these were built in the 19th century on the wrecks of earlier lights that couldn't withstand winter storms.

Begin your journey by taking Route 103, off Route 1 in Kittery, and heading north. The best place to view **Whaleback Lighthouse,** which guards the Portsmouth Harbor and the mouth of the Piscataqua River, is from Fort Foster, on Gerrish Island, which is connected to the mainland via a bridge.

Continue on Route 103 until it merges with Route 1A, then follow this north, bearing right, at the end of Long Sands Beach, on Nubble Road. The Cape Neddick Light, better known as **The Nubble,** stands just 200 yards or so off Cape Neddick Point and is easily seen from Sohier Park.

Sohier Park is also the best place to view the **Boon Island Light,** located six miles offshore. The first three lighthouses constructed on this remote pile of rock were destroyed before the current light, dating from the mid-19th century, was constructed of hand-hewn granite blocks.

Continue on 1A until it joins Route 1, then head north. Break from viewing real lighthouses for a visit to the king of lighthouse emporia, **Lighthouse Depot,** on Route 1 in Wells.

After touring, browsing, buying, and learning everything there is to know about lighthouses, continue north on Route 1 until Route 9 east splits from it, just north of Wells. Follow Route 9 through the Kennebunks and on to the village of Cape Porpoise. The town pier, at the end of Pier Road, is the best place to view the **Goat Island Lighthouse,** which has the distinction of being the last manned lighthouse in the state. It was finally automated in 1990. There's also a great view from the Vaughn's Island Preserve, in Kennebunkport, but you'll have to coordinate your visit with the tide.

Return to Route 9, and continue east until it merges with Route 208. You'll turn right, following signs for Biddeford Pool. The **Wood Island Light,** on the east end of Wood Island, marks the entrance to the Saco River. It can be seen from several points in Biddeford Pool and Hills Beach, but the best view is from the East Point Sanctuary.

(more than two dozen trolleys on display), the Seashore Trolley Museum (195 Log Cabin Rd., P.O. Box A, Kennebunkport 04046, 207/967-2800, www.trolleymuseum.org) verges on trolley-mania. Whistles blowing and bells clanging, restored streetcars do frequent trips (between 10:05 A.M. and 4:15 P.M.) on a 3.5-mile loop through the nearby woods. Ride as often as you wish, then check out the activity in the streetcar workshop and go wild in the trolley-oriented gift shop. Bring a picnic lunch and enjoy it here. Special events are held throughout the summer, including the Ice Cream and Sunset Trolley Ride, every Wednesday and Thursday at 7:30 P.M. in July and August. Cost is $3.50 and includes ice cream. Guided tours are available twice daily in July and August. And here's an interesting wrinkle: make a reservation, plunk down $50, and you can have a one-hour "Motorman" experience driving your own trolley (with help, of course).

Museum tickets are $7.50 adults, $5.50 seniors, $5 kids 6–16, and free for kids five and under. The museum is 1.7 miles southeast of Route 1. Open 10 A.M.–5 P.M. daily mid-June through Columbus Day, weekends in May and late October.

Walker's Point: The Bush Estate

There's no public access to Walker's Point, but you can join the sidewalk gawkers on Ocean Avenue overlooking George and Barbara Bush's summer compound. The 41st president and his wife lead a low-key, laid-back life when they're here, so if you don't spot them through binoculars, you may well run into them at a shop or restaurant in town. Intown Trolley's regular narrated tours go right past the house—or it's an easy, scenic family walk via Henry Parsons Park from Kennebunkport's Dock Square. On the way, you'll pass **St. Ann's Church,** whose stones came from the ocean floor, and the paths to

Spouting Rock and **Blowing Cave**—two natural phenomena that create spectacular water fountains if you manage to be there midway between high and low tides.

Wedding Cake House

The Wedding Cake House (104 Summer St., Kennebunk) is a private residence, so you can't go inside, but it's one of Maine's most-photographed buildings. Driving down Summer Street (Route 35), midway between the downtowns of Kennebunk and Kennebunkport, it's hard to miss the yellow and white Federal mansion with gobs of gingerbread and Gothic Revival spires and arches. Built in 1826 by shipbuilder George Bourne as a wedding gift for his wife, the Kennebunk landmark remained in the family until 1983.

Cape Porpoise

When your mind's eye conjures an idyllic lobster-fishing village, it probably looks a lot like Cape Porpoise—only 2.5 miles from busy Dock

© TOM NANGLE

Kennebunk's Wedding Cake House is one of Maine's most photographed buildings.

Square. Follow Route 9 eastward from Kennebunkport; when Route 9 turns north, continue straight, and take Pier Road to its end. From the small parking area, you'll see lobsterboats at anchor, a slew of working wharves, and 19th-century **Goat Island Light,** now automated, directly offshore. Cape Porpoise holds a handful of B&Bs, restaurants, galleries, historic Atlantic Hall, and the extra-friendly Bradbury Bros. Market.

Local History Museums

Occupying four restored 19th-century buildings (including the 1825 William Lord store) in downtown Kennebunk, **The Brick Store Museum** (117 Main St., Kennebunk 04043, 207/985-4802, fax 207/985-6887, www.brickstoremuseum.org, 10 A.M.–4:30 P.M. Tues.–Fri. and 10 A.M.–1 P.M. Sat.) has garnered a reputation for unusual exhibits: a century of wedding dresses, a two-century history of volunteer firefighting, life in southern Maine during the Civil War. Admission is by donation. The museum encourages appreciation for the surrounding Kennebunk Historic District with hour-long **architectural walking tours,** mid-June to mid-October (call for current schedule). Cost is $5. If this schedule doesn't suit, the museum sells a walk-it-yourself booklet for $5.

Owned and maintained by the Kennebunkport Historical Society, **The Nott House** (8 Maine St., Kennebunkport, 1–4 P.M. Tues.–Fri. and 10 A.M.–1 P.M. Sat. mid-June to Columbus Day) is a mid-19th-century Greek Revival mansion filled with Victorian furnishings. Be sure to visit the restored gardens. Tour tickets are $5 adults, under 18 free. Hour-long architectural walking tours of the Kennebunkport Historic District depart from the Nott House at 11 A.M. Thursday and Saturday in July and August, and Saturday only in September. Cost is $3 pp. At the house, you can purchase a guidebook for a do-it-yourself tour for $4.

The **Kennebunkport Historical Society** also owns and maintains a five-building History Center (125–135 North St., Kennebunkport 04046, 207/967-2751, www.kporthistory.org). The Town House School, dating from the turn of the 20th century, is the society's research center. The Pasco Exhibit Center, containing the society's

© TOM NANGLE

Shrines accent the walking trails at St. Anthony's Monastery in Kennebunk.

offices, also has permanent and rotating exhibits of local memorabilia. It's open all year (10 A.M.–4 P.M. Tues.–Fri.). Admission is $3 adults, free for children under 18. If you call ahead for an appointment, a staff member will let you into the tiny old jail on the grounds.

Dock Square

Even if you're not a shopper, make it a point to meander through the heart of Kennebunkport's shopping district, where one-time fishing shacks have been restored and renovated into upscale shops and boutiques. Some, especially those on upper floors, offer fine harbor views.

PARKS AND PRESERVES

Thanks to a dedicated coterie of year-round and summer residents, the foresighted **Kennebunkport Conservation Trust** (KCT), founded in 1974, has become a nationwide model for land-trust organizations. The KCT has managed to preserve from development several hundred acres of land (including 11 small islands off Cape Porpoise Harbor), and most of this acreage is accessible to the public, especially with a sea kayak. The trust has even assumed ownership of 7.7-acre Goat Island, with its distinctive lighthouse visible from Cape Porpoise and other coastal vantage points. Contact the KCT (P.O. Box 7028, Cape Porpoise 04014, www.thekennebunkportconservationtrust.org) for information on its holdings or to volunteer for trail maintenance.

St. Anthony's Monastery

Long ago, 35,000 Native Americans used this part of town for a summer camp. They knew a good thing. So did a group of Lithuanian Franciscan monks who in 1947 fled war-ravaged Europe and acquired the 200-acre St. Anthony's Franciscan Monastery (Beach St., Kennebunk, mailing address: P.O. Box 980, Kennebunkport 04046, 207/967-2011). From 1956 to 1969, they ran a high school here. The monks occupy the handsome Tudor great house, but the well-tended grounds (sprinkled with shrines and a recently restored sculpture created by Vytautas Jonynas for the 1964 World's Fair) are open to the public sunrise to sunset. A short path leads from the monastery area to a peaceful gazebo overlooking the

Kennebunk River. No pets or bikes. Public restrooms are available. The grounds are open 6 A.M.–8:30 P.M. in summer, closing at 6 P.M. in winter.

Vaughn's Island Preserve

Thanks to the Kennebunkport Conservation Trust, 96-acre Vaughn's Island has been saved for posterity. You'll need to do a little planning, tidewise, since the island is about 600 feet offshore. Consult a tide calendar and aim for low tide close to the new moon or full moon (when the most water drains away). Allow yourself an hour or so before and after low tide, but no longer, or you may need a boat rescue. Wear treaded rubber boots, since the crossing is muddy and slippery with rockweed. Keep an eye on your watch and explore the ocean (east) side of the island, along the beach. It's all worth the effort, and there's a great view of Goat Island Light off to the east. From downtown Kennebunkport, take Maine Street to Wildes District Road. Continue to Shore Road (also called Turbat's Creek Road), go .6 mile, jog left .2 mile more, and park in the tiny lot at the end.

Emmons Preserve

Also under the stewardship of the Kennebunkport Conservation Trust, the Emmons Preserve has two trails (blazed yellow and pink) meandering through 146 acres of woods and fields on the edge of Batson's River (also called Gravelly Brook). The yellow trail gives best access to the water. Fall colors here are brilliant, birdlife is abundant, and you can do a loop in half an hour. But why rush? This is a wonderful oasis in the heart of Kennebunkport. From Dock Square, take North Street to Beachwood Avenue (right turn) to Gravelly Brook Road (left turn). The trailhead is on the left.

Picnic Rock

About 1.5 miles up the Kennebunk River from the ocean, Picnic Rock is the centerpiece of the **Butler Preserve,** a 14-acre enclave managed by The Nature Conservancy. Well named, the rock is a great place for a picnic and a swim, but don't count on being alone. A short trail loops through the preserve. Consider bringing a canoe or kayak (or renting one) and paddling with the tide past

beautiful homes and the Cape Arundel Golf Club. From Lower Village Kennebunk, take Route 35 west and hang a right onto Old Port Road. When the road gets close to the Kennebunk River, watch for a Nature Conservancy oakleaf sign on the right. Parking is along Old Port Road; walk down through the preserve to Picnic Rock, right on the river.

Kennebunk Plains Preserve

Also linked to The Nature Conservancy is the 1,600-acre Kennebunk Plains Preserve, nesting site for the endangered grasshopper sparrow and home to dozens of other bird species. Best time to come is late July and early August, when hundreds of acres of blueberries are ripe for the picking and the rare northern blazing star carpets parts of the preserve with purple blossoms. You may even see wild turkeys. To reach Kennebunk Plains, head northwest on Route 99 from Route 9A in Kennebunk. About two miles west of I-95, watch for a small, signposted parking area.

RECREATION

Beaches

Ah, the beaches. The Kennebunks are well endowed with sand but not with parking spaces. Between mid-June and mid-September, you'll need to buy a **parking permit** ($10 a day, $20 a week, $50 a season) from the Kennebunk Town Hall (4 Summer St., 207/985-3675), the Kennebunkport Police Station (101 Maine St., 207/967-4243), or the chamber of commerce (17 Western Ave., Rte. 9, Lower Village, 207/967-0857). (The police station is open 24 hours; other locations are not.) *You need a separate pass for each town.* Many lodgings provide free permits for their guests—be sure to ask when making room reservations. Or avoid the parking dilemma altogether by hopping aboard the Intown Trolley, which goes right by the major beaches.

The main beaches in Kennebunk (east to west, stretching about two miles) are 3,346-foot-long **Gooch's** (most popular), **Kennebunk** (locally called Middle or Rocks Beach), and **Mother's** (a smallish beach next to Lords Point, where there's also a playground). Lifeguards are on duty at Gooch's and Mother's Beaches July–Labor Day. Mother's Beach is the home of the Kennebunk Beach Improvement Association. Ask locally about a couple of other beach options.

Kennebunkport's claim to beach fame is three-mile-long **Goose Rocks Beach,** one of the loveliest in the area. Parking spaces are scarce and biking on Route 9 can be dicey, so if sun and sand are your primary goals, the best solution is to book a room nearby. You'll be about five miles east of all the downtown action, however. To reach the beach, take Route 9 from Dock Square east and north to Dyke Road (Clock Farm Corner). Turn right and continue to the end (King's Highway).

The prize for tiniest beach goes to **Colony** (officially Arundel) **Beach,** near The Colony resort complex. It's close to many Kennebunkport lodgings and an easy walk from Dock Square.

Bicycling

A mandatory stop for anyone interested in bicycles and biking is **Cape-Able Bike Shop** (83 Arundel Rd., Town House Corners, Kennebunkport 04046, 207/967-4382), a local institution since 1974. The shop has all kinds of rentals and accessories, repairs your wounded gear, sponsors Saturday morning group rides, and provides a free area bike map and the best insider information. (The bike map is also available at the chamber of commerce.) One-day hybrid bike rental is $20. Mountain-bike rental is $30 a day. Map, helmet, and lock are included.

Cape-Able also offers tours. The 10–15 mile Local Beach Tour lasts 2.5–3 hours and costs $59 adults, $29 kids 15 and younger, including a snack. The four-hour Deluxe Beach Tour covers 25–30 miles and costs $89 adults, $49 kids, and includes lunch. A Singletrack Adventure moderate to advanced mountain-bike tour covers 6–8 miles, lasts about three hours, and costs $59 adults, $29 kids, including a snack. Tours include rental bike, helmet, carry bag, and water bottle; they depart at 8 A.M.

Cape-Able has information on a 10-mile Goose Rocks pedal, an eight-mile Cape Porpoise ride, and, if you can cope with a bit of congestion, an eight-mile route through downtown Kennebunkport and over to Kennebunk Beach.

At the height of midsummer traffic, the safest cycling excursion in the area follows an old trolley-line route called the **bridle path** along the Mousam River in Kennebunk. Easiest places to park are at the Sea Road School (when school isn't in session) and on Railroad Avenue, both just south of Route 35 (Summer Street). The two-mile path is also a wonderfully easy walk for the whole family, ending up not far from Kennebunk Beach.

Golf and Tennis

Three 18-hole golf courses make the sport a big deal in the area. **Cape Arundel Golf Club** (19 River Rd., Kennebunkport, 207/967-3494), established in 1897, and **Webhannet Golf Club** (8 Central Ave., Kennebunk, 207/967-2061), established in 1902, are semiprivate, open to nonmembers; call for tee times at least 24 hours ahead. At Cape Arundel, where George Bush plays, no jeans or sweatpants are allowed. In nearby Arundel, **Dutch Elm Golf Course** (5 Brimstone Rd., Arundel, 207/282-9850) is a public course with rentals, pro shop, and putting greens.

Tennis courts are scattered around town: **Kennebunk High School** (Fletcher St., Route 35, Kennebunk), **Parsons Field** (Park St., Kennebunk), and **West Kennebunk Recreation Area** (Holland Rd., West Kennebunk). The chamber of commerce can provide additional details.

Whale Watches and Lobsterboat Cruises

Whale sightings offshore include finbacks, minkes, and humpbacks, and the local cruise boats have had remarkable success. The 80-foot *Nick's Chance* (4 Western Ave., Lower Village, Kennebunk 04043, 207/967-5507 or 800/767-2628, www.firstchancewhalewatch.com) departs twice daily in July and August for 4.5-hour whale watches to Jeffrey's Ledge, weather permitting. Cost is $32 adults, $15 children (3–12). Departure is from Performance Marine in Kennebunk Lower Village (behind Bartley's Restaurant).

Under the same ownership and departing from the same location is the 65-foot open lobsterboat *Kylie's Chance,* which departs five times daily in July and August for 1.5-hour scenic lobster cruises.

A lobstering demonstration is given on most trips, but never on the evening one. Cost is $15 adults, $7.50 kids (3–12).

Sailing Excursions

For day sailing, the 37-foot yacht *Bellatrix* (95 Ocean Ave., P.O. Box 2762, Kennebunkport 04046, 207/967-8685, www.sailingtrips.com), based at the Nonantum Resort, charges $40 pp for a two-hour sail. The handsome 55-foot gaff-rigged schooner *Eleanor* (Arundel Wharf, 43 Ocean Ave., P.O. Box 572, Kennebunkport 04043, 207/967-8809, www.gwi.net/schoonersails), heads out for two-hour sails, weather and tides willing, 1–3 times daily during the summer. Cost is $38 pp.

Eco Cruise

Based at the Nonantum Resort, the *Atlantic Explorer* (95 Ocean Ave., Kennebunkport 04046, 207/967-4784 for information, 207/967-4050 for reservations, www.atlanticexposure.com), under Captain Mike Day, provides an in-your-face video view of underwater creatures and vegetation beamed back to the 49-passenger boat from an undersea robotized camera. The boat makes 3–4 1.75-hour trips daily, Memorial Day weekend to Columbus Day. Cost is $20 adults, $10 children under 12.

Sportfishing

Saltwater, light tackle, and fly sportfishing are the specialties of **Lady J Sportfishing Charters** (10 Kimball Lane, Kennebunk, 207/985-7304, www.ladyjcharters.com) aboard the *Rebecca Lynn*. Two-hour trips for kids ($175) include hauling lobster traps. Inshore trips for stripers and bluefish are $300 for four hours, $400 for six hours. Eight-hour specialty trips for shark or ground fish are $600. Trips leave from the Arundel Wharf Restaurant (Ocean Ave., Kennebunkport).

SHOPPING

Lots of small, attractive boutiques surround **Dock Square,** the hub of Kennebunkport, so gridlock often develops in midsummer. Avoid driving through here at the height of the season. Take your time and walk, bike, or ride the local trolley-bus.

Antiques and Art Galleries

English, European, and American furniture and architectural elements and garden accessories are just a sampling of what you'll find at **Antiques on Nine** (Rte. 9, Lower Village, Kennebunk, 207/967-0626). Another good place for browsing high-end antiques as well as home accents is **Hurlburt Designs** (Rte. 9, Lower Village, Kennebunk, 207/967-4110).

Jean Briggs represents nearly 100 artists at her topflight **Mast Cove Galleries** (Maine St. and Mast Cove Ln., P.O. Box 2718, Kennebunkport 04046, 207/967-3453), in a handsome Greek Revival house near the Graves Memorial Library. Prices vary widely, so don't be surprised if you spot something affordable. In July and August, the gallery sponsors 2.5-hour Wednesday evening jazz concerts ($10 donation includes light refreshments). Call for schedule.

The Gallery on Chase Hill (10 Chase Hill Rd., P.O. Box 2786, Kennebunkport, 207/967-0049), in the stunningly restored Captain Chase House, next to the Windows on the Water restaurant, mounts rotating exhibits and represents a wide variety of Maine and New England artists. **Compliments** (Dock Square, 207/967-2269) has a truly unique and fun collection of contemporary fine American crafts. More than 30 artists are represented at **Wright Gallery** (Pier Rd., Cape Porpoise, 207/967-5053).

Books, Clothing, and Gifts

The number of shops in this category in the Kennebunks is vast. You'll need to do your own exploring-and-discovering. Treasures are to be found all over the Kennebunks, but most are clustered around Dock Square (Kennebunkport) and in Lower Village (Kennebunk).

To appreciate the friendly, funky **Kennebunk Book Port** (10 Dock Sq., Kennebunkport 04046, 207/967-3815 or 800/382-2710), climb to the second floor of the antique rum warehouse and read the shop slogan: "Ice cream, candy, children, bare feet, short, long, or no hair, cats, dogs, and small dragons are welcome anytime." This place has character.

Since 1968, **Port Canvas** (9 Ocean Ave., Kennebunkport 04046, 207/985-9765 or 800/333-

Shop until you drop in Kennebunkport's famed Dock Square.

6788) has been turning out the best in durable cotton-canvas products. Need a new double-bottomed tote bag? It's here. Also golf-bag covers, belts, computer cases, day packs, and of course duffel bags.

Quilt fans should make time to visit **Mainely Quilts** (108 Summer St., Rte. 35, Kennebunk, 207/985-4250), behind the Waldo Emerson Inn. The shop has a nice selection of contemporary and antique quilts.

Most of the clothing shops clustered around Dock Square are rather pricey; not so **Arbitrage** (28 Dock Square, 207/967-9989), which combines designer consignment clothing with new fashions and other items.

Earth-Friendly Stuff

Lafayette Center, a handsomely restored mill building housing boutiques and eateries, is also home to the **Tom's of Maine Natural Living Store** (Storer St., just off Main St., Kennebunk 04043, 207/985-3874), an eco-sensitive local-turned-global firm that makes soaps, toothpaste, oils, and other products. The shop also has herbs, recycled paper, and organic cotton clothing. "Factory seconds" are real bargains.

ENTERTAINMENT

Live entertainment is featured, mostly weekends, at Federal Jack's Brewpub and Windows on the Water, and at the Kennebunkport Inn and The Colony.

Kennebunk Parks & Recreation sponsors **Concerts in the Park,** a weekly series of free concerts 6:30–7:30 P.M. Wednesdays late June to mid-August, in Rotary Park on Water Street.

On Thursday evenings at 7 P.M. in July, the **River Tree Arts Summer Concert Series** brings music to the lawn of the South Congregational Church, Kennebunkport.

Live, professional summer theater is on tap at the **Arundel Barn Playhouse** (53 Old Post Rd., Arundel, 207/985-5552, www.arundelbarnplayhouse.com), with productions staged in a renovated 1888 barn June through September; tickets are $19–24.

River Tree Arts

The area's cultural spearhead is **River Tree Arts** (RTA) (35 Western Ave., Kennebunk 04043, 207/967-9120, www.rivertreearts.org), an incredibly energetic, volunteer-driven organization that sponsors concerts, classes, workshops, exhibits, and educational programs throughout the year.

FESTIVALS AND EVENTS

Concerts and kids' activities are part of the **Summer Solstice Festival** in June. Take the kids to the **Kennebunkport Teddy Bear Show,** usually the second Saturday in August, but watch the reactions of all the grownups.

The first two weekends of December mark the festive **Christmas Prelude,** during which spectacular decorations adorn historic homes, candle-toting carolers stroll through the Kennebunks, stores have special sales, and Santa Claus shows up in a lobsterboat.

ACCOMMODATIONS

With about 1,300 beds for rent in the Kennebunks, there's plenty of choice and variety, although most are pricey and some are downright stratospheric. Don't arrive without a reservation in early August or during the Christmas Prelude; you may find yourself facing a sea of No Vacancy signs. If that happens, the best fallback is the Kennebunk & Kennebunkport Chamber of Commerce—the staff has a knack for miracle-working. Rates listed are for peak season.

Inns

Graciously dominating its 11-acre spread at the mouth of the Kennebunk River, **The Colony Resort Hotel** (140 Ocean Ave. at King's Highway, P.O. Box 511, Kennebunkport 04046, 207/967-3331 or 800/552-2363, fax 207/967-8738, www.thecolonyhotel.com/maine) springs right out of a bygone era, yet it's racing ahead as one of the state's foremost "green" resorts—the 123-room hotel has made a major recycling commitment. But green doesn't come cheap; this is a splurge choice. Doubles go for $190–435 (including breakfast but not the daily service charge—$5 pp). Higher-priced rooms have ocean views, others have garden views. There's a special feeling here, with cozy corners for reading, lawns and gardens for strolling, a beachfront swimming pool, room service, tennis privileges at the exclusive River Club, bike rentals, massage therapy, and lawn games. The hotel dining room is open to the public for breakfast, lunch, and dinner; reservations are advisable. Sunday brunch is a big winner, 11 A.M.–2 P.M. mid-June to Labor Day. The hotel is open mid-May to late October.

Innkeeper Laurie Bongiorno seems to have cornered the ultra high-end, boutique inn market, with four in this category. Most renowned is the **⚑ White Barn Inn** (37 Beach Avenue, Kennebunk, mailing address P.O. Box 560, Kennebunkport 04046, 207/967-2321, www.white barninn.com, $340–780). The empire also encompasses **The Beach House Inn** (211 Beach Ave., Kennebunk, 207/967-3850, www.beach hseinn.com, $280–500); **The Breakwater Inn and Hotel** (127 Ocean Ave., Kennebunkport, 207/967-3118, www.thebreakwaterinn.com, $290–345), **The Yachtsman Lodge and Marina** (Ocean Ave., Kennebunkport 04046, 207 /967-2511, www.yachtsmanlodge.com, $299–314), and three restaurants.

The White Barn Inn is the most exclusive, with five-diamond and Relais & Chateaux status. It's home to one of the best restaurants in the *country* (see Destination Dining). Many rooms have fireplaces and marble baths with separate steam showers and whirlpool tubs (you can even arrange for a butler-drawn bath). Service is impeccable, and nothing has been overlooked in terms of amenities. There's an outdoor heated European-style brimming pool, and spa services are available. For a truly away-from-it-all feeling, consider staying at one of the inn's ultraprivate riverfront Wharf Cottages ($585–1,270—ouch!), which face Dock Square from across the river. The inn also has two yachts, a Hinckley Talaria-44 and 50-foot Sunseeker offshore cruiser, available for charter by guests.

The Beach House Inn faces Middle Beach and is a bit less formal than the White Barn, but the service is on par. The Breakwater, at the mouth of the Kennebunk River, comprises a beautifully renovated, historical inn with wrap-around porches and an adjacent, more modern, newly renovated hotel (previously called Schooners). The complex also is home to Stripers Fish Shack. Finally, there's the Yachtsman, an innovative blend of a motel and B&B, with all rooms opening onto patios facing the river and the marina where George H. W. Bush keeps his boat. Rooms in all properties have air-conditioning, phones, satellite TV, and VCR and CD players; bikes and canoes are available for guests. Rates include bountiful continental breakfasts and afternoon tea, but check out the packages, especially if you wish to dine at one of the restaurants. All but the Beach House are within easy walking distance of Dock Square.

Innkeeper (and restaurateur and artist) Jack Nahil seems to have a magic touch with everything he undertakes. Now he's rehabbed the **⚑ Cape Arundel Inn** (208 Ocean Ave., Kennebunkport 04046, 207/967-2125, www.cape arundelinn.com), making it (and its restaurant) a prime destination. The fabulous ocean view (all but two rooms overlook the Bush estate) doesn't hurt, either. The Cape Arundel compound consists of the Shingle-style main inn building (seven rooms, most with water views; $275–345), the

Rockbound motel-style building (six rooms with sea-view balconies; $285–295), and the Carriage House Loft, a large suite on the upper floor of the carriage house ($275). An expanded continental breakfast buffet is included. Most rooms have fireplaces; Rockbound and Carriage House have TV. Open March to January 1. The inn's restaurant earns raves.

If nonstop beaching is your vacation goal, book one of the 22 rooms at **Tides Inn by-the-Sea** (252 Kings Hwy., Goose Rocks Beach, Kennebunkport 04046, 207/967-3757, www.tidesinnbythesea.com), directly across the street from superb Goose Rocks Beach. Decor at the John Calvin Stevens–designed Victorian inn is funky, whimsical (faux painting, costumed dummies, a resident ghost named Emma), and altogether fun. Next door is **Tides Too,** a modern, condo-type building with one- and two-bedroom efficiencies by the week ($3,500 for four people). Inn rooms, early June to Labor Day, go for $195–325 d, including continental breakfast. Open mid-May to mid-October. The inn's first-rate Belvidere Club serves breakfast and creative dinners.

The sprawling, riverfront **Nonantum Resort** (95 Ocean Ave., P.O. Box 2626, Kennebunkport 04046, 207/967-4050 or 800/552-5651, www.nonantumresort.com, $169–349), which dates from 1884, includes a bit of everything, from simple rooms with an old-fashioned, Victorian decor to modern family suites with kitchenettes. Some rooms have views to open ocean. Facilities include a dining room, an outdoor heated pool, and a whirlpool. All 115 rooms have air-conditioning and TV; some have refrigerators. Rates include a full breakfast. The dining room is also open for dinner and, in July and August, lunch. Packages, many of which include dinner, are a good choice. Do note: Weddings take place here almost every weekend. Open April–mid-November.

Innkeepers and chefs Brian and Shanna O'Hea (they met at the Culinary Institute of America) have created a lovely escape at **The Kennebunk Inn** (45 Maine St., Kennebunk 04043, 207/985-3351, www.thekennebunkinn.com, $110–170), a rambling 200-year-old inn in downtown Kennebunk. None of the 28 guest rooms are the same.

Some have air-conditioning or antique claw-foot tubs or fireplaces; all have TV and phones. The inn has both a dining room and pub. Rates include a continental breakfast, but a dine-and-stay package for an additional $33 pp includes a three-course meal in the dining room each night.

B&Bs

Rivaling the White Barn Inn for service, decor, amenities, and overall luxury is the three-story **M Captain Lord Mansion** (P.O. Box 800 Kennebunkport 04046, 207/967-3141 or 800/522-3141, www.captainlord.com, $215–450) which is one of the finest B&Bs anywhere. And no wonder—innkeepers Rick and Bev Littlefield have been at it for more than 25 years, and they're never content to rest on their laurels. Each year the inn improves upon seeming perfection. If you want to be pampered and stay in a meticulously decorated and historical B&B with marble bathrooms (heated floors, many with double Jacuzzis), fireplaces, original artwork, phones, and air-conditioning in all rooms and even a few cedar closets, then look no further. Even breakfast is a special affair, with fresh-squeezed orange juice made from oranges flown in daily. Bicycles and beach towels and chairs are available. Afternoon treats are provided.

The elegant, Federal-style **M Captain Jefferds Inn** (5 Pearl St., P.O. Box 691, Kennebunkport 04046, 207/967-2311 or 800/839-6844, www.captainjefferdsinn.com, $165–340), located in the historic district, provides the ambience of a real captain's house. It's so big, you might want to drop popcorn to find your way back to your room. Each of the 15 rooms and suites (11 in the main house and four more in the carriage house) has a different feel. All have plush linens, fresh flowers, down comforters, CD players, and air-conditioning; some have fireplaces, whirlpool tubs, and other luxuries. A three-course breakfast and afternoon tea are included.

The low-key, turn-of-the-20th-century **M Green Heron Inn** (126 Ocean Ave., Kennebunkport 04046, 207/967-3315, www.greenheroninn.com) sees many repeat guests. Ten rooms and a two-story cottage have TV, phones, air-conditioning, and private baths; some have fireplaces, microwaves, or refrigerators; most have cove views. Prices are $145–175 d (cottage is $250). Children are welcome; some pets are accepted ($10 per night). Also included is breakfast—one of the best in town—served in the coveside breakfast room. The inn is open mid-May to late October.

You'll awake to the drone of lobsterboat engines at **The Inn at Harbor Head** (41 Pier Rd., Cape Porpoise, Kennebunkport 04046, 207/967-5564, fax 207/967-1294, www.harborhead.com), an idyllic spot on Cape Porpoise Harbor, 2.5 miles from Dock Square. Hand-painted murals, monogrammed bathrobes, flower bouquets, a superb library, hammocks in the yard, and outstanding views are just a few of the many pluses here. There are three rooms and one good-sized suite; some have whirlpool tubs, fireplaces, or private decks. Rates are $195–325 d. Open May through October.

Here's a bargain: the nonprofit **Franciscan Guest House** (28 Beach Ave., P.O. Box 980, Kennebunkport 04046, 207/967-4865, www.franciscan guesthouse.com), on the grounds of the monastery, has rooms spread among two buildings, as well as three other Tudor-style cottages. Accommodations are basic, but do have some nice amenities, including TV, air-conditioning, and an outdoor pool. A full breakfast is included in the rates, and a buffet dinner often is available. There is no daily maid service, but fresh towels are provided daily. Rooms are $80–139, one- to three-bedroom suites are $119–249. Open mid-May to October. No credit cards.

Motels and Cottages

Patricia Mason is the 12th-generation innkeeper at **ℕ The Seaside Motor Inn & Cottages** (80 Beach Ave., Kennebunk, mailing address P.O. Box 631, Kennebunkport 04046, 207/967-4461 or 800/967-4461, www.kennebunkbeach.com, $229–239), a property that has been in her family since the mid-1600s. What a location! The 22-room motel and 10 cottages sit on 20 acres bordered by the Atlantic Ocean, the Kennebec River, and Gooch's River. It's the only truly beachfront property in the area, with a private beach for guests. Motel rooms are spacious, with TV, air-conditioning, and refrigerators. A continental

breakfast is included in the rates. The one- to four-bedroom cottages are rented by the week, with rates ranging from $965 to $2,600.

With indoor and outdoor heated pools and whirlpools and a good-sized fitness center, the **Rhumb Line Motor Lodge** (Ocean Ave., P.O. Box 3067, Kennebunkport 04046, 207/967-5457 or 800/337-4862, fax 207/967-4418, www.rhumblinemaine.com) is a magnet for families. This well-managed two-story establishment in a quiet residential area three miles from Dock Square has easy access to the trolley-bus service. Fifty-nine large rooms have private balconies or patios, phones, air-conditioning, cable TV, and small refrigerators. Free continental breakfast. From late May to mid-September, weather permitting, there are nightly poolside lobsterbakes. Rates are $145–175; kids 12 and under stay free. Special packages off-season. Open year-round except January.

Fifteen trim one- and two-bedroom cottages rim the tidal cove at **Cabot Cove Cottages** (7 S. Maine St., P.O. Box 1082, Kennebunkport 04046, 207/967-5424 or 800/962-5424, www.cabot-covecottages.com). Fully-equipped, pine-paneled, wicker-furnished efficiencies ($147–190 per night or $1,000–1,200 per week), within easy walking distance of Dock Square and Colony Beach, are just the ticket for families. Cottages have TV but no phones. Laundry facilities available. Leashed pets ($7 per night) are allowed (deposit required), as is smoking in some cottages. Rowboats, picnic tables, a grill, and laundry facilities are available. Open mid-May to mid-October.

Compared with other area properties, the **Fontenay Terrace Motel** (128 Ocean Ave., Kennebunkport 04046, 207/967-3556, www .fontenaymotel.com, $120–135) is a bargain. Innkeepers Charles an Carol Reid keep the place spotless. It borders a tidal inlet and has a private grassy and shaded lawn, perfect for retreating from the hubbub of busy Kennebunkport. Each of the eight rooms has air-conditioning, mini-fridge, cable TV, and phone; some have water views. A small beach is 300 yards away, and it's a pleasant one-mile walk to Dock Square.

Perhaps one of the best deals in the area is the clean and simple **Cape Porpoise Motel** (12 Mills

Rd., Rte. 9, P.O. Box 7218, Cape Porpoise 04014, 207/967-3370, www.capeporpoisemotel.com, $95–110). All rooms have TV and air-conditioning, some have kitchenettes; rates include a continental breakfast. Also available by the week or month are efficiencies with full kitchens, phones, and one or more bedrooms. It's an easy walk to Cape Porpoise restaurants and sights. Open May–mid-October.

Seasonal Rentals

Weekly and monthly rentals, like nightly room rates, are fairly steep in the Kennebunks. Several real-estate firms handle seasonal rentals. Start with **Kennebunk Beach Realty** (Rte. 9, P.O. Box 31, Kennebunkport 04046, 207/967-5481, fax 207/967-2940, www.kennebunkbeachrealty.com) or **Port Properties** (Cooper's Corner, Rte. 9 and Rte. 35, Lower Village, P.O. Box 799, Kennebunkport 04046, 207/967-4400 or 800/443-7678, www.portproperties.com).

FOOD

Breakfast and Picnic Fare

All Day Breakfast (55 Western Ave., Rte. 9, Lower Village, Kennebunk 04043, 207/967-5132) is a favorite meeting spot, offering such specialties as invent-your-own omelets and crepes, Texas French toast, and the ADB sandwich. ADB is open 7 A.M.–1:30 P.M. weekdays in summer (to 2 P.M. weekends). Closed mid-December to mid-January.

It's hard to choose the perfect pastry from the large selection at **Port Bakery and Café** (181 Port Rd., Kennebunk, 207/967-2263, opens at 7 A.M. daily). Hot breakfasts are also available, as are soups and sandwiches and other goodies. Eat in or outside on the deck or take it all to go.

Conveniently near the Kennebunk & Kennebunkport Chamber of Commerce, **H.B. Provisions** (15 Western Ave, Lower Village, Kennebunk 04043, 207/967-5762) has an excellent wine selection, along with plenty of picnic supplies, newspapers, and all the typical general-store inventory. It also serves breakfast and prepares hot and cold sandwiches, salads, and wraps. Open daily, all year.

The **Kennebunk Farmers' Market** sets up shop from mid-May to mid-October in the Grove Street municipal parking lot off Route 1 (behind the Mobil station). Hours are Saturday 8 A.M.–noon May–October. Vendors sell crafts, condiments, fresh produce (including organic), flowers, breads, biscotti; special events (tastings, etc.) are sometimes on the agenda.

Casual Dining

Nearest thing to being afloat is sitting at a riverfront deck table at **Arundel Wharf** (43 Ocean Ave., Kennebunkport 04046, 207/967-3444), where passing tour and lobsterboats provide plenty of lunchtime entertainment. Captain's chairs and chart-topped tables complete the nautical picture. Service is efficient and friendly. On nasty days, a fireplace warms the indoor dining area. Burgers and fries are always on the menu for kids; adults can enjoy lobster with a touch of class; dinner entrées are $14–30. Open daily at 11:30 A.M. for lunch and dinner mid-May to mid-December; reservations are wise for dinner.

Federal Jack's Restaurant and Brewpub (8 Western Ave., Lower Village, Kennebunk 04043, 207/967-4322, 11:30 A.M.–1 A.M. with late-night menu after 9 P.M., opens 10:30 A.M. Sun.) offers on tap the specialty beers of Kennebunkport Brewing Company, producers of Shipyard beers and ales—Goat Island Light, Blue Fin Stout, and several seasonal ales. An eclectic regional American lunch and dinner menu ($10–17 for entrées, plus plenty of tasty pub food; good burgers) keeps kids and adults happy at Federal Jack's (named after a locally built 19th-century schooner), and the brewery also makes nonalcoholic root beer and birch beer. There's live acoustic music on weekends, and brunch is served Sundays from 10:30 A.M. to 2 P.M.

Bush-watchers often head to **Mabel's Lobster Claw** (Ocean Ave., Kennebunkport 04046, 207/967-2562), hoping to spot the former president (the little place is just around the corner from Walker's Point). Try Mabel Hanson's chowder or a lobster roll and see why the restaurant's a favorite (entrées top off around $30); reservations are wise. During the summer, it's open 11:30 A.M.–3 P.M. and 5–9 P.M. daily.

Cherie's Bistro (7 High St., Kennebunk, 207/985-1200, 7–11 A.M. Tues.–Sat., 9 A.M.–1 P.M. Sun., and 5:30–9 P.M. Tues.–Sun.) has a dual personality. It's a cheery self-serve bakery/café by day, a stylish restaurant at night. The dinner menu (entrées $15–18) is built upon fresh and locally available foods. Kids' menu available. Whatever you do, save room for dessert.

Rustic Mediterranean cuisine is the draw at **Sam Buca's Bistro** (50 Main St., Kennebunk, 207/985-9078, 11 A.M.–3 P.M. Mon.–Fri. and 5 P.M.–close Tues.–Sat.). Entrées ($13–18) provide a taste of the Mediterranean: Greek, French, and Sicilian pastas, Portuguese mussels, moussaka, marsala, and even grilled salmon Provençal. Pizzas, pastas, soups, salads, and sandwiches are on the lunch menu.

Grab a stool at the counter, slip into a booth, or wait for a table at the **Wayfarer** (Pier Rd., Cape Porpoise, 207/967-8961), a casual restaurant that serves breakfast, lunch, and dinner to locals and in-the-know tourists (dinner entrées $10–19). Open for breakfast 7–11 A.M., for lunch 11:30 A.M.–2 P.M., and dinner 5–8 P.M. Wednesday–Saturday and 7 A.M.–noon Sunday. Good lobster stew; nightly dinner specials. Most choices are in the $10–19 range. No credit cards.

Fine Dining

While none of these restaurants require a tie or jacket, you might want to dress up a bit.

Just west of the junction of Routes 9 and 35, casually elegant **Grissini Trattoria** (27 Western Ave., Kennebunk 04043, 207/967-2211), a sibling of the White Barn Inn, has drawn nothing but bravos since it opened. Attentive service, an inspired Tuscan menu (entrées $15–27), and a bright, open-beamed space make it a winner. In nice weather, try for the sunken patio. Reservations are advisable. Open daily 5:30–9 P.M. (to 9:30 P.M. weekends).

Despite the name, **Stripers Fish Shack** (Breakwater Inn, 127 Ocean Ave., Kennebunkport, 207/967-5333), another White Barn Inn sibling, is a rather fancy dining room overlooking the Kennebunk River. It's accented by a saltwater tank with coral reef and exotic fish. Fish and seafood are the specialties, with most

entrées in the $18–28 range. Dress is casual. Valet parking is available. Hours are 5:30–9 P.M. daily (to 9:30 P.M. Fri. and Sat.) April–late October and also 11:30 A.M.–2 P.M. Memorial Day to Labor Day.

The restaurant at the **Cape Arundel Inn** (208 Ocean Ave., Kennebunkport, 207/967-2125, 5:30–9:30 P.M. early March through Dec.), where every table has an ocean view, earns raves for its intriguingly creative cuisine; entrées are $20–34. At **The Colony** (140 Ocean Ave. at King's Highway, Kennebunkport, 207/967-3331), the hotel dining room is open to the public for breakfast, lunch, and dinner; reservations are advisable. Sunday brunch is a big winner, 11 A.M.–2 P.M. mid-June to Labor Day.

The first-rate **Belvidere Club** (Tides Inn by-the-Sea, 252 Kings Hwy., Goose Rocks Beach, Kennebunkport, 207/967-3757) is open to the public Wednesday–Sunday for breakfast and creative dinners with a small but select menu (entrées $22–25). **The Kennebunk Inn** (45 Main St., Kennebunk, 207/985-3351) has both a dining room (5–9 P.M. Wed.–Sat., entrées $19–28) and pub (5–9 P.M. daily, $7–15). The menu emphasizes fresh and local foods. Lunch is served weekdays 11:30 A.M.–2 P.M.

Fusion cuisine reigns at **On the Marsh** (46 Western Ave., Rte. 9, Lower Village, Kennebunk 04043, 207/967-2299), a restored barn overlooking marshlands leading to Kennebunk Beach. Entrée range is $19–29. The decor here is astonishing, courtesy of owner Denise Rubin, an interior designer: raspberry exterior, art and antiques on both floors of the interior. Dining choices include both an "owner's table" and a "kitchen table." Entrées might include grilled tuna with French bean salad and seared sea scallops with lobster risotto. Quiet piano music adds to the elegant but unstuffy ambience; service is attentive. Reservations are essential in midsummer. Open for dinner 5:30–9:30 P.M. Closed January.

Winner of a raft of culinary awards, **Windows on the Water** (12 Chase Hill Rd., Kennebunk 04043, 207/967-3313 or 800/773-3313, 11:45 A.M.–2:30 P.M. and 5:30–9:30 P.M. daily, to 10:30 P.M. Fri. and Sat.) has been filling its screened porch, patio, and dining rooms since

1985. It's appropriately named, with big windows providing views over nearby shops to the busy harbor. Lunch entrées are $9–17; dinner entrées are $19–39, the high end for such dishes as lobster ravioli and Thai lobster. Reservations advisable—essential in midsummer.

Both the view and the food are outstanding at ⚡ **Pier 77** (77 Pier Road, Cape Porpoise 04014, 207/967-8500, 11:30 A.M.–3 P.M. and 5–9 P.M.). Chef Peter and his wife, Kate, have created an especially welcoming restaurant, where the menu ranges from lamb kebabs to lobster farfalle (entrées $13–30). Frequent live entertainment provides nice background and complements the views over Cape Porpoise Harbor, with lobsterboats hustling to and fro. Reservations advisable. Practically hidden downstairs is **The Ramp Bar & Grille** (11:30 A.M.–10 P.M.), with lighter fare and a sports-pub decor.

Destination Dining

One of Maine's biggest and best splurges is the ⚡ **White Barn Inn** (37 Beach Ave., P.O. Box 560C, Kennebunkport 04046, 207/967-2321, fax 207/967-1100, 6–9 P.M. Mon.–Thurs., 5:30–9:15 P.M. Fri.–Sun.)—haute cuisine, haute prices, haute-rustic barn. In summer, don't be surprised to run into members of ex-President George Bush's clan (probably at the back window table). Soft piano music accompanies impeccable service and chef Jonathan Cartwright's outstanding four-course prix-fixe menu ($91 pp, excluding wine). Reservations are essential—book well ahead during July and August—and you'll need a credit card (cancel 24 hours ahead or you'll have a charge). No jeans or sneakers—jackets are required. Maine's only AAA five-diamond restaurant, it's part of the Relais et Chateaux network. Closed early–late January.

Lobster-in-the-Rough

At the end of the road in Cape Porpoise is the **Cape Pier Chowder House** (79 Pier Rd., Cape Porpoise, 207/967-0123, 11 A.M.–close daily and 7–10:30 A.M. Fri.–Mon.). Most folks come for the lobster, but you can get fried seafood and fish plates ($8–24) as well as highly rated lobster rolls ($11) and sandwiches (even PB&J, $2). Order inside,

then grab one of the tables on the wharf for wowser views of Cape Porpoise out to Goat Island.

Nearby is **Nunan's Lobster Hut** (9 Mills Rd., Cape Porpoise, 207/967-4362, 5 P.M.–close), a casual dockside eatery with indoor and outdoor seating that's been serving lobsters since 1953.

INFORMATION AND SERVICES

Information

The **Kennebunk & Kennebunkport Chamber of Commerce** (17 Western Ave., Rte. 9, Lower Village, P.O. Box 740, Kennebunk 04043, 207/967-0857, fax 207/967-2867, www.visitthekennebunks.com) has an especially helpful staff; inquire about accommodations, restaurant menus, area maps, bike maps, tide calendars, recreation, and beach parking permits. Be sure to request a copy of the handsome annual chamber booklet, available each January and loaded with ads and enough useful information to plan any kind of vacation in the Kennebunks. The office is close to Meserve's Market, near the intersection of Routes 9 and 35 and about midway between Route 35 and the Kennebunk River.

Hospitals

Hospitals serving the region are: **York Hospital** (15 Hospital Dr., York 03909, emergency room 207/351-2157), **Southern Maine Medical Center** (1 Medical Center Dr., Biddeford 04005, emergency room 207/283-7100), **Goodall Hospital** (25 June St., Sanford 04073, 207/324-4310).

For minor medical problems: **Kennebunk Walk-In Clinic** (24 Portland Rd., Rte. 1, Kennebunk, 207/985-6027). York Hospital's **Tel-a-Nurse** service (800/283-7234) provides free over-the-phone advice for minor medical problems.

Local Libraries

The **Louis T. Graves Memorial Public Library** (18 Maine St., Kennebunkport, 207/967-2778) is open 1–8 P.M. Monday, Wednesday, and Thursday; 10 A.M.–8 P.M. Tuesday; 10 A.M.–5 P.M. Friday; and 9 A.M.–noon Saturday.

The **Kennebunk Free Library** (112 Main St., 207/985-2173) is open 9:30 A.M.–8 P.M.

Monday and Tuesday, 12:30–8 P.M. Wednesday, 9:30 A.M.–5 P.M. Thursday and Friday, and Saturday 9:30 A.M.–5 P.M.

Public Restrooms

Public toilets are at Gooch's and Mother's Beaches, St. Anthony's Monastery, the chamber of commerce building (17 Western Ave.), and at the chamber's Dock Square Hospitality Center.

Getting Around

From Memorial Day to mid-October, the **Intown Trolley** (207/967-3686) operates trolleybuses throughout Kennebunk and Kennebunkport, originating on Ocean Avenue (next to the Landing Restaurant) and making regular stops at beaches and other attractions. The entire route takes about 45 minutes, with the driver providing a hefty dose of local history and gossip. Seats are park-bench-style. An all-day ticket is $10 adults, $5 children 2–14. You can get on or off at any stop. The trolley operates hourly 10 A.M.–5 P.M. in July and August., to 4 P.M. in spring and fall.

Old Orchard Beach Area

A seven-mile unbroken stretch of white-sand beach has been drawing vacation-oriented folks for generations to the area stretching from Camp Ellis, in Saco, to Pine Point, in Scarborough. Cottage colonies and condo complexes dominate at the extremities, but the center of activity has always been and remains Old Orchard Beach.

In its heyday, Old Orchard Beach's Pier reached far out into the sea, huge resort hotels lined the sands, and wealthy Victorian folk (including Rose Fitzgerald and Joe Kennedy, who met on these sands in the days when men strolled around in dress suits and women toted parasols) came each summer to see and be seen.

Storms and fires have taken their toll over the years, and the grand resorts have been replaced by endless motels, many of which display *Nous parlons Français* signs to welcome the masses of French Canadians who arrive each summer. They're accompanied by young families, who come for the sand and surf, and T-shirted and body-pierced young pleasure seekers, who come for the nightlife. You'd better like people if you stop here, because this town welcomes tourists (the population expands from about 8,000 in winter to about 100,000 in midsummer).

Although town fathers are trying to alter its image, Old Orchard Beach remains somewhat gaudy and honky-tonk, and most of its visitors would have it no other way. French fries, cotton candy, and beach-accessories shops line the downtown, and as you get closer to The Pier, arcades and amusement parks crop up. There's not a kid on earth who wouldn't have fun in Old Orchard—even if some parents might find it all a bit much.

Much more sedate are the villages on the fringes. The Ocean Park section of Old Orchard, at the southwestern end of town, was established in 1881 as a religious summer-cottage community. It still offers interdenominational services and vacation Bible school, but it also has an active cultural association that sponsors concerts, Chautauquatype lectures, films, and other events throughout the summer. All are open to the public.

South of that is Camp Ellis. Begun as a small fishing village named after early settler Thomas Ellis, Camp Ellis is crowded with longtime summer homes that are in a constant battle with the sea. A nearly mile-long granite jetty—designed to keep silt from clogging the Saco River—has taken the blame for massive beach erosion in the last 20 years. But the jetty is a favorite spot for wetting a line (no fishing license needed) and for panoramic views off toward Wood Island Light (built in 1808) and Biddeford Pool. Camp Ellis Beach is open to the public, with lifeguards on duty in midsummer. Parking—scarce on hot days—is $10 a day.

Heading north from Old Orchard is Pine Point, another longtime community of vacation homes. Services are few and parking is $10 a day.

Most folks get to Old Orchard by passing through Saco and Biddeford, which have long been upstairs/downstairs sister cities, with wealthy mill owners living in Saco and their workers (and

AMUSEMENT PARKS AND AMUSING PLACES

If you've got kids or just love amusement parks, you'll find Maine's best in this region; sand and sun just seem to complement arcades and rides perfectly.

The biggie is **Funtown/Splashtown USA** (774 Portland Rd., Rte. 1, Saco, 207/284-5139 or 800/878-2900, www.funtownsplashtownusa.com). Ride Maine's only wooden roller coaster; fly down New England's longest and tallest log flume ride; free-fall 200 feet on Dragon's Descent; get wet and go wild riding speed slides, tunnel slides, and river slides or splashing in the pool. Add in a huge kiddie ride section, games, food, and other activities for a full day of family fun.

Funtown opens weekends in early May, Splashtown in mid-June; everything's up and running daily from late June to Labor Day, when Funtown is open 10 A.M.–9 P.M. (to 10 P.M. Saturdays) and Splashtown hours are 10 A.M.–6 P.M. Rates vary by height—"big" for those 48 inches and taller, and "little" for those 38–48 inches tall; kids less than 38 inches tall get in free. A Funtown USA Ride Pass provides two rides on the Grand Prix Racers and unlimited use of all other rides for $25 big, $17 little. A night special valid after 5 P.M. is $18 big and $12 little. A Splashtown unlimited slide pass is $17 big and $14 little. Combo passes for two rides on the Grand Prix Racers and unlimited use of all other rides, slides, and pools cost $32 big and $23 little. A $10 walk-around pass lets you into the park and onto the water park observation deck but doesn't include rides, slides, or pools. Minigolf is available separately for $4 big and $3.50 little. Season passes are also available.

The biggest beachfront amusement park, **Palace Playland** (1 Old Orchard St., Old Orchard, 207/934-2001, www.palaceplayland.com), has more than 25 rides and attractions packed into four acres, including a giant water slide, fun house, bumper cars, Ferris wheel, roller coaster, and a 24,000-square-foot arcade with more than 200 games. For a bird's-eye view of the area, ride the 75-foot-high gondola Sunwheel. Get soaked riding the Log Flume. Rev up the action on two roller coasters, one with a five-story drop, both with high-speed twisting turns. Kiddie Land has more than a dozen rides, including a fun house and a splashing whale. An unlimited pass is $22.95 per day, a kiddie pass good for all two-ticket rides is $15.95; two-day, season, and per ride tickets ($2–4) are available. Open Memorial Day to Labor Day.

The Pier, jutting 475 feet into the ocean from downtown Old Orchard, is a minimall of shops, arcades, and fast-food outlets. Far longer when it was built in 1898, it's been lopped off gradually by fires and storms. The current incarnation has been here since the late 1970s.

workplaces) in Biddeford. But even those personalities have always been split—congested, commercial Route 1 is part of Saco, and the exclusive enclave of Biddeford Pool is, of course, in below-stairs Biddeford. Saco still has an attractive downtown, with boutiques and stunning homes on Main Street and beyond.

Biddeford boasts a preponderance of secondhand shops downtown but is also home to the magnificent Biddeford City Theater and the University of New England. And as plans proceed for a riverfront park and other ambitious projects, Biddeford is moving quickly to try to change its blue-collar milltown image. Another Biddeford hallmark is its Franco-American tradition—thanks to the French-speaking workers who sustained the textile and shoemaking industries in the 19th century. Never is the heritage more evident than during Biddeford's annual La Kermesse festival in late June.

SIGHTS

Saco Museum

Founded in 1866, the Saco Museum, formerly the York Institute Museum (371 Main St., Saco 04072, 207/283-0684 or 207/282-3031, noon–4 P.M. Sun.–Fri., Thurs. to 8 P.M., donation) might also be one of the state's best-kept secrets. It shouldn't be. The outstanding collection, some of it rotated annually, includes 18th- and 19th-century paintings, furniture, and other household treasures. Lectures, workshops, and concerts are also part of the museum's annual schedule.

The Pier
Yes, it's honky-tonk, and yes, it's probably the most touristy place in the region, but for people-watching, you can't beat The Pier (end of Old Orchard St., over the beach, Old Orchard Beach). Fires and storms have taken their toll over the years, but it still extends about 500 feet over the ocean and it's still the heart of Old Orchard's parade of humanity. Hawkers challenge passersby to try their luck at games, shops sell trinkets and beachwear, and fast food rules. It's also the site for frequent evening entertainment and weekly fireworks.

PARKS AND PRESERVES
Saco Bay Trails, a local land trust, has produced a very helpful trail guide that includes the Saco Heath, the East Point Sanctuary, and more than a dozen other local trails. The Cascade Falls trail, for example, is a half-mile stroll ending at a waterfall. Copies are available for $5 at a number of Biddeford and Saco locations (including the Dyer Library) or from **Saco Bay Trails** (P.O. Box 7505, Ocean Park 04063, www.sacobaytrails.org).

© TOM NANGLE

An easy trail, with views to Wood Island Light, edges Maine Audubon's East Point Sanctuary, an especially popular spot for bird-watching.

East Point Sanctuary
Owned by Maine Audubon, the 30-acre East Point Sanctuary is a splendid preserve at the eastern end of Biddeford Pool. Crashing surf, beach roses, bayberry bushes, and offshore Wood Island Light are all features of the two-part perimeter trail here—skirting the golf course of the exclusive Abenakee Club. Allow at least an hour; even in fog, the setting is dramatic. During spring and fall migrations, it's one of southern Maine's prime birding locales, so you'll have plenty of company if you show up then, and the usual streetside parking may be scarce. Open sunrise to sundown, all year. It's poorly signposted (perhaps deliberately?), so here are the directions: From Route 9 (Main Street) in downtown Biddeford, take Route 9/208 (Pool Road) southeast about five miles to the Route 208 turnoff to Biddeford Pool. Go .6 mile on Route 208 (Bridge Road), then left onto Mile Stretch Road. Continue to Lester B. Orcutt Boulevard, turn left, and go to the end. For further information, contact Maine Audubon (20 Gilsland Farm Rd., P.O. Box 6009, Falmouth 04105, 207/781-2330).

The Heath
Owned by The Nature Conservancy, 870-acre **Saco Heath Preserve** is the nation's southernmost "raised coalesced bog"—where peat accumulated over eons into two above-water dome shapes that eventually merged into a single natural feature. For a bit of esoterica, it's the home of the rare Hessel's hairstreak butterfly. Pick up a map at the parking area and follow the mile-long, self-guided trail through the woods and then into the heath via boardwalk. Best time to come is early to mid-October, when the heath and woodland colors are positively brilliant and insects are on the wane. You're likely to see deer, and perhaps even spot a moose. The preserve

entrance is on Route 112, Buxton Road, two miles west of I-95. Open all year, sunrise to sunset, it's also popular with snowshoers and cross-country skiers in winter. For information, contact **The Nature Conservancy** (14 Maine St., Fort Andross, Brunswick 04011, 207/729-5181, fax 207/729-4118).

Ferry Beach State Park

When the weather's hot, arrive early at Ferry Beach State Park (Bay View Rd., off Rte. 9, Saco, 207/283-0067), a pristine beach backed by dune grass on Saco Bay. The 117-acre park offers changing rooms, restrooms, a lifeguard, picnic tables, and five easy interconnected nature trails winding through woodlands, marshlands, and dunes. (Later in the day, keep the insect repellent handy.) Admission is $3 adults, $1 children 5–11, free for seniors and kids under five. Open daily Memorial Day weekend to September 30, but accessible all year. (Trail markers are removed in winter.)

RECREATION

Golf

Opened in 1922 as a nine-hole course, the **Biddeford-Saco Country Club** (101 Old Orchard Rd., P.O. Box 448, Saco 04072, 207/282-5883) added a back nine in 1987 (toughest hole on the par-71 course is the 11th). Tee times not usually needed. Fees are moderate. Open to the public early April to mid-November.

The challenging 18-hole, par-71 **Dunegrass Golf Club** (200 Wild Dunes Way, Old Orchard Beach 04064, 207/934-4513 or 800/521-1029) covers more than 300 acres. Greens fees are a bit steep, but well worth a splurge. Tee times are essential. The sprawling modern clubhouse has a restaurant and pro shop.

Sea Kayaking

Gone with the Wind (Yates St., Biddeford Pool, 207/283-8336, www.gwtwonline.com) offers both tours (afternoon and sunset, with prices varying with the number of people on the tour; two people are about $85 pp) and rentals ($40 half day, $60 full day). Kids and seniors get a $10 pp discount.

ENTERTAINMENT

Biddeford City Theater

Designed by noted architect John Calvin Stevens in 1896, the 500-seat National Historic Register Biddeford City Theater (205 Main St., P.O. Box 993, Biddeford 04005, tel./fax 207/282-0849, www.citytheater.org) has been superbly restored, and acoustics are excellent even when Eva Gray, the resident ghost, mixes it up backstage. A respected community theater group mounts a winter drama season and showcases other talent throughout the year. Check local papers or call for schedule.

Cinema

Competing head-to-head in Biddeford and Saco are two multiplexes—**Hoyts Cinema 8** (420 Alfred Rd., Biddeford, 207/282-5995) and **Cinemagic Saco 12** (779 Portland Rd., Rte. 1, Saco, 207/282-6234)—less than five miles from each other and showing first-run films. Ticket prices keep getting lower, and both theaters have bargain matinees before 6 P.M. daily. Cinemagic, across from Funtown/Splashtown USA, has stadium seating and an arcade. They're both open year-round.

Fireworks

Fireworks are set off by The Pier, in Old Orchard Beach, every Thursday night at 9:45 P.M. from late June through Labor Day.

Live Music

You'll find plenty of it in Old Orchard Beach at places including **The Krazy Klam, Pier Patio Pub, Village Inn, PICS Pizza,** and **Surf 6.**

Free concerts are staged by The Pier at 7 P.M. every Monday and Tuesday in July and August.

Another option for family concerts and other performances is the **Old Orchard Beach Pavilion** (Union Ave. and 6th St., 207/934-2024, www.oobpavilion.org).

Ocean Park

Ocean Park's Temple, a 19th-century octagon that seats 800-plus, is the venue for Sunday-night concerts (7:30 P.M., $8 adults). The Chautauqua-style community also presents films, lectures, children's activities, and other cultural and religious programs throughout the summer. Most are open to nonmembers for a small fee. Pick up a schedule at the Old Orchard Beach chamber or visit Ocean Park's website (www.oceanpark.org).

EVENTS

La Kermesse (meaning "the fair" or "the festival") is Biddeford's summer highlight, when nearly 50,000 visitors pour into town on the last full weekend in June (Thurs.–Sun.) to celebrate the town's Franco-American heritage. Local volunteers go all out to plan block parties, a parade, games, carnival, live entertainment, and traditional dancing—most of it is centered on Biddeford's Waterhouse Field. Then there's *la cuisine franco-américaine;* you can fill up on *boudin, creton, poutine, tourtière, tarte au saumon,* and crepes (although your arteries may rebel). The camaraderie is contagious, much of it in a French you never learned in language class. As with revelers on St. Patrick's Day who adopt Irish heritage, everyone instantly becomes Franco-American during La Kermesse, but festival organizers have reached out in recent years to other ethnic groups to make this a multicultural event. For more information, call 207/283-1889.

Generally scheduled for the Saturday of the same weekend, the **Saco Sidewalk Arts Festival** involves more than 150 artists exhibiting their work all along Saco's Main Street. Strolling musicians, kids' activities, and food booths are all part of the well-organized, daylong event.

In mid-July, the parishioners of St. Demetrios Greek Orthodox Church (186 Bradley St., Saco 04072, 207/284-5651) go all out to mount the annual **Greek Heritage Festival,** a three-day extravaganza of homemade Greek food, traditional Greek music and dancing, and a craft fair. Be sure to tour the impressive $1.5 million domed church building.

Football fans might want to watch the annual **Shriner's Lobster Bowl,** an all-star high school football game to benefit Shriner's Hospitals for Children.

The beaches come to life in July. Early July brings the annual **Parade and Sandcastle Contest** to Ocean Park.

One weekend in mid-August, Old Orchard Beach's **Beach Olympics** is a family festival of games, exhibitions, and music benefiting Maine's Special Olympics program.

Mid-September brings the annual **Car Show** at Memorial Park, in Old Orchard.

ACCOMMODATIONS

The area has hundreds of beds—mostly in motel-style lodgings. The chamber of commerce is the best resource for motels, cottages, and the area's more than 3,000 campsites. Only recently have a few B&Bs popped up.

☑ The Old Orchard Beach Inn (6 Portland Ave., Old Orchard Beach 04064, 207/934-5834 or 877/700-6624, fax 207/934-0782, www.old orchardbeachinn.com) was rescued from ruin by owner Steve Cecchetti and opened in summer 2000. Built in 1730, and most recently known as the Staples Inn, the National Historic Register building seemed destined for the wrecker's ball in 1997. Now it's been transformed, with 18 antique-filled rooms with air-conditioning, phones, and TV. Continental breakfast is included in the rates—$110–185; a two-bedroom suite is $250–400. Open all year.

On a quiet side street, **The Atlantic Birches Inn** (20 Portland Ave., Rte. 98, P.O. Box 334, Old Orchard Beach 04064, 207/934-5295 or 888/934-5295) has 10 guest rooms with air-conditioning in a Victorian house and separate cottage. Breakfast is hearty continental, and there's a swimming pool. The beach is an easy walk. Rates run $89–114 d. Open all year, but call ahead off-season.

The view is everything at Dick and Patte Kessler's **Nautilus by the Sea** (2 Colby Ave., P.O. Box 7276, Ocean Park 04063, 207/934-2021 or 800/981-7018), a Victorian guesthouse about as close as you can get to the water. Thirteen comfortable rooms and suites (private and shared baths) are a very reasonable $80–160, including continental breakfast.

The view's the same at Mary and Bill Kerrigan's **Billow House Oceanfront Motel and Guesthouse** (2 Temple Ave., Box 7543, Ocean Park 04063, 207/934-2333, www.billowhouse.com).

It has 13 units including rooms, studios with kitchenettes, and apartment suites with full kitchens and private seaside decks ($100–200). All rooms have TV/VCRs, access to a free washer and dryer, use of cooking grills, umbrella tables, and beach chairs, and even robes. Cookies are baked fresh daily. All are rented by the week only in July and August.

Look out to sea from the porch or deck of **Cristina's Bed & Breakfast** (36 Main Ave., Camp Ellis Beach, Saco 04072, 207/282-7483, trahan@prexar.com, $65–110), Cristina and Paul Trahan's vintage gingerbread-trimmed cottage with three pleasant guest rooms (one with private bath), all with Victorian furnishings. Rates include continental breakfast. No credit cards.

FOOD

Old Orchard Beach

Joseph's by the Sea (55 W. Grand Ave., Old Orchard Beach 04064, 207/934-5044, fax 207/934-1862) should really be named Joseph's Oasis—a quiet, dignified shorefront restaurant amid all the hoopla. Request a table on the screened patio. The menu—French with a dash of Maine—has entrées in the $17–27 range. Try the specialty Saco Bay soup, Maine-accented bouillabaisse. Reservations advisable in midsummer. Open daily for breakfast (7–11 A.M.) and dinner (5–9 P.M. off-season, to 9:30 P.M. in summer) March–December.

Immerse yourself in a Victorian manor at **Landmark** (28 East Grand Ave., Old Orchard Beach, 207/934-0156, 5–8 P.M. daily to 9 P.M. Fri. and Sat.). Ornate tin ceilings, shining wood floors, and paintings distinguish the dining areas, which include an enclosed porch. Entrées ($15–22) range from chicken to surf and turf.

After watching seasonal restaurants come and go year after year, the building's owners took matters into their own hands and opened **Yellowfin's Restaurant** (5 Temple Ave., Ocean Park, 207/934-1100, 8–11 A.M. and 5–10 P.M. Mon.–Sat.). Plans are to serve breakfast and dinner year-round in the light yellow dining room just steps away from the beach. Dinner entrées

range from vegetable stir-fry ($15) to yellowfin ahi tuna ($23) to rack of lamb ($25); children's menu available.

Camp Ellis

Two well-seasoned family restaurants service Camp Ellis. **Wormwood's Restaurant** (16 Bay Ave., Camp Ellis Beach, Saco 04072, 207/282-9679), next to the stone jetty, still draws the crowds and keeps its loyal clientele happy with ample portions and $6–16 entrées. Cajun-style seafood is a specialty. Open 11:30 A.M.–9 P.M.

At **Huot's Seafood Restaurant** (Camp Ellis Beach, Saco 04072, 207/282-1642), portions are large, prices are not. Open at 11 A.M. for lunch and dinner.

Saco

It's no surprise that seafood is the specialty at the **New England Shrimp Co.** (148 Main St., Saco, 207/282-5100, 11:30 A.M.–9 P.M. Tues.–Sat., 4:30–9 P.M. Sun.), which overlooks the Saco River (there's patio dining, too). The huge menu lists lots of choices, from pastas to steaks, and lots of seafood, but surprisingly little shrimp (entrées $14–20).

Traditions Italian Ristorante (162 Main St., Saco, 207/282-6661, 11 A.M.–2 P.M. and 5–9 P.M. Mon.–Sat.) is a comforting trattoria with dark wood, deep booths, and a nice bar. Settle in for some fine pasta, vitello, or pollo (entrées $8–17).

INFORMATION AND SERVICES

Information

The **Biddeford-Saco Chamber of Commerce and Industry** (110 Main St., Saco 04072, 207/282-1567, fax 207/282-3149, www.biddefordsacochamber.org) oversees development and tourism in the two-town area.

The staff at the **Old Orchard Beach Chamber of Commerce** (1st St., P.O. Box 600, Old Orchard Beach 04064, 207/934-2500 or 800/365-9386, fax 207/934-4994, www.oldorchardbeachmaine.com) is especially helpful. For information on Ocean Park, contact the **Ocean Park Association** (P.O. Box 7296, Ocean Park 04063, 207/934-9068, www.oceanpark.org).

Hospitals

Hospitals serving the region are: **York Hospital** (15 Hospital Dr., York 03909, emergency room 207/351-2157), **Southern Maine Medical Center** (1 Medical Center Dr., Biddeford 04005, emergency room 207/283-7100), **Goodall Hospital** (25 June St., Sanford 04073, 207/324-4310).

For minor medical problems, York Hospital's **Tel-a-Nurse** service (800/283-7234) provides free over-the-phone advice for minor medical problems.

Local Libraries

The **Dyer Library** (371 Main St., Saco 04072, 207/282-3031), next door to the Saco Museum, attracts scads of genealogists to its vast Maine history collection. Open Monday, Wednesday, and Friday 9:30 A.M.–5 P.M., Tuesday and Thursday to 8 P.M., Saturday 9:30 A.M.–12:30 P.M.

Libby Memorial Library (Staples St., Old Orchard Beach, 207/934-4351) is open 2–8 P.M. Monday and Wednesday, 10 A.M.–5:30 P.M. Tuesday, Thursday, and Friday, and 9:30–11:30 A.M. Saturday.

Getting Around

Between late June and Labor Day, the **Old Orchard Beach Trolley** (207/282-5408) operates trolley-buses on a regular schedule, connecting restaurants and campgrounds. Service begins at 10 A.M. and ends at midnight. Cost is $1 per ride; children under five ride free.

Operated by the Biddeford-Saco-Old Orchard Beach Transit Committee, **ShuttleBus Tri-Town Service** (207/282-5408, www.shuttlebus-zoom .com) provides frequent weekday and less-frequent weekend service (except national holidays) between Biddeford, Saco, and Old Orchard Beach. One-way fare is $1. **ShuttleBus Inter-City Service** connects Biddeford, Saco, and Old Orchard with Portland, South Portland, and Scarborough, with on-request service to the Maine Mall and the Concord Trailways terminal in Portland. One-way fare on the entire one-hour route is $3; kids under five are free; seniors pay half on Tuesday. **Zoom** buses operate between Biddeford and Saco and downtown Portland with a schedule designed for commuters. Zoom buses have bicycle racks. One-way fare is $3.

Greater Portland

*Note: Please see front color maps for
Greater Portland and Downtown Portland*

Whenever national magazines have articles highlighting the 10 best places to live, Greater Portland often makes the list. The very reasons that make the area so popular with residents make it equally attractive to visitors. Small in size, but big in heart, Greater Portland entices visitors with the staples—lighthouses, lobster, and L.L. Bean—but wows them with everything else it offers. It's the state's cultural hub, with performing arts centers, numerous festivals, and varied museums; a dining destination, with nationally recognized chefs as well as an amazing assortment

and variety of everyday restaurants; and despite its urban environment, it has a mind-boggling number of recreational opportunities.

Portland's population hovers around 65,000, but when the suburbs are included, it climbs to nearly a quarter of a million souls, making it Maine's largest, by far. Take a swing through the bedroom communities of Scarborough, Cape Elizabeth, and South Portland, and you'll better understand the area's popularity: easily accessible parks, beaches, rocky ledges, and lighthouses, all minutes from downtown. Then head north, passing through suburban Falmouth and Yarmouth and on to Freeport, home of mega sports retailer L.L. Bean. If you look carefully

Must-Sees

Look for **M** to find the sights and activities you can't miss and **M** for the best dining and lodging.

M The Old Port: Plan to spend at least a couple of hours browsing the shops, dining, and enjoying the energy of this restored historic district (page 77).

M Portland Museum of Art: This museum houses works by masters such as Winslow Homer, John Marin, Andrew Wyeth, Edward Hopper, and Marsden Hartley, as well as works by Monet, Picasso, and Renoir (page 78).

© TOM NANGLE

Climb the Portland Observatory for 360-degree views of Portland, from Casco Bay to the White Mountains.

M Victoria Mansion: This house is considered one of the most richly decorated dwellings of its period remaining in the country (page 78).

M Portland Observatory: Climb the 103 steps to the orb deck of the only remaining maritime signal tower on the eastern seaboard, and be rewarded with views from the White Mountains to the Casco Bay islands (page 79).

M Portland Head Light This lighthouse, commissioned by President George Washington, is fabulously sited on the rocky ledges of Cape Elizabeth (page 81).

M Casco Bay Tour: Take a three-hour tour on the mail boat, which stops briefly at five islands en route (page 82).

M Lucky Catch Lobster Tours: Go out on a working lobsterboat in Portland Harbor, see the sights, and perhaps return with a lobster for dinner (page 89).

M L.L. Bean: The empire's flagship store is in Freeport, and no trip to this shopping mecca is complete without a visit (page 106).

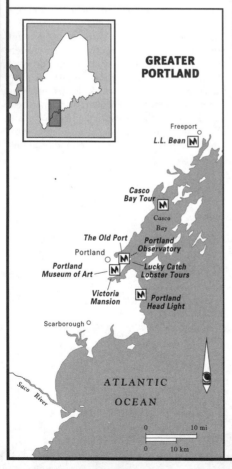

GREATER PORTLAND

Freeport
L.L. Bean **M**

Casco Bay Tour **M**

Casco Bay

The Old Port
Portland
Portland Observatory **M**
Portland
Museum of Art **M**
Lucky Catch
Lobster Tours **M**
Victoria Mansion **M**
Portland Head Light

Scarborough

Saco River

ATLANTIC OCEAN

0   10 mi
0   10 km

during your travels through suburbia, you'll still see vestiges of the region's heritage: sailboats and lobsterboats, traps and buoys piled on lawns or along driveways and, tucked here and there, farms with farmstands brimming with fresh produce.

Greater Portland also marks a transitional point on Maine's coastline. The long sand beaches of the Southern Coast begin to give way to a different coastline, one dotted with islands and edged with a jumble of rocks and ledges interrupted by rivers and coves.

July and August are the most popular times to visit, but Greater Portland is a year-round destination. Spring truly arrives by mid-May, when most summer outfitters begin operations at least on weekends. September is perhaps the loveliest month of the year weatherwise, and by mid-October, those fabled New England maples are turning crimson. No matter when you visit, pack layered clothing. Damp, foggy mornings can quickly give way to warm sunshine. Truly, there are usually only a handful of days each summer when folks wish they had an air conditioner, but for those days, you'll want to dress accordingly. A light sweater, fleece, or windbreaker is always handy when a sea breeze kicks up or after the sun sets.

While it might seem tempting to dismiss Portland in favor of seeking the Real Maine elsewhere along the coast, the truth is, the Real Maine is here. And while Portland alone provides plenty to keep a visitor busy, it's also an excellent base for day trips to places such as the Kennebunks, Freeport, Brunswick, and Bath, where more of that Real Maine flavor awaits.

PLANNING YOUR TIME

To do the region justice, spend at least three or four days here, more if your plans call for using Greater Portland as a base for day trips to more distant points. You can easily kill two days alone in downtown Portland, what with all the shops, museums, historical sites, the waterfront, and neighborhoods to explore. If you're staying in town and are an avid walker, you won't need a car to get to the in-town must-see sights: **Portland Museum of Art, Victoria Mansion, Old Port,** and **Portland Observatory.**

You simply must get out on the water. The best introduction to the islands of Casco Bay is aboard the **Mail Boat Tour** offered by Casco Bay Lines ferry service. Other options include an evening sail, an excursion to Eagle Island, or even a paddle around the islands in a kayak.

You will need a car to reach beyond the city. Allow a half day for a leisurely **lighthouse-and-parks tour** through South Portland and Cape Elizabeth, finishing (or starting) with lobster on the ledges at the Lobster Shack at Two Lights. Make it a full day and continue on to Prouts Neck in Scarborough for a few hours of sunbathing on the beach.

Avid shoppers should either stay in Freeport or allow at least a day to explore **L.L. Bean** and the 100 or so outlets nearby. If you're traveling with a super-shopper, don't despair. Freeport has parks and preserves that are light-years removed from the frenzy of its downtown, and from the fishing village of South Freeport you can take an excursion boat to Eagle Island, home of Arctic explorer Admiral Peary.

Greater Portland

Portland

Often compared to San Francisco (an oft-cited, unchallenged, but never verified statistic boasts it has more restaurants per capita than any city but San Fran), Portland is small, friendly, and easily explored on foot—although at times, it may seem that no matter which direction you head, it's uphill. The heart of Portland is the peninsula jutting into Casco Bay. It's bordered by the Eastern and Western Promenades, Back Cove, and the working waterfront. Salty sea breezes cool summer days and make winter ones seen even chillier. Unlike that other city by the bay, snow frequently blankets Portland from December into March.

Portland is Maine's most ethnically diverse city, with active refugee resettlement programs and dozens of languages spoken in the schools. Although salty sailors can still be found along the waterfront, Portland is increasingly a professional community, with young, upwardly mobile residents spiffing up Victorian houses and infusing new energy and money into the city's neighborhoods.

The region's cultural hub, Portland has a striking art museum housing three centuries of art and architecture and a world-class permanent collection, performing arts centers, active historical and preservation groups, an art school and a university, a symphony orchestra, numerous galleries, coffeehouses, and enough activities to keep culture vultures busy well into the night, especially in the thriving, handsomely restored Old Port and the up-and-coming Arts District.

Portland's also a sports- and outdoor-lovers playground, with trails for running, biking, skating and cross-country skiing, water sports aplenty, and a beloved minor league baseball team, the Sea Dogs. When city folks desire to escape, they often hop a ferry for one of the islands of Casco Bay or head to one of the parks, preserves, or beaches in the suburbs.

Still, Portland remains a major seaport. Lobsterboats, commercial fishing vessels, long-distance passenger boats, cruise ships, and local ferries dominate the working waterfront, and the briny scent of the sea—or bait—seasons the air.

PORTLAND NEIGHBORHOODS

The best way to appreciate the character of Portland's neighborhoods is on foot. So much of Portland can (and should) be covered on foot that it would take a book to list all the possibilities, but several dedicated volunteer groups have produced guides to facilitate the process.

Greater Portland Landmarks (207/774-5561, www.portlandlandmarks.org) is the doyenne, founded in 1964 to preserve Portland's historic architecture and promote responsible construction. The organization has published more than a dozen books and booklets, including *Discover Historic Portland on Foot*, a packet of four well-researched walking-tour guides to architecturally historic sections of Portland's peninsula: Old Port, Western Promenade, State Street, and Congress Street. It's available for $4.95 at local bookstores, some gift shops, and the visitor information center (245 Commercial St., 207/772-5800).

Also available at the visitor information center is a map, $1, detailing 36 significant antislavery sites in Portland. It also includes stories and information about the slave trade and what life was like for blacks during the slavery era. Six significant sites, each marked, are included in a 1.6-mile walking tour.

The **Portland Women's History Trail** details four loops—Congress Street, Munjoy Hill, State Street, and the West End—with about 20 stops on each loop. Among the sites: a long-gone chewing-gum factory where teenage girls worked 10-hour days. The trail guide is available for $8.50 in selected bookstores and at the Maine History Gallery gift shop (489 Congress St., Portland 04101, 207/879-0427).

Portland Trails (1 India St., Portland 04101, 207/775-2411, www.trails.org), a dynamic membership conservation organization incorporated in 1991, continually adds to the mileage it has mapped out for hiking and biking around Portland. The group's accomplishments include the 2.1-mile **Eastern Promenade Trail,** a landscaped bayfront dual pathway circling the base of Munjoy Hill and linking East End Beach to the Old Port, and a continuing trail connecting the Eastern Prom with the 3.5-mile Back Cove Trail, on the other side of I-295. Nearly two dozen trails are maintained, and the group also holds organized events—a great way to meet some locals. Contact Portland Trails for a colorful foldout map of Portland's entire trail and park system—including some proposed routes—a joint effort of Portland Trails and the Greater Portland Council of Governments' Kids and Transportation Program. Better still, join Portland Trails ($35 a year) and support its ambitious efforts.

The Old Port

Tony shops, cobblestone sidewalks, replica streetlights, and a casual, upmarket crowd (most of the time) set the scene for a district once filled with derelict buildings. The 1970s revival of the Old Port has infused funds, foot traffic, and flair into this part of town. Scores of unusual shops, ethnic restaurants, and spontaneous street-corner music make it a fun area to visit year-round. Nightlife centers on the Old Port, where a couple dozen bars keep everyone hopping until after midnight. Police keep a close eye on the district, but it can get a bit dicey after 11 P.M. on weekends. Caveat emptor—or maybe caveat peregrinator!

From mid-June to mid-October, at 10:30 A.M. daily, knowledgeable guides from Greater Portland Landmarks (207/774-5561, www.portlandlandmarks.org) lead a fascinating 90-minute **Old Port walking tour** in downtown Portland. No reservations needed. Buy tickets at the visitor information center (245 Commercial St.), where the tour begins and ends. Cost is $8 pp; kids under 16 with an adult are free.

Congress Street/ Downtown Arts District

Bit by bit, once-declining Congress Street is becoming revitalized, showcasing the best of the city's culture. Artists, starving and otherwise, spend much of their time here, thanks largely to encouragement from the energetic grassroots Downtown Arts District Association (DADA). Galleries, artists' studios, coffeehouses, cafés and

bistros, craft shops, two libraries, the State Theatre, the Merrill Auditorium (in City Hall), the Portland Museum of Art, the Maine College of Art, and even L.L. Bean and the Portland Public Market are all part of the ongoing renaissance.

West End

Probably the most diverse of the city's downtown neighborhoods, and one that largely escaped the Great Fire of 1866, the West End includes the historically and architecturally splendid Western Promenade, Maine Medical Center (the state's largest hospital), the city's best B&Bs, a gay-friendly community with a laissez-faire attitude, a host of cafés and restaurants, and a few niches harboring the homeless and forlorn.

Munjoy Hill/East End

A once slightly down-at-the-heels neighborhood enclave with a pull-'em-up-by-the-bootstraps attitude, Portland's East End is rapidly gentrifying. Munjoy Hill is probably best known for the distinctive wooden tower, the Portland Observatory, that adorns its summit.

Named for George Munjoy, a wealthy 17th-century resident, this district has a host of architectural and historic landmarks—well worth a walking tour. Fortunately, Greater Portland Landmarks (207/774-5561, www.portlandlandmarks.org) has produced a 24-page booklet, *Munjoy Hill Historic Guide* ($3), which documents more than 60 notable sites, including the National Historic Register Eastern Cemetery and, with spectacular harbor views, the Eastern Promenade and Fort Allen Park. From early June to early October, Landmarks also offers guided walking tours of the historic **Eastern Cemetery,** the oldest burial ground on the peninsula, on Thursdays at noon, and a **Historic Munjoy Hill Tour,** on Fridays at noon. Both begin at the Portland Observatory (138 Congress St.) and cost $5 adult, $3 under 16. Combo tickets with admission to the observatory are $8 adult, $5 under 16.

Bayside and Parkside

A Babel of languages reverberates in these districts just below Portland City Hall. Bayside experienced the arrival of refugees—Cambodian,

© TOM NANGLE

Greater Portland

The rather staid exterior of the Victoria Mansion gives no hint as to the opulence inside.

Laotian, Vietnamese, Central European, and Afghan families—from war-torn lands during the 1980s and 1990s. Nowadays, you'll hear references to Somali Town, an area named for all the resettled refugees from that shattered country. Others have come from Sudan and Ethiopia. All have been assisted by Portland's active Refugee Resettlement Program.

Beyond the Peninsula

At the western edge of Portland, close to the Portland Jetport, is the historic area known as **Stroudwater,** once an essential link in Maine water transport. The 20-mile-long **Cumberland and Oxford Canal,** hand-dug in 1828, ran through here as part of the timber-shipping route linking Portland Harbor, the Fore and Presumpscot Rivers, and Sebago Lake. Twenty-eight wooden locks allowed vessels to rise the 265 feet between sea level and the lake. By 1870, trains took over the route, condemning the canal to

oblivion. Centerpiece of the Stroudwater area today is the historic 18th-century Tate House.

SIGHTS

M Portland Museum of Art

Three centuries of art and architecture: That's what you'll discover at Maine's oldest (since 1882) and finest art museum, the Portland Museum of Art (PMA, 7 Congress Sq., Portland 04101, 207/775-6148, recorded info 207/773-2787 or 800/639-4067, www.portlandmuseum.org, 10 A.M.–5 P.M. daily, to 9 P.M. Fri., closed Mon. Columbus Day–Memorial Day, $8 adults, $6 seniors and students, $2 children 6–12, free admission 5–9 P.M. every Friday). The museum's topflight collection of American and impressionist masters and fine and decorative arts is displayed in three architecturally stunning, connected buildings: the award-winning Charles Shipman Payson building, designed by I. M. Pei and opened in 1983, the newly restored Federal-era McLellan House, and the Beaux-Arts L. D. M. Sweat Memorial Galleries, designed by noted Maine architect John Calvin Stevens. The museum also has a well-stocked gift shop and a pleasant café that's open for lunch daily (11 A.M.–4 P.M.) and for dinner Thursday and Friday (to 7:30 P.M.). Call for information about family activities, lectures, and other events.

M Victoria Mansion

Jaws literally drop upon entering the Italianate Victoria Mansion, also called the Morse-Libby Mansion (109 Danforth St., Portland 04101, 207/772-4841, www.victoriamansion.org, 10 A.M.–4 P.M. Tues.–Sat. and 1–5 P.M. Sun. May–Oct., special hours in Dec.), widely considered the most magnificently ornamented dwelling of its period remaining in the country. The National Historic Landmark is rife with Victoriana—carved marble fireplaces, elaborate porcelain and paneling, a free-standing mahogany staircase, gilded glass chandeliers, a recently restored 6- by 25-foot stained-glass ceiling window, and unbelievable trompe l'oeil touches. It's even more spectacular at Christmas, with yards of roping, festooned trees, and carolers. (This is the best time to bring kids, as they may not be particularly intrigued by the house itself.) The mansion was built in the late 1850s by Ruggles Sylvester Morse, a Maine-born entrepreneur whose New Orleans-based fortune enabled him to hire 93 craftsmen to complete the house. The interior, designed by Gustave Herter, still boasts 90 percent of the original furnishings. Guided 45-minute tours begin every half hour (on the quarter hour) in season; tours are self-guided during the holidays. Admission is $10 adults, $9 seniors, $3 students 6–17; the basement to tower tour costs $20; and holiday season admission is $20 adults, $5 students.

Portland Observatory

Providing a head-swiveling view of Portland (and the White Mountains on a clear day), the octagonal red-painted Portland Observatory (138 Congress St., Portland 04101, 207/774-5561, www.portlandlandmarks.org, 10 A.M.–5 P.M. daily Memorial Day–Columbus Day, last tour at 4:40 P.M., $5 adults, $4 kids 6–16) is the only remaining marine signal tower on the eastern

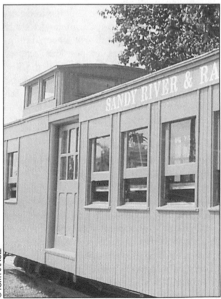

After touring the Maine Narrow Gauge Railroad Museum, a train ride along the Eastern Promenade is a must.

seaboard. Built in 1807 at a cost of $5,000 by Captain Lemuel Moody to keep track of the port's shipping activity, the tower has 122 tons of rock ballast in its base. Admission in those days (only men were allowed to climb the 103 interior steps) was 12.5 cents. Today, admission includes the small museum at the tower's base and a guided tour to the top.

The Wadsworth-Longfellow House

A few blocks down Congress Street from the PMA, you'll step back in time to the era of Portland-born poet Henry Wadsworth Longfellow, who lived in the accurately restored Wadsworth-Longfellow House (485 Congress St., Portland 04101, 207/774-1822, 10 A.M.–4 P.M. Mon.–Sat., noon– 4 P.M. Sun. May–Oct., special holiday hours Nov. and Dec., $7 adults, $6 seniors and students, $3 kids 5–17) as a child in the early 1800s—long before the brick mansion was dwarfed by surrounding high-rises. Wadsworth and Longfellow family furnishings fill the three-story house (owned by the Maine Historical Society), and savvy guides provide insight into Portland's 19th-century life. Don't miss the urban oasis—a wonderfully peaceful garden—behind the house (same hours, free admission). Purchase tickets at the adjacent Center for Maine History, which also houses the **Maine History Gallery** (489 Congress St., 207/774-1822, www.mainehistory.org, 10 A.M.–5 P.M. Mon.–Sat., noon–5 P.M. Sun., $4 adults, $3 seniors, $2 children), where you can take in the Maine Historical Society's current exhibits and find an extensive collection of Maine history books in the gift shop.

Maine Narrow Gauge Railroad and Museum

A three-mile ride along Portland's waterfront is the highlight of a visit to the Maine Narrow Gauge Railroad Company & Museum (58 Fore St., Portland 04101, 207/828-0814, www.mngrr.org). Admission is free to the museum (10 A.M.–4 P.M. daily mid-Feb. to late Dec., to 5 P.M. in late Dec., 10 A.M.–3 P.M. Mon.–Fri. in Jan. and early Feb.). The museum owns more than three dozen train cars and has others on long-term loan—most from Maine's five historic narrow-gauge railroads (the last one closed in 1943). You can board a number of the cars and see others undergoing restoration. For a fee, you can ride the two-foot rails aboard a multicar train (11 A.M.–4 P.M. on the hour daily mid-May–mid-Oct., 11 A.M.–3 P.M. weekends mid-Feb.–early May, to 4 P.M. mid-Oct.–late Nov., $6 adults, $5 seniors, $4 kids four and older). The track edges Casco Bay along the Eastern Promenade—a short but enjoyable excursion that's a real kid pleaser. Years ago, hundreds of steam engines were built here, but steam locomotives now operate only for special occasions. Trains also operate during school vacation weeks; call for schedule. At the eastern end of Fore Street, turn at the railroad-crossing sign on the water side; the museum is at the back of the complex.

Museum of African Culture

Founded in 1998, the Museum of African Culture (122 Spring St., Portland 04101, 207/871-7188, www.tribalartmuseum.com, 10:30 A.M.–4 P.M. Tues.–Fri., 12:30–4 P.M. Sat., $5 donation) is the brainchild of Nigerian-born Oscar Mokeme (the director) and Arthur Aleshire. Among the 300 or so treasures in the small but powerful museum—not all on display at once—are Nigerian tribal masks and Benin lost-wax bronzes. The museum also has an ambitious outreach program, educating the community about African art and culture.

Children's Museum of Maine

Here's the answer to parents' prayers—a whole museum in downtown Portland catering to kids (P.O. Box 4041, 142 Free St., next to the Portland Museum of Art, Portland 04101, 207/828-1234, www.kitetails.com, 10 A.M.–5 P.M. Mon.–Sat., to 8 P.M. Fri., noon–5 P.M. Sun., closed Mondays Labor Day–Memorial Day, $6, children 1 and younger free, free admission 5–8 P.M. the first Fri. of each month). Lots of hands-on displays encourage interaction and guarantee involvement for a couple of hours. What's here? A submarine, computer lab, TV studio, L.L. Bean's Discovery Woods, a space shuttle, a supermarket, bank (with an ATM), lobsterboat, a camera obscura, (one of only three in the country), and more than a dozen other activities. There's even an animal hospital. Call to check on the special-events schedule.

Shipyard Brewery

Look for the keg topping the flagpole at Shipyard Brewery (86 Newbury St., Portland, 207/761-0807, www.shipyard.com). Tours of the award-winning microbrewery are offered 3–4:30 P.M. on the half hour Monday–Friday and noon–4:30 P.M. on weekends (closed Sundays Jan. 1 to June 1). Tours begin with a short promotional video explaining the brewing process and end with a tasting. Even if you're not a beer/ale drinker, go and enjoy the root beer that's also brewed on the premises.

BEYOND THE DOWNTOWN PENINSULA

Southworth Planetarium

See stars under a 30-foot dome with comfy theater seats and a state-of-the-art laser system at the Southworth Planetarium (96 Falmouth St., Science Building, lower level, University of Southern Maine, Portland 04103, 207/780-4249, www.usm .maine.edu/~planet/, 7 P.M. Fri. and Sat., $6 adults, $4 seniors and children). Computer-savvy kids will head for the interactive computers in the exhibit area; the gift shop stocks astronaut ice cream and other science-type stuff. For recorded information on moon and planet positions, eclipses, and other astronomical happenings, call the **Skywatch Hotline** (207/780-4719). Take Exit 6B off I-295 and go west on Forest Avenue to Falmouth Street (left turn). The Science Building is on the left, after the parking lot.

Osher Map Library

Also on the university campus is the Osher Map Library (Glickman Family Library, 314 Forest Ave., Portland 04103, 207/780-4850 or 800/800-4876 ext. 4850, www.usm.maine.edu/~maps, 12:30–4:30 P.M. Tues.–Thurs., 10 A.M.–1 P.M. Sat., but call because hours may vary with academic schedule, free) The library's collection, primarily a teaching resource, documents the history of western cartography from its inception to modern times. Themed exhibits in a small display area feature highlights from the library's original maps, atlases, geographies, and globes dating from the late-15th century. Other artifacts include texts depicting explorer's narratives, accounts of early

One of the country's most photographed lighthouses, easily accessible Portland Head guards the ledgy shores of Cape Elizabeth.

travelers, and works of cosmography, astronomy, navigation, and geography.

Tate House

Just down the street from the Portland International Jetport, in the Stroudwater district, is the 1755 Tate House, a National Historic Landmark owned by the Colonial Dames of America (1270 Westbrook St., P.O. Box 8800, 207/774-6177, www.tatehouse.org, 10 A.M.- 4 P.M. Tues.–Sat. and 1–4 P.M. Sun. June 15–Sept. 30, Fri.–Sun. through Oct., $5 adults, $4 seniors, $2 children 6–12). Built by Captain George Tate, who was prominent in shipbuilding, the house has superb period furnishings and a lovely 18th-century herb garden (more than 70 varieties) overlooking the Stroudwater River. Tours last 40 minutes. Wednesdays mid-June–mid-September are "summer garden days," when tea and goodies follow tours of the garden (for an extra charge). Other

special hour-long tours focusing on the architecture and the historic Stroudwater neighborhood can be arranged by appointment. Across the street, in the Means House, is the museum's gift shop. From downtown Portland, it's 3.2 miles; take Congress Street West (Route 22), under I-295, and out as far as Waldo Street, just after the Fore River. Turn left onto Waldo and then turn right onto Westbrook Street. If you find yourself with spare time at the Portland Jetport, Tate House is an easy walk from the terminal. Ask for directions at the airport information desk.

Portland Harbor Museum

The maritime history of Casco Bay and Maine is the focus of the small Portland Harbor Museum (Fort Rd., South Portland 04106, 207/799-6337, www.PortlandHarborMuseum.org, 10 A.M.–4:30 P.M. daily Memorial Day–Columbus Day, Fri.–Sun. Apr., May., and Oct.; $4 adults, $2 children 6–16), on the waterfront campus of Southern Maine Community College (SMCC). To reach the museum, head over from downtown Portland (Route 77) and continue onto Broadway. Watch for SMCC signs. The museum now holds the title to the nearby Spring Point Ledge Lighthouse, which is open for tours periodically during the summer. Call for schedule. Also nearby are the remains of Fort Preble and the Spring Point Shoreline Walkway leading to Willard Beach (see the sidebar Lighthouses and Parks Tour).

Portland Head Light

Just four miles from downtown Portland, **Fort Williams,** in Cape Elizabeth, feels a world away. This oceanfront town park, a former military base, is home to Portland Head Light (1000 Shore Rd., Fort Williams Park, Cape Elizabeth 04107, 207/799-2661, www.portlandheadlight.com, dawn–dusk). Commissioned by President George Washington and first lighted in 1791, it has been immortalized in poetry, photography, and philately. The surf here is awesome—perhaps too awesome. The *Annie C. Maguire* was shipwrecked below the lighthouse on Christmas Eve, 1886. There's no access to the 58-foot automated light tower, but the superbly restored keeper's house has become **The Museum at Portland Head**

Light (10 A.M.–4 P.M. daily June–Oct., weekends late Apr.–May, but call first to confirm, $2 adults, $1 kids 6–18). It's filled with local history and lighthouse memorabilia. The 90-acre oceanfront park offers much else to explore, including ruins of the fort and the Goddard mansion. Walk the trails, play a game of tennis, dip your toes in the surf at the rocky beach, but be careful, there's a strong undertow here. You might even catch the Portland Symphony Orchestra, which occasionally performs here in summer. The grassy headland is a great place to watch the boat traffic going in and out of Portland Harbor. Bring a picnic lunch, and don't forget a kite. From downtown Portland, take Route 77, then Broadway, Cottage Road, and Shore Road.

TOURS

Casco Bay Tour

Casco Bay Lines (Commercial St. and Franklin St., Old Port, Portland 04101, 207/774-7871, www.cascobaylines.com), the nation's oldest continuously operating ferry system (since the 1920s), is the lifeline between Portland and six inhabited Casco Bay islands. What better way to sample the islands than to go along for the three-hour ride with mail, groceries, and island residents? The Casco Bay Lines mail boat stops—briefly—at Long Island, Chebeague, Cliff, and Little and Great Diamond Islands. Daily departures are 10 A.M. and 2:15 P.M. mid-June to Labor Day (plus 7:45 A.M. weekdays), 10 A.M. and 2:45 P.M. other months. Fares are $12.75 adults, $11 seniors, and $6 children 5–9. The longest cruise on the Casco Bay Lines schedule is a five-hour, 45-minute-narrated summertime trip (late June to Labor Day) to Bailey Island, with a two-hour stopover, departing from Portland at 10 A.M. daily ($18 adults, $16 seniors, $8 children 5–9). Dogs (on leashes) and bicycles need separate tickets—$5 for bikes, $3 for animals.

Walking Tours

The best tours of the area are offered by Greater Portland Landmarks (207/774-5561, www .portlandlandmarks.org), which sponsors neighborhood walking tours as well as an annual

© TOM NANGLE

For a close-up view of working boats in Portland Harbor, hop on a ferry or take an excursion boat into Casco Bay.

© TOM NANGLE

A tour on the Downeast Duck is a land-and-sea adventure best appreciated by kids.

summer tour program, featuring four or five walking trips and excursions to offshore islands, historic churches, revamped buildings, and gardens. Many of the destinations are private or otherwise inaccessible, so these are special opportunities. Registration is limited, and there's only one trip to each site. Tours run mid-July to mid-October, primarily on weekends.

Land and Sea Tours

Three commercial operators offer area land-and-sea tours, but frankly, none is first-rate. On each, guides often present incorrect information (and sometimes even hold passengers hostage for political rants). Still, such tours are a good way to get the city's general layout. The best of the lot is the 1.5-hour narrated sightseeing tour of Portland in a trolley-bus, by Mainely Tours (3 Moulton St., Old Port, Portland 04101, 207/774-0808, www.mainelytours.com). Cost is $14 adults, $13 seniors, $7 kids 6–12. You can combine this tour with a 90-minute Lighthouse Lover's boat tour on Casco Bay. The combined price is $22 adult, $20 senior, and $13 kids.

An alternative, especially if you're traveling with kids, is the corny land-and-sea tour in an amphibious vehicle offered by Downeast Duck Adventures (office at Communiques, 163 Commercial St., 207/774-3825, www.downeastduck.com, May–Oct., $20–45 adult, $15–40 senior or child 5–11). Prepare to do a lot of quacking on the one- to two-hour tours.

Segway Tour

Here's a completely different way to see the East End waterfront. In 2004, teacher Annie Cook found a new way to spend her summer vacation. She opened Maine Segway (207/846-3337, www.segwaymaine.com) and began offering tours of the Eastern Prom on a Segway Human Transport. The two-hour tours on the two-wheeled, gyroscope- and microprocessor-controlled stand-aboard vehicles are offered twice daily for $62. The first 20 minutes or so are spent learning to ride the Segways, including starting, stopping, and turning. It's pricey, but fun. Call for reservations and meeting place.

CASCO BAY ISLANDS

Casco Bay is dotted with so many islands that an early explorer thought there must be at least one for every day of the year and so dubbed them the Calendar Islands. Truthfully, there aren't quite that many, even if you count all the ledges that appear at low tide. No matter, the islands are as much a part of Portland life as the Old Port.

Casco Bay Lines is the islands' lifeline, providing car and passenger service daily in summer. Perhaps the best way to see the highlights is aboard the daily mail-boat run. Indeed, on hot days, it may seem as if half the city's population is hopping a ferry to enjoy the cool breezes and calming views.

Peaks Island

Peaks Island is a mere 20-minute ferry ride from downtown Portland, so it's no surprise that it has the largest year-round population. Historically a popular vacation spot—two lodges were built for Civil War veterans—it's now an increasingly popular suburb.

Although you can walk the island's perimeter in 3–4 hours, the best way to see it is to take a bike ($5 extra on the ferry) and pedal around clockwise. It can take less than an hour to do the five-mile island circuit, but plan on relaxing on the beach, savoring the views, and visiting the museums. Rental bikes are available on the island from Brad Burkholder at **Brad's ReCycled Bike Shop** (115 Island Ave., Peaks Island 04108, 207/766-5631, 10 A.M.–6 P.M. daily) for $5 an hour or $20 a day, but it's wise to call first; when he's not there, it's a self-serve honor system.

Another way to see the island is on a golf cart tour with **Island Tours** (207/653-2549, island-tours@att.net, $15 adults, $12 seniors, $8 child), which offers a variety of 90-minute island tours as well as one-hour sunset tours ($10 adults, $8 seniors, $5 child). Admission to the Fifth Maine Regiment Museum is included in longer tours.

Civil War buffs have two museums worth a visit. The **Fifth Maine Regiment Center** (45 Seashore Ave., P.O. Box 41, Peaks Island, 207/766-3330, www.fifthmainemuseum.org, 11 A.M.–4 P.M. daily, July–Labor Day, to 5 P.M. weekends late May–June and early Sept.–mid-Oct., $5 donation requested), a Queen Anne-style cottage built by Civil War veterans in 1888, now houses exhibits on the war and island history. Just a few steps away is the **Eighth Maine Regimental Memorial** (13 Eighth Maine Ave, Peaks Island, 207/766-5086, noon–3 P.M. Tues.–Sat. July–early Sept., $5 donation requested). Tours detail the building's fascinating history and its collection of artifacts pertaining to the Eighth Maine as well as material on the island, World War II, and more. Rustic lodging is available.

Another museum perhaps worthy of a visit just for its quirkiness is the **Umbrella Cover Museum** (207/766-4496), where owner Nancy 3. Hoffman (yes, 3) displays her collection.

Great Diamond Island

Great Diamond is a totally different scene. In 1891, the U.S. government began building an army post on Great Diamond, a quick ferryboat ride from the Portland harborfront. Completed in 1907, **Fort McKinley** (named after President William McKinley) became part of Portland Harbor's five-fort defense system during World Wars I and II. When peace descended, the fort's red-brick structures were left to crumble for nearly five decades. In 1984, developers stepped in, bought the derelicts, and began restoration—albeit not without financial setbacks and opposition from environmental organizations.

Today, the 193-acre **Diamond Cove** enclave boasts barracks-turned-townhomes, single-family houses, a general store (open daily late May to Labor Day), an outdoor theater, a beach bar (open mid-June to mid-September), an art gallery, no cars (only bikes and golf carts), and the first-rate **Diamond's Edge Restaurant.**

Great Chebeague

Everyone calls Great Chebeague just "Chebeague" (shuh-BIG). Yes, there's a Little Chebeague, but it's a state-owned park, and no one lives there. Chebeague is the largest of the bay's islands—4.5 miles long, 1.5 miles wide—and the relatively level terrain makes it easy to get around. Don't plan to bring a car; it's too complicated to arrange.

You can bike the leisurely 10-mile circuit of the island in a couple of hours, but unless you're in a hurry, allow time to relax and enjoy your visit. Pick up an island map at the Portland terminal or on the ferry; all the high points are listed, including two beach-access points off North Road.

If the tide is right, cross the sandspit from The Hook and explore **Little Chebeague.** Start out about two hours before low tide (preferably around new moon or full moon, when the most water drains away) and plan to be back on Chebeague no later than two hours after low tide.

Back on Great Chebeague, when you're ready for a swim, head for **Hamilton Beach,** a beautiful small stretch of sand lined with dune grass, not far from the Chebeague Island Inn. Also on this part of the island is **East End Point,** with a spectacular panoramic view of Halfway Rock and the bay.

Chebeague Transportation Company, from Cousins Island, Yarmouth, also services the island.

Eagle Island

Seventeen-acre **Eagle Island** (207/624-6080, www.pearyeagleisland.org, 10 A.M.–5 P.M. mid-June–early Sept.) juts out of Casco Bay, rising to a rocky promontory 40 feet above the crashing surf. On the bluff's crest, Robert Edwin Peary, the first man to lead a party of fellow men to the North Pole without the use of mechanical or electrical devices, built his dream home. It's now a state historic site that's accessible via excursion boats from Portland or Freeport. The half-day trip usually includes a narrated cruise to the island and time to tour the house, filled with Peary family artifacts, and wander the nature trails. (Note: Trails are usually closed until approximately mid-July to protect nesting eider ducks).

Peary envisioned the island's rocky bluff as a ship's prow and built his house to resemble a pilot house. Wherever possible, he used indigenous materials from the island in the construction, including timber drift, fallen trees, beach rocks, and cement mixed with screened beach sand and small pebbles. From the library, Peary corresponded with world leaders, adventurers, and explorers, such as Teddy Roosevelt, the Wright brothers, Roald Amundson, and Ernest Shakleton, and planned his expeditions. Peary reached the North Pole on April 6, 1909, and his wife, Josephine, was on Eagle when she received word via telegraph of her husband's accomplishment. After Peary's death, in 1920, the family continued to spend summers on Eagle until Josephine's death, in 1955. It was a unanimous family decision to donate the island to the state of Maine.

PARKS, PRESERVES, AND BEACHES

Greater Portland is blessed with green space, thanks largely to the efforts of 19th-century mayor James Phinney Baxter, who foresightedly hired the famed Olmsted brothers' firm to develop an ambitious plan to ring the city with public parks and promenades. Not all the elements fell into place, but the result is what makes Portland such a livable city.

Portland Peninsula

Probably the most visible of the city's parks, 51-acre **Deering Oaks** (Park and Forest Avenues and Deering St.), may be best known for the quaint little duck condo in the middle of the pond. Other facilities and highlights here are tennis courts, playground, horseshoes, rental paddleboats, a snack bar, the award-winning Rose Circle, a Saturday farmers' market (7 A.M.–noon), and, in winter, ice skating. After dark, steer clear of the park.

At one end of the Eastern Promenade, where it meets Fore Street, **Fort Allen Park** overlooks offshore Fort Gorges (coin-operated telescopes bring it closer). A central gazebo is flanked by an assortment of military souvenirs dating as far back as the War of 1812. All along the Eastern Prom are walking paths, benches, play areas, even an ill-maintained fitness trail—all with that terrific view. Down by the water is **East End Beach,** with parking, token sand, and the area's best launching ramp for sea kayaks or powerboats.

West of Downtown

Just beyond I-295, along Baxter Boulevard (Route 1) and tidal **Back Cove,** is a skinny green strip with a 3.5-mile trail for walking, jogging, or just watching the sailboards and the skyline. Along the way, you can cross Baxter Boulevard and spend time picnicking, playing tennis, or flying a kite in 48-acre **Payson Park.**

Talk about an urban oasis. The 85-acre **Fore River Sanctuary,** owned by Maine Audubon, has two miles of blue-blazed trails that wind through a salt marsh, link up with the historic Cumberland and Oxford Canal towpath, and pass near **Jewell Falls,** Portland's only waterfall,

protected by Portland Trails. From downtown Portland, take Congress Street West (Route 22), past I-295. From here there are two access routes: either turn right onto Stevens Avenue (Route 9), continue to Brighton Avenue (Route 25), turn left and go about 1.25 miles to Rowe Avenue, turn left and park at the end of the road; or continue past Stevens Avenue, about one-half mile to Frost Avenue, take a hard right, then left into the Maine Orthopedic Center parking lot. Portland Trails raised the funds for the handsome, 90-foot pedestrian bridge at this entrance to the sanctuary. Open daily sunup to sundown. No pets, free admission.

Scarborough

Scarborough Beach Park (Black Point Rd., Rte. 207, 207/883-2416, $3.50 adult, $1.50 child, $2 senior), a long stretch of sand, is the best beach for big waves. Between the parking area and the lovely stretch of beach, you'll pass Massacre Pond, named for a 1703 skirmish between resident Indians and resident wannabes. (Score: Indians 19, wannabes 0.) You might want to leave your car here and walk down Black Point Road to visit Prouts Neck. The park is open all year for swimming, surfing, beachcombing, and ice skating.

At 3,100 acres, **Scarborough Marsh** (Pine Point Rd., Rte. 9, 207/883-5100, www.maine audubon.org, 9:30 A.M.–5:30 P.M. daily June–Labor Day, weekends in late May and Sept.), Maine's largest salt marsh, is prime territory for birding and canoeing. Rent a canoe ($15 an hour if you're not an Audubon member or $45 per half day) at the small nature center, operated by Maine Audubon, and explore on your own. Or join one of the daily 90-minute guided tours at 10 A.M. (also Sunday at 1 P.M.). Cost is $11 adults, $9 children (subtract $1.50 pp if you have your own canoe). Guided full-moon tours ($12 per adult, $10 per child) June through September are particularly exciting; dress warmly and bring a flashlight. Other special programs, some geared primarily for children, include wildflower walks, art classes, and dawn birding trips; all require reservations and very reasonable fees. Also here is a walking tour trail of less than one mile. Pick up a map at the center.

LIGHTHOUSES AND PARKS TOUR

Whether in a car or on a bike, it's easy to loop through South Portland and Cape Elizabeth on a route that takes in lighthouses, forts, beaches, and parks.

Begin just over the Casco Bay Bridge from downtown Portland (Route 77); take Broadway and continue to the end at **Southern Maine Community College** (SMCC), overlooking the bay. (Best time to come here is evenings and weekends, when there's ample parking.) Unless it's foggy (when the signal is deafening) or thundering (when you'll expose yourself to lightning), walk out along the 1,000-foot granite breakwater to the **Spring Point Ledge Lighthouse,** with fabulous views in every direction. Also here are picnic benches, the remains of Fort Preble, the Portland Harbor Museum, and the Peter A. McKernan Hospitality Center. At the southern edge of the SMCC campus is the **Spring Point Shoreline Walkway,** a scenic three-mile pathway with views off to House, Peaks, and Cushings Islands. At the end of the shoreway, you'll reach crescent-shaped **Willard Beach,** a neighboroody sort of place with lifeguards, a changing building, a snack bar, and those same marvelous views.

From the SMCC campus, return on Broadway to the major intersection with Cottage Road and bear left. Cottage Road becomes Shore Road at the Cape Elizabeth town line. Loop into Fort Williams Park and make a pilgrimage to **Portland Head Light** before continuing on Shore Road to its intersection with Route 77. Bear left and follow to Two Lights Road and follow signs to 40-acre **Two Lights State Park.** Almost a vest-pocket park, it has picnicking and restroom facilities, but its biggest asset is the panoramic ocean view from atop a onetime gun battery. Summer admission is $3 adults 12-64, $1 kids 5-11.

Before or after visiting the park, take a left just before the park entrance (continuation of Two Lights Road; the sign says Lighthouses). Continue to the parking lot at the end, where you'll see the signal towers for which Two Lights is named. (There's no access to either one; only one still works.) If you haven't brought a picnic for the state park, enjoy the food and the view at **The Lobster Shack.**

To eke out some beach time, return to Route 77 and continue to **Crescent Beach State Park,** a 243-acre park with changing rooms, lifeguard, restrooms, picnic tables, and a snack bar. Admission is $3.50 adults 12-64, $1 kids 5-11. Directly offshore is Saco Bay's **Richmond Island,** a 200-acre private preserve with a checkered past dating to the 17th century.

Falmouth (North of Portland)

Nearly a dozen of Falmouth's parks, trails, and preserves, official and unofficial, are described and mapped in the *Falmouth Trail Guide,* a handy little booklet published by the Falmouth Conservation Commission. Copies are available at Gilsland Farm, Falmouth Town Hall, and local bookstores. Two of the best options are described here.

A 65-acre wildlife sanctuary and environmental center on the banks of the Presumpscot River, **Gilsland Farm** (20 Gilsland Farm Rd., 207/781-2330, www.maineaudubon.org, dawn–dusk daily) is state headquarters for Maine Audubon. More than two miles of easy, well-marked trails wind through the grounds, taking in salt marshes, rolling meadows, woodlands, and views of the estuary. Observation blinds allow inconspicuous spying during bird-migration season. In the edu-

cation center (9 A.M.–5 P.M., Mon.–Sat. and 1–4 P.M.) are hands-on exhibits, a nature store, and classrooms and offices. Fees are charged for special events, but otherwise it's all free. The visitor center is one-quarter mile off Route 1.

Once the summer compound of the prominent Baxter family, Falmouth's 100-acre **Mackworth Island,** reached via a causeway, is now the site of the Governor Baxter School for the Deaf. Limited parking is just beyond the security booth on the island. On the 1.5-mile, vehicle-free perimeter path (great Portland Harbor views), you'll meet bikers, hikers, and dog walkers. Just off the trail on the north side of the island is the late Governor Percival Baxter's stone-circled pet cemetery, maintained by the state at the behest of Baxter, who donated this island as well as Baxter State Park to the people of Maine. From downtown

Portland, take Route 1 across the Presumpscot River to Falmouth Foreside. Andrews Avenue (third street on the right) leads to the island. Open sunup to sundown, all year.

RECREATION

Bicycling

The **Bicycle Coalition of Maine** (P.O. Box 5275, Augusta 04332, 207/623-4511, www.bike maine.org) has an excellent website that lists nearly two dozen trails in Greater Portland. You'll also find info on events, organized rides, bike shops, and more. Another good resource is **Casco Bay Bicycle Club** (www.cascobaybicycleclub), a recreational cycling club with rides several times weekly. Check its website for details.

For rentals (hybrids are $20 a day) and repairs visit **Cycle Mania** (59 Federal St., 207/774-2933, www.cyclemania1.com). A number of shops offer weekly rides, including **Back Bay Bicycle** (333 Forest Ave., 207/773-6906) and

Allspeed Bicycle & Ski (1041 Washington Ave., www.allspeed.com, 207/878-8741). **Summerfeet.Maine Coast Cycling Adventures** (P.O. Box 10822, Portland 04104, 207/828-0342 or 866/857-9544, www.summerfeet.net, daily June–Sept.) leads three half-day cycling trips in Portland over flat and rolling terrain. Rates include a Portland history guide, bike and helmet rental, souvenir water bottle, snacks, and ferry passage where applicable. Choose from Peaks and the Prom, a four-hour 14-mile trip, $40 for adults, $25 children 12 and under; Portland End to End, a three-hour, 14-mile trip, $28 adults, $20 children; or To the Lighthouses, a four-hour, 25-mile pedal, $40 adults, $25 children. Call for info on full-day trips.

The best locales for island bicycling—fun for families and beginners but not especially challenging for diehards—are Peaks and Great Chebeague Islands (see the Casco Bay Islands sidebar), but do remember to follow the rules of the road.

© TOM NANGLE

Governor Percival Baxter donated Mackworth Island to the state, which maintains the stone-circled cemetery, a final resting place for his beloved pets.

Golf

You'll have no problem finding a place to tee off in Greater Portland. Some of the best courses are private, so if you have an "in," so much the better, but there are still plenty of public and semiprivate courses for every skill level. Free advice on helping you choose a course is offered by Maine's Golf Concierge (info@golfme.com).

Let's just consider Greater Portland's 18-hole courses. For all, it's a smart move to reserve tee times. **Sable Oaks Golf Club** (505 Country Club Dr., South Portland, 207/775-6257, www.sableoaks.com) is considered one of the toughest and best of Maine's public courses. Since 1998, **Nonesuch River Golf Club** (304 Gorham Rd., Rte. 114, Scarborough 04074, 207/883-0007 or 888/256-2717, www.nonesuchgolf.com) has been drawing raves for the challenges of its par-70 championship course and praise from environmentalists for preserving wildlife habitat; there's a full-size practice range and green, too. A bit less challenging than these is **Val Halla Golf and Recreation Center** (1 Val Halla Rd., off Rte. 9, Cumberland Center, 207/829-2225, www.valhallaglf.com). **Willowdale Golf Club** (52 Willowdale Rd., Scarborough, 207/883-9351 or 207/883-6504, www.willowdalegolf.com) is opposite Scarborough Downs racetrack. Scarborough Marsh is visible from a couple of the holes. The City of Portland's **Riverside Municipal Golf Course** (1158 Riverside St., Portland, 207/797-3524) has an 18-hole par-72 course (Riverside North) and a nine-hole par-35 course (Riverside South). Opt for the 18-hole course. The clubhouse is just west of I-95, between Exits 8 and 9.

When lousy weather sets in, the local alternative is **Fore Season Golf** (1037 Forest Ave., Portland 04104, 207/797-8835), where you can play virtual golf at nearly two dozen famous courses with regulation clubs and balls, thanks to computerized simulators. A snack bar keeps you going, and beer and wine are available.

Tennis

Portland's 31 free municipal tennis courts, open dawn to dusk, are scattered all over the city. Best ones are in Deering Oaks, Payson Park, and on the Eastern Promenade. It's first-come, first-served, though, so you may have to wait. The **City of Portland Recreation Division** (207/874-8793) manages them all; call for other locations.

Swimming

Besides the saltwater beaches listed under *Parks, Preserves, and Beaches,* Portland has two indoor municipal pools open to the public: **Reiche Pool** (166 Brackett St., in the West End, 207/874-8874) and **Riverton Pool** (1600 Forest Ave., Route 302, west of I-295, 207/874-8456). Both are part of community center/school complexes. **South Portland's municipal pool** (21 Nelson Rd., 207/767-7655) also has open swim times. Hours vary, so call for schedules.

Sea Kayaking

With all the islands scattered through Casco Bay, Greater Portland has become a hotbed of sea-kayaking activity. The best place to start is out on Peaks Island, 15 minutes offshore via Casco Bay Lines ferry. **Maine Island Kayak Company** (MIKCO, 70 Luther St., Peaks Island 04108, 207/766-2373 or 800/796-2373, www.maine islandkayak.com) is a successful tour operation that organizes half-day, all-day, and multiday local kayaking trips as well as national and international adventures. An introductory half-day tour in Casco Bay is $60 pp; a full day is $95, including lunch. Reservations are essential. MIKCO also does private lessons and group courses and clinics (some require previous experience). MIKCO's owner, Tom Bergh, has a flawless reputation for safety and skill. Send for the extensive trip schedule. In early October (usually Columbus Day weekend), there's a daylong sale of used boats and gear—lots of real bargains.

Lucky Catch Lobster Tours

Learn all kinds of lobster lore and maybe even catch your own dinner with Lucky Catch Lobster Tours (170 Commercial St., 207/233-2026 or 888/624-6321, www.luckycatch.com, $20 adult, $18 seniors or juniors ages 13–18, $12 ages 12 and younger). Captain Tom Martin offers five different 80- to 90-minute cruises on his 37-foot lobsterboat, with options including seal-watching,

White Head passage, and Portland Head Light. On each (except late Saturday and all day Sunday, when state law prohibits it), usually 10 traps are hauled and the process and gear are explained. You can even help, if you're willing. Any lobsters caught are available for purchase after the cruise for wholesale boat price (and you can have them cooked nearby for a reasonable rate). Now wouldn't that make a nice story to tell the folks back home?

Sailboat and Powerboat Excursions

Down on the Old Port wharves are several excursion-boat businesses. Each has carved out a niche, so choose according to your interest and your schedule. Dress warmly and wear rubber-soled shoes. Remember that all cruises are weather-dependent.

Bay View Cruises operates the 66-foot *Bay View Lady* (184 Commercial St., Fisherman's Wharf, Old Port, 207/761-0496, www.bayviewcruisesme.com, daily late June–Sept. 1, reduced schedule in spring, $10 adults, $9 seniors, $7 children; the lunchtime cruise is $3, altitude adjustment cruise is $5). Six different cruises vary from 40 minutes (lunchtime) to 90 minutes (morning and afternoon) to two hours (sunset). On longer cruises, you can feast on lobster for an extra fee. The main deck is enclosed and heated; the upper deck has the best views.

The **Olde Port Mariner Fleet** (Long Wharf, Commercial St., 207/775-0727 or 207/642-3270 or 800/437-3270, mailing address 634 Cape Rd., Standish 04084, www.marinerfleet.com) operates three boats with seemingly endless possibilities for getting afloat. Choose from hour-long harbor cruises, half-day and full-day deep-sea-fishing and bay-fishing excursions, and sunset and dinner cruises. Seven-hour whale-watching cruises are a specialty aboard the *Odyssey,* departing daily at 10 A.M. from late June to Labor Day, plus spring and fall weekends. (Don't overload on breakfast that day, and take preventive measures if you're motion-sensitive.) Tickets are $28–38 pp.

The **Coast Watch & Guiding Light Navigation Company** (Long Wharf, Old Port, 207/774-6498, www.eagleislandtours.com, no credit cards) offers several excursion options, but the best is the four-hour trip to 17-acre **Eagle Island** (departing 10 A.M. daily mid-June to Labor Day then weekends until the island is closed, $24 adults, $22 seniors, $13 kids), where Arctic explorer Admiral Robert Peary built his summer home. The state-owned house is open daily late June to Labor Day, plus weekends into September. The cruise allows time on the island to visit the house and wander the grounds. Pack a picnic, or order a box lunch 24 hours in advance.

Portland Schooner Company (Maine State Pier, Commercial St., 207/766-2500, www.portlandschooner.com, May–Oct., $25–35 adult, $12 child) offers four, two-hour sails daily on the 72-foot schooner *Bagheera,* designed by John G. Alden and built in East Boothbay in 1924. On Tuesdays in July and August, the boat sails from Peaks Island.

Spectator Sports

A pseudo-fierce mascot named Slugger stirs up the crowds at baseball games played by the **Portland Sea Dogs** (Hadlock Field, 271 Park Ave., 207/879-9500 or 800/936-3647, www.portlandseadogs.com), a AA Boston Red Sox farm team. Ever since the team arrived, in 1994, loyal local fans have made tickets scarce, so it's wise to reserve well ahead (you'll pay a minimal reservation surcharge) with a major credit card. The season schedule (early April through August) is available after January 1. General-admission tickets are $6 adults, $3 seniors (62 and over) and kids 16 and under. Reserved seats are $7 adults, $6 all others. For hassle-free parking, leave your car at the USM parking lot on Bedford Street, off I-295 Exit 6B, and take the continuous Metro Shuttle service ($1 pp) to the ballpark.

For ice hockey action, the **Portland Pirates** (207/775-3458, www.portlandpirates.com, $10–25 adults, $8–25 children 12 and under), a farm team for the American Hockey League Washington Capitals, play winter and spring home games at the 8,700-seat Cumberland County Civic Center.

The civic center is also the locale for year-round special sporting events and exhibition games, ice shows, concerts, and college hockey games. Check the *Portland Press Herald* for schedules or call the center.

Indoor Fun and Games

If you're traveling with kids, **Jokers** (512 Warren Ave., 207/878-5800, www.jokersfunandgames.com, 10 A.M.–10 P.M. daily—closing at 9 P.M. Sun.—July 4–Labor Day, to 9 P.M. Mon.–Thurs. and to 8 P.M. Sun. the rest of the year) is a godsend, especially on a rainy day. The 28,000-square-foot indoor play area has laser tag, a train and mini Ferris wheel, rock climbing, jumpshot trampoline basketball, three-story playhouse, animated rock and roll show, more than 120 arcade and video machines, an inflatable bounce area, and a giant slide, plus an outdoor 18-hole miniature golf course. Food is available, and on Friday nights there's an all-you-can-eat family pizza buffet with karaoke 6–9 P.M. for $3.99 per person.

SHOPPING

The Portland peninsula—primarily Congress Street and the Old Port waterfront district—is thick with non-cookie-cutter shops and galleries. This is just a taste to spur your explorations.

Antiquarian Bookstores

Carlson-Turner Books (241 Congress St., 207/773-4200 or 800/540-7323), based on Munjoy Hill, seems to have Portland's largest used-book inventory. Look for unusual titles and travel narratives. For good reads, contemporary fiction, and a big selection of cookbooks, visit **Cunningham Books** (199 State St., Longfellow Sq., 207/775-2246). Antique maps and atlases are the specialty at the Old Port's **Emerson Booksellers** (18 Exchange St., 207/874-2665), but it has an excellent used-book selection as well.

Antiques

Antique and junktique shops are dotted throughout the city, with clusters along Congress Street in the Old Port. Here are a few offering the real thing. **Nelson Rarities** (2 Monument Square, seventh floor, 207/775-4150 or 800/882-3150, www.nelsonrarities.com) specializes in estate jewelry and carries a huge selection of antique engagement rings. **Portland Antiques & Fine Art** (223 Commercial St., 207/773-7052 or 800/896-8824) specializes in 18th- to 20th-century

furniture as well as nautical antiques and marine art. **The Clown** (123 Middle St., 207/756-7399) carries an unusual mix of European antiques and art and a huge wine selection (specializing in Italian).

Art Galleries

In-town Portland's galleries host a **First Friday Artwalk** on the first Friday evening of each month, with exhibition openings, open houses, meet-the-artist gatherings, and other such artsy activities.

Galleries specializing in contemporary art are clustered in the Arts District. These include **Hay Gallery** (594 Congress St., 207/773-2513), **Aucocisco** (615 Congress St., 207/874-2060), **Aucocisco at the Eastland** (157 High St., 207/775-2227), **June Fitzpatrick Gallery** (112 High St., 207/879-5742), and **Institute for Contemporary Art** (Maine College of Art, Congress St., 207/879-5742), with walk-in tours at 12:15 P.M. every Wednesday.

Carrying reasonably priced prints and original art, the **Bayview Old Port Gallery** (75 Market St., Old Port, 207/773-3007) is eminently affordable. Prints by three generations of Wyeths are a specialty. Just around the corner is **Greenhut Galleries** (146 Middle St., 207/772-2693), another well-respected gallery showing contemporary Maine art and sculpture. Also in the Old Port is **The Stein Gallery Contemporary Glass** (195 Middle St., Old Port, 207/772-9072), which displays works by more than 100 American glass and jewelry artists.

Crafts and Gifts

More than 15 Maine potters—with a wide variety of styles and items—market their wares at the **Maine Potters Market** (376 Fore St., 207/774-1633), an attractive shop in the heart of the Old Port. Established in 1980, the cooperative remains a consistently reliable outlet for some of Maine's best ceramic artisans.

For the kid in all of us, there's **Northern Sky Toyz** (388 Fore St., 207/828-0911 or 800/611-6047), probably the best kite shop you've ever seen. Price range is vast—$10 to several hundreds—and owners Bob and Nancy Ray can recommend the best places to try out your purchase.

Just around the corner is **Abacus** (44 Exchange St., 207/772-4880), where craft rises to a high art. Whimsy is the byword here; if you don't arrive smiling, you'll leave that way. Open all year. Abacus has branches in Kennebunkport and Freeport, and a seasonal shop in Boothbay Harbor.

Gourmet Treats

For "gourmet goodies" don't miss **Browne Trading Market** (Merrill's Wharf, 262 Commercial St., 207/775-7560). Owner Rod Mitchell became the Caviar King of Portland by wholesaling Caspian caviar, and he's now letting the rest of us in on it. Ultimately fresh fish and shellfish fill the cases next to the caviar and cheeses. The mezzanine is wall-to-wall (literally) wine, specializing in French. Much less fancy is **Micucci's Grocery Store** (45 India St., 207/775-1854), which has been servicing Portland's Italian community since 1949. Great stop for picnic fixings and a nice selection of inexpensive wines.

Don't fail to miss the **Portland Public Market** (see Food).

Offbeat Shopping

Trustmi, you have to see **Suitsmi** (35 Pleasant St. 207/772-8285), which carries wearables (including jewelry) perfect for rock concerts, funky cafés, and, if you're dying to make a statement, your class reunion. Top it all off with a hat from **Queen of Hats** (560 Congress St., 207/772-2379). **Shipwreck and Cargo** (207 Commercial St., Old Port, 207/775-3057) stocks a wide assortment of marine-related items—boat models, barometers, navy surplus stuff, and more.

ENTERTAINMENT AND NIGHTLIFE

The best places to find out what's playing at area theaters, cinemas, concert halls, and nightclubs are *The Portland Phoenix* and the *Go* supplement in the Thursday edition of the *Portland Press Herald.* Both are available at bookstores and supermarkets; the *Phoenix* is free.

Also free are some outdoor concert series. Portland Parks & Recreation sponsors **Summer in the Parks** (207/7566-8275, www.ci.portland

WINSLOW HOMER

Discovering Maine in his early 40s, Winslow Homer (1836–1910) was smitten—enough to spend the last 27 years of his life in Prouts Neck (Scarborough, south of Portland), a small fishing village gradually morphing into an exclusive summer enclave. Here, in a cluttered, rustic studio converted from a onetime stable (recently acquired by the Portland Museum of Art, but not open to the public), he produced his finest works, the seascapes that have become so familiar to us all. He painted the sea in every mood, the rocks in every light, the snow in all its bleakness, the hardy trees bent to the wind. Occasional forays to the Bahamas, the Adirondacks, and the Canadian wilderness inspired other themes, but Prouts Neck always lured him back. Homer's last work, an oil titled *Driftwood,* painted in 1909 when his health was in major decline, depicts once again the struggle of man against the roiling surf that Homer knew so intimately from his life on the coast of Maine.

.me.us/summer.htm, July and August, free), comprising evening concert series, a noontime kids' series, and even movies in downtown parks.

Center for Cultural Exchange

In the heart of the Downtown Arts District, the Center for Cultural Exchange (1 Longfellow Sq., Portland, 207/761-0591, box office 207/761-1545, www.centerforculturalexchange.org) exposes Portlanders to multicultural arts—music and dance performers from throughout the world, as well as Portland's own ethnic community. Lectures, classes, and other special events are also on the agenda; the center acts as a clearinghouse for an impressive array of activities.

State Theatre

After an astonishing renovation that produced a stunning gilded, painted performance space, the 1929 State Theatre (609 Congress St., Portland, 207/780-8265, www.liveatthestate.com) has had financial ups and downs. Nonetheless, it's the focal point of Congress Street's Downtown Arts District; the city and private citizens have worked hard to keep it afloat. Plays, big-name rock concerts, and classical performances have all contributed to the theater's renown in the past, and it's still a happening place.

St. Lawrence Arts and Community Center

Proof of what enthusiastic, determined activists can accomplish is the new St. Lawrence Arts and Community Center (76 Congress St., Portland, 207/775-5568, www.stlawrencearts.org), formerly St. Lawrence Congregational Church. Built in 1897 in Queen Anne style, the church is a distinctive landmark with more than 90 stained-glass windows. On the same street as the Portland Observatory, on Munjoy Hill, the center has become a vibrant venue for professional and semiprofessional theater and concerts.

Merrill Auditorium

The magnificently restored Merrill Auditorium (20 Myrtle St., Portland, box office 207/874-8200) is a 1,900-seat theater inside Portland City Hall (on Congress Street) with two balconies and one of the country's only municipally owned pipe organs, the **Kotzschmar Organ.** A summer classical organ concert series with guest artists is held at 7:30 P.M. most Tuesdays from mid-June through August, $10 donation.

Special events and concerts are common at Merrill, and the auditorium is also the home to a number of the city's arts organizations. The **Portland Symphony Orchestra** (207/842-0800, www.portlandsymphony.org) and **PCA Great Performances** (207/773-3150, www.pcagreatperformances.org) have extensive, well-patronized fall and winter schedules; the PSO presents three summer Independence Pops concerts as well. The **Portland Opera Repertory Theatre** (437 Congress St., Portland 04101, 207/879-7678, www.portopera.org) performs a major opera each summer, usually in late July. In addition, there are films, lectures, and other related events throughout July. Tickets for the PSO, PCA, and PORT are available through PortTix (207/942-0800, www.porttix.com). Call for more information on the Pops series, 207/883-9525.

Drama

Innovative staging and controversial contemporary dramas are typical of the **Portland Stage Company** (Portland Performing Arts Center, 25A Forest Ave., Portland, 207/774-0465, www.portlandstage.com), established in 1974 and going strong ever since. Equity pros present a half dozen plays each winter season in a 290-seat performance space.

Cinemas

Downtown Portland's two movie theaters, with a total of seven screens, aren't quite highest-tech, but they'll do just fine, especially since ticket prices are reasonable. At the six-screen **Nickelodeon** (Temple St. and Middle St., 207/772-9751), tickets are inexpensive and the seats are comfy. The place is casual enough that you can bring your own popcorn (don't make a huge deal of it; just carry it in); buy it there and you'll pay through the nose. **The Movies** (10 Exchange St., 207/772-9600) screens esoterica, and its seats are guaranteed to keep you awake, but tickets and popcorn are cheap and there are weekend matinees.

Beyond downtown are the garden-variety multiplexes: **Clarks Pond 8** (888 Clarks Pond Pkwy., behind Maine Mall, South Portland, 207/879-1511) and **Falmouth Cinemas** (206 Rte. 1, Falmouth, 207/781-5616). Most of the biggies have daily matinees, cheaper than evening screenings.

Brewpubs and Bars

Not only is **Gritty McDuff's** (396 Fore St., Old Port, Portland, 207/772-2739, 11:30–1 A.M.) one of Maine's most popular breweries, its brewpub was the state's first—opened in 1988. The menu includes pub classics such as fish and chips and shepherd's pie, as well as burgers, salads, and sandwiches. Among the Gritty's beers and ales on tap are Sebago Light and Black Fly Stout. Gritty's also books live entertainment fairly regularly. Tours by appointment. Gritty's has a branch in Freeport.

Sebago Brewing Company (164 Middle St., Old Port, Portland, 207/775-2337, 11:30–1 A.M.) is newer on the scene, but prolific, with brewpubs also in Gorham and at the Maine Mall. The Portland location has seating indoors and out and a menu that ranges from munchies to steak and lobster. Tours on request.

A longtime favorite pub, **$3 Dewey's** (241 Commercial St., Old Port, 207/772-3310) is so authentic that visiting Brits, Kiwis, and Aussies often head here to assuage their homesickness. Inexpensive fare, 36 brews on tap, free popcorn, and live music on Sunday, Tuesday, Wednesday, and Thursday make it a very popular spot. Especially popular in the late afternoon and early evening is **J's Oyster** (5 Portland Pier, Portland, 207/772-4828, 11:30–1 A.M.) a long-time fixture on the waterfront known for its raw bar and for pouring a good drink.

Of all Portland's neighborhood hangouts, **Ruski's** (212 Danforth St., 207/774-7604, Mon.–Sat. 7–12:45 A.M., Sun. 9–12:45 A.M.) is the most authentic—a small, usually crowded onetime speakeasy that rates just as high for breakfast as for nighttime schmoozing. Basic, homemade fare goes for well under $10. Darts and big-screen TV, too. Dress down or you'll feel out of place. No credit cards.

For more upscale tippling, head for **Top of the East** (157 High St., near Congress Square, Portland, 207/775-5411), the lounge at the top of the Eastland Park Hotel, where all of Portland's at your feet. Happy hour is 4–6 P.M. weekdays; the lounge is open until 1 A.M. Thursday–Saturday, till midnight other nights. Live jazz Friday and Saturday begins at 9:30 P.M. A few blocks away, down toward the Old Port, is the elegant, relaxing **Armory Lounge** at the Portland Regency Hotel (20 Milk St., Portland 04101, 207/774-4200).

Comedy

Portland's forum for stand-up comedy is the **Comedy Connection** (6 Custom House Wharf, Portland, 207/774-5554, open Thurs.–Sun. evenings at 8:00 or 8:30 P.M., depending on the night), a crowded space that draws nationally known pros. Avoid the front tables unless you're inclined to be the fall guy/guinea pig, and don't bring anyone squeamish about the F-word. Bring your sense of humor, enjoy the show, and patronize the waitstaff; they have a tough job. Reservations advised on weekends.

Live Music

So many possibilities are in this category, but not a lot of veterans. The Portland club scene is a volatile one, tough on investors and reporters. The best advice is to scope out the scene when you arrive; the *Portland Phoenix* has the best listings. Most clubs have cover charges. Here's a sampling of some Portland options. **Asylum** (121 Center St., 207/772-8274) caters to a young crowd with dance jams, CD release parties, DJ nights, and live bands. **The Alehouse** (30 Market St., 207/253-5100, www.thealehouserocks.com) boasts of being named one of the top 20 dive bars in America (don't say they didn't warn you). **Geno's** (13 Brown St., 207/772-7891) has been at it for years—an old reliable for rock.

Another local favorite is **Brian Boru** (57 Center St., Old Port, 207/780-1506, www.bboru .com), an Irish pub with live Irish music and $2 pints of Guinness on Sundays. **Bull Feeney's** (375 Fore St., 207/773-7210, www.bullfeeneys.com) and the **Free Street Taverna** (128 Free St., 207/774-1114) are eclectic venues. Much more classy is **Meritage** (24 Preble St., 207/828-0900). Settle into one of the couches, order from the tapas menu, and select one of 40 wines available by the glass. Go Thursday nights for jazz and Saturday nights for fondue. Feeling blue? Check out **Big Easy Blues Club** (55 Market St., 207/871-8817).

From October through early April, the Portland Conservatory of Music presents free, weekly **Noonday Concerts** at First Parish Church (425 Congress St., 207/773-5747) Thursdays (excluding late November) at 12:15 P.M. The music ranges widely, from saxophone to Scottish fiddle and dance, a string quartet to Irish baroque.

FESTIVALS AND EVENTS

Pick up a free copy of the *Portland Area Arts & Events Calendar* at Portland shops and cafés, the visitor information center, or City Hall (389 Congress St.).

June brings a host of events. The **Old Port Festival** (one of Portland's largest festivals), usually the first weekend, has entertainment, food and craft booths, and impromptu fun in Portland's Old Port. The **Greek Heritage Festival**, usually the last weekend, features Greek food, dancing, and crafts at Holy Trinity Church (133 Pleasant St., Portland).

Some of the world's top runners join upwards of 500 racers in the **Beach to Beacon Race,** held in late July/early August. The 10K course goes from Crescent Beach State Park to Portland Head Light, in Cape Elizabeth.

In mid-August, the **Italian Street Festival** showcases music, Italian food, and games at St. Peter's Catholic Church (72 Federal St., Portland).

Artists from all over the country set up in 350 booths along Congress Street for the annual **Sidewalk Arts Festival,** in late August.

The **Maine Brewers' Festival,** the first weekend in November at the Portland Exposition Building, is a big event that expands every year, thanks to the explosion of Maine microbreweries. Samples galore. And from Thanksgiving weekend to Christmas Eve, **Victorian Holiday,** in downtown Portland, harks back with caroling, special sales, concerts, tree lighting, horse-drawn wagons, and Victoria Mansion tours and festivities.

On December 31, **New Year's/Portland** is a city-wide chem-free celebration with music, dance, and family entertainment.

ACCOMMODATIONS

Downtown Portland

Portland's peninsula doesn't have an overwhelming amount of sleeping space, but it does have good variety in all price ranges.

Inns/B&Bs Railroad tycoon John Deering built **The Inn at St. John** (939 Congress St., 207/773-6481 or 800/636-9127, www.innatstjohn.com, $55–180) in 1897. The clean, comfortable, moderately priced 37-room hostelry welcomes children and pets and even has bicycle storage. Cable TV, air-conditioning, free local calls, free parking, free airport pickup, and continental breakfast are provided. Most rooms have private baths (some are detached). The only downside is the lackluster neighborhood, although even that is beginning to change as fun restaurants and antique shops open.

M The Danforth (163 Danforth St. at Winter St., 207/879-8755 or 800/991-6557, www

.danforthmaine.com, $139–329) is a gracious, beautifully restored, 21-room Federal-style mansion with magnificent architectural detailing. Innkeeper Barbara Hathaway has 10 guest rooms, each with fax service and data ports, cable TV, air-conditioning, and phones, and most with working fireplaces. Climb to the cupola for a great view of the Portland Harbor sunrise, hunker down in the cozy library, and don't miss the gardens or the billiards room. The self-serve continental breakfast usually includes a hot entrée, and afternoon tea and snacks are served.

Staying at **M The Pomegranate Inn** (49 Neal St. at Carroll St., 207/772-1006 or 800/356-0408, www.pomegranateinn.com, $175–285) is an adventure in itself, with faux painting, classical statuary, art, antiques, and whimsical touches everywhere. The elegant 1884 Italianate mansion has seven guest rooms and a suite, all with private baths, air-conditioning, TV, and phones; some have fireplaces. Afternoon refreshments are served.

Sue and Phil Cox (and their two Maine Coon cats) are especially hospitable hosts at **M The Inn on Carleton** (46 Carleton St., 207/775-1910 or 800/639-1779, www.innoncarleton .com, $179–225). The 17-room National Historic Register mansion has six attractively decorated second- and third-floor guest rooms with majestic antique beds. Breakfast is a feast.

Former travel writer Dale Northrup put his experience to work in opening the **Percy Inn** (15 Pine St., 207/871-7638 or 888/417-3729, www.percyinn.com, $89–139), just off Longfellow Square. You can easily hole up in the guest rooms, which are furnished with phones, fax machines, CD players, TVs with VCRs, wet bars, and stocked refrigerators and have air-conditioning. It's best suited for independent-minded travelers, who don't desire much contact with the host or other guests, as public rooms are few. Breakfast is a continental buffet.

The Wild Iris Inn (273 State St., 207/775-0224 or 800/600-1557, www.wildirisinn.com, rates are $99–135) provides seven comfortable rooms, all with air-conditioning, five with private baths. You'll get your exercise: all rooms are on the second and third floors of a Victorian house; it's a short, but uphill, walk to the Arts District.

A buffet continental breakfast is served. An office provides a computer, fax, printer, and WiFi at no charge. Free local calls and free parking.

Built in 1877, the handsome Georgian-style **West End Inn** (146 Pine St. at Neal St., 207/772-1377 or 800/338-1377, www.westendbb.com, $159–209) has six nicely decorated second- and third-floor guest rooms with private baths and TV, and a first-floor room with private porch. A full breakfast is served.

Full-Service Hotels: Grander accommodations are provided by three in-town hotels, one in the Arts District and two in the Old Port.

The beautifully renovated **Eastland Park** (273 State St., 207/775-5411 or 888/671-8008, www.eastlandparkhotel.com, $139–229), one of Portland's oldest hotels, is practically a steal for an in-town hotel. It's right across from the Portland Museum of Art. Facilities include a restaurant, top-floor lounge with fabulous views, free WiFi, and fitness room. Do ask for one of the renovated rooms.

You might have trouble finding **The Portland Regency** (20 Milk St., 207/774-4200 or 800/727-3436, www.theregency.com, $199–249). That's because this lovely hotel is secreted in a renovated armory in the heart of the Old Port. Local calls are free, WiFi and laptop rentals are available, and free shuttles are provided to all major Portland transportation facilities. A restaurant and fitness center are on-site.

Newest and most luxurious of the three is the ꟽ **Portland Harbor Hotel** (468 Fore St., 207/775-9090 or 888/798-9090, www.portlandharborhotel.com, $249–299), an upscale, boutique hotel in the Old Port built around a garden courtyard with fountain. Rooms are plush, with chic linens, duvets, down pillows on the beds, WiFi and digital cable TV, and bathrooms with separate soaking tubs and showers. The restaurant gets high marks from locals, although service can be almost surly.

Beyond Downtown

South of Portland are numerous inns and resorts, some right on the ocean, others within walking distance.

The **Peter A. McKernan Hospitality Center** (Southern Maine Technical College, Fort Road, South Portland 04106, 207/741-5672 front desk, 207/741-5662 reservations, www.hospitality.smccme.edu, $165) provides a different twist on the inn experience. In fact, it's the proving ground for students in the Lodging and Restaurant Management Program at Southern Maine Community College. The center, a 1902 brick building that once served as officers' quarters, has spectacular views of Casco Bay and the offshore islands. Students staff the inn, and they all aim to please. Shorefront walking/biking trails are nearby. The center keeps a low profile, yet rooms are booked far ahead. Rates include continental breakfast.

You'll get a sense of the **Black Point Inn Resort** (510 Black Point Rd., Prouts Neck, Scarborough 04074, 207/883-2500 or 800/258-0003, www.blackpointinn.com, $450–630 d, including breakfast, dinner and afternoon tea) as soon as you eyeball the honeymooners, yuppies, dowagers, and sedate film stars rubbing shoulders here. Many guests are repeats. Many also never leave Prouts Neck during their stay—everything's here for a real getaway, including tennis courts, an 18-hole golf course, indoor and outdoor pools, bicycles to borrow, fitness room, wicker chairs on the glassed-in veranda, sand beach, local library, gift shop, and walking paths. Guest rooms range from surprisingly plain to downright elegant. The inn's dining room is open to the public by reservation only; don't show up without a jacket. (Children's dining and movies are offered each evening.) The inn and cottages comprise 84 rooms and suites, most with water views.

Seven miles south of downtown Portland, ꟽ **Inn by the Sea** (40 Bowery Beach Rd., Route 77, Cape Elizabeth 04107, 207/799-3134 or 800/888-4287, www.innbythesea.com, $319–639 d) is a well-managed modern complex with the stylishly casual feel of an upscale summer house. Forty-three one- and two-bedroom suites and cottages have kitchen facilities and spectacular water views. Best of all, a boardwalk winds down through the salt marsh to the southern end of Crescent Beach State Park. Facilities at the inn, built in 1986, include a tennis court, outdoor pool, croquet lawn, and bicycles. By reservation, pets are honored guests here (they even have their own room-service menu). Make reservations early; the inn is incredibly popular. Priceless Audubon prints cover the walls in the appropriately named **Audubon Room** (207/767-0888), where moderate-to-expensive breakfasts, lunches, and excellent dinners are served daily to guests—and to the public by reservation. (Entrée range is $19–29; try the crab cakes.)

Island Lodging

Peaks Island: The **Inn on Peaks Island** (33 Island Ave., Peaks Island 04108, www.theinnonpeaks island.com, $199–299) overlooks the ferry dock and has jaw-dropping sunset views over the Portland skyline. No island roughing it here. The spacious cottage-style guest rooms have fireplaces, sitting areas, whirlpool baths, TV and VCR, and refrigerators, and rates include a continental breakfast. Lunch and dinner are also served in the inn's restaurant (dinner entrées $14–22). Access is via Casco Bay Lines.

On the other end of the Peaks Island luxury scale is the extremely informal and communal **Eighth Maine Living Museum and Lodge** (13 Eighth Maine Ave., Peaks Island 04108, 207/766-5086 mid-May–mid-Sept., 914/237-3165 off-season, $61–73), a shorefront, rustic, living-history lodge overlooking White Head Passage. Shared baths and a huge shared kitchen (in which every room is allocated a two-burner gas stove, cabinet space, dining table, and access to full kitchen facilities) allow you to rusticate in much the same manner as did the Civil War vets who built this place, in 1891, with a gift from a veteran who had won the Louisiana Lottery. Bring your own linens, or rent for $8 per bed, per stay.

Overlooking the Stone Pier and the golf course, **The Cheabeague Island Inn** (61 South Rd., Chebeague Island 04017, 207-836-5155, www .chebeagueislandinn.com, $185–315) is an imposing three-story hotel with a spectacular sunset-view veranda. The inn's been here since the early 20th century, but it was renovated in 2004 with completely new furnishings. Although the inn is decidedly new-fashioned now, there are still no TVs or phones in the rather-smallish rooms. The dining room serves breakfast and dinner daily, lunch Monday–Saturday, and Sunday brunch June–Thanksgiving. Access is via Cheabeague Transportation, in Yarmouth, or Casco Bay Lines.

The **Chebeague Orchard Inn** (453 North Rd., Chebeague Island 04017, 207/846-9488, http://web.nlis.net/~orchard/orchard.html, $90–120) doubles as Vickie and Neil Taliento's comfortable, antique-filled home. Five rooms have handmade quilts (three have private baths and two share a bath); some have water views. The congenial Talientos are big supporters of the Maine Island Trail Association, so you'll get a discount if you arrive by kayak (the trail begins near Chebeague). Coffee's ready at 7 A.M.; breakfast is a feast, overlooking the backyard's bird feeders and apple orchard. There are bikes for guests, a fireplace in the common room, and tons of helpful advice about the island.

FOOD

Downtown Portland alone has more than a hundred restaurants, so it's impossible to list even all the great ones—and there are many. The city's proximity to fresh foods, from both farms and the sea, makes it popular with chefs, and its Italian roots and growing immigrant population mean a good choice of ethnic dining, too. Below is a choice selection, by neighborhood, with open days and hours provided for peak season. Call in advance, from September through June. You'll note that some restaurants don't list a closing time; that's because they shut the doors when the crowd thins, so call ahead if you're heading out much after 8 P.M., just to be safe.

If you'll be in Maine for more than a few days, check out the **Portland Dine Around Club** (P.O. 15338., Portland 04112, 207/775 4711 or 877/732-2582, www.dineportland.com, $29.95). This discount card gets you two-for-the-price-of-one meals (usually dinner entrées) at more than 150 restaurants with a wide variety of menus, decor, and price ranges as well as discounts at numerous attractions, museums, performing arts venues, and even lodging, statewide. Check the website to see if the discounts are valid where and when you want them.

In addition to the many restaurant options listed here, check the *Community News* listings in each Wednesday's *Portland Press Herald.* Under "Potluck," you'll find listings of **public meals,** usually benefiting nonprofit organizations. Prices are always quite low (under $10 for adults, $2–4 for children), mealtimes quite early (5 or 6 P.M.), and the flavor quite local.

Old Port and the Waterfront

Destination Dining: Plan well in advance to get a reservation at 🅼 **Fore Street** (288 Fore St., Old Port, 207/775-2717, 5–10 P.M. Sun.–Thurs., to 10:30 P.M. Sat. and Sun.). Chef Sam Hayward, a fixture on the Maine food scene who is well known for his creative use of Maine-sourced ingredients, won the James Beard Award for Best Chef in the Northeast in 2004 and has been featured in most of the foodie publications. Even though the copper-topped tables, open kitchen, and the industrial decor create a din in this ex-warehouse, no one seems to mind much. Game is roasted on a spit, seafood is grilled over apple wood or roasted in the wood oven. Appetizers are particularly imaginative. Entrées are in the $18–28 range. The restaurant is a joint project with Street & Company owner Dana Street.

In 2004, *Food and Wine* named Rob Evans as one of America's Ten Best New Chefs, making 🅼 **Hugo's** (88 Middle St., corner of Franklin St., 207/774-8538, 5:30–9 P.M. Tues.–Thurs., to 9:30 P.M. Sat. and Sun.) a destination unto itself. Not that savvy Portlanders hadn't already been beating a path to his door for his outstanding New American cuisine. The fixed price menu, around $45 for three courses, changes weekly. For a real splurge, call at least 24 hours in advance for the 10-course Chef's Menu, which draws from the freshest Maine ingredients available. For just a taste of this renowned chef's food, sit at the bar and choose from a limited tapas-style bar menu. Reservations are essential.

Fabulous! and Outstanding! are just a few of the exclamations you'll hear from diners about 🅼 **Bandol** (90 Exchange St., 207/347-7155, 5–10 P.M. Tues.–Sat.). Chef Erik Desjarlais's intimate and très French restaurant is a must for foodies or anyone who enjoys lingering over a truly fine dining experience. The five-course, fixed price menu is $74; the nine-course tasting

menu is $89, but it usually includes a few extras from the kitchen. Not a place to rush through a meal—not that you'll want to anyway. Every bite is meant to be savored. Service is excellent. Reservations are a must.

Okay, it's not exactly on the city's waterfront, but you take a Casco Bay Lines ferry from there to get to **Diamond's Edge Restaurant** (207/766-5850, Great Diamond Island, 11 A.M.–2:30 P.M. and 5–9 P.M. Mon.–Sat., 11 A.M.–3 P.M. Sun., late May–late Sept.). You'll need to coordinate your dining with the ferry schedule, but it's worth it. The citrus tea-rubbed salmon, seared peppered tuna, and roasted rack of lamb are all superb. Entrées run $20–32. The restaurant, in a renovated Fort McKinley Quartermaster Corps building, is elegant without being at all stuffy. In fine weather, you can dine outside.

Fish and Seafood: Ask around, and everyone will tell you the best seafood in town is at 🅼 **Street & Company** (33 Wharf St., Old Port, 207/775-0887, 5–9:30 P.M. daily, to 10 P.M. Fri. and Sat.) Fresh, beautifully prepared fish (entrées $16–26) is what you get, often with a Mediterranean flair—in an informal, brick-walled environment that's been here since 1989 (mercifully expanded in 2001). Don't show up without a reservation.

For lobster-in-the-rough, head to **Portland Lobster Company** (180 Commercial St., 207/775-2112, 11 A.M.–9 P.M. daily). There's a small inside seating area, but it's much more pleasant to sit out on the wharf and watch the excursion boats come and go. Expect to pay in the low $20 range for a one-pound lobster with french fries and slaw. Other choices ($6–17) and a kids' menu are available.

Ethnic Fare: If you like sushi, beat a path to the sushi bar at **Benkay Sushi Bar and Japanese Restaurant** (2 India St., 207/773-5555, 11:30 A.M.–2 P.M. weekdays, 5–9:30 P.M. Sun.–Thurs., 5–10 P.M. Fri.–Sat., with rock and roll sushi 10 P.M.–12:30 A.M. Fri.–Sat.). This is Maine's best Japanese eatery. No reservations, so you may have to wait. Parking is free, but if you don't feel like going out, delivery is free. Running a close second is Maine's most enduring Japanese restaurant, **Sapporo** (230 Commercial

St., Union Wharf, Old Port, 207/772-1233, 11:30 A.M.–2 P.M. and 5–10 P.M. Mon.–Fri., noon–10 P.M. Sat., weekend nights to 1 A.M. for sushi and music). Kids gravitate to the tempura and teriyaki ($10–16)—and of course they're entranced by the in-your-face, table-side preparation. Reservations advisable on weekends.

Primo rustic Italian fare is the rule at **Ribollita** (41 Middle St., 207/774-2972, 5–9 P.M. Tues.–Sat., to 10 P.M. Fri. and Sat.). You'll want reservations at this small, casual, restaurant that's justly popular for delivering fabulous food at fair prices ($11–18); just be in the mood for a leisurely meal. Handmade pastas, such as white bean and romano ravioli or pan-seared gnocchi, and choices such as radicchio-wrapped salmon with pesto and roast pepper sauce are typical.

Top-notch for northern Italian is **Cinque Terre Ristorante** (36 Wharf St., 207/347-6154, 5–9 P.M. daily, to 10 P.M. Fri. and Sat.). Chef Lee Skawinski is committed to sustainable farming, and much of the seasonal and organic produce used comes from the restaurant owners' Laughing Stock Farm and other Maine farms. The restaurant is housed in a former ship's chandlery that's been transformed into a comfortable, Tuscan-accented dining area, with an open kitchen and seating either on the main floor or a second-floor balcony that rims the open space. Choose from half- or full-size portions ranging $12–28. Do begin with the antipasto plate, and don't miss the handmade pastas or the lobster risotto. More than 100 Italian wines are on the award-winning list.

A family-oriented restaurant, and one that's endured since 1936, is the Reali family's **Village Café** (112 Newbury St., 207/772-5320, 11 A.M.–10 P.M. Mon.–Thurs., 11 A.M.–11 P.M. Fri. and Sat., 11:30 A.M.–8 P.M. Sun.—to 9:30 in July and Aug.). The huge place has a moderate menu of respectable Italian food (entrées $10–23), healthful specials, and free crayons for the kids. Fried clams are a major specialty.

Irish fare with a Maine accent fills the menu at **Ri-Ra** (72 Commercial St., Old Port, 207/761-4446, 11:30 A.M.–10 P.M.). How about beef stew made with Guinness? Or grilled salmon with leeks? Entrées in the glass-walled second-floor dining room (overlooking the Casco Bay Lines ferry terminal) are $11–29. Appetizers and desserts are superb, too. The ground-floor pub, elegantly woody, with an enormous bar, is inevitably stuffed to the gills on weekends—a great spot for such traditional fare as corned beef and cabbage (pub entrées $8–16), as long as you can stand the din. No reservations, so be prepared to wait, especially on weekends.

Eclectic Dining: At **Natasha's** (82 Exchange St., Old Port, 207/774-4004, 11 A.M.–2:30 P.M. Mon.–Fri., 5–10 P.M. Mon.–Sat.), the dinner menu might include Maine haddock with prosciutto-wrapped scallops, crispy Laos orange whitefish with lime, or udon noodles and shiitake mushrooms. Lunch fare is equally creative. Dinner entrées are in the $18–28 range. In 2004, chef Natasha Carleton opened the more casual and less pricey **Mim's Brasserie** (205 Commercial St., Old Port, 207/345-7478, 8 A.M.–10 P.M. Mon.–Thurs., 9 A.M.–10:30 P.M. Fri. and Sat., 9 A.M.–9 P.M. Sun.). The à la carte French-inspired menu features naturally raised meats and simple yet stunning preparations. Small plates run $7–14, entrées $13–23; side dishes are extra and designed to be mixed, matched, and shared. The whole roasted branzino is a knockout. At breakfast, omelet possibilities include duck confit, lobster, artichokes, and white anchovy. Dine indoors or outside on the patio or deck.

Just up the street, **Walter's** (15 Exchange St., 207/871-9258, 11 A.M.–3 P.M. Mon.–Sat. and 5–9 P.M. daily, to 10 P.M. Fri. and Sat.) has been serving creative fusion fare since 1990s, and despite the longevity, it's never tiresome. The two-level dining room can be noisy. Entrées run around $18–22.

You never know what'll be on the menu (Indonesian chicken, North African stuffed peppers, maybe Caribbean shrimp cakes?) at funky **Pepperclub** (78 Middle St., east of Franklin St., 207/772-0531, 5–9 P.M. Mon.–Thurs., 5–10 P.M. Sat. and Sun.) but take the risk. Vegetarian and vegan specials are always available, as are local and organic meats and seafood. If your kids are even vaguely adventuresome, they'll find food to like here—and prices to match (entrées $11–15).

Local Favorites: You can usually get out for less than $10 from any of these, significantly less at most.

Best known for the earliest and most filling breakfast, **Becky's Diner** (Hobson's Wharf, 390 Commercial St., Old Port, 207/773-7070, 4 A.M.–9 P.M. daily) has more than a dozen omelet choices, just for a start. It also serves lunch and dinner, all at downright cheap prices.

The color's a lot more local just down the street at ◼ **The Porthole** (20 Custom House Wharf, Commercial St., Old Port, 207/774-6652, 6 A.M.–9 P.M. Mon.–Sat., 8 A.M.–3 P.M. Sun.), a one-time dive that's been gussied up a bit. The all-you-can-eat Friday fish fry pulls in *real* fisherfolk, in-the-know locals, and fearless tourists. Eat inside or on the wharf.

Mmmmm, mmmm. For finger-lickin' barbe-cued ribs and chicken, fried chicken, blackened catfish, and pulled pork or beef brisket sand-wiches, it's **Norm's East End Grill** (37 Middle St., 207/253-1700, 11:30 A.M.–10 P.M. Mon.–Sat., 4–9 P.M. Sun.). All barbecue items are smoked on premises with hickory and apple wood. Of course, this being Maine, clam and corn chowder, homemade fishcakes, and lobster stew are also available.

Pizza with a view is on tap at **Flatbread Company** (72 Commercial St., 207/772-8777, 11:30 A.M.–close daily). The all-natural pizza is baked in a primitive, wood-fired clay oven and served in a dining room with a wall of windows overlooking the ferry terminal and Portland Har-bor. Half and whole pizzas include choices such as nitrate-free pepperoni, vegan (dairy-free) flat-bread, cheese and herb, and you-choose combos.

Mainers love their Italian sandwiches, and **Amato's** (71 India St., 207/773-1682, 6:30 A.M.–11 P.M. Mon.–Sat., 7 A.M.–11 P.M. Sun.) is cred-ited with creating this drool-worthy sub, made with ham, cheese, tomatoes, green peppers, black olives, and onions (or various other combina-tions), all wrapped in a doughy roll and drizzled with olive oil. Also available are calzones, salads, and other Italian-inspired foods. Amato's has outlets throughout southern Maine. This one has outdoor patio seating.

Healthful fast food? Stonyfield Farm CEO Gary Hirshberg proved it wasn't an oxymoron with **O'Natural's** (88 Exchange St., 207/321-2050, 10:30 A.M.–8 P.M. Sun.–Thurs., to 9 P.M. Fri. and Sat.). The emphasis is on fresh, local, and organic, with choices including flatbread sandwiches, tossed salads, Asian noodles, soups, and even a kids' menu. Wheat-free, dairy-free, and veggie choices available. It's all served in a his-torical bank building, where the huge safe is now a safe play area for kids.

Hands down, the Old Port's favorite and cheapest fast food comes from **Granny's Bur-rito's** (420 Exchange St., 207/761-0751, 11 A.M.–10 P.M. Sun.–Thurs., to midnight Fri. and Sat.). Burritos and quesadillas dominate the menu, with plenty of vegan and vegetarian op-tions. Take-out and counter service are down-stairs. Upstairs has table service, beer and wine, and live music Friday and Saturday nights and an open mic on Sunday night.

Sweet Treats: When you're craving carbs, want pastries for breakfast, or need to boost your en-ergy with a sweet, follow your nose to **Standard Baking Company** (75 Commercial St., 207/773-2112, 7 A.M.–6 P.M. Mon.–Fri., to 5 P.M. Sat. and Sun.), deservedly famous for its hand-crafted breads and pastries. Stephen Lanzalotta, the chef/owner of **Sophia's** (81 Market St., 207/879-1869, 9 A.M.–4 P.M. Tues.–Fri., or until sold out), created the DaVinci Diet, which re-ceived national acclaim. Choose from an an-tipasto menu or sandwiches, all made on fabulous breads. Chocoholics take note: When a craving strikes for scrumptious homemade chocolates or ice cream, head to **Fuller's** (432 Fore St., 207/253-8010).

Arts District

Fun, whimsical, and artsy best describe most restaurants in the Arts District, but not **Five Fifty-Five** (555 Congress St., 207/761-0555, 5–10 P.M. Wed.–Mon. and 10:30 A.M.–2:30 P.M. Sun.). The bilevel dining area is bright and ele-gant. Fresh, local, and seasonal are the menu's promise. Artisanal cheeses have a page unto them-selves, while the rest of the menu is divided into small plates, greens (grilled Caesar), and savory plates, perhaps pepper-crusted, pan-seared day-boat scallops or two peppers, two ways. Entrées cost $17–24.

How about rainbow trout with Drambui-lobster cream sauce or a grilled center-cut pork chop? Both share the menu at **Cafe Uffa** (190 State St. 207/775-3380, 11:30 A.M.–2:30 P.M. and 5:30–10 P.M. Wed.–Sat., also 8 A.M.–noon Sat. and 9 A.M.–2 P.M. Sun.). High ceilings, mismatched chairs, and a changing selection of art are in keeping with its location across from the Portland Museum of Art, but the draped tables indicate the quality and price (entrées $17–29). Uffa is also renowned for its weekend brunch (entrées $9–11). Choose from more than 12 items to create an omelet, or select from traditional, steak, or lobster eggs Benedict.

Next door is **Local 188** (188 State St., 207/761-7909, 11 A.M.–2 P.M. Tues.–Fri., 5–10 P.M. Tues. and Wed., 5–10:30 P.M. Sat. and Sun., 11 A.M.–2 P.M. Sun.). Don't be put off by the flea market furnishings; this place serves fabulous Mediterranean-inspired food with a tapas-heavy menu. It doubles as an art gallery, with rotating exhibits. Spend lunch, Sunday brunch, or an evening grazing through marinated mushrooms, vegetable salads, imaginative soups, mussel stew, even paella. A few more substantial entrées are available, but most menu items are under $13. Free parking behind Joe's Smoke Shop.

Be sure to have a reservation if you're going, pre-theater, to **M BiBo's Madd Apple Café** (23 Forest Ave., 207/774-9698, 11:30 A.M.–2 P.M. Wed.–Fri., 5:30–9 P.M. Wed.–Sat., 11 A.M.–2 P.M. and 4–8 P.M. Sun.)—it's right next to the Portland Performing Arts Center. On the other hand, it's popular any time, thanks to chef Bill Boutwell (BiBo). There's no way of predicting what will be on the bistro-fusion menu, although the sweet soy marinated salmon is so popular that it's almost always available. Dinner entrée range is $15–20.

Local Favorite: Even the name, **M Norm's Bar & Grill** (617 Congress St., 207/828-9944, 11:30 A.M.–10 P.M. daily), is reminiscent of Cheers. Locals would prefer this neighborhood eatery were kept secret, but the food is too good not to share. One of the reasons Norm's is so popular is that you can cobble together a meal that meets your ap-

petite from a menu that includes selections for tapas, sandwiches, salads, entrées, and sides in addition to chalkboard specials. Norm's doesn't take reservations, so you'll probably have to relax in the equally popular bar while waiting for a table. Norm also operates the tavern across the street and a barbecue joint in the Old Port.

Ethnic Fare ¡Olé! Healthful Mexican is served at **Mesa Verde** (618 Congress St., 207/774-6089, 11:30 A.M.–9 P.M. Tues.–Thurs., to 9:30 P.M. Fri. and Sat., to 8:30 P.M. Sun.), a colorful restaurant and juice bar that also rightfully famous for its margaritas.

Easy on-the-budget Vietnamese food has earned **Saigon Thinh Thanh** (608 Congress St., 207/773 2932, 11:30 A.M.–2:30 P.M. daily, 4:30–9 P.M. Sun.–Wed., to 10 P.M. Thurs.–Sat.) a strong local following. Choices are plentiful, and many allow you to create dishes just the way you like.

Elsewhere in Portland

Fine Dining: For an elegant meal, look no further than the **Back Bay Grill** (65 Portland St., near the main post office, 207/772-8833, 5–9 P.M. Mon.–Thurs., to 9:30 P.M. Fri. and Sat.). The serene dining room is accented by a colorful mural, and arts-and-crafts wall sconces cast a soft glow on the white linen-raped tables. The menu, which highlights fresh, seasonal ingredients, ranks among the best in the city, and the wine list is long and well chosen. Service is professional. Entrée range is $19–34. Reservations are needed on weekends.

Casual Dining: In-the-know Portlanders have long favored **Bintliff's American Café** (98 Portland St., Portland, 207/774-0005, 7 A.M.–2 P.M. daily and 5–9 P.M. Wed.–Sat.) for its fabulous brunches ($7–12); the menu is humongous. In 2004, it began serving a much smaller dinner menu (entrée s $15–23) to equally rave reviews. No reservations for brunch, so expect to wait in line on weekends (it's worth it).

Blue Spoon (89 Congress St., 207/773-1119, noon–9 P.M. Tues.–Thurs., to 9:30 P.M. Fri. and Sat., and 9 A.M.–2 P.M. Sun.) is one of the first upscale eateries on Portland's gentrifying East End. Chef-owner David Iovino, who studied at the French Culinary Institute, has created a warm, welcoming, and inexpensive bistro (entrées $9–13), where one of the best-sellers is roast chicken that's pan seared, then roasted beneath a hot brick. Vegetarian and vegan selections are available.

Local Favorites: Tiny **Dogfish Cafe** (953 Congress St., 207/253-5400, 11:30 A.M.–10 P.M. Mon.–Sat.) packs 'em in for salads and sandwiches and grilled goodies, averaging around $8, with heartier dinner specials ($11–18) served Wednesday–Saturday evenings. It's just a couple of doors down from the Inn on St. John.

Keep it really cheap by picking up delicious and healthful sandwiches, pizzas, salads, sushi, or deli selections at **Wild Oats** (87 Marginal Way, 207/699-2626), a natural foods supermarket with indoor and outdoor seating. You can even pick up meat or fish and nuke it in a microwave.

Eclectic Choices: When everyone in your party wants something different, head to the **Portland Public Market** (25 Preble St., 207/228-2000, www.portlandmarket.com, 9 A.M.–7 P.M. Mon.–Sat., 10 A.M.–4 P.M. Sun.) It's modeled on Seattle's famous Pike Place; you can nibble your way through more than a dozen Maine food vendors peddling everything from sushi to lobster, homemade soup to artisanal cheese. Seating is available. Two hours of parking is free in the attached garage. Attractions include frequent demonstrations, classes, and entertainment. In 2004, renowned chefs Dana Street and Sam Hayward, of Fore Street fame, opened a combo seafood market and restaurant, **Scales** (Portland Public Market, 25 Preble St., 207/228-2010, 11 A.M.–7 P.M. Mon.–Sat., to 5 P.M. Sun.). As might be expected, fish and seafood, all at market prices, are served along with a lone choice for meat eaters—a hot dog. It's all very casual—order at the register, pay, then grab a table—and very good. There's also a small raw bar. Plans call for the restaurant part to be enlarged and for dinner to be served later than market hours.

The 'Burbs

Great sunset views over Portland's skyline, a casual atmosphere, and excellent fare have earned **Saltwater Grille** (231 Front St., South Portland, 207/799-5400, www.saltwatergrille.com, 11 A.M.–3 P.M. and 5–9 P.M.) an excellent reputation. Dine inside or on the waterfront deck. Dinner entrées run $15–22.

Pizza: Ricetta's Brick Oven Pizzeria (29 Western Ave., Rte. 9, South Portland, between Maine Mall and Portland Jetport, 207/775-7400, and 240 Rte. 1, Falmouth, 207/781-3100, 11:30 A.M.–10 P.M. Sun.–Thurs., to 11 P.M. Fri. and Sat.) is regularly voted Greater Portland's best pizza palace. Not surprising when you see the lunchtime-only pizza smorgasbord—all the pizza you can eat, plus salad and soup. Specialty pizzas are outstanding, or you can invent your own combo. Also on the menu are antipasti, calzones, giant salads, soups, pasta dishes, and high-calorie desserts.

Lobster-in-the-Rough: Every Mainer has a favorite lobster eatery (besides home), but **The Lobster Shack** (222 Two Lights Rd., Cape Elizabeth, 207/799-1677, 11 A.M.–8 P.M. daily mid-Apr. to mid-Oct., to 8:30 P.M. in July and Aug.) tops an awful lot of lists. Seniority helps—it's been here since the 1920s. Scenery, too—a panoramic vista in the shadow of Cape Elizabeth Light. Plus the menu—seafood galore (and hot dogs for those who'd rather). Choose a lobster from the tank, indulge in the lobster stew, grab a table on the ledges, and watch the world sail by. Opt for a sunny day; the lighthouse's foghorn can kill your conversation when the fog rolls in.

A sure bet for a splurge is the handsome **Audubon Room** at Inn by the Sea (40 Bowery Beach Rd., Rte. 77, Cape Elizabeth, 207/767-0888, entrées $19–29), where breakfasts, lunches, and excellent dinners are served daily to guests—and to the public by reservation.

INFORMATION AND SERVICES

The **Visitor Information Center of the Convention and Visitors Bureau of Greater Portland** (245 Commercial St., Portland 04101, 207/772-5800, www.visitportland.com, 8 A.M.–6 P.M. Mon.–Fri., 10 A.M.–3 P.M. Sat. and holidays, to 5 P.M. mid-May–mid-Oct.) The office has tons of brochures, plenty of restaurant menus, and public restrooms.

The Portland Downtown District (94 Free

St., 207/772-6828, www.portlandmaine.com), an independent merchants' association, instituted a very successful **Downtown Guides** program in the summer of 1996. Between early June and Labor Day, a handful of young, enthusiastic guides, wearing yellow shirts and khaki shorts, patrol a 65-acre rectangular downtown area bounded by Congress, Franklin, Commercial, and State Streets. The Old Port District and Congress Street are their busiest locations. Carrying maps, brochures, and cell phones, they're on the streets Monday–Saturday 11:30 A.M.–8 P.M., Sunday 9:30 A.M.–5 P.M. Ask them anything; they love the challenge and, as one visitor noted, they're "relentlessly friendly." The organization's website has tons of info.

For **time** and **temperature information,** call 207/775-4321; for the current **weather report,** call 207/688-3210. For **winter parking-ban information,** call 207/879-0300.

Hospitals

The state's largest hospital, **Maine Medical Center** (22 Bramhall St., Portland 04101, emergency 207/871-2381), offers round-the-clock emergency-room care and a cafeteria that can turn out cheap and tasty made-to-order omelets any hour of the day or night. Also in downtown Portland is Catholic **Mercy Hospital** (144 State St., Portland 04101, emergency 207/879-3265), with a first-rate reputation for its caring staff.

Libraries

The **Portland Public Library** (5 Monument Sq., Portland 04101, 207/871-1700, www.portland library.com, 9 A.M.–6 P.M. Mon. and Wed., noon–9 P.M. Tues. and Thurs., 9 A.M.–5 P.M. Fri. and Sat.) can be a useful stop.

Public Restrooms

In the **Old Port** area, you'll find restrooms at the Convention and Visitors Bureau Visitor Information Center (245 Commercial St.), the Spring Street parking garage (45 Spring St.), the Fore Street parking garage (419 Fore St.), and the Casco Bay Lines ferry terminal (Commercial St. and Franklin St.).

On **Congress Street,** you can use the rest-

rooms at Portland City Hall (389 Congress St.) and the Portland Public Library (5 Monument Sq.). In **Midtown,** head for the Cumberland County Civic Center (1 Civic Center Sq.). In the **West End,** use Maine Medical Center.

GETTING THERE

The best overall source for planning your transportation is the website www.transportme.org. It lists schedules, fares, and other information for airlines, buses, ferries, and trains. The ultra clean and comfortable **Portland Transportation Center** (100 Thompson Point Rd., Portland 207/828-3939) is the base for Concord Trailways bus line and Amtrak's Downeaster service. Parking is $2 per day, and the terminal has free coffee, free newspapers (while they last), and vending machines. The Metro, The Portland Explorer, and the Zoom buses stop here. If you show your Trailways or Amtrak ticket stub to the Metro bus driver, you'll have a free ride downtown.

By Air

The **Portland International Jetport** terminal (207/774-7301, www.portlandjetport.org) underwent a multimillion-dollar facelift in 1996, and another one is planned, perhaps starting as early as 2005. The terminal contains all the amenities—including offices of Thomas Cook travel and Alamo, Avis, Budget, Hertz, and National car-rental agencies. Visitor information is available at a desk (not always staffed; 207/775-5809) between the gates and the baggage-claim area. Baggage-handling offices surround the luggage carousels, but if you have an emergency, contact the jetport manager at 207/773-8462. Do give yourself plenty of time to get through security, especially during rush periods, such as first thing in the morning. There are restrooms, a snack bar, and small newsstand in the gate area.

Expect the fare to be about $13 on a metered **taxi** from the jetport to the Portland waterfront. The airport website has a useful **Ground Transportation Guide** with a list of taxi fares and other relevant information. (Also see Getting Around.)

By Train

Amtrak's Downeaster (800/872-7245, www.the-downeaster.com, $21 one-way) makes four daily round-trip runs between Boston's North Station and Portland Transportation Center, with stops at Wells and Saco and seasonally in Old Orchard Beach. Call or check the website for discounted fares and special rates for children and seniors. From the station, Portland's Metro municipal bus service will take you gratis to downtown Portland; just show your Amtrak ticket stub. For information, call Amtrak at 800/872-7245 or check www.thedowneaster.com.

By Bus

Concord Trailways (Portland Transportation Center, Thompson Point Rd., Portland, 800/639-3317, www.concordtrailways.com) departs downtown Boston (South Station Transportation Center) and Logan Airport for the 100-mile trip to Portland about 10 times daily, making pickups at all Logan airline terminals (lower level). A free movie is shown along the way. The fare is $23 one-way, $37 round-trip. Three daily nonexpress Concord Trailways buses continue from Portland along the coast, making about 10 stops before heading inland to the Trailways terminal in Bangor. If you show your Trailways ticket stub to the Metro bus driver, you'll have a free ride downtown.

Vermont Transit Lines (950 Congress St., Portland, 207/772-6587 or 800/552-8737), a division of Greyhound Bus Lines, serves Maine, the rest of New England, and beyond, connecting with Greyhound routes. The schedule is slightly less convenient than that of Concord Trailways, but rates are slightly lower.

By Boat

If you're coming from Nova Scotia (or if you want to include it in your travels), you can save about 850 miles of driving (along the coasts of Maine and New Brunswick, then back) by boarding the 475-foot cruise liner MS *Scotia Prince* (International Marine Terminal, 468 Commercial St., P.O. Box 4216, Portland 04101, 207/775-5616 or 800/341-7540, www.scotiaprince.com). Departures are at 8 P.M., early May to late Octo-

ber, arriving Yarmouth, Nova Scotia, at 8 A.M. (9 A.M. Atlantic time). After an hour's layover, the ship returns to Portland, arriving at 8 P.M., only 23 hours after you left. (Another Maine–Nova Scotia boat connection is *The Cat,* a huge catamaran ferry departing daily for Yarmouth from Bar Harbor; see the *Acadia Region* chapter. *The Cat* is working toward operating from Portland, too.) You won't lack for entertainment: the *Scotia Prince* has all the hyperactivity of typical cruise ships, including a casino, floor show, and duty-free shopping. Fares vary, depending on the season and whether you're taking a car or want an overnight cabin. Special packages are available, including round-trip super savers with cabin and meals.

Van Service

Mermaid Transportation (P.O. Box 10676, Portland 04104, 207/772-2509 or 800/696-2463, www.gomermaid.com) operates the best van service between Boston and Portland (and vice versa). Pickup and drop-off, five times daily, are at Portland Jetport and Logan Airport, by reservation only. Pickup and drop-off can be arranged for Falmouth Shopping Center, just north of Portland. Mermaid also will pick up and drop off customers at three Maine Turnpike exits south of Portland. The company also runs daily van service between Manchester, New Hampshire (primarily for Southwest Airlines), and the Portland Jetport.

Highway Access

The major highway access to Portland is the **Maine Turnpike,** which links with the I-95 interstate highway system at the New Hampshire border. I-295, a spur of I-95, runs through Portland, allowing easy access to the Old Port district.

GETTING AROUND

Parking garages and lots are strategically situated all over downtown Portland, particularly in the Old Port and near the civic center. Unless you're lucky, you'll probably waste a lot of time looking for on-street parking (meters start at $.25 a half hour), so a garage or lot is the best option. If you land in a garage or lot with a Park & Shop sticker, you can collect free-parking stamps, each good for an hour, from participating shops and restaurants. You could even end up parking for free. A day of parking generally runs $8–14. The Casco Bay Lines website, www.cascobaylines .com, has a very useful parking map, listing parking lots and garages and their hourly and daily rates. Good for comparison shopping.

Bus and Ferry Service

Again, the website www.transportme.org is a good one-stop resource for area transportation schedules. **The Portland Explorer** (207/774-9891 or 800/377-4457, www.portlandexplorer .org, free) connects the Portland Transportation Center, Portland Jetport, Scotia Prince Ferry, Vermont Transit terminal, Casco Bay Lines, Old Port, Monument Square, and the Maine Mall, as well as various hotels along the routes.

Portland's bus network, **Metro** (114 Valley St., P.O. Box 1097, Portland 04104, 207/774-0351, $1 exact change, $.75 students with ID, two kids under five are free with paying adult), is well planned and often underused. Metro produces a colorful, easy-to-read route map and schedule that facilitates getting around. Buses have wheelchair lifts and bike racks (room for two of each). Free transfers are available between routes. Sunday bus service is very limited, and there's no service on major national holidays.

Casco Bay Lines ferry service provides transport to the Casco Bay islands. Great Chebeague Island is on the Casco Bay Lines route, but you can also get there from Yarmouth via **Chebeague Transportation Company** (CTC, Chebeague Island 04017, 207/846-3700, www.chebeaguetrans.com, $10 round-trip adult, $2.50 kids 1–12, $2.50 dogs, $6 bikes, no charge for infants). For this service, drive to the CTC Parking Lot on Route 1, between Tuttle Road and I-95 Exit 15. (Take Exit 15 off I-95 and head south on Route 1.) Park your car ($10 per day) and board a van or bus for the 20-minute ride to the Cousins Island dock at the southeastern edge of Yarmouth. The bus departs Cumberland *precisely* 30 minutes before boat time. The boat makes 8–10 round-trips daily, beginning at 6:40 A.M. on Chebeague and 7 A.M. in Yarmouth. Last boat from Chebeague departs at 10:30 P.M. on summer weekends, but you'll need to return earlier on other days. Pay your way either on the bus or on the boat.

All Casco Bay Lines tickets are round-trip, and they're collected when you board in Portland, so if you manage to get to one of the islands by some other means, such as via the CTC, there's no charge for going from island to island or returning to Portland on a Casco Bay Lines vessel.

Taxis

Portland and South Portland have a dozen taxi fleets, most radio-operated. You won't have much luck trying to flag one down on the street. Reliables in Portland are **ABC Taxi** (207/772-8685), **Airport Limo & Taxi** (207/773-3433), and **Town Taxi** (207/773-1711). In South Portland, call **South Portland Taxi** (207/767-5200). **Jetport Taxi** (888/891-3299) provides service as far as Boston and Manchester, New Hampshire.

Freeport

Freeport has a special claim to historic fame— it's the place where Maine parted company from Massachusetts in 1820. The documents were signed on March 15, making Maine its own separate state.

At the height of the local mackerel-packing industry here, countless tons of the bony fish were shipped out of South Freeport, often in ships built on the shores of the Harraseeket River. Splendid relics of the shipbuilders' era still line the streets of South Freeport, and no architecture buff should miss a walk, cycle, or drive through the village. Even downtown Freeport still reflects the shipbuilder's craft, with contemporary shops tucked in and around handsome historic houses. Some have been converted to B&Bs, others are boutiques, and one even disguises the local McDonald's franchise.

Today, Freeport is best known as the mecca for the shop-till-you-drop set. The hub, of course, is sportswear giant L.L. Bean, which has been here since 1912, when founder Leon Leonwood Bean began making his trademark hunting boots (and also unselfishly handed out hot tips on where the fish were biting). More than 120 retail operations now fan out from that epicenter, and you can find almost anything in Freeport (pop. about 7,700)—except maybe a parking spot in midsummer.

When (or if) you tire of shopping, you can always find quiet refuge in the town's preserves and parks—Mast Landing Sanctuary, Wolfe's Neck Woods State Park, and Winslow Memorial Park—and plenty of local color at the Town Wharf in the still honest-to-goodness fishing village of South Freeport.

An orientation note: Don't be surprised to receive directions (particularly for South Freeport) relative to "the Big Indian"—a 40-foot-tall landmark at the junction of Route 1 and South Freeport Road. If you stop at the Maine Visitor Information Center in Yarmouth and continue on Route 1 toward Freeport, you can't miss it, just north of the Freeport Inn and the Casco Bay Inn.

SHOPPING

Logically, this category must come first in any discussion of Freeport, since shopping's the biggest game in town. It's pretty much a given that anyone who visits Freeport intends to darken the door of at least one shop.

L.L. Bean

If it's *only* one, it's likely to be "Bean's." The whole world beats a path to L.L. Bean, (95 Main St., Rte. 1, 207/865-4761 or 800/341-4341, www.llbean.com)—or so it seems in July, August, and December. Established as a hunting/fishing supply shop, this giant sports outfitter now sells everything from kids' clothing to cookware. Hunting and fishing gear has been moved to a separate store behind the mother ship.

The Bean reputation rests on a savvy staff,

© TOM NANGLE

In a version of "build a better mousetrap," Leon Leonwood Bean built a better boot. Since then, avid outdoorspeople have been beating a path to the L.L. Bean, the gigantic Freeport sporting goods emporium he founded.

MAINE WILDLIFE PARK

If you want to see where Maine's wild things are, venture a bit inland to visit the Maine Wildlife Park (Shaker Rd./Rte. 26, Gray 04039, 207/657-4977, www.state.me.us/ifw/education/wildlifepark.htm). Nearly 25 native species of wildlife can be seen at this state-operated wildlife refuge, including such ever-popular species as moose, black bear, white-tailed deer and bald eagle. The park began in 1931 as a state-run game farm. For more than 50 years, the Department of Inland Fish and Game reared pheasants here for release during bird-hunting season. At the same time, wildlife biologists and game wardens with the state's Department of Inland Fisheries and Wildlife needed a place to care for orphaned or injured animals.

In 1982, the farm's mission was changed to that of a wildlife and conservation education facility. Today the park is a temporary haven for wildlife, but those who cannot survive in the wild reside here permanently.

Among the wildlife that have been in residence at the park are lynx, deer, opossums, black bears, bobcats, porcupines, raccoons, red-tailed hawks, barred and great horned owls, mountain lions, bald eagles, ravens, skunks, woodchucks, and coyotes. Other frequent guests include wild turkeys, fishers, gray foxes, kestrels, turkey vultures, wood turtles, and box turtles. Most are here for protection and healing, and while they're in residence, visitors are able to view them at close range.

In addition to the wildlife, there are numerous interactive exhibits and displays to view, nature trails to explore, a nature store, snack shack, and even picnic facilities. Special programs and exhibits are offered on Sundays from mid-May through mid-September. In summer and fall, there are full-moon "night walks," 8–10 P.M. (6–8 P.M. in October). Bring a flashlight covered with red cellophane, or buy one when you arrive.

The park is 3.5 miles north of downtown Gray and Maine Turnpike Exit 63. From the coast, take Route 115 from Main Street in downtown Yarmouth, continuing through North Yarmouth (with stunning old houses) to Gray, then head north on Route 26 for 3.5 miles. Hours are 9:30 A.M.–5:30 P.M. mid-April–Veterans' Day—no entry after 4 P.M. Admission is $5 ages 13–60, $4 seniors, $3.25 kids 4–12.

high quality, an admirable environmental consciousness, and a no-questions-asked return policy. Bring the kids—for the indoor trout pond, the clean restrooms, and the "real deal" outlet store, across the street behind Polo Ralph Lauren. The store's open-round-the-clock policy has become its signature, and if you show up at 2 A.M., you'll have much of the store to yourself, and may even spy vacationing celebrities or the rock stars who often visit after Portland shows.

Outlets and Specialty Stores

After Bean's, it's up to your whims and your wallet. The stores stretch for several miles up and down Main Street and along many side streets. Pick up a copy of the *Official Map & Visitor Guide* at any of the shops or restaurants, at one of the visitor kiosks, or at the Hose Tower Information Center (23 Depot St., two blocks east of L.L. Bean).

Among downtown Freeport's big names are **Banana Republic, Brooks Brothers, Coach, Cole-Haan, Crabtree & Evelyn, Dansk, Burberry, Gap, J. Crew, Levi's, North Face, Patagonia, Ralph Lauren, J. L. Coombs,** and **Samsonite.**

But don't overlook the small shops tucked on the side streets, such as **Earrings and Co., Wilbur's of Maine Chocolate Confections,** and **Edgecomb Potters.** Christmas fans shouldn't miss **Christmas Magic,** just south of downtown Freeport on Route 1.

PARKS, PRESERVES, AND OTHER ATTRACTIONS

Mast Landing Sanctuary

More than two miles of easy, yellow-blazed trails wind through the 140-acre Mast Landing Sanctuary, an area that ages ago was the source of masts for the Royal Navy. Pick up a trail map at the parking area and start watching for birds. Best (and longest) route is the 1.6-mile Loop Trail, which passes fruit trees, hardwoods, and an old milldam. (Keep the kids off the dam.) The sanctuary is owned by Maine Audubon (207/781-2330, www.maineaudubon.org). The sanctuary is open sunrise to sunset, year-round, and is popular in winter with cross-country skiers. Admission is free. From downtown Freeport (Route 1), take Bow Street (opposite L.L. Bean) one mile east to Upper Mast Landing Road. Turn left (north) and go 500 feet to the parking area.

Wolfe's Neck Woods State Park

Five miles of easy to moderate trails meander through 233-acre Wolfe's Neck Woods State Park (Wolfe's Neck Rd., 207/865-4465, $3 ages 11–64, $1 children 5–11), just a few minutes' cycle or drive from downtown Freeport. You'll need a trail map, available near the parking area. Easiest route (partly wheelchair-accessible) is the Shoreline Walk, about three-quarters of a mile, starting near the salt marsh and skirting Casco Bay. Sprinkled along the trails are helpful interpretive panels explaining various points of natural history—bog life, osprey nesting, glaciation, erosion, and tree decay. Guided tours are offered at 2 P.M. daily, mid-July through late August, weather permitting. Leashed pets are allowed. Adjacent **Googins Island,** an osprey sanctuary, is off-limits. From downtown Freeport, follow Bow Street (across from L.L. Bean) for 2.25 miles; turn right onto Wolfe's Neck Road (also called Wolf Neck Road) and go another 2.25 miles.

Wolfe's Neck Farm

The best time to visit Wolfe's Neck Farm (10 Burnett Rd., 207/865-4469, www.wolfesneck farm.org) is March and April for the annual **Calf Watch,** when about 60 calves and 15 lambs join the herd on the 620-acre farm. During calving season, the farm is open daily 9 A.M.–5 P.M., and kids can see the latest newborns as well as chickens, turkeys, pigs, and other creatures. Sustainable agriculture and environmental sensitivity are the overriding philosophies at this working farm owned and operated by the nonprofit Wolfe's

Neck Farm Foundation. Nature trails lace the property, and a small retail shop in the farmhouse (open weekdays 9 A.M.–4:30 P.M.) sells naturally raised beef, lamb, pork, and eggs.

Also part of the farm is **Recompence Shore Campsites** (134 Burnett Rd., Freeport 04032, 207/865-9307, www.freeportcamping.com, $14–24)—an eco-sensitive campground with 175 wooded tent sites (a few hookups are available), many on the farm's three-mile-long Casco Bay shorefront. For anyone seeking peace, quiet, and low-tech camping (outhouses and hot showers) in a spectacular setting, this is it. Ice, firewood, and snacks are available at the camp store. Quiet time begins at 9 P.M. As with Winslow Memorial Park, swimming depends on the tides; check the tide calendar in a local newspaper. Take Bow Street (across from L.L. Bean) to Wolfe's Neck Road, turn right, and go 1.6 miles to Burnett Road, a left turn.

Winslow Memorial Park

Owned by the town of Freeport, Winslow Memorial Park (Staples Point, South Freeport, 207/865-4198, Memorial Day weekend–late. Sept., $2) is a spectacular 90-plus-acre seaside park, overlooking the islands of upper Casco Bay. Swim off the beach (changing house, restrooms, but no lifeguards), picnic on the shore, walk the three-quarter-mile nature trail and perch on the point, launch a canoe or kayak, or reserve one of the 100 inland or waterfront campsites ($18–20, no hookups, but some sites can take RVs). The boat landing and beach area are tidal, so boaters and swimmers should plan to be here two hours before and two hours after high tide; otherwise, you're dealing with mudflats. From the Big Indian on Route 1, take South Freeport Road one mile to Staples Point Road and continue to the end.

Desert of Maine

Okay, so maybe it's a bit hokey, but talk about sands of time. More than 10,000 years ago, glaciers covered the region surrounding the Desert of Maine (95 Desert Rd., 207/865-6962, www .desertofmaine.com, early May–mid-Oct., $7.75 adults, $5.25 ages 13–16, $4.25 ages 6–12).

When they receded, they scoured the landscape, pulverizing rocks and leaving behind a sandy residue that was covered by a thin layer of topsoil. Jump forward to 1797, when William Tuttle purchased 300 acres and moved his family here, as well as his house and barn, and cleared the land. Now jump forward again to the present and tour where a once-promising farmland has become a desert wasteland. The guided, safari-style tram tours combine history, geology, and environmental science and an opportunity for children to hunt for "gems" in the sand. Decide for yourself: Is the desert a natural phenomenon? a man-made disaster? or does the truth lie somewhere in the middle. The Desert Dunes of Maine Campground has a pool, laundry, convenience store, and campsites under towering pines. Rates range from $28 for a tent site to $36 for an RV site with water, electric, and sewer.

Harrington House

A block south of L.L. Bean is the Harrington House (45 Main St., Rte. 1, 207/865-3170, www .freeporthistoricalsociety.org, 10 A.M.–2:30 P.M. Tues., Thurs., and Fri., 10 A.M.–7 P.M. Wed., free),

home base of the Freeport Historical Society. You can pick up walking maps detailing Freeport's architecture for a small fee and tour the house. Exhibits pertaining to Freeport's history and occasionally ones by local artists are presented in two rooms in the restored 1830 Enoch Harrington House, a National Historic Register property.

RECREATION AND SPORTS

L.L. Bean Outdoor Discovery Schools

Since the early 1980s, the sports outfitter's Outdoor Discovery Schools (888/552-3261 www.llbean .com/odp) have trained thousands of outdoors enthusiasts to improve their skills in fly-fishing, archery, hiking, canoeing, sea kayaking, winter camping, cross-country skiing, orienteering, and even outdoor photography. Here's a deal that requires no advance planning. **Walk-On Adventures** provide a 1.5–2.5-hour lessons in sports such as kayak touring, fly casting, archery, clay shooting, snowshoeing, and cross-country skiing for $12, including equipment. All of the longer programs, plus canoeing and camping trips, require preregistration, well in advance because of their popularity.

Poor agricultural practices turned promising farmland into what's now Freeport's Desert of Maine. Tours combine history, geology, and environmental science along with a bit of hokiness.

Some are held in the mountains and on the rivers of western Maine, others are in Maryland and Virginia. Some of the lectures, seminars, and demonstrations held in Freeport are free, and a regular catalog lists the schedule. The new, waterfront campus on Flye Point, which hosts many of the kayaking, saltwater fly fishing, and guiding programs, is expected to become home to the annual PaddleSports Festival in June, with demonstrations, seminars, vendors, lessons and more, most of which are free.

Atlantic Seal Cruises

Atlantic Seal Cruises (207/85-6112), owned and operated by Captain Tom Ring, makes two or three 2.5-hour cruises daily from the nearby Freeport Town Wharf (in South Freeport) to 17-acre **Eagle Island,** a State Historic Site once owned by Admiral Robert Peary of North Pole fame. The trip includes a lobstering demonstration (except Sunday, when lobstering is banned). Captain Ring also does day-long excursions Wednesday and Sunday to **Seguin Island,** off the Phippsburg Peninsula, where you can climb the light tower and see Maine's only first-order Fresnel lens, the largest on the coast. (This trip, which costs $35, is not for the unsteady; you'll be off-loaded from a small boat.) A Seal and Osprey Watch cruise is offered at twilight.

Golf

Those who prefer to hit a few balls rather than shop can head to the nine-hole, par-3 **Freeport Country Club** (2 Old County Rd., 207/865-0711, 7 A.M.–dusk daily). On weekends, play one round for $18 adult, $12 student, or two for $22/$15. Weekday rates are $15 adult, $10 student for one round, $10/$12 for two. After 5 P.M. anytime, play as many holes as you like for $12. Gas carts ($10 per nine), pull carts ($2), and club rentals ($10) are available. (For more challenging courses, see Portland).

ENTERTAINMENT

Shopping seems to be more than enough entertainment for most of Freeport's visitors, but don't miss the **L.L. Bean Summer Concert Series.**

From early July to Labor Day weekend, at 7:30 P.M. each Saturday, Bean's hosts free big-name, family-oriented events in Discovery Park, in the Bean's complex. Arrive early (these concerts are *very* popular) and bring a blanket or a folding chair. For more info, call 800/341-4341, ext. 37222.

ACCOMMODATIONS

If you'd prefer to drop where you shop, Freeport has a large country inn, several motels, and more than two dozen B&Bs, so finding a pillow is seldom a problem, but it's still wise to have reservations. Rates listed are for peak season, double occupancy.

For camping, see Parks, Preserves, and Other Attractions.

Downtown

One of Freeport's pioneering B&Bs is on the main drag yet away from much of the traffic, in a restored house where Arctic explorer Admiral Donald MacMillan once lived. The 19th-century **White Cedar Inn** (178 Main St., Freeport 04032, 207/865-9099 or 800/853-1269, www.white-cedarinn.com, $120–155) has seven attractive guest rooms with antiques, air-conditioning, and private baths; some have gas fireplaces.

Two blocks north of L.L. Bean, the **M Harraseeket Inn** (162 Main St., Freeport 04032, 207/865-9377 or 800/342-6423, www.harraseeketinn.com, $199-279) is a splendid 84-room country inn with an indoor pool, cable TV, air-conditioning, phones, and data ports; many rooms have fireplaces and hot tubs. Decor is colonial reproduction in the two antique buildings and a modern addition. Rates include a hot-and-cold buffet breakfast and afternoon tea—a refreshing break from power shopping—with finger sandwiches and sweets. Ask about packages, which offer excellent value. Children 12 and younger stay free. (See Food for information on its two excellent restaurants.)

Three blocks south of L.L. Bean, on a quiet side street shared with a couple of other B&Bs, is **The James Place Inn** (11 Holbrook St., Freeport 04032, 207/865-4486 or 800/964-9086, www

.jamesplaceinn.com, $135–155). Darcy and Bill James and their two dogs are immediately welcoming, sharing their enthusiasm for all the area's activities. They'll even organize a free round of golf at the local club. Seven comfortable rooms have private baths, air-conditioning, and TV; some have whirlpool tubs and/or fireplaces.

Beyond Downtown

In South Freeport you'll find the **Atlantic Seal Bed & Breakfast** (25 Main St., South Freeport 04078, 207/865-6112 or 877/285-7325, $125–200), a mid-19th-century Cape-style house with stupendous harbor views and lots of fascinating maritime collectibles. Four pleasant rooms have private baths. From late May to late October, owner Tom Ring operates **Atlantic Seal Cruises** (see Recreation).

Here's a throwback. Three miles north of downtown is the **Maine Idyll** (1411 Rte. 1, 207/865-4201, www.maineidyll.com, $55–95), a tidy cottage colony operated by the Marstaller family for three generations. Twenty cottages are tucked under the trees. All have fireplaces and TV, and most have limited cooking facilities. A free light breakfast is served. There are two children's playsets, and well-behaved pets are welcome.

The family-run **Casco Bay Inn** (107 Rte. 1, Freeport 04032, 207/865-4925 or 800/570-4970, www.cascobayinn.com, $90–115) is a bit fancier than most motels. It has a pine-paneled lounge with fieldstone fireplace, an Internet station for guest usage, and spacious rooms with double sinks in the bath area.

FOOD

Freeport has an ever-increasing number of places to eat, but nowhere enough to satisfy hungry crowds at peak dining hours on busy days. Go early or late for lunch, and make reservations for dinner.

Casual Dining

The Harraseeket Inn's woodsy-themed **M Broad Arrow Tavern** (162 Main St., 207/865-9377 or 800/342-642, 11:30 A.M.–10 P.M. daily, to 11 P.M. Fri. and Sat.), just two blocks north of L.L. Bean but seemingly a world away, is a perfect place to

escape shopping crowds and madness. The food is terrific, with everything made from organic and naturally raised foods, with prices running $9–23. Can't decide? Opt for the extensive lunch buffet ($13.95) that highlights a bit of everything.

Good wine and fine martinis are what reels them into **Conundrum** (117 Rte 1, Freeport, 207/865-0303, 4:30–10 P.M. Tues.–Sat.), near Freeport's Big Indian, but the food is worth noting, too. Dozens of wines by the glass, more than 20 martinis, and 20 champagnes will keep most oenophiles happy. The food, ranging from patées and cheese platters to cheeseburgers and maple-barbecued chicken, helps keep them sober ($5–15).

Ethnic Fare

Dine indoors or out on the tree-shaded patio at **Azure Italian Café** (123 Main St., 207/865-1237, 11 A.M.–3 P.M. and 5–8 P.M. Sun.–Thurs., to 9 P.M. Fri. and Sat.). Go light, mixing selections from antipasto, insalate, and zuppa choices, or savor the heartier entrées ($12–26), such as lasagna formaggio, veal saltimbocca or Tuscan chicken. The service is pleasant and the indoor dining areas are accented by well-chosen contemporary Maine artwork. Live jazz is a highlight some evenings.

Two surprisingly good, easy-on-the-budget Asian restaurants share the same building on the south end of town. **China Rose** (23 Main St., 207/865-6886, 11 A.M.–9:30 P.M. Sun.–Thurs., 11 A.M.–10 P.M. Fri. and Sat.) serves Sichuan, Mandarin, and Hunan specialties in a pleasant first-floor dining area. Upstairs is **Miyako** (207/865-6888, 11 A.M.–10 P.M. Sun.–Thurs., 11 A.M.–11 P.M. Fri. and Sat. in summer, shorter hours in winter). It has an extensive sushi bar menu and also serves other Japanese specialties, including tempura, teriyaki, nabemono, and noodle dishes. Luncheon specials are available at both.

Fine Dining

Priciest and worth every penny is the Harraseeket Inn's cloth-and-candles **M Maine Dining Room** (207/865-1085, 6–9 P.M. daily to 9:30 P.M. Fri. and Sat.) The service is excellent, and chef Theda Lyden's commitment to natural and organic foods is impressive. Tableside preparations (for 2–7), such as Caesar salad, Chateaubriand, and flaming desserts, add an understated note of theater. Dinner entrées are $24–38. Sunday brunch (11:45 A.M.–2 P.M., $24.95) is a seemingly endless buffet, with whole poached salmon and Belgian waffles among the highlights.

Lobster

Two blocks south of L.L. Bean is the **Lobster Cooker** (39 Main St., 207/865-4349, 11 A.M.–9 P.M. daily in season, to 7 P.M. off-season). Lobster rolls are predictably good and not overpriced for the neighborhood; try the award-winning chowder. It's a popular place where you order at the counter, so expect to stand in line. Beer and wine available; no credit cards.

In South Freeport, order lobster-in-the-rough at **M Harraseeket Lunch & Lobster Company** (Main St., Town Wharf, South Freeport, 207/865-4888, 11 A.M.–7:45 P.M. daily May–mid-June; 11 A.M.–8:45 P.M. mid-June–mid-Oct.). Grab a waterfront picnic table, place your order, and go at it. (There's also inside dining.) Be prepared for a wait in midsummer. Fried clams are particularly good here, and they're prepared two ways. Order both and decide for yourself which is better, battered or breaded. Another option: If you're camping nearby, call ahead and order boiled lobsters to go. BYOL; no credit cards.

INFORMATION AND SERVICES

With shopping being Freeport's occupation and preoccupation, the best source of information is the **Freeport Merchants Association** (Hose Tower, 23 Depot St., Freeport 04032, 207/865-1212 or 800/865-1994, www.freeportusa.com, 9 A.M.–9 P.M. Mon.–Sat., 10 A.M.–6 P.M. Sun. in summer, 10 A.M.–6 P.M. daily in winter). The association annually produces an invaluable foldout map/guide showing locations of all the shops, plus sites of lodgings, restaurants, visitor kiosks, pay phones, restrooms, and car and bike parking. If you're serious about "doing" Freeport, send for one of these guides before you arrive so you can plan your attack and hit the ground running.

Just south of Freeport is the **Maine Visitor Information Center** (Rte. 1, at I-95 Exit 17, Yarmouth 04096, 207/846-0833), part of the statewide tourism-information network. Staffers are particularly attuned to Freeport and Yarmouth, but the center has brochures and maps for the entire state. Also here are restrooms, phones, picnic tables, vending machines, and a dog-walking area.

Getting Around

The Freeport Explorer (V.I.P. Tour & Charter Bus Co., 129-137 Fox St., Portland 04101, 207/772-4457 or 800/337-4457, www.vipcharter coaches.com, Sat. and Sun. May.–Dec., $10 each way, kids under 10 free, purchase tickets on board) provides service from the Portland Transportation Center to in downtown Freeport (100 Main St.). The buses coordinate with Amtrak's Downeaster train, departing Portland at 12:30 and 3 P.M. and returning at 1:15, 4:15, and 5:30 P.M.

Free parking is plentiful in Freeport. The most crowded lots are behind L.L. Bean.

Mid-Coast Region

In contrast to the Southern Coast's gorgeous sandy beaches, the Mid-Coast Region features a deeply indented shoreline with snug harbors and long, gnarled fingers of land. Even though these fingers are inconvenient for driving and bicycling, this is where you'll find picture-book Maine in a panorama format. Drive to the tips of the peninsulas and come upon lighthouses, fishing villages, country inns, and lobster wharves. The Mid-Coast, as defined in this chapter, stretches from Brunswick through Waldoboro.

Visitors come for Brunswick's Bowdoin College, Bath's marine museum, Wiscasset's historic homes, the jumbled shops of Boothbay Harbor, Pemaquid Point's lighthouse, and, of course, lob-

ster. The Bath-Brunswick area is one of the least touristy areas of the coast. Not that visitors don't come, but this area has a strong and varied economic base other than tourism, which means that no matter when you visit, you'll find shops, restaurants, and lodgings open and activities scheduled. Bowdoin College, Bath Iron Works, and the Brunswick Naval Air Station also contribute to a population more ethnically diverse than most of Maine and draw an active retiree population. Still, as you drive down the peninsulas that reach seaward from Bath and Brunswick, the vibrancy gives way to traditional fishing villages pressed by the hard realities of maintaining such lifestyles in a modern world

Must-Sees

Look for **M** to find the sights and activities you can't miss and **M** for the best dining and lodging.

M Bowdoin College: This beautiful, shady campus is home to the Peary-MacMillan Arctic Museum and the Bowdoin College Museum of Art (page 117).

M Maine Maritime Museum: It's easy to while away a half day touring the exhibits or just enjoying the riverfront setting (page 131).

M Popham Beach: Often winning accolades as Maine's prettiest beach, Popham is a long stretch of

© TOM NANGLE

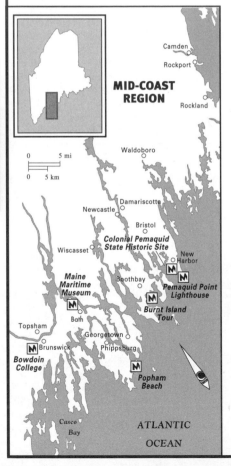

MID-COAST REGION

Three forts protected John's Bay between 1677 and the late 18th century. The rebuilt western tower of Fort William Henry dates from 1692. It's part of the eight-acre Colonial Pemaquid state and national historic site, which also comprises a museum, remnants of a village, an 18th century cemetery, and the beautifully restored Fort House.

sand anchored by a fort at one end and seabird colonies at the other (page 134).

M Burnt Island Tour: Step back in history and visit with a lighthouse keeper's family circa 1952 on a living history tour (page 152).

M Pemaquid Point Lighthouse: Hard to say which is Maine's prettiest lighthouse, but Pemaquid is right up there. It's also depicted on the Maine state quarter (page 166).

M Colonial Pemaquid State Historic Site: A beautiful setting overlooking John's Bay, a partially reconstructed fort, and remnants from archaeological digs from one of the first English settlements in America make this well worth a visit (page 167).

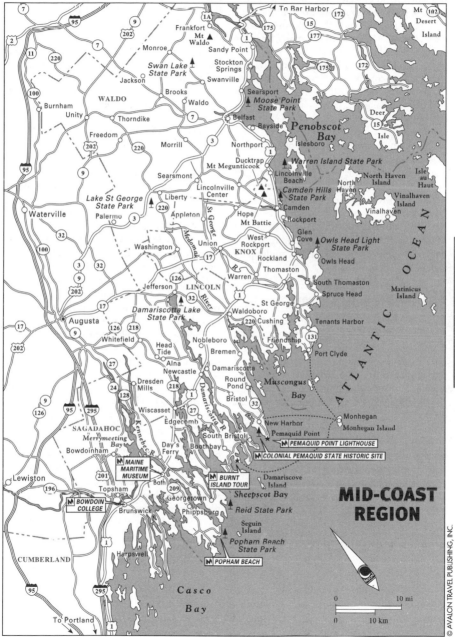

and hanging on to waterfront properties in the face of rapidly rising real estate prices.

Wiscasset still clings to the nickname "Prettiest Village in Maine," but for many travelers heading through it on Route 1, Wiscasset is nothing but an expletive-deleted headache. Traffic often backs up for miles, inching forward through the bottleneck village. Although many are just glad to get through it, those who take time to explore Wiscasset are rewarded with a multitude of antique shops and lovely architecture.

The tempo changes northeast of Wiscasset. Traffic eases and there's less roadside development. Detour down the Boothbay and Pemaquid Peninsulas, and you'll be rewarded with the Maine of postcards. These two peninsulas appear unchallenged as home to more lobster-in-the-rough spots than elsewhere on the coast, and Maine's creative economy is blossoming here, as evidenced by the artists' and artisans' studios that pepper these peninsulas.

PLANNING YOUR TIME

Route 1 is the primary artery connecting all the points in the Mid-Coast region, and Wiscasset, a major bottleneck, is smack dab in the middle. For that reason, it's best to split your lodging and explorations into two parts: south of Wiscasset and north of Wiscasset. Even then, driving down the long fingers of land requires patience. The towns south of Wiscasset are less touristy than those on the Boothbay or Pemaquid Peninsula.

Begin in downtown Brunswick, touring **Bowdoin College** and the Peary-MacMillan Museum (and the Museum of Art, if it has reopened). If you're a Civil War buff, the Joshua L. Chamberlain Museum is a must-stop. If you enjoy scenic drives and exploring, noodle your way around the Harpswells, including Orr's and Bailey Islands, and be rewarded with small towns, fishing villages, and spectacular ocean vistas at the end of each point. If not, head north to Bath and spend the afternoon at **Maine Maritime Museum,** perhaps arranging for a cruise down the Kennebec River.

Allow at least a half day to loop down the Phippsburg Peninsula, meandering along Parker Head Road and on to **Popham Beach,** where you can sunbathe, brave a swim, walk the beach, and prowl around the remains of two forts.

Serious and not-so-serious shoppers can easily spend a day or more browsing all the antique shops in Bath and Wiscasset and the group shops and flea market in between. And if you're a fan of historic houses and fine architecture, plan time for a walking tour in both towns.

To appreciate Boothbay Harbor, you need to get on the water, and the best way to do that is with a morning or afternoon **Burnt Island tour** to the lighthouse (do make reservations). Afterward, shop downtown, visit the Coastal Maine Botanical Gardens, or take a scenic drive out to East Boothbay and on to Ocean Point.

Allow at least a full day for exploring the Pemaquid Peninsula, looping down to **Colonial Pemaquid/Fort William Henry** and **Pemaquid Point Lighthouse** and allowing time to appreciate the small fishing villages along the way and hike in a preserve. Finish the day with **lobster-in-the-rough** at one of the two dueling lobster pounds in Round Pond.

To cover the region, you'll need 4–5 days. Of course, if you're an avid or even aspiring kayaker, you'll want time to puzzle through the nooks and crannies of the coastline in a boat, and if you value parks and preserves, this region offers plenty worth your time.

Brunswick Area

Brunswick (pop. 20,520), straddling Route 1, relies partly on modern defense dollars—but it was incorporated in 1738 and is steeped in history. The town is home to both prestigious Bowdoin College and the sprawling Brunswick Naval Air Station—an unusual and sometimes conflicting juxtaposition that makes this a college town with a difference. You'll find lots of classic homes and churches, several respected museums, and year-round cultural attractions.

Brunswick and Topsham face each other across roiling waterfalls on the Androscoggin River. The falls, which Native Americans knew by the tongue-twisting name of Ahmelahcogneturcook ("place abundant with fish, birds, and other animals"), were a source of hydropower for 18th-century sawmills and 19th- and 20th-century textile mills. Franco-Americans arrived in droves to beef up the textile industry in the late 19th century (but lost their jobs eventually in the Depression). Those once-derelict mills now house shops, restaurants, and offices.

Brunswick is also the gateway to the stunning Harpswells, a peninsula/archipelago complex linked by causeways, several bridges, and one unique granite cribstone bridge. Scenic back roads on Harpswell Neck inspire detours to the fishing hamlets of Cundy's Harbor, Orr's Island, and Bailey Island.

SIGHTS

ⓜ Bowdoin College

Bowdoin College got its start here nearly 150 years before the Naval Air Station landed on the nearby Brunswick Plains. Founded in 1794 as a boys' college with a handful of students, Bowdoin (coed since 1969) now has 1,550 students. The college has turned out such noted graduates as authors Nathaniel Hawthorne and Henry Wadsworth Longfellow, sex pioneer Alfred Kinsey, U.S. president Franklin Pierce, Arctic explorers Robert Peary and Donald MacMillan, U.S. senators George Mitchell and William Cohen, and a dozen Maine governors. Massachusetts Hall, the oldest building on the 110-acre campus, dates from 1802. The stately Bowdoin pines, on the northeast boundary, are even older. The striking **David Saul Smith Union,** occupying 40,000 square feet in a former athletic building on the east side of the campus, has a café, pub, lounge, and bookstore open to the public. For admissions and campus-tour information, call 207/725-3100, or write to Bowdoin College, Brunswick 04011. For information on campus concerts, lectures, and performances open to the public, call 207/725-3375. (The website is www.bowdoin.edu and the main switchboard number is 207/725-3000.)

Photos and artifacts bring Arctic expeditions to life at the small but fascinating **Peary-MacMillan Arctic Museum** (Hubbard Hall, Bowdoin College, Brunswick 04011, 207/725-3416, http://academic.bowdoin.edu/arcticmuseum). Among the specimens are stuffed animals, a skin kayak, fur clothing, snow goggles, and Inuit carvings—most collected by Arctic pioneers Robert E. Peary and Donald B. MacMillan, both Bowdoin grads. Permanent exhibits highlight the natural and cultural diversity of the Arctic. The small gift shop specializes in Inuit books and artifacts. Admission is free, but donations are welcomed (Tues.–Sat. 10 A.M.–5 P.M., Sun. 2–5 P.M.).

An astonishing array of Greek and Roman artifacts is only one of the high points at the **Bowdoin College Museum of Art** (Walker Art Building, Bowdoin College, Brunswick 04011, 207/725-3275, Tues.–Sat. 10 A.M.–5 P.M., Sun. 2–5 P.M.). The building alone is worth a look. Designed in the 1890s by Charles McKim of the famed McKim, Mead & White firm, it's a stunning neoclassical edifice with an interior rotunda and stone lions flanking the entry. Also here is an impressive permanent collection of 19th- and 20th-century American art. Admission is free, but donations are welcomed. The museum will be closed for 2005 and most of 2006 for a controversial renovation. Tentative plans call for some of the museum's works to be relocated to the Bliss Room in Hubbard Hall.

Pejepscot Historical Society Museums

Side by side in an unusual, cupola-topped du-plex facing Brunswick's Mall (village green), the **Pejepscot Museum** (159 Park Row) and the **Skolfield-Whittier House** (161 Park Row) are both operated by the Pejepscot Historical Society (207/729-6606), founded in 1888 and headquartered at the museum. Focusing on local history, the museum, in the left-hand sec-tion, has a collection of more than 50,000 arti-facts and mounts an always-interesting special exhibit each year. Admission is free; there's a small gift shop. Open 9 A.M.–5 P.M. Tues-day–Friday year-round and 9 A.M.–4 P.M. Sat-urday (to 8 P.M. Thurs. June–Sept.). The 17-room Skolfield-Whittier House, on the right-hand side of the building, looks as though the owners just stepped out for the afternoon. Unused from 1925 to 1982, the onetime sea captain's house has elegant Victorian furnish-ings and lots of exotic artifacts collected on global seafaring stints. Hour-long guided tours (on demand) are available at 10 and 11:30 A.M., 1 and 2:30 P.M. Admission is $5 adults, $2.50 children 6–16. Open Tuesday–Saturday late May to mid-October.

Also operated by the Pejepscot Historical So-ciety, the **Joshua L. Chamberlain Museum** (226 Maine St., Brunswick, 207/729-6606), across from First Parish Church, commemo-rates the Union Army hero of the Civil War's Battle of Gettysburg, who's now gaining long-overdue respect. The partly restored house where Chamberlain lived in the late 19th century (and Henry Wadsworth Longfellow lived 30 years earlier) is a peculiar architectural hodgepodge with six rooms of exhibits of Chamberlain mem-orabilia, much of it Civil War–related. A gift shop stocks lots of Civil War publications, es-pecially ones covering the Twentieth Maine Vol-unteers. Guided tours are offered twice an hour; the last tour is at 4:15 P.M. Tickets are $5 adults, $2.50 children 6–16. Open Tuesday–Saturday 10 A.M.–5 P.M. late May to mid-October. A com-bination ticket for all three society holdings is $8 adults, $4 children.

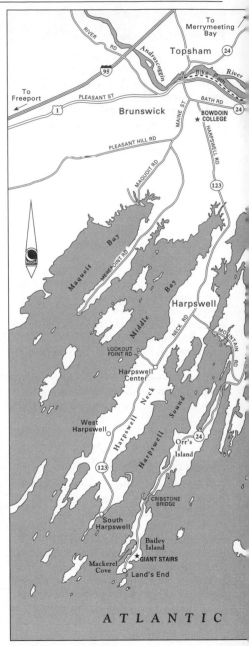

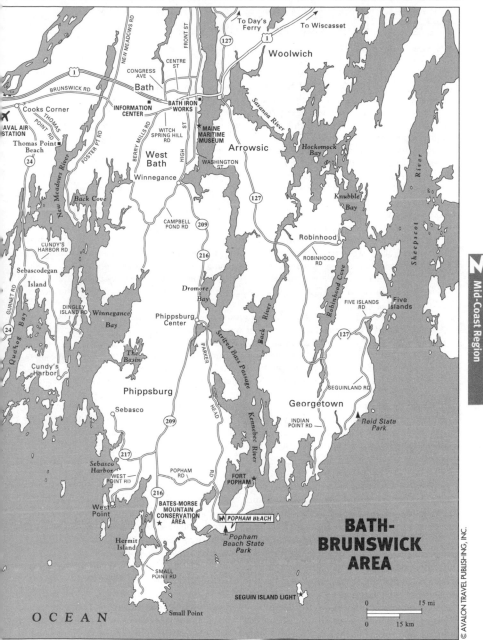

JOSHUA L. CHAMBERLAIN, CIVIL WAR HERO

When the American Civil War began in 1861, Joshua Chamberlain was a 33-year-old logic instructor at Bowdoin College in Brunswick; when it ended, in 1865, Chamberlain earned the Congressional Medal of Honor for his "Daring heroism and great tenacity in holding his position on the Little Round Top." He was designated by Ulysses S. Grant to formally accept the official surrender of Confederate general John Gordon (both men represented the infantry). He later became governor of Maine (1867–1871) and president of Bowdoin College, but Chamberlain's greatest renown, ironically, came more than a century later—when 1990s PBS filmmakers focused on the Civil War and highlighted his strategic military role.

Joshua Lawrence Chamberlain was born in 1828 in Brewer, Maine, the son and grandson of soldiers. After graduating from Bowdoin in 1852, he studied for the ministry at Bangor Theological Seminary, then returned to his alma mater as an instructor.

With the nation in turmoil in the early 1860s, Chamberlain signed on to help, receiving a commission as a lieutenant colonel in the Twentieth Maine Volunteers in 1862. After surviving 24 encounters and six battle wounds and having been promoted to general (brigadier, then major), Chamberlain was elected Republican governor of Maine in 1866—by the largest margin in the state's history—only to suffer through four one-year terms of partisan politics. In 1871, Chamberlain became president of Bowdoin College, where he remained until 1883. He then dove into speechmaking and writing, his best-known work being *The Passing of the Armies*, a memoir of the Civil War's final campaigns. From 1900 to 1914, Chamberlain was surveyor of the Port of Portland, a presidential appointment that ended only when complications from a wartime abdominal wound finally did him in. He died at the grand old age of 86.

Brunswick's Joshua L. Chamberlain Museum (226 Maine St.), in his one-time home, commemorates this illustrious Mainer, and thousands of Civil War buffs annually stream through the door in search of Chamberlain "stuff." To make it easier, the Pejepscot Historical Society has produced a helpful map titled *Joshua Chamberlain's Brunswick*, highlighting town and college ties to the man—his dorm rooms, his presidential office, his portraits, even his church pew (number 64 at First Parish Church). Chamberlain's gravesite, marked by a reddish granite stone, is in Brunswick's Pine Grove Cemetery, just east of the Bowdoin campus.

In odd years, the museum celebrates **Chamberlain Days** with a symposium that concentrates on his roles in the war and in Maine. Typically, events include lectures by authors and scholars; field trips to places of interest connected with Chamberlain's life; tours of his home, concentrating on the most recent restoration work; musical or dramatic performances; and group discussions.

Uncle Tom's Church

Across the street from the Chamberlain museum is the historic 1846 **First Parish Church** (9 Cleaveland St. at Bath Rd., Brunswick 04011, 207/729-7331), a Gothic Revival (or carpenter Gothic) board-and-batten structure crowning the rise at the head of Maine Street. Scores of celebrity preachers have ascended this pulpit, and Harriet Beecher Stowe was inspired to write *Uncle Tom's Cabin* while listening to her husband deliver an antislavery sermon here. If you're a fan of organ music, arrive here before noon any Tuesday, early July to early August (or call ahead for details),

when guest organists present 40-minute lunchtime concerts (12:10–12:50 P.M.) on the 1883 Hutchings-Plaisted tracker organ. Admission is free, but a small donation is requested. Stick around for the post-concert church tour. At other times, the church is open by appointment.

Brunswick's Noted Women

With more than 20 points of interest, the **Brunswick Women's History Trail** covers such national notables as authors Harriet Beecher Stowe and Kate Douglas Wiggin and lesser-known lights including naturalist Kate Furbish, pioneering Maine pediatrician Dr. Alice Whittier, and the Franco-American women who slaved away in the textile mills at the turn of the 20th century. Purchase the walking-tour booklet at the Pejepscot Museum gift shop ($2). Then set out to follow the fascinating story. The museum offers guided tours lasting about one hour once a month in June, July, and August. (donation requested).

Go, Fish!

If you're in town between mid-May and late June, plan to visit Central Maine Power's **Brunswick Hydro** generating station, straddling the falls on the Androscoggin River (Lower Maine St., next to Fort Andross, Brunswick-Topsham town line, 207/729-7644 or 207/623-3521, ext. 2116, weekdays, or 800/872-9937). A glass-walled viewing room lets you play voyeur during the annual ritual of anadromous fish heading upstream to spawn. Amazingly undaunted by the obstacles, such species as alewives (herring), salmon, and smallmouth bass make their way from saltwater to fresh via a 40-foot-high, 570-foot-long man-made fish ladder. The viewing room, which maxes out at about 20 people, is open 1–5 P.M. Wednesday–Sunday during the brief spring spawning season.

RECREATION

Hiking/Walking

In the village of Bailey Island, there's a miniwalk to the **Giant Stairs,** a waterfront stone stairway of mammoth proportions. To get there, take Route 24 from Cooks Corner toward Bailey Island and Land's End, keeping an eye out for Washington Avenue, on the left about 1.5 miles after the cribstone bridge. (Or drive to Land's End, park the car with the rest of the crowds, survey the panorama, and walk .8 mile back along Route 24 to Washington Avenue from there.) Turn onto Washington Avenue, go .1 mile, and park at the Episcopal Church (corner of Ocean Street). Walk along Ocean Street to the shorefront path. Watch for a tiny sign just before Spindrift Lane. Don't let small kids get close to the slippery rocks on the

surf-tossed shoreline. (The same advice, by the way, holds for Land's End, where the rocks can be treacherous.)

Thanks to the **Brunswick-Topsham Land Trust,** founded in 1985, two nature preserves (one on Harpswell Neck, one in Topsham) are open to the public for hiking, birding, and cross-country skiing. Both are free and accessible from sunrise to sunset; no bikes or pets are allowed. Be a conscientious trail-keeper and carry a litter bag when you go. The 11-acre **Captain Alfred Skolfield Nature Preserve** has two blue-blazed nature-trail loops; one skirts a salt marsh, where you're apt to see egrets, herons, and osprey in summer. Adjacent to the preserve is an ancient Indian portage site that linked Middle Bay and Harpswell Coves when Native Americans spent their vacations here. (No dopes, they!) Dr. Alice Whittier donated the preserve in memory of her seafaring grandfather. Take Route 123 (Harpswell Road) south from Brunswick about three miles; when you reach the Middle Bay Road intersection (on the right), continue on Route 123 for 1.1 miles. Watch for a small sign, and a small parking area, on your right.

In Topsham, the 163-acre **Bradley Pond Farm Preserve** has two well-laid-out nature loops (a total of 2.5 miles) that let you sample marshes, woodlands, fields, and the pond—all astonishingly close to civilization. Farm owners Florence and Fred Call have generously agreed to share their special turf, so heed the rules and stay on the trails. From Maine Street in Brunswick, cross the river to Topsham's Main Street. At the junction of Routes 196 and 201, take 201 four miles to Bradley Pond Road (on the left). Turn in and park (or leave your bike) in the designated parking areas on the left. For further information on these and other reserved lands, or even to volunteer some trail-maintenance time, contact the Brunswick-Topsham Land Trust (108 Maine St., Brunswick 04011, 207/729-7694).

The 103-acre **Cox Pinnacle,** owned by the town of Brunswick, comprises wooded hills, rocky ledges, and wetlands laced with about 1.5 miles of old logging and farming roads. The trails lead to Cox Pinnacle, the highest point of land in Brunswick (350 feet). Take Durham

Road, then turn right at the blinking light onto Hacker Road and drive .3 mile to the parking lot on the left.

Also owned by the town of Brunswick is the **Town Commons,** granted by vote of the Pejepscot Proprietors on May 8, 1719. The one-mile Pitch Pine Barren Loop starts and finishes at the picnic area, by the main entrance just on Route 123. The trail passes through swamp lands and by a peat heath.

Besides the hikes discussed, be sure to consider the **Androscoggin River Bicycle Path,** which also has a lane for walkers.

Bicycling

A particularly attractive place for biking in the Brunswick area is the 2.6-mile **Androscoggin River Bicycle Path** running between downtown Brunswick and Cooks Corner, meandering along the scenic Androscoggin River and paralleling Route 1. (Unfortunately, the traffic noise often makes the route less than tranquil.) The landscaped asphalt path, also popular with joggers, strollers, and in-line skaters, deserves to be a model for many other Maine communities where biking is likely to be hazardous to your health. To reach the path from the lower end of Maine Street in downtown Brunswick, take Mason Street and then the next left onto Water Street. Continue about two blocks to the parking area (often very crowded) next to the boat-launching site. The path has no loop, so return back along the path.

Center Street Bicycles (11 Center St., just off Maine St., Brunswick 04011, 207/729-5309) does repairs and sells bikes and a good range of accessories. Bike rentals begin at $20. The knowledgeable staff also act as a clearinghouse for route information. (For instance, they strongly urge every customer to avoid biking the Harpswells, especially Route 123; the scenic rewards are outstanding, but the risks are many on the shoulderless roads.) Between February and early October, the shop is open weekdays 9 A.M.–5:30 P.M. and Saturday 9 A.M.–3 P.M. From early October through December, it's open weekdays noon–5:30 P.M. and Saturday 9 A.M.–3 P.M. Closed in January.

Swimming

Thomas Point Beach (29 Meadow Rd., Brunswick 04011, 207/725-6009 or 877/872-4321, www.thomaspointbeach.com) is actually 85 acres of privately owned parkland with facilities for swimming (lifeguard on duty; bathhouses), fishing, field sports, picnicking (500 tables), and camping (75 tent and RV sites at $20; no water or sewer hookups, but electricity and dump station available). No pets, skateboards, or motorcycles are allowed. The sandy beach is tidal, so the swimming "window" is about two hours before high tide until two hours afterward; otherwise, you're wallowing in mudflats. (The same rule holds for kayakers or canoeists.) Toddlers head for the big playground; teenagers gravitate to the arcade and the ice cream parlor. For adults, there's a gift shop (which also carries paper plates and such). The park is also the site of several annual events, including the Maine Highland Games and the Bluegrass Festival. Parking is ample. At Cooks Corner, where Bath Road meets Route 24 South, go 1.5 miles on Route 24, then turn left and follow signs for less than two miles to the park. Open mid-May through September 9 A.M.–sunset. Admission to the park is $3.50 adults, $2 children 3–12.

If the tide is low and freshwater swimming appeals, head to town-owned **Coffin Pond** (River Rd., Brunswick, 207/725-6656), a man-made swimming hole with a sandy beach, lifeguards, water slide, picnic tables, playground, changing rooms, and snack bar. Kids' swimming lessons (ages 5–14) are held in August. It's a popular spot, so expect plenty of company. Open 10 A.M.–7 P.M. mid-June to Labor Day. Nonresident admission is $3.50 adult, $2 age 12 and younger. Heading west on Route 1 (Pleasant Street), turn right onto River Road and go about a half mile to the parking area (on the right).

Another terrific but nonsecret spot for freshwater swimming is **White's Beach** (White's Beach and Campground, Durham Rd., Brunswick 04011, 207/729-0415, www.geocities.com/whites beachbluegrass). The sandy-bottomed pond maxes out at nine feet, so it's particularly good for small kids. In mid-July, the campground hosts a popular family bluegrass festival. Park facilities include a snackbar, playground, hot showers, and campsites. Admission is $3 adults, $2 kids 12 and under. Campsites (45) are $15–25. Open mid-May to mid-October. From Route 1 just south of the I-95 exit into Brunswick, take Durham Road 2.2 miles northwest.

Golf

Established in 1901 primarily for Bowdoin College students, the **Brunswick Golf Club** (River Rd., Brunswick 04011, 207/725-8224) is now an especially popular 18-hole public course, so call for a starting time. Heading west on Route 1 (Pleasant Street), turn right onto River Road and go three-quarters of a mile. Open April to mid-November. If you can stand the runway backdraft challenging your swing, the nine-hole **Brunswick Naval Air Station Golf Club** (Bath Rd., Brunswick, 207/921-2155) is open to the public. You'll have access to the pro shop, snack bar, and driving range. Call for tee times.

Boating Excursions

Departing at noon from the Cook's Lobster House wharf (Cook's Landing) in Bailey Island (end of Route 24), a large, sturdy **Casco Bay Lines ferry** does a 1.75-hour nature-watch circuit of nearby islands, including Eagle Island, the onetime home of Admiral Robert Peary (there are no stopovers on these circuits; for excursions to Eagle Island, see Recreation in the Portland section of the Greater Portland chapter). The nature-watch cruise operates daily except Saturday, late June through Labor Day. Reservations aren't needed. Cost is $11.50 adults, $9 seniors, $5 children 5–9; under five are free. To confirm the schedule when weather is iffy, call Casco Bay Lines (207/774-7871) or Cook's Landing (207/833-6641).

For a more intimate excursion in a smaller boat, Captain Les McNelly, owner of **Sea Escape Charters** (Box 7, Bailey Island 04003, 207/833-5531, www.seaescapecottages.com) operates two-hour on-demand sightseeing cruises throughout the summer (weather permitting) for $65 pp (two people) or $35 pp (four people). Or he'll take you out to Eagle Island for $120 a couple (lower rate if there are more passengers). He also offers fishing trips for $275 for

four hours, including bait and tackle; no fishing license required; bring your own lunch. Call to schedule a trip. Trips operate out of Sea Escape Cottages, one- and two-bedroom cottages, with full kitchens and oceanside decks and use of bicycles, that rent for $130–150 per night or $795–955 per week, including linens and one change of towels.

Once a week, usually on Tuesdays, from mid-July through August, the grandson of Admiral Robert E. Peary, the first explorer to reach the North Pole, leads an **Eagle Island Adventure** (Friends of Peary's Eagle Island, P.O. Box 70, Bailey Island 04003, 207/833-2310, $35). The half-day excursion leaves from Dolphin Marina, Harpswell, at 9:30 A.M., returning at noon. Trips are limited to 26 passengers, and reservations must be made in advance by mail; write or call for details.

Sea Kayaking

H2Outfitters (P.O. Box 72, Orr's Island 04066, 207/833-5257 or 800/205-2925, fax 207/833-6606) has been a thriving operation since 1978. Based in a wooden building on the Orr's Island side of the famed cribstone bridge, this experienced company organizes multiday trips, including island camping, for $395 pp and up; all gear is included.

Newer on the scene is **Seaspray Kayaking** (207/443-3646 or 888/349-7772, www.seaspray kayaking.com), with bases on the New Meadows River, in Brunswick; at Sebasco, in Phippsburg; and Bay Point, in Georgetown. The New Meadows base is particularly good for those nervous about trying the sport, as it isn't open ocean and there are no waves. Rentals and tours are available. Rentals are $10–20 for the first hour, $5–10 for additional hours, $25–50 per day. Equipment options include solo and tandem kayaks, recreational kayaks, surf kayaks, and canoes. Tours, led by Registered Maine Guides, range from sunset paddles to three-day expeditions and include moonlight paddles, island-to-island tours, and inn-to-inn tours. Rates begin at $40/adult, $20 kids for shorter tours. A striper fishing kayak tour, including tackle and instruction, is $75. Reserve early for the popular moonlight paddles ($40).

Mid-Coast Region

If you're an experienced sea kayaker, consider exploring Harpswell Sound from the boat launch on the west side of the cribstone bridge; kayaks can also put in at Mackerel Cove, near Cook's Lobster House. There's also a boat launch with plentiful parking at Sawyer Park on the New Meadows River, on Route 1, just before you cross the river heading north.

SHOPPING

Downtown Brunswick invites leisurely browsing, with most of the shops concentrated on Maine Street. Do take special care when crossing the four-lane-wide street, and do so only at marked crosswalks, very carefully.

A handful of small shops are part of the **Tontine Mall** (149 Maine St., Brunswick); the mall entrance is right in the middle of downtown.

Art, Craft, and Antiques Galleries

The **Bayview Gallery** (58 Maine St., Brunswick 04011, 800/244-3007) mounts half a dozen superb shows annually, specializing in contemporary New England artists.

Facing the Mall, **Day's Antiques** (153 Park Row, Brunswick 04011, 207/725-6959) occupies five rooms and the basement of the handsome historic building known as the Pumpkin House. Quality is high at David Day's shop; prices are fair.

More than 140 dealers show and sell their wares at **Cabot Mill Antiques** (14 Maine St., 207/725-2855), in the renovated Fort Andross mill complex next to the Androscoggin River.

Along Route 123 in South Harpswell, south of Mountain Road, watch for distinctive blue-heron signs that mark the studios of **Harpswell Art and Craft Guild** members—nearly a dozen artisans who welcome visitors to see (and buy) their pottery, sculpture, jewelry, and chocolate (yes!). Appointments are necessary for some studios. Membership varies from year to year, so call 207/833-6081 for details.

Part gallery, part resource center **Maine Fiberarts** (13 Maine St., Topsham, 207-721-0678, www.mainefiberarts.org) is a must-stop for anyone interested in fiber-related artwork: knitting, quilting, spinning, basketry. If you're really interested in finding artists and resources statewide, purchase a copy of its resource book.

Twenty artists exhibit their works in varied media at **Sebascodegan Artists Gallery** (Rte. 24, Great Island, Harpswell, 207/833-6260).

Bookstores

Bet you can't leave Brunswick without buying a book! Bookstores are plentiful. In addition to the ones described, there's also the Bowdoin College Bookstore in the campus's David Saul Smith Student Union.

With an eclectic new-book inventory that includes lots of esoterica, **Gulf of Maine Books** (134 Maine St., Brunswick 04011, 207/729-5083) has held the competition at bay since the early 1980s. The fiction selection is particularly good, as are the religion, health, and poetry sections. Poet/publisher/Renaissance man Gary Lawless oversees everything. Open all year.

Upstairs from Gulf of Maine is Clare Howell's **Old Books** (136 Maine St., Brunswick 04011, 207/725-4524), another long-standing operation, specializing in literary classics and other out-of-print titles. Count on her prices being fair.

Bookland (Cooks Corner Shopping Center, Bath Rd. and Rte. 24 S, Brunswick 04011, 207/725-2313), a thriving independent emporium, was the largest bookstore north of Boston when it opened in 1994. That's no longer true, but no matter. This is a terrific store with an especially helpful staff. Inside its 20,000 square feet are a zillion books, new and used (plus CDs and cards) and the very popular Hardcover Cafe. At *least* try one of the desserts.

ENTERTAINMENT

Brunswick's extremely active arts organization, **Brunswick Area Arts & Cultural Alliance** (BAACA, 108 Main St., Brunswick, 207/798-6964, www.baaca.org), maintains a calendar of area concerts, gallery openings, art shows, lectures, exhibits, and other arts-related events and also sponsors a few key events. Listings also appear on www.midcoastmaine.com/events.

There's no lack of classical music in Brunswick each summer, but for lighter fare, the **Maine State Music Theatre** (Pickard Theater, Bowdoin College, mailing address 14 Maine St., Suite 109, Brunswick 04011, box office 22 Elm St., 207/725-8769, www.msmt.org) has been a summer tradition since 1959. The renovated, state-of-the-art, air-conditioned theater brings real pros to its stage for four musicals (mid-June to late Aug.). Loyal subscribers book the same seats year after year, and performances tend to sell out, so call ahead for the schedule and reservations. (Nonsubscription tickets go on sale May 1.) Performances are Tuesday–Saturday at 8 P.M.; matinees are staged at 2 P.M. on an alternating schedule—each week has matinees on different days. (No children under four are admitted, but special family shows are performed during the season.) Ticket range is $29–44.

From late June through early August, the **Bowdoin International Music Festival** is a showcase for musical talent of all kinds. Guest artists, faculty, and music students perform Friday and Wednesday classical concerts in the state-of-the-art Crooker Theater at Brunswick High School. Friday MusicFest concerts, with renowned guest musicians, are at 8 P.M. ($25); Wednesday Upbeat! concerts are at 7:30 P.M. ($20 adult, $5 under 21 or free with adult). A festival-within-the-festival, the Gamper Festival of Contemporary Music features the works of 20th-century contemporary American composers. It usually takes place in late July, with concerts held at Kresge Auditorium at Bowdoin College ($10 suggested donation; call for details). Also open to the public are frequent student concerts, also held at Kresge at 7:30 P.M. (suggested donation $5). For a full schedule, check with the festival box office (12 Cleveland St., mailing address 6300 College Station, Brunswick, 207/725-3895, www.bowdoinmusic.org).

From May into November, **Second Friday Art Walks** (207/725-4366) take place in downtown Brunswick 5–7:30 P.M. Gallery openings, wine tastings, light refreshments, and other activities are usually part of the mix.

Wednesday evenings (Thursday if it rains) July and August, **Music on the Mall** presents family band concerts at 7 P.M. on the Brunswick Mall (the lovely park in the center of town).

Eveningstar Cinema (Tontine Mall, Brunswick, 207/729-5486) screens first-run as well as lesser-known art and second-run films. It also offers inexpensive matinees of PG-rated kids' movies. Open all year.

FESTIVALS AND EVENTS

The first full week of August, the **Topsham Fair** is a weeklong agricultural festival with exhibits, demonstrations, live music, ox pulls, contests, harness racing, and fireworks at the Topsham Fairgrounds.

The third Saturday of August, the **Maine Highland Games,** sponsored by the St. Andrew's Society of Maine, mark the annual wearing of the plaids—but you needn't be Scottish to join in the games or watch the highland dancing or browse the arts and crafts booths. (Only a Scot, however, can appreciate that unique concoction called haggis.) If you're seeking your clan roots, this is the place; lots of genealogical networking goes on here. It all happens at Thomas Point Beach in Brunswick.

Also at Thomas Point Beach, September's **Annual Bluegrass Festival** is a four-day event with nonstop bluegrass, including big-name artists. Kickoff is Thursday noon.

The **Family Arts Festival** (207/798-6964), in September, has hands-on workshops, music, dance, and storytelling for all ages under tents on the Town Mall.

In early November, **Arts Downtown & All Around,** presented by BAACA (207/798-6964), is a weekend of open studios, performances, exhibitions, and demonstrations throughout Brunswick and Harpswell.

ACCOMMODATIONS

Hotels, Motels, Inns

Combining a Federal-style manse with a new hotel wing, **The Captain Daniel Stone Inn** (10 Water St., Brunswick 04011, 207/725-9898 or 877/573-5151, www.someplacesdifferent.com) has 34 guest rooms and suites with reproduction furnishings and a country-hotel feel. Private baths, air-conditioning, phones, cable TV; no pets. In summer, rooms are $170–290, suites are $220–255, including continental breakfast; rates are lower other months, and special packages are available. The inn's casually elegant Narcissa Stone Restaurant serves dinner, lunch, and a mean Sunday brunch.

Set back from the road on park-like grounds, but right near all the action in Cooks Corner, is **The Parkwood Inn** (71 Gurnet Rd., Rte. 24, P.O. Box 92, Brunswick 04011, 207/725-5251 or 800/349-7191, www.parkwoodinn.com, $139–249). Rooms range from basic motel style to fancier units with fireplaces and/or whirlpool tubs. All rooms have a refrigerator, microwave, and satellite TV. Facilities include a lounge with fireplace open only to guests, an indoor pool, a small fitness center, guest laundry, and ATM. A deluxe continental breakfast and afternoon refreshments are included in the rate.

A dozen miles down Route 24 from Cooks Corner is the turnoff for the **Little Island Motel** (44 Little Island Rd., Orr's Island 04066, 207/833-2392, www.littleislandmotel.com), an eight-unit complex on its own spit of land with deck views you won't believe. Basic rooms have cable TV and small fridges. Doubles go for $118–138 in midsummer (lower rates early and late season), including buffet breakfast and use of bikes, boats, and a little beach. No credit cards. Open mid-May to mid-October.

Continue another mile down Route 24, cross the cribstone bridge, and you'll come to the **Bailey Island Motel** (Rte. 24, P.O. Box 4, Bailey Island 04003, 207/833-2886, www.baileyislandmotel.com), a congenial, clean, no-frills waterfront spot with 11 rooms that go for $85–115 d, depending on the month. Kids under 10 are free, 10 and older are $15. Continental breakfast is included, and rooms have cable TV. A dock is available for boat launching. Open mid-May to late October.

Looking rather like an old-fashioned tear-jerker film set, the family-run **Driftwood Inn** (81 Washington Ave., P.O. Box 16, Bailey Island 04003, 207/833-5461) has 25 very basic rooms in four buildings (some with private toilet and sink; all with shared showers), six housekeeping cottages, a saltwater pool, a stunning view, a dining room, and a determinedly rustic ambience. No frills, period, but ocean-front porches, games, and a old-fashioned simplicity that you rarely find anymore, and you'll sleep at night listening to the waves crash on the rocky shore. It's all on three oceanfront acres near the Giant Stairs. The dining room serves a set, home-cooked meal nightly (usually with a fish-of-the-day alternative) from late June to Labor Day for $16.50–18. Breakfast is $6.50. Rooms are $85–120 d; all meals are extra, but room and meal rates are available ($450 pp/week). Open mid-May to early October.

B&Bs

Right downtown, facing the tree-shaded Mall, is Mercie (an occupational therapist) and Steve (an architect) Normand's **M Brunswick Bed & Breakfast** (165 Park Row, Brunswick 04011, 207/729-4914 or 800/299-4914, www.brunswickbnb.com), a handsome, 30-room Greek Revival mansion built in 1849. Special touches are the twin parlors (with fireplaces), lots of antiques, and the Normands' extensive collection of antique and modern quilts. Fifteen elegant guest rooms are split between the main house (including a great family suite), the Garden Cottage (with kitchen), and the newly renovated Carriage House (with two fully accessible rooms). Breakfast is a treat. Doubles are $110–170; the Garden Cottage is $255. Open February through December.

On the outskirts of town, in a rural location smack dab on Middle Bay, is the beautifully renovated **M Middle Bay Farm Bed & Breakfast** (287 Pennellville Rd., Brunswick 04011, 207/373-1375, www.middlebayfarm.com, $150–170). Four water-view guest rooms in the 1834 farmhouse are lovingly decorated with antiques and have TV/VCRs. Also in the main house is a living room with fireplace and grand piano. Two suites in the sail loft each have a living room with kitchenette and two bedrooms. All guests receive a full breakfast in the water-view dining room. Canoes and bicycles are available to guests. Bring a sea kayak to launch from the dock.

A super bed-and-breakfast-cum-boat operation, slightly off the beaten track, has a mouthful of a name: **The Captain's Watch at Cundy's Harbor B&B and Sail Charter** (2476 Cundy's Harbor Rd., Cundy's Harbor, Brunswick 04011, 207/725-0979). In the National Historic Register Cupola House—an inn since Civil War days—the B&B has five guest rooms, including a suite, all with private baths and unusual features (two share access to the head-swiveling octagonal cupola). Energetic hosts Donna Dillman and Ken Brigham, innkeepers since 1986, took the reins here in 1996. Ken captains the 37-foot sloop *Symbion* for day sails (up to four people; cost depends on the time and itinerary); Donna produces the gourmet breakfasts and goes sailing off-season. Doubles are $115–175. Credit cards are accepted but cash and checks are preferred. Open all year, by reservation off-season. From Cooks Corner, go 4.5 miles on Route 24, turn left and go another 4.4 miles to Cundy's Harbor, near the "fingertips" of Great Island's easternmost "arm."

After many years as an extremely popular dining destination 13 miles south of Cooks Corner, **The Log Cabin** (Rte. 24, P.O. Box 41, Bailey Island 04003, 207/833-5546, www.logcabin-maine.com) in 1996 added lodging to its repertoire and now serves meals only to guests. Nine nicely decorated rooms have phones, TV/VCRs, private decks facing the bay, and, weather permitting, splendid sunset views to the White Mountains. Four rooms have kitchen facilities; some have gas fireplaces or whirlpool tubs. There's also an outdoor heated pool. Rates are $139–299 d in midsummer, lower early and late in the season. Full breakfast is included; dinner ($15–29) is available only to guests 6–6:30 P.M. Open April through October.

Across the Androscoggin in Topsham is the **Black Lantern Bed & Breakfast** (6 Pleasant St., Topsham 04086, 207/725-4165 or 888/306-4165, www.blacklanternbandb.com). Judy and Tom Connelie spent a year restoring this handsome Federal home, which was built in 1810 and expanded in 1839. Three second-floor rooms have private baths (one detached) and quilts. (Judy's an avid quilter.) Rooms are $85–90. The Connelies light a fire each night in the cozy parlor,

where *The New York Times* appears every morning (coffee is ready for early risers). An unusual touch is the "book exchange"—a handy swap service where you leave one and take one. Bikes are available for guests to use. Open all year.

Seasonal Rentals

For weekly and monthly rentals on Great, Orr's, and Bailey Islands, contact Becky-Sue Betts at **Your Island Connection** (P.O. Box 300, next to the cribstone bridge, Bailey Island 04003, 207/833-7779, www.mainerentals.com). Rob Williams, at **Harpswell Property Management** (Bailey Island, 207/833-7795) has been in the business for more than 20 years and has a wide range of summer and year-round rentals. The Southern Midcoast Maine Chamber of Commerce also keeps a list of seasonal cottage rentals.

Campgrounds

Campsites are available at Thomas Point Beach and White's Beach (see Recreation). Also, **Orr's Island Campground** (44 Bond Point Rd., Orr's Island 04066, 207/833-5595, www.orrsisland .com, $24–35) is a 42-acre campground with a half-mile pebble beach and 70 wooded and open sites. Canoe rentals available.

FOOD

Brunswick has an abundance of inexpensive cafés, delis, coffeehouses, and ethnic restaurants lining its main and side streets as well as seasonal vendors operating cart stands on the Mall. At most, you order at the counter, then select your table.

Breakfast, Lunch, Miscellany

Wild O.A.T.S. Bakery and Café (149 Maine St., Tontine Mall, Brunswick 04011, 207/725-6287, 7:30 A.M.–5 P.M. Mon.- Sat., 8 A.M.–3 P.M. Sun. year-round) turns out terrific made-from-scratch breads and pastries, especially the breakfast kind, in its cafeteria-style place. (Just so you know, the name stands for Original And Tasty Stuff.) Inside and outside tables, moderate prices, good-for-you salads, and great sandwiches (try the Club Med or the curried chicken melt).

For food on the run—no-frills hot dogs straight from the cart—head for Brunswick's Mall, the village green where **Danny's on the Mall** (no telephone) has been cooking dirt-cheap tube steaks since the early 1980s.

Fat Boy Drive-In (Bath Rd., Old Route 1, Brunswick 04011, 207/729-9431) is a genuine throwback—a landmark since 1955, boasting carhops, window trays, and a menu guaranteed to clog your arteries. Fries and frappes are specialties. If you insist, there are five booths indoors. No credit cards. Open—get this—the third Tuesday in March to the second Sunday in October, daily 11 A.M.–8:30 P.M. The second Saturday in August, about 700 people show up, many in 1950s get-ups, for the annual sock hop. Only pre-1970 cars can park in the lot that night (if you have one, stop in ahead of time for a pass).

One of Maine's best farmers' markets is the **Brunswick Farmers' Market,** which sets up, rain or shine, on the Mall (village green) Tuesday and Friday 8 A.M.–3 P.M. May–November (Friday is the bigger day). On Saturday, the market moves to Crystal Spring Farm, Pleasant Hill Road, between 8 A.M. and 1 P.M. Produce, cheeses, crafts, condiments, live lobsters, and serendipitous surprises—depending on the season.

Eclectic

At the upper end of the downtown drag is Doug and Colleen Lavallee's **Scarlet Begonias** (212B Maine St., Brunswick 04011, 207/721-0403, 11 A.M.–8 P.M. Mon.–Thurs., to 9 P.M. Friday, noon–9 P.M. Sat.), an especially cheerful place with a bistro-type pizza-and-pasta menu. Order at the counter and look for a table. How could anyone resist a $9.95 pasta *puttanesca* dubbed Scarlet Harlot? You can't go wrong here; everything's a winner. No credit cards. BYOL.

Sophisticated yet casual, **M Henry and Marty** (61 Maine St., P.O. Box 147, Brunswick 04011, 207/721-9141) has grown into a European-style bistro with an excellent reputation. Eclectic art adds pizzazz to the sunshine yellow dining room. Owners Henry Holbrook and Martin Perry with chef Paul Verhoeven concentrate on preparing the best local meat, fish, and produce—and vegetarian specialties every day. Entrées are $14–26. Reservations recommended; lots of loyal customers show up here. It's also a great place for a light after-theater or -concert meal in summer. Open 5–9 P.M. Tuesday–Saturday; a light menu is available until midnight during the summer season.

At The Captain Daniel Stone Inn (10 Water St., 207/725-9898), the casually elegant **Narcissa Stone Restaurant** (open daily year-round for dinner 5–9 P.M. and weekdays for lunch 11:30 A.M.–2 P.M.) serves a mean Sunday brunch 10 A.M.–2 P.M. Dinner entrées are $11–24.

The dining room at the **Driftwood Inn** (81 Washington Ave., 207/833-5461), open to the public by reservation, serves a set, home-cooked meal nightly (usually with a fish-of-the-day alternative) from late June to Labor Day for $16.50–18. Breakfast is $6.50.

Ethnic

Generous portions, moderate prices, efficient service, and narrow aisles are the story at **The Great Impasta** (42 Maine St., Brunswick 04011, 207/729-5858, 11 A.M.–9 P.M. Mon.–Sat., to 10 P.M. Fri. and Sat.), a cheerful, informal eatery where the garlic meets you at the door. No reservations, so expect to wait, although you can call ahead and add your name to the waiting list. Dinner entrées are $10–17. There's a small but varied wine list and a "bambino menu" for the kids.

If you'd rather go a bit more ethnic, try **Rosita's Mexican Food** (212 Maine St., Brunswick 04011, 207/729-7118)—Tex-Mex with a veggie slant. Order at the counter and grab a table. Prices are incredibly reasonable: deluxe nachos ($4.95) are topped with homemade guacamole, combo plates are $4.50–6.50, and Mexican pizza is $2.25–4.25; the beans are lard- and oil-free. No credit cards; beer license only. Open Monday–Friday 11 A.M.–8:30 P.M. (to 9 P.M. Friday), Saturday noon–8:30 P.M., Sunday noon–8 P.M.

Chef Richard Gnauck has been serving authentic German fare in the area for nearly 20 years, and recently he's been joined by sons Erik and Wilhelm at his **Richard's Restaurant** (115 Maine St., Brunswick, Mon.–Sat. 11 A.M.–2 P.M. and 5–9 P.M., to 9:30 P.M. Fri. and Sat.). German favorites such as wienerschnitzel and sauerbraten share the menu with American-style fare; heartsmart and petite portions are available ($8–20). A German sampler plate is $16.

Pizza and Brewpub Fare

The area's best pizza is at **Benzoni's Brick-Oven Pizza & Back Street Bistro** (11 Town Hall Pl., Brunswick 04011, 207/729-2800), where you can also have calzones, pasta entrées, and soup-and-salad combos—indoors or on the deck. Or get it all to go. Try the Greek Odyssey specialty pizza. Full liquor license. Open daily at 4 P.M., Benzoni's is next to the fire station in the center of town.

Just over the bridge from Brunswick, in the renovated Bowdoin Mill complex overlooking the Androscoggin River, is the **Sea Dog Brewery** (1 Main St., Topsham, 207/725-0162, 11:30–1 A.M.). Lunch and dinner are served daily and Sunday brunch is served 9 A.M.–2 P.M. There's seating inside and on a deck hanging over the river. The menu ranges from burgers and sandwiches to full plate entrées ($11–18). Frequent acoustic entertainment includes open-mike nights on Thursdays. There are also games for kids and a game room with a video arcade and pool tables.

Vegan

Everything at the vegan restaurant **Little Lads Bakery and Café** (25 Mill St., Brunswick, 11:30 A.M.–7 P.M. Mon.–Thurs., 11:30 A.M.–3 P.M. Fri. and Sun.), including the all-you-care-to-try buffet, is less than $5. Absolutely no atmosphere, but a warm, friendly staff.

Seafood

Arguments rage endlessly about who makes the best chowder in Maine, but **The Dolphin Chowder House** (Dolphin Marina, 515 Basin Point Rd., South Harpswell, 207/833-6000) heads lots of lists for its fish chowder, accompanied by a blueberry muffin. Plus you can't beat the scenic 13-mile drive south from Brunswick and the spectacular water views at the tip of Harpswell Neck. This popular spot, with two walls of windows overlooking the water, is open daily 11 A.M.–8 P.M. May 1–November 1.

Seafood is king at the ◼ **Star Fish Grill** (100 Pleasant St., Rte. 1, Brunswick 04011, 207/725-7828), where you feel like you're in an aquarium as soon as you walk in the door. Everything carries out the marine theme. No starfish on the menu, but everything else is, depending on what's fresh and in season—including a fabulous lobster paella. Entrées are $14–25; the paella is $45, supposedly for two, but you'd better be hungry. Don't like fish? Not to worry, there are choices for you, too. The restaurant is open Tuesday–Saturday at 5 P.M., all year. Reservations are essential. Finding it can be a bit tricky, even though it's on the main road. Coming from the south (Freeport, Portland), watch for it on your left, next to a video store, at the southern end of Brunswick just before Route 1 takes a 90-degree left turn. Unfortunately, it shares a building with Modern Pest Control, which has the bigger sign.

A Bailey Island landmark since the 1950s, the sprawling **Cook's Lobster House** (Garrison Cove Rd., Rte. 24, Bailey Island 04003, 207/833-2818) is one of the most reliable of several seafood places near the peninsula's tip. The fish is predictably fresh, service is efficient, and the view is unbeatable. Besides, meat freaks can even order a steak. Most entrées are $16–23, but sandwiches and pasta are less. The restaurant overlooks the hamlet's unique cribstone bridge—a massive latticelike structure that's been allowing tides to ebb and flow since 1928. Open all year, daily 11:30 A.M.–9 P.M. in summer, reduced hours in winter. No reservations, so you may have to wait.

Lobster-in-the-Rough

After a few seasons of so-so food and service, new leasees at **Holbrook's Wharf and Snack Bar** (984 Cundy's Harbor Rd., 207/729-0848, 11:30 A.M.–sunset) have given new life to this popular spot at the end of the Cundy's Harbor Road. Nothing fancy here at all. Order at the window, then choose a picnic table on the wharf, some under cover. Seafood baskets, hot dogs, and burgers also available. Locals complain that the lobster's a bit pricey, but really, what a location. BYOL.

INFORMATION AND SERVICES

Information

Contact the **Southern Midcoast Maine Chamber of Commerce** (207/725-8797) for information on lodgings, restaurants, and area activities (the office will have a new Topsham location in 2005; call for address and hours). The particularly useful *Bath/Brunswick Region Map and Guide* is $2.50. A seasonal information center operated by volunteer members is on Route 1 at Witch Spring Hill (right side northbound from Brunswick to Bath, about a mile south of Bath). It's open weekends in May and daily all summer. Request copies of the *City of Bath Downtown Map and Guide* and the *Bath/Brunswick Region Map and Guide.*

For information on Harpswell, visit www.harpswellmaine.org or pick up the free brochure produced by the Harpswell Maine Business Association.

Hospitals

Two Brunswick hospitals serve the Bath-Brunswick region. **Mid-Coast Hospital** (Bath Rd., Cooks Corner, Brunswick, 207/729-0181) and the Seventh Day Adventist **Parkview Hospital** (329 Maine St., a mile south of Bowdoin College, Brunswick, 207/373-2000).

Local Library

The **Curtis Memorial Library** (23 Pleasant St., Brunswick 04011, 207/725-5242, www.curtislibrary.com), one of the state's best public libraries, has recently undergone an impressive 21st-century overhaul. It also has an especially friendly children's department and a lovely little reading garden. From late June to Labor Day, the library is open 9:30 A.M.–8 P.M. Monday–Thursday, 9:30 A.M.–6 P.M. Friday, and 9:30 A.M.–1 P.M. Saturday. Other months, it's also open Saturday to 5 P.M. and Sunday noon–4 P.M. The all-volunteer Friends of the Curtis Memorial Library has produced the *Children's Resource Handbook,* a periodically updated booklet containing dozens of well-organized ideas for entertaining the under-14 set. Copies are available free at the library and on the library's website.

Getting Around

Concord Trailways (800/639-3317, www.cocordtrailways.com) stops in Brunswick, Bath, Wiscasset, Damariscotta, and Waldoboro on its three daily nonexpress trips up the coast.

Bath Area

One of the smallest in area of Maine's cities, Bath—with a population of about 9,920 in only nine square miles—has many similarities to Brunswick. It sits astride Route 1 and a river, relies on modern military funding, yet has centuries of historical and architectural tradition. The defense part is impossible to ignore, since giant cranes dominate the riverfront cityscape at the huge Bath Iron Works complex, source of state-of-the-art warships—your tax dollars at work. Less evident (but not far away) is the link to the past: just south of Bath, in Popham on the Phippsburg Peninsula, is an unmarked site where a trouble-plagued English settlement predated the Plymouth Colony by 13 years. (Of course, Champlain arrived before that, and Norsemen allegedly left calling cards even earlier.) In 1607 and 1608, settlers in the Popham Colony managed to build a 30-ton pinnace, *Virginia of Sagadahoc,* designed for transatlantic trade, but they lost heart during a bitter winter and abandoned the site. (A replica is under construction at the Maine Maritime Museum, with a targeted launch date of August 2006. For details, visit www.mainesfirstship.org.)

Bath is the jumping-off point for two peninsulas to the south—Phippsburg (of Popham Colony fame) and Georgetown. Both are dramatically scenic, with glacier-carved farms and fishing villages. Drive or cycle a dozen miles down any of these fingers and you're in different worlds, ones where artists and photographers, hikers and historians go crazy with all the possibilities.

SIGHTS

Bath Iron Works

Only during one of its relatively infrequent launchings is Bath Iron Works (BIW) open to the public, and then it's a mob scene, with hordes of politicos, townsfolk, and military pooh-bahs in their scrambled eggs and brass. But the launchings are exciting occasions, with flags flying everywhere. BIW, under the umbrella of giant defense contractor General Dynamics, employs thousands in its Bath and smaller Brunswick sites. When BIW talks, everyone listens. And when BIW's afternoon shift changes, everyone from Brunswick to Wiscasset feels the gridlock. Avoid approaching Bath on a weekday between 3:25 and 4 P.M.; be forewarned and plan your schedule around the witching hour. Despite the construction of the brand-new Sagadahoc Bridge, which has definitely eased the situation, traffic still backs up at shift-change time.

⚓ Maine Maritime Museum

Spread over 20 acres on the Kennebec River, the Maine Maritime Museum (243 Washington St., Bath 04530, 207/443-1316, fax 207/443-1665, www.mainemaritimemuseum.org) is the state's premier marine museum. On the grounds are relics of the 19th-century Percy & Small Shipyard (1897–1920) and a hands-on lobstering exhibit,

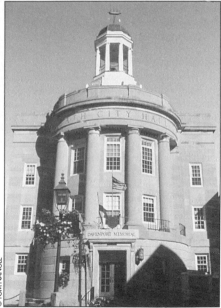

© TOM NANGLE

Smack in the middle of Bath's historic shopping district is the handsome City Hall.

Kids of all ages can explore the waterfront ruins of 19th-century Fort Popham, on the Phippsburg peninsula.

but the first thing you see is the architecturally dramatic Maritime History Building, locale for permanent and temporary displays of marine art and artifacts and a shop stocked with nautical books and gifts. Bring a picnic and let the toddlers loose in the children's play area. Then join one of the three daily hour-long guided shipyard tours or the special themed tours offered weekdays at 2 P.M. (all tours Memorial Day–Columbus Day). Shipyard demonstrations are held on a rotating schedule, and brown-bag lectures are often given. In summer, weather permitting, the museum sponsors special river cruises; call for information. Open 9:30 A.M.–5 P.M. daily year-round; Percy & Small Shipyard is open all year as long as the weather holds. Admission is $9.75 adults, $8.75 ages 65 and up, $6.75 children 7–17, or $28 per family (two adults, two kids).

Bath History Preserved

Sagadahoc Preservation Inc. (SPI), founded in 1971 to rescue the city's architectural heritage, has produced *Architectural Tours: Self-Guided Walking and Driving Tours of the City of Bath,* a terrific foldout brochure (with maps) to guide you—

via car, ankle express, or bicycle—around Bath. Pick up a copy at a local business or contact SPI (Box 322, Bath 04530).

Phippsburg Peninsula

Thanks to an impressive map/brochure produced by the Phippsburg Historical Society and the Phippsburg Business Association, you can spend a whole day—or, better still, several days—exploring the peninsula that drops from Bath. Along the way are campgrounds, B&Bs, an updated traditional resort, restaurants, a unique state park, hiking trails, secluded coves, spectacular scenery, and tons of history.

About two miles south of Bath is a causeway known as **Winnegance,** an Abnaki name usually translated as "short carry" or "little portage." Native Americans crossed here from the Kennebec to the New Meadows River. Early settlers erected nearly a dozen tide-powered mills to serve the shipbuilding industry, but they're long gone. Just before the causeway, on the Bath-Phippsburg boundary, is the **Winnegance General Store** (36 High St., Bath 04530, 207/443-9805), a local favorite for the miscellanea that general stores offer, including inexpensive sandwiches. About 1.5 miles farther is a left turn onto Fiddler's Reach Road, leading to the **Morse Cove Public Launching Facility,** one of the state's most scenic boat-launch sites. If you have a kayak, plan to go downriver on the ebb tide and return on the flow (otherwise, you'll be battling the strong Kennebec River current). There's plenty of paved parking here, plus a restroom.

Back on Route 209, it's another 1.3 miles to the **Dromore Burying Ground** (on the right), with great old headstones; the earliest is dated 1743. The next mile opens up with terrific easterly views of Dromore Bay. Right in the line of sight is 117-acre Lee Island (which the owners sold to the state in 1995). From May through mid-July, the island is off-limits to protect nesting eagles and waterfowl.

Next you're in **Phippsburg Center,** alive with shipbuilding from colonial days to the early 20th century. Hang a left onto Parker Head Road (but avoid this detour if you're on a bicycle; it's too narrow and winding). After the Phippsburg Historical Museum (in an 1859 schoolhouse) and the Alfred Totman Library, turn left onto Church Lane to see the **Phippsburg Congregational Church,** built in 1802. Out front is a "Constitution Tree," a huge English linden planted in 1774.

Parker Head Road continues southward and meets up with Route 209, which takes you to **Popham Beach State Park.** Continue to the end of Route 209 for **Fort Popham Historic Site,** where parking is woefully inadequate in summer (and costs an exorbitant $5 at nearby Percy's Store). The fort is accessible Memorial Day through September. Youngsters love this place—they can fish from the rocks, climb to the third level of the 1865 stone fortress (although the chicken-wire fencing is annoying for photographers), picnic on the seven-acre grounds, and create sandcastles on the tiny beach next to the fort. Resist the urge to swim, though; the current is dangerous, and there's no lifeguard. Across the river is Bay Point, a lobstering village at the tip of the Georgetown Peninsula. **Percy's Store** (207/389-2010), by the way, with a handful of tables, is the best place down here for pizza, picnic fare, and fishing tackle. On weekends, if your arteries can tolerate it, sample the fried dough. Across the cove from the fort is Fort Baldwin

Road, a narrow, winding road leading to the unmarked shorefront site of the 1607 Popham Colony. Excavations are ongoing here each summer, so you may arrive to find some activity. Climb the path up Sabino Hill to World War I–era **Fort Baldwin,** the best vantage point for panoramic photos.

Backtrack about four miles on Route 209, turn left onto Route 216, and head toward **Small Point.** On the left, watch for the sign marking the parking area for the **Bates-Morse Mountain Preserve.** Farther south are Head Beach and Hermit Island.

Returning northward on Route 216, you'll hook up with Route 209 and then see a left turn (Route 217) to Sebasco Harbor Resort (see Accommodations). Take the time to go beyond the resort area. When the paved road goes left (to the Water's Edge Restaurant), turn right at a tiny cemetery and continue northward on the Old Meadowbrook Road, which meanders for about four miles along the west side of the peninsula. About midway along is **the Basin,** regarded by sailors as one of the Maine coast's best "hurricane holes" (refuges in high winds). As you skirt the Basin and come to a fork, bear right to return to Route 209; turn left and return northward to Bath.

Woolwich Historical Society Museum

Next to a Route 1 flashing caution light, 2.5 miles north of Bath, the two-story Woolwich Historical Society Museum (Rte. 1 at Nequasset Rd., P.O. Box 98, Woolwich 04579, 207/443-4833, 10:30 A.M.–2:30 P.M. Tues.–Sat. in July and Aug., $3 adults, $1 children over six), admirably well organized, has rooms full of early 19th- to early 20th-century quilts, clothing, tools, and tradesmen's wares. The oldest part of the building dates from the early 19th century.

PARKS, BEACHES, AND PRESERVES
Bath's In-Town Parks
An old unchipped gazebo, just right for hanging out with a book (bring a cushion), is the centerpiece of **Library Park,** the manicured space

fronting the Patten Free Library, Summer and Washington Streets.

Waterfront Park, bordering the Kennebec on Commercial Street, has covered picnic tables, restrooms, and Friday-night concerts in summer.

At the end of High Street is the **Thorn Head Preserve,** maintained by the Lower Kennebec Regional Land Trust. Allow a half hour for the easy walk to the headland and its stone "picnic" table with views toward Merrymeeting Bay. Allow longer if you wish to explore any of the side trails.

Hamilton Sanctuary

Owned by Maine Audubon, Hamilton Sanctuary (Foster Point Rd., West Bath, no phone, sunrise–sunset all year, free) is a peaceful site for walking and nature study on the New Meadows River, with 1.5 miles of trails winding through meadows and forests and along the Back Cove shoreline. From Route 1 between Bath and Brunswick, take the New Meadows Road exit. Head south on New Meadows. When it becomes Foster Point Road, go four miles to the sanctuary entrance. For more information, contact Maine Audubon (20 Gilsland Farm Rd., Falmouth 04105, 207/781-2330).

Popham Beach

On hot July and August weekends, the parking lot at Popham Beach State Park (Rte. 209, Phippsburg 04562, 14 miles south of Bath, 207/389-1335) fills up by 10 A.M., so plan to arrive early at this huge crescent of sand. Even when the parking lot is full, however, if you're willing to walk a bit, you'll find a spot to call your own. The beach is backed by sea grass, beach roses, and dunes. Depending on the tide, there are tidepools and sandbars to explore. The water is warmest when the tide comes in over sun-warmed sands. Be forewarned: There's a nasty undertow. Facilities include changing rooms, outside showers, restrooms, seasonal lifeguards. Admission is $3 adults, $1 children 5–11. Officially open April 15–October 30, but the beach is accessible all year (no winter contact number).

Bates-Morse Mountain Conservation Area

Consider visiting the lovely, 600-acre Bates-Morse Mountain Conservation Area (Routes 209 and 216, Small Point, Phippsburg Peninsula) *only* if you are willing to be extra-conscientious about the rules for this private preserve. A relatively easy four-mile round-trip hike takes you through marshland (you'll need insect repellent) and to the top of 210-foot Morse Mountain, with panoramic views, then down to privately owned Seawall Beach. On a clear day, you can see New Hampshire's Mount Washington from the summit. No dogs or vehicles; no recreational facilities; stay on the preserve road and the beach path at all times (side roads are private). Least terns and piping plovers—both endangered species—nest in the dunes, so avoid this area, especially mid-May to mid-August. Birding hint: Morse Mountain is a great locale for spotting hawks during their annual September migration southward. Pick up a map (and the rules) from the box in the parking area, Morse Mountain Road, off Route 216 (just under a mile south of the Route 209 turnoff to Popham Beach). No admission fee; open sunrise to sunset.

Head Beach

Just off Route 216, about two miles south of the Route 209 turnoff to Popham Beach, is Head Beach, a sandy crescent that's open until 10 P.M. A day-use fee ($5) is payable at the small gatehouse; there's a restroom on the path to the beach and a store within walking distance.

Phippsburg Hiking Trails

The town of Phippsburg and the Phippsburg Land Trust have prepared a handy free brochure with map that describes nine preserves with trails. Three, Center Pond, Spirit Pond, and Ridgewell Preserve, have detailed maps and field guides available at trailhead boxes.

Reid State Park

Reid State Park, on the Georgetown Peninsula (Seguinland Rd., Georgetown 04548, 207/371-2303), is no secret, so plan to arrive early on summer weekends, when parking is woefully inadequate. Highlights of the 765-acre park are 1.5 miles of splendid beach (in three distinct sections), marshlands, sand dunes, and tidepools. Kids love the tidepools, treasure troves left by the receding tide. Facilities include changing rooms (with showers), picnic tables, restrooms, and snack bars. Test the water before racing in; even in midsummer, it's breathtakingly cold. In winter, bring cross-country skis and glide along the shoreline. The park—14 miles south of Route 1 (Woolwich) and two miles off Route 127—is open daily all year. Admission is $3.50 adults, $1 children 5–11, free for kids under five.

Just half a mile beyond the Reid State Park entrance is **Charles Pond,** where the setting is unsurpassed for freshwater swimming in the long, skinny pond. You'll wish this were a secret, too, but it isn't. No facilities.

Josephine Newman Sanctuary

A must-see for any nature lover, the 119-acre Josephine Newman Sanctuary (Rte. 127, Georgetown, no phone) has 2.5 miles of blazed loop trails winding through 110 wooded acres and along Robinhood Cove's tidal shoreline. Josephine Oliver Newman (1878–1968), a respected naturalist, bequeathed her family's splendid property to Maine Audubon, which maintains it today. The .6-mile Self-Guiding Trail is moderately difficult, but the rewards are 20 informative markers highlighting special features: glacial erratics, reversing falls, mosses, and marshes. Easiest route is the three-quarter-mile Horseshoe Trail, which you can extend for another mile or so by linking into the Rocky End Trail. The sanctuary is open daily, all year, sunrise to sunset; free admission. No pets or bikes. The best way to appreciate it is to buy *Forests, Fields, and Estuaries,* a 60-page sanctuary guide ($3.50), with lots of natural-history information useful for other preserves. Contact Maine Audubon (20 Gilsland Farm Rd., Falmouth 04105, 207/781-2330) or stop in at the society's environmental center in Falmouth. To reach the Newman sanctuary, take Route 127 from Route 1 in Woolwich (the road to Reid State Park) for

9.1 miles. Turn right at the sanctuary sign and continue up the narrow, rutted, dirt road (pray no one's coming the other way) to the small parking lot. A map of the trail system is posted at the marsh's edge and available in the box.

Montsweag Preserve

Owned and managed by the Chewonki Foundation, 45-acre Montsweag Preserve (Montsweag Road, Woolwich, no phone) is a peaceful estuarine microcosm on the shore of tidal Montsweag Brook. A 1.5-mile, blue-blazed loop trail meanders through fields and woods, tidal frontage, and salt marsh. Wear long pants and waterproof shoes or boots. Open all year sunrise to sunset. From Bath, take Route 1 northwest about 6.5 miles to Montsweag Road (not well marked). Turn right and go 1.3 miles to the preserve on the left (also not well marked). Park alongside the road and do the trail clockwise.

Robert P. Tristram Coffin Wildflower Sanctuary

The New England Wildflower Society owns this lovely 128-acre preserve, with more than 200 species of flowers, grasses, trees, and shrubs. Well-marked trails lace the sanctuary. It's located just north of the Chops Point Road, before the Dresden town line.

RECREATION

Golf

The 18-hole **Bath Country Club** (Whiskeag Rd., Bath, 207/442-8411) has moderate greens fees, a particularly well-stocked pro shop, and a restaurant serving lunch and dinner. Starting times are needed on weekends. Open early April through October. From Route 1 in West Bath, take New Meadows Road, then Ridge Road, north two miles to Whiskeag Road and the club.

The **Sebasco Harbor Resort** has a nine-hole course (expanding to 18 holes) open to nonguests on a space-available basis; call the resort's pro shop (207/389-9060) to inquire. Each hole has two sets of tees. Watch out for the infamous second hole, which gives new meaning to the term water hole, and be sure to say "Morning, Sarah," on the sixth tee. If you look nearby, you'll find a gravestone inscribed "Sarah Wallace—1862." A local rhyme goes:

> *Show respect to Sarah*
> *You golfers passing by;*
> *She's the only person on this course*
> *Who can't improve her lie.*

The course, called Shore Acres, is open early May to late October.

Bicycling

Bath-area headquarters for anything to do with bikes is **Bath Cycle and Ski** (Rte. 1, opposite Route 127 North, Woolwich 04579, 207/442-7002 or 800/245-3626). Rentals are $18 a day (including helmet and lock), route maps are available, and the shop sponsors weekly road and mountain-bike rides (Mon., Tues., and Sun. at 6 P.M.).

A relatively easy nine-mile loop recommended by the bike shop begins at the downtown Bath post office (750 Washington St.; parking available). Go north on Washington Street to North Street, turn left and go one-half mile to Oak Grove Avenue. Turn sharply right at the five-way intersection and continue about one mile to Whiskeag Road; turn left. Go another .7 mile and turn right, continuing for 1.6 miles. Turn left at Hawkes Farm and go about two miles (part unpaved) to Old Brunswick Road; turn left. Continue 2.3 miles back toward town (Old Brunswick becomes Lincoln Street) to Centre Street; turn left and continue down the hill to Washington Street. Turn right to return to the post office.

Canoeing and Kayaking

Close to civilization, yet amazingly undeveloped, 392-acre **Nequasset Lake** is a great place to canoe. You'll see a few fisherfolk, a handful of houses, and near-wilderness along the shoreline. Personal watercraft and motors over 10 hp are banned. Take Route 1 from Bath across the bridge to Woolwich. Continue to the flashing caution light at Nequasset Road; turn left and continue to Route 127. Turn right and go about 1.5 miles to Old Stage Road. Turn right and go

about a half mile to the Nequasset Brook bridge. The hand-carry launch is west of the bridge, while the trailer launch is east of the bridge; parking is limited. Canoe the lake itself and/or paddle upstream along Nequasset Brook for a mile or so until you reach a small waterfall.

In 1996, town fathers in their wisdom established an even more convenient launch site, close to Route 1. At the flashing caution light, turn *right* and go .1 mile. Turn left, and left again, into the parking area for the Nequasset Stream Waterfront Park, a popular swimming hole. Launch your canoe and head upstream, under Route 1, to the lake.

Paddle the relatively calm and safe waters of Winnegance Creek with a rental boat from **Up the Creek Kayak and Canoe Rentals** (Rte. 209, Phippsburg, 207/443-4845, www.rentkayaks .com). Canoe and kayak rentals are $10 pp for three hours.

Excursion Boats

The 50-foot *Yankee* operates out of Small Point's Hermit Island Campground Monday–Saturday throughout the summer. You can go on nature cruises, enjoy the sunset, or visit Eagle Island; the schedule is different each day and rates vary widely by trip. For information and reservations, call 207/389-1788.

The M/V *Ruth*, a 38-foot excursion boat, runs cruises out of Sebasco Harbor Resort from late June through Labor Day. You don't need to be a Sebasco guest to take the trips, but reservations are essential. The schedule changes weekly, but possible options are a harbor and nature cruise (1.5 hours), Cundy's Harbor cruise (two hours), lobstering demos (one hour), sunset cruise (1.5-hours), and Pirate Island (one hour). Price for nonguests is $12 adults, $7 kids 3–12. Resort guests pay about $1 less per cruise. Call the Sebasco Harbor Resort (207/389-1161) for the schedule, which is available a week in advance. Also sailing from Sebasco Harbor Resort is *Sail Magic* (207/650-3293, www.sailmagic.com), a Tartan 41 ocean racer built in 1974.

Long Reach Cruises (207/442-0092 or 888/538-6785, www.longreachcruises.com) offers one- to three-plus-hour cruises, departing from the Maine Maritime Museum or Bath's waterfront. Options include narrated history, lighthouses, seal-watching, eagle-watching, and sunset cruises. Prices range $18–40 adult, $10–25 child. Cruises departing from the museum include museum admission.

The **Maine Maritime Museum** runs excursion boats to Seguin Island in summer, weather permitting, allowing you about three hours to explore the island, where you can climb the hill to the lighthouse, then climb the 53-foot light tower for a fabulous view from the deck. Afterward, visit the three-room **Seguin Museum,** loaded with lighthouse memorabilia. The nonprofit Friends of Seguin maintains the island's buildings and subsidizes the summertime caretakers, in residence from Memorial Day to mid-September. The Coast Guard maintains the automated light, which has an 18-mile range. There's no dock, so you'll be off-loaded by dinghy—not an experience recommended for the unsteady.

Kennebec Sporting Clays

Brooks Mitchell, a former L.L. Bean wingshooting instructor, has a range for shooting sporting clays, sometimes referred to as "golf with a shotgun" (Rte. 217, Phippsburg, 800/933-0674, 10 A.M.–5 P.M. Wed. and Sat., and 9 A.M.–1 P.M. Sun.). Each target simulates the flight of a different game bird. Rates are $20 for 50 targets, $35 for 100 targets. Gun rental is $10 and an ammo box of 25 is $5. Individual lessons are $25 per hour, plus ammo and targets; all-inclusive group lessons are $85. Note: Mitchell was considering adding archery.

Fishing Charters

Captain Tom Ackerman, a Registered Maine Guide and former director of the L.L. Bean Fly Fishing School, now operates **Maine Coast Charters** (888/729-8645). Fish the Kennebec River for striped bass and bluefish aboard an 18-foot center-console Parker. Cost is $400 full day, $300 half day.

Another outfitter offering guided fishing trips for stripers, bluefish, pike trout, and smallmouth bass is **Kennebec Tidewater Charters** (207/737-

4695, www.kennebectidewater.com). Captain Robin Thayer, a Master Maine Guide, offers freshwater and saltwater cruises, beginning at $250 for four hours. Tackle is provided, instruction is available. Catch and release is encouraged.

SHOPPING

Front and Center Streets are lined with fun, independent shops, including a number of antique shops clustered on lower Front Street.

Bath is home to yet another good independent bookstore successfully bucking the megastore trend. The **Bath Book Shop** (96 Front St., Bath 04530, 207/443-9338) has friendly, hometown service and a discerning taste in books.

Right in the shadow of the Route 1 overpass is an incredible resource for knitters and weavers. **Halcyon Yarn** (12 School St., Bath 04530, 207/442-7909 or 800/341-0282), a huge warehouse of a place, carries domestic and imported yarns, looms, spinning wheels, how-to videos, kits, and pattern books.

And, while you're in town, there's the well-stocked, marine-oriented gift shop at the Maine Maritime Museum.

About nine miles down Route 127, you'll come to **Georgetown Pottery** (Rte. 127, Georgetown 04548, 207/371-2801), a top-quality ceramics studio/shop.

Anyone who appreciates fine woodworking tools *has* to visit the Shelter Institute's **Woodbutcher Tools** (873 Rte. 1, Woolwich 04579, 207/442-7938) retail shop and bookstore, five miles north of Bath.

Flea Market

One of Maine's biggest and most-enduring flea markets is right on Route 1 north of Bath, often creating near-accidents as rubbernecking motorists slam to a halt. **Montsweag Flea Market** (Rte. 1 at Mountain Rd., P.O. Box 252, Woolwich 04579, 207/443-2809) is a genuine treasure trove about seven miles northeast of Bath's Sagadahoc Bridge. Open weekends in May, September, and October; open Wednesday, Friday, Saturday, and Sunday June through August. Sales begin at 6:30 A.M.

Farmers' Market

In Waterfront Park, Commercial Street, the **Bath Farmers' Market** operates 8:30 A.M.–12:30 P.M. every Thursday and Saturday May–October, featuring crafts, plants, condiments, baked goods, and cheeses in addition to seasonal produce.

ENTERTAINMENT AND FESTIVALS

Bath's most diversified entertainment setting is the **Center for the Arts at the Chocolate Church** (804 Washington St., Bath 04530, 207/442-8455, www.chocolatechurch.com)—a chocolate-brown board-and-batten structure built in 1846 as the Central Congregational Church. Year-round activities at the arts center include music and dance concerts, dramas, exhibits, and children's programs.

Every Friday, June through Labor Day, the **Downtown Concert Series** brings live entertainment to Bath's Waterfront Park and outside City Hall. The week of the Fourth of July, **Bath Heritage Days** fills three or four days with art exhibits, a carnival, entertainment, a parade, a triathlon, and fireworks.

Throughout the summer, the **Maine Maritime Museum** (207/443-1316) schedules special events, often hinging on visits by tall ships and other vessels. Some of the visiting boats are open to the public for an extra fee. Call the museum to check.

From November through April, 60 dealers show their wares at the monthly **Bath Antiques Shows** (207/443-8983, www.bathantiquesshows.com, $4), held at Bath Middle School.

ACCOMMODATIONS

Bath

Most of Bath's in-town B&Bs and inns are in historic residences built by shipping magnates and their families, giving you a chance to appreciate the quality of craftsmanship they demanded in their ships and their homes alike.

The flamboyant pink, plum, and teal Italianate **Ⓜ Galen Moses House** (91009 Washington St., Bath 04530, 207/442-8771 or 888/442-8771,

www.galenmoses.com, $119–199) is a standout in the city's Historic District. Original architectural features—soaring ceilings, friezes, chandeliers, elaborate woodwork, stained glass windows—and period antiques make it equally appealing inside, as do hosts Jim Haught and Larry Kieft. All rooms have air-conditioning. Plenty of common rooms to relax, including one with TV and VCR. A fancy full breakfast and afternoon refreshments are included.

Innkeeper Elizabeth Knowlton purchased the **Inn at Bath** (969 Washington St., Bath 04530, 207/443-4294 or 800-423-0964, www.innat-bath.com, $125–200) in 2004, adding the hospitality and culinary skills she honed as chef and co-owner of a Montana fly-fishing lodge to the already highly regarded inn. Guest rooms in the 1810 Greek Revival-style inn each have air-conditioning, TV, VCR, and phone. Five have wood-burning fireplaces, and two have two-person Jacuzzi tubs.

Just a few miles from downtown Bath, yet feeling a world away, is the **Fairhaven Inn** (118 North Bath Rd., Bath 04530, 207/443-4391 or 888/443-4391, www.mainecoast.com/fairhaven, $80–140). Antiques and country pieces furnish Dave and Susie Reed's truly rambling 1790 colonial, built on 16 country acres with views over the Kennebec River. Open year-round.

Phippsburg Peninsula

Ⓜ Sebasco Harbor Resort (Rte. 217, Sebasco Estates 04565, 207/389-1161 or 800/225-3819, www.sebasco.com), on the saltwater New Meadows River, is a self-contained seaside resort on 575 acres 12 miles south of Bath. Families have come here year after year—since 1930, when Sebasco opened. Many guests stay for a week. Sebasco changed hands in 1997, and the enthusiastic new owners began a major overhaul, with astonishing speed and success, but they've kept the emphasis on families, and you'll have to look far and wide to find a better family resort. Scattered around the well-tended property are the main lodge and 23 widely varying cottages (from 1–6 bedrooms; the two-bedroom units with shared living room are a great choice for families). All have private baths, phones, and cable TV; many have water views;

some have refrigerators or kitchenettes. Pets are not allowed. Most intriguing (and most expensive; $275–315 d in July and Aug.) is The Lighthouse, a four-story, multisided, cupola-topped building right on the harbor; it's worth the splurge. Otherwise, in July and August, room rates range $189–275; cottage rates are $355–1,999 ($15 per extra person; kids 10 and under are free). MAP plan is an additional $35 pp, and special packages (and lower rates) are available spring and fall. The Pilot House restaurant serves breakfast and dinner. The casual Ledges Pub offers lunch and dinner and is a late-day magnet, with indoor and outdoor seating. Weekly summer events include a Sunday evening reception and grand buffet, lobsterbakes, family barbecues, bingo, live entertainment, and the free Camp Merrit Children's Program. Recreational facilities include two all-weather tennis courts ($6 an hour), a nine-hole championship golf course ($22 nine holes, $33 for 18, $14 after 4 P.M.), a three-hole regulation course for beginners and families, the state's largest outdoor saltwater pool, sea kayak rentals and tours, cruises, candlepin bowling, horseshoes, a play-

ground, a well-equipped fitness center, and as much or as little organized activity as you want. Spa services also are available. Sebasco Harbor Resort is open early May to late October.

Right on the beach between Popham Beach State Park and Fort Popham is the  **Popham Beach Bed & Breakfast** (4 Ocean View Ln., Popham Beach, Phippsburg 04562, 207/389-2409), a unique hostelry in a partly restored 1883 Coast Guard station. Innkeeper Peggy Johannessen takes guests to the rooftop lookout tower and shares the building's history as a maritime lifesaving center. Three rooms and a suite, two with gas fireplaces, go for $175–215 d. A two-course breakfast is served in the dining room each morning, and guests can hang out in the large oceanfront living room. Open all year.

Just south of the turnoff to Popham Beach, and close to the access for Morse Mountain, is **Edgewater Farm Bed & Breakfast** (71 Small Point Rd., Route 216, Sebasco Estates 04565, 207/389-1322 or 877/389-1322, www.edgewaterfarmbedandbreakfast.com), Carol and Bill Emerson's restored 19th-century farmhouse. Six

Mid-Coast Region

No, it's not a real lighthouse, but the views from rooms in Sebasco Harbor Resort's lighthouse building are real enough.

© TOM NANGLE

rooms and two suites with private baths go for $95–200 d. A brunch-sized breakfast served in the many-windowed solarium benefits from lots of organic produce grown on the four-acre grounds. (The Emersons always plant extra to donate to the Bath food pantry each summer.) And then there's the four-foot-deep *indoor lap pool*, a hot tub outside on the deck, and the Benedictine labyrinth Bill created in a wooded grove. English, Spanish, a bit of French, and German are all spoken.

Rock Gardens Inn (Rte. 218, Sebasco Estates, Phippsburg 04562, 207/389-1339, www.rockgardensinn.com) hosts numerous artists' workshops, and no wonder. It sits on its own peninsula, and the pretty grounds are landscaped with wild and cultivated flowers. Guests stay in one of three inn rooms or 10 cottages and have use of an outdoor heated pool and sea kayaks. Cottage rates begin at $120 pp and include breakfast and dinner—and the weekly lobster cookout. Sebasco Harbor Resort is just steps away, and guests have access to its facilities, too.

Joe and Debbie Braun have done a masterful job restoring **The 1774 Inn at Phippsburg** (44 Parker Head Rd., Phippsburg Center 04562, 207/389-1774, www.1774inn.com, $115–175), a four-square Georgian Colonial National Historic Register property with an ell and barn. Many Colonial details have been preserved, including window shutters with peep-holes and strong bars to defend against attack, paneled wainscoting, ceiling moldings, fluted columns, and wide pine floors. Most of the seven rooms (four in the main house, three in the ell, all but two with private bath), have views of the Kennebec River. Rooms are furnished with antiques or tasteful reproductions. Also on the premises is the Riverside Guest House, a four-bedroom, two-bath cottage available for $1,600 per week.

Georgetown Peninsula

Staying at Ⓜ **The Grey Havens Inn** (Seguinland Rd., P.O. Box 308, Georgetown 04548, 207/371-2616 or 800/431-2316, winter 517/439-4115, www.greyhavens.com) is like holing up at a classic seacoast summer home: National Historic Register Shingle-style building, huge screened veranda, tongue-and-groove paneling, lounge decorated in the style I usually call "early relative," honor bar. Bill and Haley Eberhart and their children keep everything up and running. They have 10 rooms; water views are especially spectacular from the turret rooms ($200 d). An oceanfront room with balcony is $230; other rooms (private and shared baths) are $100–145 d. There's a private dock with rowboats. Open early May to late October.

Almost next door and sharing the same fabulous island-studded view is **The Mooring Bed & Breakfast** (132 Seguinland Rd., Georgetown 04548, 207/371-2790 or 866/828-7348, www.themooringb-b.com, $150–180), the original home of Walter Reid, who donated Reid State Park to the state. It's been beautifully restored by his great-granddaughter and family. Each room has a water view and air-conditioning. Plenty of room to spread out, including the appropriately named Spanish room. A full breakfast is served.

Campgrounds

Plan to book a site in January if you want a waterfront campsite in midsummer at the Phippsburg Peninsula's **Hermit Island Campground** (6 Hermit Island Rd., Phippsburg 04566, 207/443-2101, www.hermitisland.com, winter mailing address 42 Front St., Bath 04530, same phone). With 275 campsites (no vehicles larger than pickup campers; no hookups) spread over a 255-acre causeway-linked island, this is oceanfront camping at its best. The well-managed operation has a store, snack bar, seasonal post office, boat rentals, boat excursions, trails, and seven private beaches. The hub of activity (and registration) is the Kelp Shed, next to the campsite entrance. No washing machines, but dryers are available. Rules are strictly enforced (no visitors allowed in the camping area). Open and wooded sites run $29–40 (two adults and two kids) mid-June to Labor Day, $27 a site early and late in the season. No credit cards. Reservations for a week's stay or longer and Memorial and Labor Day weekends can be made by mail beginning in early January and by phone in early February (call for exact date). Reservations for stays of less than one week are accepted as of March 1. Open mid-May through Columbus Day, but full operation is really June to Labor Day. The campground is at the tip of the Phippsburg Peninsula.

On Georgetown's Molly Point is Pat and Eric Kosalka's **Sagadahoc Bay Campground** (P.O. Box 171, Georgetown 04548, 207/371-2014, www.sagbaycaping.com), with both oceanfront and wooded sites, some with platforms ($30–47.50). Also on the premises is an oceanfront rental cabin ($125) and two cute-as-a-button fully equipped wood cabins, with bath, kitchenette, gas fireplace, and screened porch ($100). The campground has a small beach, rental kayaks, boat launch, and shorefront grills and picnic tables.

FOOD

Breakfast, Lunch, and Miscellany

For breakfast or lunch, drop into the **Starlight Café** (15 Lambard St., 207/443-3005, 7 A.M.–2 P.M. Mon.–Fri.), a too cute and too tiny daylight-basement space across a side street from the Customs House. Out front you might see a couple of old L.L. Bean boots planted with marigolds.

Here's a wonderful, multifaceted find. Susan Verrier and Kai Jacob's **M North Creek Farm** (24 Sebasco Rd., Phippsburg, 207/389-1341, 9 A.M.–6:30 P.M., lunch served 11:30 A.M.–3:30 P.M.) is an 1850s saltwater farm with fabulous organic gardens, including ornamental display gardens and lots of rugosa roses (a specialty—Susan has written two books). Visitors can meander down to a waterfall, creek, and salt marsh. Inside the barn is a small store stocked with garden and gourmet goodies and a small café, where Susan makes delicious soups and sandwiches to order ($5–7). There are tables indoors, but there also are chairs and tables scattered in the gardens. Pick up one of their illustrated catalogs, a fun read and you're almost guaranteed to find something you want. German spoken.

Pizza and Barbecue

Bath's best pizza comes from **The Cabin** (552 Washington St., Bath 04530, 207/443-6224, 10 A.M.–10 P.M. daily, to 11 P.M. Thurs.–Sat. year-round)—a local landmark since 1973. The white garlic sauce is outstanding, and the cheesesteak is about the best outside of Philly. A large three-topping pizza is $15. Order food to go or eat in at this decidedly casual place across from Bath Iron Works. Beer and wine license only. Reservations are wise Friday and Saturday evenings.

And its best barbecue comes from **Beale Street Barbeque & Grill** (215 Water St., Bath, 207/442-9514, 11 A.M.–9 P.M., to 10 P.M. July and Aug.). Finger-licking good, Memphis-style barbecue along with other Southern specialties, all served in big quantities and made on the premises, is served at this tiny spot, next to the municipal parking lot.

Casual Dining

Kate Winglass, a 10-year employee at Kristina's Restaurant and Bakery, purchased the operation with her husband, Andy, in 2004, changing its name to **M Mae's Café & Bakery** (160 Centre St., at High Street, Bath, 207/442-8577, 8 A.M.–9 P.M. Tues.–Sat. and 9 A.M.–3 P.M. Sun.). She actually improved upon the already super-successful operation. The menu has been slightly simplified, which has practically eliminated the lag between ordering and eating. Service is improved, prices have been slightly reduced, and the already pleasant dining areas seem even more so, with local art on the walls. The menu has retained its creative touches, and it's still *the* place to go for brunch (reservations essential on weekends). Dinner entrées are $14–20, but lighter fare and gourmet pizzas also begin at $8. There's often jazz in the upstairs lounge.

The Mediterranean theme at **M Maryellenz & Co.** (99 Commercial St., Bath, 207/442-0960, Tues.–Sat. beginning at 5 P.M.) allows for some whiffs of Maine (sautéed lobster tarragon, for instance, and fresh fish); there's a good selection of creative pasta dishes. Dine inside or on the patio. Entrée range is $8–24. Don't feel like dining in? Pick up a meal to go at Maryellenz Fresh Food Emporium (10 A.M.–6 P.M. Mon.–Fri.).

The View's the Thing

Gaze out at seals playing in the Kennebec River, over to Fort Popham, and out to open ocean from **Spinney's Restaurant** (Rte. 209, Popham

Mid-Coast Region

Beach, 207/389-2052, 8 A.M.–8:30 P.M., entrées $10–26). Food varies in quality from year to year (best advice: keep it simple), but you can't beat the view. Open mid-May to late October.

Bright, airy, and right on the riverfront, **Kennebec Tavern** (119 Commercial St., Bath, 207/442-9636, 11 A.M.–10 P.M. daily, to 11 P.M. Fri. and Sat.) is pleasant and informal, with a wide-ranging menu, entrées $12–22. Try for a table on the deck and watch the boats come and go.

The Sebasco Harbor Resort's **Pilot House** restaurant (Rte. 217, 207/389-1161, 7:30–9:30 A.M. and 6–9 P.M.), with a dramatic sunset water view, is also open to the public; dinner entrée range is $17–27. Below it, the patio at the casual **Ledges Pub** (11:30 A.M.–2 P.M. and 5–9 P.M., $6–18) is a late-day magnet, with indoor and outdoor seating.

Lobster-in-the-Rough

Phippsburg Peninsula: Overlooking the New Meadows River, **The Water's Edge Restaurant** (75 Black's Landing Rd., off Route 217, Sebasco Estates 04565, 207/389-1803, daily 11 A.M.–9 P.M. mid-May to Labor Day) is aptly named—and well worth a bit of effort to find it. The unassuming red-shingled place has indoor and deck dining, plus waterside picnic tables. Besides the usual lobster fare, you'll find steak and chicken dinners, sandwiches, and even salad plates. Unlike many lobster places, Water's Edge has a full liquor license and takes credit cards. Dining-room reservations are wise on weekends. Take Route 209 south from Bath 11 miles, then turn right onto Route 217. Continue beyond Sebasco Harbor Resort and make two left turns to the restaurant.

Back on Route 209, continue south and pick up Route 216. About 2.5 miles south of the Route 217 turnoff stands the rustic, buoy-draped **Lobster House** (395 Small Point Rd., Route 216, Small Point, 207/389-1596 or 207/389-2178, Tues.–Sat. 5–9 P.M., Sun. noon–8:30 P.M. mid-May to Labor Day). The windowed eating area, with open beams, overlooks a scenic tidal cove; the view is best when the tide's in.

Georgetown Peninsula: Just over a mile beyond the turnoff to Reid State Park, you'll reach the end of Route 127—at Five Islands. Here you'll find **Five Islands Lobster Company** (1447 Five Islands Rd., Five Islands, Georgetown 04548, 207/371-2990, 11:30 A.M.–8 P.M. daily Memorial Day–Sept.), known for its great slogan: "Eat on the dock with the fishermen but best avoid the table by the bait-shack door." Here you can pig out on lobster rolls, better-than-usual onion rings, even crab cakes. It even takes credit cards, a rarity among lobster wharves. Dress down, BYOL, and enjoy the end-of-the-road ambience of this idyllic spot.

Destination Dining

The building alone is worth a visit to the **Robinhood Free Meetinghouse** (210 Robinhood Rd., HC 33, Box 1469A, Georgetown 04548, 207/371-2188, www.robinhood-meetinghouse .com), a multistar restaurant in a beautifully restored 1855 building on the Georgetown Peninsula. Most tables are on the main floor; overflow diners go to the second floor, where many of the pews remain. The enormous (more than two dozen entrées, a dozen appetizers) high-quality menu makes it even more enticing. Noted chef Michael Gagne presides over the kitchen. Creativity is the menu byword for Gagne. If you're a chocoholic, save room for Gagne's to die for signature obsession in three chocolates with chocolate sauce. Entrées are in the $20–28 range, and portions are large. This isn't a setting for children, but the kitchen can come up with chicken fingers or fettuccine if necessary. Reservations are essential. Open daily 5:30–9 P.M. mid-May–mid-October, Thursday–Saturday mid-October through mid-May. In winter, ask about special "theme" nights. The restaurant is on the left, about a mile east of Route 127.

INFORMATION AND SERVICES

Information

The **Southern Midcoast Maine Chamber of Commerce** (207/725-8797) is good for information on lodgings, restaurants, and area activities (the office will have a new Topsham location in 2005; call for location and hours). The particularly useful *Bath/Brunswick Region Map and Guide* is

$2.50. A seasonal information center operated by volunteer members is on Route 1 at Witch Spring Hill (right side northbound from Brunswick to Bath, about a mile south of Bath). It's open weekends in May and daily all summer. Request copies of the *City of Bath Downtown Map and Guide* and the *Bath/Brunswick Region Map and Guide*. **Main Street Bath** (4 Centre St., Bath 04530, 207/442-7291, www.visitbath.com) produces a guide and has an informative website.

Local Library

Bath's **Patten Free Library** (33 Summer St., Bath 04530, 207/443-5141) has one of the state's most comfortable and elegant library reading rooms. It's entirely too easy to spend a rainy day hanging out here with the huge supply of newspapers and magazines. The library's outstanding Sagadahoc History and Genealogy Room draws genealogists from all over (open Mon.–Fri. noon–4 P.M.), and the Children's Room is especially kid-friendly. The library is open Monday–Friday 10 A.M.– 5 P.M. (to 8 P.M. Tues. and Thurs.).

Getting Around

The **Bath CityBus** circulates through the city, with each one-way trip costing $.60. Route 2 stops at the Maine Maritime Museum. All buses stop at City Hall, intersection of Front and Center Streets. For a schedule, visit City Hall (www.cityofbath.com).

Public Restrooms

Public restrooms are at Bath City Hall (55 Front St.), Patten Free Library (33 Summer St.), Sagadahoc County Courthouse (752 High St.), and (summer only) Waterfront Park, Commercial Street.

Wiscasset Area

Billing itself "The Prettiest Village in Maine," Wiscasset works hard to live up to its slogan, with quaint street signs, well-maintained homes, and an air of attentive elegance. Behind the scenes, however, it's actually a rather workaday community—not overrun with deep-pocketed retirees. The interesting mix includes artists, antique dealers, state government workers, worm diggers, and blue-collar types. And it seems to work.

Just east of Wiscasset, across the Donald Davey Bridge, is Edgecomb, a tiny town that primarily serves as a funnel to the Boothbay Peninsula. (Except for Route 1 Edgecomb locations, most of Edgecomb's handful of attractions and facilities are described in the *Boothbay Peninsula* section.)

The Davey Bridge, built in 1983, is the most recent span over the Sheepscot. The earliest, finished in 1847, was a toll bridge that charged a horse and wagon $.15 to cross, pedestrians $.03 each, and pigs $.01 apiece. Before that, ferries carried passengers, animals, and vehicles between Wiscasset and Edgecomb's Davis Island (then named Folly Island).

North and a bit east of Wiscasset are the lovely rural communities of Sheepscot and Alna, definitely worth a detour.

Wiscasset is notorious for midsummer gridlock. Especially on weekends, traffic backs up on Route 1 for miles in both directions—to the frustration of drivers, passengers, and Wiscasset merchants. The state Department of Transportation has tested traffic medians, stoplights, and other devices, but nothing seems to solve the problem. A bypass has been under discussion for years, but not-in-my-backyard opposition to every route has halted progress. (When you stop in town, try to park pointed in the direction you're going; it's impossible to make turns across oncoming traffic.)

HISTORIC SIGHTS AND MUSEUMS

In 1973, a large chunk of downtown Wiscasset was added to the National Register of Historic Places, and a walking tour is the best way to appreciate the Federal, Classical Revival, and even pre-Revolutionary homes and commercial buildings in the Historic District. Below are a few of the prime examples. If you do nothing else, be sure to swing by the homes on High Street.

Castle Tucker

Once known as the Lee-Tucker House, Castle Tucker (Lee St. and High St., Wiscasset 04578, 207/882-7169, Fri.–Sun. June to Oct. 15) is a must-see for historical house buffs. Built in 1807 by Judge Silas Lee, and bought by sea captain Richard Tucker in 1858, the imposing mansion has Victorian wallpaper and furnishings, Palladian windows, an amazing elliptical staircase, and a dramatic view over the Sheepscot River. In early 1997, Jane Tucker, Richard's granddaughter, magnanimously deeded the house to the Society for the Preservation of New England Antiquities (SPNEA). Tours begin on the hour 11 A.M.– 4 P.M. Admission is $5.

Nickels-Sortwell House

Also owned by SPNEA, the three-story Nickels-Sortwell House (Main St., Rte. 1, Wiscasset 04578, 207/882-6218, Fri.–Sun. June to Oct. 15) looms over Route 1, yet it's so close to the road many motorists miss it. Don't. Sea captain William Nickels commissioned the mansion in 1807 but died soon after its completion. For 70 or so years, it was the Belle Haven Hotel, before Alvin and Frances Sortwell's meticulous Colonial Revival restoration in the early 20th century. Tours begin on the hour 11 A.M.–4 P.M. Admission is $5.

Lincoln County Jail and Museum

Wiscasset's Old Jail, completed in 1811, was the first prison in the District of Maine (then part of Massachusetts). Amazingly, it remained a jail—mostly for short-termers—until 1953. Two years after that, the Lincoln County Historical Association took over, so each summer you can check out the 40-inch-thick granite walls, floors, and ceilings; the 12 tiny cells; and historic graffiti penned by the prisoners. Attached to the prison is the 1837 jailer's house, now the Lincoln County Museum, containing antique tools, the original kitchen, and various temporary exhibits. The complex is open 10 A.M.–4 P.M. Tuesday–Saturday and noon–4 P.M. Sunday July to Labor Day.

© TOM NANGLE

Sea captain William Nickels commissioned the mansion that bears his name in 1807. Alvin and Frances Sortwell meticulously restored the downtown Wiscasset landmark in the early 20th century. It's now open for tours.

RURAL RAMBLINGS

S urrounding Wiscasset are the lovely rural inland communities of Dresden, Sheepscot, and Alna, definitely worth a detour.

Begin in Dresden at the **Pownalborough Court House,** a pre-Revolutionary riverfront courthouse (River Rd., Rte. 128, Dresden Tues.–Sat. 10 A.M.–4 P.M. and Sun. noon–4 P.M. July and Aug., weekends only June and Sept., $4 adults, $2 kids 7–17). President John Adams once handled a trial here—in a mid-18th-century frontier community (named Pownalborough) established by French and German settlers. During the 30-minute tour of the three-story courthouse, guides delight in pointing out the restored beams, paneling, and fireplaces, as well as the on-site tavern that catered to judges, lawyers, and travelers. Walk a few hundred feet south of the dramatically sited courthouse and you'll find a cemetery with Revolution-era graves. Along the river is a nature trail developed by local Eagle Scouts. For more information, call or write **Lincoln County Historical Association** (Federal St., P.O. Box 61, Wiscasset 04578, 207/882-6817, www.lincolncountyhistory.org). From Route 1 in Wiscasset, take Route 27 about nine miles north to the junction with Route 128. Turn left (south) and go 2.5 miles to the courthouse sign. The courthouse is also an easy drive from Bath.

Return to Wiscasset and follow Route 218 north for about eight miles to **Head Tide Village,** an eminently picturesque hamlet at the farthest reach of Sheepscot River tides. From the late 18th century to the early 20th, Head Tide (now part of the town of Alna) was a thriving mill town, a source of hydropower for the textile and lumber industries. All that's long gone, but hints of that era come from the handful of well-maintained 18th- and 19th-century homes in the village center.

Up the hill, the stunning 1838 **Head Tide Church,** another fine example of local prosperity, is usually open 2–4 P.M. Saturday in July and August. Volunteer tour guides point out the original pulpit, a trompe l'oeil window, a kerosene chandelier, and walls lined with historic Alna photographs. An annual service is held at the church, usually the first Sunday in August.

Head Tide's most famous citizen was the poet **Edwin Arlington Robinson,** born here in 1869. His family home, at the bend in Route 194 and marked by a plaque, is not open to the public. Perhaps his Maine roots inspired these lines from his poem "New England":

Here where the wind is always north-north-east
And children learn to walk on frozen toes.

Just upriver from the bend in the road is a favorite swimming hole, a millpond where you can join the locals on a hot summer day. Not much else goes on here, and there are no restaurants or lodgings, so Head Tide can't be termed a destination, but it's a village frozen in time—and an unbeatable opportunity for history buffs and shutterbugs.

Also historic, but a bit more lively and fun for kids is the **Wiscasset, Waterville, and Farmington Railway** (97 Cross Road, off Rte. 218, Sheepscot, 207/882-4193, www.wwfry.org, 9 A.M.–5 P.M. Sat. year-round and Sun. late May to mid-Oct.). This museum commemorates a two-foot gauge common carrier railroad that operated in the early part of the 20th century, from Wiscasset in the south to Albion and Winslow in the north. The grounds hold a museum in the old station (free admission) and train rides along the mainline track running north from Cross Road, on the original roadbed ($5 adult, $3 kids 4–12). Trains run hourly on weekends 10 A.M.–4 P.M. Take Route 218 north 4.7 miles from Route 1 in Wiscasset to a four-way intersection and go left on Cross Road to the museum.

Admission is $4 adults, $2 ages 7–17. A Victorian gazebo, overlooking the Sheepscot River, is a great spot for a picnic. From Route 1 (Main Street) in downtown Wiscasset, take Federal Street (Route 218) 1.2 miles. For more information, contact **Lincoln County Historical Association** (Federal St., P.O. Box 61, Wiscasset 04578, 207/882-6817, www.lincolncountyhistory.org).

Musical Wonder House

The treasures in the Musical Wonder House (18 High St., P.O. Box 604, Wiscasset 04578, 207/882-7163, www.musicalwonderhouse.com), an 1852 sea captain's mansion, are indeed astonishing, and eccentric Austrian-born museum founder Danilo Konvalinka delights in sharing them—for a price. The best way to appreciate the collection of hundreds of 19th-century European music boxes, player pianos, and musical rarities is to take a guided tour (available 10 A.M.–5 P.M. late May–Oct., reduced schedule spring and fall), including two dozen player-piano and music-box demonstrations. A 35-minute tour is $8; the 75-minute tour is $15; a three-hour tour, by appointment only, is $30. A web-order sideline, offering music boxes and music-box and player-piano cassettes and CDs, continues year-round.

PARKS AND FARMS

Sunken Garden

Across Federal Street from the Nickels-Sortwell House in downtown Wiscasset is the lovely Sunken Garden, an almost-unnoticed pocket park created around the cellar hole of a long-gone inn. Bring a book or a picnic (or buy one across the street at Treat's) and ignore the traffic streaming by on Main Street.

Morris Farm

In 1995, a group of civic-minded citizens managed to stave off developers and buy the Morris Farm (Rte. 27, Gardiner Rd., P.O. Box 136, Wiscasset 04578, 207/882-4080, fax 207/882-7390, www.morrisfarm.org). Thanks to the energy of Morris Farm Trust members and the resident caretakers, the 60-acre working farm has become a community center for agriculture-related education and recreation, including workshops, a summer day-camp program, and an organic farmstand. Arrive here any day at 4:30 P.M. and you can watch the milking of the Jersey herd. In winter, there's a workshop and lecture series in the farm's Learning Center. In spring, there's an Easter egg hunt ($5 per child), including egg coloring with natural dyes, visiting all the spring newborns in the barn, and the hunt itself. In summer, there's a pick-your-own raspberry patch. Always, dawn to dusk, the farm is open for walking, hiking, and picnicking. The trails connect to the 83-acre Sortwell Memorial Forest trails. A popular annual event is the **Tour de Farms,** which attracts dozens of bike riders for several different routes. Along the way are stops at various local farms, followed by a wrap-up barbecue at the Morris Farm. The ride takes place mid- to late August. The Morris Farm is three-quarters of a mile from Route 1 (turn onto Route 27 next to the Wiscasset Municipal Building).

Winters Gone Farm

Everything you wanted to know about alpacas is presented at the Winters Gone Farm (245 Alna Rd., Rte. 218, Wiscasset, 207/882-9191 or 800/645-0188, www.wintersgonefarm.com, 10 A.M.–6 P.M.). Begin with an informative video, then walk the trails around the pastures to see these funky critters. Bring a lunch to enjoy in the picnic area by the pond. In the store you can buy alpaca apparel and merchandise and even ask about buying an alpaca—talk about a unique souvenir! To get to the farm from Route 1 in Wiscasset, take Federal Street/Route 218, opposite the post office, and follow it 2.5 miles.

RECREATION

Sports Outfitter

Registered Maine Guide and Sea Kayak Guide Kurt Geib is the man behind **Frozen Paddler** (271 Old Bath Rd., Wiscasset, 207/882-9066, www.frozenpaddler.com), which offers canoeing, kayaking, winter camping, hiking, skiing, and snowshoeing adventures. Here's a sampling. A two-hour lake tour via canoe, kayak, or rowing canoe is $25, four hours is $45, and a full day is

$90, including boat and snacks or lunch. A four-hour river tour is $50, a full day is $95. Sea kayak tours are $35 for two hours (family oriented), $75 for four hours, and $95 for a full day. Canoe or sea kayak overnights are $125 per day. Winter snowshoe tours range from $30 for two hours to $70 for a full day. Winter overnights are $130 per day. Geib also rents equipment for those who want to do it themselves. Canoes are $25–40 per day; sea kayaks are $40–55 (experience required), snowshoes are $8–12. He also rents all manner of camping gear.

SHOPPING

Antiques and Collectibles

It's certainly fitting that a town filled end-to-end with antique homes should have more than two dozen solo and group antique shops. Most are at the eastern end of town, between High Street and the Sheepscot River; a few are at the western end of town. Most do cooperative advertising, so newspapers and shops have ads and brochures listing them all.

Right downtown, **The Marston House** (Main St. and Middle St., Wiscasset 04578, 207/882-6010) specializes in textiles, furniture, and accessories and caters to serious dealers and collectors. The owners travel to France each year and return with all sorts of finds.

High-quality American antiques are the specialty at **Priscilla Hutchinson** (62 Pleasant St., Wiscasset 04578, 207/882-4200), in an attractive carriage house half a block from Route 1.

Art Galleries

European and American 19th- and 20th-century painters are the broad focus at **Wiscasset Bay Gallery** (67 Main St./Rte. 1, P.O. Box 309, Wiscasset 04578, 207/882-7682 or 888/622-9445), which schedules high-quality rotating shows throughout the season.

In the handsome open spaces of an early-19th-century brick schoolhouse, the **Maine Art Gallery** (Warren St., P.O. Box 315, Wiscasset 04578, 207/882-7511) was founded in 1957 as a nonprofit corporation to showcase contemporary Maine artists.

Gifts, Crafts, and Miscellany

The oldest commercial building in town is **Wiscasset Hardware** (Water St., Wiscasset 04578, 207/882-6622), built in 1797 as a ship chandlery on the east side of Water Street. Since 1949, the Stetson family has run this hardware-plus business. (The "plus" part is a general store with antiques, souvenirs, and Maine products. Do your gift shopping here; there's plenty of variety.) Request a free town map and check out the great view from the river-view deck, where you can buy sandwiches, hot dogs, ice cream, and coffee.

The Butterstamp Workshop (55 Middle St., Wiscasset 04578, 207/882-7825) not only creates and sells designs copied from antique molds, but is also a source of hard-to-find gravestone-rubbing supplies. Plus sometimes you can watch the workshop operation, which produces butter and cookie molds, beeswax ornaments, even magnets.

Rock, Paper, Scissors (78 Main St., Wiscasset, 207/882-9930) is a stylish paper store with a terrific selection and interesting array of products.

Sinks, serving bowls, vases, and lamps are just some of the finely glazed objects available at **Sheepscot River Pottery** (Rte. 1, Davis Island, Edgecomb 04556, 207/882-9410 or 800/659-4794), just across the river from Wiscasset. The Maine Island pattern is especially striking.

Discount Shopping

Carving out a unique niche is **Big Al's Super Values** (Rte. 1, Wiscasset 04578, 207/882-6423), a catchall emporium specializing in odd lots, closeouts, funky souvenirs, and half-priced birthday cards. Bargains galore, plus free coffee, restroom, and a gift. Some tourism brochures are also available here. Three miles south of Wiscasset, across from The Sea Basket Restaurant.

FESTIVALS AND EVENTS

Wiscasset's daylong **Annual Strawberry Festival and Country Fair** celebrates with tons of strawberries, plus crafts and an auction at St. Philip's Episcopal Church (Hodge St., 207/882-7184), the last Saturday in June.

In early July, the daylong **Morris Farm Fair** takes place at the nonprofit community Morris

Farm on Route 27 and includes animal exhibits, farm tours, crafts, games, and food. St. Philip's Episcopal Church on Hodge Street is the site of **Monday night fish-chowder suppers,** mid-July to mid-August. Reservations are advised (207/882-7184) for these very popular 5:30 P.M. suppers.

ACCOMMODATIONS

B&Bs

Wiscasset isn't loaded with B&Bs, but the choices are intriguing.

Named after a famous Maine clipper ship, the **Snow Squall B&B** (5 Bradford Rd. at Rte. 1, P.O. Box 730, Wiscasset 04578, 207/882-6892 or 800/775-7245, www.snowsquallinn.com) is a renovated mid-19th-century house with four lovely rooms and two suites, all with phones, most with air-conditioning, two with fireplaces ($100–220, including full breakfast). Rooms are named for clipper ships, and the gathering room even has a glass case with a *Snow Squall* relic, retrieved from the ship's Falkland Islands wreckage. The suites, in the adjacent carriage house, each sleep four. Open all year, but only by reservation November through April.

Attached to The Marston House antique shop, **M The Marston House B&B** (Main St. and Middle St., Wiscasset 04578, 207/882-6010, www.marstonhouse.com) has two good-sized rooms for $90 d in the carriage house out back (away from Route 1 traffic noise). Each has a fireplace, private bath, and private entrance on Middle Street. The rooms can be connected to form a suite. A breakfast basket is delivered each morning, which you can enjoy in the garden. Open May through October.

Then there's a major getaway—**The Squire Tarbox Inn** (1181 Main Rd., Route 144, Westport Island 04578, 207/882-7693 or 800/818-0626, www.squiretarboxinn.com), an elegantly casual B&B/inn. Accomplished Swiss chef-owner Mario De Pietro and his wife, Roni, have continued the inn's reputation for dining excellence. Eleven lovely rooms, some with fireplaces, are divided between the late-18th-century main house and the early-19th-century carriage house.

Doubles are $95–190, including breakfast. Three-course dinners (open to the public by reservation; $32–38) are memorable and preceded by hors d'oeuvres. Also on the property are walking paths, a rowboat, mountain bikes, a working pottery, and a working farm, with organic vegetable gardens, chickens, and goats. Open April through December. From downtown Wiscasset, head southwest four miles on Route 1 to Route 144. Turn left and go about 8.5 scenic miles to the inn.

Motels

Fairly close to Route 1 but buffered a bit by century-old hemlocks, the **Wiscasset Motor Lodge** (Rte. 1, R.R. 3, Box 911, Wiscasset 04578, 207/882-7137 or 800/732-8168, www.wiscassetmotorlodge.com) is a comfortable, well-maintained motel/cottage colony. The 10-acre complex, open April–November, has six tiny cottages and 19 motel rooms for $60–105. Cable TV and air-conditioning in all units; phones in motel rooms; free light breakfast in summer. Ask for a room in the back building if you're sensitive to noise.

FOOD

Lunch and Miscellany

Red's Eats (Main St. and Water St., Wiscasset 04578, 207/882-6128, 11 A.M.–11 P.M. Mon.–Sat. and noon–6 P.M. Sun. early May to mid-Oct.) is a takeout stand, but don't let that dissuade you. It's been here for decades (formerly Al's Eats), and there's always a line for hot dogs, lobster rolls, pocket sandwiches, and more. If you're planning on one of Red's lobster rolls, ask someone who's just purchased one the price before you get in line and make sure you have enough cash (no credit cards). It can be expensive, especially if you're ordering lobster rolls for a group. The few tables on the sidewalk and behind the building, overlooking the river, are seldom empty (except in bad weather), but it's only a quick walk across Main to picnic tables (and a public restroom) on the Town Wharf.

Tucked behind Wiscasset Bay Gallery is **River Dog** (54-D Water St., Wiscasset, 207/882-5444,

Pick up lunch or dinner at Red's Eats, a popular downtown Wiscasset take-out stand, then head for the waterfront.

Mid-Coast Region

7:30 A.M.–2 P.M., to 9 P.M. Thurs.–Sun.), a pleasant café serving soups, sandwiches, and other inexpensive fare.

Back up the street, across from the post office, is **Treat's** (Main St., Box 156, Wiscasset 04578, 207/882-6192, 10 A.M.–6 P.M. Mon.–Sat., 10 A.M.–5 P.M. Sun. all year), a superb source of gourmet picnic fixings: sandwiches, soups, wine, cheese, condiments, and artisanal breads. You won't leave here empty-handed, even when you aren't hungry.

Two miles southwest of downtown Wiscasset, **The Sea Basket Restaurant** (Rte. 1, Wiscasset 04578, 207/882-6581, 11 A.M.–8 P.M. daily, reduced hours and days off-season) has been serving hearty bowls of lobster stew and good-sized baskets of eminently fresh seafood since 1981. Three hundred pounds of scallops get devoured here each week, and the lobster stew is so popular it's available by mail order. There's always a crowd—locals eat here, too—so expect to wait. Picnic tables are outside, a few tables inside. Best plan is to order lunch to go, wait for your number to be called, and head for the picnic tables on the Wiscasset waterfront. (If traffic looks heavy, though, stay here; it could take ages to get to the waterfront.)

Casual Dining

Two waterfront restaurants get high marks for their views.

In a high-visibility location across Route 1 from Red's Eats, **Sarah's Cafe** (Main St. and Water St., Rte. 1, Wiscasset 04578, 207/882-7504, 11 A.M.–8 P.M. Mon.–Fri., 7:30 A.M.–9 P.M. Sat. and Sun.) is the home of huge "whaleboat" and "dory" sandwiches, homemade soups (self-serve), pizza, vegetarian specials, and an ice cream fountain. Lobster meat shows up in salads, burritos, quesadillas, wraps, croissants, and more. The deck has front-row seats on the Sheepscot River. Beer and wine license, air-conditioning.

Also overlooking the water is **Le Garage** (15 Water St., Wiscasset 04578, 207/882-5409, 11:30 A.M.–2:30 P.M. and 5–8:30 P.M. Tues.–Sat., 11 A.M.–8 P.M. Sun.), which has upper and lower enclosed porch/decks. Request a porch/deck table, and dine by candlelight. Lamb is a specialty, as is finnan haddie (entrée range is $10–20); light suppers are thrifty choices. Reservations are wise on weekends; this is an enduringly popular spot. The restaurant is two blocks off Route 1.

INFORMATION AND SERVICES

Information

The **Wiscasset Regional Business Association** (WRBA, P.O. Box 150, Wiscasset 04578, www.wiscassetmaine.com) is the local information clearinghouse. The best place to find the annual WRBA booklet is the display rack at Big Al's Super Values, three miles southwest of downtown. Once you get into town, stop at Wiscasset Hardware for a free walking map of the downtown area. Another resource is the **Wiscasset Town Hall** (Rte. 1, Wiscasset 04578, 207/882-8205), in the brick municipal building at the western end of town. It's open weekdays.

Local Library

The brick **Wiscasset Public Library** (High St.,

Wiscasset 04578, 207/882-7161), built as a bank in 1805, is a lively year-round operation, with book-discussion groups, children's story hours, a small art collection, and an annual used-book sale. Hours are 10 A.M.–5 P.M. Tuesday–Friday (to 7 P.M. Wednesday) and 9 A.M.–2 P.M. Saturday from Labor Day to July 1.

Public Restrooms

The Town Wharf, Water Street, and the Lincoln County Court House, on Route 1 next to the sharp curve as you come down the hill from the south, have public restrooms.

Getting Around

Concord Trailways (800/639-3317, www.concordtrailways.com) stops in Brunswick, Bath, Wiscasset, Damariscotta, and Waldoboro on its three daily nonexpress trips up the coast.

Boothbay Peninsula

East of Wiscasset, en route to Damariscotta, only a flurry of signs along Route 1 in Edgecomb (pop. around 1,000) hints at what's down the peninsula bisected by Route 27. Drive southward down the Boothbay Peninsula between Memorial Day and Labor Day and you'll find yourself in one of Maine's longest-running summer playgrounds.

The four peninsula towns of Boothbay (pop. 2,675), Boothbay Harbor (pop. 2,165), East Boothbay, and, connected by a bridge, Southport Island (pop. 590) have sightseeing and whale-watching excursions, a first-rate small aquarium, an antique-railway museum, wall-to-wall shops, scads of restaurants and beds, and quiet preserves for escaping the inevitable mid-summer crowds.

When Route 27 arrives at the water, having passed through Boothbay Center, you're at the hub, Boothbay Harbor ("the Harbor"), scene of most of the action. The harbor itself is a boat fan's dream, loaded with working craft and pleasure yachts. Ashore, you'll face one-way streets, traffic congestion, and pedestrians everywhere. But there's plenty in this area to appreciate. Parking areas are noted on the Boothbay Harbor Re-

gion Chamber of Commerce's walking map; just be prepared to shell out about $3–5 for the day.

Try to save time for quieter spots: East Boothbay, Ocean Point, Southport Island, or even just over the 1,000-foot-long footbridge stretching across one corner of the harbor. Cross the bridge and walk down Atlantic Avenue to the Fishermen's Memorial, a bronze fishing dory commemorating the loss of hardy souls who've earned a rugged living here by their wits and the sea. Across the street is Our Lady Queen of Peace Catholic Church, with shipwright-quality woodwork and its own fishing icon—a lobster trap next to the altar.

In the 1870s, when many scenic coastal areas experienced an influx of steamboat-borne rusticators from the Boston area and beyond, the Boothbay region entered its tourism phase—an era that shows no indication of coming to a close.

SIGHTS

Fort Edgecomb

Before turning off Route 1 for the Boothbay Peninsula, make a quick, interesting detour in Edgecomb, immediately east of the Wiscasset bridge, to historic Fort Edgecomb—perfect for a riverfront picnic. Afterward, back roads can connect you to Route 27 for Boothbay and Boothbay Harbor, but it's less confusing to return to Route 1, continue a bit east, and turn onto Route 27.

Built in 1808 to protect the Sheepscot River port of Wiscasset, the Fort Edgecomb State Historic Site (Eddy Rd., Edgecomb, 207/882-7777, $2 adults, $1 children 5–11) occupies a splendid, three-acre riverfront spread ideal for picnicking and fishing (no swimming). Many summer weekends, the Revolutionary encampments on the grounds of the octagonal blockhouse make history come alive with reenactments, period dress, craft demonstrations, and garrison drills. The fort officially is open 9 A.M.–5 P.M. daily Memorial Day weekend to Labor Day, but the grounds are easily accessible all year. From Route 1 at the Sheepscot River Inn, take Eddy Road and go one-half mile to Fort Road.

Ride the Rails

Boothbay Railway Village (Rte. 27, Boothbay, 207/633-4727, www.railwayvillage.org, $8 adults, $4 children under 16) feels like a life-sized train set. More than two dozen old and new buildings have been assembled here since the museum was founded, in 1964, and a restored narrow-gauge steam train makes a 1.5-mile, 20-minute circuit throughout the day. Among the structures are a toy shop, a one-room schoolhouse, a chapel, a barbershop, a 19th-century town hall, two railroad stations, and a firehouse. You'll also find more than four dozen antique cars and trucks. The gift shop stocks train-oriented

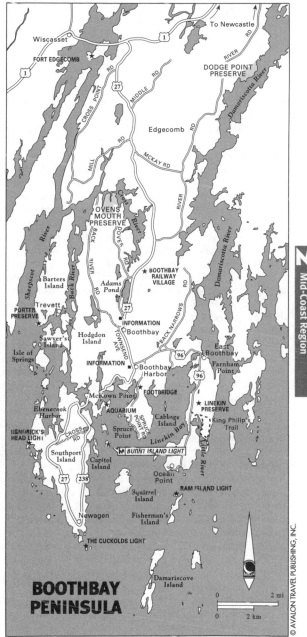

items. During the summer, special events include an antique auto meet (mid-July weekend), Children's Day (third Sunday in August), and the Columbus Day weekend fall foliage festival. The village is open 9:30 A.M.–5 P.M. daily mid-June to Columbus Day; train rides also operate on Memorial Day weekend, early June weekends, and the last weekend in October (a ghostly Halloween ride). The village is 3.5 miles north of downtown Boothbay Harbor, 7.5 miles south of Route 1.

Feel the Fish

A 20-foot touch tank, with slimy but pettable specimens, is a major kid magnet at the **Marine Resources Aquarium** (McKown Point Rd., West Boothbay Harbor, 207/633-9559, www.maine.gov /dmr, $5 adults, $3 ages 5–18 and 60 and older), operated by the state Department of Marine Resources. Exhibits in the hexagonal aquarium include rare lobsters (oversize, albino, and blue) and other Gulf of Maine creatures, and new residents arrive periodically. Self-guiding leaflets are available. In July and August, marine scientists present free daily programs. The aquarium is open daily 10 A.M.–5 P.M. Memorial Day weekend through September. Consider bringing a picnic—it's a great setting. At the height of summer, parking is limited, and it's a longish walk from downtown around the west side of the harbor, so plan to take the free local trolley-bus, departing on the half hour from the Meadow Mall (many locals still call it the Small Mall, its former name) or from one of the downtown trolley-bus stops.

Southport Island Highlights

A historic 1810 Cape-style building, carefully restored, is the home of the **Hendricks Hill Museum** (Rte. 27, West Southport, 207/633-4831), a community attic filled with all kinds of workaday tools and utensils and fascinating maritime memorabilia. The 11-room museum is open 11 A.M.– 3 P.M. Tuesday, Thursday, and Saturday July to Labor Day. During September, call for an appointment. Admission is free, but donations are welcomed. The museum is about two miles south of the Southport Island bridge, on the right, in the center of West Southport.

Continuing down Route 27 toward Cape

Newagen, stop at the **Southport Memorial Library** (207/633-2741). Here's a rare, surprising treat: a huge collection of beautifully mounted butterflies once owned by Dr. and Mrs. Stanley Marr. The library is open 9 A.M.–4 P.M. and 7–9 P.M. Tuesday and Thursday, plus 1–4 P.M. Saturday, all year.

Also worthy of a stop is the **Kenneth E. Stoddard Shell Museum** (Rte. 27, 207/633-4828, 10 A.M.–10 P.M. May–mid-Sept.). Inside are thousands of shells, including many from the Pacific.

Ⓜ Burnt Island Tour

Explore an island, visit with a lighthouse-keeper's family, and climb the tower into the lantern room during this living- and natural-history program presented by the **Maine Department of Marine Resources** (207/633-9580, www.maine.gov /dmr/education/lighthousetour.htm, $20 adult, $12 kids under 12). The tour is offered twice daily from late June to early September. Travel via excursion boat from 21st-century Boothbay Harbor to Burnt Island, circa 1950, where actors portray the family of lighthouse-keeper Joseph Muise, who lived here 1936–1951. During the three-hour program, you'll spend time with the lightkeeper, his wife, and each of his children while learning about their lifestyle and views on island life. Historical documents, photographs, and lenses, from 1821 to the present, are displayed in the 45-foot covered walkway between the house and tower. You may climb the spiral stairway up to the lantern room to see how the lighthouse actually functions. On an easy hike, a naturalist explains the island's flora, fauna, and geology and recounts legends, including one about a sea serpent. During free time, you may hike other trails, listen to a program on present-day lobstering and Maine fisheries, go beachcombing, fish for mackerel off the dock, or just relax and enjoy it all.

PARKS AND PRESERVES

Boothbay Region Land Trust

Courtesy of the very active Boothbay Region Land Trust (BRLT), about 900 acres on the peninsula and nearby islands have been preserved for wildlife, residents, and visitors. Twenty miles of trails are open to the public in various preserves. Individual preserve maps, as well as a general brochure/map with driving directions, are available at the information centers or at the BRLT office (1 Oak St., P.O. Box 183, Boothbay Harbor 04538, 207/633-4818, www.bbrlt.org, 9 A.M.–noon Mon., Wed., and Fri. all year). Inquire at the office about summertime guided walks in the various preserves. Kiosks at the trailheads hold preserve maps. There are no trash receptacles, so carry a litterbag and help the BRLT and everyone who follows you. To do even more, make a cash donation to the BRLT (any amount is welcome).

Most popular is the **Porter Preserve,** a 19-acre property bordering the Sheepscot River. Follow the moderately easy .86-mile loop trail and be rewarded with spectacular views, especially at sunset. You might even spy some seals lolling in the ledges at low tide. To get there, take Route 27 south to the monument in Boothbay Center. Bear right on Cory Lane and go .3 mile, bearing right again on Barters Island Road. Follow it 12.2 miles (perhaps stopping at the Barters Island General Store for lobster rolls or subs to go), then go left on Kimballtown Road. Go 0.5 miles and turn left at the fork onto Porter Point Road. Park in the small lot just beyond the cemetery.

Also popular is the 146-acre **Ovens Mouth Preserve,** with almost 5 miles of trails on two peninsulas linked by a 93-foot bridge (wear insect repellent). The 1.6-mile trail on the east peninsula is much easier than the 3.7 miles of trails on the west peninsula. To get there, from the monument in Boothbay Center, travel 1.7 miles north, then go left on Adams Pond Road. Bear right at the fork, then continue 2.2 miles. To get to the east peninsula, bear right at the junction onto the Dover Road Extension. Proceed to the end of the tarred road to the parking lot on the left. To get to the west peninsula, bear left and the junction and continue .15 miles to the parking area on the right.

In East Boothbay, on the way to Ocean Point, is the 95-acre **Linekin Preserve,** stretching from Route 96 to the Damariscotta River. The 2.3-mile, white-blazed River Loop (best done clock-

wise) takes in an old sawmill site, a beaver dam, and great riverfront views. You'll meet a couple of moderately steep sections on the eastern side, near the river, but otherwise it's relatively easy. To get there, take Route 96 3.8 miles and look for the parking area and trailhead on the left.

Coastal Maine Botanical Gardens

Still in its embryonic phase but growing quickly are these shorefront gardens (Barters Island Rd., Boothbay, office at Old Firehouse, Rte. 27, Boothbay, 207/633-4333, www.mainegardens.org), a nonprofit project designed to preserve more than 125 acres of woodlands with a trail network and landscaped pocket "theme" gardens. A visitors center is scheduled to open in 2006; in the meantime, follow signs to visitor parking, then look for mailboxes, which contain maps and brochures. There are portable toilets near the parking areas. Entrance to the preserve (watch for two stone pillars and a sign) is on Barters Island Road, about 1.3 miles west of Boothbay Center.

Damariscove Island

Summering Wabanakis knew it as Aquahega, but Damerill's Cove was the first European name attributed to the secure, fjordlike harbor at the southern tip of 209-acre Damariscove Island in 1614, when Captain John Smith of the Jamestown Colony explored the neighborhood. By 1622, Damerill's Cove fishermen were sharing their considerable codfish catch with starving Plimoth Plantation colonists desperate for food. Fishing and farming sustained resident Damariscovers during their up-and-down history, and archaeologists have found rich deposits for tracing the story of this early island settlement about seven miles south of Boothbay Harbor.

Rumors persist that the ghost of Captain Richard Pattishall, decapitated and tossed overboard by Indians in 1689, still roams the island, accompanied by the specter of his dog. The fog that often overhangs the low-slung, bleak, almost-treeless island makes it easy to fall for the many ghost stories about Pattishall and other onetime residents. In summer, the island is awash with wildflowers, bayberries, raspberries, black-berries, and rugosa roses.

Since 1966, most of 1.7-mile-long Damariscove has been owned by The Nature Conservancy. Day-use visitors are welcome on the island any-time, but the northern section (called Wood End) is off-limits March 15–August 15 to protect the state's largest nesting colony of eiders—nearly 700 nests. Damariscove Island became a National His-toric Landmark in 1978. Dogs are not allowed.

Access to the island is most convenient if you have your own boat. Enter the narrow cove at the southern end of the island and disembark at the Nature Conservancy dock on the west side of the harbor. Summertime caretakers live in the small cabin above the dock, where a trail map is available. Stay on the trail (watch out for poison ivy) or on the shore and away from any aban-doned structures; the former Coast Guard station is privately owned.

For information about Damariscove Island, contact **The Nature Conservancy** (Fort An-dross, 14 Maine St., Suite 401, Brunswick 04011, 207/729-5181, fax 207/729-4118). The Booth-bay Harbor Region Chamber of Commerce (Rte. 27, P.O. Box 356, Boothbay Harbor 04538, 207/633-2353, fax 207/633-7448, www.booth-bayharbor.com) can provide information on get-ting to the island.

Sherman Lake Rest Area

About four miles east of Wiscasset on Route 1 (in the town of Newcastle) is the state-operated Sher-man Lake Rest Area, a scenic spot with picnic ta-bles, toilets, and a dog-walking area. Bring a kayak or canoe and paddle around the mile-long lake. Birders should have good luck spotting wa-terfowl. Open all year.

RECREATION

The **Boothbay Region YMCA** (Rte. 27, Booth-bay Harbor, 207/633-2855), an impressive com-plex, has a pool, fitness center, sauna, racquetball and tennis courts, indoor jogging track, and aer-obics classes. Scuba certification classes are held in June and July, and the summer sports camps for kids (preregistration required) are terrific. Call

the Y for racquetball reservations or to reserve one of the municipal tennis courts, just south of the Boothbay Region High School. Daily guest passes ($10 adult, $15 family) are available.

Bicycling

If you haven't brought your own bike, the local rental source is **Tidal Transit Company** (Chowder House Bldg., Boothbay Harbor, 207/633-7140, www.kayakboothbay.com), near the footbridge. Cost is $25 a day, $15 a half-day; helmet and lock are included.

When you're ready to take your bike on the road, head for one of the chamber of com-merce information centers and pick up a copy of the bike route for the 31-mile Barters Is-land/Southport loop (also a fine driving itin-erary). Pack a picnic. Allow a full day to bike it, including stops and detours. The terrain is mostly easy and relatively level, but many stretches are narrow and winding, with poor shoulders, so it's *essential* to follow biking rules and exercise caution.

An alternate loop route, about 15 miles long, follows only the Southport Island section, from downtown Boothbay Harbor. If you're biking with kids, opt for this itinerary—but make sure they know the rules of the road, too. Again, take a picnic, or plan to stop at the Southport General Store (Rte. 27, 207/633-6666), about two miles south of the bridge. Also check out the nearby historic cemetery, the Hendricks Hill Museum, and the Hendricks Head Light (go west on Beach Road from the general store; the light is privately owned, so don't trespass).

When crossing the swing bridge that spans Townsend Gut, between West Boothbay Har-bor and Southport Island, be especially cautious. The surface can be a bear trap for bike tires.

Another good biking (and driving) route begins at the junction of Routes 27 and 96, going through East Boothbay, then on down to Ocean Point, where the Shore Road loop skirts the rocky shoreline. (Ocean Point is about six miles from the Route 27/96 crossroads.) About halfway down Linekin Neck toward Ocean Point, hang a left onto King Philip's Trail, then left onto the loop road, clockwise, through the hamlet of Little

River, returning to Route 96. Like the Southport Island route, the roads are narrow and winding along Linekin Neck, and traffic can be heavy at the height of summer. Early morning is a great time to bike here; park your car in the Hannaford supermarket lot, the Meadow Mall, or the YMCA, back on Route 27 at the entrance to Boothbay Harbor.

Excursion Boats

Two major fleet operators provide practically every type of sea adventure imaginable. Boothbay Harbor's veteran excursion fleet is **Cap'n Fish's Cruises** (Pier 1, Wharf St., Boothbay Harbor, 207/633-3244 or 207/633-2626 or 800/636-3244). In addition to whale-watching trips, Cap'n Fish's 150-passenger boats do nine varied, mostly two- to three-hour cruises. There's bound to be a length and itinerary (seal-watching, lobster-trap hauling, lighthouses, Damariscove, puffin cruises, and more) that piques your interest. Pick up a schedule at one of the information centers and call for reservations.

The harbor's other big fleet is **Balmy Days Cruises** (Pier 8, Commercial St., Boothbay Harbor, 207/633-2284 or 800/298-2284, www.balmy dayscruises.com), operating three vessels. The *Novelty* does about seven one-hour **harbor tours** daily from late June to Labor Day; cost is $10 adults, $5 children. Reservations usually are unnecessary. The 31-foot Friendship sloop *Bay Lady* does five 90-minute **sailing trips** daily in summer. Cost is $18 pp. Reservations are wise for the *Bay Lady* as well as for the fleet's most popular cruise, a daylong trip to Monhegan Island on the *Balmy Days II*, departing daily at 9:30 A.M. and returning at 4:15 P.M., early June through September, plus weekends in late May and early October. The three-hour round-trip allows about 3.5 hours ashore on idyllic Monhegan Island. Cost is $30 adults, $18 children 3–11. You're headed 12 miles offshore on the Monhegan trip, so be sure to dress warmly, wear sturdy walking/hiking shoes, and take a camera and binoculars.

Sailing

Sail aboard *Schooner Eastwind*, a 65-foot traditional wooden schooner built in 2004, with

Appledore Cruises (20 Commercial St. Boothbay Harbor, 207/633-6598, www.fishermans wharfinn.com). Herb and Doris Smith take passengers on 2.5-hour cruises to the outer islands and Seal Rocks, up to four times daily, for $22. The boat departs from Fisherman's Wharf.

Whale-Watching

Variations in Gulf of Maine whale-migration patterns have added whale-watching to the list of Boothbay Harbor boating options as the massive mammals travel northeastward within reasonable boating distance. **Cap'n Fish's** (Pier 1, Wharf St., Boothbay Harbor 04538, 207/633-3244 or 207/633-2626, or 800/636-3244) is the best choice. Three- to four-hour trips depart daily mid-June to mid-October. Cost is $28 adults, $15 kids 6–12, with a raincheck if the whales don't show up. Reservations are advisable, especially early and late in the season and on summer weekends. No matter what the weather on shore, dress warmly and carry more clothing than you think you'll need. Motion-sensitive children and adults need to plan for appropriate medication.

Sea Kayaking

From Memorial Day weekend through September, **Tidal Transit** (18 Granary Way, Chowder House Bldg., Boothbay Harbor, 207/633-7140), near the footbridge, will get you afloat with a two- to three-hour guided lighthouse or wildlife tour for $35. A sunset tour concluding with a lobsterbake is $65. No experience is necessary. Reservations are required. For do-it-yourselfers, Tidal Transit rents single kayaks for $15 an hour or $50 a day, tandems for $25 an hour, $75 a day; other time options are available.

On the other side of the harbor, **East Boothbay Kayak Co.** (Rte. 96, East Boothbay, 207/633-7411 or 866/633-7411, www.eastboothbaykayaks .com) provides rentals and gives guided tours. Rentals range from $12 single to $20 tandem per hour; $50–75 per day. Delivery is available in the Boothbay region for $20, including pickup. Tours are $35 for two hours, $50 for four hours; sunset tours are $25. Private tours also are available beginning at $40 pp for two hours. The shop is next to the post office.

SHOPPING

Artisans' galleries pepper the peninsula. Galleries, boutiques, T-shirt stores, and novelty shops crowd Boothbay Harbor, providing plenty of browsing for all budgets and tastes. Here's just a sampling.

Art and Craft Galleries

Gleason Fine Art (31 Townsend Ave., Boothbay Harbor, 207/633-6849) is one of Maine's top retail venues for 19th- through 21st-century painting and sculpture.

The nonprofit **Boothbay Region Art Foundation** (7 Townsend Ave., Boothbay Harbor, 207/633-2703) mounts five juried shows of members' work, plus a student art show during the season.

Also downtown is the **Gold/Smith Gallery** (41 Commercial St., Boothbay Harbor, 207/633-6252), featuring intriguing gold jewelry and contemporary paintings.

The area's veteran craft shop is **Abacus** (12 McKown St., Boothbay Harbor, 207/633-2166 or 800/206-2166). Great stuff—functional items, wearable art, and charming doodads—high-end American crafts from several hundred artisans.

Three miles south of Route 1 is the **Iron and Silk Forge and Gallery** (Rte. 27, Edgecomb, 207/882-4055), the 400-square-foot retail shop for Elizabeth Derecktor's hand-painted silk scarves and clothing and Peter Brown's high-end handwrought weathervanes, chandeliers, and fireplace tools.

It's hard not to stop at the wonderful **Edgecomb Potters Gallery** (Rte. 27, Edgecomb, 207/882-9493), filled with amazingly beautiful pottery as well as high-end crafts.

Juried works from 25 Maine artists are shown at **Boothbay Harbor Artisans** (11 Granary Way, Boothbay Harbor, 207/633-1152).

The working metalsmiths at **A Silver Lining** (17 Townsend Ave., 207/633-4103) create beautiful original jewelry in gold, sterling, brass, copper, and titanium.

Books, Etc.

You're bound to find something at the two-story **Sherman's Book & Stationery (& Music) Store** (5 Commercial St., Boothbay Harbor, 207/633-7262 or 800/371-8128). Cards and cassettes, games and gifts, books and more books, kitchenware and kitsch.

Antiques

Antique store or museum, you decide. The **Palabra Shop** (53 Commercial St., Boothbay Harbor, 207/633-4225) has 10 chock-full rooms of antiques and collectibles. It's also home to the world's largest collection of Moses bottles.

ENTERTAINMENT

The renovated 1894 **Opera House** (86 Townsend Ave., Boothbay Harbor, 207/633-6855, www.opera-house.org) is now the site of concerts, lectures, dramas, and special events.

Arrive early for a movie at the **Harbor Theatre** (Meadow Mall, Rte. 27 and Rte. 96, Boothbay Harbor, 207/633-0438) and listen to the 1946 Wurlitzer jukebox.

Your waiter turns into a performer at the **Carousel Music and Dinner Theatre** (Rte. 27, Boothbay Harbor, 207/633-5297 or 800/757-5297, www.carouselmusictheatre.com, $28). After your meal, sit back and enjoy the cabaret-style performance of American popular music.

Live entertainment, especially on weekends, can be found at three Pier 1 restaurants. **Gray's Wharf** (207/633-5629) has live weekend entertainment, a dance floor, and pinball and video games. Pub-style food is available 11 A.M.–8:30 P.M.; bar is open to 1 A.M. **J.H. Hawk** (207/633-5589) serves food 11 A.M.–11 P.M. **McSeagull's** (207/633-5900) serves food 11 A.M.–10 P.M.

The **Lincoln Arts Festival** (207/633-3913, www.lincolnartsrestival.org) presents half a dozen or more concerts—classical, pops, choral, and jazz—and other arts-related events at various locations on the Boothbay Peninsula from late March to early October.

Early July through August is a great time for music in Boothbay Harbor. Free Thursday night **band concerts** at 8 P.M. are performed on the Memorial Library lawn, Boothbay Harbor. Bring a blanket or folding chair.

EVENTS

The **Fishermen's Festival** is a locally colorful early-season celebration, held the third weekend of April, beginning with a Friday Miss Shrimp Princess pageant. Saturday brings a lobster-crate race and afternoon contests such as trap hauling, scallop- and clam-shucking, fish-filleting, and net mending (plus a real steal—a lobster-eating contest you can enter for $5). Saturday night, church suppers feature fish and shellfish, and Sunday, a chowder luncheon precedes the blessing of the fleet to ensure a successful summer season.

June is the month for **Windjammer Days,** two days of festivities centering on traditional windjammer schooners. Highlights are the Windjammer Parade, harborfront concerts, plenty of food, and a fireworks extravaganza.

A summer highlight at Watershed Center for the Ceramic Arts is its annual **Salad Days,** a fund-raising event held on a July Saturday. For a $15 donation, you choose a handmade pottery plate, fill it from a piled-high buffet of fruit and veggie salads, and be part of an old-fashioned picnic social—and you even get to keep the plate! Afterward, there's plenty of time to explore the center's 32 acres. Call ahead to confirm the date.

Columbus Day weekend marks the **Fall Foliage Festival,** featuring craft and food booths, a petting zoo, live entertainment, train rides, and more at Boothbay Railway Village.

ACCOMMODATIONS

Boothbay Harbor's longevity as a holiday destination means beds galore—more than anyone cares to count. Even so, from late June to mid-August, you'll meet a blur of No Vacancy signs. If that's when you decide to show up here, make reservations. Here's a hint: If you want to concentrate your time in downtown Boothbay Harbor, shopping or taking boating excursions, stay in town and avoid the parking hassles.

Although the town practically rolls up the sidewalks in the winter, a few businesses do stay open year round. Lodgings that usually do so are noted; others are seasonal (usually mid-May

© TOM NANGLE

Windjammers fill Boothbay Harbor during the annual Windjammer Days, but you'll see working and pleasure boats, kayaks and excursion boats anytime.

Mid-Coast Region

through mid-October). You'll often find great rates before July and after August.

Classic Inns

To get away from it all, book at the **Newagen Seaside Inn** (Rte. 27, Southport 04576, 207/633-5242 or 800/654-5242, www.newagen seasideinn.com, $169–250), a full-service, unstuffy inn with casual fine dining and views that go on forever. Recently renovated rooms are split between the Main Inn, the Little Inn (where rooms have private decks, TV, and kitchenettes), and three cottages ($1,400 per week, with breakfast). Plus there's a long rocky shore, a nature trail, tennis courts, heated oceanfront saltwater pool and hot tub, guest rowboats, game room, candlepin bowling, and porches just for relaxing. Rates include a generous buffet breakfast. The dining room serves dinner 6–9 P.M. Sunday-

Friday; entrées run $15–25. Several cottages are available by the week. Open mid-May through September. The inn is six miles south of downtown Boothbay Harbor.

The **Lawnmeer Inn** (Rte. 27, Southport Island, 207/633-2544 or 800/633-7645, mailing address P.O. Box 505, West Boothbay Harbor 04575, www.lawnmereinn.com, $164–199), only two miles from downtown Boothbay Harbor, is the Newagen's sister property. Built in 1898 on Southport Island, overlooking Townsend Gut, the traditional inn has 13 comfortable rooms, about half with water views. A separate modern motel building has 18 rooms. Children are welcome. The inn's multistar **water-view restaurant** offers breakfast and dinner. Dinner reservations are essential; it's a popular spot. The inn is open mid-May through Columbus Day.

Over in East Boothbay, the oceanfront **M Ocean Point Inn** (Shore Rd., P.O. Box 409, East Boothbay 04544, 207/633-4200 or 800/552-5554, www.oceanpointinn.com, $120–200) wows guests with spectacular sunset views and an easy-going ambience that keeps guests returning generation after generation. The sprawling complex includes numerous lodging buildings: an inn, lodge, motel, apartments, cottages, and others. All rooms have mini-fridge, phone, cable TV, and air-conditioning, and some have kitchenettes. A well-respected dining room, a pier, an outdoor heated pool, and Adirondack-style chairs set just-so on the water's edge round out the facilities. The best deals are the packages.

Fanciest option is the **Spruce Point Inn and Spa** (Atlantic Ave., P.O. Box 237, Boothbay Harbor 04538, 207/633-4152 or 800/553-0289, www.sprucepointinn.com, $155–505), which has expanded dramatically in recent years, adding modern condos to its already extensive complex of traditional inn rooms and cottages, all with private decks, mini fridges, and TV; some have fireplaces, kitchenettes, and whirlpool tubs. Decor and prices vary widely. The inn holds big weddings on many weekends, so try for midweek. For MAP, add $54 per adult a day, $15 per child. Amenities at the 15-acre resort include a full-service spa and fitness center, freshwater and saltwater pools, tennis courts, rocky

shorefront, and a shuttle bus to downtown (about 1.5 miles, although it seems farther). A children's program is available 9:30 A.M.–2:30 P.M. Tuesday–Saturday for $35 per day, including lunch and snack. Also available is an evening program 6–9 P.M. Thursday–Saturday for $15 for ages 4–12. Dining choices range from poolside to pub-style to fine dining, with prices to match each setting. The inn is open Memorial Day weekend to mid-October.

B&Bs

Escape the hustle-bustle of Boothbay Harbor at the **M Five Gables Inn B&B** (107 Murray Hill Rd., P.O. Box 335, East Boothbay 04544, 207/633-4551 or 800/451-5048), which began life as a no-frills summer hotel in the late 19th century. It's gone steadily upmarket since then, and well-traveled innkeepers De and Mike Kennedy, owners since 1995, have added their unique touches, including wonderful murals throughout and window seats in the gable rooms. Fifteen of the light and airy 16 rooms have Linekin Bay views, and five have fireplaces. The living room is congenial, the gardens are gorgeous, and the porch goes on forever. Rates are $135–200, including Mike's gourmet buffet breakfast. Book well ahead at this popular spot. The inn, on a side road off Route 96 in the traditional boatbuilding hamlet of East Boothbay, is 3.5 miles from downtown Boothbay Harbor. Arriving by boat? One mooring is available for guests.

Square in the middle of downtown, overlooking the harbor and close to everything, the **M 1830 Admiral's Quarters Inn** (71 Commercial St., Boothbay Harbor 04538, 207/633-2474) is an 1830 sea captain's home renovated by personable innkeepers Les and Deb Hallstrom, who work hard to put everyone at ease. Every room has cable TV, air-conditioning, phones, water views, gas fireplaces, and private decks and entrances. A laundry is available. Rates ($165–195) include a bountiful breakfast buffet and afternoon refreshments. Open year-round.

Across the street from the Admiral's Quarters is **The Greenleaf Inn** (65 Commercial St., Boothbay Harbor 04538, 207/633-7346 or 888/950-7724, fax 207/633-2642), Jeff Teel's mid-19th-century home. Seven brightly decorated rooms all have harbor views, phones, air-conditioning, fireplaces, TV, even small refrigerators; five also have private decks. Guests have use of a comfy living/dining room with fireplace, a sunroom, and an outdoor hot tub. Rates are $175–185, including a fancy full breakfast. Open year-round.

Just up the hill is **The Welch House** (56 Mc Kown St., Boothbay Harbor 04538, 207/633-3431 or 800/279-7313, www.welchhouseinn.com), with stunning 180-degree views from the third-floor deck (and not-shabby ones from the lower deck). This 14-room B&B (all private baths, but some are down the hall) is an elegant getaway in an 19th-century shipbuilder's home. All of the rooms have air-conditioning, cable TV/VCR, and phone; many have water views; some have fireplaces or whirlpool tubs. Breakfast in the solarium is a treat. Rates are $125–195. Open year-round.

Views, views, views. On the oceanfront, with a private dock (moorings available for guests), and views past the islands to open ocean is **Sur La Mer Inn** (18 Eames Rd., P.O. Box 663, Boothbay Harbor 04538, 207/633-7400 or 800/791-2026, www.surlamerinn.com), a rather modern house in which most of the elegant rooms have private baths and water views. Rates are $85–265, except for the third-floor penthouse, with its own hot tub and private deck ($295), and the water's edge boathouse cottage ($300). Host Gene Damon also owns The Boat House Bistro (if you can tear yourself away from the magnificent terrace with huge hot tub). Breakfast is a hearty buffet. Open year-round.

In town and on the water, the **Blue Heron Inn** (65 Townsend Ave., Boothbay Harbor 04538, 207/633-7020 or 866/216-2300, www.blueheron seasideinn.com, $150–215) opened in 2003 and quickly made a name for itself. The Victorian vintage belies the clean, bright interior. Large rooms are accented with antiques and collectibles from Phil and Laura Chapman's years overseas. Each room has a waterfront deck, air-conditioning, fridge, microwave, TV, and phone; some also have a fireplace and Jacuzzi. Rates include a continental breakfast buffet. Open year-round.

Staying at the **Hodgdon Island Inn** (Barters Island Rd., P.O. Box 492, Boothbay 04571, 207/633-7474, 800/314-5160, www.hodgdon-islandinn.com) is a peaceful alternative to being in town. The 1810 sea captain's house is 10 minutes from downtown Boothbay Harbor. Hosts Steve and Sherri Matte have eight beautifully decorated rooms on three floors with views of a small cove; you'll inevitably gravitate to the Adirondack chairs on the shore. There are gorgeous gardens and a heated outdoor pool. Rates are $125–175. Open year-round.

Marti Booth and Larry Brown give guests a warm welcome to their **Linekin Bay Bed & Breakfast** (531 Ocean Point Rd., 207/633-9900 or 800/596-7420, www.linekinbaybb .com, $130–180). No wonder, considering all the work they did to transform the 1878 home overlooking the bay into an inn. Begin the day with full breakfast on the deck, perhaps watching lobsterers pull their traps. Afternoon refreshments also are served. Guest rooms are spacious and beautifully decorated; three have ocean views and two have fireplaces. Open year-round.

Motels

The gray-shingled **Cod Cove Inn and Cottages** (22 Cross Rd., P.O. Box 117, Edgecomb 04556, 207/882-9586 or 800/882-9586, www.codcove inn.com) is perched high on a hill overlooking tidal Cod Cove and Wiscasset beyond. Thirty rooms have balconies or patios, air-conditioning, cable TV, mini-fridges, and telephones; some have microwaves and gas fireplaces. Best views are from second-floor rooms. Within the inn's lovely gardens await an outdoor heated pool and hot tub. Also part of the inn are 14 cottages built in the early 1930s but tastefully updated. The inn is a mile east of Wiscasset, at the turnoff to the Boothbay Peninsula. Rates are $114–229, including continental breakfast. Open year-round.

A great location just 100 feet from the footbridge, a good dining room, a fun lounge, an indoor pool, and harbor views combine to make the **Rocktide Inn** (35 Atlantic Ave., Boothbay Harbor 04538, 207/633-4455 or 800/762-8433, www.rocktideinn.com, $129–144) a popular spot. Rooms are spread out among four buildings, with rates varying according to the view. All have air-conditioning, cable TV, and phone, and a full buffet breakfast is included. Even if you don't stay here, pop over for a drink in the tastefully decorated tiki bar-style lounge (open 4–11 P.M.) or on the expansive decks overhanging the harbor. The dining room, open to the public for dinner (5:30–9 P.M.), has both casual and formal areas; men must wear jackets in the latter.

Hidden away in a quiet neighborhood on West Harbor Pond is a vintage 1960s motel that welcomes families, the **Lakeview Inn** (48 Lakeview Rd., P.O. Box 516, West Boothbay Harbor 04575, 207/633-0353 or 866/851-0450, www.thelakeviewinn.com, $89–119). Swim in the lake or the heated pool or use one of the inn's canoes or rowboats to explore the lake or to go fishing. Every room has a lake view, air-conditioning, cable TV, and phone. Those on the upper balcony are nicest and largest and have mini-fridges; some have kitchenettes. Two connecting rooms for families are $160. Pets are allowed in some rooms for $15 per pet, per day. Rates include a continental breakfast. Also available are two apartments ($105–125). The appropriately named Greenhouse Restaurant has earned a reputation for good food at a fair price; entrées $10–24, half servings available on most. It's only one mile into downtown Boothbay Harbor.

Campgrounds

With 150 well-maintained wooded and open sites on 45 acres, **Shore Hills Campground** (Rte. 27, P.O. Box 448, Boothbay 04537, 207/633-4782, www.shorehills.com) is a popular destination where reservations are essential in midsummer. Rates are $22–32. Be sure to request a wooded site away from the biggest RVs. Leashed pets are allowed. Facilities include coin-operated showers and laundry, free use of canoes. On the tidal Cross River, 7.5 miles south of Route 1 and close to the Boothbay Railway Village, Shore Hills is open mid-April to mid-October.

Much smaller and right on the ocean is the **Gray Homestead Oceanfront Camping** (21 Homestead Rd., Southport 04576, 207/633-4612, www.graysoceancamping.com, $21–32), a family-run campground with 40 RV and tenting sites, as well as cottages and apartments. Amenities include a stone beach, pier, laundry facilities, kayak rentals, and lobsters, live or cooked.

Seasonal Rentals

For a long-term rental, start with the **Cottage Connection of Maine** (P.O. Box 662, Boothbay Harbor 04538, 207/633-6545 or 800/823-9501, www.cottageconnection.com), which has a free catalog of more than 150 rental properties. The annual tourism booklet published by the Boothbay Harbor Region Chamber of Commerce includes cottage-rental listings.

FOOD

No one starves in the Boothbay area, thanks to food emporia varying from sidewalk hot-dog vendors to sandwich shops to pizza palaces to tearooms, lobster wharves, and a handful of nicer dining rooms. However, the vast majority of restaurants are overpriced for the quality and dining experience. Boothbay's short season and the difficulty of finding qualified help account for most of this, but not all. Those two reasons and changing ownership account for the lack of continuity in dining from year to year. The choices below have been reliably good, but it's best to ask locally to see what's new, changed, and worth your dollar.

General Stores and Miscellany

Wood floors and a braided rug are welcoming touches at the **East Boothbay General Store** (255 Ocean Point Rd., Rte. 96, East Boothbay, 207/633-4503), which has been serving locals since 1893. Choose from pastries and hand-cut doughnuts for breakfast; sandwiches, lobster rolls, and pizza the rest of the day ($4–7); finish it off with homemade goodies. Eat inside or on the porch, or get it to go for a picnic on the point.

Close to the harbor, **Eastside Market and Deli** (26 Atlantic Ave., Boothbay Harbor 04538, 207/633-4616) is an old-fashioned Maine market morphed into a New York deli selling thick sandwiches (most $5–6), creative salads, veggie items, pizza, wine, and anything else you might need for a designer picnic. Breakfast—egg sandwiches, wraps, waffles, bagels, is available 8:30–10:30 A.M.

The market is at the end of the footbridge, on the east side of downtown.

Right in the center of all the action, **Village Market** (24 Commercial St., Boothbay Harbor, 207/633-0944) makes sandwiches and pizzas to order. Absolutely no atmosphere, but it's cheap and convenient.

It's worth the drive over to Trevett to indulge in a lobster roll from the **Barters Island General Store** (207/633-1140), just before the bridge connecting Hodgdon and Barters Islands.

Lots of variety is the lure at the small **Boothbay Farmers' Market**, operating 9 A.M.–noon each Thursday from mid-June to late August. Set up at the high school ballfield on Route 27 in Boothbay Harbor, a dozen or so vendors have goat cheese, lamb, preserves, breads, and, of course, fresh produce.

Watch local papers and bulletin boards for notices of **public suppers** and **chowder suppers,** great opportunities for sampling local home cooking and local color. Most start relatively early, do not include liquor, and cost under $10 for all you can eat. Such a deal.

Breakfast and Lunch

The Boothbay region even has a Scottish tearoom. *Tea: A Magazine* gives a thumbs-up to **MacNab's Tea Room** (5 Lu Yu Tea Ln., off Back River Rd., P.O. Box 206, Boothbay 04537, 207/633-7222 or 800/884-7222, fax 207/633-4691), near the center of Boothbay (not the harbor). Tartans and terriers are the dominant motifs in this informal, folksy place, where Frances Browne inquires about your tea choice as soon as you settle in. Homemade soups, Highland pie, and sandwiches are all on the lunch menu ($9–10), served 11 A.M.–3 P.M. Also available are typically Scottish sweets. A proper afternoon or high tea is available by arrangement. Even if you can't get here, send for the entertaining mail-order catalog. MacNab's, .4 mile off Route 27, is open Tuesday–Saturday 10 A.M.–5 P.M. July and August, to 4 P.M. the rest of the year.

Ask any local where to go for a reliably good and reasonably priced breakfast or lunch, and you'll be directed to the **M Blue Moon Café**

(54 Commercial St., Boothbay Harbor 04538, 207/633-2349). Order at the counter, then grab one of the handful of tables inside or on the harbor-view deck or in the overflow garden seating behind the restaurant. Homemade soups and salads, great sandwiches, and sinful pastries ($4–10). If you're headed out for a picnic, the café will fix you up with a box lunch. "The Moon" is open 7:30 A.M.–2 P.M. May to mid-November.

Another locals' favorite serving breakfast, lunch, and dinner is the unassuming **Ebb Tide Restaurant** (43 Commercial St., Boothbay Harbor, 207/633-5692, 6:30 A.M.–9 P.M.). Booths line the tiny pine-paneled dining area, where some mighty good homestyle cooking is served. The chowders are renowned, and breakfast is served all day. Look for the red-and-white awning.

Casual Dining

The Boat House Bistro (12 The By-Way, Boothbay Harbor 04538, 207/633-7300), under the same management as Sur La Mer B&B, is offers several options. The first floor dining room serves primarily a northern Italian dinner menu, with entrées in the $15–30 range. No reservations, so you may have to wait (enjoy drinks on the deck). Lunch and dinner are also served upstairs inside and on the deck of **The Grille & Crow's Nest Bar.** Open all year for lunch noon–3 P.M. daily (designer pizzas and $6–13 sandwiches) and dinner 6–9 P.M.

Fresh fish simply prepared has earned **The Daily Catch** (93 Townsend Ave., Boothbay Harbor, 207/633-0777, 11:30 A.M.–9:30 P.M. Mon.–Thurs., to 10:30 P.M. Fri. and Sat.) a solid reputation. Nothing fancy at this family friendly place (except an award-winning lobster risotto) and no view, but the dining room is pleasant, there's a kids' menu, and the desserts are homemade. An early-bird special is served daily 4–6 P.M., otherwise prices range $14–20.

Also reliable and a long-timer on the scene is the **Tugboat Inn** (80 Commercial St., Boothbay Harbor, 207/633-4434), with two options for dining, both with great views. The inn serves lunch 11:30 A.M.–2:30 P.M. and dinner 5:30–9 P.M. daily; dinner entrées $9–22. The more casual **Marina**

Lounge & Café serves 11:30 A.M.–11 P.M. ($6–13), with light entertainment Tuesday–Sunday nights.

Real Italian fare prepared by a real Italian chef is on the menu at **Ports of Italy** (47 Commercial St., Boothbay Harbor, 207/633-1011, 5–9:30 P.M. Mon.–Thurs., to 10 P.M. Fri. and Sat., to 9 P.M. Sun.), an upper-level restaurant with deck seating. Great food, but as one local noted: "Big plates, small portions, big price." Entrées $15–26.

Fine Dining

One of the most reliable fine dining experiences in town is at 🔟 **The Thistle Inn** (55 Oak St., Boothbay Harbor, 207/633-3541, 5–9 P.M. daily, to 10 P.M. Fri. and Sat.), although service can be inconsistent. The dining room is reminiscent of an old tavern. The menu emphasizes fresh and local, whenever possible, and ranges from an open-flame grilled Angus burger ($9) to herb-crusted rack of lamb ($29). On a cold night, ask for a table by one of the fireplaces; on a warm night, ask for one on the porch.

For spectacular sunset views and reliably good food, take a spin out to the **Ocean Point Inn** (Shore Rd., East Boothbay, 207/633-4200 or 800/552-5554, 6–9 P.M.). Every table in the two-tiered, pine-paneled dining room has a view. Most entrées are in the $17–22 range; children's menu available.

Newagen Seaside Inn (Rte. 27, Southport, 207/633-5242) offers casual fine dining and views that go on forever. The dining room is open to the public by reservation for dinner 6–9 P.M. Sunday–Friday; entrées run $15–25.

The multistar water-view restaurant at the **Lawnmeer Inn** (Rte. 27, Southport Island, 207/633-2544) is open to the public beginning late May, for breakfast (7:30–10 A.M. Mon.–Sat., to 11 A.M. Sun.) and dinner (6–9 P.M.). Seafood is predominant on the extensive menu, which is imaginative and well prepared; entrées run $15–30. Dessert specialty is Key limepie. Dinner reservations are essential; it's a popular spot.

Lobster-in-the-Rough

Boothbay Harbor and East Boothbay seem to have more eat-on-the-dock lobster shacks per square inch than almost anywhere else on the coast. If you're a lobster fanatic, you've reached nirvana, heaven, ground zero, whatever. Two excellent choices are Robinson's Wharf and Lobsterman's Wharf. On the Southport Island side of the harbor, overlooking Townsend Gut next to the swing bridge, **Robinson's Wharf** (Rte. 27, Southport Island, 207/633-3830) is a sprawling place with tons of indoor and outdoor seating. Lobster dinners, lobster stew, fried seafood, steamed clams, mussels—it's all here. Plus burgers, dogs, fries, pasta salad, even BLTs and grilled cheese sandwiches. Save room for homemade pie with Round Top ice cream. Beer and wine are available. The restaurant is open 11:30 A.M.– 8 P.M. daily mid-June to Labor Day (to 9 P.M. July and Aug.).

Around the other side of the harbor, facing the Damariscotta River in East Boothbay, is the **Lobsterman's Wharf** (Rte. 96, East Boothbay, 207/633-3443). Everything from ties to T-shirts adorns the clientele, usually a mix of locals and flatlanders. The lobsters are great; so are the baby-back ribs and the crab melt; dinner entrées are $14–22. Nearly 200 seats inside and out. Mid-summer hours are 11:30 A.M.–10 P.M. Tuesday–Sunday. Open mid-May to late October. From the junction of Routes 27 and 96 in Boothbay Harbor, take Route 96 three miles to the wharf, on the left.

Cabbage Island Clambakes (Pier 6, Fisherman's Wharf, Boothbay Harbor, 207/633-7200, www.fishermanswharfinn.com) deserves a category all its own. Touristy, sure, but it's a delicious adventure. You board the 126-passenger excursion boat *Argo* at Pier 6 in Boothbay Harbor; cruise for about an hour past islands, boats, and lighthouses; and disembark at 5.5-acre Cabbage Island. Watch the clambake in progress, if you like, explore the island, or play volleyball. When the feast is ready, pick up your platter, find a picnic table, and dig in. A cash bar is available in the lodge, as are restrooms. When the weather's iffy, the lodge and covered patio have seats for a hundred. For $44.95, you'll get two lobsters (or half a chicken), chowder, clams, corn, potatoes, dessert, beverage, and the boat ride.

No credit cards. Clambake season is late June to mid-September. The 3.5-hour trips depart Monday–Friday at 12:30 P.M.; Saturday trips depart at 12:30 and 5 P.M.; Sunday trips are at 11:30 A.M. and 1:30 P.M.

INFORMATION AND SERVICES

Information

The **Boothbay Harbor Region Chamber of Commerce** (Rte. 27, P.O. Box 356, Boothbay Harbor 04538, 207/633-2353, fax 207/633-7448, www.boothbayharbor.com, open weekends throughout the summer, 10 A.M.–6 P.M. Mon.–Sat. from Labor Day to Columbus Day) also maintains one seasonal and one year-round information center. The seasonal center (mid-June to mid-October) is on Route 1, at the Route 27 junction (10 A.M.–7 P.M. Mon.–Thurs. and Sat., 10 A.M.–9 P.M. Fri., and 10 A.M.–5 P.M. Sun.). Down Route 27, 10.8 miles from Route 1, is the chamber's main office, next to Hannaford (8 A.M.–5 P.M. Mon.–Fri. all year). There's an information kiosk outside if the office is closed.

All three centers stock brochures for the entire peninsula; wherever you stop, be sure to request the handy annual *Boothbay Harbor walking map*, the Boothbay Region Land Trust hiking brochure, and the tourism booklet covering the whole peninsula.

Hospitals

The Boothbay region is served by the nonsectarian **St. Andrews Hospital and Healthcare Center** (3 St. Andrews Ln., Boothbay Harbor, 207/633-2121).

Local Library

The handsome Greek Revival **Boothbay Harbor Memorial Library** (Oak St., Boothbay Harbor 04538, 207/633-3112) has a summertime "used bookstore." Summer library hours are 10 A.M.–4:30 P.M. Tuesday–Saturday (to 7 P.M. Wednesday). Bookstore hours are 10:30 A.M.–4:30 P.M. Monday–Saturday mid-June to mid-September. Thursday evenings in July and August there are band concerts on the lawn.

Public Restrooms

At the municipal parking lot on Commercial Street (next to Pier 1) and at the municipal lot at the end of Granary Way there are public restrooms. St. Andrews Hospital, the town offices, the library, and the Marine Resources Aquarium also have restrooms.

Getting Around

Concord Trailways (800/639-3317, www.concordtrailways.com) stops in Brunswick, Bath, Wiscasset, Damariscotta, and Waldoboro on its three daily nonexpress trips up the coast.

The Rocktide Inn operates free trolley-buses on continuous scheduled routes during the summer. Approaching Boothbay Harbor on Route 27, you can pick up a trolley-bus at the Flagship Motor Inn or at the Meadow Mall, across from the Boothbay Harbor Region Chamber of Commerce. The Rocktide trolley-bus makes special hourly trips (on the half hour) from the Meadow Mall to the Marine Resources Aquarium, alleviating the parking problem there. Check at any of the information centers to confirm the trolley-bus schedule, usually 10 A.M.–5 P.M. mid-June to Labor Day (aquarium runs are 10:30 A.M.–2:30 P.M.).

Mid-Coast Region

Pemaquid Region

The two riverfront towns of Damariscotta and her Siamese twin, Newcastle, anchor the southern end of the Pemaquid Peninsula; Waldoboro anchors the northeastern end. Towns along the peninsula include New Harbor (probably Maine's most photographed fishing village), Pemaquid Point (site of one of Maine's most photographed lighthouses), and historic ports reputedly used by Captain John Smith, Captain Kidd, and assorted less-notorious types. Here, too, are Native American historic sites, a restored fortress, craft shops galore, a thriving cultural center, boat excursions to offshore Monhegan, and one of the best pocket-size sand beaches in Mid-Coast Maine.

On Christmas Day 1614, famed explorer Captain John Smith anchored on Rutherford Island, at the tip of the peninsula, and promptly named the spot Christmas Cove. And thus it remains

today. Christmas Cove is one of three villages belonging to the town of South Bristol, the southwestern finger of the Pemaquid Peninsula. South Bristol and Bristol (covering eight villages on the bottom half of the peninsula) were named after the British city.

As early as 1625, settler John Brown received title to some of this territory from the Abnaki sachem (chief) Samoset, an agreeable fellow who learned snippets of English from British codfishermen. Damariscotta (dam-uh-riss-COT-ta), in fact, is Abnaki for "plenty of alewives [herring]." The settlement here was named Walpole but was incorporated, in 1847, under its current name.

Newcastle, incorporated in 1763, earned fame and fortune from shipbuilding and brickmaking—which explains the extraordinary number of

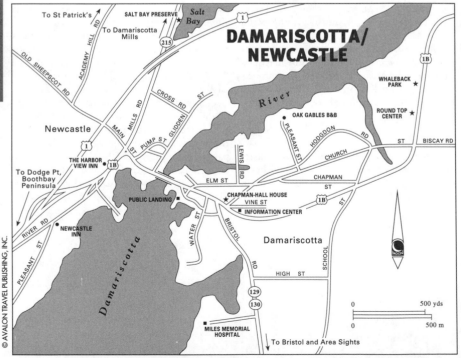

© TOM NANGLE

Mid-Coast Region

Few places are as typically New England as the twin towns of Damariscotta and Newcastle in autumn.

brick homes and office buildings throughout the town. In the 19th century, Newcastle's shipyards sent clippers, Downeasters, and full-rigged ships down the ways and around the world.

On the other northeastern end of the peninsula is Waldoboro. Route 1 cuts a commercial swath through Waldoboro without revealing the attractive downtown—or the lovely Friendship Peninsula, south of the highway. Duck into Waldoboro, then follow Route 220 south 10 miles to Friendship for an off-the-beaten-track drive.

Waldoboro's heritage is something of an anomaly in Maine. It's predominantly German, thanks to 18th-century Teutons who swallowed the blandishments of General Samuel Waldo, holder of a million-acre "patent" stretching as far as the Penobscot River. In the cemetery at the Old German Church, on Route 32, is a 19th-century marker whose inscription sums up the town's early history:

This town was settled in 1748, by Germans who emigrated to this place with the promise and expectation of finding a popu-

lous city, instead of which they found nothing but a wilderness; for the first few years they suffered to a great extent by Indian wars and starvation. By perseverance and self-denial, they succeeded in clearing lands and erecting mills. At this time [1855] a large proportion of the inhabitants are descendants of the first settlers.

(Sure makes you wonder why Waldo's name stuck to the town.)

After the mill era, the settlers went into shipbuilding in a big way, establishing six shipyards and producing more than 300 wooden vessels, including the first five-masted schooner, the 265-foot *Governor Ames,* launched in 1888. Although the *Ames*'s ill-supported masts collapsed on her maiden voyage, repairs allowed her to serve as a coal hauler for more than 20 years, and many more five-masters followed in her wake. It's hard to believe today, but Waldoboro once was America's sixth-busiest port. At the Town Landing, alongside the Medomak River, a marker describes the town's shipyards and shipbuilding heritage.

RETURN OF THE ALEWIVES

I f you're in the Damariscotta area in May and early June, don't miss a chance to go to Damariscotta Mills to see the annual Alewife Run. More than 250,000 alewives (*Alosa pseudoharengus,* a kind of herring) make their way during this time from Great Salt Bay to their spawning grounds in freshwater Damariscotta Lake, 42 feet higher. Waiting eagerly at the top are ospreys, gulls, cormorants, and sometimes eagles, ready to feast on the weary fish. Connecting the bay and the lake is a man-made stone-and-masonry "fish ladder," a zigzagging channel where you can watch the foot-long fish wriggle their way onward and upward. The ladder was built in 1807 and restored in the early 1990s. A walkway runs alongside the route, and informative display panels explain the event. It's a fascinating historical ecology lesson. To reach the fishway, take Route 215 for 1.5 miles west of Route 1. When you reach a small bridge, cross it and take a sharp left down a slight incline to a small parking area. Walk behind the barn to follow the path to the fish ladder. Try to go on a sunny day—the fish are more active and their silvery sides glisten as they go.

SIGHTS

Pick up *A Walking Tour of the Early Dwellings of Damariscotta, Maine* at the chamber of commerce office. The book by the Damariscotta Historical Society (207/563-8441) covers sites in the Main Street Historic District and details their histories. Most are privately owned and not open for tours.

Chapman-Hall House

Damariscotta's oldest surviving building is the Cape-style Chapman-Hall House (270 Main St., 207/563-3001, 1–5 P.M. Tues.–Sun. July and Aug., $2), built in 1754 by Nathaniel Chapman, whose family tree includes the legendary John Chapman, a.k.a. Johnny Appleseed. Highlights are a 1754 kitchen and displays of local shipbuilding memorabilia. The National Historic Register house has been meticulously restored by the Chapman-Hall House Preservation Society in the styles of three different eras. Don't miss the antique roses in the back garden.

Pemaquid Point Lighthouse

One of the icons of the Maine coast, the Pemaquid Point Lighthouse has been captured for posterity by many photographers and even is depicted on the Maine state quarter. The lighthouse, adjacent keeper's house, and picnic grounds are a town park. Also on the premises is an art gallery. Admission to the grounds, payable at the gatehouse, is $2 for age 12 and older. The

lighthouse grounds are accessible all year, even after the museum closes for the season, when admission is free. The point is 15 miles south of Route 1, via winding, two-lane Route 130.

Lighthouses are irresistible, and the setting here makes it even more so. Commissioned in 1827, Pemaquid Point Light stands sentinel over some of Maine's nastiest shoreline—rocks and surf that can reduce any wooden boat to kindling. Now automated, the light tower is licensed to the American Lighthouse Foundation and is managed by the Friends of Pemaquid Point Lighthouse (www.lighthousefoundation.org /pemaquid.cfm). Volunteers *aim* to open the tower 1–5 P.M. daily during the summer season. There is no charge for the tower, but donations are appreciated.

The adjacent **Fisherman's Museum** in the former lightkeeper's house (207/677-2494, 9 A.M.– 5 P.M. mid-May–mid-Oct., free, donations appreciated) points up the pleasures and perils of the lobstering industry and also has some lighthouse memorabilia. While here, you should also visit the **Pemaquid Art Gallery** (207/644-2752, 10 A.M.–5 P.M. Mon.–Sat., 1–5 P.M. Sun., mid-May–mid-Oct.). It's operated by the Pemaquid Group of Artists, which has displayed its juried members works since 1928.

Bring a picnic and lounge on the rocks below the light tower, but don't plan to snooze. You'll be busy protecting your food from the dive-bombing gulls and your kids from the treacherous surf.

Colonial Pemaquid State Historic Site

At the Colonial Pemaquid State Historic Site (end of Huddle Rd., 207/677-2423, www.friendof-colonialpemaquid.org, 9 A.M.–5 P.M. Memorial Day–Labor Day, $2 adults, $1 kids 5–11), visitors can gain a basic understanding of what life was like in an English frontier settlement. The eight-acre complex, listed on the National Historic Register, comprises a museum/visitor center, Fort William Henry, the Fort House, the remnants of a village, an 18th-century cemetery, picnic area, a pier and boat ramp, and restrooms, all spread out on a grassy point sloping to John's Bay and bordered by McCaffrey's Brook, the Pemaquid River, and Pemaquid Harbor. Bring a picnic, bring a kite, bring a kayak, let the kids run, but do take time to visit the historic sites. Demonstrations, tours, lectures, and reenactments are part of the

Colonial battle reenactments are just one of many activities scheduled at Colonial Pemaquid from late spring through early autumn.

site's summer schedule. Sadly, a monstrous house, perhaps appropriate in another setting, now dominates the view from the fort, lessening the historic feel of the experience.

Four national flags fly over the ramparts of **Fort William Henry**, a reconstruction of a fort dating from 1692, the second of three that stood here between 1677 and the late 18th century. The forts were built to defend the English settlement of Pemaquid, settled between 1625 and 1628, from the French. From the rebuilt western tower, you'll have fantastic views of John's Bay and John's Island, named for none other than Captain John Smith; inside are artifacts retrieved from archaeological excavations of the 17th-century trading outpost.

The square, white **Fort House,** which dates back to the late 1800s, houses a research library and archaeology lab as well as a gift shop.

Exhibits at the **Museum/Visitor Center** focus on regional history, from early Native American life through the Colonial period. Selections from the more than 100,000 artifacts uncovered during archaeological digs here are displayed, along with a diorama of Pemaquid Village.

Take time to wander the **Village,** 14 cellar holes of 17th- and 18th-century dwellings, a forge, trading post, jail, and other early buildings, all marked with interpretive signs. Also visit the burying ground. Note that no rubbings are permitted, as they could damage the fragile old stones.

Historic Houses of Worship

One of the oldest houses of worship in Maine that still holds services, **The Old Walpole Meeting House** (Rte. 129, Bristol Rd., Walpole, 207/563-5554), built in 1772, remains remarkably unchanged, with original hand-shaved shingles and handmade nails and hinges. The balcony—where black servants once were relegated—is paneled with boards more than two feet wide. A nondenominational service is held each Sunday in August (3 P.M.), but better still is the annual candlelight concert, a dramatic occasion in this building with no electricity and splendid acoustics. It's at 7 P.M. on a September Sunday (usually the second Sunday, but call ahead to confirm the date). It's always a sellout,

© TOM NANGLE

Mid-Coast Region

© TOM NANGLE

Mid-Coast Region

Inside Waldoboro's Old German Church, built in 1772, are a box of pews and a hanging pulpit; outside is an ancient cemetery.

but the acoustics are so good that attendees outside can hear every note. The meeting house is 3.5 miles south of Damariscotta and a quarter mile south of where Routes 129 and 130 fork.

The **Harrington Meeting House** (Old Harrington Rd., off Rte. 130), begun in 1772 and completed in 1775, now serves as Bristol's local-history museum—town-owned and run by the Pemaquid Historical Association. Behind it is an old cemetery that's fascinating to explore—if you're a fan of that sort of thing. The museum is open Monday, Wednesday, Friday, and Saturday 2–4:30 P.M. July and August. No admission fee, but donations are welcomed.

A remnant of Waldoboro's German connection is the **Old German Church** and its cemetery (Rte. 32, Waldoboro 04572, 207/832-5369 or 207/832-7742). The Lutheran church, built in 1772 on the opposite side of the Medomak River, was moved across the ice in the winter of 1794. Inside are box pews and a huge hanging pulpit. One of the three oldest churches in Maine, it lost its flock in the mid-19th century, when new generations no longer spoke German. The church is open daily 1–3 P.M. in July and August.

Built in 1808, **St. Patrick's Catholic Church** (Academy Hill Rd., Damariscotta Mills, Newcastle 04553, 207/563-3240), a solid brick structure with 18-inch-thick walls and a Paul Revere bell, is New England's oldest surviving Catholic church. Open daily 9 A.M. to sundown. Academy Hill Road starts at Newcastle Square, downtown Newcastle; the church is 2.25 miles from there, and one mile beyond Lincoln Academy.

St. Andrew's Episcopal Church (Glidden St., Newcastle 04553, 207/563-3533), built in 1883, is nothing short of exquisite, with carved oak beams, stenciled ceiling, and, for the cognoscenti, a spectacular Hutchings organ.

Darling Marine Research Center

Not far beyond the Old Walpole Meeting House is the turnoff to the **Ira C. Darling Center for Marine Research, Teaching, and Service** (193 Clark's Cove Rd., off Route 129, Walpole 04573, 207/563-3146, http://server.dmc.marine.edu/), part of the University of Maine system. Generally known as the Darling Center, it's the hands-on laboratory for the university's marine-biology students. From mid-July to late August, the Gulf of

Maine Foundation sponsors a weekly lecture series. Held in the waterfront conference center, the programs (Thursday at 7:30 P.M.) focus on maritime history, ecology, and marine biology. Suggested donation is $5; call ahead for schedule details. Tours of the 136-acre campus occur Wednesday at 1 P.M. and Friday at 11:30 A.M. during July and August. Call extension 252 to sign up. Also on the premises are six miles of trails through fields, woodlands, and along the river and cove. Pick up a free map and detailed guide ($2) at the kiosk next to the administrative building. From downtown Damariscotta, take Route 130 two miles to Route 129. Continue five miles on Route 129 to Clark's Cove Road; turn right and go about one mile to the campus.

The Iceman Cometh

In the years before refrigeration was common, ice cutting was a winter ritual for most communities and was even big business in a few. On a February Sunday morning (weather and ice permitting), several hundred helpers and onlookers gather at Thompson Pond, next to **The Thompson Ice House** (Rte. 129, South Bristol 04568, 207/644-8551 or 207/644-8120), to reenact the annual ice harvest. Festivity prevails as a crew of robust fellows marks out a grid and saws out 12-inch-thick ice cakes, which are pushed up a ramp to the ice-storage house. More than 60 tons of ice are harvested each year. Sawdust-insulated 10-inch-thick walls keep the ice from melting in this National Historic Register building first used in 1826. In 1990, the house became part of a working museum, open 1–4 P.M. Wednesday, Friday, and Saturday in July and August; $1 adults, $.50 kids. The grounds are accessible free all year, including a photographic display board depicting a 1964 harvest. The museum (with ice tools and a window view of the stored ice cakes) is open 1–4 P.M. Wednesday, Friday, and Saturday in July and August. Suggested donation is $1 adults, $.50 kids. The site is on Route 129, 12 miles south of Damariscotta. Roadside parking is allowed.

The Gut

At the foot of a hill on Route 129 is the tiny community of **South Bristol,** the heart of the town that stretches along the western edge of the Pemaquid Peninsula. In the village center is a

© TOM NANGLE

Every winter, local volunteers reenact traditional ice cutting on Thompson Pond, storing the ice in the historic Thompson Ice House, a working museum.

green-painted swing bridge (swinging sideways) spanning a narrow waterway quaintly named The Gut. Separating the mainland from Rutherford Island, The Gut is a busy thoroughfare for local lobsterboat traffic, so the bridge opens and closes often. No one is in much of a hurry in this sleepy hamlet, so the frequent stoppages never seem to bother anyone, and the scenery is worth it all. So be patient.

Waldoborough Historical Society Museum

The Waldoborough Historical Society Museum (1164 Main St., Waldoboro 04572, 207/832-4725), is a three-building roadside complex just .1 mile south of Route 1, at the eastern end of town. The grounds hold the one-room 1857 **Boggs Schoolhouse,** the 1819 **Town Pound** (to detain stray livestock), and two buildings filled with antique tools, toys, and utensils, plus period costumes, antique fire engines, and artifacts from the shipbuilding era. The museum is open daily 1–4:30 P.M. July through Labor Day, as well as occasional weekends in September and October. While you're here, ask about the nature trail out back.

Maine Antique Toy and Art Museum

Indulge your inner child at the Maine Antique Toy & Art Museum (Rte. 1, Waldoboro, 207/832-7398, 10 A.M.–4 P.M. Thurs.–Mon. Memorial Day–Columbus Day, noon–4 P.M. Sat. and Sun. to Christmas, $4). The museum houses an extensive collection of antique toys and original comic art. See how Mickey Mouse first appeared. Browse a collection of Lone Ranger memorabilia. You'll find all the old favorites, from Popeye to Felix the Cat, Betty Boop to Snow White, Pogo to Yoda. Note: This museum is geared to adults, not kids.

PARKS AND PRESERVES

Residents of the Pemaquid Peninsula region are incredibly fortunate to have several foresighted local conservation organizations, each with its own niche and mission: Damariscotta River Association, Pemaquid Watershed Association,

Damariscotta Lake Watershed Association, and Medomak Valley Land Trust. In addition, The Nature Conservancy, Maine Audubon, and National Audubon all have holdings on the peninsula, a natural-resource bonanza. For good descriptions of trails throughout Lincoln county, purchase a copy of Paula Roberts's *On the Trail in Lincoln County* ($15.75), which describes and provides directions to more than 60 area walking trails. It's available at Salt Bay Farm, which benefits from its sale.

Salt Bay Farm

Headquarters of the **Damariscotta River Association** (DRA), founded in 1973, is the Heritage Center, a late-18th-century farmhouse on 90-acre DRA Salt Bay Farm (Belvedere Rd., P.O. Box 333, Damariscotta 04543, 207/563-1393). Here you can pick up maps, brochures, and other information on the hundreds of acres of land protected and managed by the DRA—notably the Dodge Point Preserve, Menigawum (Stratton Island) Preserve, and the Salt Bay Preserve. More than two miles of trails cover Salt Bay Farm's fields, salt marsh, and shore frontage and are open to the public from sunrise to sunset daily, year-round; the office is open weekdays, usually 8 A.M.–4 P.M. No camping or fires. To reach the farm from downtown Newcastle, take Mills Road (Route 215) to Route 1. Turn right (north) and go 1.4 miles to the blinking light (Belvedere Road). Turn left and go .4 mile.

Salt Bay Preserve Heritage Trail

Across Great Salt Bay from the DRA Salt Bay Farm is the trailhead for the Salt Bay Preserve Heritage Trail, a relatively easy three-mile loop around Newcastle's Glidden Point that touches on a variety of habitat and also includes remnants of oyster-shell heaps ("middens") going back about 2,500 years. This part of the trail is protected by the feds; do *not* disturb or remove anything. Better still, carry a litterbag and help maintain the path.

This is a super family hike, and leashed dogs are allowed. Along the trail, watch for eagles, osprey, herons, river otters, Indian pipes, several stands of rare white oaks, and open views of

© TOM NANGLE

The Salt Bay Preserve Heritage Trail is a relatively easy loop that edges the Great Salt Bay estuary, where it flows into the Damariscotta River.

Great Salt Bay. Best time to come is close to low tide, as some parts of the trail require slight detours at high tide—especially during the new or full moon. In any case, rubberized shoes or boots are a good idea. To reach the preserve from Newcastle Square, take Mills Road (Route 215) about two miles to the offices of the *Lincoln County News* (just after the post office). The newspaper allows parking in the northern end of its lot, but stay to the right, as far away from the buildings as possible, and be sure not to block vehicles or access ways. Walk across Route 215 to the trailhead and pick up a brochure/map.

Whaleback Park

After a decade of push-me, pull-you struggling, the Damariscotta River Association, in conjunction with Maine's Bureau of Parks and Lands,

finally acquired all the requisite permits in 2001 to create Whaleback Park, an eight-acre public preserve designed to highlight what remains of the "Glidden Midden," ancient oyster-shell heaps across the river from the park viewpoint. (The midden is also visible, but not as easily, from the Salt Bay Preserve Heritage Trail.) Informational signs explain the history of the midden, allegedly the largest such man-made artifact north of Florida. The "mini-mountain" of castoffs was even more vast until the 1880s, when a factory harvested much of it for lime. It's on the river (west) side of Route 1 opposite and between the Great Salt Bay School and the CLC YMCA. For information about the park, contact the DRA (207/563-1393).

Dodge Point Preserve

In 1989, the state of Maine acquired the 506-acre Dodge Point Preserve—one of the stars in its crown—as part of a $35 million bond issue. The Damariscotta River Association (DRA), which initiated its protection, helps manage and maintain the property. To sample what the Dodge Point Preserve has to offer, pick up a map at the entrance and follow the Old Farm Road loop trail, then hook into the Shore Trail (Discovery Trail), heading clockwise, with several dozen highlighted sites. Consider stopping for a riverside picnic and swim at Sand Beach before continuing back to the parking lot. Hunting is permitted in the preserve, so November isn't the best time for hiking here (unless you hike on Sunday, when hunting is banned). Winter brings out ice-skaters and cross-country skiers. The Dodge Point parking area is on River Road, 2.6 miles southwest of Route 1 and 3.5 miles southwest of downtown Newcastle. Open all year for day use only, closing at sunset. Admission is free. For more information, contact the DRA.

Menigawum Preserve (Stratton Island)

Owned by the Damariscotta River Association, 30-acre Stratton Island is also known locally as Hodgdon's Island. You'll need your own small boat, canoe, or kayak to get here—it's at the entrance to Seal Cove on the west side of the South

Mid-Coast Region

Bristol peninsula. Closest public boat launch is at The Gut, about four miles downriver—a trip better done *with* (in the same direction as) the tide. Best place to land is Boat House Beach, in the northeast corner—also a great spot for shelling. Pick up a map in the small box at the north end of the island and follow the perimeter trail clockwise. At the northern end, you'll see osprey nests; at the southern tip are Native American shell middens—discards from hundreds of years of marathon summer lunches. (Needless to say, do *not* disturb or remove anything.) You can picnic in the pasture, but camping and fires are not allowed. Stay clear of the abandoned homesite on the island's west side. The preserve is accessible from sunrise to sunset.

Witch Island Preserve

Named for a 19th-century local woman dubbed "The Witch of Wall Street" for her financial wizardry, Witch Island Preserve is owned by Maine Audubon. The wooded, 19-acre island has two beaches, a perimeter trail, and the ruins of the "witch's" house. A quarter of a mile offshore, it's accessible by canoe or kayak from the South Bristol town landing, just to the right after the swing bridge over The Gut. Put in, paddle under the swing bridge, and go north to the island. For more information, contact Maine Audubon (20 Gilsland Farm Rd., Falmouth 04105, 207/781-2330).

Tracy Shore Preserve

Walk through a woodland wonderland that extends to ledgy shorefront along Jones Cove, in South Bristol. Old cellars, moss-covered trails, lichen-covered rocks, a vernal pool, old pasture grounds, and spectacular views highlight this little-known gem, owned by The Nature Conservancy. Cliffs and slippery rocks abound, so be extra watchful of children. You can connect to another preserve, the Library Preserve, on a link crossing busy Route 129. Trailhead and parking is at the intersection of Route 129 and the S Road, 8.7 miles south of the split from Route 130.

Rachel Carson Salt Pond/ La Verna Preserve

If you've never spent time studying the variety of sealife in a tidal pool, the Rachel Carson Salt Pond is a great place to start. Named after the famed author of *Silent Spring* and *The Edge of the Sea*, who summered in this part of Maine, the salt pond was a favorite haunt of hers. The whole point of visiting a tidepool is to see what the tide leaves behind, so check the tide calendar (in local newspapers, or ask at your lodging) and head out a few hours after high tide. Wear rubber boots and beware of slippery rocks and rockweed. Among the many creatures you'll see in this quarter-acre pond are mussels, green crabs, periwinkles, and starfish. Owned by The Nature Conservancy, the salt pond is on Route 32 in the village of **Chamberlain,** about a mile north of New Harbor. Parking is limited. Across the road is a trail into a 78-acre inland section of the preserve, most of it wooded. Brochures are available in the registration box.

About two miles farther north on Route 32 (or four miles south of Round Pond) is the 119-acre **La Verna Preserve,** also owned by The Nature Conservancy. Behind the 3,600-foot-long Muscongus Bay shorefront (spectacular views from the cliffs) are woodlands, marshlands (wear insect repellent and rubberized shoes or boots), and old cellar holes. Park on Route 32 and walk into the preserve on half-mile-long Tibbitts Road, an unpaved private road that begins opposite the red North Country barn. (Keep right when Tibbitts Road forks.) A trail leads through woodlands to the shore, with intriguing geological formations and spectacular views.

For additional information about both preserves, which are accessible from sunrise to sunset year-round, contact The Nature Conservancy, Maine Chapter (14 Maine St., Fort Andross, Brunswick 04011, 207/729-5181).

Todd Wildlife Sanctuary

The mainland section of a 345-acre Audubon Society property, the Todd Wildlife Sanctuary (11 Audubon Rd., Bremen 04551, 207/529-5148) includes a visitors center and gift shop (open 10 A.M.–4 P.M. daily June–Aug.) and the **Hockomock Nature Trail,** winding through the woods and down to the shore (open year-round). Pick up a trail guide at the center and follow the informative signs. Allow about an hour. Don't forget a picnic so you can have lunch on the beach. Just offshore is 333-acre **Hog Island,** site of the summertime **Audubon Ecology Camp** for youth and adults. If you have your own boat, you can walk the island's beautiful perimeter trail (no camping). Allow about three hours for the hike. Just check in beforehand at the office near the dock at the north end of the island.

Osborn Finch Preserve

Even if you can't squeeze in a visit to the Osborn Finch Preserve (Dutch Neck Rd., Waldoboro), at least allow time for a drive down **Dutch Neck.** If you can hike the 11-acre preserve, so much the better, as you'll end up on the shores of the Medomak River (bring a picnic and enjoy it on the rocks). Terrain is easy, through fields and woods. To reach the preserve—owned by the Pemaquid Watershed Association (207/563-2196)—from Route 1, go 2.7 miles south on Route 32 and turn left onto Dutch Neck Road. Continue 3.1 miles to the small preserve sign (on left). Park along the road, pulling off as far as possible.

About 500 feet before you reach the preserve, you'll see a public boat landing, a fine place to launch a sea kayak or other small boat.

RECREATION

Tennis

Central Lincoln County YMCA (Business Rte. 1, 207/563-3427) has inexpensive one-day memberships for access to tennis courts and fitness facilities.

Golf

The nine-hole **Wawenock Country Club** (Rte. 129, Walpole, 207/563-3938), established in the 1920s, is a challenging and very popular public course about midway down the Pemaquid Peninsula from Damariscotta. The par-3 eighth hole features a treacherous bunker named Big Bertha. Starting times are needed on summer weekends.

Bicycling

As with so many other parts of Maine, bike lanes

on the Pemaquid Peninsula are poor to nonexistent, so exercise the utmost caution. Roads are narrow, winding, and poorly shouldered.

Swimming

Best bet (but also most crowded) on the peninsula for saltwater swimming is town-owned **Pemaquid Beach Park,** a lovely, tree-lined sandy crescent. No lifeguard, but there are showers (cold water) and bathrooms, and the snack bar serves decent food. No alcohol is allowed on the beach. Admission is $3 for anyone over 12, free for anyone younger. At 7 P.M., the gates close (restrooms close at 5 P.M.). The beach is just off Snowball Hill Road, west of Route 130.

A much smaller beach is the pocket-size sandy area in Christmas Cove, on Rutherford Island. Take Route 129 around the cove and turn to the right, then right again down the hill.

One of the area's most popular freshwater swimming holes is **Biscay Pond,** a long, skinny body of water in the peninsula's center. From Business Route 1 at the northern edge of Damariscotta, take Biscay Road (turn at McDonald's) three miles to the pond (on the right, heading east). On hot days, this area sees plenty of cars; pull off the road as far as possible.

Farther down the peninsula, on Route 130 in **Bristol Mills,** is another roadside swimming hole, between the dam and the bridge.

Boat Excursions

At 9 A.M. each day between early June and late September, the 60-foot powerboat *Hardy III* departs for **Monhegan,** a Brigadoon-like island a dozen miles offshore, where passengers can spend the day hiking the woods, picnicking on the rocks, birding, and inhaling the salt air. At 3:15 P.M., everyone reboards, arriving in New Harbor just over an hour later. The boat has toilets and a snack bar. Dress warmly and wear rubber-soled shoes. Cost is $27 adults, $15 children under 12. Reservations are required, and they're held until 20 minutes before departure, but plan to arrive 30 minutes ahead of time (or 45 minutes if you have luggage). Trips operate rain or shine, but heavy seas can affect the schedule. Go light on breakfast beforehand. From late June through

Mid-Coast Region

late September, there's also a second Monhegan trip—used primarily for overnighters—departing New Harbor at 2 P.M. daily. In late May and early October, Monhegan trips operate only Wednesday, Saturday, and Sunday. The *Hardy III* also operates daily 1.5-hour **puffin-watching tours** (5:30 P.M. daily mid-June to late Aug., Wed., Sat., and Sun. mid-May–mid-June, $18 adults, $11 kids), one-hour **seal-watching tours** (noon daily late June to Labor Day and weekends in Sept., $10 adults, $7 kids), and one-hour **lighthouse cruises** (7:30 P.M. late June to Labor Day, $10 adults, $7 kids). **Hardy Boat Cruises** is 19 miles south of Route 1, based at Shaw's Fish and Lobster Wharf (Rte. 32, New Harbor 04554, 207/677-2200 or 800/278-3346). Parking is free, at the baseball field near Shaw's.

Sea Kayaking

Sea Spirit Adventures (www.seaspiritadventures.com), with two locations (Schooner Landing, 47 Main St., Damariscotta, 207/563-7532, and 1440 Rte. 32, Round Pond, 207/529-4732), has rentals and offers guided tours and lessons on Muscongus Bay and the Damariscotta River. Three- to seven-hour tours range $35–95 and include introductory, adventure, sunset, night, and gourmet lunch tours. If you would rather do it yourself, sea kayaks with rudders rent for $45 per day, $30 per half day; recreational kayaks rent for $35 per day, $25 per half day; and tandem sea kayaks rent for $64 per day, $45 per half day.

Canoeing

Experienced canoeists may want to take the **Damariscotta-Pemaquid River Canoe Trail,** a 40-mile clockwise loop that begins in Damariscotta and follows some of the region's traditional Indian canoe routes. Although few portages are required, one, fairly close to the beginning, is about a mile long over private land. For a route map, contact Mike Krepner at **Native Trails** (P.O. Box 240, Waldoboro 04572, 207/832-5255, www.nativetrails.org).

Cane & Canvas (Bristol Mills, 207/563-1280) rents canoes and kayaks for use on the Pemaquid River. Paddle upstream from its launch site to

Biscay, Pemaquid, and Duckpuddle Ponds or south to a recently restored, early-19th-century stone arch bridge that was built without mortar. Lots of wildlife can be seen in the area. Canoes rent for $22 half day, $35 full day; kayaks for $15 half day, $25 full day. Multiple day and weekend rates are available.

If you have your own canoe, or just want to paddle the three-mile length of **Biscay Pond,** you can park at the beach area and put in there (see Swimming). Another good launching site is a state ramp off Route 1 in **Nobleboro,** at the head of eight-mile-long **Lake Pemaquid.**

SHOPPING

Since many of the shops listed are downtown, a parking advisory is in order. Downtown parking in Damariscotta in summer is a major headache; the municipal lot, behind the storefronts, has a three-hour limit, and it's almost always full. You'll usually find spots on some of the side streets.

Antiques and Antiquarian Books

Antique shops are numerous along the Bristol Road (Route 130), where many barns have been turned into shops selling everything from fine antiques to old stuff. Serious antiques aficionados will find plenty to browse and buy along this stretch of road.

Two Route 1 shops are worth a stop. Just south of the turnoff for Damariscotta/Newcastle is **Antiques with Attitude** (Rte. 1 and Hopkins Rd., 207/563-2651), a fun shop with a wide range of goods, from French country antiques to American primitives, filling a pre-Revolutionary house and much-newer barn.

Continue north on Route 1 to find **Nobleboro Antique Exchange** (104 Atlantic Hwy., Rte. 1, Nobleboro, 207/563-6800). This multidealer antique mall is housed in a light blue building that goes on and on, with more than 100 display areas on three levels. The selection is diverse, from period antiques to 20th-century collectibles.

Based in a screen-fronted antique carriage house just south of Round Pond village, **Jean Gillespie Books** (1172 Route 32, Round Pond, 207/529-

5555) has separate rooms and alcoves, all very user-friendly. Specialties are cookbooks, nautical and Maine titles, and illustrated children's books; the "Royalty" category fills six shelves.

Art Galleries

Worth a visit for the building alone, the **Stable Gallery** (26 Water Street, Damariscotta, 207/563-1991), just off Main Street, was built in the 19th-century clipper-ship era and still has original black-walnut stalls—providing a great foil for the work of dozens of Maine craftsmen. Lining the walls are paintings and prints from the gallery's large "stable" of artists.

In his **River Gallery** (Main St., Damariscotta, 207/563-6330), dealer Geoff Robinson specializes in 19th- and early-20th-century European and American fine art—a connoisseur's inventory.

Showing a high profile ever since it opened in the renovated antique fire station, **The Firehouse Gallery** (1 Bristol Rd., Damariscotta, 207/563-7299) has a tasteful, well-displayed selection of paintings, sculpture, prints, and jewelry. The gallery mounts half a dozen shows during its season (May–Oct.).

The works of more than 50 Maine craft artisans can be seen in the 15 rooms of the **Pemaquid Craft Co-op** (Rte. 130, New Harbor, 207/277-2077). Lots of stuff to see here: iron art, woodwork, needlework, quilts, bears, candles, jewelry, and much, much, more.

The **Round Top Center for the Arts** (Business Rte. 1, Damariscotta, 207/563-1507), in addition to putting on all kinds of cultural activities, has a gift shop with especially unusual arts and crafts—members of the respected Maine Crafts Association display and sell their wares here.

If you especially interested in arts and crafts, make Round Pond part of your itinerary. The small village is home to about a dozen galleries and studios, most within walking distance of one another. Just north of "downtown" Round Pond is the **Scottish Lion Blacksmith** and the **Village Weaver** (1486 Rte. 32, 207/529-5523), where skilled smith Andrew Leck turns out all kinds of attractive wrought-iron accessories—wall brackets, fireplace tools, and more—and Phyllis Leck hand looms beautiful blankets and other textiles.

Books, Gifts, and Clothing

The Pemaquid Peninsula is fertile ground for crafts and gifts, and many of the shop locations provide opportunities for exploring off the beaten path.

The inventory at the **Maine Coast Book Shop and Café** (Main St., 207/563-3207) always seems to anticipate customers' wishes, so you're unlikely to walk out empty-handed. There's a superb children's section, a large magazine selection, a helpful staff, and always something tempting in the café.

Whimsy is the theme at **2fish** (44 Main St., Damariscotta, 207/563-2220), a small gift shop stocked with appealing jewelry, clothing, and trinkets from here and abroad

Just off Main Street (turn at Reny's), is **Weatherbird** (1168 Elm St., Damariscotta, 207/563-8993), a terrifically eclectic shop with an inventory that defies description. Housewares, wines, toys, cards, gourmet specialties, and intriguing women's clothing are all part of the mix. Above it is **Tin Fish Etc.** (207/563-8204). Dana Moses's shop features brilliantly handpainted tin *objets* made from recycled roofing metal. She also accepts commissions.

All those upscale home-and-garden catalogs come to life at **Brambles** (Main St., Damariscotta, 207/563-2800). You'll find unusual birdhouses, whimsical garden ornaments, wind chimes, great garden tools, plus books and cards.

Whatever you do, don't leave downtown Damariscotta without visiting **Reny's** (207/563-5757 or 207/563-3011), with stores on each side of Main Street; one sells clothing, the other everything else. This is Reny's hometown, so the selection is huge in both. If you can recognize the edges of cut-out labels, you'll find clothes from major retailers at way discounted prices. Stock up on housewares, munchies, puzzles, shoes, and whatever else floats your boat; the prices can't be beat.

Down the peninsula, there's no question that the **Granite Hall Store** (9 Backshore Rd., off Rte. 32, Round Pond, 207/529-5864) is unique. Eric and Sarah Herndon's eclectic inventory is tough to describe but always fascinating. The first floor of this mid-19th-century emporium carries pottery,

CDs, paper dolls, fudge, baskets, even catnip mice and cookie cutters. The "penny" candy, ice cream, and the old-fashioned peanut-roasting machine capture the kids. Upstairs, their parents usually succumb to books, antiques, and stunning handwoven Scottish and Irish woolens. Adding to the flavor are old ship models, hardwood floors, and a ship's bell that tolls the time. The shop is in "downtown" Round Pond, 11 miles south of Route 1.

Puzzle fans come from all over the country to shop at **I'm Puzzled** (246 Lower Cross Rd., Nobleboro, 207/563-5719), on the inland side of Rte. 1. Robert Havenstein stocks more than 650 jigsaw puzzles.

ENTERTAINMENT

The region is blessed with dynamic cultural centers. **Round Top Center for the Arts** (Business Rte. 1, Round Top Ln., Damariscotta 04543, 207/563-1507, www.roundtoparts.org) has concerts, plays, workshops, classes, and exhibits as well as a gallery shop. It also sponsors a summer lecture series (usually 7 P.M. Wednesday, in the Darrows Barn, $7) with nationally recognized speakers.

The neoclassic **Waldo Theatre** (916 Main St., P.O. Box 587, Waldoboro 04572, 207/832-6060, www.waldotheatre.org) was built as a cinema in 1936. Restored in the mid-1980s, it now operates as a nonprofit organization, presenting first-rate concerts, plays, films, lectures, and other year-round community events.

Lincoln County Community Theater (Theater St., Damariscotta, 207/563-3424, www.lcct.org) owns and operates the historic Lincoln Theater, dating from 1867. It also presents musicals and dramas, concerts, films, and more.

FESTIVALS AND EVENTS

July brings the annual **House and Garden Tour,** a peek into some lovely private homes and gardens, and the **St. Andrew's Lawn Party and Auction,** a fun event that always draws a crowd.

The second weekend in August, **Olde Bristol Days** features a craft show, a parade, road and boat races, live entertainment, and fireworks. At Fort William Henry, in Pemaquid, it's a summer highlight on the peninsula.

In late August, hundreds of diehard shoppers turn out for the annual three-day **Miles Memorial Hospital League Rummage Sale,** held under tents on Business Route 1 (close to the junction with Route 1) in Damariscotta.

And in October, during the **Round Pond Round About,** local galleries hold open houses and demonstrations.

ACCOMMODATIONS

Inns

Along a scenic side road and overlooking the Damariscotta River is **M The Newcastle Inn** (River Rd., Newcastle 04553, 207/563-5685 or 800/832-8669, www.newcastleinn.com, $150–250), an 1860s' sea captain's home. Ideal for a romantic getaway, the lovely hostelry (main inn and carriage house) has 15 elegant guest rooms and suites (some with fireplaces and whirlpool tubs), riverfront gardens, and an upscale country-inn ambience. Special packages are available off-season. The inn's excellent restaurant, **Lupines,** is open to the public by reservation. Chef Josh DeGroot specializes in French cuisine utilizing primarily fresh and local ingredients. Guests gather for hors d'oeuvres at 6 P.M. before sitting down for five-course dinners ($46) at 7 P.M. Tuesday–Sunday in summer, Thursday–Sunday in winter. Open all year.

Within easy walking distance of Pemaquid Light and 16 miles south of Route 1, **The Bradley Inn** (3063 Bristol Rd., Rte. 130, Pemaquid Point, New Harbor 04554, 207/677-2105 or 800/942-5560, fax 207/677-3367, www.bradleyinn.com, $155–275) is a beautifully restored, century-old three-story building with rooms and a suite (with full kitchen and fireplace) in the inn and carriage house, a separate cottage, and lovely gardens—a great location for a quiet weekend getaway. The inn's restaurant, overlooking the gardens and open to the public, has an ambitious and pricey menu (entrées $25–32). Don't miss the granite bar in the adjoining pub. Room rates include full breakfast and afternoon tea. Open all year.

On Rutherford Island, just off the end of the South Bristol peninsula, **Coveside** (105 Coveside Rd., Christmas Cove, South Bristol 04568, 207/644-8282, lincoln.midcoast.com/~coveside/, $85–100) has been run by the Mitchell family since 1969. The red-clapboard main building, built in the 1880s, has five rooms (private baths attached or across the hall). Across the lawn is the 10-room motel-style Shorefront building, with skylights, decks overhanging the water, and unbeatable views of the cove. Coveside caters to yachters, providing guest moorings, dock space, and fuel; the pennant-draped Dory Bar and the Shorefront Restaurant attract a steady stream of boaters and summer vacationers during the cruising season. Continental breakfast is included. The restaurant, serving lunch and dinner (entrées $18–22) daily during the season, usually closes Labor Day.

Almost on top of Pemaquid Light is the rambling **M Hotel Pemaquid** (3098 Bristol Rd., Rte. 130, New Harbor 04554, 207/677-2312, www.hotelpemaquid.com, $85–145). Seventeen miles south of Route 1 but just 450 feet from the lighthouse (you can't see it from the inn, but you sure can hear the fog horn!), the hotel has been welcoming guests since 1900; it's fun to peruse the old guest registers. Hang out in the large, comfortable parlor or the wraparound veranda. The owners have gently renovated the property, updating and improving everything without losing the Victorian charm of an old seaside hotel. The inn building has rooms with private and shared baths ($70–85) and suites ($145). Other buildings have motel-style units with private baths ($85–100); apartments in the annex rent for ($170–190). A beautiful second-floor suite in the carriage house, with full kitchen and deck, is $230. For the Victorian flavor of the place, request an inn room or suite. No restaurant, but The Bradley Inn and The Sea Gull Shop are nearby. No credit cards. Open mid-May to mid-October.

Up the eastern side of the peninsula, in the middle of New Harbor, **The Gosnold Arms** (146 Route 32, New Harbor 04554, 207/677-3727, off-season 561/575-9549, www.gosnold.com) has been here since 1925 and remains deliberately old-fashioned, with pine-paneled rooms and a country-cottage common room. Customers return year after year. The family-owned operation includes the inn building and eight other buildings (with 14 units), so there's variety in layout, location, and decor. Many of the 11 inn rooms (private baths) include water views, but the loudspeaker at the lobster wharf across the street (Shaw's) can preclude an afternoon nap in front rooms. Cottage units are $95–177, inn rooms are $95–117, including breakfast. Open mid-May to mid-October.

B&Bs

A lovely water-view living room with piano and harp sets the tone for **The Harbor View Inn** (Business Rte. 1, P.O. Box 791, Newcastle 04553, 207/563-2900, www.theharborview.com, $135–190). Another selling point is the huge deck overlooking the twin towns and the river. Joe McEntee's family antiques fill the three beautifully decorated first- and second-floor suites. All rooms have phones, cable TV, and comfortable chairs; two have fireplaces. Breakfast is a four-course extravaganza in the formal dining room with a printed menu, thanks to one of Joe's former careers as an executive chef (he was also a publishing executive). Open all year.

Martha Scudder provides a warm welcome for her guests at **Oak Gables Bed & Breakfast** (Pleasant St., P.O. Box 276, Damariscotta 04543, 207/563-1476 or 800/335-7748, www.oakgablesbb.com, $95). At the end of a pretty lane, this 13-acre hilltop estate overlooks the Damariscotta River. Despite a rather imposing setting, everything's homey, informal, and hospitable. Four second-floor rooms, which can be joined in pairs, share a bath; a guest wing ($875) has a full kitchen, private bath, and separate entrance. The heated swimming pool is a huge plus, as is the boathouse deck, on the river. Guests can harvest blackberries from scads of bushes. The grounds also hold a three-bedroom cottage ($1,20) and two attractive riverfront apartments ($875–980 a week all year), usually booked up well ahead. Open all year.

Wake up with a dip, after a restful sleep at the **M Mill Pond Inn** (50 Main St., Rte 215, Damariscotta Mills, Nobleboro 04555, 207/563-8014, www.millpondinn.com, $120). The 1780 Colonial was restored and converted into an inn in 1986 by delightful owners Bobby and Sherry Whear. After a full breakfast, snooze in a hammock, watch for eagles and great blue herons, pedal a bicycle into nearby Damariscotta, or canoe the pond, which connects to 14-mile long Damariscotta Lake. Bobby, a Registered Maine Guide, offers fishing trips and scenic tours of the lake in his restored, antique Lyman lapstrake boat. Use of bicycles and canoe is free to guests. The inn is just a five-minute drive from downtown Damariscotta, but a world away. No credit cards.

The Mansard-roofed **Inn at Round Pond** (1442 Rte 32, Round Pond 04564, 207/529-2004, www.theinnatroundpond.com, $130–190) commands a sea captain's view of the harbor as it presides over the lovely village of Round Pond. It's an easy walk to a waterfront restaurant, two dueling lobster pounds, an old-timey country store, and a handful of galleries and shops. Sea Spirit Adventures is next door. Each of the good-sized rooms has harbor views and sitting areas. A full breakfast is included. The inn is open Memorial Day through Columbus Day.

Globetrotters Robin and Bill Branigan have made the in-town Victorian **Roaring Lion Bed and Breakfast** (995 Main St., Waldoboro 04572, 207/832-4038, fax 207/832-7892) an informal home away from home for their many guests. Three rooms share a bath (with clawfoot tub); the Rose Room has a private bath. Doubles are $80–90. Bill's hearty breakfasts (often lion eggs—a secret recipe) are served in the tin-walled, tin-ceilinged dining room; he's a whiz with vegetarian/macrobiotic diets. Maine crafts, paintings, and Bill's superb photos are sold in the screened-porch "gallery." Children are welcome. Open all year.

Just up the hill from the Waldo Theatre, hospitable Libby Hopkins has been running the **Broad Bay Inn and Gallery** (1014 Main St., P.O. Box 607, Waldoboro 04572, 207/832-6668 or 800/736-6769, www.broadbayinn.com) since 1984, and she's an energetic breakfast chef (she attended Le Cordon Bleu cooking school in Paris). Four antique-filled rooms share three baths—$75–110, including afternoon tea or sherry. Guests can play the piano, browse through the huge art-book collection, or watch old films. The barn gallery—stocked with watercolors and some crafts—is in July and August, when Libby also organizes art workshops run by professional teachers. Open May to mid-October.

Motels and Cottage Colonies

You'll have to plan well in advance to snag one of the rustic **Ye Olde Forte Cabins** (18 Old Fort Rd., Pemaquid Beach 04554, 207/677-2261, $80–126 per day, $410–595 per week). These simple cabins have edged a grassy lawn dropping to John's Bay since 1922. Each has at least a toilet and sink, but a shower house and a well-equipped cookhouse are part of the colony. Although guests are expected to clean up after themselves when using the kitchen facilities, manager Julie Powell keeps the place spotless. No frills, unless you count the private small beach. Great place to bring a kayak. The cabins are less than 25 yards from Colonial Pemaquid and Fort William Henry. No credit cards.

Now here's a bargain. Up a long winding driveway behind Moody's Diner is **Moody's Motel** (Rte. 1, Waldoboro 04572, 207/832-5362, www.moodysdiner.com, $38–55), in biz since 1927, and likely little has changed in the meantime. Nothing fancy here, but it's clean and well run. The motel and tourist cabins all have screened porches and TV, and a few have kitchenettes. Open mid-May–mid-October.

Campgrounds

The area's best-run campground is 150-acre **Lake Pemaquid Camping** (off Biscay Rd., P.O. Box 967, Damariscotta 04543, 207/563-5202, www.lakepemaquid.com, $24–41), with 280 tent and RV sites, many right on the seven-mile-long lake. It's a lively operation, with tennis, pool and lake swimming, fishing (licenses available), playground, game room, store (lobsters available), laundry, sauna, Jacuzzi, and canoe, kayak, and boat rentals. Also plenty of entertainment, including train and hay rides, dances, movies, and performances. Rustic cabins and cottages, with full baths, are $650–950 per week. The campground is open Memorial Day weekend to Columbus Day.

FOOD

Breakfast, Lunch, and Miscellany

For breakfast, look no farther than **The Breakfast Place and Bakery** (Business Rte. 1, Main St., Damariscotta, 207/563-5434, 7 A.M.–1 P.M.), a small place that turns out big breakfasts. Homemade breads, muffins, and biscuits, eggs, omelets, pancakes, waffles, and more are all reasonably priced, most $4–6. A few specials, such as crab cakes and eggs or shrimp Creole omelet, are closer to $8.

For baked goods, sandwiches, soups, and gourmet goodies to go, head to **Weatherbird** (1168 Elm St., Damariscotta, 207/563-8993, 8 A.M.–5:30 P.M. Mon.–Sat.). Eat at one of the handful of tables out front or take it to the waterfront.

Just off Main Street, in the alley below Sheepscot River Pottery, is **Paco's Tacos** (207/563-5355, 11 A.M.–4 P.M. Mon.–Fri.), a hole-in-the-wall restaurant, where you order at the counter, then grab one of the few tables or take your meal to the waterfront. TexMex-style tacos, burritos, chimichangas, and fajitas, with most choices less than $7. Enchiladas are the specialty on Fridays.

In a barn-style building at the northern edge of Damariscotta is the area's best homemade ice cream—about four dozen flavors, including some unusual ones you'd never dream up. **Round Top Ice Cream** (Business Rte. 1, Damariscotta 04543, 207/563-5307), in business since 1924, is open daily 11:30 A.M.–10 P.M. May to Columbus Day, fewer hours off-season.

A New Harbor landmark since 1928, **C. E. Reilly & Son** (Village Center, New Harbor 04554, 207/677-2321, 8 A.M.–6 P.M. daily, to 8 P.M. Fri. and Sat.) is one of those local markets that has nearly everything: pizza, sandwiches, meat, first-rate produce, roast chicken, baked goods, liquor, lottery tickets, video rentals, upscale goodies, a few hardware items, and daily New York and Boston newspapers.

At the corner of Routes 1 and 220 in Waldoboro, opposite Moody's Diner, is the warehousey building that turns out superb **Borealis Breads** (1860 Atlantic Hwy., Rte. 1, Waldoboro, 207/832-0655, 8:30 A.M.–5:30 P.M. Mon.–Fri., 9 A.M.–4:30 P.M. Sat. and Sun.). Using sourdough starters (and no oils, sweeteners, eggs, or dairy products), owner Jim Amaral and his crew produce baguettes, olive bread, lemon fig bread, rosemary focaccia, and about a dozen other inventive flavors (each day has its specialties). A refrigerated case holds a small selection of picnic fixings (sandwich spreads, juices). Great soups and salads and excellent sandwiches are available to go.

The **Waldoboro 5&10** (Friendship St., Waldoboro 04572, 207/832-4624, 8 A.M.–5 P.M. Mon.–Sat.) is one of those old-fashioned, little-of-everything variety stores that disappeared ages ago. Inside are antiques, penny candy, and a deli serving excellent sandwiches and Round Top ice cream. It's a one-man operation, so service can be slow at peak times.

Each fall, around mid-September, a tiny, cryptic display ad appears in local newspapers: "Kraut's Ready." Savvy readers recognize this as the announcement of the latest batch of **Morse's sauerkraut**—an annual ritual since 1918. The homemade kraut is available in stores and by mail order, but it's more fun (and cheaper) to visit the shop, the **Kraut House** (3856 Washington Rd., Rte. 220, Waldoboro, 207/832-5569 or 800/486-1605), which also has a small café serving traditional German fare. Sandwiches, such as a classic Reuben, liverwurst, or Black Forest ham are $6; homemade pierogies are $5; a sausage plate is $7; and stuffed cabbage rolls are $8. Big serve-yourself jars of Morse's pickles are on the tables. The red-painted farm store also carries Aunt Lydia's Beet Relish, baked beans, mustard, maple syrup, and other Maine foods. Eight miles north of Route 1, it's open 9 A.M.–6 P.M. with food served to to 5 P.M.

Pizza, Pasta, Subs

For pizza, subs, and pasta, the choice is **Romeo's Pizza** (Business Rte. 1, Damariscotta, 207/563-1563, 11 A.M.–9 P.M.). The gourmet pizzas are superb (try the Aegean); most are around $8.50 small, $15.50 large. Dinners and pasta dishes, served with garlic bread and small tossed salad, are a steal at less than $8.

Also making good pizza is **Rosario's Café and Pizzeria** (South Side Rd., New Harbor, 207/677-6363, 4–8 P.M. daily, opens at noon Sat.). Pick your own toppings or go with one of the fancier offerings (12-inch pizzas begin at $6.75). Any pizza can be made into a calzone. There are a few tables inside and two on the tiny deck. Rosario's is behind Gifford's Ice Cream and across from C.E. O'Reilly store in the heart of New Harbor.

Diner Fare

Truck drivers, tourists, locals, and notables have been flocking to  **Moody's Diner** (Routes 1 and 220, Waldoboro 04572, 207/832-7785) since the early 1930s, when the Moody family established this classic diner on a Waldoboro hilltop. The antique neon sign has long been a Route 1 beacon, especially on a foggy night, and the crowds continue, with new generations of Moodys and considerable expansion of the premises. It's gone beyond diner-dom. Expect hearty, no-frills fare and such calorific desserts as peanut-butter or walnut pie. After eating, you can buy the cookbook. Open 4:30 A.M.–11 P.M.

Monday–Friday, 5 A.M.–11 P.M. Saturday, and 6 A.M.–11 P.M. Sunday.

Natural Foods/Farmers' Market

Rising Tide Natural Foods Market (Business Rte. 1, Damariscotta, 207/563-5556, 8 A.M.–7 P.M. Mon.–Sat. all year) at the northern end of town has been a thriving co-op organization since 1978, and it keeps on growing. Bulk items are available, plus books, cosmetics, and all kinds of preservative-free organic food. A self-service deli section has soups, sandwiches, salads, and entrées; you may be lucky enough to snag one of the handful of tables in the dining area.

From mid-May through October, 9 A.M.–noon on Friday, the **Damariscotta Area Farmers' Market** sets up at the Lincoln County Assembly of God parking lot on Business Route 1, Damariscotta. Condiments, baked goods, cheeses, local shellfish, and crafts are always available from about two dozen vendors, and you never know

© TOM NANGLE

The antique neon sign at Moody's Diner, in Waldoboro, has been a beacon in the night for generations of weary travelers. Stop in for no-frills fare, cheap prices, and fabulous pie.

what else will turn up at this major market. From late June through August, 9 A.M.–noon on Monday, a smaller market operates in the same location.

Casual Dining

A reliable standby in downtown Damariscotta, next to the Damariscotta Bank & Trust, the **Salt Bay Café** (Main St., Damariscotta 04543, 207/563-1666) has a loyal following—thanks to its imaginative, reasonably priced cuisine and cheerful, plant-filled setting. Vegetarians will love the two-dozen-plus choices. Dinner entrées are $11–19; hearty lunch sandwiches run $6–8. Liquor license. Open for breakfast (at 7:30 A.M.), lunch, and dinner Monday–Saturday (usually closing around 8:30 P.M. or so).

The view's the thing at **Schooner Landing** (Main St., Damariscotta, 207/563-7447, 11:30 A.M.–8 P.M.). The restaurant sits on the water's edge, with views way down the Damariscotta River. The menu has a bit of everything, with heftier choices priced $9–16. Evening entertainment is often on the schedule.

Same river, different view; near-to-impossible to find, but worth finding. **Backstreet Landing** (17 Elm St., Damariscotta, 207/563-5666, 11:30 A.M.–8 P.M. daily, to 8:30 P.M. Fri. and Sat. in summer, off-season hours vary) is a bit fancier and more creative (entrées $12–19) than Schooner Landing. To find it, head down the lane by the theater to the parking lot and plaza beyond, then veer right and continue behind that plaza to the restaurant, which sits right on the river's edge (you won't see it until you're almost there).

One of the best meal deals in the area is the ⛵ **Anchor Inn** (Harbor Rd., Round Pond 04564, 207/529-5584), tucked away on the picturesque harbor in Round Pond, on the eastern side of the peninsula. Informal and rustic, with a menu that'll surprise you (entrées $14–22), the place always attracts a crowd. Reservations are advisable on summer weekends. Open for lunch and dinner mid-May to mid-October. (After Labor Day, the schedule can be a bit erratic; call to confirm.) **Damariscotta River Grill** (155 Main St., Damariscotta, 207/563-2992), under the same ownership as the Anchor Inn, delivers a similar menu at a similar price. The artichoke fondue

is worth fighting over. Choose a table in the back with a river view, if available. The summer schedule is 11 A.M.–3 P.M. daily and 5–8 P.M. Sunday–Thursday, to 9 P.M. Friday and Saturday, and 9 A.M.–2:30 P.M. Sunday (for a very popular brunch). Open all year.

Location, location. Right next to Pemaquid Light is **The Sea Gull Shop** (Pemaquid Point, 207/677-2374), an oceanfront place with touristy prices ($7 for a cheese omelet, $17 for a lobster salad roll) but decent food—pancakes and muffins, for instance, overflowing with blueberries. Open 7:30 A.M.–7:30 P.M. the second Sunday in May to Columbus Day. BYOL.

Fine Dining

Most of the restaurants in this category are eateries in lodgings. The Bradley Inn, Coveside, and The Newcastle Inn are all good options (see Accommodations).

Lobster-in-the-Rough

The Pemaquid Peninsula must have more eat-on-the-dock places per capita than anyplace in Maine. Some are basic, no-frills operations, others are big-time commercial concerns. Each has a loyal following.

The biggest and best-known lobster wharf is **Shaw's Fish and Lobster Wharf** (Rte. 32, New Harbor, 207/677-2200 or 800/772-2209), where you place your order, take a number, and wait for it to come booming back at you over the loudspeaker. (You can also order steak here. And margaritas. And oysters at the wharf raw bar.) Fried seafood dinners run $8–17. Open mid-May to mid-October. Summer hours are 11 A.M.–9 P.M. daily; in spring and fall, Shaw's closes at 8 P.M. Sun.–Thurs. and at 9 P.M. on weekends.

Facing each other across the dock in the hamlet of Round Pond are the ⛵ **Round Pond Lobster Co-Op** (207/529-5725) and ⛵ **Muscongus Bay Lobster** (207/529-5528). Hard to say which is better; both are good, and competition keeps prices low. Muscongus has enlarged in recent years, so it even has covered seating; Round Pond is tiny but oh-so-fresh. Both are usually open 10 A.M.–7 P.M. in July and August, but Muscongus stays open later in the season.

Other seasonal lobster wharves on the peninsula are the **New Harbor Co-Op** (Rte. 32, New Harbor, 207/677-2791), **Pemaquid Fishermen's Co-Op** (Pemaquid Harbor Rd., Pemaquid Harbor, 207/677-2801), **South Bristol Fishermen's Co-Op** (Thompson Inn Rd., South Bristol, 207/644-8224 or 207/644-8246), and **Broad Cove Marine Services** (off Route 32, Medomak, 207/529-5186), a low-key sleeper with a wowser view.

INFORMATION AND SERVICES

Information

The **Damariscotta Region Chamber of Commerce** (P.O. Box 13, Damariscotta 04543, 207/563-8340, www.damariscottaregion.com) publishes a free annual information booklet about the area. Its office, just off Main Street, is open 9 A.M.–5 P.M. weekdays. The **Pemaquid Area Association** (Chamberlain 04541, no telephone) produces a very useful annotated map covering the lower half of the Pemaquid Peninsula. Both publications are available by mail and at the information bureaus. Also ask for a copy of *The Upper River Region Field Guide,* a foldout map/brochure produced by the Damariscotta River Association and containing excellent information about the area's preserves and natural history.

Hospitals

Just south of downtown Damariscotta is **Miles Memorial Hospital** (Bristol Rd., Route 130, Damariscotta, 207/563-1234).

Local Libraries

The **Skidompha Library** (Main St., Damariscotta, 207/563-5513) is open 9 A.M.–5 P.M. Tuesday–Friday, to 7 P.M. Thursday, and 9 A.M.–1 P.M. Saturday. (Incidentally, if you're puzzled by the name, it comes from the names of the members of a local literary society who founded the library at the turn of the 20th century.)

The **Waldoboro Public Library** (Main St., Waldoboro 04572, 207/832-4484) is in an 1855 Italianate building that once was a thriving customs house (a new building planned for a site just a few doors up the street is in the fund-raising stage). It's open 9:30 A.M.–8 P.M. Monday, 9:30 A.M.–4:30 P.M. Wednesday–Friday, and 9:30 A.M.–noon Saturday.

Getting Around

Concord Trailways (800/639-3317, www.concordtrailways.com) stops in Brunswick, Bath, Wiscasset, Damariscotta, and Waldoboro on its three daily nonexpress trips up the coast.

Penobscot Bay

Although considered part of the Mid-Coast, the region edging Penobscot Bay has a different feel. Coastal mountains in Camden and Lincolnville and an abundance of islands frame views. These island-studded waters are renowned by sailors, so it's no surprise that Maine's famed windjammer fleet is based here.

From Thomaston through Searsport, no two towns are alike except that all are changing, as traditional industries give way to arts- and tourism-related businesses and clean, modern enterprises such as the credit-card giant MBNA, with bases in Rockland and Belfast.

Thomaston's Museum in the Streets, Rockland's art galleries, Camden's picturesque mountainside harbor, Lincolnville's pocket beach, Belfast's inviting downtown, and Searsport's sea captains' homes all invite exploration, as do offshore islands. From Port Clyde, take the ferry to Monhegan, an offshore idyll known

© TOM NANGLE

Must-Sees

Look for **M** to find the sights and activities you can't miss and **M** for the best dining and lodging.

M Monhegan Museum: View an impressive art collection in this museum located beside the Monhegan Lighthouse, at the highest point on unique Monhegan Island (page 197).

M The Farnsworth Art Museum and Wyeth Center: Three generations of Wyeths are represented in this recently expanded museum, which also boasts an excellent collection of works by Maine and American masters (page 202).

During frequent special events at the Owls Head Transportation Museum, volunteers fly the planes, ride the bicycles, and drive the automobiles.

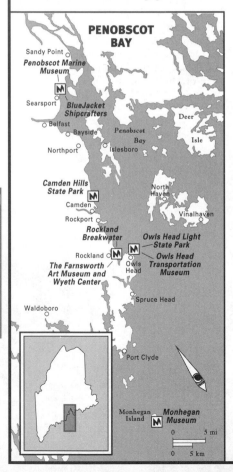

M Owls Head Transportation Museum: View a fabulous collection of vintage airplanes, automobiles, and even bicycles, many of which are flown, driven, or ridden during special weekend events (page 203).

M Rockland Breakwater: Take a walk on this nearly mile-long breakwater to the lighthouse at the end (open on weekends). It's an especially fine place to watch the windjammers sail in and out of Rockland Harbor (page 203).

M Owls Head Light State Park: The views of Penobscot Bay are spectacular, and it's a great place for a picnic lunch (page 204).

M Camden Hills State Park: If you have time, hike the moderate trail to the summit for a gull's-eye view over Camden Harbor and Penobscot Bay. If not, take the easy route and drive (page 221).

M Penobscot Marine Museum: Learn what life was *really* like during the Great Age of Sail in a town renowned for the number and quality of its sea captains (page 249).

M BlueJacket Shipcrafters: Even if you have no inclination whatsoever to build a model ship, stop by and view some of the museum-quality models built at the oldest model company in the country (page 249).

as the Artists' Island. From Rockland and Lincolnville Beach, car and passenger ferries head to Vinalhaven, North Haven, Matinicus, and Islesboro. All are occupied year-round by hardy souls and joined in summer by less-hardy ones. Except for Matinicus, they're great day-trip destinations. If what appeals to you about a ferry trip is traveling on the water, you can get a taste of the great age of sail by booking a three- or six-day cruise on one of the classic windjammer schooners berthed in Rockland, Rockport, and Camden. Or simply book a day sail or sea kayak excursion.

In July and August, try to avoid arriving in this region without a reservation. Helpful chamber of commerce staffers in prime locations often can work last-minute miracles, but special events and festivals can fill up all the beds for miles around.

PLANNING YOUR TIME

To hit just the highlights, you'll need at least four days. If you want to relax a bit and enjoy the area, plan on four or five days. Make it a full week if you plan on overnighting on any of the offshore islands. In general, lodging is less expensive in Rockland, Belfast, and Searsport than it is in Camden. Here's a suggested itinerary, but

make plans according to the weather. Head for Monhegan on a good day and save the museums for inclement ones.

Day one, in Rockland, visit The Farnsworth Art Museum in the morning, allowing an hour or so in town to browse galleries. Then, pick up a picnic lunch and aim for Owls Head. Begin at the Owls Head Light, where you can enjoy your lunch along with the view, then head over to the Owls Head Transportation Museum. Finish the day with a walk along the Rockland Breakwater.

Day two, head for Monhegan. Catch the early boat (pick up breakfast at the Port Clyde General Store), so you'll have most of the day to hike and visit artists' studios.

On day three, concentrate on Camden. Begin with a hike or drive to the summit of Mount Battie in Camden Hills State Park. Explore the downtown shops and galleries, perhaps breaking for a picnic lunch in Harbor Park. Plan an afternoon sailing or sea kayaking excursion. On your drive to Belfast, detour off Route 1 to the villages of Bayside and Temple Heights.

Day four, explore Belfast. Spend the morning taking a self-guided walking tour through the town, allowing plenty of time to shop downtown. Spend the afternoon in Searsport immersing yourself in maritime history at the Penobscot Marine Museum and BlueJacket Shipcrafters.

Thomaston Area

Thomaston is a little gem of a town, and getting more so each year thanks to the razing of the old Maine State Prison. It's also the gateway to two lovely fingers of land bordering the St. George River and jutting into the Gulf of Maine—the Cushing and St. George Peninsulas.

In 1605, British adventurer Captain George Waymouth sailed up the river now named after him (it was originally called the Georges River). A way station for Plymouth traders as early as 1630, Thomaston was incorporated in 1777 and officially named after General John Thomas, a Revolutionary War hero.

Industry began with the production of lime, which was used for plaster. A growing demand for

plaster, and the frequency with which the wooden boats were destroyed by fire while carrying loads of extremely flammable lime, spurred the growth of shipbuilding and all its related infrastructure. Thomaston's slogan became "the town that went to sea."

Seeing the sleepy harborfront today, it's hard to visualize the booming era when dozens of tall-masted wooden ships slid down the ways. But the town's architecture is a testament and tribute to the prosperous past—all those splendid homes on Main and Knox Streets were funded by wealthy shipowners and shipmasters who well understood how to occupy the idle hands of off-duty carpenters.

If you're in the area in December, you're in for a treat: Thomaston's holiday decorations are stunning. All over town, but especially in the Historic District, huge wreaths, tiny white lights, and (usually) a blanket of snow create a scene lifted right out of a Currier & Ives print.

SIGHTS AND RECREATION

Montpelier

As you head out of Thomaston on Route 1, toward Rockland, you'll come face to face with an imposing colonial hilltop mansion at the junction with Route 131 South. (Behind it, unfortunately, is the rather ugly outline of a huge cement plant.) Dedicated to the memory of General Henry Knox, President George Washington's secretary of war, Montpelier (Routes 1 and 131, P.O. Box 326, Thomaston 04861, 207/354-8062, www.generalknoxmuseum.org, 10 A.M.–4 P.M. Tues.–Sat. June–Sept.) is a 1930s replica of Knox's original Thomaston home. The mansion today contains Knox family furnishings and other period antiques—all described with great enthusiasm during the hour-long tours, beginning on the hour and half hour. A gift shop run by the Friends of Montpelier carries books and other relevant items. Concerts and other special events occur here periodically throughout the summer; General Knox's birthday is celebrated with considerable fanfare in early July. Admission is $6 adults, $5 seniors, $3 children 5–13, or $15 per family.

The Museum in the Streets

Montpelier is the starting point for a walking, cycling, or, if you must, driving tour (about three miles) of nearly 70 sites in Thomaston's National Historic District. Pick up a copy of the tour brochure at one of the local businesses. Included are lots of stories behind the facades of the handsome 19th-century homes that line Main and Knox Streets; the architecture here is nothing short of spectacular. Much of this history is also recounted in The Museum in the Streets, a walking tour taking in 25 informative plaques illustrated with old photos throughout town.

SHOPPING

Thomaston has a block-long shopping street (on Route 1), with ample free parking out back behind the stores. No big businesses here, but you'll find an especially choice collection of book, antique, and gift shops.

Books

If you arrive at Marti Reed's **Personal Book Shop** (78 Main St., Thomaston 04861, 207/354-8058) at the right time, you're likely to run into local writers' groups that gather frequently to swap tips and gossip. That's just the kind of place this is—an independent bookstore with a warm, nurturing feel. Not to mention a dog in residence. Lots of unusual titles, too—you won't leave empty-handed. Just give Marti an idea of the type of books you enjoy, and she's bound to steer you toward winners. It's all part of her personal service. She also has a 100 percent success record, to date, for finding out-of-print books.

Gifts—From Behind Bars

The **Maine State Prison Showroom Outlet** (Main St., Rte. 1, corner of Wadsworth St., Thomaston 04861, 207/354-3131, fax 207/354-3132) markets the handiwork of inmate craftsmen. Some of the souvenirs verge on kitsch; the bargains are wooden bar stools, toys (including dollhouses), and chopping boards. You'll need to carry your purchases with you; prison-made goods cannot be shipped.

Antiques

High-end 17th- and 18th-century American furniture and accessories are the stock-in-trade of **David C. Morey American Antiques** (103 Main St., 207/354-6033).

If you're more of a rumble-around-and-see-what-you-can-find type, **Thomaston Antiques** (179 Main St., 207/354-0600) is a group shop with a bit of this and a lot of that.

At the southern end of Thomaston, in a renovated chicken barn, is **Thomaston Place Auction Gallery** (51 Atlantic Hwy., Rte. 1, Thomaston 04861, 207/354-8141 or 888/834-5538, fax 207/354-9523), the home of Kaja Veilleux Antiques, a longtime dealer, appraiser, and auctioneer.

Auctions occur frequently throughout the summer (also in winter), with previews beforehand. The auctions are catered; call to reserve a place. You never know what you'll find. Check *Maine Antique Digest* for the current schedule.

ENTERTAINMENT, FESTIVALS, AND EVENTS

On Thomaston's northern flank, the 10-screen **Flagship Cinema** (Rte. 1, Thomaston 04861, 207/594-2100) draws customers from a wide area.

Thomaston's **Fourth of July**, an old-fashioned hometown celebration reminiscent of a Norman Rockwell painting, draws huge crowds. A spiffy parade—with bands, veterans, kids, and pets—starts off the morning (11 A.M.), followed by races, craft and food booths, and lots more. If you need to get *through* Thomaston on July 4, do it well before the parade or well after noon; the marchers go right down Main Street, Route 1, and gridlock forces a detour.

ACCOMMODATIONS

For lodgings nearby, see the St. George Peninsula and Rockland Area sections.

The best campground is on the Thomaston/Cushing town line at **Saltwater Farm Campground** (Wadsworth St./Cushing Rd., Cushing, mailing address P.O. Box 165, Thomaston 04861, 207/354-6735, www.midcoast.com/~sfc/), a 35-acre Good Sampark 1.5 miles south of Route 1. Thirty-seven open and wooded tent and RV sites ($28–35) overlook the St. George River. Cabins go for $40 a day. On-site trailers are $50. Facilities include a bathhouse, freshwater pool, laundry facilities, store, and play area. The river is tidal, so swimming is best near high tide; otherwise, you're dealing with mudflats. Open mid-May to mid-October.

FOOD

Casual Dining

Often overlooked by visitors (but certainly not by locals) is casual **N Thomaston Café & Bakery** (154 Main St., Rte. 1, Thomaston 04861,

207/354-8589). German-born chef Herb Peters is one of Mid-Coast Maine's best-known culinary pros. He and his wife, Eleanor, produce superb pastries, breads, and desserts (eat here or take out). Everything's homemade, there are children's options, and the café uses only organic poultry. Try the incredible wild mushroom hash. Beer and wine only. Open all year (7 A.M.–2 P.M. Mon.–Sat. and 8:30 A.M.–2 P.M. Sun. for brunch, 5:30–8 P.M. Fri. and Sat. for dinner). Entrées range $16–22; reservations are essential.

Hidden away on Thomaston's waterfront is the **Harbor View Restaurant** (Thomaston Landing, Water St., Thomaston 04861, 207/354-8173). Try for a table in the back, where you'll have a front-row seat on the harbor or out on the deck. The decor is disconnected: painted cement floors, cloth tablecloths and napkins, blaring TV in the bar area, orange chairs that look as if they were purchased from a 1970s lounge, and old mirrors on the wall, but the food, although a bit pricey, is good. Seafood is the specialty. (entrées $10–21). From Route 1 in Thomaston, take Knox Street to Water Street. The restaurant is a half mile off Route 1. Open daily 11:30 A.M.–2:30 P.M. and 5–8:30 P.M., to 9 P.M. Friday and Saturday, year-round; call ahead off-season.

INFORMATION AND SERVICES

Information

The **Rockland-Thomaston Area Chamber of Commerce** (P.O. Box 508, Rockland 04841, 207/596-0376 or 800/562-2529, www.therealmaine.com, 9 A.M.–5 P.M. Mon.–Fri. and 10 A.M.–2 P.M. Sat.), currently facing Harbor Park, will move into the new Gateway Center on Rockland's waterfront in mid- to late 2005. Until then, it's across the parking lot, but still on the waterfront.

Hospitals

Two major hospitals service the region. **Penobscot Bay Medical Center** (Rte. 1, Rockport 04856, 207/596-8000) and **Waldo County General Hospital** (118 Northport Ave., Belfast, 207/338-2500 or 800/649-2536), a community-oriented private (despite its name) institution.

Local Library

The **Thomaston Public Library** (42 Main St., Thomaston 04861, 207/354-2453) occupies part of the Greek Revival Thomaston Academy, once the town's elementary school (until 1982). Now the library shares the space with the Thomaston branch of the University of Maine's Thomaston Center; college classes are held here throughout the school year.

Getting Around

Concord Trailways (800/639-3317, www .concordtrailways.com) stops in Rockland, Camden-Rockport, Belfast, and Searsport on its three daily nonexpress trips up the coast.

Camden-based **Mid-Coast Limo** (800/937-2424 or 207/236-2424, www.midcoastlimo.com) provides van service, by reservation, between towns as far northeast as Belfast and Portland International Jetport.

Cushing Peninsula

Cushing's recorded history goes back at least as far as 1605, when someone named "Abr [maybe Abraham] King"—presumably a member of explorer George Waymouth's crew—inscribed his name here on a ledge (now private property). Since 1789, settlers' saltwater farms have sustained many generations, and the active Cushing Historical Society keeps the memo-ries and memorabilia from fading away. But the outside world knows little of this. Cushing is better known as "Wyeth country," the terrain depicted by the famous artistic dynasty of N. C., Andrew, and Jamie Wyeth (and assorted talented other relatives).

Even though several Wyeths still spend time here, you're not likely to meet any members of the family (unless you hang out near Fales's Store for days on end). However, if you're an Andrew Wyeth fan, visiting Cushing will give you the feeling of walking through his paintings. The flavor of his Maine work is here—rolling fields, wildflower meadows, rocky tidal coves, broad vistas, character-filled farmhouses, and some well-hidden summer enclaves. The only retail businesses are a general store, a few farmstands, and a seasonal takeout—plus a campground on the Cushing/Thomaston town line.

SIGHTS

Cushing's town boundary begins 1.3 miles south of Route 1 (take Wadsworth Street at the Maine State Prison Showroom Outlet). Two miles farther, you'll pass giant wooden sculptures in the yard of late artist **Bernard Langlais,** who died in 1977.

Six miles from Route 1 is the **A. S. Fales & Son Store** (locally, just "Fales's Store"), Cushing's heart and soul—source of fuel, film, gossip, and groceries. Built in 1889, the store has been in the Fales family ever since. Just beyond the store, take the left fork, continuing down the

© TOM NANGLE

Fans of Andrew Wyeth will recognize the Olson House, depicted in many of his paintings, including *Christina's World.*

Penobscot Bay

BEANHOLE BEANS

"To be happy in New England," wrote one Joseph P. MacCarthy at the turn of the 20th century, "you must select the Puritans for your ancestors . . . [and] eat beans on Saturday night." There is no better way to confirm the latter requirement than to attend a "beanhole" bean supper—a real-live legacy of colonial times, with dinner baked in a hole in the ground.

Generally scheduled, appropriately, for a Saturday night (check local newspapers), a beanhole bean supper demands plenty of preparation from its hosts—and a secret ingredient or two. (Don't even think about trying to pry the recipe out of the cooks.) The supper always includes hot dogs, cole slaw, relishes, home-baked breads, and homemade desserts, but the beans are the star attraction. (Typically, the suppers are also alcohol-free.) Not only are they feasts, they're also bargains, never setting you back more than about $8.

The beans at the Broad Cove Church's annual mid-July beanhole bean supper, served family style at long picnic tables, are legendary—attracting nearly 200 eager diners. Minus the secrets, here's what happens:

Early Friday morning: Church volunteers load 10 pounds of dry pea and soldier (yelloweye) beans into each of four large kettles and add water to cover. The beans are left to soak and soften for six or seven hours. Two or three volunteers uncover the churchyard's four rock-lined beanholes (each about three feet deep), fill the holes with hardwood kindling, ignite the wood, and keep the fires burning until late afternoon, when the wood is reduced to red-hot coals.

Early Friday afternoon: The veteran chefs parboil the beans and stir in the seasonings. Typical additions are brown sugar, molasses, mustard, salt, pepper, and salt pork (much of the secret is in the exact proportions). When the beans are precooked to the cooks' satisfaction, the kettle lids are secured with wire and the pots are lugged outdoors.

Friday midafternoon: With the beans ready to go underground, some of the hot coals are quickly shoveled out of the pits. The kettles are lowered into the pits and the coals replaced around the sides of the kettles and atop their lids. The pits are covered with heavy sheet metal and topped with a thick layer of sand and a tarpaulin. The round-the-clock baking begins, and no one peeks before it's finished.

Saturday midafternoon: Even the veterans start getting nervous just before the pits are uncovered. Was the seasoning right? Did too much water cook away? Did the beans dry out? Not to worry, though—failures just don't happen here.

Saturday night: When a pot is excavated for the first of three seatings (about 5 P.M.), the line is already long. The chefs check their handiwork and the supper begins. No one seems to mind waiting for the second and third seatings—while others eat, a sing-along gets under way in the church, keeping everyone entertained.

peninsula toward the Broad Cove Church and the Olson House.

Broad Cove Church

Wyeth aficionados will recognize the Broad Cove Church as one of his subjects—alongside Cushing Road en route to the Olson House. Most days, it's open, so step inside and admire the classic New England architecture. The church is also well known as the site of one of the region's best beanhole bean suppers, held on a mid-July Saturday and attracting several hundred appreciative diners (see the sidebar, Beanhole Beans). Bear left at the fork after Fales's Store; the church is .4 mile farther, on the right.

The Olson House

Many an art lover makes the pilgrimage to the Olson House, a famous icon near the end of Hathorn Point Road. The early-19th-century farmhouse appears in Andrew Wyeth's 1948 painting *Christina's World* (which hangs in New York's Museum of Modern Art), his best-known image of disabled Christina Olson, who died in 1968. In 1991, two philanthropists donated the Olson House to The Farnsworth Art Museum in Rockland, which has retained the house's sparse, lonely, and almost mystical ambience. The clapboards outside remain unpainted, the interior walls bear only a few Wyeth prints (hung close to the settings they depict), and it is easy to sense

Wyeth's inspiration for chronicling this place. The house is open 11 A.M.–4 P.M. daily Memorial Day weekend through Columbus Day. Admission is $4 adults and seniors, free for anyone under 18. (An $11 combination ticket includes admission to The Farnsworth Art Museum.)

From Route 1 in Thomaston, at the Maine State Prison Showroom Outlet, turn onto Wadsworth Street and go six miles to Fales's Store. Take the left fork after the store, go 1.5 miles, and turn left onto Hathorn Point Road. Go another 1.9 miles to the house.

St. George Peninsula

Even though the Cushing and St. George Peninsulas face each other across the St. George River, they differ dramatically. Cushing is far more rural, seemingly less approachable—with little access to the surrounding waters; St. George has a whole string of things to do and see, and places to sleep and eat—plus shore access in various spots along the peninsula.

The St. George Peninsula is actually better known by some of the villages scattered along its length: Tenants Harbor, Port Clyde, Wiley's Corner, Spruce Head—plus the smaller neighborhoods of Martinsville, Smalleytown, Glenmere, Long Cove, Hart's Neck, and Clark Island. Each has a distinct personality, determined partly by the different ethnic groups—primarily Brits, Swedes, and Finns—who arrived to work the granite quarries in the 19th century. Wander through the Seaview Cemetery in Tenants Harbor and you'll see the story: row after row of gravestones with names from across the sea.

A more famous former visitor was 19th-century novelist Sarah Orne Jewett, who holed up in an old schoolhouse in Martinsville, paid a weekly rental of $.50, and wrote *The Country of the Pointed Firs,* a tale about "Dunnet's Landing" (Tenants Harbor).

Today the picturesque peninsula has saltwater farms, tidy hamlets, a striking lighthouse, spruceedged tidal coves, an active yachting harbor, and, at the tip, a tiny fishing village (Port Clyde), which serves as the springboard to offshore Monhegan Island.

Port Clyde, in fact, may be the best-known community here. (Fortunately, it's no longer called by its unappealing 18th-century name—Herring Gut.) George Waymouth explored Port Clyde's nearby islands in 1605, but you'd never suspect its long tradition. It's a sleepy place, with a general store, an inn, a couple of shops, and expensive parking. (Enterprising locals charge $4 a day, mostly to capture visitors heading to car-free Monhegan.)

SIGHTS
Lighthouse Museum
Not many settings can compare with the spectacular locale of the **Marshall Point Lighthouse Museum** (Marshall Point Rd., P.O. Box 247, Port Clyde 04855, 207/372-6450), a distinctive 1857 lighthouse and park overlooking Port Clyde, the harbor islands, and the passing lobsterboat fleet. Bring a picnic and let the kids run on the lawn (but keep them well back from the shoreline). The tiny museum, in the 1895 keeper's house, displays local memorabilia. Admission is free, but donations are welcomed. Open 1–5 P.M. Sunday–Friday, 10 A.M.–5 P.M. Saturday, Memorial Day weekend through September, and occasional weekend afternoons in May and October. The grounds are accessible year-round. Take Route 131 to Port Clyde and watch for signs to the museum.

RECREATION
Swimming and Beachcombing
Drift Inn Beach, on Drift Inn Beach Road (also called Candy's Cove Road), isn't a big deal as beaches go, but it's the best public one on the peninsula, so it gets busy on hot days. The name comes from the Drift Inn, a summer hotel situated here early in the 20th century. Drift Inn Beach Road parallels Route 131, and the parking lot is accessible from both roads. Heading south on the peninsula, about 3.5 miles after the junction with Route 73, turn left at Drift Inn Beach

Road. The sign frequently disappears; watch for an imposing square granite house and a red farm on your left. Go .2 mile from the turn.

Bicycling

Bicycling in this region is hazardous. Roads are narrow and at times rather heavily traveled, especially in July and August, and shoulders are poor-to-nonexistent.

Tennis

Public courts, available on a first-come, first-served basis, are behind the municipal building in **South Thomaston,** about three-quarters of a mile south of the Keag Store (Rte. 73, Village Center, South Thomaston).

Sea Kayaking

The St. George Peninsula is especially popular for sea kayaking, with plenty of islands to add interest and shelter. **Port Clyde Kayaks** (440 Glenmere Rd., Port clyde, 207/372-8128, www.portclydekayaks.com) offers 2.5-hour ($45) and 4-hour ($59) guided tours around the tip of the peninsula, taking in Marshall Point Lighthouse and the islands.

If you've had experience, you can launch on the ramp just before the causeway that links the mainland with Spruce Head Island, in Spruce Head (Island Rd., off Rte. 73) Parking is limited. A great paddle goes clockwise around Spruce Head Island and nearby Whitehead (there's a lighthouse on its southeastern shore) and Norton Islands. Duck in for lunch at Waterman's Beach Lobster. Around new moon and full moon, plan your schedule to avoid low tide near the Spruce Head causeway, or you may become mired in mudflats.

Boat Tours

The best boating experience on this peninsula is a passenger-ferry trip from Port Clyde to offshore **Monhegan Island**—for a day, overnight, or longer. (See Monhegan: Offshore Idyll for more information.) Perhaps because the private ferry company has a monopoly on this harbor, the trip isn't cheap, and parking adds to the cost, but it's a "must" excursion, so try to factor it into the budget. Port Clyde is the nearest mainland harbor to

Monhegan; this service operates all year (summer-only boats depart from New Harbor and Boothbay Harbor). **Monhegan-Thomaston Boat Line** (P.O. Box 238, Port Clyde 04855, 207/372-8848, www.monheganboat.com) uses two boats, the *Laura B.,* 70 minutes each way, and the newer *Elizabeth Ann,* 50 minutes. Round-trip tickets are $27 adults, $14 kids 2–12. (Leave your bicycle in Port Clyde; you won't need it on the island.) Reservations are essential in summer, especially for the 10:30 A.M. boat; a $5 pp fee holds the reservation until 75 minutes before departure, so you have to get to the dock early. No deposit is needed for other boats, but show up 30 minutes before departure. Parking in Port Clyde is $4 a day. If a summer day trip is all you can manage, aim for the first or second boat and return on the last one; don't go just for the boat ride.

In May, before Memorial Day weekend, there's only one daily boat, so you'll need to stay overnight unless you just do the round-trip. There are three boats daily (except Sunday) in June, then three trips every day July through Labor Day. From Labor Day to mid-October, there are three daily (except Sunday) trips, then one trip the rest of October. November–April, trips are Monday, Wednesday, and Friday only (except postal holidays).

During the summer months, the Monhegan-Thomaston Boat Line also offers sightseeing cruises on a varied schedule, including a Puffin/Nature Cruise, a Lighthouse Cruise, and, from mid-August through mid-September, a Fall Fins and Feathers Cruise. Each lasts about 2.5 hours and costs $24 adult, $12 child.

SHOPPING

Art Galleries

The St. George Peninsula has been attracting artists for decades, so it's no surprise that galleries seem to be everywhere you look. Some have been here for years, others started yesterday; most are worth a stop, so keep an eye out for their signs.

The Drawing Room Gallery (863 River Rd., St. George 04860, 207/372-6242) mounts several theme-based group shows each summer. Philip and Barbara Anderson's gallery is just north of

Fine wine and tire sealer, the *New York Times* and *Commercial Fisheries News* share shelf space at the Port Clyde General Store, a perfect place to pick up goodies before taking the boat to Monhegan Island.

the junction with Route 73, about five miles south of Route 1.

Overlooking the reversing falls in downtown South Thomaston, **The Old Post Office Gallery** (Spruce Head Rd., Rte. 73, P.O. Box 356, South Thomaston 04858, 207/594-9396) focuses on marine art and antiques: ship models, prints, paintings, sculpture, scrimshaw, and jewelry. The price range is broad.

Pottery

Since 1972, Tony Oliveri has been the inspiration and the artisan behind **Keag River Pottery** (Westbrook St., P.O. Box 227, South Thomaston 04858, 207/594-7915), a small shop attached to his home just .1 mile off Route 73 (or 2.2 miles east of Route 131). He produces brilliantly glazed functional wares, such as bowls, dishes, and lamps, and readily accepts commissions.

Used Books

Drive up to the small parking area at **Lobster**

Lane Book Shop (Island Rd., Spruce Head 04859, 207/594-7520) and you'll see license plates from everywhere. Owner Vivian York's tiny shop, a crammed but well-organized shed that's been here since the 1960s, has 50,000 or so treasures for used-book fans. For a few dollars, you can stock up on a summer's worth of reading. The shop is just under a mile east of Route 73, with eye-catching vistas in several directions (except, of course, when Spruce Head's infamous fog sets in).

Miscellany

Despite periodic ownership changes, **Port Clyde General Store** (Rte. 131, Port Clyde 04855, 207/372-6543) remains a character-ful destination, a two-century-old country store with a few yuppie touches. Stock up on groceries, pick up a newspaper, order a pizza, or buy a sweatshirt (you may need it on the Monhegan boat). Open daily 6 A.M.–9 P.M. in summer, shorter hours the rest of the year. Out back is the Dip Net restaurant, a great place to eat on the dock.

ACCOMMODATIONS

Inns

The East Wind Inn (Mechanic St., Rte. 131, P.O. Box 149, Tenants Harbor 04860, 207/372-6366 or 800/241-8439, www.eastwindinn.com) is the perfect rendition of an old-fashioned country inn—some parts of it more old-fashioned than others. Built in 1860 and originally used as a sail loft, it has a huge veranda, a cozy parlor, harbor-view rooms, and a quiet dining room with a creditable New England menu. Of the 26 traditional rooms in the main inn building, 19 have private baths; the others share four baths. Next door, the inn's spiffed-up 19th-century Meeting House, a former sea captain's home, has 10 modern rooms and suites, all with great views, and one apartment; $129–189. Also on the premises, the Ginny Wheeler Cottage has three superb apartments—$199–279. All rates include a full breakfast. The water-view dining room serves breakfast and dinner. Reservations are wise. Lunch is available in summer at the dockside Chandlery. Children are welcome; pets are $10 per visit. The inn is open all year; the dining room is open April–November.

If you stay at the **Ocean House** (Rte. 131, P.O. Box 66, Port Clyde 04855, 207/372-6691 or 800/269-6691, www.oceanhousehotel.com), you can plan to roll out of bed, eat breakfast, and roll down the hill to the Monhegan boat. It's ultra-convenient, and you can leave your car here (free). Several of the 10 unpretentious inn rooms (seven with private bath) have great harbor views (especially number 11). Doubles are $75–105, plus $5 for a single-night stay. No credit cards. Open mid-May through October. Breakfast, served 7 A.M.–noon, is a big deal in the 40-seat dining room, and Sunday it's filled with locals. Before the boat, try the "Monhegan quickie" ($4.50), a variation on an Egg McMuffin.

B&Bs

The **Blue Lupin** (372 Waterman's Beach Rd., South Thomaston 04858, 207/594-2673) has an out-of-this-world view in an off-the-beaten-track locale. Three rooms and a suite, all with private bath and TV/VCR, go for $75–160 d, mid-May through October, less off-season. Breakfast is a feast. You're right on the water, so bring a sea kayak and launch it from the beach. Or bring a bicycle to explore the area. Next door is Waterman's Beach Lobster. Open all year, but call ahead off-season.

In the center of South Thomaston village but overlooking the reversing falls on the tidal Wessaweskeag River, the 1830 **Weskeag at the Water** (14 Elm St., Rte. 73, P.O. Box 213, South Thomaston 04858, 207/596-6676 or 800/596-5576, www.midcoast.com/weskeag) has nine rooms, of which four have private baths, for $85–150 d in summer. This place is especially relaxing; congenial innkeepers Gray and Lynne Smith provide guests with games, puzzles, books, a huge video library, a great deck, and a lawn stretching to the river. Bring your sea kayak and bicycles. It's 1.5 miles from the Owls Head Transportation Museum (the Smiths love vintage cars) and a few more miles from the restaurants of downtown Rockland. Open all year.

FOOD

Picnic Fare

Don't be surprised to see the handful of tables occupied at the **Keag Store** (Rte. 73, Village Center, South Thomaston, 207/596-6810, 6 A.M.–9 P.M. Mon.–Sat. and 7 A.M.–8 P.M. Sun. year-round), one of the most popular lunch stops in the area. (Keag, by the way, is pronounced "gig"—short for "Wessaweskeag.") Roast-turkey sandwiches with stuffing ($3.99) are a big draw, as is the pizza, which verges on the greasy but compensates with its flavor—no designer toppings, just good pizza. Order it all to go and head across the street to the public wharf, where you can hang out and observe all the comings and goings.

Other good spots for picnic fare are the **Port Clyde General Store** (Rte. 131, Port Clyde 04855, 207/372-6543), the **Schoolhouse Bakery** (Rte. 131, Tenants Harbor 04860, 207/372-9608), and the **Off Island Store** (Island Rd., Spruce Head 04859, 207/594-7475).

Casual Dining

Farmer's Restaurant (Main St., Rte. 131, P.O. Box 240, Tenants Harbor 04860, 207/372-6111), a longtime neighborhoody place, is unfancy but reliable, with fresh seafood, steaks, and such. Open daily 7 A.M.–9 P.M. (to 9:30 P.M. Fri. and Sat.), all year. The menu has a bit of everything, with most choices in the $9–15 range. The restaurant is in Tenants Harbor village.

Seafood is everything at **The Harpoon** (Drift Inn Rd. and Marshall Point Rd., Port Clyde 04855, 207/372-6304), and it's about as fresh as it gets. Steaks are also on the menu, along with Cajun dishes ($17–23). Lobster's available, but save that for an outdoor deck. Rebuilt from the ashes of an early-1990s fire, the informal restaurant is just over a low hill from the center of Port Clyde. Open daily 5–9 P.M. (to 10 P.M. Fri. and Sat.) mid-May to mid-October.

The decidedly old-fashioned **Craignair Inn Restaurant** (Clark Island Rd., off Rte. 71, Spruce Head, 207/594-7644), built in 1928 to house granite workers, serves dinner in its waterview dining room daily except Sunday, entrées $16–24. No surprise that seafood is the specialty. Also in the Main Inn and Vestry Annex are rooms, some with shared baths, $65–140, with breakfast.

At **The East Wind Inn** (Mechanic St., Rte. 131, Tenants Harbor, 207/372-6366), the water-view dining room is open to the public April–November for breakfast (7:30–9:30 A.M., to 10 A.M. in July and Aug.) and dinner (5:30–8:30 P.M., to 9 P.M. in July and Aug.). Dinner entrées are $16–26. Reservations are wise. Lunch is available in summer at the dockside Chandlery.

Mediterranean

You might think you've ventured into Italy upon entering chef Kevin M. Kieley's ◼ **Sul Mare** (13 River Rd., Rte. 131, Tenants Harbor, 207/372-9995, 5–10 P.M. daily in summer, closed Mon. and Tues. in winter), an intimate bistro, with tile floors, a rustic ambience, a fireplace to ward off the chill on chilly nights, and a hearty menu that seals the deal (entrées $16–22).

Lobster-in-the-Rough

These open-air lobster wharves are the best places in the area to get down and dirty and manhandle a steamed or boiled lobster.

With outside picnic tables overlooking the harbor, **Cod End** (Commercial St., next to the town dock, Tenants Harbor 04860, 207/372-6782) is the right kind of rustic. Dig into lobster, fried clams, chowders, and delicious homemade pies; beer and wine available. Dinner entrées run $11–15, but inexpensive sandwiches, clam rolls, and burgers are available. Bring the kids: Peanut butter and jelly and hot dogs are each about $1.50. The market, selling fresh fish and seafood, is open daily 7 A.M.–7 P.M., the cookhouse is open 11 A.M.–8:30 P.M. Memorial Day through September. Take Route 131 south 9.5 miles from Route 1 in Thomaston; turn left about 30 yards beyond Hall's Market.

Out back behind the Port Clyde General Store, and overlooking the Port Clyde lobsterboat fleet, is the **Dip Net** (Rte. 131, Port Clyde 04855, 207/372-6543, 11 A.M.–10 P.M. mid-May to mid-Sept.), with indoor and outdoor seating. It's all quite casual. The menu emphasizes seafood, with light fare ($4.50–8) and more substantial choices ($11–20) available. Great place for a shore dinner: lobster, clams, mussels, corn, and bread, at market price.

Poking right into Wheeler's Bay, **Miller's Lobster Company** (Eagle Quarry Rd., off Rte. 73, Spruce Head 04859, 207/594-7406) is the quintessential lobster pound, a well-run operation that draws crowds all summer long. Lobster rolls, steamed clams, crabmeat rolls, homemade pies—the works. Even hot dogs if you need them. Several picnic tables are under cover for chilly or rainy weather. BYOL. Open 11 A.M.–7 P.M. late June to Labor Day.

A broad view of islands in the Mussel Ridge Channel is the bonanza at ◼ **Waterman's Beach Lobster** (343 Waterman's Beach Rd., South Thomaston 04858, 207/596-7819, 11 A.M.–7 P.M. Thurs.–Sun. mid-June to Labor Day). This tiny operation has a big reputation: It has won a James Beard Award. It turns out well-stuffed lobster and crabmeat rolls and superb pies. Step up to the window and place your order. Service can be slow, but why rush with a view like this? Choose a good day; there's no real shelter from bad weather. BYOL; no credit cards. Next door to the Blue Lupin B&B, the wharf is on a side road off Route 73 between Spruce Head Village and South Thomaston; watch for signs on Route 73.

Monhegan: Offshore Idyll

Eleven or so miles from the mainland lies a unique island community with gritty lobstermen, close-knit families, a can-do spirit, a long-standing summertime artists' colony, no cars, astonishingly beautiful scenery, and some of the best birding on the eastern seaboard. Until the 1980s, the island had only radiophones and generator power; with the arrival of electricity and real phones, the pace has quickened a bit—but not much. Welcome to Monhegan Island.

But first a cautionary note: Monhegan has remained idyllic largely because generations of residents, part-timers, and visitors have been ultrasensitive to its fragility. When you buy your ferry ticket, you'll receive a copy of the regulations, all very reasonable, and the captain of your ferry will reiterate them. *Heed them or don't go.*

Many of the regulations have been developed by The Monhegan Associates, an island land trust founded in the 1960s by Theodore Edison, son of the inventor. Firmly committed to preservation of the island in as natural a state as possible, the group maintains and marks the trails, sponsors natural-history talks, and insists that no construction be allowed beyond the village limits.

The origin of the name Monhegan remains up in the air; it's either a Maliseet or Micmac name meaning "out-to-sea island" or an adaptation of the name of a French explorer's daughter. In any case, Monhegan caught the attention of Europeans after English explorer John Smith stopped by in 1614, but the island had already been noticed by earlier adventurers, including John Cabot, Giovanni da Verrazzano, and George Waymouth. Legend even has it that Monhegan fishermen sent dried fish to Plimoth Plantation during the Pilgrims' first winter on Cape Cod. Captain Smith returned home and carried on about Monhegan, snagging the attention of intrepid souls who established a fishing/trading outpost here in 1625. Monhegan has been settled continuously since 1674, with fishing as the economic base.

In the 1880s, lured by the spectacular setting and artist Robert Henri's enthusiastic reports, gangs of artists began arriving, lugging their easels here and there to capture the surf, the light, the tidy cottages, the magnificent headlands, fishing boats, even the islanders' craggy features. American, German, French, and British artists have long (and continue to) come here; well-known signatures associated with Monhegan include Rockwell Kent, George Bellows, Edward Hopper, James Fitzgerald, Andrew Winter, Alice Kent Stoddard, Reuben Tam, William Kienbusch, and Jamie Wyeth.

Officially called Monhegan Plantation (part of Lincoln County), the island has about 105 year-rounders. Several hundred others summer here. A handful of students attend the tiny school through eighth grade; high schoolers have to pack up and move "inshore" to the mainland during the school year.

As if the isolation weren't rigorous enough, Monhegan's lobster-fishing season—a legislatively sanctioned period—perversely begins on December 1 (locally known as Trap Day). An air of nervous anticipation surrounds the dozen or so lobsterers after midnight the day before, as they prepare to steam out to set their traps on the ocean floor. Of course, with the lack of competition from mainland fisherfolk that time of year, and a supply of lobsters fattening up since the previous June, there's a ready market for their catch. But success still depends on a smooth "setting." Meetings are held daily during the month beforehand to make sure everyone will be ready to "set" together. The season ends on June 25.

Almost within spitting distance of Monhegan's dock (but you'll still need a boat) is whale-shaped **Manana Island,** once the home of an ex-New Yorker named Ray Phillips. Known as the Hermit of Manana, Phillips lived a solitary shepherding existence on this barren island for more than half a century until his death in 1975. His story had spread so far afield that even *The New York Times* ran a

TEN RULES FOR MONHEGAN VISITORS

1. Smoking is banned everywhere except in the village.
2. Rock climbing is not allowed on the wild headlands on the back side of the island.
3. Preserve the island's wild state—do not remove flowers or lichens.
4. Bicycles and strollers are not allowed on island trails.
5. Camping and campfires are forbidden islandwide.
6. Swim only at Swim Beach, just south of the ferry landing—if your innards can stand the shock. Wait for the incoming tide, when the water is warmest (and this warmth is relative). It's wise not to swim alone.
7. Dogs must be leashed; carry a pooper-scooper to remove their waste.
8. Be respectful of private property; stay on the trails. (As the island visitor's guide puts it, "Monhegan is a village, not a theme park.")
9. If you're staying overnight, bring a flashlight; the village paths are very dark.
10. Carry the island trail map when you go exploring; you'll need it.

A strong suggestion: Carry a trash bag, use it, and take it off the island when you leave.

front-page obituary when he died. (Photos and clippings are displayed in the Monhegan Museum.) In summer, youngsters with skiffs often hang around the harbor, particularly Fish Beach and Swim Beach, and you can usually talk one of them into taking you over, for a fee. (Don't try to talk them down too much or they may not return to pick you up.) Some curious inscriptions on Manana (marked with a yellow X near the boat landing) have led archaeologists to claim that Vikings even made it here, but cooler heads attribute the markings to Mother Nature.

When to Go

If a day trip is all your schedule will allow, visit Monhegan between Memorial Day weekend and mid-October, when ferries from Port Clyde, New Harbor, and Boothbay Harbor operate daily, allowing 5–9 hours on the island—time enough to do an extensive trail loop, visit the museum and handful of shops, and picnic on the rocks. Other months, there's only one ferry a day from Port Clyde (only three a week Nov.–April), so you'll need to spend the night—not a hardship, but definitely requiring planning.

Almost any time of year, but especially in spring, fog can blanket the island, curtailing photography and swimming (although usually not the ferries). A spectacular sunny day can't be beat, but the fog lends an air of mystery you won't forget, so don't be deterred. Rain, of course, is another matter; some island trails can be perilous even in a misty drizzle.

Other Points to Consider

Monhegan has no bank, but there's an ATM in the Barnacle Café. Credit cards are not accepted everywhere. Personal checks, traveler's checks, or cash will do. The few **public telephones** in the village require phone credit cards.

The only **public restroom** unconnected to a restaurant or lodging is on Horn Hill, at the southern end of the village (near the Monhegan House), and it will cost you $1 to use it. Outrageous, perhaps, but the restroom was installed to protect the woods and trails and deter daytrippers from bothering innkeepers. Unfortunately, the fee inspires some people to spurn these facilities and head for the woods. Please spend the dollar and preserve the island.

Whitetail deer used to overrun the island, leading to a relatively high incidence of Lyme disease (transmitted by deer ticks), but elimination of the herd (don't ask how) in recent years seems to have alleviated the situation. Nonetheless, birders and hikers should err on the side of caution and wear long pants rather than shorts, and tuck pant legs into socks. Check for ticks after hiking. (See Health and Safety in the Know Coastal Maine chapter.)

SIGHTS AND RECREATION

Monhegan is a getaway destination, a relaxing place for self-starters, so don't anticipate organized entertainment beyond the occasional lecture or narrated nature tour. Bring sturdy shoes (maybe even an extra pair in case trails are wet), a windbreaker, binoculars, a camera, and perhaps a sketch pad or a journal. If you're staying overnight, bring a flashlight for negotiating the unlighted island

© TOM NANGLE

Monhegan's nickname "Artists' Island" is appropriate, given the amount of artwork visible on the island and the number of artists opening their studios to visitors.

walkways, even in the village. For rainy days, bring a book. (If you forget, there's an amazingly good library.) In winter, bring ice skates for use on the Ice Pond.

Monhegan Museum

The National Historic Register **Monhegan Lighthouse**—activated in July 1824 and automated in 1959—stands at the island's highest point, Lighthouse Hill, an exposed summit that's also home to the Monhegan Museum (207/596-7003, www.monheganmuseum.org), in the former keeper's house and adjacent buildings. Overseen by the **Monhegan Historical and Cultural Museum Association** (Monhegan 04852), the museum contains an antique kitchen, lobstering exhibits, and a fine collection of paintings by noted and not-so-noted artists. Two outbuildings have tools and gear connected with fishing and ice-cutting, traditional island industries. The assistant lightkeeper's house, recently restored top-to-bottom as a handsome art gallery, provides a climate-controlled environment for the museum's impressive art collection. A volunteer usually is on hand to answer questions. Museum hours, coordinated with the ferry schedule, are 11:30 A.M.–3:30 P.M. July and August, 12:30–2:30 P.M. June and September. Admission is technically free, but donations are encouraged.

Artists' Studios

Nearly 20 artists' studios are open to the public during the summer (usually July and August), but not all at once. At least five are open most days—most in the afternoon (Monday has the fewest choices). Sometimes it's tight timewise for day-trippers who also want to hike the trails, but most of the studios are relatively close to the ferry landing. An annually updated map/schedule details locations, days, and times. It's posted on bulletin boards in the village and is available at lodgings and shops.

Shopping

Galleries and shops in the village include **Winter Works** (craft co-op), **Lupine Gallery** (207/594-8131, works by Monhegan artists and artists' supplies), **Black Duck** (gifts), and the **Carina Shop** (bread, produce, coffee, wine, newspapers, gourmet specialties).

Hiking/Walking

Just over a half mile wide and 1.7 miles long, barely a square mile in area, Monhegan has 18 numbered hiking trails, most easy to moderate, covering about 17 miles. All are described in the *Monhegan Associates Trail Map* (www.monheganassociates.org), available at mainland ferry offices and island shops and lodgings or on the website. (The map is not to scale, so the hikes can take longer than you think.)

Dress in layers, including long pants, and wear hiking boots or sturdy walking shoes. Even if you're warm in the village, you'll feel the wind on the island's backside and up at the lighthouse. Do bring water and a picnic lunch or snack.

The footing is uneven everywhere, so Monhegan can present major obstacles to those with disabilities, even on the well-worn but unpaved village roads. Maintain an especially healthy respect for the ocean here, and don't venture too close; over the years, rogue waves on the island's backside have claimed victims young and old.

A relatively easy **day-tripper loop,** with a couple of moderate sections along the backside of the island, takes in several of Monhegan's finest features, starting at the southern end of the village, opposite the church. To appreciate it, allow at least two hours. From the Main Road, go up Horn Hill, following signs for the **Burnthead Trail** (no. 4). Cross the island to the **Cliff Trail** (no. 1). Turn north on the Cliff Trail, following the dramatic headlands on the island's backside. Lots of great picnic rocks in this area. Continue to Squeaker Cove, where the surf is the wildest, but be cautious. Then watch for signs to the **Cathedral Woods Trail** (no. 11), carpeted with pine needles and leading back to the village.

When you get back to Main Road, detour up the **Whitehead Trail** (no. 7) to the museum. If you're spending the night and feeling energetic, consider circumnavigating the island via the **Cliff Trail** (nos. 1 and 1-A). Allow at least five or six hours for this route; don't rush it.

Birding

One of the East Coast's best birding sites during spring and fall migrations, Monhegan is a migrant trap for exhausted creatures winging their way north or south. Avid birders come here to add rare and unusual species to their life lists, and some devotees return year after year. No birder should arrive, however, without a copy of the superb *Birder's Guide to Maine* (see Suggested Reading in the Know Coastal Maine chapter).

Predicting exact bird-migration dates can be dicey, since wind and weather aberrations can skew the schedule. Generally, the best times are mid- to late May and most of September, into early October. If you plan to spend a night (or more) on the island during migration seasons, don't try to wing it—reserve a room well in advance.

Around-the-Island Tour

On most days, the Balmy Days excursion boat makes a half-hour circuit around the island 2–2:30 P.M. for $2. Ask at the ferry dock.

ACCOMMODATIONS

The island has a variety of lodgings from rustic to comfortable; none qualify in the multistar category. Pickup trucks of dubious vintage meet all the ferries and transport luggage to the lodgings. For cottage renters, Monhegan Trucking charges $2 for the first piece of luggage, $1 for each additional piece.

Best lodging is the **Island Inn** (P.O. Box 128, Monhegan 04852, 207/596-0371, www.islandinnmonhegan.com), an imposing three-story mid-19th-century building with an expansive veranda and lawns overlooking the ferry landing. Thirty-four harbor- and meadow-view rooms and suites (most with private baths) are $105–295, including full breakfast, plus a $2 pp charge for a one-night stay. The inn's restaurant, open to the public for breakfast, lunch, and dinner, has developed an excellent dinner menu with creative entrées for $15–27; the only negative is a $3 corkage fee for the wine and $1 for the beer that *you* have to supply. Children are welcome. Cash, checks, or traveler's checks are preferred. Open late May to early October.

In the heart of the village, **Monhegan House** (P.O. Box 345, Monhegan 04852, 207/594-7983 or 800/599-7983, fax 207/596-6472, www .monheganhouse.com), built in 1870, is a large four-story building with 33 rooms (shared baths, not always on the same floor as your room), which go for $99–125. Don't miss the loose-leaf notebook in the lobby. Labeled *A Monhegan Novel*, it's the ultimate in shaggy-dog sagas, created by a long string of guests since 1992. Children are welcome. Islanders and visitors flock to the inn's airy **Monhegan House Café**, overlooking the village, for breakfast, lunch, and dinner (entrées $13–20). The café will pack a picnic if you want to hit the trails. Order the lobster stew—it's justifiably famous. Open late May to Columbus Day.

A more modernized hostelry, **Shining Sails** (P.O. Box 346, Monhegan 04852, 207/596-0041, www.shiningsails.com), lacks the quaintness of the other inns, but it's very comfortable, convenient to the dock, stays open all year, and has private baths. Breakfast (included only in season) is continental. Seven first- and second-floor rooms and efficiencies (some with water

views) go for $95–180, May to mid-October; lower rates for multiple nights and off-season stays. "Well-supervised" children are welcome.

Funkiest lodging, and not for everyone, is **The Trailing Yew** (P.O. Box 98, Monhegan 04852, 207/596-0440 or 800/592-2520), owned for eons by colorful islander Josephine Davis Day, who remained omnipresent until 1996, when she died at the age of 99. Spread among five rustic buildings south of the village on the road to Lobster Cove, the 35 rooms are $62 a person; $10–55 for kids under 12 (shared baths, averaging five rooms per bath, not always in the same building), including breakfast and dinner. The old-fashioned, low-key 50-seat dining room is also open to the public for dinner at 5:45 P.M., served family-style by reservation, and for breakfast at 7:45 A.M. Bring a sleeping bag in spring or fall; rooms are unheated. Only the main building has electricity. No credit cards. Open late May to early October.

Seasonal Rentals

More than two dozen weekly-rental cottages and apartments—categorized as very rustic, fair, very good, and excellent—are managed by **Shining**

The mid-19th century Island Inn, a classic summer hotel that's been recently updated, is situated right next to the ferry dock. Many rooms have awesome ocean views.

© TOM NANGLE

Penobscot Bay

Sails Real Estate (P.O. Box 346, Monhegan 04852, 207/596-0041, www.shiningsails.com). About half have electricity; the others have gas lights and appliances. Some sleep up to six people; kids, pets, and smoking may be limited. Peak-season (July and Aug.) weekly rates range $700–2,500, lower off-season. Credit cards are accepted. A few are available by the night, space permitting, especially off-season. To rent one of the better seasonal places, you may need to make a two-week commitment.

FOOD

Most visitors don't arrive on Monhegan expecting gourmet cuisine, and except for the Island Inn dining room, they won't find it. Everything is quite casual, and food is hearty and ample. None of the eateries have liquor licenses, so buy beer or wine at the Carina Shop, North End Market, or the Barnacle Café, or bring it from the mainland. All of the restaurants and food sources are in or close to the village.

As you disembark from the ferry, you'll see the **Barnacle Café** (207/596-0371), under the same ownership as the nearby Island Inn. From mid-May to mid-October, this casually upscale operation is open daily 8 A.M.–5 P.M., offering picnic-ready sandwiches and salads, plus croissants, scones, and designer coffees. There's also an ATM, and you can buy wine.

North End Market (207/594-5546) dishes up pizza (whole or by the slice), sandwiches (great subs), salads, and soups. It's a popular day-trippers' lunch spot, so if you need to organize a lunch, beat the crowd by making this your first stop after getting off the ferry. Go up the hill from the wharf and turn right; it's ahead on your left. You can always backtrack to the galleries afterward. It's open daily in summer only.

You can't get much rougher for lobster-in-the-rough than **Fish House Fish** (on Fish Beach, 11:30 A.M.–1:30 P.M. and 4–6 P.M.). Lobster and crabmeat rolls, locally smoked fish, and home-made stews and chowders are on the menu as well as fresh lobster. Take it to the picnic table on beach and enjoy.

Sandwiches, pizzas, and baked goodies are available at **The Novelty,** located behind and operated by The Monhegan House.

(Also see Accommodations for information on meals served at Monhegan House, the Island Inn, and The Trailing Yew.)

INFORMATION AND SERVICES

Information

Several free brochures and flyers, revised annually, will answer most questions about planning a day trip or overnight visit to Monhegan. At the ferry ticket office in Port Clyde, pick up the 12-page *Visitor's Guide to Monhegan Island* and the *Monhegan Associates Trail Map.* Both are also available at island shops, galleries, and lodgings, and at the New Harbor and Boothbay Harbor ferry offices. To obtain copies beforehand, contact **Monhegan-Thomaston Boat Line** (P.O. Box 238, Port Clyde 04855, 207/372-8848, fax 207/372-8547, www.monheganboat.com) around mid-April. Also request a copy of the **ferry schedule.** For fastest service, send a self-addressed stamped envelope. The Rockland-Thomaston Area Chamber of Commerce also has some information about lodgings and other facilities on Monhegan. Monhegan info is also available on the website www.monhegan.com.

Also check the **Rope Shed,** the community bulletin board next to the meadow, right in the village. Monhegan's version of a bush telegraph, it's where everyone posts flyers and notices about nature walks, lectures, excursions, and other special events. You'll also see the current map of *Monhegan Artists Studio Locations.*

Hospitals

Monhegan has an **emergency rescue squad,** but the island has no doctor or medical facility, so watch your step while hiking—broken bones can make the boat ride to the mainland excruciating. Locations of several **fire boxes** are noted on the island's trail map.

Library

Monhegan's pleasant little library, the **Jackie and Edward Library,** was named after two children who drowned in the surf in the 1920s. The fic-

© TOM NANGLE

Find out what's happening on Monhegan Island by visiting the Rope Shed, which serves as a community bulletin board.

tion collection is especially extensive, and it's open to everyone. At the head of Wharf Hill, it's usually open Tuesday, Thursday, and Saturday 1–4 P.M., plus two or three evenings a week; check when you arrive.

Getting There and Around

Ferries travel to Monhegan from **Port Clyde** year-round. Seasonal service to the island is provided from **New Harbor** by Hardy Boat Cruises and from **Boothbay Harbor** by Balmy Days Cruises.

Part of the daily routine for many islanders and summer folk is a stroll to the harbor when the ferry comes in, so don't be surprised to see a good-sized welcoming party when you arrive. You're the live entertainment.

Monhegan's only vehicles are a handful of pickup trucks owned by local lobsterers and li'l ol' trucks used by **Monhegan Trucking.** If you're staying a night or longer and your luggage is too heavy to carry, they'll be waiting when you arrive at the island wharf.

The latest wrinkle in island transport is a hand-ful of shiny golf carts, adding a different "feel" to the well-trod village paths. At least it eases the ac-cess for long-termers who, despite infirmities, insist on returning annually to the island. But they're not available for the casual visitor.

Penobscot Bay

Rockland Area

A "Share the Pride" campaign—kicked off in the 1980s to boost sagging civic self-esteem and the local economy—was the first step in the transformation of Rockland. Once a run-down county seat best known for the aroma of its fish-packing plants, the city has undergone a sea change—most of it for the better. The expansion of The Farnsworth Art Museum and the addition of its Wyeth Center was a catalyst. Benches and plants line Main Street (Route 1), stores offer appealing wares, coffeehouses and more than a dozen art galleries attract a diverse clientele, and Rockland Harbor boasts more windjammer cruise schooners than neighboring Camden (which had long claimed the title "Windjammer Capital"). If you haven't been to Rockland in the last decade, prepare to be astonished.

Foresighted entrepreneurs had seen the potential of the bayside location in the late 1700s and established a tiny settlement here called "Shore Village" (or "the Shore"). Today's commercial-fishing fleet is one of the few reminders of Rockland's past, when multimasted schooners lined the wharves, some to load volatile cargoes of lime destined to become building material for cities all along the eastern seaboard, others to head northeast—toward the storm-racked Grand Banks and the lucrative cod fishery there. Such hazardous pursuits meant an early demise for many a local seafarer, but Rockland's 5,000 or so residents were enjoying their prosperity in the late 1840s. The settlement was home to more than two dozen shipyards and dozens of lime kilns, was enjoying a construction boom, and boasted a newspaper and regular steamship service. By 1854, Rockland had become a city.

Today, Rockland remains a commercial hub—with Knox County's only shopping plazas (not quite malls, but Wal-Mart and other big-box stores have arrived), a fishing fleet that heads far offshore, ferries that connect nearby islands, and firms that manufacture clothing, snowplows, and leather goods. Rockland also claims the title of "Lobster Capital of the World"—thanks to Knox County's shipment nationally and internation-

ally of 10 million pounds of lobster each year. (The weathervane atop the police and fire department building is even a giant copper lobster.)

Present-day entrepreneurs, carried along on a whole new wave of enthusiasm, are quickly making Rockland an interesting place to live, work, and play. And, with just over 8,000 souls, Rockland is more year-round community than tourist town. But visitors pour in during two big summer festivals—the North Atlantic Blues Festival in mid-July and the Maine Lobster Festival in early August. Highlight of the Lobster Festival is King Neptune's coronation of the Maine Sea Goddess—carefully selected from a bevy of local young women—who then sails off with him to his watery domain.

SIGHTS

ⓜ The Farnsworth Art Museum and Wyeth Center

Anchoring downtown Rockland is the nationally respected Farnsworth Art Museum (356 Main St., Rockland, 207/596-6457, www.farnsworthmuseum.org), established in 1948 through a trust fund set up by Rocklander Lucy Farnsworth. With an ample checkbook, the first curator, Robert Bellows, toured the country, accumulating a splendid collection of 19th- and 20th-century Maine-related American art—the basis for the permanent Maine in America exhibition.

The 6,000-piece collection today includes work by Fitz Hugh Lane, Gilbert Stuart, Eastman Johnson, Childe Hassam, John Marin, Maurice Prendergast, Rockwell Kent, George Bellows, and Marsden Hartley. Best known are the paintings by three generations of the Wyeth family (local summer residents) and sculpture by Louise Nevelson, who grew up in Rockland. Sculpture, jewelry, and paintings by Nevelson form the core of the third-floor Nevelson-Berliawsky Gallery for 20th Century Art. (The only larger Nevelson collection is in New York's Whitney Museum of American Art.) The new **Wyeth Center,** across Union Street in a former church, contains the work of Andrew, N. C., and Jamie Wyeth. In the summer of 2000, The Farnsworth opened its 6,000-square-foot **Jamien Morehouse Wing**, an elegant venue for rotating exhibits.

In The Farnsworth's library—a grand, high-ceilinged oasis akin to an English gentleman's reading room—browsers and researchers can explore an extensive collection of art books and magazines. The museum's hyperactive education department annually sponsors hundreds of lectures, concerts, art classes for adults and children, poetry readings, and field trips. Most are open to nonmembers; some require an extra fee. A glitzy gift shop stocks posters, prints, notecards, imported gift items, and art games for children.

Next door to the museum is the mid-19th-century Greek Revival **Farnsworth Homestead**, with original high-Victorian furnishings. Looking as though William Farnsworth's family just took off for the day, the house has been preserved rather than restored.

The Farnsworth also owns the **Olson House**, 14 miles away in nearby Cushing, where the whole landscape looks like a Wyeth diorama. (See details in the Cushing Peninsula section.) Pick up a map at the museum to help you find the house—definitely worth the side trip.

The Farnsworth is open year-round, including summer holidays. Farnsworth summer hours are 10 A.M.–5 P.M. (to 7 P.M. Wed.–Fri.). Winter museum hours are 10 A.M.–5 P.M. Tuesday–Sunday. Call the museum for its current definition of summer and winter. The Homestead and the Olson House are open daily, 11 A.M.–4 P.M. for the Olson House, 10 A.M.–5 P.M. for the Homestead, Memorial Day weekend to Columbus Day. Admission to the museum and the Homestead is $9 adults, $8 seniors, $5 students 18 and older, free for kids under 18 and for Rockland residents. A special $11 combination ticket, valid only Memorial Day through Columbus Day, covers entry to all properties.

Owls Head Transportation Museum

Don't miss this place, even if you're not an old-vehicle buff. A generous endowment has made the Owls Head Transportation Museum a premier

facility for celebrating wings and wheels; it draws more than 75,000 visitors a year (Rte. 73, Owls Head, 207/594-4418, www.ohtm.org, 10 A.M.–5 P.M. Apr.–Oct., to 4 P.M. Nov.–March, $7 adults, $5 ages 5–11, $18 for a family, special events extra). Scads of eager volunteers help restore the vehicles and keep them running. On weekends, May–October, the museum sponsors air shows (often including aerobatic displays) and car and truck meets for hundreds of enthusiasts. The highlight of the season is the annual rally and aerobatic show (early August), when more than 300 vehicles gather for two days of festivities. Want your own vintage vehicle? Attend the antique, classic, and special-interest auto auction (third Sunday in August). The gift shop carries transportation-related items. If the kids get bored (unlikely), there's a play area outside, with picnic tables. In winter, groomed cross-country-skiing trails wind through the museum's 60-acre site. (Ask for a map at the information desk.)

Maine Lighthouse Museum

In 2005, the Maine Lighthouse Museum (previously known as the Shore Village Museum) plans to reopen in its new digs in the waterfront Gateway Center (1 Park Dr., Rockland, 207/594-3301, www.mainelighthousemuseum.com), which it will share with the chamber of commerce and other organizations. The museum claims to have the nation's largest collection of lighthouse and Coast Guard memorabilia: foghorns, ships' bells, nautical books and photographs, marine instruments, ship models, scrimshaw, even a giant lens built for Maine's tallest lighthouse. Call for updated information.

Rockland Breakwater

Protecting the harbor from wind-driven waves, the 4,346-foot-long Rockland Breakwater took 18 years to build, with 697,000 tons of locally quarried granite. In the late 19th century, it was piled up, chunk by chunk, from a base 175 feet wide on the harbor floor (60 feet below the surface) to the 43-foot-wide cap. The Breakwater Light—now automated—was built in 1902 and added to the National Historic Register in 1981. The city of Rockland owns the keeper's house, and the

Friends of the Rockland Breakwater Lighthouse maintain it. Member volunteers usually open the lighthouse to the public 10 A.M.–5 P.M. Saturday and Sunday late May to mid-October. The breakwater provides unique vantage points for photographers, and a place to picnic or catch sea breezes or fish on a hot day, but it is extremely dangerous during storms, when anyone on the breakwater risks being washed into the sea or struck by lightning (ask the local hospital staff: it *has* happened!). Do not take chances when the weather is iffy.

To reach the breakwater, take Route 1 north to Waldo Avenue and turn right. Take the next right onto Samoset Road and drive to the end, to **Marie Reed Memorial Park** (tiny beach, benches, limited parking). Or go to the Samoset Resort and take the path to the breakwater from there.

Main Street Historic District

Rocklanders are justly proud of their Main Street Historic District, lined with 19th- and early-20th-century Greek and Colonial Revival structures, as well as examples of mansard and Italianate architecture. Most now house retail shops on the ground floor; upper floors have offices, artists' studios, and apartments. The district starts at the corner of Winter and Main Streets and runs north to the alley just after Kelsey's Appliances. The chamber of commerce has a map and details.

PARKS AND RECREATION

Harbor Park

If you're looking for a park with more commotion than quiet green space, spend some time at Harbor Park. Boats, cars, and delivery vehicles come and go; the chamber of commerce office has a steady stream of visitors; and you can corner a picnic table or a bench or a patch of grass and watch all the action. Public restrooms (open late May to mid-Oct.) are available. The park is just off Main Street.

Owls Head Light State Park

On Route 73, about 1.5 miles past the junction of Routes 1 and 73, you'll reach North Shore Road in the town of Owls Head. Turn left, toward Owls

Head Light State Park. Standing 3.6 miles from this turn, Owls Head Light occupies a dramatic promontory with panoramic views over Rockland Harbor and Penobscot Bay. Don't miss it. The keeper's house and the light tower are off-limits, but the park surrounding the tower has easy walking paths, picnic tables, and a pebbly beach where you can sunbathe or check out Rockland Harbor's boating traffic. (If it's foggy or rainy, don't climb the steps toward the light tower: the view evaporates in the fog, the access ramp can be slippery, and the foghorn is dangerously deafening.) Follow signs to reach the park. From North Shore Road, turn left onto Main Street, then left onto Lighthouse Road, and continue along Owls Head Harbor to the parking area. This is also a particularly pleasant bike route—about 10 miles round-trip from downtown Rockland—although, once again, the roadside shoulders are poor along the Owls Head stretch.

Rockland Harbor Trail

You can walk for more than four miles along this public footpath that edges Rockland Harbor, passes along streets, cuts through parks, and connects major waterfront points. Signs show the way from Snow Marine Park.

Swimming

Lucia Beach is the local name for **Birch Point Beach State Park,** one of the best-kept secrets in the area. In Owls Head, just south of Rockland—and not far from Owls Head Light—the spruce-lined sand crescent (free; outhouses but no other facilities) has rocks, shells, tidepools, and very chilly water. There's ample room for a moderate-sized crowd, although parking and turnaround space can get a bit tight on the access road. From downtown Rockland, take Route 73 one mile to North Shore Drive (on your left). Take the next right, Ash Point Drive, and continue past Knox County Regional Airport to Dublin Road. Turn right, go .8 mile, then turn left onto Ballyhac Road (opposite airport landing lights). Go another .8 mile, fork left, and continue .4 mile to the parking area.

If frigid ocean water doesn't appeal, head for freshwater **Chickawaukee Lake,** on Route 17, two miles inland from downtown Rockland. Don't expect to be alone, though; on hot days, **Johnson Memorial Park**'s pocket-size sand patch is a major attraction. A lifeguard holds forth; there are restrooms, picnic tables, a snack bar, and a boat-launch ramp. (In winter, iceboats, snowmobiles, and ice-fishing shacks take over the lake.) A signposted bicycle path runs alongside the busy highway, making the park an easy pedal from town.

Golf

The **Rockland Golf Club** (606 Old County Rd., Rockland 04841, 207/594-9322, Apr.–Oct.), an 18-hole course .2 mile northeast of Route 17, ranks high on many a Maine golfer's list. In July and August, you'll need to reserve a starting time a day or so in advance if you plan to tee off anytime after 7 A.M. The modern clubhouse—rebuilt after a disastrous fire in the late 1980s—has a full bar and serves breakfast and lunch at reasonable prices. Parking is plentiful.

For an 18-hole course in an unsurpassed waterfront setting (but steep rental and greens fees), check out the links at the **Samoset Resort,** technically in Rockport but most often reached via Rockland. Resort guests receive golf discounts, and the course often has a longer season than others in the area.

Bicycling and Kayaking

Veteran Maine Guide and naturalist Mark DiGirolamo is the spark plug behind **Breakwater Kayak** (Rockland Public Landing, Rockland, 207/596-6895 or 877/559-8800, www.breakwaterkayak.com), which has a full range of tours, even multiday ones. A two-hour Rockland Harbor tour (usually offered three times a day at the height of summer) is $35, and the all-day Owls Head Light tour is $95, including lunch. Reservations are advisable. This outfit is particularly eco-sensitive, definitely worth supporting. Maine Audubon often taps Mark to lead natural-history field trips. Dress warmly for these tours and be sure to bring your own water bottle (filled). Also available are half-day biking ($45) and hiking ($35) tours. (See also Bicycling and Kayaking under Camden-Rockport Area.)

Boating Excursions

Marine biologist Captain Bob Pratt is the skipper of *A Morning in Maine,* a classic 55-foot ketch designed by noted naval architect R. D. (Pete) Culler and built by Concordia Yachts. June–October, *Morning* departs from the Middle Pier at the Rockland Public Landing at 10 A.M. and 1 and 4 P.M. for two-hour day sails ($30), with plenty of knowledgeable commentary from Captain Pratt. A 6 P.M. sunset sail is available in July and August. For details, contact Captain Bob Pratt (207/691-7245, www.morninginmaine.com). Inquire about boat-and-breakfast overnights, which run $325 per couple and include a sail, lobster dinner, and continental breakfast.

Watch Captain Steve Hale set and haul lobster traps on a cruise aboard the *Captain Jack* (Rockland Harbor, 207/594-1048) during a 75-minute cruise aboard a 30-foot working lobsterboat. Cruises depart five times daily Monday–Saturday May–September; $20 adult, $14 kids under 12. Note: There are no toilets aboard.

Maine State Ferry Service

Car and passenger ferries service the islands of Vinalhaven, North Haven, and Matinicus. The Vinalhaven and North Haven routes make fantastic day trips (especially with a bike), or you can spend the night; the Matinicus ferry is much less predictable.

Scenic Flights

Maine Atlantic Aviation (207/596-5558 or 800/780-6071, www.maineatlanticaviation.com), a division of Telford Aviation, offers flightseeing over the coast and islands, with rates beginning at $65 for 15 minutes. It operates from Knox County Regional Airport in Owls Head, just south of Rockland.

SHOPPING

Art Galleries

Piggybacking on the fame of The Farnsworth Art Museum, or at least working symbiotically, more than a dozen art galleries have opened in Rockland since 1990, with more likely to come. Ask around and look around. During the summer, many of

Penobscot Bay

them coordinate monthly openings (usually a Wednesday evening) so you can meander and munch (and sip) from one gallery to another.

Across from The Farnsworth's side entrance, the **Caldbeck Gallery** (12 Elm St., Rockland, 207/594-5935) has gained a top-notch reputation as a "must-see" (and "must-be-seen") space. Featuring the work of contemporary Maine artists, the gallery mounts more than half a dozen solo and group shows each year, May–September.

Also gaining a high profile is **The Gallery at 357 Main** (357 Main St., 207/596-0084, 10 A.M.–5 P.M. Mon.–Sat., 1–5 P.M. Sun. May–late Dec.).

Other eminently browsable downtown-Rockland galleries are **Harbor Square Gallery** (374 Main St., 207/594-8700 or 877/594-8700), **Elements Gallery** (431 Main St., 207/596-6010), **Élan Fine Arts** (8 Elm St., 207/598-9933), **Nan Mulford Gallery** (313 Main St., 207/594-8481), and **Gallery One** (365 Main St., 207/594-5441), above Huston-Tuttle.

Books, Crafts, Gifts, and Clothing

Plenty of interesting shops dot downtown Rockland. Here's just a selection.

An independent bookstore with inventories of best-sellers, cookbooks, kids' books, remainders, magazines, and CDs, **The Reading Corner** (408 Main St., Rockland, 207/596-6651) occupies two full rooms in downtown Rockland.

The Grasshopper Shop (400 Main St., Rockland, 207/596-6156) is an eclectic emporium filled with jewelry, clothing, shoes, accessories, cards, toys, and unusual gifts, all tastefully displayed beneath a handsome antique tin ceiling.

Archipelago (Main St., Rockland, 207/596-0701), on the ground floor of the Island Institute (a nonprofit steward of Maine's 4,617 offshore islands), is an attractive retail outlet for talented craftspeople from 14 year-round islands. The shop also carries island-related books.

Appropriately labeling its wares "elegant necessities and practical indulgences," **Meander** (373 Main St., Rockland, 207/596-6781) has all those splurge items you'd love to own but can't quite bring yourself to buy. Lamps, ties, leather items, jewelry, even furniture—it's all here.

ENTERTAINMENT

For live entertainment, head to **Waterworks Pub** (7 Lindsey St., Rockland, 207/596-2753, 11:30 A.M.–9 P.M. daily, to 10 P.M. Fri. and Sat.), home of Rocky Bay Brewing. The English-style pub has live music Wednesday–Sunday. Another good choice is the **Breakwater Lounge** at the Samoset Resort.

Stop by the **Lincoln Street Center for Arts & Education** (24 Lincoln St., Rockland, 207/594-6490, www.lincolnstreetcenter.org), a community arts center with exhibitions, performances, and classes, to see what's on the schedule.

The historic **Strand Theater** (339 Main St., 207/594-7266), opened in 1923, is expected to reopen in 2005 after an extensive restoration. Films as well as live entertainment are planned.

FESTIVALS AND EVENTS

In mid-July, the **North Atlantic Blues Festival** means a weekend of festivities featuring big names in blues. Thousands of fans jam Harbor Park for the nonstop music.

August's **Maine Lobster Festival** is a five-day lobster extravaganza, with live entertainment, the Maine Sea Goddess pageant, a lobster-crate race, craft booths, boat rides, a parade, lobster dinners, and megacrowds (the hotels are full for miles in either direction). Tons of lobsters bite the dust during the weekend—despite annual protests by the People for the Ethical Treatment of Animals. (The protests, however, only seem to increase the crowds.)

ACCOMMODATIONS

If you're planning an overnight stay in the Rockland area the first weekend in August—during the Maine Lobster Festival—*be sure* to make reservations well in advance. Festival attendance runs close to 100,000, No Vacancy signs extend from Waldoboro to Belfast, and there just aren't enough beds or campsites to go around.

Samoset Resort

The 221-acre waterfront Samoset Resort (220

Warrenton St., Rockport 04856, 207/594-2511 or 800/341-1650, www.samoset.com) straddles the boundary between Rockland and Rockport, the next town to the north. Most guests get to it via Rockland, from the south. Built on the ashes of a classic, 19th-century summer hotel, the Samoset is a top-of-the-line modern resort with knockout ocean views from most of its 178 rooms and suites, plus 72 separate condos. Peak-season (early July–Labor Day) doubles go for $199–399, suites are $299–549. Rooms, suites, and condos have phones, cable TV, air-conditioning, and lots of other amenities; no pets. Conferences go on here throughout the year, but it's also a great family place, particularly off-season—with special package rates, indoor and outdoor swimming pools, fitness center, lighted tennis courts, cross-country skiing, kids' programs, golf simulator, and a fabulous 18-hole waterfront golf course. The elegant, bay-view Marcel's Restaurant (7–10:30 A.M. and 6–9 P.M.) has an ambitious, pricey menu; jackets are suggested for dinner, and reservations are a good idea; entrées are $19–34. The best deal is Sunday brunch (10 A.M.–2 P.M.)—a huge, all-you-can-eat buffet for $19.95. More casual is the Breakwater Lounge, with light fare ($10–20), live entertainment (Wed. and Fri. nights mid-June–early Sept.), and a fabulous water-view patio area (weather permitting). The lounge is open 11:30 A.M.–9 P.M. for lunch and dinner, to midnight for drinks.

Motels

Directly opposite the ferry terminal for boats going to the islands of Vinalhaven, North Haven, and Matinicus, the 81-room **Navigator Motor Inn** (520 Main St., Rockland 04841, 207/594-2131 or 800/545-8026, www.navigatorinn.com, $99–115) is a five-story shingled place with cable TV, air-conditioning, phones, refrigerators, and laundry facilities. Rooms are basic motel-style, but upper-floor ones have plenty of space and great views of the harbor (be prepared for traffic noise from the parking lot and street). Pets are allowed in some rooms. The bright, modern Portsider Grill and Pub is open 6:30 A.M.–9:30 P.M., but you're just steps from Rockland's Main Street restaurants. Open all year.

B&Bs

These B&Bs are in Rockland's historic district, within easy walking distance of downtown attractions and restaurants. All are members of **Historic Inns of Rockland Maine** (www.historicinnsofrockland.com).

Most elegant is **M The Berry Manor Inn** (81 Talbot Ave., P.O. Box 1117, Rockland 04841, 207/596-7696 or 800/774-5692, www.berrymanorinn.com, $135–235), on a quiet side street a few blocks from downtown. Cheryl Michaelsen and Michael LaPosta have totally restored the manse built in 1898 by wealthy Rocklander Charles Berry as a wedding gift for his wife (thoughtful fellow). High ceilings and wonderful Victorian architectural touches are everywhere, especially in the enormous front hall and two parlors. Eight second- and third-floor Victorian-decor rooms and four ultra-luxurious suites in the adjacent Carriage House have private baths, gas fireplaces, air-conditioning, hair dryers, data ports, journals, and more; many have whirlpools. In-room TV upon request. A guest pantry is stocked with free soda and juices and sweets, not that you'll be hungry after the extravagant breakfasts. Open all year.

Opened in 1996, the **Captain Lindsey House Inn** (5 Lindsey St., P.O. Box 864, Rockland 04841, 207/596-7950 or 800/523-2145, www.lindseyhouse.com, $140–190) is more like a boutique hotel than a B&B. The Barnes family gutted the 1835 brick structure and restored it dramatically, adding such modernities as phones, air conditioning, and TV. The decor is strikingly handsome, not at all fussy or frilly. Don't miss the 1926 safe in the front hall or the hidden-from-the-street garden patio—not to mention the antiques from everywhere that fill the nine comfortable rooms, all with TV, phones, and air-conditioning. A few have glimpses of the water. Rates include an extensive hot-and-cold breakfast buffet and afternoon refreshments. Open all year.

Filled with reproduction furnishings and unusual touches, **The Limerock Inn** (96 Limerock St., Rockland 04841, 207/594-2257 or 800/546-3762, www.limerockinn.com, $125–215) is a lovely painted lady. The 1890s' Queen

Anne mansion, listed on the National Historic Register, faces on a quiet street. Each of the eight rooms has its own distinctive flavor—such as the Turret Room with a wedding canopy bed and the Island Cottage Room with a private deck overlooking the back gardens. Open all year.

Across the street from the ferry terminal (and next door to the Navigator Motor Inn), the mid-19th-century **Old Granite Inn** (546 Main St., Rockland 04841, 207/594-9036 or 800/386-9036, www.oldgraniteinn.com, $140–170) couldn't be more convenient for island-goers. Innkeepers Ragan and John Cary are very knowledgeable about the area. They display their art collection throughout the inn, including the nine guest rooms. The inn is on Route 1, but thick granite walls subdue traffic noise, so most rooms are quiet. (Request a back or side room if you're particularly noise-sensitive.) Open all year, but call ahead off-season.

FOOD

Once a wasteland for foodies, Rockland has evolved to offer interesting choices for all budgets and tastes. Poke around a bit, and you're sure to find something that suits.

Breakfast, Lunch, and Miscellany

A winner for creative breakfasts and lunches is **The Brown Bag** (606 Main St., Rockland, 207/596-6372 or 800/287-6372, bakery 207/596-6392, 6 A.M.–4 P.M. Mon.–Sat.). It's *the* place for breakfast, especially weekends, with fantastic baked goods and a full blackboard of other options. Lunches include a half dozen veggie choices and imaginative salads. Order at the counter; no table service. The Brown Bag is at the junction of Routes 1 and 17.

Hot diggity dog! Backed up against an outside wall of The Brown Bag is a long-standing Rockland lunch landmark—**Wasses Hot Dogs** (2 N. Main St., Rockland, 207/594-7472, 10:30 A.M.–6 P.M. Mon.–Sat. and 11 A.M.–4 P.M. Sun.), source of great chili dogs and creative ice cream (in waffle cones). This onetime lunch wagon is now a permanent modular building—only for takeout, though. It's open all year. Branch "wagons" carry

on the tradition in Camden, Belfast, Thomaston, and the south end of Rockland.

Lots of Rockland-watchers credit **Second Read Books & Coffee** (328 Main St., Rockland, 207/594-4123, 7 A.M.–6 P.M. Mon.–Fri., 8 A.M.–6 P.M. Sat.) with sparking the designer-food renaissance in town. In 1995, it outgrew its original space and moved into this high-ceilinged room in a historic downtown block. Order coffee (regular and fancy) and pastries or one of the lunch specials at the counter, then peruse the shelves of "pre-read books" while you wait. In a relatively short time, Second Read has become an institution. About once a month, there's an evening of Irish music. Open all year.

Hands down, the best doughnuts in the area come from the tiny **Willow Street Bake Shoppe** (49 Willow St., Rockland, 207/596-0564, 6–11 A.M. Mon.–Fri.). Betcha can't eat just one. Note: The shop will be moving in late 2005, but will not change its name. Ditto for the barbecue served at **Texas Outlaw BBQ** (Rte. 1, Rockland, 207/594-0600, 11 A.M.–6 P.M. Mon.–Fri.), a take-out stand just north of Thomaston that specializes in Texas-style barbecue slow-cooked over a wood fire.

Great bread, yummy pastries, and grab-and-go sandwiches (about $5) have made **Atlantic Baking Co.** (351 Main St., Rockland, 207/596-0505, 7 A.M.–6 P.M. Mon.–Sat.) a popular spot for a quick, informal lunch. There are plenty of tables to enjoy your treats.

Remember when every pharmacy had a soda fountain? There's still one at **Goodnow's Pharmacy** (300 Main St., Rockland, 207/594-5131).

At the end of a day exploring Rockland, relax at **In Good Company** (415 Main St., 207/593-9110, opens at 4:30 P.M. Tues.–Sat.), a casual wine bar with a tapas-style menu that also lists a few heartier choices.

If you're craving a decent breakfast (or lunch or snack) and are up for a little foray "down the peninsula," head for the **Owls Head General Store** (2 South Shore Dr., Owls Head, 207/596-6038), where the atmosphere is friendly and definitely contagious. If you get lost, they'll steer you the right way, and the helpful staff will even take your photograph in front of the store. Despite all the competition from lobster-in-the-rough places, the lobster roll here is among the best around. Summer hours are 5:30 A.M.–7 P.M. Monday–Saturday (to 8 P.M. Fri. and Sat.) and 7 A.M.–3 P.M. Sunday. The store is quite close to Owls Head Light.

The **Rockland Farmers' Market** gets under way each Thursday 9 A.M.–1 P.M. June–September, at Harbor Park, on Rockland's Public Landing. Wares from more than a dozen vendors include produce, crafts, syrup, poultry, mushrooms, baked goods, and cheeses. Every week, there's a special event—music, dancers, lectures, special giveaways, and occasionally a llama or goat for the kids to pet.

Ethnic Fare

When you're *really* famished, the place to go is **Conte's Fish Market & Restaurant** (Harbor Park, off Main St., Rockland, 207/596-5579), where portions are humongous and prices are not ($10–20). John Conte moved here from New York in 1995, bringing his family's century-old restaurant tradition. Specialties are pasta and seafood—Italian all the way, loaded with garlic. Beer and wine only. The decor is wildly funky—fishnets, marine relics, old books, even stacks of canned plum tomatoes—all with a terrific view of Rockland Harbor. Menus are handwritten on paper-towel rolls and in-your-face at the door (order before you sit down), table coverings are yesterday's newspapers, and Edith Piaf *chansons* or operatic arias sometimes play in the background. Bring your sense of humor and don't be put off by the exterior or the attitude; there's life behind the doors. No credit cards. Open daily at 4 P.M. for dinner, all year (usually).

Amalfi (421 Main St., Rockland, 207/596-0012, 5–9 P.M. Tues.–Sat., to 8 P.M. Sun.) is a Mediterranean oasis in the middle of downtown. Only three dozen seats, so it fills up quickly; reservations are advisable. Most entrées are in the $16–21 range. Excellent wine list and hard-to-resist desserts.

East meets West at **Oh! Bento** (10 Leland St., Rockland 04841, 207/593-9216, 11 A.M.–2:30 P.M. and 5:30–8:30 P.M. Tues.–Sat.), where Bay Bigelow, a Japanese American, and his Japanese wife, Keiko Takahashi, have created a local destination for Japanese cuisine, with plenty of choices for vegetarians and vegans. Named after the traditional Japanese box lunches, the restaurant fills small rooms and niches on the first floor of a backstreet house. Japanese family treasures are everywhere. Service is excellent. Reservations are wise—this is no longer a secret. Entrées average $14; it's hard to resist the appetizers and great sushi choices ($3–6). Oh! Bento is a block off Route 1, on the street behind The Brown Bag.

Southwest fare dominates the menu at **The Park Street Grille** (279 Main St. at Park St., Rte. 1, Rockland, 207/594-4944, 11:30 A.M.–2 P.M. Mon.–Sat. and 5–9 P.M. Mon.–Sun., to 10 P.M. Fri. and Sat.). Steaks and seafood are also specialties at this casual, bright spot at the southern end of the main drag. The margaritas are huge and the nacho platter could make a whole meal. Entrée range is $5–14.

A small dining area decorated in avocado and gold is the appropriate setting for the Mexican food dished out at **Sunfire Mexican Grill** (488 Main St., Rockland, 207/594-6196, 11 A.M.–3 P.M. Tues.–Wed., to 8 P.M. Thurs.–Sat.). You'll find all the usuals, from tacos ($2.95) to chipotle shrimp tostada ($11.75).

Casual Dining

Half restaurant and half gourmet market, **Market on Main** (315 Main St., Rockland, 207/594-0015, 10:30 A.M.–8 P.M. Mon.–Thurs., to 8:30 P.M. Fri. and Sat., and 10 A.M.–3 P.M.—brunch—and 5–8 P.M. Sun.) is a good choice for a casual lunch or dinner or for a meal to go. Owned by the energetic entrepreneurs of Café Miranda, "MOM's" has homemade soups, ethnic munchies and salads, chili, burgers, and super sandwiches made with hot-from-the-oven focaccia. Dinner choices include black bean burritos and fish cakes. Most prices range $7–13, although specials can go much higher. Sunday brunch includes such creativity as Thai eggs and Italian French toast. Open all year.

Fresh fish, simply prepared is the hallmark of **Kate's Seafood Restaurant** (Rte. 1, Rockland,

207/594-2626, 11:30 A.M.–8 P.M.). Order at the counter, than find a table. Don't miss the homemade chowders. Most choices $8–12.

In 2004, Damariscotta's ever-popular **Salt Bay Café** (227 Park St., Rockland, 207/593-9179, 7 A.M.–9 P.M. Mon.–Sat.) opened a second location offering its wide-ranging menu to a new audience. It has a separate vegetarian menu, and at dinner offers choices for both light and heavy eaters (entrées $8–21).

M Café Miranda (15 Oak St., Rockland, 207/594-2034, 5:30–9 P.M., closed Sun. offseason) is summed up in one of its slogans, "We do not serve the food of cowards." This popular, casual place is terrific—and moderately priced—with a huge and eminently adventurous menu. Lots of pastas, smoked items, veggies, olive oil, greens, and way-out combinations. Entrées are $15–20, but many of the appetizers ($3–9) are enough for a meal. Freshfrom-the-brick-oven focaccia comes with everything. If you sit at the counter, you can watch chef Kerry Altiero's creations emerging from the oven. Beer and wine only. Reservations are essential throughout the summer and on weekends off-season.

Fine Dining

See Samoset Resort for information about Marcel's.

Destination Dining

Arriving in Rockland trailing a James Beard award-winning reputation, chef Melissa Kelly opened **M Primo** (Rte. 73, Rockland, 207/596-0770, 5:30–10 P.M. daily in summer) in the spring of 2000 and hasn't had time to breathe. With six rooms in an air-conditioned Victorian home, the aptly named Primo has first-rate cuisine (and presentation). Fresh local ingredients (many from the restaurant's gardens) are a high priority, and unusual fish specials appear every day. Appetizers are especially imaginative; entrée range is $16–30. Kelly's partner, Price Kushner, produces an impressive range of breads and desserts. Reservations are essential, usually at least a week ahead on midsummer weekends—and you still may have to wait when you get there. Open all year (closed Tues. and Wed. in

winter). The restaurant is at the southern end of Rockland, on the Owls Head boundary.

INFORMATION AND SERVICES

Information

The **Rockland-Thomaston Area Chamber of Commerce** (P.O. Box 508, Rockland 04841, 207/596-0376 or 800/562-2529, www.therealmaine.com, 9 A.M.–5 P.M. Mon.–Fri. and 10 A.M.–2 P.M. Sat.), currently facing Harbor Park, will move into the new Gateway Center on Rockland's waterfront in mid- to late 2005. Until then, it's across the parking lot but still on the waterfront.

Hospitals

Penobscot Bay Medical Center (Rte. 1, Rockport 04856, 207/596-8000) serves this region.

Local Library

The handsome stone **Rockland Public Library** (80 Union St., Rockland, 207/594-0310, 9 A.M.–9 P.M. Mon., Tues., and Thurs., to 5 P.M. Wed., Fri., and Sat.), has been a local landmark since 1904, when townsfolk received a $20,000 Carnegie grant to jump-start its construction. It's now the beneficiary of a multimillion-dollar renovation, with state-of-the-art facilities.

Public Restrooms

You'll find public restrooms at the Gateway Center, the Knox County Court House, Union and Masonic Streets, the Rockland Recreation Center, across from the courthouse, next to the playground, Union and Limerock Streets, the Rockland Public Library, and the Maine State Ferry Service terminal.

Getting Around

Concord Trailways (800/639-3317, www.concordtrailways.com) stops in Rockland, Camden-Rockport, Belfast, and Searsport on its three daily nonexpress trips up the coast.

All Aboard Trolley Co. (21 Limerock St., 207/594-9300) departs from Park Drive, next to the Tradewinds Motor Inn. From late June through Labor Day, the trolley circulates through Rockland 9 A.M.–5 P.M., making stops at the public landing, along Main Street, the ferry and bus terminal, local marinas, the big box stores, and the Samoset. The fare is $2. Pick up a schedule at the chamber office.

Coastal Trans (207/596-6605 or 800/289-6605), a nonprofit organization, operates a weekday, wheelchair-accessible van service throughout Rockland and the surrounding region, but you must call one day in advance to schedule rides.

An efficient **taxi** service is active in Rockland and the surrounding areas. **Schooner Bay Limo & Taxi** (207/594-5000) provides round-the-clock service. Taxis meet ferries in peak season at the Maine State Ferry Service terminal (where Concord Trailways buses from Boston and Portland stop), and there's a pay phone outside when the terminal is closed. The Rockland taxis are accustomed to making runs to Port Clyde for the ferry to Monhegan.

Camden-based **Mid-Coast Limo** (800/937-2424 or 207/236-2424, www.midcoastlimo.com) provides van service, by reservation, between towns as far northeast as Belfast and Portland International Jetport.

Vinalhaven and North Haven Islands

Vinalhaven and neighboring North Haven have been known as the Fox Islands ever since 1603, when English explorer Martin Pring sailed these waters and allegedly spotted gray foxes in his search for sustenance. Nowadays, you'll find reference to that name only on nautical charts, identifying the passage between the two islands as the Fox Islands Thorofare—and there's nary a fox in sight.

Each island has its own distinct personality. To generalize, Vinalhaven is the largest and busiest, while North Haven is sedate and exclusive. The Rockland terminal of the Maine State Ferry Service serves both.

GETTING THERE

The Maine State Ferry Service (207/596-2202, www.exploremaine.com) operates six round trips daily between Rockland and Vinalhaven (75-minute crossing) in summer and three round-trips between Rockland and North Haven (70-minute crossing). Round-trip tickets are $12 adults, $5.25 kids. Both ferries take cars ($34.50 round-trip), but a bicycle ($11.50 round-trip per adult bike, $5.75 per child's bike) will do fine unless you have the time or inclination to see every corner of the island. Getting car space on the ferry during midsummer can be a frustrating—and complicated—experience, so *avoid taking a car to the island.* If you're not spending the night on the island, watch the clock so you don't miss the last boat back to Rockland.

No official ferry service travels between Vinalhaven and North Haven, even though the two islands are almost within spitting distance. Fortunately, the J. O. Brown & Sons boat shop on North Haven provides shuttles most days from 7 A.M. on. Call the boat shop (207/867-4621) to arrange a pickup on the Vinalhaven side. (A handy outdoor pay phone is at the north end of Vinalhaven—at the end of the North Haven Road.) Don't let anyone convince you to return to Rockland for the ferry to North Haven.

Charter air service (not inexpensive) is available to the islands via **Maine Atlantic Aviation** (207/596-5558 or 800/780-6071, www.maineatlanticaviation.com), a division of Telford Aviation. It operates from Knox County Regional Airport in Owls Head, just south of Rockland. You'll need to arrange for a pickup beforehand.

VINALHAVEN

Five miles wide, 7.5 miles long, and covering 10,000 acres, Vinalhaven is 13 miles off the coast of Rockland—a 75-minute ferry trip. The shoreline has so many zigs and zags that no place on the island is more than a mile from water.

The island is famed for its granite. Vinalhaven granite first headed for Boston around 1826, and within a few decades, quarrymen arrived from as far away as Britain and Finland to wrestle out and shape the incredibly resistant stone. Schooners, barges, and "stone sloops" left Carver's

Penobscot Bay

VINALHAVEN

North Haven

Fox Islands Thorofare

Perry Creek

Zeke Point

Carver Cove

POLLY COVE PRESERVE

BROWN'S HEAD LIGHT

Perry Creek

Preserve

Calderwood Neck

Tip-Toe Mountain

Middle Mountain

Seal Cove

Crockett Point

Crockett Cove

Long Cove

NORTH HAVEN

Mill River

Winter Harbor

Penobscot Island

Seal Bay

Smith Cove

Coombs Neck

Round Pond

NECK RD

Leadbetter Island

The Basin

Folly Pond

Otter Pond

ROUND

Vinal Cove

THE ISLAND FARM

POOR FARM

COOMBS RD

Lairey

Narrows

RD

Isle-au-Haut Mountain

LAWSON'S QUARRY

Carver's Pond

Geary's Beach

Big Garden Island

SUNSET ROCK PARK

Old Harbor Pond

HIGH ST

VINALHAVEN HISTORICAL SOCIETY

BOOTH QUARRY

Arey Cove

NARROWS PARK

OLD HARBOR RD

Hurricane Sound

The Reach

MAIN ST

Sands Cove

PEQUOT RD

ROBERTS CEMETERY RD

Narrows Island

Big White Island

Greens

Carver's Harbor

ARMBRUST HILL TOWN PARK

FERRY LANDING

Roberts Harbor

Sheep Island

Hurricane Island

Island

SANDS COVE RD

ATLANTIC AVE

LANE'S ISLAND PRESERVE

Indian Creek

Penobscot   Bay

0   1 mi
0   1 km

© AVALON TRAVEL PUBLISHING, INC.

Harbor carrying mighty cargoes of granite destined for government and commercial buildings in Boston, New York, and Washington, D.C. In the 1880s, nearly 4,000 people lived on Vinalhaven, North Haven, and Hurricane Island. After World War I, demand declined, granite gave way to concrete and steel, and the industry petered out and died. But Vinalhaven has left its mark—ornate columns, paving blocks, and curbstones in communities as far west as Kansas City.

With a full-time population of about 1,300 souls, Vinalhaven is a serious working community, not primarily a playground. Nearly 600 island residents depend on the lobster and fishing industry. Shopkeepers cater to locals as well as

visitors, and increasing numbers of artists and artisans work away in their studios. For day-trippers, there's plenty to do—shopping, picnicking, hiking, biking, swimming—but an overnight stay provides a chance to sense the unique rhythm of life on a year-round island.

Sights

One Main Street landmark that's hard to miss is the three-story, cupola-topped **Odd Fellows Hall,** a Victorian behemoth with assorted gewgaws in the streetfront display windows. Artist Robert Indiana, who first arrived as a visitor in 1969, owns the structure, built in 1885 for the IOOF Star of Hope Lodge. It's not open to the public.

At the top of the hill just beyond Main Street (corner of School St. and East Main St.) is a greenish-blue replica **galamander,** a massive reminder of Vinalhaven's late-19th-century granite-quarrying era. Galamanders, hitched to oxen or horses, carried the stone from island quarries to the finishing shops. (By the way, the origin of the name remains unexplained.) Next to the galamander is a colorful wooden bandstand, site of very popular evening band concerts held sporadically during the summer.

The unusually energetic **Vinalhaven Historical Society** (207/863-4410, 11 A.M.–3 P.M. Wed.–Sun. early June to mid-Oct., or by appointment, free) operates a museum in the onetime town hall on High Street, just east of Carver's Cemetery. The building itself has a tale, having been floated across the bay from Rockland, where it served as a Universalist church. The museum's documents and artifacts on the granite industry are particularly intriguing, and special summer exhibits add to the interest. Donations are welcomed. At the museum, request a copy of *A Self-Guided Walking Tour of the Town of Vinalhaven and Its Granite-Quarrying History,* a handy little brochure that details 17 in-town locations related to the late-19th and early-20th-century industry.

Built in 1832 and now owned by the town of Vinalhaven, **Brown's Head Light** guards the southern entrance to the Fox Islands Thorofare. To reach the grounds (no access to the light itself; the keeper's house is a private residence for the town manager), take the North Haven Road about six miles, at which point you'll see a left-side view of the Camden Hills. Continue to the second road on the left, Crockett River Road. Turn and take the second road on the right, continuing past the Brown's Head Cemetery to the hill overlooking the lighthouse.

Parks and Preserves

Vinalhaven is loaded with wonderful hikes and walks, some deliberately unpublicized. Since the mid-1980s, the foresighted **Vinalhaven Land Trust** (207/863-2543) has expanded the opportunities. When you reach the island, pick up maps at the land trust's office at **Skoog Memorial**

Park (Sands Cove Rd.), west of the ferry terminal, or inquire at the town office or the Paper Store. The trust also offers a seasonal series of educational walks and talks.

Some hiking options are the **Perry Creek Preserve** (terrific loop trail), **Middle Mountain Park, Tip-Toe Mountain, Polly Cove Preserve, Isle au Haut Mountain, Arey's Neck Woods, Huber Preserve,** and **Sunset Rock Park.**

The Maine chapter of **The Nature Conservancy** (207/729-5181) owns or manages several islands and island clusters near Vinalhaven. **Big Garden** (formerly owned by Charles and Anne Morrow Lindbergh) and **Big White Islands** are easily accessible and great for shoreline picnics if you have your own boat. Other Conservancy holdings in this area are fragile environments, mostly nesting islands off-limits from mid-March to mid-August. Contact the Conservancy for specifics.

No, you're not on the moors of Devon, but you could be fooled in the 45-acre **Lane's Island Preserve,** one of the Nature Conservancy's most utilized island preserves. Masses of low-lying ferns, rugosa roses, and berry bushes cover the granite outcrops of this sanctuary—and a foggy day makes it even more moorlike and mystical, a Brontë novel setting. Best (albeit busiest) time to come is early August, when you can compete with the birds for blackberries, raspberries, and blueberries. Easy trails wind past old stone walls, an aged cemetery, and along the surf-pounded shore. The preserve is a 20-minute walk (or five-minute bike ride) from Vinalhaven's ferry landing. Set off to the right on Main Street, through the village. Turn right onto Water Street, then right on Atlantic Avenue. Continue across the causeway on Lane's Island Road and left over a salt marsh to the preserve. The large white house on the harbor side of Lane's Island is privately owned.

Next to the ferry landing in Carver's Harbor is **Grimes Park,** a wooded, vest-pocket retreat with a splendid view of the harbor. Owned by the American Legion, the 2.5-acre park is perfect for picnics or for hanging out (especially in good weather) between boats.

Just behind the Island Community Medical

Penobscot Bay

Center, close to downtown, is 30-acre **Armbrust Hill Town Park,** once the site of granite-quarrying operations. Still pockmarked with quarry pits, the park has beautifully landscaped walking paths and native flowers, shrubs, and trees— much of it thanks to late island resident Betty Roberts, who made this a lifelong endeavor. From the back of the medical center, follow the trail to the summit for a southerly view of Matinicus and other offshore islands. If you're with children, be especially careful about straying onto side paths, which go perilously close to old quarry holes. Before the walk, lower the children's energy level at the large playground off to the left of the trail.

Recreation

Swimming: Abandoned quarries are all over the island, and most are on private property, but two town-owned ones are easy to reach from the ferry landing. **Lawson's Quarry,** on the North Haven Road, is about a mile from downtown; **Booth Quarry** is on Pequot Road, 1.5 miles from downtown. Both are signposted. You'll see plenty of swimmers and sunbathers-on-the-rocks on a hot day, but there are no lifeguards, so swimming is at your own risk. There are no restrooms or changing rooms. *Note:* Pets and soap are not allowed in the water; camping, fires, and alcohol are not allowed in the quarry areas.

Down the side road beyond Booth Quarry is **Narrows Park,** a town-owned space looking out toward Narrows Island, Isle au Haut, and, on a clear day, Mount Desert Island.

For saltwater swimming, continue along Pequot Road about 1.5 miles beyond Booth Quarry. At the crossroads, you'll see a whimsical bit of local folk art—the Coke lady sculpture. Turn right (east) and go a half mile to **Geary's Beach** (also called **State Beach**), where you can picnic and scour the shoreline for shells and sea glass.

Bicycling: Even though Vinalhaven's 40 or so miles of public roads are narrow, winding, and poorly shouldered, they're relatively level, so a bicycle is a fine way to tour the island. Bring your own, preferably a hybrid or mountain bike, or rent one at the **Tidewater Motel** (207/863-4618), on Main Street near the ferry landing ($10 a day or $5 a half-day). A wide selection of rental bikes

Vinalhaven Island is a favorite destination for sea kayakers and bicyclists, as can be seen on this ferry approaching the Carvers Harbor landing.

is available on the mainland in Rockport at **Maine Sport Outfitters** (Rte. 1, Rockport, 207/236-8797 or 888/236-8796; see also Bicycling and Kayaking under Camden-Rockport Area), but you have to pay extra to bring one on the ferry.

A 10-mile, 2.5-hour bicycle route begins on Main Street and goes clockwise out the North Haven Road (rough pavement), past Lawson's Quarry, to Round the Island Road (some sections are dirt), then Poor Farm Road to Geary's Beach and back to Main Street via Pequot Road and School Street. Carry a picnic and enjoy it on Lane's Island; stop for a swim in one of the quarries; or detour down to Brown's Head Light. If you're here for the day, keep track of the time so you don't miss the ferry.

Sea Kayaking: Kayak tours and instruction as well as biking and hiking tours are available through **SeaEscape Kayak** (W. Main St., Vinalhaven, 207/863-9343, www.seaescapekayak.com). An Island Picnic Tour, $85, includes a gourmet picnic lunch on an island. If you're not that gung ho, try the Harbor Tour, $45, which is a good introduction to sea kayaking. Combination biking/hiking tours are $20–65, depending upon length and inclusions.

Shopping

Vinalhaven's shops change regularly, but a few have stood the test of time. **The Paper Store** (Vinal's News Stand, Main St., 207/863-4826) carries newspapers, gifts, film, maps, and odds and ends. **Port O' Call** (Main St., 207/863-2525) is much more than a hardware store. Poke around to see what you'll find. **New Era Gallery** (Main St., 207/863-9351) has a well-chosen selection of art in varied media representing primarily island artisans.

The Saturday morning **flea markets** held in the open field next to the galamander are an island must, as much for the browsing and buying as for the gossip.

Entertainment

No one visits Vinalhaven for nightlife, but concerts (Fox Island series and others) and lectures (most organized by the Vinalhaven Land Trust or the Vinalhaven Historical Society) are frequent.

Islanders expect most will be held at the brand-spanking new $12 million school, opened in autumn 2004. Check *The Wind* to see what's on the docket during your visit.

Accommodations

Vinalhaven isn't overrun with spare beds, so if you plan to spend the night (or stay longer), especially between mid-July and mid-August, be sure to make a reservation. If you're going for the day, pay attention to the ferry schedule and allow enough time to get back to the boat. Islanders may be able to find you a bed in a pinch, but don't count on it. The island has no campsites. Rates listed are for peak season.

Your feet practically touch the water when you spend the night at the **M Tidewater Motel and Gathering Space** (12 Main St., Carver's Harbor, P.O. Box 546, Vinalhaven 04863, 207/863-4618, www.tidewatermotel.com, $115–256), a well-maintained motel in two buildings cantilevered over the harbor. Owned by Phil and Elaine Crossman (she operates the New Era Gallery across the street), the 19-room motel was built by Phil's parents in 1970. It's the perfect place to sit on the deck and watch the lobsterboats do their thing. Be aware, though, that commercial fisherfolk are early risers, and lobsterboat engines can rev up as early as 4:30 A.M. on a summer morning—all part of the pace of Vinalhaven. Phil Crossman is practically a one-man chamber of commerce. He can recommend hikes and other activities and, since he maintains the island's calendar of events, he always knows what's happening and when. A continental breakfast and use of bicycles are included in the rates. Kids 10 and under are free; seven units are efficiencies. Open all year. Also on the premises is **Island Spirits,** a small gourmet foods store stocked with wines, beers, cheeses, breads, and other goodies, even picnic baskets to pack it all in. About once a month, the motel hosts a wine tasting in the second-floor Gathering Space, overlooking the harbor. And if all that's not enough, there's the **Toggle,** a wine bar with a tapas-style menu that usually also includes lobster. If you want to get a better sense of island life, pick up a copy of Phil's book *Away Happens,* a collection of humorous essays about island living. You can read a sample from it on the motel's website.

Two seasonal B&Bs convenient to downtown are **The Libby House** (Water St., Vinalhaven 04863, 207/863-4696, $70–150, open summer only) and the **Payne Homestead at the Moses Webster House** (Atlantic Ave., P.O. Box 216, Vinalhaven 04863, 207/863-9963 or 888 /863-9963, $90–145), most rooms with shared baths, breakfast daily in midsummer, weekends in shoulder months. Open May–October; no credit cards.

Food

Hours listed are for peak season. Expect reduced hours and fewer days of operation at other times.

Baked bean suppers are regularly held at a couple of island locations. Check *The Wind.*

The island's best dinner spot is the harbor-side room at **The Haven** (Main St., 207/863-4969, Tues.–Sat.), with a great view and a creative menu that changes nightly in summer. Two seatings—6 and 8:15 P.M.—by reservation. The restaurant's streetside room (5:30–9:30 P.M.) is more casual and less creative (they call it "pub style"), but the walls are lined with artwork on a rotating basis; no reservations, so you may need to wait, especially on summer weekends. The restaurant is a one-woman show, and Tori Pratt doubles as a local caterer and the girl's basketball coach, so hours can be sporadic.

New in 2004 was **Tibbs** (Main St., 207/863-4475), which got off to a rocky start but earned a reputation for good Mediterranean-influenced food by summer's end, only to close for renovations and to open a TV sports lounge. Ask locally about its current reputation.

Opposite the municipal parking lot is the **Harbor Gawker** (Main St., 207/863-9365, 10:30 A.M.–8 P.M., to 9 P.M. July and Aug.), a local landmark since 1975, but now with a nice indoor dining area. On the menu are burgers, lobster rolls, sandwich baskets, fried seafood, terrific fish chowder (by the cup, pint, or quart), and soft ice cream. Dine in or take out.

Originally opened as an ice cream spot, **Annabelles** (Main St., 207/863-2789, 8 A.M.–9 P.M. daily, to 10 P.M. Fri. and Sat.), now serves pastries for breakfast and sandwiches and soups for lunch and dinner.

For pizza, head to **The Pizza Pit** (Harbor Wharf, 207/863-4311, 11:30 A.M.–2 P.M. and 4–8 P.M. Wed.–Mon.), which probably has the best view of any pizza place, anywhere. Pizza, calzones, pasta, and even some Tex-Mex specialties, such as quesadillas and nachos, are on the menu. In the off-season, heartier fare is served on weekend nights.

Sharing space on the wharf is the island's best breakfast place, **Surfside** (Harbor Wharf, 207/863-4311, 4:30–10 A.M. daily, to 11 A.M. Sun.). Eat inside or out on the wharf. From June into September, the restaurant also serves lunch, and it began dabbling with serving dinner in fall 2004.

Getting Around

I can't stress this enough: Don't bring a car unless it is absolutely necessary. If you're coming over for a day trip, you can get to parks and quarries, shops, restaurants, and the historical society museum on foot. If you want to explore farther, a bicycle is an excellent option or you can rent a car for $40 a day from the Tidewater Motel (207/863-4618) or Phil will meet you at the ferry landing. Only a few are available, so call well ahead to reserve.

Information and Services

For information on Vinalhaven, write the **Vinalhaven Chamber of Commerce** (P.O. Box 703, Vinalhaven 04863, www.vinalhaven.org). The website is poorly maintained, but the chamber produces a helpful little flyer/map showing locations in the Carver's Harbor area. Also helpful for planning a trip to Vinalhaven is a guidebook published by Phil Crossman at the Tidewater Motel (207/863-4618, $3.50).

Vinalhaven's weekly newsletter, *The Wind* (P.O. Box 194, Vinalhaven 04863, 207/863-2158), named after the island's original newspaper, first published in 1884, is loaded with island flavor: news items, public-supper announcements, editorials, and ads. A year's subscription is $25; single copies are available free at most downtown locales.

The **Vinalhaven Public Library** (E. Main St. and Chestnut St., 207/863-4401), a distinctive,

Carnegie-funded granite building built in 1906, is open Tuesday and Thursday 1–5 P.M. and 6–8 P.M., Wednesday and Friday 9 A.M.–noon and 1–5 P.M., and Saturday 9 A.M.–1 P.M.

Public restrooms are at the ferry landing and the town office (weekdays only).

NORTH HAVEN

Eight miles long by three miles wide, North Haven is 12 miles off the coast of Rockland—an hour by ferry. The island boasts sedate summer homes, open fields where hundreds of sheep once grazed, about 350 year-round residents, a yacht club called the Casino, and a village gift shop that's been here since 1954.

Originally called North Island, North Haven had much the same settlement history as Vinalhaven, but, being smaller (about 5,280 acres) and more fertile, it has developed—or not developed—differently. In 1846, North Haven was incorporated and severed politically from Vinalhaven, and by the late 1800s, the Boston summer crowd began buying traditional island homes, building tastefully unpretentious new ones, and settling in for a whole season of sailing and socializing. Several generations later, "summer folk" now come for weeks rather than months, often rotating the schedules among slews of siblings. Informality remains the key, though—now more than ever.

The island has two distinct hamlets—North Haven Village, on the Fox Islands Thorofare, where the state ferry arrives, and Pulpit Harbor, particularly popular with the yachting set.

North Haven doesn't offer a lot for the day visitor, and islanders don't welcome them with open arms, unless they give something back. If you choose to venture much beyond North Haven Village, do your part by picking up any litter as you walk or cycle along.

North Haven Village

Fanning out from the ferry landing is a delightful cluster of substantial, year-round clapboard homes—a marked contrast to the weathered-shingle cottages typical of so many island communities. It won't take long to stroll Main Street, but you'll want a camera.

Anchoring the cluster of shops "downtown" is the **North Haven Gift Shop** (Main St., 207/867-4444), a rabbit warren of rooms that June Hopkins has been running since 1954. No problem spending money here—everything's tastefully selected, from the pottery to the notecards to the books, jewelry, and gourmet condiments. One room is a gallery, with work by Maine artists.

Next door (connected via an elevated corridor) is the **Eric Hopkins Gallery** (Main St., 207/867-2229), owned by June Hopkins's son, a megatalented painter who's gained repute far beyond Maine. If you can't spring for an original (figure on several thousand dollars), his distinctive work—luminous bird's-eye views of island, sea, and forest—now appears also on notecards, postcards, T-shirts, and one-of-a-kind sweaters.

The four-story, early-20th-century **Calderwood Hall** (Main St., 207/867-2265) is artist Herb Parsons's eclectic gift shop/art gallery, with many works by island artists and artisans

The new **Waterman's Community Center** (Main St., 207/867-2029, www.watermans.org), opened in a renovated market, provides a place for island residents and visitors to gather for entertainment, events, and even coffee and gossip. Check the schedule on its website to see what's planned.

Bicycling

North Haven has about 25 miles of paved roads, but, just as on most other islands, they are narrow, winding, and nearly shoulderless. Starting near the ferry landing in North Haven Village, take South Shore Road eastward, perhaps stopping en route for a picnic at town-owned Mullin's Head Park (also spelled Mullen Head) on the southeast corner of the island. Then follow the road around, counterclockwise, to North Shore Road and Pulpit Harbor. Be conscientious and obey the rules of the road and do carry out any trash (yours, or whatever you find along the way).

Sailing

If you have your own boat, this area is a sailor's nirvana. Be sure to have on board a copy of *A Cruising Guide to the Maine Coast* (see Suggested Reading in the Know Coastal Maine chapter).

Boat fanatics will enjoy peeking into the **J. O.**

Brown & Sons boat shop (207/867-4621), on the Thorofare in North Haven Village. It's a remnant of a bygone era, with the scents and feel of traditional craftsmanship. The fifth generation now works here. In the late 19th century, Brown's built the first North Haven Dinghy, a 14.5-foot wooden sailboat, and followed it with dozens more. The fleet has had a summer racing season here since the 1880s. The boatyard, by the way, has a launderette and showers and also rents moorings. If you need boat transportation across the Thorofare to Vinalhaven, someone at the shop may be able to help you out. It's open all year.

Accommodations and Food

Guest beds are scarce on North Haven; other than the summer folk, most visitors are day-trippers.

Food choices are also slim. Picnic fixings are available at Brown's Market. For a sit-down lunch (or breakfast or dinner), head for the **Coal Wharf Restaurant** (Main St., 207/867-4739), next to Brown's boat shop. A rustic seasonal eatery that can serve 60 at a time, it's open 6 A.M.–9 P.M. Tuesday–Sunday in July and August, weekends in June, September, and early October. Reservations are wise.

Information and Services

The best source of information is the **North Haven Town Office** (Upper Main St., North Haven 04853, 207/867-4433). It's open weekdays, all year. The shops closest to the ferry landing are accustomed to fielding questions, so try them for answers.

Camden-Rockport Area

Contributing to Camden's image as a picture-perfect New England seaside village are white churches with steeples piercing the sky.

Driven apart by a local squabble in 1891, Camden and Rockport have been separate towns for more than a century, but they're inextricably linked. They share school and sewer systems and an often-hyphenated partnership. On Union Street, just off Route 1, a white wooden arch reads Camden on one side and Rockport on the other. These days, this area is one of the Mid-Coast's—even Maine's—prime destinations.

Camden, the better known of the two, has a year-round population of about 5,390, but that triples during the summer; Rockport, with a much lower profile, doubles in summer from about 3,210 year-round. While Rockport's harbor is relatively peaceful—with yachts, lobsterboats, and a single windjammer schooner— Camden Harbor is a summer-long madhouse, jammed with dinghies, kayaks, windjammers, megayachts, minor yachts, and a handful of fishing craft.

Much of Camden's appeal is its drop-dead-gorgeous setting—a deeply indented harbor with parks, a waterfall, and a dramatic backdrop of low mountains. It is views of Camden that typify Maine nationwide, even worldwide, on calendars and postcards, in photo books, you name it.

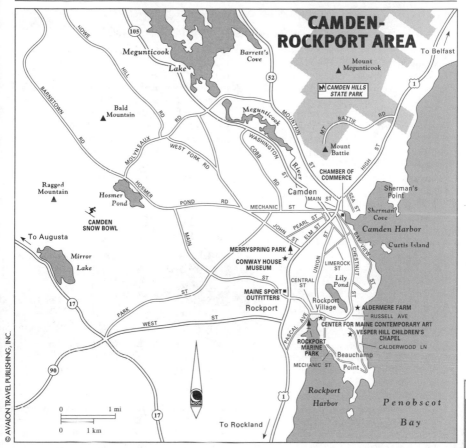

CAMDEN-
ROCKPORT AREA

To Belfast

Megunticook Lake

Barrett's Cove

Mount Megunticook

CAMDEN HILLS STATE PARK

Bald Mountain

Megunticook River

MT. BATTIE RD

WASHINGTON

COBB ST

Mount Battie

Ragged Mountain

Hosmer Pond

POND RD

CHAMBER OF COMMERCE

Sherman's Point

CAMDEN SNOW BOWL

Camden

MAIN ST

MECHANIC ST

Sherman Cove

To Augusta

MERRYSPRING PARK

JOHN ST PEARL ST ELM ST

Camden Harbor

Curtis Island

Mirror Lake

CONWAY HOUSE MUSEUM

LIMEROCK ST

Lily Pond

MAINE SPORT OUTFITTERS

CENTRAL ST

Rockport Village

Rockport

ALDERMERE FARM

RUSSELL AVE

CENTER FOR MAINE CONTEMPORARY ART

VESPER HILL CHILDREN'S CHAPEL

CALDERWOOD LN

ROCKPORT MARINE PARK

Beauchamp

MECHANIC ST Point

Rockport Harbor

Penobscot

To Rockland

Bay

0   1 mi
0   1 km

© AVALON TRAVEL PUBLISHING, INC.

Penobscot Bay

SIGHTS

Self-Guided Historical Tour

The **Camden-Rockport Historical Society,** supported by the Whitehall Inn, has produced a handy little flyer, *A Walking Tour and Bicycle or Car Tour,* detailing more than 50 significant historic sites (mostly private residences) in downtown Camden, Camden's High Street and Chestnut Street Historic Districts, and downtown Rockport. To cover it all, you'll want a car or bike; to cover segments, and really appreciate the architecture, don your walking shoes. Pick up a copy of the flyer at the chamber of commerce.

Old Conway Homestead and Museum

Just inside the Camden town line from Rockport, the Old Conway Homestead and Museum (Conway Rd., Camden, 207/236-2257, 10 A.M.– 4 P.M. Tues.–Fri. July–Aug., $5 adults, $2 children) is a five-building complex owned and run by the Camden-Rockport Historical Society. The 18th-century Cape-style **Conway House,** on the National Register of Historic Places, contains fascinating construction details and period furnishings; in the barn are carriages and farm tools. Two other buildings—a blacksmith shop and a 19th-century sap house used for making maple syrup—have been moved to the grounds and restored. In the contemporary **Mary Meeker**

WINDJAMMING

In 1936, Camden became the home of the "cruise schooner" (sometimes called "dude schooner") trade when Captain Frank Swift restored a creaky wooden vessel and offered sailing vacations to paying passengers. He kept at it for 25 years, gradually adding other boats to the fleet—and the rest, as they say, is history. Windjammers have become big business on the Maine coast, with Camden and Rockland sparring for the title of Windjammer Capital. Rockland wrested it from Camden in the mid-1990s and, so far, has held onto it.

Named for their ability to "jam" into the wind when they carried freight up and down the New England coast, windjammers trigger images of the Great Age of Sail. Most are rigged as schooners, with two or three soaring wooden masts; their lengths range from 64 to 132 feet. Nine are National Historic Landmarks; four were built for the trade.

These windjammers head out for 3–6 days late May to mid-October, tucking into coves and harbors around Penobscot Bay and its islands. The mostly engineless craft set their itineraries by the wind, propelled by stiff breezes to Buck's Harbor, North Haven, and Deer Isle. Everything's totally informal, geared for relaxing.

You're aboard for the experience, not for luxury, so expect basic accommodations with few frills, although newer vessels were built with passenger trade in mind and tend to be a bit more comfy. Down below, cabins typically are small and basic, with paper-thin walls—sort of a campground afloat (earplugs are often available for light sleepers). It may not sound romantic, but be aware that the captains keep track of postcruise marriages. Most boats have shared showers and toilets. If you're Type-A, given to pacing, don't inflict yourself on the cruising crowd; if you're flexible, ready for whatever, go ahead and sign on. You can help with the sails, eat, curl up with a book, inhale salt air, shoot photos, eat, sunbathe, bird-watch, eat, chat up fellow passengers, sleep, eat, or just settle back and enjoy spectacular sailing you'll never forget.

When you book a cruise, you'll receive all the details and directions, but for a typical six-day trip, you arrive at the boat by 7 P.M. for the captain's call to meet your fellow passengers. You sleep aboard at the dock that night, then depart midmorning Monday and spend five nights and days cruising Penobscot Bay, following the wind, the weather, and the whims of the captain. (Many of the windjammers have no engines, only a motorized yawlboat used as a pusher and a water taxi.) You might anchor in a

© TOM NANGLE

Windjammers, working boats, and excursion boats are among the many vessels in Camden's harbor.

deserted cove and explore the shore, or you might pull into a harbor and hike, shop, and bar-hop. Then it's back to the boat for chow—windjammer cooks are legendary for creating three hearty, all-you-can-eat meals daily, including at least one lobster feast! When the cruise ends on Saturday morning, most passengers find it hard to leave.

On the summer cruising schedule, several weeks coincide with special windjammer events, so you'll need to book a berth far in advance for these: mid-June (Boothbay Harbor's Windjammer Days), July Fourth week (Great Schooner Race), Labor Day weekend (Camden's Windjammer Weekend), and the second week in September (WoodenBoat Sail-In).

Most windjammers offering three- to six-day sails out of Camden, Rockland, and Rockport are members of the **Maine Windjammer Association** (P.O. Box 1144, Blue Hill 04614, 800/807-9463, www.sailmainecoast.com), a one-stop resource for vessel and schedule information.

Cramer Museum (named for the prime bene-factor) are displays from the historical society's collection of ship models, old documents, and period clothing. For local color, don't miss the Victorian outhouse. The museum and sap house are also open for maple-syrup demonstrations on Maine Maple Sunday (fourth Sunday in March).

Vesper Hill

Built and donated to the community by a local benefactor, the rustic, open-air **Vesper Hill Children's Chapel** is dedicated to the world's children. Overlooking Penobscot Bay and surrounded by gardens and lawns, the nondenominational chapel is an almost mystical oasis in a busy tourist region. Except during weddings or memorial services, there's seldom a crowd, and if you're lucky, you might have the place to yourself. From Central Street in downtown Rockport, take Russell Avenue east to Calderwood Lane (fourth street on right). On Calderwood, take the second right (Chapel Street) after the (private) golf course. If the sign is down, look for a boulder with Vesper Hill carved in it. From downtown Camden, take Chestnut Street to just past Aldermere Farm; turn left at Calderwood Lane and take the second right after the golf course.

Aldermere Farm, by the way, is the home of America's original herd of Belted Galloway cattle—Angus-like beef cattle with a wide white midriff. First imported from Scotland in 1953, the breed now shows up in pastures all over the United States. The animals' startling "Oreo-cookie" hide pattern never fails to halt passersby—especially in spring and early summer, when the calves join their mothers in the pastures. The 135-acre farm is owned by Maine Coast Heritage Trust, a state conservation organization based in Brunswick.

Center for Maine Contemporary Art

Once a local firehouse, this attractive building has been totally rehabbed to provide display space for the work of Maine's best contemporary artists. The nonprofit Center for Maine Contemporary Art (62 Russell Ave. Rockport, 207/236-2875, www.artsmaine.org, 10 A.M.–5 P.M. Tues.–Sat., 1–5 P.M. Sun., $3), mounts as many as a dozen shows each summer, along with special lectures, a wildly popular art auction (early August), an annual juried art exhibition featuring more than 100 selections, and an annual juried craft show (mid-October) spotlighting several dozen artisans. An exceptional gift shop carries high-end crafts.

PARKS AND PRESERVES

For more than a century, the Camden-Rockport area has benefited from the providence of conscientious year-round and summertime conservationists. Thanks to their benevolence, countless acres of fragile habitat, woodlands, and scenic viewpoints have been preserved. Nowadays, the most active organization is the **Coastal Mountains Land Trust** (CMLT, 101 Mt. Battie St., Camden 04843, 207/236-7091, www.coastal-mountains.org), founded in 1986. It owns 1,900 acres. Maps and information about trails open to the public are available from CMLT.

A Rockland-based group, **The Georges River Land Trust** (207/594-5166, www.grlt.org), whose territory covers the Georges (St. George) River watershed, is the steward for **The Georges Highland Path,** a low-impact hiking trail that reaches Rockport and Camden from the back side of the surrounding hills (see Recreation).

Camden Hills State Park

A five-minute drive and a small fee gets you to the top of **Mount Battie,** the centerpiece of 5,650-acre Camden Hills State Park (Belfast Rd., Rte. 1, 207/236-3109, $3 adults, $1 children 5–11), and the best place to understand why Camden is "where the mountains meet the sea." The summit panorama is, well, breathtaking, and reputedly the inspiration for Edna St. Vincent Millay's poem "Renascence" (a bronze plaque marks the spot); information boards identify the offshore islands. Climb the summit's stone tower for an even better view. The 20 miles of hiking trails (some for every ability) include two popular routes up Mount Battie—an easy, hour-long hike from the base parking lot (Nature Trail) and a more strenuous 45-minute one from the top of Mount Battie Street in Camden (Mount Battie Trail). Or drive up the paved Mount Battie Auto

Road. The park has plenty of space for picnics, and the 112-site camping area (no hookups) is wheelchair-accessible. The nonresident camping fee is $20 per site per night. In winter, ice climbers use a rock wall near the Maiden's Cliff Trail, reached via Route 52 (Mountain Street). The park entrance is two miles north of downtown Camden. Request a free trail map. The park is open mid-May–mid-October. Hiking trails are accessible all year, weather permitting.

Merryspring Park

Straddling the Camden-Rockport boundary, 66-acre Merryspring Park (Conway Rd., Camden, 207/236-2239, www.merryspring.org) is a magnet for nature lovers. More than a dozen well-marked trails wind through woodlands, berry thickets, and wildflowers; near the preserve's parking area are lily, rose, and herb gardens. Admission is free, but donations are welcomed. Special programs (fee charged) include lectures, demonstrations, and a summer Ecology Camp for youngsters. Most programs are held in the park's modern Ross Center (9 A.M.–2 P.M. Tues.–Fri.), named for Merryspring founders Mary Ellen and Ervin Ross. The entrance is on Conway Road, .3 mile off Route 1, at the southern end of Camden. Trails are open daily dawn to dusk.

In-Town Parks

Just behind the Camden Public Library is the **Camden Amphitheatre** (also called the Bok Amphitheatre, after a local benefactor), a sylvan spot resembling a set for *A Midsummer Night's Dream* (which, yes, has been performed here). Concerts, weddings, and all kinds of other events take place in the park. Across Atlantic Avenue, sloping to the harbor, is **Camden Harbor Park,** with benches, a couple of monuments, and some of the best waterfront views in town. The noted landscape firm of Frederick Law Olmsted designed the park in 1931, and it is listed on the National Register of Historic Places. Both the park and amphitheater were restored to their original splendors in 2004.

Rockport's in-town parks include **Marine Park,** off Pascal Avenue, at the head of the harbor; **Walker Park,** on Sea Street, west side of

In Marine Park, a statue memorializes André the Seal, Rockport's one-time honorary harbormaster and the subject of several books and a movie.

the harbor; **Mary-Lea Park,** overlooking the harbor next to the Rockport Opera House; and **Cramer Park,** alongside the Goose River just west of Pascal Avenue. At Marine Park are the remnants of 19th-century lime kilns, an antique steam engine, picnic tables, a boat-launching ramp, and a polished granite sculpture of André, a harbor seal adopted by a local family in the early 1960s. André had been honorary harbormaster, ringbearer at weddings, and the subject of several books and a film—and even did the honors at the unveiling of his statue—before he was fatally wounded in a mating skirmish in 1986, at the age of 25.

Curtis Island

Marking the entrance to Camden Harbor is town-owned Curtis Island, with a 26-foot automated light tower (and adjoining keeper's house) facing into the bay. Once known as Negro Island, it's a sight (and site) made for photo ops; the views are stunning in every direction. A kayak or dinghy will get you out to the island, where you can picnic (take water; there are no facilities), wander around, gather berries, or just watch the passing fleet. Land on the Camden (west) end of the island, allowing for tide change when you beach your boat. Respect the privacy of the keeper's house in summer; it's occupied by volunteer caretakers.

G. W. Hodson Park

Another good picnic spot is a tiny little town park just outside of Camden, overlooking the Megunticook River outlet from Megunticook Lake. G. W. Hodson Park is a serene, pine-needled space with a riverfront picnic table. From downtown Camden, take Route 105 (Washington Street) 2.6 miles to Molyneaux Road. Turn right and go a half mile to the park, on the right. Alternatively, take Route 52 (Mountain Street) 1.8 miles to Beaucaire Road; turn left and go .6 mile to the park.

Fernald's Neck

Three miles of Megunticook Lake shoreline, groves of conifers, and a large swamp ("the Great Bog") are features of 315-acre Fernald's Neck Preserve, on the Camden-Lincolnville line (and the Knox-Waldo County line). Shoreline and mountain views are stupendous, even more so during fall foliage. Easiest trail is the Blue and White Loop, at the northern end of the preserve; the longer Orange Loop begins at the same point, goes past the Great Bog, and loops around the southern end of the preserve. Yellow Trails connect the loops. While on the Blue and White Loop, take the Green offshoot for a great view of the lake and hills. Some sections can be wet; wear boots or rubberized shoes, and use insect repellent. From Route 1 in Camden, take Route 52 (Mountain Street) about 4.5 miles to Fernald's Neck Road, about .2 mile beyond the Youngtown Inn. Turn left, then bear left at the next fork. Go past the gray farmhouse at the road's end, continue into the hayfield, and park near the woods. Head into the woods (look for signs bearing the Nature Conservancy oak leaf) and pick up a map/brochure at the trailhead register. A map is also available at the chamber of commerce office.

Avena Botanicals Medicinal Herb Garden

Visitors are welcome to visit Deb Soule's one-acre medicinal herb gardens (519 Mill St., Rockport, 207/594-2403, www.avenainstitute.org, 9 A.M.–5 P.M. Mon.–Thurs. May–Oct., free), which is part of an herbal and healing arts teaching center. Pick up a garden map and guide at the kiosk, then stroll the paths. More than 120 species of medicinal herbs are planted, and everything is labeled. It's both a teaching garden and a working garden, as herbs are harvested for various preparations made by Avena Botanicals. During the same hours, the herbal apothecary is open for purchases. Better yet, check on the multitude of courses offered by the Avena Institute, which range from women's health to cooking, healing to feng shui. A real gold mine, for those who are open to such ideas. Mill Street is just shy of one mile south of the intersection of Routes 17 and 90 in West Rockport. Turn left on Mill Street and continue for almost one mile. Avena is on the right, down a long dirt driveway.

RECREATION

Recreation Centers

The new **Penobscot Bay YMCA** (116 Union St., Rockport, 207/236-3375, www.penbayymca.org) has an indoor pool, fitness center, therapy pool, indoor track, gymnasium, and indoor rock climbing center, as well as numerous programs for all ages.

Kudos to the town of Rockport for establishing a first-rate recreation area, with ballfields, a playground, picnic tables, basketball court, horseshoe pits, and tennis courts. Open sunrise to sunset, the **Rockport Recreation Park** is on Route 90, 1.2 miles west of Route 1 (watch for the sign on the right).

Also in Rockport is **MidCoast Recreation Center** (535 West St., Rte. 90, 207/236-9400, www.midcoastrec.com), an indoor ice arena and tennis facility.

More than an alpine ski area, the **Camden Snow Bowl** (207/236-3438, www.camdensnowbowl.com) is a four-season recreation area with tennis courts, public swimming in Hosmer

Pond, and hiking trails as well as alpine trails for day and night skiing and riding and the only to-boggan chute in Maine.

Bicycling and Sea Kayaking

Local entrepreneurs Stuart and Marianne Smith have made **Maine Sport** (Rte. 1, Rockport, 207/236-8797 or 888/236-8796, www.maine sport.com) a major destination for anyone interested in outdoor recreation. The knowledgeable staff can lend a hand and steer you in almost any direction, for almost any summer or winter sport. Nothing seems to stump them. The store sells and rents canoes, kayaks, bikes, skis, and tents, plus all the relevant clothing and accessories. A bicycle rents for $18 per day, calm-water canoes and kayaks are $30–40 per day. Sea kayaks are $50 per day single, $65 per day tandem.

Maine Sport Outdoor School (800/722-0826, a division of the Maine Sport) has a full schedule of canoeing, kayaking, and camping trips. A two-hour guided Camden Harbor tour departs three times daily in summer and costs $45 adult, $35 ages 10–15. A four-hour, guided harbor-to-harbor tour (Rockport to Camden) is offered once each day for $85 adult, $75 child, including a picnic lunch. An intensive day-long guided natural history tour is offered once a week for $125 adult, including lunch. The store is a half mile north of the junction of Routes 1 and 90.

Another contact for guided kayak tours is **Riverdance Outfitters** (207/763-3139 or 800/770-3139, www.riverdanceoutfitters.com). An easy 2.5-hour tour using tandem sea kayaks, with a stop on Curtis Island, is $60, a half-day trip is $85, including a picnic. Freshwater tours on Megunticook Lake are $60 for 2.5 hours or $85 for a half day with lunch. (See also Recreation in the Lincolnville section for an outfitter that organizes three-hour afternoon tours for families on Megunticook Lake.)

If you have your own canoe, kayak, rowboat, or whatever, there are a number of boat-launching sites, both saltwater (Eaton Point, at the end of Sea Street, in Camden; and, even better, Marine Park, in Rockport) and freshwater (Megunticook Lake, west and east sides; Bog Bridge, on Route 105, about 3.5 miles from downtown Camden; and

Barrett's Cove, on Route 52, also about 3.5 miles from Camden).

Despite a scarcity of designated bike routes, cycling is popular in the Camden-Rockport area. It's partly the scenery, partly exercise, and partly a solution to summer auto gridlock. At the chamber of commerce, pick up a bike-route map, which has lots of suggestions for short and long rides.

Brown Dog Bikes (53 Chestnut St., Camden, 207/236-6664) is a full-service rental (and sales) shop in downtown Camden; it'll even deliver the wheels to your lodging. The shop also does repairs, sponsors group rides, and serves as a very helpful local clearinghouse for bike-related information. Also renting bikes is **Ragged Mountain Sports** (46 Elm St., Camden, 207/236-6664). Ragged makes deliveries for a fee and also offers weekly rides.

Hiking

There's enough hiking in **Camden Hills State Park** to fill any vacation, but many other options exist as well. For instance, there's **Bald Mountain,** northwest of downtown Camden, for magnificent views of Penobscot Bay. From Route 1 at the southern end of town (between Subway and Exxon), take John Street for .8 mile. Turn left and go .2 mile to a fork. Continue on the left fork (Hosmer Pond Road) for two miles. Bear left onto Barnestown Road (passing the Camden Snow Bowl) and go 1.4 miles to the trailhead on the right, signposted Georges Highland Path Barnestown Access. Maps are available in the box; the parking lot holds half a dozen cars. The blue-blazed trail is relatively easy, requiring just over an hour round-trip; the summit views are spectacular, especially in fall. Carry a picnic and enjoy it at the top. Avoid this in late May and early June, however, when the blackflies take command. Depending on the season, you may encounter squishy areas, although trail stewards have installed some well-placed boardwalks.

The Georges Highland Path eventually will wind through the Georges (St. George) River watershed from the source in Liberty to the outlet in Port Clyde. For now, however, more than 15 miles of trails have been cleared and blazed (blue). Spearheaded by members of the Georges River Land Trust, the trail now has five access points on the outskirts of Camden and West Rockport. Contact the Rockland-based land trust (207/594-5166) for an up-to-date map, or pick it up from a box at one of the trailheads. The easiest access point is on Route 17 about 10 miles from downtown Rockland. Just past Mirror Lake (on your right) is a well-signposted parking area. The Ragged Mountain direction (north) is more strenuous than the Spruce Mountain/Mount Pleasant section (south; across Route 17). The latter is a great three-hour round-trip. Views are spectacular in either direction; Ragged Mountain gets you closer to the ocean panorama. **River-dance Outfitters** (800-770-3139, www.river danceoutfitters) offers half-day guided hiking tours along the path for $85, including a trail-side lunch.

Swimming

The Camden area is blessed with several locales for freshwater swimming—a real boon, since Penobscot Bay can be mighty chilly, even at summer's peak. **Shirttail Point,** with limited parking, is a small sandy area on the Megunticook River. It's shallow enough for young kids and has picnic tables and a play area. From Route 1 in Camden, take Route 105 (Washington Street) 1.4 miles; watch for a small sign on the right. **Barrett's Cove,** on Megunticook Lake, has more parking space, usually more swimmers, and restrooms, picnic tables, and grills, as well as a play area. Diagonally opposite the Camden Public Library, take Route 52 (Mountain Street) about three miles; watch for the sign on the left. To cope with the parking crunch on hot summer days, bike to the beaches. You'll be ready for a swim after the uphill stretches, and it's all downhill on the way back.

Camden and Rockport both have saltwater swimming but no major sandy beaches. In Camden, it's **Laite Beach Park,** on Bay View Street about 1.5 miles from downtown Camden. Right on Camden Harbor, the park has great views, a strip of sand, picnic tables, a playground, and children's musical events every Wednesday (1–3 P.M.) in July and August. Check the local papers or contact Camden Parks & Recreation (207/236-3438) for the schedule. Rockport has **Walker Park,** tucked away on the west side of the harbor. From Pascal Avenue, take Elm Street, which becomes Sea Street. Walker Park is on the left, with picnic tables, a play area, and a small, pebbly beach.

Indoor-pool options are the **Penobscot Bay YMCA** and the **Samoset Resort,** on the Rockport-Rockland boundary (see the Rockland Area section).

Golf

On a back road straddling the Camden-Rockport line, the **Goose River Golf Club** (50 Park St., Rockport, 207/236-8488) competes with the best for outstanding scenery. A second set of tees in the nine-hole layout makes the course virtually an 18-holer. Starting times are needed on weekends and holidays. Snack bar, cart and club rentals, moderate greens fees.

Day Sails and Excursions

Most day sails and excursion boats operate late May into October, with fewer trips in the spring and fall than in July and August. You can't compare a two-hour day sail to a weeklong cruise on a Maine windjammer (see the sidebar Windjamming), but at least you get a hint of what could be—and it's a far better choice for most kids, who aren't allowed on most windjammer cruises. Several excursion boats operate out of Camden in summer. Most weekdays, you can just show up at the dock and find a space, but on weekends, better call for a reservation. Several are based at Bay View Landing, formerly known as Sharp's Wharf.

The classic wooden schooner ***Olad*** (207/236-2323, www.maineschooners.com) does several two-hour sails daily from Camden's Public Landing, weather permitting, late May to mid-October. Call to check on the sailing schedule and/or make reservations. Tickets are $27 adults, $15 for kids under 12; snacks are served.

Another historic Camden daysailer is the 57-foot, 18 passenger schooner ***Surprise*** (207/236-4687, www.camdenmainesailing.com), built in

1918 and skippered by congenial educator Jack Moore and his wife, Barbara. Between May and October, they do daily two-hour sails, departing from Camden's Public Landing. Cost is $25–28, including snacks.

The 49-passenger *Appledore* (207/236-8353, www.appledore2.com), built in 1978 for round-the-world cruising, sails from Bay View Landing three or four times daily June to October, beginning around 10 A.M. Most cruises last two hours and cost $25. Cocktails, wine, and soft drinks are available.

Over in Rockport, the schooner *Heron* (207/236-8605 or 800/599-8605, www.wooden boatco.com) is a 65-foot, John Alden–designed wooden yacht launched in 2003. Sailing options include a lobster-roll lunch sail ($65), lighthouse sail ($38), and sunset sails with hors d'oeuvres ($50).

For a short cruise—but a great way to see Camden and Rockport, their lighthouses and shorelines—head down to the Camden Public Landing and buy a ticket for the 30-passenger converted lobsterboat *Betselma* (207/236-4446, www.betselma.com). Reservations usually aren't

needed. Retired schooner captain Les Bex knows these waters, the wildlife, and the history. He does about eight hour-long trips daily, beginning at 10:30 A.M., June through September, for $10 adults, $5 children under 12. Last trip is at 7:30 P.M. He also does two two-hour trips—one in the morning, one in the afternoon—for $20 adults, $10 children under 12. A three-hour combo ($30 adults, $15 kids) also is available.

If the kids are bombarding you with FAQs about lobsters, here's the solution. Take a two-hour trip aboard Captain Alan Philbrick's *Lively Lady Too* (207/236-6672), berthed at Camden's Bay View Landing. He hauls in a trap, takes out a lobster, explains all its parts, and generally provides all the answers. As a former biology teacher, he's a whiz at natural history, so there's also information about seabirds, seals, and lots more. Trips depart three times a day Monday–Saturday. Cost is $20 adults, $5 kids under 15. The Philbricks also organize four-hour sunset cruise/lobsterbakes on an unpredictable schedule (usually Tuesday, Thursday, and Saturday at 4 P.M.); call for details. Cost is $50 for adults (for clams, mussels, corn, and *two* lobsters), $20 for the children's menu.

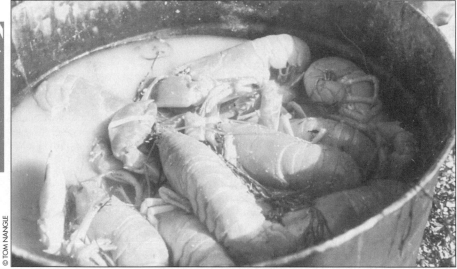

© TOM NANGLE

An island lobster bake is a highlight of most windjammer cruises on Penobscot Bay.

SHOPPING

Downtown Camden is a tough place to find socks or thread, but it's a boutique-shopper's paradise if gifts are your goal. Rockport has a handful of unusual gift and antiques shops and galleries.

New and Old Books

The Owl and Turtle Bookshop (32 Washington St., Camden, 207/236-4769 or 800/876-4769), one of Maine's best new-books stores, with thousands of books and a wonderful children's room, moved to spacious new digs in the Knox Mill Center in 2004. Replacing it in its old location is **Sherman's** (8 Bay View St., Camden, 207/236-2223), another excellent bookstore with shops up and down the coast.

For antiquarian books, **ABCD Books** (23 Bay View St., Camden, 207/236-3903 or 888/236-3903) maintains an excellent stock of rare books and first editions (prices are a bit steep).

Crammed floor to ceiling with used books, **Stone Soup Books** (33 Main St., Camden, no phone), a tiny second-floor shop across from the Lord Camden Inn, is Camden's best source for contemporary used fiction.

Gifts and Crafts

You'll need to wander the streets to take in all the gift and craft shops, particularly in Camden. Some are obvious, others are tucked away on side streets and back alleys. Explore.

Planet Emporium (31 Main St., Camden, 207/236-9022) and **Planet World Marketplace** (10 Main St.). face each other across Main Street in downtown Camden. It bills itself as a contemporary department store, with fine clothing, shoes, housewares, and lots of toys and gadgets. Guard your wallet—there's lots of tempting stuff here.

A downtown Camden landmark since 1940, **The Smiling Cow** (41 Main St., Camden, 207/236-3351 or 800/646-6169) is as good a place as any to pick up Maine souvenirs—a few slightly kitschy, but most reasonably tasteful. Before or after shopping here, head for the rear balcony for coffee and a knockout view of the harbor and the Megunticook River waterfall.

© TOM NANGLE

Stone Soup Books, at a second-floor location in downtown Camden, is a great place to pick up used contemporary fiction or to chat about literature or local politics with co-owner Paul Joy.

The name tells it all at **Once a Tree** (46 Bay View St., 207/236-3995 or 800/236-0440). Wood is everywhere: cutting boards, clock faces, vases, game boards, spoons, furniture. It's an education in the versatility of wood.

Follow West Street (Route 90) from Route 1 for almost three miles and you'll come to **Danica Candleworks** (Rte. 90, West Rockport, 207/236-3060), producers of the loveliest candle colors you've ever seen. Owner Erik Laustsen learned the hand-dipping trade from his Danish relatives, and Danica now ships its work all over the country. The Scandinavian-style shop also carries other gift items.

Clothing and Sporting Gear

Established in 1976, **The Admiral's Buttons** (36 Bay View St., Camden, 207/236-2617) stocks a carefully selected line of classic, high-end men's and women's clothing and accessories

Penobscot Bay

(bow ties, foul weather gear, cuff links, Tilley hats, great sweaters), plus Maine-created Shard pottery and Thomas Moser furniture.

Sturdy, well-designed, homemade (by knitting machine) wool and cotton sweaters are the specialty at **Unique One** (2 Bay View St., Camden, 207/236-8717). Or you can pick out yarn and make your own.

Discount Shopping

With a name like **Heavenly Threads** (57 Elm St., Rte. 1, Camden, 207/236-3203), how can anyone resist this thrift shop? Established by Camden's community-oriented First Congregational Church (next door to the shop), Heavenly Threads carries high-quality pre-owned clothing, books, and jewelry. Staffed by volunteers, with proceeds going to such local ecumenical causes as Meals-on-Wheels.

ENTERTAINMENT

Thursday and Friday evenings at 8 P.M. in July and August, and once a month the rest of the year, **Bay Chamber Concerts** (207/236-2823 or 888/707-2770, www.baychamberconcerts.org) draw sell-out audiences to the beautifully restored (and air-conditioned) Rockport Opera House. Founded in the 1960s as a classical series, the summer concerts feature a resident quartet, prominent guest artists, and outstanding programs. The series has expanded to include world music, jazz, and dance. The first week in August ("Next Generation Week") is devoted to classes and concerts for and by talented teenagers. Seats are reserved for summer concerts ($22 for adults in July, $25 in August); open seating is the rule in winter, when tickets are less expensive and programs vary from classical to pops to jazz. (Season tickets and flex passes are available.) In a praiseworthy effort to foster music appreciation among youngsters, the Bay Chamber organization makes free student tickets available at the door before each concert on a space-available basis.

Fans of art flicks would scream if **The Bayview Street Cinema** (10 Bay View St., Camden, 207/236-8722) ever closed its doors (it's been a tradition since 1975), but there's seldom a mob at this second-floor movie house in downtown Camden. The management screens all sorts of esoterica, as well as films already available at the local video store. Biggest turnouts are for movies filmed in the area—*Peyton Place, Man without a Face, Thinner.* Two screenings nightly, usually 7 and 9 P.M.; some Sunday matinees (3 P.M.). Tickets are $6.50 adults, $5.50 seniors, $4.50 children.

The beautifully renovated **Camden Opera House** (29 Elm St., Camden, 207/236-7963, 207/236-4884 box office, www.camdenopera house.org) is the site of many performances by renowned performers. It's also home to the **Camden Civic Theatre** (207/236-2281), which presents impressively creditable performances, thanks to lots of fine local talent, and **Maine Grand Opera** (207/230-6737 or 866/595-6737, www .mainegrandopera.org).

FESTIVALS AND EVENTS

One weekend in February is given over to the **Camden Conference,** an annual three-day foreign-affairs conference with nationally and internationally known speakers. The first weekend in February marks the **National Toboggan Championships,** two days of races and fun at the nation's only wooden toboggan chute at the Camden Snow Bowl.

The third Thursday of July is **House and Garden Day,** when you can take a self-guided tour (10 A.M.–4:30 P.M.) of significant homes and gardens in Camden and Rockport. Proceeds benefit the Camden Garden Club. And **HarborArts,** on the third weekend in July, draws dozens of artists and craftspeople displaying and selling their wares at the Camden Amphitheatre, Harbor Park.

Labor Day weekend is also known as **Windjammer Weekend** here, with cruises, windjammer open houses, fireworks, and all kinds of live entertainment in and around Camden Harbor. Twenty top artisans open their studios for the annual **Country Roads Artists and Artisans Tour** in September.

Dozens of artists and craftspeople display and sell their wares at the **Fall Festival and Arts and Crafts Show,** the first weekend in October at the Camden Amphitheatre, Harbor Park.

Christmas by the Sea is a family-oriented early-December weekend featuring open houses, special sales, concerts, and a visit from Santa Claus.

ACCOMMODATIONS

The Camden-Rockport area (including Lincolnville) is loaded with lodgings—from basic motels to cottage complexes to elegant inns and B&Bs. Many of Camden's most attractive accommodations (especially B&Bs) are on Route 1 (variously disguised as Elm Street, Main Street, and High Street), heavily trafficked in summer. If you're unusually sensitive to nighttime noises, request a room facing away from the street.

The chamber of commerce is very helpful with lodging information and also maintains a lengthy list of seasonal rentals. A private firm, **Camden Accommodations** (43 Elm St., Rte. 1, Camden 04843, 207/236-6090 or 800/344-4830, www.camdenac.com), arranges reservations at all kinds of lodgings in Camden and surrounding communities—for a week or all summer. In July and August, it's best to reserve far in advance. Toughest time to find a last-minute bed is the first weekend in August, when the Maine Lobster Festival is under way in next-door Rockland.

Camden

A baker's dozen of Camden's finest B&Bs have banded together in the **Camden Bed and Breakfast Association** (P.O. Box 553, Camden 04843, www.camdeninns.com), with an attractive brochure and website. Some of them are described here.

One of Maine's most unusual (and priciest) B&Bs, **Norumbega** (61 High St., Rte. 1, Camden 04843, 207/236-4646 or 877/363-4646, $185–475) is an 1886 turreted stone castle overlooking Camden's outer harbor. Provided your wallet can stand the crunch, splurge for a night (or two) here—if only to feel like temporary royalty. Honeymooners are frequent guests. Thirteen rooms and suites are strikingly decorated, filled with antiques, and have air-conditioning, TV, phones, and data ports. Rates include gourmet breakfast and afternoon tea; lower rates and special packages are available off-season.

Opened for guests in 1901 and operated since the 1970s by the Dewing family, the **Whitehall Inn** (52 High St., Rte. 1, P.O. Box 558, Camden 04843, 207/236-3391 or 800/789-6565, $110–170) retains its century-old genteel air. Lovely gardens, rockers on the veranda, a tennis court, and attentive service all add to the appeal of this historic country inn. Ask to see the Millay Room, commemorating famed poet Edna St. Vincent Millay, who graduated from Camden High School and first recited her poem "Renascence" to Whitehall guests in 1912. Fifty comfortable, unpretentious rooms (45 with private baths) are spread throughout the inn and two separate buildings (Maine House and Wicker House). The dining room is open to the public for breakfast (8–9:30 A.M.) and dinner (6–8:30 P.M.); dinner entrées are $17–18. Open mid-May to late October.

New innkeepers Bob and Juanita Topper, the hospitable hosts at **Camden Maine Stay** (22 High St., Rte. 1, Camden 04843, 207/236-9636, www.camdenmainstay.com, $125–205), do everything right, from the elegant decor to the delicious breakfasts to the welcoming window candles. The stunning residence, built in 1802 and known as the Bass-Huse House, faces busy Route 1 and is just a bit uphill from downtown, but inside and out back, behind the carriage house and barn, you'll feel worlds away. (Request a rear room if you're worried about traffic noise.)

Just off busy Route 1 and two blocks from downtown Camden, in the National Historic District, **The Nathaniel Hosmer Inn** (4 Pleasant St., Camden 04843, 207/236-4012 or 800/423-4012, www.nathanielhosmerinn.com, $125–165), built in the early 1800s, earns high marks for comfort, convenience, and quiet ambience. Breakfast is a feast, served under a real chandelier.

A block away from the Hosmer Inn is the **M Hartstone Inn** (41 Elm St., Camden 04843, 207/236-4259 or 800/788-4823, www.hartstoneinn.com, $125–235), Michael and Mary Jo Salmon's imposing mansard-roofed Victorian close to the heart of downtown. Although some rooms face on the street (and these are insulated with triple-pane windows), most do not, and all have air-conditioning. Once inside, you're away from it all. Be *sure* to make reservations for dinner:

Michael is an award-winning chef, and the five-course dinners are a fine-dining experience blending New England fare with international style. And for guests, the next morning, there's the incredible breakfast. If you get hooked, the Salmons organize culinary classes during the winter.

The eye-grabbing **Captain Swift Inn** (72 Elm St., Camden 04843, 207/236-8113 or 800/251-0865, www.swiftinn.com, $95–155) is named after Frank Swift, who launched Penobscot Bay's windjammer trade. Three of the four rooms have four-poster beds; all have private baths and air-conditioning. Good-for-you breakfasts are served in the antique keeping room, and there's tea in the afternoon.

In the heart of downtown Camden, **The Lord Camden Inn** (24 Main St., Rte. 1, Camden 04843, 207/236-4325 or 800/336-4325, www.lordcamdeninn.com, $160–220) is a hotel alternative in a historic, four-story downtown building (with elevator). Decor is reproduction colonial with exposed brick walls and scads of old framed photos in rooms and hallways. (The brick moderates the noise level.) All 31 rooms and suites have phones, air-conditioning, and cable TV; a full breakfast buffet is provided. Top-floor rooms have harbor-view balconies.

A fine choice for families is **The Lodge at Camden Hills** (Rte. 1, P.O. Box 794, Camden 04843, 207/236-8478 or 800/832-7058, www.thelodgeatcamdenhills.com, $125–225), with 20 modern suites and cottages in an especially attractive modern enclave a mile uphill from downtown Camden. Facilities include air-conditioning, phones, cable TV, some kitchens, some fireplaces.

A hybrid of an inn, B&B, motel, and cottage three miles north of town, **The High Tide Inn on the Ocean** (Rte. 1, Camden 04843, 207/236-3724 or 800/788-7068, www.hightideinn.com, $75–215) has enough variety for every budget—all in an outstanding, seven-acre oceanfront setting with a private pebbly beach. The two-story, eight-unit "Oceanfront" motel unit is closest to the water and farthest from Route 1. Rates include continental breakfast on the water-view porch. Pets can be accommodated in some rooms.

In a town full of high-end lodgings, **The Good Guest House** (50 Elm St., Rte. 1, Camden 04843,

207/236-2139, $60–90) may be the biggest bargain. Two no-frills rooms have private baths, and rates include breakfast. Children are welcome.

Rockport

Although the elegant, award-winning **Samoset Resort** is technically in Rockport, most guests reach it from the south, via Rockland. (See details in the Rockland Area section.)

Step back in time at the oceanfront **M Oakland Seashore Motel & Cottages** (112 Dearborn Ln., Rockport, 207/594-8104, $55–125), a low-key throwback on 75 mostly wooded acres that dates back more than a century. Originally a recreational park operated by a trolley company, its heyday passed with the arrival of the automobile. In the late 1940s, shorefront cabins were added, and in the 1950s, the dance pavilion was renovated into a motel. Nothing fancy here, but the rooms and cabins are comfortable, clean, and right on the ocean's edge; some have kitchenettes, one has a full kitchen. No phones or TVs, but if you're desperate, a black-and-white TV can be rented for $1 per day. Note: This place isn't for those who need attentive service or fluffy accommodations; rather, it's best for those who appreciate quiet simplicity with a big view.

One of the area's spiffiest motels also has terrific Penobscot Bay views. In the Glen Cove section of Rockport (three miles south of downtown Rockport, three miles north of downtown Rockland, next door to Penobscot Bay Medical Center), the **Glen Cove Motel** (Rte. 1, P.O. Box 35, Glen Cove 04846, 207/594-4062 or 800/453-6268, $129–200) sits on a 17-acre bluff with a lovely trail leading to the rocky shore. Many of the 34 units boast water views; all have air-conditioning, phones, and cable TV. The pool is heated. Request a room set back from Route 1.

Camping

Megunticook Campground by the Sea (Rte. 1, P.O. Box 375, Rockport 04856, 207/594-2428 or 800/884-2428, www.campgroundbythesea.com, $32–41) is the area's best-run commercial campground, a 17-acre facility with 87 wooded sites. Also on the premises are 10 camping cabins ($70). Amenities include hot showers, a playground, snack bar, heated pool, laundry, and kayak rentals. Weekly lobsterbakes ($20) are held at the oceanfront picnic area. Noise rules are strictly enforced; pets are allowed. Open mid-May to mid-October. The campground is three miles south of Camden, five miles north of Rockland.

FOOD

Farmers' Markets and Fresh Foods

The best source for health foods, homeopathic remedies, and fresh, seasonal produce is **Fresh Off the Farm** (Rte. 1, Rockport, 207/236-3260, 8 A.M.–7 P.M. Mon.–Sat. and 9 A.M.–5:30 P.M. Sun.), an inconspicuous red-painted roadside place that looks like an overgrown farmstand (it is). Watch for one of those permanent/temporary signs highlighting latest arrivals (Native Blueberries, Native Corn, etc.). The shop is 1.3 miles south of the junction of Routes 1 and 90.

At the southern entrance to Rockport, a sprawling red building is the home of **The State of Maine Cheese Company** (461 Commercial St., Rte. 1, Rockport, 207/236-8895 or 800/762-8895), makers of a dozen varieties of cows'-milk hard cheeses, all named after Maine locations (Aroostook Jack, Allagash Caraway, St. Croix Black Pepper, and so on). Under the cheese company's umbrella (and roof) is the Maine-Made Products Center, covering 9,500 square feet. Among the items are blueberry chutneys, maple syrup, designer breads, great jams—a one-stop-shopping—and tasting—site. November–April, the about a dozen members of the Camden Farmers' Market peddle their products here on Saturdays 9 A.M.–noon.

The **Camden Farmers' Market,** one of the best in the state, holds forth in a parking lot at Colcord and Limerock Streets, across from Tibbetts Industries. Temporary signs are posted on Route 1 on market days—Wednesday 4:30–6:30 P.M. mid-June to mid-September, Saturday 9 A.M.–noon mid-May through October. The market goes on, rain or shine. Besides an unusually good selection of produce, you'll find jams, cheeses, exotic edible mushrooms, plants, crafts, breads, spreads, Korean and Chinese foods, scarves, baskets, and skin products.

Breakfast, Lunch, and Miscellany

The **Camden Bagel Cafe** (Brewster Mill, 26 Mechanic St., Camden, 207/236-2661, 6:30 A.M.–2 P.M. Mon.–Sat., 7:30 A.M.–2 P.M. Sun.) has a hugely loyal clientele, drawn by *real* coffee, fresh bagels, fast service, daily newspapers, and a casual air. No credit cards.

Good coffee is also a draw at the **Camden Deli** (37 Main St., Camden, 207/236-8343, 6 A.M.–10 P.M.), in the heart of downtown, but its biggest asset is the windowed seating overlooking the Megunticook River waterfall. The view doesn't get much better than this (go upstairs for the best angle). Made-to-order sandwiches and wraps, homemade soups, veggie burgers, and subs all add to the mix. Beer and wine only for takeout.

Since the early 1970s, **Scott's Place** (85 Elm St., Rte. 1, Camden, 207/236-8751, 10 A.M.–7 P.M. Mon.–Fri., to 4 P.M. Sat.), a roadside lunch stand near Harbor Audio-Video at the Camden Marketplace, has been dishing up inexpensive ($2–6) burgers and dogs, nowadays adding veggie burgers and salads. Call ahead and it'll be ready.

Peek behind the old-fashioned facade at **N** **Boynton-McKay Food Company** (30 Main St., Camden, 207/236-2465) and you'll see an old-fashioned soda fountain, early-20th-century tables, antique pharmacy accessories, and a thoroughly modern café menu. Restored and rehabbed in 1997, Boynton-McKay had been *the* local drugstore for more than a century. The new incarnation features bagels, creative salads, homemade soups, superb wrap sandwiches, an espresso bar, and the whole works from the soda fountain. Open for breakfast and lunch (7 A.M.–6 P.M. Mon.–Sat. and 8 A.M.–5 P.M. Sun.).

Facing downtown Camden's five-way intersection, **French & Brawn** (1 Elm St., Camden, 207/236-3361, 6 A.M.–8 P.M. Mon.–Sat. and 8 A.M.–8 P.M. Sun.) is an independent market that earns the description *super.* Ready-made sandwiches, soups, and other goodies complement the oven-ready take-out meals, high-cal frozen desserts, esoteric meats, and a staff with a can-do attitude.

The **Rockport Corner Shop** (Main St. and Central St., Rockport, 207/236-8361), a bright, clean, airy place, is the ultimate local hangout, so seats can be hard to come by. Lunch menu is basic American, always reliable—sandwiches, burgers, soups, salads. No credit cards. Open all year (6:30 A.M.–2 P.M. Mon.–Fri., 7 A.M.–2 P.M. Sat., and 7 A.M.–1 P.M. Sun.).

At the junction of Routes 1 and 90, a colorfully painted barn is the home of **The Market Basket** (Rte. 1, Rockport 04856, 207/236-4371, 7 A.M.–6:30 P.M. Mon.–Fri. and 8 A.M.–6:30 P.M. Sat.), the best take-out source for creative sandwiches, homemade soups, cheeses, exotic condiments, pastries, wine (large selection), beer, and entrées-to-go. The market will also do boat provisioning. Regular customers receive the daily menu by fax; in winter, The Market Basket sponsors weeklong cooking classes. Also open Sundays in peak season.

Ethnic Dining

Sonny G's (Elm St., Rte. 1, 207/236-4477, 5–9 P.M.) has been voted the best Italian restaurant in a local poll. The menu changes monthly but usually includes such classic choices as piccatas, marsalas, pastas, and unconventional ones such as pesto-encrusted salmon. Most entrées are in the $9–24 range.

Zaddik's Pizza, Pasta & Mex (20 Washington St., Rte. 105, Camden, 207/236-6540, 5–9 P.M.), a kid-friendly place, has one foot in Mexico and one in Italy—an extensive menu with pizza, bruschetta, paninis, fajitas, calzones, and quesadillas ($8–18). The New York–style pizza is tops. Beer and wine available. It's tucked behind the Opera House.

Seafood and Chowder

In the heart of Camden, **Cappy's** (1 Main St., 207/236-2254, 11 A.M.–9 P.M. Sun.–Thurs., to 10 P.M. Fri. and Sat.) is small, a bit cramped, reliably good (it's been here for 25 years), and very popular with locals and out-of-towners alike. In summer, request a table in the second-floor Crow's Nest, where you'll be less squished; micro-brew tastings are held here 5–7 P.M. daily in season. The burger-and-sandwich menu offers some heartier seafood choices ($8–19); clam chowder is a specialty. During summer, Cappy's operates a

bakery with take-out pastries, sandwiches, and other goodies underneath, facing on the alley that runs down to the public parking lot.

Just down the street, **The Village Restaurant** (7 Main St., Camden, 207/236-3232) gets raves for an equally fine view and, say aficionados, the town's best chowder ($5.95 for a bowl of seafood chowder). At lunchtime, locals throng to this longtime no frills standby along with the tour-bus crowd. Try to hold out for a window table. Open all year for lunch and dinner, with choices for both light and hungry eaters, $7–20.

Casual Dining

Chefs/owners Lindsey Schechter and Brian Hill have created one of the region's hottest restaurants with **M Francine Bistro** (55 Chestnut St., Camden, 207/230-0083, 5:30–10 P.M. Tues.–Sat.), in a house on a residential street. The well-chosen menu (entrées $19–23) is short and focused on whatever's fresh and usually locally available that day. In addition to the dining room, there's also seating at the bar and, when the weather cooperates, on the front porch.

Since 1974, **Peter Ott's** (16 Bay View St., Camden, 207/236-4032, 5:30–9:30 P.M.) has been a mainstay of the Camden restaurant scene—an informal spot where you can count on excellent steaks, seafood, a salad bar, heart-healthy entrées ($17–29), and heart-unhealthy (but award-winning) desserts. No reservations, so expect to wait in July and August, but the comfortable lounge eases the anxiety. The bar is also a local watering hole for the after-work crowd.

Down on the harbor behind Peter Ott's is the informal, art-filled **Atlantica Grille** (1 Bay View Landing, Camden, 207/236-6011 or 888/507-8514, 5:30–9:30 P.M. Wed.–Mon.), two floors of culinary creativity. In summer, try for a table on the deck hanging over the water. The luncheon chicken salad is particularly tasty; you can't go wrong with any of the dinner entrées ($20–27), which concentrate on seafood.

M The Waterfront Restaurant (Bay View St., Camden, 207/236-3747, 11:30 A.M.–2 P.M. and 5–10 P.M.) has the biggest waterside dining deck in town, but you'll need to arrive early to snag one of the tables. Lunches are the most fun, overlooking lots of harbor action; at high tide, you're eye-to-eye with the boats. Most entrées run $16–25. About three blocks from the town center, the Waterfront is behind the Once a Tree shop.

For a special evening, make reservations at the **N Hartstone Inn** (41 Elm St., Camden 04843, 207/236-4259 or 800/788-4823, www.hartstone inn.com). Chef-owner Michael Salmon, named Caribbean chef of the year when they lived in Aruba, produces five-course prix-fixe dinner extravaganzas for $42.50 a person. Even Julia Child has dined here. The menu changes daily to use the freshest ingredients.

The **Whitehall Inn** dining room (52 High St., Rte. 1, Camden, 207/236-3391) is open to the public for breakfast (8–9:30 A.M.) and dinner (6–8:30 P.M.); dinner entrées are $17–18.

In Rockport, **The Helm** (Rte. 1, Rockport, 207/236-4337, 11:30 A.M.–9 P.M.) has a good reputation and a wide-ranging menu. You'll find everything from chopped hamburger to bouillabaisse ($8–17), as well as an extensive and good salad bar.

Food as art seems to be the idea behind the **Gallery Café** (297 Commercial St., Rte. 1, Rockport, 207/230-0061, 11 A.M.–3 P.M. and 5–9 P.M. Wed.–Sat., 10 A.M.–3 P.M. Sun.), across from Hoboken Gardens. Chef Pierre Labonte serves fine fare in a restaurant that's part of **Prismglass**, a fine art glass gallery and working studio representing more than 50 glass artists. Dinner entrées range $16–30; brunch is $8–18.

INFORMATION AND SERVICES

Information

The **Camden-Rockport-Lincolnville Chamber of Commerce** (P.O. Box 919, Camden 04843, 207/236-4404 or 800/223-5459, www .visitcamden.com) is at the Public Landing. Request a copy of its map of area streets and businesses and the official chamber guide. The gray building, facing the parking lot and the harbor at Camden's Public Landing, is open daily in summer, Monday–Saturday the rest of the year.

Hospitals

Penobscot Bay Medical Center (Rte. 1, Rockport 04856, 207/596-8000) serves this region.

Local Libraries

Both Camden and Rockport have undertaken major expansions of their libraries in the last several years—and the results themselves are worth a visit. A $2.3 million expansion at the **Camden Public Library** (Main St., Rte. 1, Camden, 207/236-3440, 9:30 A.M.–5 P.M. Mon.–Sat., to 8 P.M. Tues. and Thurs., and 1–5 P.M. Sun.) created a state-of-the-art facility with a subterranean lecture room. Don't miss the wonderful children's garden, with stone bench supports made to look like books (all classic Maine children's titles). If you're a fan of Edna St. Vincent Millay, pick up a biographical brochure here that notes key sites in Camden. The library often holds lecture series, including the Maine Authors Series in autumn. The **Rockport Public Library** (1 Limerock St., Rockport, 207/236-3642, 10 A.M.–5 P.M. Mon.–Sat., to 8 P.M. Wed.) is a smaller but very user-friendly oasis at the head of Rockport's main drag. Even the gardens are conducive to a good read.

Public Restrooms

With the number of visitors who arrive in Camden each summer, merchants and restaurateurs tend to be reluctant to allow use of their restrooms to noncustomers. Fortunately, the town provides public facilities—in the gray building across the parking lot from the chamber of commerce on Camden's Public Landing. There are also restrooms at the Camden Public Library. In Rockport, there are restrooms at Marine Park.

Getting Around

Concord Trailways (800/639-3317, www.concordtrailways.com) stops in Rockland, Camden-Rockport, Belfast, and Searsport on its three daily nonexpress trips up the coast.

Camden-based **Mid-Coast Limo** (800/937-2424 or 207/236-2424, www.midcoastlimo.com) provides van service, by reservation, between towns as far northeast as Belfast and Portland International Jetport.

Downtown Camden, at the height of summer, is a traffic nightmare. Route 1 bisects the village, and getting across it on foot or by car can be perilous. It's not Boston or Rome or Istanbul, but it's still aggravating. The scarcity of parking creates a musical-cars situation with drivers circling endlessly to find a space. At the chamber of commerce, be sure to request local maps, which show locations of two-hour and all-day parking areas.

Better still, bring or rent a bike and use that to get around. There are few bike lanes, so safety is an extra concern; be cautious.

Lincolnville

Since the early 1990s, the town of Lincolnville, in Waldo County just north of Camden, has outpaced all the surrounding communities in population growth. An influx of new residents has pushed the census to the 2,000 mark. Two distinct enclaves make up the town—oceanfront Lincolnville Beach ("the Beach") and, about five miles inland, Lincolnville Center ("the Center"). Lincolnville is laid-back and mostly rural; the major activity center is a short strip of shops and restaurants at the Beach, and few visitors realize there's anything else.

About a mile north of Lincolnville Beach is a part of town with the quaint name of Ducktrap. Near the mouth of the Ducktrap River, where shoreline trees screen the water, ducks used to gather as ducks do. During molting season, when the ducks shed their feathers and were unable to fly, foraging Native Americans would sneak up on them and capture them for dinner. Or so the story goes.

Directly offshore from Lincolnville Beach, almost within spitting distance, is the island of Islesboro, a fine day-trip destination from Lincolnville and the Camden-Rockport area. The car ferry departs from the southern end of Lincolnville Beach.

SIGHTS

Microbrewery and Winery

A ride into rural country inland from Camden ends up at Andrew Hazen's farm-cum-brewery, **Andrew's Brewery** (High St., Lincolnville, 207/763-3305). Except on major national holidays, Andrew will give a free, 15-minute tour—by appointment only—any time of year. While you tour the operation, the kids can visit the donkeys in the barn. Brewery specialties are Andrew's Old English Ale, Andrew's Brown Ale, and St. Nick Porter. From Camden, take Washington Street (Route 105) to Route 235. Go .6 mile and turn left onto Moody Mountain Road. Continue 1.6 miles and turn right onto High Street. The brewery is one mile ahead, on the left.

Riesling, chardonnay, cabernet sauvignon, and blended wines are just a few of the more than a dozen wines handcrafted at the **Cellardoor Winery and Vineyards** (367 Youngtown Rd., Lincolnville, 207/763-4478, www.mainewine.com, 11 A.M.–5 P.M. mid-May–mid-Oct.). The grapes are grown on the property, and visitors are welcome to walk in the vineyards. Tastings are available. Bring a picnic to enjoy in the gardens. There's also a nice gift shop.

RECREATION

Swimming

Penobscot Bay flirts with Route 1 at **Lincolnville Beach,** a sandy stretch of shorefront in the congested hamlet of Lincolnville Beach. This is about as close as the road gets to the ocean. On a hot day, the sand is wall-to-wall people; during one of the coast's legendary northeasters, it's quite a wild place. There's **freshwater swimming** at several area ponds (most people would call them lakes). On Route 52 in Lincolnville Center is Breezemere Park, a small town-owned swimming/picnic area on **Norton Pond.** The Lincolnville Band, one of the oldest town bands in the country, often plays in the park's Bicentennial Bandstand, built to commemorate the town's 200th birthday. Other swimming ponds are **Coleman Pond, Pitcher Pond,** and **Knight's Pond.**

Sea Kayaking and Canoeing

Ducktrap Kayak (Rte. 1, Lincolnville Beach, 207/236-8608) runs 2.5-hour harbor tours ($25–35) and half-day guided tours ($60–70; bring your own lunch). Three-hour family outings on Megunticook Lake usually begin about 1 P.M. daily; rates are $25–45, depending on the kayaker's age. No experience is needed, but be sure to call for reservations. Rentals are also available for $20–50, depending upon type and size. If you decide you need your own kayak, Ducktrap will even sell you one. If you're around in October, inquire about the date for the annual fall clearance sale—a good chance to pick up an affordable kayak.

Best places to canoe are Norton Pond and Megunticook Lake, and you can even canoe (or kayak) all the way from the head of Norton Pond to the foot of Megunticook Lake. The only tricky part is navigating the drainage culvert between the pond and the lake.

Hiking

The boundaries of both Camden Hills State Park and Fernald's Neck extend into Lincolnville, where the major state-park hike follows the **Ski Shelter Trail** to the **Bald Rock Trail**. From Route 1 in Lincolnville Beach, take Route 173 west about 2.5 miles to the marked parking area just beyond the junction of Youngtown Road. The 1,200-foot summit—with great views of Penobscot Bay (weather permitting)—is about two miles one way, easy to moderate hiking. The route links up with the rest of the state-park trail network, but unless you've arranged for a shuttle, it's best to do Bald Rock as a round-trip hike.

Cross-Country Skiing

Tanglewood 4-H Camp and Learning Center (Lincolnville, 207/789-5868) spreads out over 830 acres. In winter, Tanglewood has more than 10 miles of cross-country trails, the best network in this part of the Mid-Coast. Some winters, Mother Nature provides scanty snow cover here, but when she obliges, the trails are superb. Some trails are also used by snowmobiles. No pets. To reach Tanglewood from Route 1, continue .8

mile north of Lincolnville Beach and turn left at the Tanglewood sign; go .7 mile and turn right onto an unpaved road; continue .8 mile to the camp and park on the right side. At the gate, pick up a trail map.

SHOPPING

Art, craft, and souvenir shops are clustered along the Route 1 strip at Lincolnville Beach; just north of town are a couple of unusual shops and galleries worth a visit.

Handsome, dark wood buildings .2 mile north of the Beach are home to **Windsor Chairmakers** (Rte. 1, Lincolnville, 207/789-5188 or 800/789-5188). You can observe the operation, browse the display area, or order some of the well-made chairs, cabinets, and tables.

Professional boatbuilder Walt Simmons has branched out into decoys and wildlife carvings, and they're just as outstanding as his boats. Walt and his wife, Karen, run **Duck Trap Decoys** (Duck Trap Rd., Lincolnville, 207/789-5363), a gallery/shop that also features the work of nearly five dozen other woodcarvers.

Miscellany

The **Center General Store** (Rte. 52, Lincolnville Center, 207/763-3666) is more than just a market—it's an experience. At this old-fashioned, early-20th-century place, you can pick up baked goods, ice-cream cones, animal feed, liquor, fuel, lottery tickets, bait, and a fishing license. Stock up for a picnic or eat it here and watch the comings and goings.

ACCOMMODATIONS

B&Bs

About four miles north of Camden and a mile south of Lincolnville, **The Victorian by the Sea** (Seaview Dr., Lincolnville Beach, mailing address P.O. Box 1385, Camden 04843, 207/236-3785 or 800/382-9817, www.victorianbythesea.com, $160–235) overlooks the bay at the end of a winding lane from Route 1. It's a dreamy Victorian with numerous fireplaces and a dining room in the turret, where a four-course breakfast is served.

The **Inn at the Ocean's Edge** (Rte. 1, Lincolnville Beach, mailing address P.O. Box 704, Camden 04843, 207/236-0945, www.innat oceansedge.com, $195–295), built in turn-of-the-20th-century Shingle style on seven acres, is well camouflaged from the highway. In 2004, Tim and Joan Porta, owners of the exclusive Migis Lodge, on Sebago Lake, purchased it to complement their inland resort. Often booked for wedding groups or small conferences, the inn has laundry and exercise rooms and is wheelchair-accessible. The rooms have reproduction furniture, cable TV, phones, air-conditioning, double hot tubs, and gas fireplaces—and superb ocean views. There's also a guest-only pub.

About midway between Camden and Lincolnville, down an oceanward lane, **The Inn at Sunrise Point** (Rte. 1, FR 9, Lincolnville, mailing address P.O. Box 1344, Camden 04843, 207/236-7716 or 800/435-6278, www.innat sunrisepoint.com, $260–470) has three handsome rooms in the main lodge, four separate cottages, and two suites. Decor is tastefully elegant; breakfast in the conservatory is spectacularly good. Each cottage has a double hot tub, phone, fireplace, TV/VCR, minibar, and private bay-view deck.

Just across Route 1 from the Islesboro ferry landing and a two-minute walk to the Lobster Pound is the **Spouter Inn** (2506 Atlantic Hwy., Rte. 1, Lincolnville Beach, 207/789-5171 or 866-787-5171, www.spouterinn.com, $115–195). Paul and Catherine Lippmann have filled this 19th-century home with antiques. Most rooms have ocean views; two have wood-burning fireplaces. A full breakfast chosen from an extensive menu is included.

Motels and Cottages

Motels and cottage complexes are strung all along Route 1 between Camden and Lincolnville Beach. Rates vary widely, depending on amenities.

Pine Grove Cottages (2076 Atlantic Hwy., Rte. 1, Lincolnville 04849, 207/236-2929 or 800/530-5265, $65–150) is a neat, comfortable, no-frills cottage complex with bay views. Nine one- and two-bedroom cottages have kitchens, phones, and

cable TV. Children are welcome and pets are allowed in some cottages for a fee. Pine Grove is four miles north of Camden, set back from the highway. Open mid-April to mid-November.

The family-run **M Mount Battie Motel** (2298 Atlantic Hwy., Rte. 1, Lincolnville 04849, 207/236-3870 or 800/224-3870, www.mount-battie.com, $89–120), a particular favorite of Islesboro residents, has 22 charming motel-style rooms with air-conditioning, TV, phone, fridge, and a continental breakfast.

Snow Hill Lodge (Rte. 1, HC 60, Box 550, Lincolnville Beach 04849, 207/236-3452 or 800/476-4775, www.midcoast.com/~theview, $65–99) is an unpretentious, well-maintained motel with a splendid view of Penobscot Bay. Hospitable hosts Sitki and Marie Kocak have 30 rooms with TV and phones. Breakfast is available at the on-site café at an additional charge.

FOOD
Lobster-in-the-Rough

Lincolnville's best-known landmark is **The Lobster Pound Restaurant** (Rte. 1, Lincolnville Beach, 207/789-5550, 11:30 A.M.–8 P.M., to 9 P.M. in July and Aug.). About 300 people—some days, it looks like more than that—can pile into the main restaurant, an enclosed patio, and a separate oceanfront eating area, so be sure to make reservations on summer weekends. Despite the crowds, food and service are reliably good. Lobster, of course, is king, and unless you're allergic, it's crazy not to order it here. The huge menu also includes other seafood, poultry, and steaks. Entrées are $9–24; a one-pound lobster with salad, potato, rolls, and butter is $16.95.

INFORMATION AND SERVICES
Information

The **Camden-Rockport-Lincolnville Chamber of Commerce** (P.O. Box 919, Camden 04843, 207/236-4404 or 800/223-5459, www .visitcamden.com) is at the Public Landing. Request a copy of its map of area streets and businesses and the official chamber guide. The gray building, facing the parking lot and the harbor at Camden's Public Landing, is open daily in summer, Monday–Saturday the rest of the year.

Also handy is a directory published by the **Lincolnville Business Group** (P.O. Box 202, Lincolnville 04849, www.lincolnville.org) and a free annual map/brochure called *The Island of Islesboro*, available at the ferry landings in Lincolnville Beach and Islesboro, and the **Town Office** (Municipal Building, Main Rd., P.O. Box 76, Islesboro 04848, 207/734-2253, 8:30 A.M.–4:30 P.M. Mon.–Fri.).

Hospitals
Two major hospitals service the region. **Penobscot Bay Medical Center** (Rte. 1, Rockport 04856, 207/596-8000) and **Waldo County General Hospital** (118 Northport Ave., Belfast, 207/338-2500 or 800/649-2536), a community-oriented private (despite its name) institution.

Getting Around
Concord Trailways (800/639-3317, www.concordtrailways.com) stops in Rockland, Camden-Rockport, Belfast, and Searsport on its three daily nonexpress trips up the coast.

Camden-based **Mid-Coast Limo** (800/937-2424 or 207/236-2424, www.midcoastlimo.com) provides van service, by reservation, between towns as far northeast as Belfast and Portland International Jetport.

Islesboro

Lying three miles offshore from Lincolnville Beach, via 20-minute car ferry, is 12-mile-long Islesboro, a year-round community with a population of about 600—beefed up annually by a sedate summer colony. Time was when islanders and summer rusticators barely intermingled—except that many islanders served as caretakers, kitchen staff, and general gofers for wealthy visitors in their grand mansions, primarily in the enclave of Dark Harbor. The summer social scene remains exhaustingly active, and many islanders still have jobs as caterers and property managers, but apartheid has diminished. Year-rounders and summer folk roll up their sleeves and work together for worthy island causes—land trust, churches, school, library, and historical society—and there's even gentle joshing about the island culture.

Car ferries are frequent enough to make Islesboro an ideal day-trip destination—and that's the choice of most visitors, partly because lodging is pretty scarce. The only camping is on nearby Warren Island State Park—and you have to have your own boat to get there. If you're not spending the night, keep an eye on the time so you don't miss the last ferry (4:30 P.M.) back to the mainland.

SIGHTS

Views from the Road
The best way to get an island overview (besides flying into the tiny airstrip) is to do an end-to-end auto tour. You won't see all the huge "cottages" tucked down long driveways, and you won't absorb island life and its rhythms (that requires a longer stay), but you'll scratch the surface of what Islesboro is about. Drive off the ferry, which docks about a third of the way down the island, and go one mile to a stop sign. Turn right and go 1.2 miles to another stop sign. Turn right, onto Main Road, and go 4.3 miles south to the Town Beach at the bottom of the island. Then backtrack on Main Road, past the turnoff to the ferry dock, heading "up island" (as it's known locally) and covering 12 miles to northernmost Pripet and Turtle Head. En route, you'll pass exclusive summer estates, workaday homes, spectacular seaside vistas, and a smattering of shops for crafts, books, and take-out food. On the up-island circuit, watch for a tiny marker on the west side of the road (.8 mile north of the Islesboro Historical Society building). It commemorates the 1780 total eclipse witnessed here—the first recorded in North America. At the time, British loyalists still held Islesboro, but they temporarily suspended

Penobscot Bay **M**

hostilities, allowing Harvard astronomers to lug their instruments to the island and document the eclipse.

Sailors' Memorial Museum

As the ferry glides into the western side of Gilkey Harbor, you can't miss the squat little **Grindle Point Light** (207/734-2253), built in 1850, rebuilt in 1875, and now automated. Next to it, in the former keeper's house, is the town-owned Sailors' Memorial Museum, filled with seafaring memorabilia and allegedly home to a benevolent ghost or two. The volunteer-staffed museum is open 9 A.M.–4:30 P.M. Tuesday–Sunday, late June through Labor Day (closed for lunch at midday). Admission is free, but donations are welcomed.

Islesboro Historical Society

Right about the center of the island, 3.8 miles from the ferry and just south of the aptly named Narrows, stands the two-story Islesboro Historical Society (corner of Main Rd. and West Side Rd., 207/734-6733), in the former town hall. On the first floor are rotating temporary exhibits throughout the summer, while the second-floor museum contains the permanent collection of island memorabilia. The society also sponsors frequent programs/meetings with guest lecturers. The building generally is open 12:30–4:30 P.M. five days a week, July to Labor Day, usually Sunday–Thursday, but call ahead to be sure. Or call for an appointment; volunteers often are in the building even when it's closed. Admission is free, but donations are welcomed.

PARKS AND RECREATION

Warren Island State Park

Why is 70-acre Warren Island State Park the most underused of Maine's state parks? There's no organized transportation to the island. If you want to hike, camp, or picnic on Warren, you'll need a boat—but it's well worth the effort. Besides, it'll give you a chance to see some of Islesboro's shorefront homes. A painless way to do this is to lash a kayak, canoe, or skiff atop your vehicle, take the ferry from Lincolnville Beach, park at the Islesboro ferry landing, and paddle the protected quarter mile to the east side of the island. Ten well-spaced, wooded campsites (some oceanfront) and two Adirondack shelters have picnic tables and plenty of potable water and firewood; no reservations accepted. For information, contact the Camden Hills State Park manager (207/236-3109). Day-use fees are $3 adults, $1 children 5–11, free for seniors and children four and under. Camping is $19 pp per site per night for nonresidents. The park is open Memorial Day weekend to mid-September.

Town Beach

At Pendleton Point, Islesboro's southern tip, the Town Beach has two sandy pockets, tidepools, unique rock formations, wooded paths, well-spaced picnic tables, blackberry bushes (in season), and

Seventy-acre Warren Island State Park, off Islesboro, is an excellent destination for sea kayakers.

great views. The beach is 2.5 miles south of Dark Harbor Village.

Bicycling and Hiking

Islesboro is fairly level, and walking end to end is unrealistic for a day trip, so a bicycle would seem to be the perfect solution. Not exactly. Bicycles are very controversial here—hardly surprising, since the shoulderless roads are narrow and too many cyclists have failed to heed commonsense rules. A safer solution is to take leisurely drives to both ends of the island, then park the car (in summer, there's room near the Islesboro Central School) and walk along the road through Dark Harbor Village to the Town Beach at the southern end of the island.

SHOPPING

A handful of shops and galleries dot the island. At **Seven Knots Gallery** (300 Main Rd., 207/734-8877), in the old Pendleton schoolhouse, across from the library, Paula McNamara and Jack McConnell have created a space that invites leisurely browsing. Rotating shows feature guest artists working in varied media.

ENTERTAINMENT

Churches, the library, and the historical society manage to organize impressive schedules of concerts, lectures, craft fairs, public suppers, and other events during July and August—when the population is at its height and fund-raising is most successful. Check the *Islesboro Island News* for listings.

ACCOMMODATIONS AND FOOD

Both lodging and dining are limited on Islesboro. The only public campsites are on Warren Island, accessible only by boat.

Dark Harbor Bed and Breakfast (119 Derby Rd., Islesboro 04848, 207/734-9772, www.islesboromaine.com, $125) is in a renovated 1890s farmhouse not far from the Dark Harbor Shop and about 100 yards from the water. Four warmly decorated rooms have private baths.

Elegant seasonal accommodations are available at the bright yellow **Dark Harbor House** (P.O. Box 185, Dark Harbor, Islesboro 04848, 207/734-6669, $115–185)—and what a place it is. Built in the late 19th century by a Philadelphia banker, the Georgian Revival mansion (on the National Historic Register) has 11 rooms, all with private baths, some with fireplaces and balconies (the penthouse suite with roof terrace is $275). Despite the pomp, the ambience is casual. Dinner (5:30–8 P.M.; open to the public by reservation only) is served in the oval dining room. The inn has bikes for guests to use, and it'll arrange access to the island's private golf club. Full breakfast. Open April–October.

The Dark Harbor Shop (Dark Harbor, 207/734-8878, 8 A.M.–5 P.M., to 7 P.M. in July and Aug.) is the hub for local gossip over breakfast, lunch, snacks, sandwiches, or just an ice-cream cone. Kids love the penny candy, and there's a selection of gifts. When the late Senator Margaret Chase Smith cruised to Islesboro on her namesake ferry, she lunched at the counter here. Bill Warren, the Dark Harbor Shop's owner, also operates Warren Realty; if you're interested in a **seasonal rental,** check with him.

Islesboro's two markets sell sandwiches and other picnic fare in summer—much easier than packing lunch ahead of time. **Durkee's General Store** (Main Rd., corner of Ryder's Rd., 207/734-2201, 8 A.M.–6 P.M. Mon.–Sat., 10 A.M.–2 P.M. Sun.) sells a full line of groceries, plus burgers, pizza, sandwiches, hardware, fuel, newspapers, T-shirts, and liquor. Near the post office and the municipal building, **The Island Market** (207/734-6672, 7 A.M.–5:30 P.M. Mon.–Fri., 8 A.M.–5:30 P.M. Sat.), run by Shake and Loony Mahan, carries a similar inventory (beer and wine, but no liquor), plus Loony's terrific baked goods.

INFORMATION AND SERVICES

Information

A handy directory is published by the **Lincolnville Business Group** (P.O. Box 202, Lincolnville 04849, www.lincolnville.org), and a free annual map/brochure called *The Island of Islesboro* is available at the ferry landings in Lincolnville Beach and Islesboro and the **Town Office** (Municipal Building, Main Rd., P.O. Box 76, Islesboro 04848, 207/734-2253, 8:30 A.M.–4:30 P.M. Mon.–Fri.).

Hospitals

Islesboro Health Center (in the municipal building, 207/734-2213) is open 9 A.M.–4:30 P.M. weekdays.

Two major hospitals service the region. **Penobscot Bay Medical Center** (Rte. 1, Rockport 04856, 207/596-8000) and **Waldo County General Hospital** (118 Northport Ave., Belfast, 207/338-2500 or 800/649-2536), a community-oriented private institution.

Local Library

The handsome stone **Alice L. Pendleton Memorial Library** (corner of Main Rd. and Hewes Point Rd., 207/734-2218, 10 A.M.–noon Mon. and Wed., 1:30–4:30 P.M. Mon., Wed., Sat., and Sun., to 7 P.M. Wed. in July and Aug.). The library also has a "port-o-call" branch at the ferry terminal on Gilkey Harbor. Inside the waiting room is a carousel of paperbacks available for the borrowing. A long wait for the ferry? No problem—borrow a book to pass the time. Or take it

away and return it (or something else) next time. It's all on the honor system—and it *works*.

Public Restrooms

There are public toilets at the ferry terminal in Gilkey Harbor and at the Town Beach.

Getting There

The car ferry *Margaret Chase Smith* departs Lincolnville Beach almost every hour on the hour, 8 or 9 A.M. to 5 P.M., and Islesboro on the half hour, 7:30 A.M.–4:30 P.M. Round-trip fares are $17.50 for car, $6 adults, $2.50 children, $5.75 adult bicycles, and $3 kids' bikes. Reservations are $5 extra. A slightly reduced schedule prevails late October to early May. The 20-minute trip crosses a stunning three-mile stretch of Penobscot Bay, with views of islands and the Camden Hills. In summer, avoid the biggest bottlenecks: Friday afternoon (to Islesboro), Sunday afternoon and Monday holiday afternoons (from Islesboro). The *Smith* remains on Islesboro overnight, so don't miss the last run to Lincolnville Beach. For more information contact **Maine State Ferry Service** (P.O. Box 214, Lincolnville 04849, 207/789-5611, Islesboro 207/734-6935, www.exploremaine.com).

Belfast Area

With a population of about 6,400, Belfast is relatively small as cities go, but changes have been occurring at lightning speed—courtesy of gigantic credit-card company MBNA (the nation's largest in affinity cards), which established a major presence here in 1996. Even before MBNA arrived, Belfast was becoming one of those off-the-beaten-track destinations popular with tuned-in travelers. Chalk that up to its status as a magnet for leftover back-to-the-landers and enough artistic types to earn the city a nod for cultural cool. Belfast boasts a curling club, meditation centers, a clutch of art galleries and boutiques, dance and theater companies, the oldest shoe store in America, and half a dozen different 12-step self-help groups. It's also emerging as a dining destination with a range of good restaurants at moderate prices.

This eclectic city is a work in progress, a study in Maine-style diversity. It's also a gold mine of Federal, Greek Revival, Italianate, and Victorian architecture. Take the time to stroll the well-planned backstreets, explore the shops, and hang out at the newly gussied-up waterfront.

Separating Belfast from East Belfast, the Passagassawakeag River is pronounced "puh-sag-gus-uh-WAH-keg," but fortunately it is known more familiarly as "the Passy." The Indian name has been translated as both "place of many ghosts" and the rather different "place for spearing sturgeon by torchlight." You choose.

Many travelers make Belfast a day stop on their way between Camden and Bar Harbor. Truly, Belfast is worth more time than that. Spend a full day or two here, and it's likely you'll

OFF THE BEATEN PATH IN LIBERTY

Seventeen miles west of Belfast, off Route 3, is Liberty, a tiny town with a funky tool store, quirky museum, a bargain T-shirt shop, and a great state park. Everything is seasonal, running mid-May or so through mid-October or so. Call before visiting, if you want to be sure everything's open. It's a store! It's a museum! It's amazing! More

Liberty Tool Company is part store, part museum. More than 10,000 tools, as well as antique furniture, used books, prints, and bric-a-brac, fill this eclectic emporium 17 miles west of Belfast.

than 10,000 "useful" tools—plus used books and prints and other tidbits—fill the three-story **Liberty Tool Company** (Main St., Liberty, 207/589-4771). Drawn by nostalgia and a compulsion for hand-made adzes and chisels, thousands of vintage-tool buffs arrive at this eclectic emporium each year; few leave empty-handed. Nor do the thousands of everyday home hobbyists looking to pick up a hammer or find a missing wrench to fill out a set. Nor do the antique-seekers, who browse the trash and treasures on the upper floors. The collection is beyond amazing, especially in its organization. Owner Skip Brack brings back vanloads of finds almost every week, and after sorting and cleaning, many make it into this store.

The best-of-the-best make it into Brack's **Davistown Museum** (Main St., 207/589-4900, www.davistownmuseum.org), on the third floor

of the building housing Liberty Graphics, across the street. The museum houses not only a history of Maine and New England hand tools, but also local, regional, Native American and environmental artifacts and information and an amazing collection of contemporary art, highlighted by works by artists such as Louise Nevelson (who used to purchase tools across the street), Melitta Westerlund, and Phil Barter.

Downstairs is **Liberty Graphics Outlet Store** (1 Main St., 207/589-4035), selling the eco-sensitive company's overstocks, seconds, and discontinued-design T-shirts. Outstanding silkscreened designs are done with water-based inks, and many of the shirts are organic cotton; prices begin at $5.

Just down Main Street is the old **Liberty Post Office**, a unique octagonal structure that looks like an oversized box. It was built in 1867 as a harness-maker's shop and later used as the town's post office.

Two miles west of downtown, **Lake St. George State Park** (Rte. 3, 207/589-4255, $3 adults, $1 kids 5–11) is a refreshing find. This 360-acre park has wooded picnic sites with grills along the lake, a beach, rental boats, a playground, volleyball and basketball courts, and five miles of hiking trails. Also available are campsites, $20 for nonresidents.

If you're up for more inland exploring, weave your way along the **Georges River Scenic Byway**, a 50-mile auto route along the St. George River (a.k.a. Georges River) from its inland headwaters to the sea in Port Clyde. The official start is at the junction of Routes 3 and 220 in Liberty, but you can follow the trail in either direction or pick it up anywhere along the way. Road signs are posted, but it's far better to obtain a map/brochure at a chamber of commerce or other information locale. Or contact the architects of the route, **The Georges River Land Trust** (328 Main St., Rockland, 207/594-5166, www.grlt.org).

Penobscot Bay

be charmed like many of the other urban refugees into resettling here.

SIGHTS

Historic Walking Tour

No question, the best way to appreciate Belfast's fantastic architecture is to tour by ankle express. At the Belfast Area Chamber of Commerce, pick up the well-researched *Belfast Historic Walking Tour* map/brochure. Among more than 40 highlights on the mile-long, self-guided route are the 1818 Federal-style **First Church,** handsome residences on **High** and **Church Streets,** and the 1840 **James P. White House** (corner of Church Street and Northport Avenue, now an elegant B&B), New England's finest Greek Revival residence. Amazing for a community of this size, the city actually has three distinct National Historic Districts: Belfast Commercial Historic District (47 downtown buildings), Church Street Historic District (residential), and Primrose Hill Historic District (also residential). Another walking tour is presented by the Belfast Historical Society's **Museum in the Streets,** comprising two large panels and 30 smaller ones highlighting historic buildings and people. Signs are in English and French.

Bayside

Continuing the focus on architecture, just south of Belfast, in Northport, is the Victorian enclave of Bayside, a neighborhoody sort of place with small, well-kept, gingerbreaded cottages cheek-by-jowl on pint-sized lots. Formerly known as the Northport Wesleyan Grove Campground, the village took shape in the mid-1800s as a summer retreat for Methodists. In the 1930s, the retreat was disbanded and the main meeting hall was razed, creating the waterfront park at the heart of the village. Today, many of the colorfully painted homes are rented by the week, month, or summer season, and their tenants are more likely to indulge in athletic rather than religious pursuits. The camaraderie remains, though, and a stroll (or cycle or drive) through Bayside is like a visit to another era. Bayside is four miles south of Belfast, just east of Route 1.

Temple Heights

Continue south on Shore Road from Bayside to **Temple Heights Spiritualist Camp** (Shore Rd., Northport, 207/338-3029, www.temple heightscamp.org, mailing address P.O. Box 311, Lincolnville 04849), yet another religious enclave—this one still going. Founded in 1882, Temple Heights has become a shadow of its former self, reduced primarily to the funky, 12-room Nikawa Lodge on Shore Road ($35 d, $25 s, shared bath, some rooms with ocean view), but the summer program continues, thanks to prominent mediums from all over the country. Even a temporary setback in 1996—when the camp president was suspended for allegedly putting a hex on Northport's town clerk—failed to derail the operation. Camp programs, late June through Labor Day, are open to the public; a schedule is published each spring. Spiritualist church services and group healing sessions are free; Saturday-morning workshops are $20. Better yet, sign up for a 1.5-hour or longer **group message circle,** when you'll sit with a medium and a dozen or so others and receive insights—often uncannily on-target—from departed relatives or friends. Message circles occur Wednesday and Saturday at 7:30 P.M. (arrive a half-hour early). Suggested donation is $10 pp and reservations are necessary. Private readings can be arranged for a donation of $30.

The Bull Moose Railroad

And now for something completely different. On the Belfast waterfront, climb aboard the **Belfast and Moosehead Lake Railroad** (800/392-5500, www.belfastrailroad.com) and roll off into the countryside. Affectionately called the Bull Moose Railroad, the B&ML has been operating excursion trains through rural Waldo County for decades—and since the late 1980s in its most recent incarnation. From June to mid-October, a diesel engine pulls vintage Swedish cars along a 1.5-hour route ($15 adults, $10 children 3–15), usually departing at 12:30 P.M. The schedule is bit complicated, so call for current info. Special excursions include occasional lobster-dinner trains ($42) and murder-mystery trains ($50).

PARKS AND RECREATION

One of the state's best municipal parks is just on the outskirts of downtown. Established in 1904, **Belfast City Park** (87 Northport Ave., 207/338-1661) has lighted tennis courts, an outdoor pool, a pebbly beach, plenty of picnic tables, an unusually creative playground, lots of green space for the kids, and fantastic views of Islesboro, Blue Hill, and Penobscot Bay. For more action, right in the heart of Belfast, head for **Heritage Park**, at the bottom of Main Street, with front-row seats on waterfront happenings. Bring a picnic, grab a table, and watch the yachts, tugs, and lobsterboats.

Golf

Just south of Belfast is the nine-hole **Northport Golf Club** (581 Bluff Rd., Northport, Belfast, 207/338-2270), established in 1916. Operating out of a classic shingled clubhouse, the club is open mid-April through October. Snacks and carts are available; starting times usually aren't necessary.

Boat Excursions

Sail aboard the Friendship sloop *Amity* (207/469-0849 evenings, 207/323-1443 daytime, www.friendshipsloopamity.com), based at the Belfast Public Landing, for 90-minute morning ($20) or 2.5-hour afternoon or sunset ($30) sails. The classic Friendship sloop, built in 1901 in Friendship, was originally used for lobstering. These days, it's been beautifully restored and carries up to six passengers. Home-baked cookies, hot coffee, and tea are served on all cruises. Captain Stephen O'Connell, a former journalist, explains the boat's history and its role in lobstering and regales passengers, when asked, with tales of his experiences living in exotic locations around the world.

Take a day trip to Castine aboard the *Good Return,* operated by Belfast Bay Cruises (207/322-5530, www.belfastbaycruises.com), departing from Thompson Wharf (by the railroad). Captain Melissa Terry, a fifth-generation descendent of a whaling captain from New Bedford, Massachusetts, is a Maine Maritime Academy graduate who enjoys sharing her love of the sea. The Castine Lunch Cruise ($25 adults, $20 seniors 65 and older, and $15 kids 3–16) provides time for exploring Castine and lunch (on your own). Other options include an educational lobstering cruise during which traps are hauled ($20 adults, $15 seniors, $12 kids), harbor cruises ($15 adults, $12 seniors, $10 kids), Saturday lobster dinner ($35, including lobster and fixings), and a family cruise up the Penobscot River to Fort Point ($25 pp or $70 for a family of four; lunch available for an extra fee).

If you don't have your own kayak, Harvey Schiller's **Belfast Kayak Tours** (207/382-6204), based at the Belfast Public Landing, operates two-hour, three-mile harbor excursions, which include a paddling lesson. Cost is $30 adults, $15 kids 6–12. When boats are available, he'll rent kayaks to experienced kayakers for $25 for two hours, $60 per day. For reservations, call before 7:30 A.M. or after 8 P.M. If you're at all squeamish, go in the morning—the harbor tends to be less choppy then.

Recreation Centers

The **Waldo County YMCA** (157 Lincolnville Ave., Belfast, 207/338-4598) has a walk-track, fitness room, gymnasium, weight room, and other facilities.

Winter Sports

The Scottish national sport of curling has dozens of enthusiastic supporters at Maine's only curling rink, the **Belfast Curling Club** (Belmont Ave., Rte. 3, Belfast, 207/772-3140), an institution here since the late 1950s. Leagues play regularly on weeknights, and the club holds tournaments (*bonspiels*) and open houses several times during the season, which runs early November to early April.

SHOPPING

It's easy and fun to shop in downtown Belfast, a town that has so far managed to keep the big boxes away, providing fertile ground for entrepreneurs. Downtown shops reflect the city's population, with galleries and boutiques, thrift and used-goods stores, and eclectic shops.

Penobscot Bay

Art Galleries

Exactly midway between Lincolnville Beach and Belfast (five miles in each direction), the **Saturday Cove Fine Art Gallery** (608 Atlantic Hwy., Rte. 1, Northport, 207/338-3654) is a retired post office/gas station transformed into a dramatically cheerful gallery featuring Maine artists in excellent rotating exhibits.

Books

Belfast's independent bookstore is a friendly place with good intentions but not a huge inventory. The quaintly named **Fertile Mind Bookshop** (105 Main St., Belfast, 207/338-2498) has a particularly good children's section and also carries magazines.

Clothing, Gifts, and Crafts

Even if shoes aren't on your shopping list, stop in at "the oldest shoe store in America." Founded in the 1830s (!), **Colburn Shoe Store** (81 Main St., Belfast, 207/338-1934 or 877/338-1934) may be old, but it isn't old-fashioned—all the latest brands and styles are here.

Coyote Moon (54 Main St., Belfast, 207/338-5659) is an especially attractive New Age-y boutique carrying natural-fiber clothing, jewelry, recycled-paper items, and, of course, incense.

Cooks should just head straight for **The Good Table** (68 Main St., Belfast, 207/338-4880), source of cookbooks galore and almost any kitchen tools and gadgets you can think of.

Perhaps it's not surprising in a city named Belfast, but **Shamrock, Thistle & Rose** (48 Main St., Belfast, 207/338-1864) is a find for lovers of Irish goods. Clothing, jewelry, original art, and even music are found here.

About two miles east of Belfast's bridge, on the right, is the small roadside shop of **Mainely Pottery** (181 Searsport Ave., Rte. 1, Belfast, 207/338-1108). Since 1988, Jeannette Faunce and Jamie Oates have been marketing the work of more than two dozen Maine potters, each with different techniques, glazes, and styles. It's the perfect place to select from a wide range of reasonably priced work. Peek into the adjacent studio and you'll find Jamie, who specializes in lamps (under the name of Pequog Pottery) and is happy to answer questions. Don't miss Jeannette's lovely garden out back.

The Green Store

Calling itself a "general store for the 21st century," The Green Store (71 Main St., Belfast, 207/338-4045) carries a huge selection of environmentally friendly products. Whether you're thinking of going off the grid, need a composting toilet, want natural-fiber clothing or other natural-living products, this is the place. An very knowledgeable staff can answer nearly any question on environmentally sustainable lifestyles.

ENTERTAINMENT

It's relatively easy to find nightlife in Belfast—not only are there theaters and a cinema, but there usually are a couple of bars open at least until midnight, and sometimes later. Some spots also feature live music, particularly on weekends.

If you don't feel like searching out a newspaper to check the entertainment listings, just go to the **Belfast Co-op Store** (123 High St., 207/338-2532) and study the bulletin board. You'll find notices for more activities than you could ever squeeze into your schedule.

An old-fashioned downtown cinema—recently restored to its Art Deco splendor—shows first-run films for moderate ticket prices. The **Colonial Theatre** (163 High St., Belfast, 207/338-1930) has three screens, each with one or two showings a night and matinees Saturday, Sunday, and sometimes Wednesday. Open all year.

Check local papers for the schedule of the **Belfast Maskers,** a community theater group that never fails to win raves for its interpretations of contemporary and classical dramas. Performances are held throughout the year near the waterfront, in the minimalist Waterfront Theatre (43 Front St., Belfast, 207/338-9668). In winter, wear an extra pair of socks; the floor is drafty.

Just south of Belfast, the funky **Blue Goose Dance Hall** (Rte. 1, Northport, 207/338-3003) has to be seen to be believed. This low-slung roadside establishment is the site of folk concerts, contra dances, auctions, and more. Most events occur Saturday nights. Check local papers or the Belfast Co-op Store bulletin board.

FESTIVALS AND EVENTS

Belfast is a hive of activity, but lots of the surrounding Waldo County communities also put on some ambitious fairs, festivals, and public suppers. Check the newspapers for schedules.

In early July, soon after July 4, the **Arts in the Park** festival gets under way at Heritage Park, on the Belfast waterfront. It's a weekend event, with two days of music, juried arts and crafts, children's activities, and lots of food booths. The **Belfast Bay Festival,** usually the third week of July, has music, carnival rides, fireworks, food, and more.

Downtown Belfast comes alive the first Saturday in October with the **Church Street Festival** and its food booths, art and craft exhibits and sales, unique parade, and kids' events. And the annual **New Year's by the Bay** is a nonprofit, chem-free family event, with music, dancing, puppetry, theater, performance art, and more.

ACCOMMODATIONS

B&Bs

On a quiet side street, **The Jeweled Turret** (40 Pearl St., Belfast 04915, 207/338-2304 or 800/696-2304, www.jeweledturret.com, $105–155) is one of Belfast's pioneer B&Bs. Carl and Cathy Heffentrager understand the business and go out of their way to make guests comfortable. The 1898 Victorian inn is loaded with handsome woodwork and Victorian antiques—plus an astonishing stone fireplace. Carl can even fix your bike, if necessary, and he's up on all the local byways.

The White House (1 Church St., Belfast, 207/338-1901 or 888/290-1901, www.mainebb .com, $115–175), the handsomest manse in Belfast, is the star of the Church Street Historic District. Built in the mid-19th century, the Greek Revival building is elegant inside and out—parlors, library, guest rooms, and gardens dominated by a giant copper beech tree. Hosts Terry Prescott and Robert Hansen will lend you a tandem bike, pack you a picnic lunch,

make dinner reservations—more than the comforts of home.

Marble fireplaces, tin ceilings, antiques, and ornate woodwork fill the public and guest rooms of the 1840 **M Alden House Bed & Breakfast** (63 Church St., Belfast, 207/338-2151 or 877/337-8151, www.thealdehouse .com, $95–130), in the Church Street Historic District. The inn has seven rooms (five with private baths) and offers a hearty breakfast. Some rooms have VCRs.

Even infants are welcome at the **M Mad Captain's House** (66 Congress St., Belfast, 207/338-2343 or 866/338-2343, www.midcoastbb.com $95–150). Linda Briggs Hause and her husband, Thomas, give an especially warm welcome to children, with a special room decorated with toys, books, a crib, and child-sized beds. Not that grown-ups don't have their own places to relax in the Victorian home. Linda has added her artistic touches to many rooms, which are comfortably furnished with antiques, hand-painted furniture, and other pieces. Her skills extend to the kitchen; a lovely full breakfast is served. Bikes and beach towels are available.

On the inland side of Route 1 is **Londonderry Inn** (133 Belmont Ave., Rte. 3 Belfast, 207/338-2763 or 977/529-9566, www.londonderry-inn .com, $95–140), a big house with rambling rooms and a huge country kitchen. Innkeepers Marsha and Fletcher Oakes have restored the farmhouse into a welcoming B&B. All rooms have TV/VCR, phone, air-conditioning, and mini-fridge. A full farmer's breakfast and complimentary evening beverages and dessert are served.

The back lawn of the **Belfast Bay Meadows Inn** (192 Northport Ave., Belfast 04915, 207/338-5717 or 800/335-2370 www.baymeadowsinn .com, $85–165) rolls down to the water, and some of the 19 rooms share that view over the gardens. All have air-conditioning, phones, and TV. A full breakfast is served on the back deck, when the weather is fine. Afterward, walk down the grassy paths to the private beach. Also on the premises is Oliver's restaurant.

Motel

The 61 rooms at the oceanfront **Belfast Harbor**

Penobscot Bay

Inn (91 Searsport Ave., Belfast 04915, 207/338-2740 or 800/545-8576, www.belfastharborinn.com, $79–149) have cable TV, air-conditioning, and phones; there's an outdoor heated pool. Pets and children are welcome. Rates include a continental breakfast. Rooms in the back face the ocean, a much nicer and quieter view than Route 1.

Campground

Every one of the 44 sites at the **Moorings Oceanfront RV Resort** (191 Searsport Ave., Rte. 1, Belfast 04915, 207/338-6860, www.mooringscamp.com) has an ocean view and hookups. Views are fabulous, and the rocky beach has a pocket of sand; swimming is only for the hardy. Sites in midsummer are $34–40 (two adults plus three kids under 17). Coffee is available every morning, a free Sunday newspaper is delivered to your site, concierge services are available, and special events are often held, including lobster shore dinners, barbecues, and deep-fried turkey fests. Facilities include laundry, play area, kayak launch, game room, and on-site restaurant, serving breakfast, lunch, and dinner. Extra fees for air-conditioning or heat hookup, pumpout, dogs, and day or overnight visitors. Open mid-May through October.

Seasonal Rentals

Most of the Belfast area's seasonal rentals are in Northport, specifically the charming Victorian enclave of Bayside. For info, contact **Blair Agency** (Bayside, mailing address P.O. Box 368, Belfast 04915, 207/338-2257) or **Bayside Cottage Rentals** (539 Bluff Rd., Northport 04948, 207/338-5355, www.baysidecottagerentals.com).

FOOD

Belfast is emerging as a dining destination, with a good choice of restaurants with moderate prices.

Lunch and Miscellany

In downtown Belfast, occupying a wonderful Victorian Gothic building with tin ceilings and unusual wainscoting, is **M The Gothic** (108 Main St., Belfast, 207/338-9901), a Lilliputian coffeehouse owned by Lisa Whiting, a European-

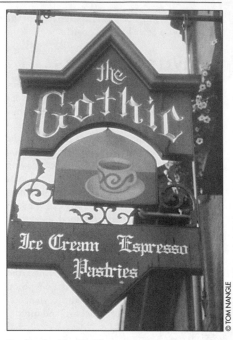

© TOM NANGLE

Don't miss The Gothic, a European-style pastry shop in Belfast that in summer also makes to-die-for ice cream.

trained pastry chef. The pastries are divine. During summer, Whiting also makes ice cream from scratch using only the purest ingredients, such as Belgian chocolate, jasmine, Earl Grey teas, and lavender flowers, creating unusual flavors, such as chocolate jasmine. It is to die for. Open 8 A.M.–8 P.M. Monday–Saturday in summer; spring and fall hours are 8 A.M.–5 P.M. Monday–Friday and 9 A.M.–3 P.M. Saturday. Closed mid-December through April.

Wraps are fast food at **Bay Wrap** (20 Beaver St., Belfast, 207/338-9757, 11 A.M.–7 P.M. Mon.–Fri., to 4 P.M. Sat.). There's no limit to what the staff can stuff into various flavors of tortillas. Go for the adventure. Wraps are in the $6 range. Eat here or get them to go.

The **Belfast Co-op Store** (123 High St., Belfast 04915, 207/338-2532, 7:30 A.M.–8 P.M.) is an experience in itself. You'll have a good impression of Belfast after one glance at the clientele and the bulletin board. Open to members and nonmembers alike (with lower prices for members), the co-op store has local organic produce, fresh and frozen pesto, baked goods, teas and coffees, bulk grains and nuts, a great deli, meat and fish, dozens of cheeses, camping foods, wine and beer, and a deli-café serving lunches daily 11:30 A.M.–2:30 P.M. and weekend brunches 9 A.M.–2 P.M.

Ethnic

Don't be put off by the lackluster exterior of **N Seng Thai** (160 Searsport Ave., Rte. 1, Belfast, 207/338-0010, 11 A.M.–9 P.M. Tues.–Sun.), a small, low building across from the Comfort Inn. Inside, the ambience is pleasant, the service is good, everything's available for takeout if you prefer, and best of all, it's really good Thai food (entrées $8–14).

Who'd expect big crowds at an unpretentious, brightly painted building advertising south-of-the-border cuisine alongside Route 1? **Dos Amigos' Mexican Restaurant and Cantina** (144 Bayside Rd., Rte. 1, Northport, 207/338-5775, 11:30 A.M.–9 P.M. Tues.–Sun., to 10 P.M. Fri. and Sat.) has earned a reputation as purveyor of the area's best Tex-Mex cuisine. Or is it the ambience? Margaritas are jumbo; nachos are loaded. Thirteen miles north of Camden, about three miles south of Belfast. Open mid-March to mid-December.

Judy's Eggroll (Lincolnville Ave., Rte. 52, Belfast, 207/338-1400, 4–8 P.M. Wed.–Sun.) operates out of a small prefab building next to Judy's house, a mile south (feels like west) of the Route 1 bypass. Plastic is the dominant theme (as in flowers, tablecloths, menus), but this folksy place has homemade Chinese and Korean sauces (no MSG), top-notch egg rolls (and other Asian goodies), large portions, and down-to-earth prices. Eat in or order to go.

Casual Dining

A longtime standby for creative (including vegetarian) world cuisine, **N Darby's Restaurant & Pub** (155 High St., Belfast, 207/338-2339, 11:30 A.M.–3:30 P.M. and 5–9 P.M.) served tofu before tofu was cool. This place has been providing food and drink since just after the Civil War; the tin ceilings and antique bar are reminders of that. Reservations are wise on weekends and Belfast Maskers performance nights; entrées cost $11–20.

Fresh food prepared in creative ways has earned **N Chase's Daily** (96 Main St., Belfast, 207/338-0555, 7–10:30 A.M. and 11:30 A.M.–2:30 P.M. Tues.–Sat., 8 A.M.–1 P.M. Sun., and 5:30–8 P.M. Fri.) a devoted local following. The emphasis is on vegetarian fare, with most of the vegetables coming from the Chase family farm in nearby Freedom. Trust me, you won't miss meat at this spot. Most choices are in the $4–7 range; dinner entrées are $13 and $14.

Techy-cool, casual, and laid-back best describe **Three Tides** (2 Pinchy Ln., on Marshall Wharf, Belfast, 207/338-1707, 7 P.M.–1 A.M.). Grab a booth inside, a seat at the bar, or a table on the deck overlooking the working harbor, then choose from the tapas-style menu ($3.50–10.50). Also part of the operation is **LB,** a lobster pound.

The Twilight Café (70-72 Main St., Belfast 04915, 207/338-0937, 5:30–9 P.M. Mon.–Sat.) doubles as the NTWH Art Gallery, complementing the menu and making the dining experience especially pleasant. Entrées such as pecan-crusted lobster cakes, stuffed portobello mushrooms, and lime-glazed sesame chicken range $16–25. Everything is prepared fresh, so this is not a place to be in a hurry.

Noted local chef Oliver Outerbridge is now at **Oliver's** at the Belfast Bay Meadows Inn (192 Northport Ave., Belfast 04915, 207/338-6846, 5:30–9 P.M. Fri.–Mon.). Choose from either small plates ($5–10) or grande ones ($15–21), all designed to make your palate dance. How about jambalaya with grilled chicken, Maine shrimp, or Moroccan beef pastry with harissa?

Seafood with a View

Lobster pie and fried Maine shrimp are specialties at the **Maine Chowder & Steak House** (139 Searsport Ave., Rte. 1, Belfast, 207/338-5225, 11 A.M.–8 P.M., to 9 P.M. in July and Aug.), a modern eatery with spectacular panoramic views of Penobscot Bay. Most entrées are $10–16, although some can go much higher. Dine on the

N Penobscot Bay

deck or even order takeout and eat at picnic tables. Chowder & Steak House is about two miles from downtown Belfast (1.5 miles east of the bridge), en route to Searsport. Open April through November.

Lobster-in-the-Rough

Young's Lobster Pound (2 Fairview St., Belfast, 207/338-1160, 8 A.M.–8 P.M. May–Nov.) is a classic eat-on-the-dock lobster place overlooking the bay. Dress down, relax, and pile into the crustaceans. BYOL. No credit cards. From downtown, cross the bridge to East Belfast and turn right at Jed's Restaurant. Continue to the end of the street.

Farmers' Market

Twice weekly, **The Belfast Farmers' Market** (Washington St. parking lot, downtown Belfast, daily 9 A.M.–1 P.M. Fri. and 3–6 P.M. Tues.) provides the perfect opportunity for stocking up for a picnic. In addition to plentiful veggies, you'll find honey, sweets, eggs, chicken pies, goat cheeses, breads, berries and apples in season, jams, medicinal and culinary herbs, jams, salsa, dillybeans, Asian vegetables, ready-to-eat Korean specialties, even sushi.

INFORMATION AND SERVICES

Information

The **Belfast Area Chamber of Commerce** (P.O. Box 58, Belfast 04915, 207/338-5900, www .belfastmaine.org) and **Waldo County Marketing Association** (P.O. Box 139, Searsport 04974, 800/870-9934, www.waldocountymaine.com) both have information about the Belfast area. The chamber operates a seasonal visitor information center (15 Main St.). In Searsport, a small, volunteer-run information center is open on an unpredictable schedule—it's in a shedlike building on Route 1 (at Norris Street), across from the Pumpkin Patch antique shop. On weekdays, you

can check at the **Searsport Town Office** (207/548-6372) on Reservoir Street (just after the Penobscot Marine Museum).

Hospitals

Waldo County General Hospital (118 Northport Ave., Belfast, 207/338-2500 or 800/649-2536), a community-oriented private institution, serves this area.

Local Library

Founded in 1888, the **Belfast Free Library** (106 High St., Belfast, 207/338-3884, 9:30 A.M.–8 P.M. Mon., 9:30 A.M.–6 P.M., Tues., Thurs., and Fri., noon–8 P.M. Wed., 10 A.M.–2 P.M. Sat.), in addition to normal library activities, has an active community-service program with terrific lectures and concerts in the 200-seat Abbott Auditorium.

Public Restrooms

Facilities are at the waterfront Public Landing, in the railroad station, at the Waldo County Court House, and at the Waldo County General Hospital.

Getting Around

Concord Trailways (800/639-3317, www .concordtrailways.com) stops in Rockland, Camden-Rockport, Belfast, and Searsport on its three daily nonexpress trips up the coast.

Camden-based **Mid-Coast Limo** (800/937-2424 or 207/236-2424, www.midcoastlimo.com) provides van service, by reservation, between towns as far northeast as Belfast and Portland International Jetport.

Downtown Belfast parking is limited to two hours, so if you're hanging around longer, head for the municipal parking lot on Lower Main Street, convenient to the waterfront and the chamber of commerce.

For taxis, contact the **Belfast Taxi Company** (207/338-2943).

Searsport Area

Five miles northeast of downtown Belfast, you're in the heart of Searsport, a name synonymous with the sea, thanks to an enduring oceangoing tradition that's appropriately commemorated here in the state's oldest maritime museum. The seafaring heyday occurred in the mid-19th century, but settlers from the Massachusetts Colony had already made inroads here 200 years earlier. By the 1750s, Fort Pownall, in nearby Stockton Springs, was a strategic site during the French and Indian War (the American phase of Europe's Seven Years' War).

Shipbuilding was under way by 1791, reaching a crescendo between 1845 and 1866, with six year-round shipyards and nearly a dozen more seasonal ones. By 1885, 10 percent of all full-rigged American-flag ships on the high seas were under the command of Searsport and Stockton Springs captains—many bearing the name of Pendleton, Nichols, or Carver. Many of these were involved in the perilous China trade, rounding notorious Cape Horn with great regularity.

All this global contact shaped Searsport's culture, adding a veneer of cosmopolitan sophistication. Imposing mansions of seafaring families were filled with fabulous Oriental treasures, many of which eventually made their way to the Penobscot Marine Museum. Brick-lined Main Street is more evidence of the mid-19th-century wealth, and local churches reaped the benefits of residents' generosity. The Second Congregational Church, known as the Safe Harbor Church and patronized by captains and shipbuilders (most ordinary seamen attended the Methodist church), boasts recently restored Tiffany-style windows and a Christopher Wren steeple.

Another inkling of this area's oceangoing superiority comes from visits to local burial grounds: check out the headstones at Gordon, Bowditch, and Sandy Point cemeteries. Many have fascinating tales to tell.

Today, with a population of just under 2,600, the Searsport area's major draws are the Penobscot Marine Museum, the still-handsome brick Historic District, several B&Bs, a couple of special state parks, and wall-to-wall antique shops and flea markets.

The Maine Historic Preservation Commission considers the buildings in Searsport's Main Street Historic District the best examples of their type outside of Portland—a frozen-in-time, mid-19th-century cluster of brick and granite structures. The ground floors of most of the buildings are shops or restaurants; make time to stop in and admire their interiors.

SIGHTS

Ⓜ Penobscot Marine Museum

Exquisite marine paintings, ship models, and unusual China-trade *objets d'art* are just a few of the 10,000 treasures at the Penobscot Marine Museum (5 Church St., at Rte. 1, Searsport, 207/548-2529, www.penobscotmarinemuseum.org, 10 A.M.–5 P.M. Mon.–Sat., noon–5 P.M. Sun., $8 adults, $6 seniors, $3 kids 7–15, or $18 per family). Maine's oldest maritime museum was founded in 1936. Allow several hours to explore the 13 old and new buildings just east of downtown. For a start, you'll see one of the nation's largest collections of paintings by marine artists James and Thomas Buttersworth. And the 1830s Fowler-True-Ross House is filled with exotic artifacts from foreign lands. Check out the exhibits, have a picnic, then visit the particularly well-stocked museum store on Main Street (Route 1). Pick up tickets at the Museum Admissions Building (restrooms are here, as well as in the museum store and the library), first building on your left on Church Street. Call or check the web for the schedule of lectures, concerts, and temporary exhibits. This isn't a very sophisticated museum, but it is a treasure. Open Memorial Day weekend to mid-October.

Ⓜ BlueJacket Shipcrafters

Complementing the collections at the museum are the classic and contemporary models built by BlueJacket Shipcrafters (160 E. Main St., Rte. 1, Searsport, 800/448-5567, www.bluejacketinc.com), which boasts Maine's largest selection of

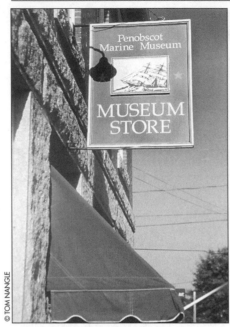

By 1885, 10 percent of all full-rigged American-flag ships on the high seas were under the command of Searsport and Stockton Springs captains. See artifacts, maritime art, and related exhibits at the Penobscot Marine Museum.

ship models and nautical gifts. Even if you're not a hobbyist, stop in to see the incredibly detailed models on display. Shipcrafters is renowned for building one-of-a-kind museum-quality custom models—it's the official model maker for the U.S. Navy—but don't despair, there are kits here for all abilities (and budgets). It's easy to find: just look for the inland lighthouse on Route 1.

PARKS AND RECREATION

Moose Point State Park

Here's a smallish park with a biggish view—183 acres wedged between Route 1 and a dramatic Penobscot Bay panorama. Moose Point State Park (Rte. 1, Searsport, 207/548-2882, $2 adults, $1 children 5–11) is 1.5 miles south of downtown Searsport. Bring a picnic, let the kids hang

out and play (there's no swimming), walk through the woods. Moose-crossing signs are posted on the highway, but don't count on seeing one. Open Memorial Day weekend to October 1, but since it's alongside the highway, the park is accessible, weather permitting, all year.

Mosman Park

Southeast of busy Route 1, the four-acre, town-owned Mosman Park has picnic tables, a traditional playground, lots of grassy space, a pocket-size pebbly beach, seasonal toilets, and fabulous views of the bay. Turn off Route 1 at Water Street and continue to the end.

Sears Island

After almost two decades of heavy-duty squabbling over a proposed cargo port on Searsport's 940-acre Sears Island, the state bought the island for $4 million in November 1997. Discussions are ongoing about the establishment of visitor facilities, but for now, the only improvement on this lovely, causeway-linked island is a road. It's a fine place for biking, picnicking, walking, fishing, and cross-country skiing. From downtown Searsport, continue northeast on Route 1 two miles to Sears Island Road (on your right). Turn and go 1.2 miles to the beginning of the island, where you can pull off and park before a gate (cars aren't allowed on the island). An easy 1.5-mile walk will take you to the other side of the island, overlooking Mack Point (site of a rather unattractive cargo port) and hills off to the left. Bring a picnic and binoculars—and a swimsuit if you're hardy enough to brave the water.

Fort Point State Park

Continuing northeast on Route 1 from Sears Island will get you to the turnoff for Fort Point State Park (Fort Point Rd., Stockton Springs, 207/567-3356, $2 adults, $1 children 5–11) on Cape Jellison's eastern tip. Within the 154-acre park are the earthworks of 18th-century **Fort Pownall** (a British fortress built in the French and Indian War), **Fort Point Light** (a square, 26-foot, 19th-century tower guarding the mouth of the Penobscot River), shoreline trails, and a 200-foot pier where you can fish or bird- or boat-watch. (Birders can spot waterfowl—especially ruddy ducks, but also eagles and osprey.) Bring picnic fixings, but stay clear of the keeper's house—it's private. At the Route 1 fork for Stockton Springs, bear right onto Main Street and continue to Mill Road, in the village center. Turn right and then left onto East Cape Road, then another left onto Fort Point Road, which leads to the parking area. Officially, the park is open Memorial Day weekend through Labor Day, but it's accessible all year, weather permitting.

Bicycling

One of the state's most hyperactive bicycle shops is about a mile north of downtown Searsport. **Birgfeld's Bicycle Shop** (184 E. Main St., Rte. 1, Searsport, 207/548-2916 or 800/206-2916), in business since the 1970s, is a mandatory stop for any cyclist, novice or pro. Local information on about 15 biking loops, supplies, maps, weekly group rides, sales (also skateboards and scooters), and excellent repair services are all part of the Birgfeld's mix. Free parking is behind the shop, which is headquarters for the Waldo County International Cycling and Dining Society—an informal group that gets together for rides and follow-up food. Inquire about its schedule.

An especially good ride in this area is the **Cape Jellison** loop in Stockton Springs, even though it means biking from Birgfeld's about four miles along congested Route 1 (be extremely cautious). If you have your own bike or a car to transport the rental, park at Stockton Springs Elementary School and do the loop from there. Including a detour to Fort Point, the ride totals less than 10 miles from downtown Stockton Springs.

Golf

Searsport Pines (240 Mt. Ephraim Rd., Searsport, 207/548-2854) is a nine-hole par-4 course on the inland side off Route 1.

SHOPPING

The word "shopping" in Searsport usually applies to antiques—from 25-cent flea-market collectibles to well-used tools to high-end china, furniture, and glassware. The town has more than a dozen separate businesses—and some of *those* are group shops with multiple dealers. Searsport vies with Wiscasset as Maine's "Antiques Capital."

More than two dozen dealers supply the juried inventory for Bob and Phyllis Sommer's **Pumpkin Patch** (15 W. Main St., Rte. 1, Searsport, 207/548-6047)—with a heavy emphasis on Maine antiques. Specialties include quilts (at least 80 are always on hand), silver, paint-decorated furniture, Victoriana, and nautical and Native American items.

More than 70 dealers sell their antiques and collectibles at **Searsport Antique Mall** (149 E. Main St., Rte. 1, Searsport, 207/548-2640), making it another worthwhile stop for those seeking oldies but goodies.

Crafts and Gifts

Close to the highway in a farmstand-style building about a mile east of downtown Searsport, the **Waldo County Craft Co-op** (1778 E. Main St., Rte. 1, Searsport, 207/548-6686) features the work of about 30 Mainers: quilts, jams, bears, dolls, jewelry, baskets, pottery, floor cloths, and lots else.

Hooked rugs as well as Victorian and country gifts and crafts are the specialties at **Silkweeds** (191 E. Main St., Rte. 1, Searsport, 207/548-6501), in the midst of antique shops and flea markets at the eastern end of town. You'll find 17 rooms to explore, including a special area for rug hooking (if you're a hooker —rugs, that is—ask about special workshops). Don't miss the potpourri corner—where you serve yourself from a clawfoot tub.

Teddy bear fans must stop at **Cranberry Hollow** (157 W. Main St., Rte. 1, Searsport, 207/548-2647), a shop filled with stuffed bears, quilts, and other country folk items. You can also order a custom bear.

Used Books

A local fixture in Stockton Springs since 1960, **Victorian House Books/Book Barn** (E. Main St., Stockton Springs, 207/567-3351) is jam-packed with used and antiquarian books.

Penobscot Bay

ACCOMMODATIONS

B&Bs

The veteran B&B in town is **The Homeport Inn** (121 E. Main St., Rte. 1, P.O. Box 647, Searsport 04974, 207/548-2259 or 800/742-5814, www.homeportbnb.com, $85–115), a fabulous 1861 sea captain's mansion presided over since 1978 by genial Edith Johnson. Her fascination with antiques and British royalty is evident everywhere, creating an unstuffy, user-friendly museum of a place: four-poster and canopied beds, fireplaces, Spode pottery, Oriental carpets, even wallpaper copied from Queen Victoria's bedroom. Breakfast is served on the glassed-in porch overlooking gardens beautifully landscaped by Edith's husband, George. Guests can play darts or do puzzles in the pub-style family room on the lower level. Six first-floor rooms (private baths) and four second-floor rooms (sharing one bath). Also on the premises are three two-bedroom, waterfront Victorian cottages for $750–850 per week; a good choice for families.

Across Route 1 is the impressive **M Carriage House Inn** (120 E. Main St., Searsport 04974, 207/548-2167 or 800/578-2167, www.carriagehouseinmaine.com, $90–125), a National Historic Register sea captain's home that's been most recently restored by Marcia Mackwardt. Built in 1874 by Captain John McGilbery, it later became home to impressionist painter Waldo Pierce, whose friend Ernest Hemingway visited the inn often. The architectural detailing and 12-foot ceilings add elegance to this grand property. The three guest rooms and the public rooms are decorated with Victorian-era antiques and family heirlooms. A multicourse breakfast and afternoon snacks are included.

Waving pennants mark the entrance to **1794 Watchtide** (190 W. Main St., Rte. 1, Searsport 04974, 207/548-6575 or 800/698-6575, www.watchtide.com, $135–198), in a sprawling late-18th-century sea captain's home formerly known as The College Club Inn. Each of the three rooms and two suites has a historic-name connection; the Eleanor Roosevelt Suite acknowledges visits by former First Ladies in decades past. Amenities are endless, from air-conditioning and white-noise clock radios (the inn is on a busy highway) to hot and cold drinks to unusual snacks. Two rooms have whirlpool tubs. Rooms in the back have the nicest views and are most quiet. Nancy-Linn Nellis was a designer/decorator in a previous life; it's evident here. (She and husband Jack Elliott have become such pros in this business they give three-day innkeeping seminars.) Breakfasts are fabulous. Collapse on the 60-foot sun porch, overlooking the bay, and you may never want to leave. In the barn is an antique and gift shop with lots of great treasures. The inn is open all year, while the shop is open as long as the weather holds out.

Motel

The **Yardarm** (172 East Main St., Rte. 1, P.O. Box 246, Searsport 04974, www.searsportmaine.com, $68–110), a small motel set back from the road, is next door to BlueJacket Shipcrafters. Each of the 18 pine-paneled units has TV and phone; suites (perfect for families) have a dinette, microwave, and small fridge. A continental breakfast is served in a cheery breakfast room in the adjacent farmhouse. Open May to late October.

Campgrounds

How can you beat 1,100 feet of tidal oceanfront and unobstructed views of Islesboro, Castine, and Penobscot Bay? **Searsport Shores Camping Resort** (216 W. Main St., Rte. 1, Searsport 04974, 207/548-6059, www.campocean.com) gets high marks for its fabulous six-acre setting. About 120 good-sized sites (including a wilderness camping area) go for $30–45 a day. Facilities include a private beach, small store, free showers, laundry, play areas, recreation hall, nature trails, and volleyball court. Request a site away from organized-activity areas. Bring a sea kayak and launch it here. Leashed pets are allowed. The campground is slightly more than a mile southwest of downtown Searsport, about four miles east of downtown Belfast. Open mid-May to Columbus Day.

FOOD

Whether you're up for a splurge or hunting for a bargain, restaurants in Searsport and Stockton Springs are few in number but run the gamut.

Casual Dining

The ☒ **Anglers Restaurant** (215 E. Main St., Rte. 1, Searsport, 207/548-2405, 11 A.M.–8 P.M.) is probably the least assuming and one of the most popular restaurants around. Expect hearty New England cooking, hefty portions, local color, no frills, and a bill that won't dent your wallet Big favorites are the chowders and stews ($4–9) and lobster rolls ($11). Dinner entrées are $9–14, although lobsters are higher. The "minnow menu" for smaller appetites runs $6–13. Desserts are a specialty: the gingerbread with whipped cream is divine ($1.99); kids love the "bucket o' worms" ($2.99). If it's not too busy, and you've ordered a lobster, ask owner Buddy Hall if he'll demonstrate hypnotizing it. Next to a small roadside motel, the restaurant is 1.5 miles northeast of downtown Searsport.

Chocoholics, meet your match at **The Chocolate Grille** (1 E. Main St., Rte. 1, Searsport, 207/548-2555, 11 A.M.–11 P.M., to 12:30 A.M. Fri. and Sat., to 10 A.M. Sun.). As its name suggests, there's plenty of chocolate on the dessert menu as well as in coffees and in cocktails. The wide-ranging menu includes salads, pizza, sandwiches, burgers, meat, seafood, and pasta; most choices in the $8–19 range. Food's good, but service can be painfully slow.

Fine Dining

Screened from the highway behind bushes, **The Rhumb Line** (200 E. Main St., Rte. 1, Searsport, 207/548-2600) occupies two rooms on the first floor of an imposing Victorian house. Chef/owners Charles and Diana Evans have created an excellent "new American" menu with such entrées as orange-glazed and roasted Long Island half duck and spicy seared pork medallions (entrées are $21–25). The main room, with its hardwood floors, can be noisy if a group shows up, but it's

brighter than the smaller back room. Reservations are essential, especially on weekends, at this popular place. Open all year for dinner, not every day in winter. Watch for the sign across from the Irving gas station.

INFORMATION AND SERVICES

Information

Waldo County Marketing Association (P.O. Box 139, Searsport 04974, 800/870-9934, www.waldocountymaine.com) has information about the area. In Searsport, a small, volunteer-run information center is open on an unpredictable schedule—it's in a shedlike building on Route 1 (at Norris Street), across from the Pumpkin Patch antique shop. On weekdays, you can check at the **Searsport Town Office** (207/548-6372) on Reservoir Street (just after the Penobscot Marine Museum).

Hospitals

Waldo County General Hospital (118 Northport Ave., Belfast, 207/338-2500 or 800/649-2536), a community-oriented private institution, serves this area.

Local Library

The handsome fieldstone **Carver Memorial Library** (Mortland Rd. at Union St., Searsport, 207/548-2303) was built in 1910. The library is a block off Route 1 (11 A.M.–5 P.M. Mon.–Fri., to 7 P.M. Tues. and Thurs., and 9 A.M.–noon Sat.).

Getting Around

Concord Trailways (800/639-3317, www.concordtrailways.com) stops in Rockland, Camden-Rockport, Belfast, and Searsport on its three daily nonexpress trips up the coast.

Blue Hill Peninsula

The Blue Hill Peninsula, once dubbed "The Fertile Crescent," is unique. Few other Maine locales harbor such a high concentration of artisans, musicians, and on-their-feet retirees juxtaposed with top-flight wooden boat builders, lobsterers, and umpteenth-generation Mainers. Perhaps surprisingly, the mix seems to work.

Anchored by the towns of Bucksport to the east and Ellsworth to the west, the peninsula comprises several enclaves with markedly distinctive personalities: Blue Hill, Castine, Deer Isle and Isle au Haut, and Brooklin, Brooksville, and Sedgwick. These towns are stitched together by a network of narrow, winding country roads. Thanks to the mapmaker-challenging coastline and a handful of freshwater ponds and rivers, there's a view of water around nearly every bend.

You can watch the sun set from atop Blue Hill Mountain; tour the home of the fascinating Jonathan Fisher; stroll through the village of Castine (charming verging on precious), whose streets are lined with dowager-like homes; visit *WoodenBoat* magazine's world headquarters in tiny Brooklin; browse galleries throughout the peninsula; and visit a remote section of Acadia National Park on Isle au Haut.

© TOM NANGLE

Must-Sees

M Fort Knox: Ongoing restoration, frequent events, and secret passages to explore makes this late-19th-century fort one of Maine's best (page 258).

M The Parson Fisher House: More than just another historic house, the Parson Fisher House is a remarkable testimony to one man's ingenuity (page 261).

M The Good Life Center: Remember the back-to-the-land movement of the '60s? Refresh your

Galleries, including the highly regarded Blue Heron Gallery, abound on Deer Isle, thanks in part to the Haystack Mountain School of Crafts.

memory and learn how you can live a sustainable life as founders Helen and Scott Nearing did (page 268).

M Flash in the Pans Community Steel Band Concerts: Close your eyes, and you might think you're on a Caribbean island rather than in Maine when you hear this phenomenal steel pan band (page 269).

M Castine Historic Tour: You might just think you've stepped into a movie set in Castine, a small town with a fascinating history and gorgeous architecture that's easily explored on foot (page 274).

M Deer Isle Art and Craft Galleries: Thanks in part to the presence of the renowned Haystack Mountain School of Crafts, high-end galleries dot Deer Isle (page 285).

M Acadia National Park: Avoid the millions in Bar Harbor and Mount Desert Island by being one of the 48 people a day allowed to visit the remote section of the park on sparsely populated **Isle au Haut** (page 290).

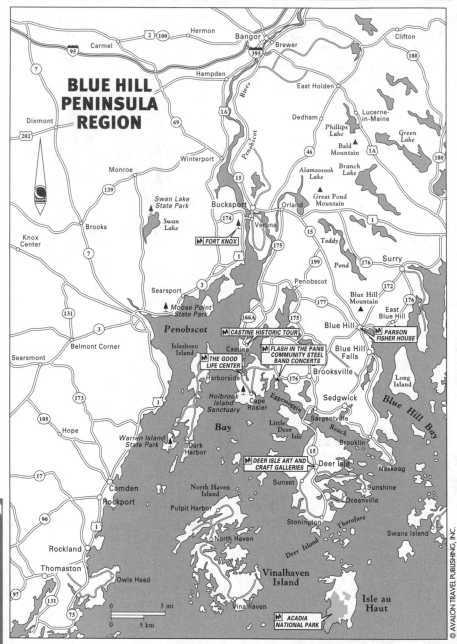

BLUE HILL PENINSULA REGION

Hermon
Bangor
Brewer
Clifton
Carmel
Hampden
East Holden
Lucerne-in-Maine
Dixmont
Dedham
Phillips Lake
Green Lake
Bald Mountain
Winterport
Monroe
Alamoosook Lake
Branch Lake
Great Pond Mountain
Swan Lake State Park
Bucksport
Orland
Swan Lake
Brooks
Verona
Toddy
Knox Center
FORT KNOX
Pond
Penobscot
Surry
Searsport
Moose Point State Park
Blue Hill Mountain
East Blue Hill
Belmont Corner
Penobscot
CASTINE HISTORIC TOUR
Blue Hill
PARSON FISHER HOUSE
Searsmont
Islesboro Island
Castine
FLASH IN THE PANS COMMUNITY STEEL BAND CONCERTS
Blue Hill Falls
THE GOOD LIFE CENTER
Harborside
Brooksville
Long Island
Holbrook Island Sanctuary
Cape Rosier
Sedgwick
Blue Hill Bay
Hope
Warren Island State Park
Bay
Little Deer Isle
Sargentville
Reach
Brooklin
Dark Harbor
DEER ISLE ART AND CRAFT GALLERIES
Deer Isle
Naskeag
Camden
Rockport
North Haven Island
Sunset
Sunshine
Oceanville
Pulpit Harbor
Stonington
Thorofare
Swans Island
Rockland
North Haven
Deer Island
Thomaston
Owls Head
Vinalhaven Island
Isle au Haut
Vinalhaven
ACADIA NATIONAL PARK

0   5 mi
0   5 km

The peninsula, including Deer Isle, is home to some of Maine's finest traditional inns and lodges and a surprising number of excellent restaurants.

PLANNING YOUR TIME

To truly enjoy this region, spend at least three or four days here, perhaps splitting your lodging between two or three locations. The region is designed for leisurely exploring; you won't be able to zip from one location to another. Traveling along the winding roads, discovering galleries and country stores, and lodging at traditional inns are all part of the experience.

Arts fans will want to concentrate their efforts in Blue Hill, Deer Isle, and Stonington, possibly spending a night or two in Blue Hill and again in Deer Isle or Stonington. Outdoor-oriented folks should consider Deer Isle, Stonington, or Castine as a base for sea kayaking or exploring the area preserves. Architecture buffs and fans of good restaurants should consider Castine for a few nights. Or just settle into a cottage at one of the traditional lodges for a week, enjoying breakfast and dinner at the main inn and using your days to explore all the region has to offer.

On your way to or from the peninsula, be sure to visit **Fort Knox.** The views over Bucksport and up and down the Penobscot River are outstanding, and ongoing restoration has recaptured the fort's spirit. Another spirit not to be missed is that of **The Parson Fisher House,** an architectural gem in Blue Hill that was home to a man of incredible ingenuity. Allow a half day to tour the house and visit nearby galleries. Spirit of yet another type is demonstrated almost weekly around the region by the not-to-be-missed **Flash in the Pans,** a community steel pan band that performs in street concerts.

Quiet pleasures await history and architecture buffs in **Castine.** Allow the better part of a day to follow the historical markers throughout town and admire the houses and public buildings. Better yet, immerse yourself in it by staying in one of the lovely inns.

Another day is easily spent browsing through **Deer Isle's galleries,** and perhaps allowing a wee bit of time for a walk in a coastal preserve.

No visit to this region is complete without at least a cruise by if not a visit to **Isle au Haut,** an offshore island that's home to a remote section of Acadia National Park. Allow at least a few hours for a ride on the mail boat, but if you can afford the time, spend a full day hiking the park's trails. Don't forget to pack food and water.

Finding tourism information about the East Penobscot Bay area can be frustrating, so it's wise to check the website of the **East Penobscot Bay Association** (www.penobscotbay.com) and request a copy of its handy flyer/map. Once you've landed on Route 172 or 175, pop into one of the small roadside convenience stores and start asking questions. The clerks—often the owners—know it all cold, and these markets always have a fair share of local color. Of course, they won't object if you also buy something while you're there.

Bucksport Area

Working hard and well to gentrify its longtime rough-and-ready river-port image, Bucksport changes even as you watch. Long dominated by a giant International Paper mill, Bucksport has in recent years striven to become more than a mill town—and it's succeeding. New businesses have arrived, a marina has been built, and the local newspaper has improved communications and sparked community spirit.

Bucksport is no upstart. Native Americans first gravitated to these Penobscot River shores in summers, finding here a rich source of salmon for food and grasses for basketmaking. In 1764, it was officially settled by Colonel Jonathan Buck, a Massachusetts Bay Colony surveyor who modestly named it Buckstown and organized a booming shipping business here. His remains are interred in a local cemetery, where his tombstone bears the distinct outline of a woman's leg; this is allegedly the result of a curse by a witch Buck ordered executed, but in fact it's probably a flaw in the granite. Most townsfolk prefer not to discuss the matter, but the myth refuses to die—and it has immortalized a man whose name might otherwise have been consigned to musty history books. (The monument is across Route 1 from the Hannaford supermarket, on the corner of Hinks Street; a sign tells the tale, and a new sidewalk has improved access and visibility.)

Papermaking came to Bucksport in 1930, and the International Paper mill on Indian Point still dominates the riverfront.

Just south of Bucksport, at the bend in the Penobscot River, Verona Island is best known as the mile-long link between Prospect and Bucksport. Just before you cross the bridge from Verona to Bucksport, hang a left, then a quick right to a small municipal park with a boat launch and broad views of Bucksport Harbor (and the paper mill). In the Buck Memorial Library is a scale model of Admiral Robert Peary's Arctic exploration vessel, the *Roosevelt,* built on this site.

Route 1 east of Bucksport leads to Orland, whose idyllic setting on the banks of the Narramissic River makes it a magnet for shutterbugs. It's also the site of a unique service organization called H.O.M.E.

(Homeworkers Organized for More Employment). East Orland (officially part of Orland) claims the Craig Brook National Fish Hatchery and Great Pond Mountain (you can't miss it, jutting from the landscape on the left as you drive east on Route 1).

SIGHTS

M Fort Knox

Looming over Bucksport Harbor, the *other* Fort Knox (Rte. 174, Prospect, 207/469-7719, www.fortknox.maineguide.com, 9 A.M.–sunset, May 1–Nov. 1, $3 adults, $1 children 5–11) is a 125-acre state historic site, just off Route 1. Named for Major General Henry Knox, George Washington's first secretary of war, the sprawling granite fort was begun in 1844. Built to protect the upper Penobscot River from attack, it was never finished and never saw battle. Still, it was, as guide Kathy Williamson said: "very well thought out and planned, and that may have been its best defense." Begin your visit at the Visitor and Education Center, operated by the Friends of Fort Knox, a nonprofit group that has partnered with the state to preserve and interpret the fort. Guided tours are available from Memorial Day through Labor Day, and well worth it, as guides point out some of the fort's distinguishing features. Wear rubberized shoes and bring a flashlight to explore the underground passages; you can set the kids loose. Bring a picnic; views over the river to Bucksport are fabulous. An observatory is planned for the top of the 420-foot high west tower of the new bridge spanning the Penobscot River. It will be open to the public via Fort Knox. Civil War reenactments occur here several times a summer (check with the chamber of commerce). The Halloween Fright at the Fort is a ghoulish event for the brave. The grounds are accessible all year.

Old-Time Flicks

Phoenixlike, the 1916 **Alamo Theatre** (85 Main St., Bucksport 04416, 207/469-0924 or 800/639-1636, event line 207/469-6910, www.alamotheatre.org) has been retrofitted for a new life—focusing on films about New England produced and/or revived by unique **Northeast Historic Film** (NHF), which is headquartered here. Stop in, survey the restoration, visit the displays (donation requested), and browse the Alamo Theatre Store for antique postcards, T-shirts, toys, and reasonably priced videos on ice harvesting, lumberjacks, maple sugaring, and other traditional New England topics. One-half mile west of Route 1, it's open 9 A.M.–4 P.M. weekdays all year. The Alamo has also become an active cinema, screening classic and current films regularly in the 120-seat theater, usually weekends. Tickets are $6. Each summer there's also a silent film festival.

H.O.M.E.

Adjacent to the flashing light on Route 1 in Orland, H.O.M.E. is tough to categorize. Linked with the international Emmaus Movement founded by a French priest, H.O.M.E. (Homeworkers Organized for More Employment) was started in 1970 by Lucy Poulin, still the guiding force, and two nuns at a nearby convent. The quasi-religious organization shelters refugees and the homeless, operates a soup kitchen and a car-repair service, runs a day-care center, and teaches work skills in a variety of hands-on cooperative programs. Seventy percent of its income comes from sales of crafts, produce, and services. At the Route 1 store (corner of Upper Falls Rd.; open 9 A.M.–4:30 P.M. daily), you can buy handmade quilts, organic produce, maple syrup, and jams—and support a worthwhile effort. To volunteer time in the workshops, store, or learning center, write P.O. Box 10, Orland 04472, or call 207/469-7961.

PARKS AND RECREATION

For a day of hiking, picnicking, swimming, canoeing, and a bit of natural history, pack a lunch and head for 135-acre **Craig Brook National Fish Hatchery** (306 Hatchery Rd., East Orland, 207/469-2803), on Alamoosook Lake. Turn off Route 1 six miles east of Bucksport and continue 1.4 miles north to the parking area just above the visitor center (open 8 A.M.–3:30 P.M. weekdays and most weekends in summer; no charge; maps

and restroom), with interactive displays on Atlantic salmon (don't miss the downstairs viewing area). The grounds are accessible all year, 6 A.M. to sunset daily. Established in 1871, the U.S. Fish and Wildlife Service hatchery raises sea-run Atlantic salmon for stocking seven Maine rivers, and each river has a different strain, so they're kept separate. The birch-lined shorefront has picnic tables, a boat-launching ramp, Atlantic salmon display pool, additional parking, and a spectacular cross-lake view. Watch for eagles, osprey, and loons. Also on the premises is the small Atlantic Salmon Museum, operated by the Friends of Craig Brook, with salmon and fly-fishing artifacts and memorabilia. Hiking options include two to three miles of nature trails through old-growth woods between Alamoosook and Craig ponds and an easy-to-moderate two-hour (round-trip) hike up Great Pond Mountain.

Great Pond Mountain's biggest asset is its 1,038-foot summit, with 360-degree views and lots of space for panoramic picnics. On a clear day, Baxter State Park's Katahdin is visible from Great Pond Mountain's north side. In fall, watch for migrating hawks. Access to the mountain is via gated private property beginning about a mile north of the hatchery parking area. Roadside parking is available near the trailhead, but during fall-foliage season, you may need to park at the hatchery. Pick up a brochure from the box at the trailhead, stay on the trail, and respect the surrounding private property. The **Great Pond Mountain Conservation Trust** (P.O. Box 266, Orland 04472, 207/326-8472 or 207/469-3003) acts as conscientious local steward for Great Pond Mountain and surrounding wild lands.

Stroll the half-mile walkway along the restored Bucksport waterfront, from the Bucksport/Verona Bridge to Sprague Point. Along the way are historical markers, picnic tables, a gazebo, a restroom, and expansive views of the harbor and Fort Knox.

Canoeing

If you've brought a canoe, **Silver Lake,** just two miles north of downtown Bucksport, is beautiful place for a paddle. There's no development along its shores, and the birding is excellent. No swimming ($500 fine); this is Bucksport's reservoir.

To get to the public launch, take Route 15 north off Route 1 after crossing the Verona-Bucksport Bridge. Go .5 mile and turn right on McDonald Road, which becomes Silver Lake Road, follow it 2.1 miles to the launch site.

Golf

Bucksport Golf Club (Duck Cove Rd., Route 46, 1.5 miles north of Rte. 1, 207/469-7612, mid-April–Sept.) prides itself on having Maine's longest nine-hole course. Greens fees are moderate; facilities include pro shop, snack bar, driving range, and carts.

ACCOMMODATIONS

B&B

The most attractive B&B in this area is **The Sign of the Amiable Pig** (74 Castine Rd., Rte. 175, P.O. Box 232, Orland 04472, 207/469-2561), once a hideout on the Underground Railroad. Three rooms (one with a private bath) are $60 and $75 d, including an imaginative breakfast. A separate guest house, sleeping five, goes for $550 a week, not including breakfast. Guests have the run of Charlotte and Wes Pipher's very comfortable home with parlor, keeping room, and lots of fireplaces. The oldest house section dates from 1765. Oriental carpets and fresh flowers are everywhere. The Amiable Pig (named for the weathervane atop the barn) is open all year, but be sure to call ahead and reserve space off-season.

Motel

In downtown Bucksport, the award for best view goes to the **Jed Prouty Motor Inn** (64 Main St., P.O. Box 826, Bucksport 04416, 207/469-3113 or 800/528-1234, $99–159), a four-story Best Western motel nudged right up to the harbor's edge. Forty modern rooms have phones, air-conditioning, and cable TV. Be sure to request a water view, or you'll be facing a parking lot.

Campgrounds

The rivers, lakes, and ponds in the area between Bucksport and Ellsworth make it especially ap-

pealing for camping, and sites tend to be cheaper than in the Bar Harbor area. During July and August, especially weekends, reservations are wise.

Six miles east of Bucksport, across from Craig Pond Road, is Back Ridge Road, leading to **Balsam Cove Campground** (P.O. Box C, East Orland 04431, 207/469-7771 or 800/469-7771, www.balsamcove.com, $18–25). From Route 1, take Back Ridge Road 1.5 miles to the left turn for the campground, on the shores of 10-mile-long Toddy Pond. Facilities on the 50 acres include 60 wooded tent and RV sites, a one-room rental cabin ($50), on-site rental trailers ($65–80), dump station, store, laundry, free showers, boat rentals, and freshwater swimming. Open late May to late September. The same season holds for 10-acre **Whispering Pines Campground** (Rte. 1, East Orland 04431, 207/469-3443, www.campmaine.com /whisperingpines/, $26), also on Toddy Pond but with access directly from Route 1. Facilities include 50 tent and RV sites (request one close to the pond), canoes and rowboats, freshwater swimming, playground, free showers, and rec hall. Whispering Pines is 6.5 miles east of Bucksport.

FOOD

MacLeod's (Main St., Bucksport, 207/469-3963, opens at 4:30 P.M. daily) is Bucksport's most popular restaurant. The menu is varied, children are welcome, it has a liquor license, and it's air-conditioned. French chocolate silk pie is a specialty. Dinner entrées are $9–16. Reservations are wise for Saturday dinner.

The **Bucksport Riverfront Market** (9 A.M.–5 P.M. Sat.), a farmers' market on the waterfront behind the Town Office, has artwork, fresh produce, baked goods, crafts, food, and more.

INFORMATION AND SERVICES

Information

The **Bucksport Bay Area Chamber of Commerce** (52 Main St., P.O. Box 1880, Bucksport 04416, 207/469-6818, www.bucksportchamber

.org) is right next to the municipal office in downtown Bucksport. Office hours are 9 A.M.– 5 P.M. Monday–Friday, but the side door is always open for access to an extensive array of brochures, newspapers, and other publications, plus bulletin-board notices. Bucksport information is also available at the **Gateway Mobil Station,** at the traffic light on the corner of Route 1, between the bridge and the Hannaford supermarket. The local *Enterprise* newspaper and the Bucksport Chamber of Commerce produce a very helpful annual, *The Guide,* covering Bucksport, Orland, and Verona Island. Be sure to request a copy.

Public Restrooms

In Bucksport, public restrooms next to the town dock (behind the Bucksport Historical Society) are open spring, summer, and fall. Restrooms are open year-round in the Gateway Mobil gas station (at the Route 1 traffic light next to the Bucksport bridge) and in the Bucksport Municipal Office (weekdays) on Main Street.

Blue Hill

Twelve miles south of Route 1 is the hub of the peninsula, Blue Hill (pop. 2,500), exuding charm from its handsome old homes to its waterfront setting to the shops, restaurants, and galleries that boost its appeal.

Eons back, Native American summer folk gave the name Awanadjo ("small, hazy mountain") to the minimountain that looms over the town and draws the eye for miles around. The first permanent settlers arrived after the French and Indian War, in the late 18th century, and established mills and shipyards. More than 100 ships were built here between Blue Hill's incorporation, in 1789, and 1882—bringing prosperity to the entire peninsula.

Critical to the town's early expansion was its first clergyman, Jonathan Fisher, a remarkable fellow who's been likened to Leonardo da Vinci. In 1803, Fisher founded Blue Hill Academy (predecessor of today's George Stevens Academy), then built his home (now a museum) and eventually left an immense legacy of inventions, paintings, engravings, and poetry.

Throughout the 19th century and into the 20th, Blue Hill's granite industry boomed, reaching its peak in the 1880s. Scratch the Brooklyn Bridge and the New York Stock Exchange and you'll find granite from Blue Hill's quarries.

At the height of industrial prosperity, tourism took hold, attracting steamboat-borne summer boarders. Many succumbed to the scenery, bought land, and built waterfront summer homes. Thank these summer folk and their offspring for the fact that music has long been a big deal in Blue Hill. The Kneisel Hall Chamber Music School, established in the late 19th century, continues to rank high among the nation's summer music colonies. New York City's Blue Hill Troupe, devoted to Gilbert and Sullivan operettas, was named for the longtime summer home of the troupe's founders.

SIGHTS
Ⓜ The Parson Fisher House

Named for a brilliant Renaissance man who arrived in Blue Hill in 1794, the Parson Fisher House (Rte. 15/176, Mines Rd., Blue Hill, 207/374-2459, www.jonathanfisherhouse.org, 1–4 P.M. Mon.–Sat. July–mid-Sept., $5) immerses visitors in period furnishings and Jonathan Fisher lore. And Fisher's feats are breathtaking: he was a Harvard-educated preacher who also managed to be an accomplished painter, poet, mathematician, naturalist, linguist, inventor, cabinetmaker, farmer, architect, and printmaker. In his spare time, he fathered nine children. Fisher also pitched in to help build the yellow house on Tenney Hill, which served as the Congregational Church parsonage. Now it contains intriguing items created by Fisher, memorabilia that volunteer tour guides delight in explaining, including a camera obscura. Don't miss it.

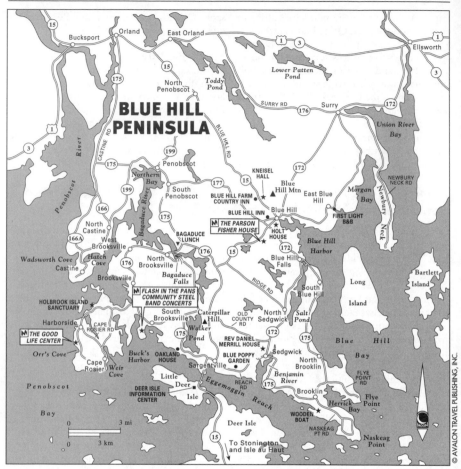

Historic Houses

A few of Blue Hill's elegant houses have been converted to museums, inns, restaurants, even some offices and shops, so you can see them from the inside out. To appreciate the private residences, you'll want to walk, bike, or drive around town.

In downtown Blue Hill, a few steps off Main Street, stands the **Holt House** (3 Water St., Blue Hill, 207/326-8250, 1–4 P.M. Tues. and Fri. and 11 A.M.–2 P.M. Sat. July–mid-Sept., $3 adults, free for kids 12 and under), home of the Blue Hill Historical Society. Built in 1815, the Fed-

eral-style building contains restored stenciling, period decor, and masses of memorabilia contributed by local residents.

Walk or drive up Union Street (Route 177), past George Stevens Academy, and wander **The Old Cemetery,** established in 1794. If gnarled trees and ancient headstones intrigue you, there aren't many good-sized Maine cemeteries older than this one.

Bagaduce Music Lending Library

At the foot of Greene's Hill in Blue Hill is one of Maine's more unusual institutions, a library where

GALLERY HOPPING IN BLUE HILL

Perhaps it's Blue Hill's location near the renowned Haystack Mountain School of Crafts. Perhaps it's the way the light plays off the rolling countryside and onto the twisting coastline. Perhaps it's the inspirational landscape. Whatever the reason, numerous artists and artisans call Blue Hill home, and top-notch galleries are abundant.

Contemporary art is the focus of the **Leighton Gallery** (207/374-5001), an airy two-story-plus-basement space in a converted barn on the Parker Point Road, with a spectacular backyard sculpture garden. The **Liros Gallery** (207/374-5370 or 800/287-5370), also on the Parker Point Road, is noted for Russian icons, but it also sells Currier & Ives prints, antique maps, and 18th- and 19-century paintings. The newest addition to Blue Hill's galleries is the **Blue Hill Bay Gallery** (207/374-5773), which represents contemporary art in various media.

Jud Hartmann (207/374-9917 or 207/359-2544) displays and sells his detailed bronze sculptures as well as works by other artists at his gallery on Main Street. Also on Main Street is **Handworks Gallery** (207/374-5613), along with **L. Balombini's** (207/374-5142) and **North Country Textiles** (207/374-2715). Handworks sells a range of fun, funky, utilitarian and fine art crafts by more than 50 Maine artists and craftspeople, including jewelry, furniture, rugs, wall hangings, and clothing. L. Balombini creates handwoven storytellers and other creative and colorful figures and also maintains a studio off Route 177 on Mattson Lane. Browse North Country Textiles for fine handwoven throws, rugs, clothing, and table linens as well as other fine crafts. Just off Main Street, on Water Street overlooking Blue Hill Bay, is **The Fairie Ring** (207/374-2545), which displays Tracy Johnson's handworked 18k and 22k gold and silver jewelry as well as paintings, wool felt appliqué, and handblown glass.

Outside of the downtown, you'll find **Peninsula Weavers** (Rte. 172 on Green's Hill, 207/374-2760), another resource for table linens, scarves, rugs, and other hand-woven pieces. On Beach Hill Road is **Gallery 66** (207/374-8853), where you can browse fine art digital images.

Pottery is abundant in Blue Hill. **Rowantrees Pottery** (Rte. 177, 207/374-5535) and **Rackliffe Pottery** (Rte 172, 207/374-2297 or 888/631-3321) both have well established reputations. Rowantrees Pottery's kiln was first fired in 1934. The handmade pottery is made from local marine clay accented by rich glazes derived from local sources. Rackliffe, noted for its vivid blue wares, also makes its own glazes and has been producing lead-free pottery since 1969. Newer in the neighborhood is **Mark Bell Pottery** (Rte. 15 on Tenney Hill, 207/374-5881). Bell's award-winning fine porcelain has been displayed at the Smithsonian Institution's Craft Fair as well as other juried shows across the country.

you can borrow by mail or in person from a collection of 625,000 scores and sheet music (3 Music Library Ln., Rte. 172, P.O. Box 829, Blue Hill 04614, 207/374-5454, www.bagaducemusic.org, 10 A.M.–3 P.M. or by appointment). Somehow this seems so appropriate for a community that's a magnet for music lovers. Annual membership is $10 ($5 for students); the library publishes six catalogs of its holdings; fees range from $1 to $2.50 per piece—and you can keep it for up to two months.

Scenic Route

Parker Point Road (turn off Route 15 at the Blue Hill Library) takes you from Blue Hill to Blue Hill Falls the back way, with vistas en route toward Acadia National Park. For other great views, drive the length of **Newbury Neck,** in nearby Surry, or head west on Route 15/176 toward Sedgwick, Brooksville, and beyond.

PARKS AND RECREATION

Blue Hill Mountain

Mountain seems a fancy label for a 943-footer, yet Blue Hill stands alone, visible from Camden and even beyond. On a clear day, head for the summit and take in the wraparound view. Climb the fire tower and you'll see even more. In mid-June, the lupines along the way are breathtaking; in fall, the colors are spectacular—with reddened blueberry barrens added to the variegated foliage. Go early

Blue Hill Peninsula

in the day; it's a popular easy-to-moderate hike, 1.5–2 hours round-trip. A short loop on the lower slopes takes only half an hour. Take Route 15 (Pleasant Street) to Mountain Road. Turn right and go .8 mile to the trailhead (on the left) and the small parking area (on the right). You can also walk (uphill) the mile from the village. The trail can be squishy, especially in the wooded sections, so you'll want rubberized or waterproof shoes or boots.

Blue Hill Town Park
At the end of Water Street is a small park with a terrific view. It has picnic tables and a creative playground. Pick up picnic fixings at Pain de Famille or the Blue Hill Co-Op and bring it all here.

MERI Center
A great way to raise kids' environmental consciousness is to enroll them in summer activities sponsored by the **MERI Center for Marine Studies** (55 Main St., Blue Hill, 207/374-2135, www.meriresearch.org). MERI (Marine Environmental Research Institute), a nonprofit marine-ecology organization, schedules daylong island boat trips, "eco-cruises," and island walks, plus a variety of naturalist-led morning and afternoon programs, each geared to different age groups or groupings ($25–35). The MERI Center has a touch tank, a marine lending library, and exhibit space. It's open Monday–Saturday all year.

SHOPPING
Boutiques, antiques, galleries, and even two downtown bookstores make shopping a pleasure in Blue Hill, especially if you're looking for the unusual. (See the sidebar Gallery Hopping in Blue Hill.)

Antiques
Historical and cottages goods are the specialty at **Salt Air Primitives** (5 Main St., Blue Hill, 207/374-8886). **Blue Hill Antiques** (8 Water St., Blue Hill, 207/374-2199 or 207/326-4973) specializes in 18th- and 19th-century French

and American furniture—it attracts a high-end clientele. The same patrons seek out Brad Emerson's **Emerson Antiques** (Water St., Blue Hill, 207/374-5140), concentrating on early Americana, such as hooked rugs and ship models. Also worth a browse for antique fiends is **Stephen Rowe Antiques** (138 Main St., Blue Hill, 207/374-3811), in front of the Blue Hill Wine Shop, which is always a fun stop, too. Just outside of town is the new location of **Belcher's Antiques** (232 Ellsworth Rd., Rte. 172, Blue Hill, 207/374-3751).

Books
Blue Hill's literate population manages to support two full-service, year-round, independent bookstores. Best selection is at **Blue Hill Books** (2 Pleasant St., Rte. 15, Blue Hill, 207/374-5632), thanks to knowledgeable owners Nick Sichterman and Mariah Hughs. Around the corner, **North Light Books** Main St., Blue Hill, 207/374-5422) carries a healthy inventory of Maine and children's books.

Eclectic
The Himalayas meet Blue Hill at Jeff Kaley's **Asian World Imports** (Pleasant St., Rte. 15, Blue Hill, 207/374-2284). A Nepal Peace Corps veteran, Kaley seeks out eco-sensitive suppliers using fair-trade practices, bringing back custom-made Nepalese, Tibetan, Indian, and Thai clothing, jewelry, and artifacts, as well as organic Himalayan tea. The shop is loaded with treasures. Jeff also leads small-group cultural tours and treks in Nepal and Tibet; contact him for details.

ENTERTAINMENT AND EVENTS
Variety and serendipity are the keys here. Check local calendar listings and tune in to radio station **WERU** (89.9 and 102.9 FM), www.weru.org), the peninsula's own community radio; there might be announcements of concerts by local resident pianist Paul Sullivan or the Bagaduce Chorale, or maybe a contra dance or a tropical treat from Carl Chase's Atlantic Clarion Steel Band or Flash in the Pans Community Band. The George Stevens Academy also has a weekly lecture series.

Music

Since 1922, chamber-music students have been spending summers perfecting their skills and demonstrating their prowess at the **Kneisel Hall Chamber Music School** (Pleasant St., Rte. 15, Blue Hill 04614, 207/374-2811, www.kneisel .org). Faculty concerts run Friday evenings (8:15 P.M.) and Sunday afternoons (4 P.M.) late June to mid-August. The concert schedule is published in the spring, and reserved-seating tickets ($26 inside, $19 on the veranda outside; nonrefundable) can be ordered by phone. There is also unreserved tent seating ($10) for the Friday evening and Sunday afternoon concerts. Kneisel Hall is about a half mile from the center of town.

Chamber music continues in winter thanks to the volunteer **Blue Hill Concert Association** (P.O. Box 140, Blue Hill 04614). Five concerts are performed between January and March at the Congregational Church, a handsome, traditional New England spired edifice on Main Street.

Fairs and Festivals

The first weekend in August, the **Academy Antiques Show** draws a huge crowd to the George Stevens Academy on Union Street in Blue Hill. Admission is $6, and lunch and tea are available.

WERU's annual Full Circle Fair is usually held in mid-August at the Blue Hill Fairgrounds (Rte. 172, north of downtown Blue Hill). Expect world music, good food, crafts, and socially and environmentally progressive talks.

On Labor Day weekend, the **Blue Hill Fair** (Blue Hill Fairgrounds, Rte. 172, Blue Hill, 207/374-9976) is one of the state's best agricultural fairs. Besides the food booths (good-for-you fare competes with fried dough), a carnival, fireworks, sheepdog trials, and live musical entertainment, you can check out the blue-ribbon winners for finest quilt, beefiest bull, or largest squash.

ACCOMMODATIONS

Inns and B&Bs

On a quiet side street close to town, **Ⓜ The Blue Hill Inn** (Union St., Rte. 177, P.O. Box 403, Blue Hill 04614, 207/374-2844 or 800/826-

7415, www.bluehillinn.com, $148–195, mid-May–late Oct.) has been welcoming guests since 1840. If you're trying to imagine a classic country inn, this would be it. Hosts Mary and Don Hartley do everything right. Stay here if you enjoy antiques, warm hospitality, and classic New England inns; don't stay if you're on a tight budget or have small children. Ten rooms and a suite, all with air-conditioning, boast real chandeliers, four-posters, down comforters, fancy linens, and braided and Oriental rugs; three have wood-burning fireplaces. The third-floor garret suite is ideal for families with well-behaved children; a first-floor room is wheelchair-accessible. Rear rooms overlook the extensive cutting garden, with chairs and a hammock. The library, dominated by a Persian chandelier, has masses of local information on an old country-store counter. Refreshments are available all day; superb hors d'oeuvres are served 6–7 P.M. in two elegant parlors or the garden. An adjacent suite in the elegant Cape House—the ground floor of a tiny dwelling—is $165–285, depending on season. Twice each year, usually May and October, the inn puts on gala wine-dinner weekends; the multicourse gourmet dinners are outstanding. The innkeepers will arrange for Kneisel Hall tickets, kayak rentals, cruises, massages, and more.

Two miles north of town, at the **Blue Hill Farm Country Inn** (Rte. 15, P.O. Box 437, Blue Hill, 207/374-5126, www.bluehillinn.com, $85–99), a huge refurbished barn serves as the gathering spot for guests. If the weather is lousy, you can plop down in front of the oversize woodstove and start in on cribbage or other games. Antique sleigh-runner banisters lead to the barn's seven second-floor rooms—all with private baths, skylights, hooked rugs, and quilts. A wing of the farmhouse has seven more rooms with shared baths and more quilts. Breakfast is generous continental. During the summer, visiting jazz or classical musicians sometimes entertain in the barn, but it all eases off early. On the inn's 48 acres are well-cleared nature trails, an 18th-century cellar hole, and a duck pond.

Okay, it's not a *real* lighthouse, but the waterfront **First Light B&B** (821 E. Blue Hill Rd., East Blue Hill 04614, 207/374-5819, www.firstlightbandb.com, $105–135) is close enough to fool many folks. Huge windows frame views that, on a clear day, extend for five miles. If you're a lighthouse buff, reserve the Lighthouse Suite, in the tower. Two other rooms share a bath or can be connected as a suite. Guests can climb the tower for 360-degree views. A comfortably cluttered common room, with fireplace, plentiful books, and a grand piano, faces McHeard's Cove. Breakfast is served either in the dining room or on the patio.

Motel

Blue Hill's only motel is the **Heritage Motor Inn** (Rte. 172, P.O. Box 453, Blue Hill 04614, 207/374-5646, www.bhheritagemotel.com, $95–108), a clean, no-frills, 23-room year-round place on Greene's Hill. Rooms have cable TV, air-conditioning, coffeemakers, and views of Blue Hill Bay, but no phones. Also available are housekeeping-style apartments ($1,150/week), with well-equipped kitchen and living room on one floor, bedroom, bath, and laundry on the second floor. Open all year.

Seasonal Rentals

Weekly rentals (or longer) can pay off if you have a large family or are planning a group vacation. The Blue Hill Peninsula has lots of rental cottages, camps, and houses, but the trick is to plan ahead. This is a popular area in summer, and many renters sign up for the following year before they leave town. For information, contact **Peninsula Property Rentals** (Main St., P.O. Box 611, Blue Hill 04614, 207/374-2428, www.peninsula propertyrentals.com).

FOOD

Picnic Fare and Pizza

Picnic fare is available at **Merrill & Hinckley** (Union St., Blue Hill, 207/374-2821, 7 A.M.–9 P.M. Mon.–Sat., 8 A.M.–9 P.M. Sun.), a quirky, 150-year-old, family-owned grocery/general store.

The **Blue Hill Co-Op and Café** (Greene's Hill, Rte. 172, Blue Hill, 207/374-2165, café 207/374-8999, 8 A.M.–7 P.M. Mon.–Fri., to 6 P.M. Sat., 10 A.M.–5 P.M. Sun.) sells organic and hydroponic

produce and grains, cheeses, organic coffee, and more. Breads are terrific here. Sandwiches, salads, and soups—many with ethnic flavors—are available in the café. The staff will pack it all up for a picnic, too.

On the other side of the village, **Pain de Famille** (Main St., Blue Hill, 207/374-3839, 7 A.M.–6 P.M. Mon.–Fri., to 7 P.M. Fri., and 9 A.M.–1 P.M. Sat. and Sun.) has earned an outstanding reputation for its unusual selection of breads. You can pick up Greek pockets or ready-made sandwiches and designer juices. Obviously, bread is the thing (fantastic focaccia). It's wise to call ahead for the Friday Night Pizza Plus, when two sizes of pizza are offered with about two dozen possible toppings.

Best pizza in the area is at **Oven Works** (37 Water St., Blue Hill, 374-5775, 9 A.M.–9 P.M. Tues.–Sat.).

Local gardeners, farmers, and craftspeople peddle their wares at the **Blue Hill Farmers' Market** (9–11:30 A.M. Sat.) It's a particularly enduring market, well worth a visit. Demonstrations are often on the agenda. The major effort is late June through September at the Blue Hill Fairgrounds (Rte. 172, just north of downtown).

Lobster and Fried Fish

For lobster, fried fish, and the area's best lobster roll ($9.95), head to **The Fish Net** (Main St., Blue Hill, 207/374-5240, 11 A.M.–8 P.M. Mon.–Thurs., to 9 P.M. Fri. and Sat.). Dine outdoors on picnic tables or inside. A cheeseburger is $2.60 and a fried clam dinner is $12.95.

Casual to Fine Dining

Here's a double header: **M Arborvine and The Vinery** (Main St., Blue Hill, www.arborvine .com). For a light lunch or dinner, head to The Vinery (207/374-2441, noon–2 P.M. Wed.–Sat. and 5–9 P.M. Wed.–Sun.), in a beautifully renovated bar, where there's often evening entertainment, too. Entrées are $6.50–12. If you're up for something fancier, make reservations at the Arborvine (207/374-2119, 5:30–9 P.M. Tues.–Sun. summer, Fri.–Sun. winter), a conscientiously renovated two-century-old Cape-style house with four dining areas, each with a different feel and understated decor. Most entrées are in the $19–24 range; there's always at least one for vegetarians. The wine list is small but select. Chef/owner John Hikade and his wife, Beth, operate both.

First choice for families is **The Blue Moose** (50 Main St., Blue Hill, 207/374-3274, 10:30 A.M.–9:30 P.M. Mon.–Fri., 8 A.M.–10 P.M. Sat. and Sun.), which has a wide-ranging menu and welcomes kids. Most choices are in the $8–12 range. Kids'/small appetite menu ranges $3–5.

INFORMATION AND SERVICES

Information

The **Blue Hill Peninsula Chamber of Commerce** (28 Water St., Box 520, Blue Hill 04614, 207/374-

2281, www.bluehillpeninsula.org, 9 A.M.–4 P.M. Mon.–Fri., to 1 P.M. Sat., 11 A.M.–3 P.M. Sun.) is stocked with brochures, menus, and other information on Blue Hill and the surrounding area.

Public Library

At the **Blue Hill Public Library** (Main St., 207/374-5515, 10 A.M.–6 P.M. Tues.–Fri., to 8 P.M. Thurs., 10 A.M.–1 P.M. Sat.) ask to see the suit of armor, which *may* have belonged to Magellan.

Public Restrooms

In season, there's a portable toilet behind the chamber of commerce building. Public buildings that have restrooms are the Blue Hill Town Hall (Main St.), Blue Hill Public Library (Main St.), and Blue Hill Memorial Hospital (Water St.).

Brooklin/Brooksville/Sedgwick

Nestled near the bottom of the Blue Hill Peninsula and surrounded by Castine, Blue Hill, and Deer Isle, this often-missed area offers superb hiking, kayaking, and sailing, plus historic homes and unique shops, studios, lodgings, and personalities.

Best-known town is Brooklin (pop. just over 1,000), thanks to two magazines: *The New Yorker* and *WoodenBoat.* Wordsmiths extraordinaire E. B. and Katharine White "dropped out" to Brooklin in the 1930s and forever afterward dispatched their splendid material for *The New Yorker* from here. (The Whites' former home, a handsome colonial not open to the public, is on Route 175 in North Brooklin, 6.5 miles from the Blue Hill Falls bridge.) In 1977, *WoodenBoat* magazine moved its headquarters to Brooklin, where its 60-acre shoreside estate attracts builders and dreamers from all over the globe. Nearby Brooksville (pop. 970) drew the late Helen and Scott Nearing, whose *Living the Good Life* made them role models for back-to-the-landers. Their compound now verges on "must-see" status. Buck's Harbor, a section of Brooksville, is the setting for *One Morning in Maine,* one of Robert McCloskey's beloved children's books. Oldest of the three towns is Sedgwick (pop. 1,175, incor-

porated in 1789), which once included all of Brooklin and part of Brooksville. Now wedged *between* Brooklin and Brooksville, it includes the hamlet of Sargentville, the Caterpillar Hill scenic overlook, and a well-preserved complex of historic buildings. The influx of pilgrims continues in this area—many of them artist wannabes bent on capturing the spirit that has proved so enticing to creative types.

SIGHTS

WoodenBoat Publications

On Naskeag Point Road, 1.2 miles from downtown Brooklin (Route 175), a small sign marks the turn to the world headquarters of the *Wooden-Boat* empire (Naskeag Point Rd., P.O. Box 78, Brooklin 04616, 207/359-4651, www.wooden boat.com). Buy magazines and books at the office, stroll the grounds, or sign up for one of the dozens of one- and two-week spring, summer, and fall courses in seamanship, navigation, boatbuilding, sailmaking, marine carving, and more. Special courses are geared to kids, women, pros, and all-thumbs neophytes; the camaraderie is legendary, and so is the cuisine. One-week tuition runs $550–1,000, plus materials in some courses. Room

Blue Hill Peninsula

and board is $400. School visiting hours are 8 A.M.–5 P.M. Monday–Saturday June–October.

Historical Sights

Now used as the museum/headquarters of the Sedgwick-Brooklin Historical Society, the 1795 **Reverend Daniel Merrill House** (Rte. 172, P.O. Box 171, Sedgwick 04676, 207/359-8086, 2–4 P.M. Sun. in July and Aug., or by appointment, donations welcomed) was the parsonage for Sedgwick's first permanent minister. Inside the house are period furnishings, old photos, toys, and tools; a few steps away are a restored 1874 schoolhouse, an 1821 cattle pound (for corralling wandering bovines), and a hearse barn. Pick up a brochure during open hours and guide yourself around the buildings and grounds. The **Sedgwick Historic District,** crowning Town House Hill, comprises the Merrill House and its outbuildings, plus the imposing 1794 Town House and the 23-acre Rural Cemetery (oldest headstone dates from 1798) across Route 172.

⋈ The Good Life Center

Forest Farm, home of the late Helen and Scott Nearing, is now the site of The Good Life Center (372 Harborside Rd., Box 11, Harborside, 207/326-8211, www.goodlife.org). Advocates of simple living and authors of 10 books on the subject, the Nearings created a trust to perpetuate their farm and philosophy. Resident stewards lead tours 1–5 P.M. Thursday–Tuesday in July and August (Thurs.–Mon. the rest of the year, but call ahead). Copies of Nearing books are available for sale. From mid-June to mid-September, Monday night meetings (7 P.M.) at the farm feature free programs by gardeners, philosophers, musicians, and other guest speakers. Occasional work parties, workshops, and conferences are also on the center's schedule. The farm is on Harborside Road, just before it turns to dirt. From Route 176 in Brooksville, take Cape Rosier Road, go 8 miles, passing Holbrook Islands Sanctuary. At the Grange Hall, turn right and follow it 1.9 miles to the end. Turn left onto Harborside Road and continue 1.8 miles to Forest Farm, across from Orrs Cove.

PARKS, PRESERVES, AND RECREATION

In the early 1970s, foresighted benefactor Anita Harris donated to the state 1,230 acres in Brooksville that would become the **Holbrook Island Sanctuary** (207/326-4012, free). From Route 176, between West Brooksville and South Brooksville, head west on Cape Rosier Road, following brown-and-white signs for the sanctuary. Trail maps and bird checklists are available in boxes at trailheads or at park headquarters. The easy Backshore Trail (about 30 minutes) starts here, or go back a mile and climb the steepish trail to **Backwoods Mountain** for the best vistas. Other trails include one around a beaver flowage. Other attractions include shorefront picnic tables and grills, four old cemeteries, and super birding during spring and fall migrations. Leashed pets are allowed, but no bikes on the trails and no camping. Officially open May 15–October 15, but the access road and parking areas are plowed for cross-country skiers.

Or you can take a picnic to the **Bagaduce Ferry Landing,** in West Brooksville off Route 176, where there are picnic tables and cross-river vistas toward Castine.

A small, relatively little-known beach is Brooklin's **Pooduck Beach.** From the Brooklin General Store (Route 175), take Naskeag Point Road about half a mile, watching for the Pooduck Road sign on the right. Drive to the end. You can also launch a sea kayak into Eggemoggin Reach here.

Bicycling

Bicycling in this area is hazardous. Roads here are particularly narrow and winding, with poor shoulders.

Scenic Routes

No one seems to know how **Caterpillar Hill** got its name, but its reputation comes from a panoramic vista of water, hills, and blueberry barrens—with a couple of convenient picnic tables where you can stop for lunch, photos, or a ringside view of sunset and fall foliage. The signposted rest area is on Route 175/15, between

Brooksville and Sargentville, next to a small gift shop; watch out for the blind curve when you pull off the road. Between Sargentville and Sedgwick, Route 175 offers nonstop views of Eggemoggin Reach, with shore access to the Benjamin River just before you reach Sedgwick village.

Two other scenic routes are **Naskeag Point,** in Brooklin, and **Cape Rosier,** westernmost arm of the town of Brooksville. Naskeag Point Road begins off Route 175 in "downtown" Brooklin, heads down the peninsula for 3.7 miles past the entrance to WoodenBoat Publications, past Amen Farm (home of the late author Roy Barrette, 207/359-8982, gardens and 10-acre arboretum open for viewing), to a small shingle beach (limited parking) on Eggemoggin Reach where you'll find picnic tables, a boat launch, a seasonal toilet, and a marker commemorating the 1778 Battle of Naskeag, when British sailors came ashore from the sloop *Gage,* burned several buildings, and were run off by a ragtag band of local settlers. Cape Rosier's roads are poorly marked, perhaps deliberately, so keep your DeLorme atlas handy. The Cape Rosier loop takes in Holbrook Island Sanctuary, Goose Falls, the hamlet of Harborside, and plenty of water and island views.

Boat Excursions

Captain LeChain Smith sails *Perelandra* (Buck's Harbor, 207/326-4279), a 44-foot ketch, in the waters of Penobscot Bay. Rates begin at $35 pp for a two-hour trip and increase to $55 pp for a four-hour sail and $95 for a full day. The boat holds a maximum of six passengers.

SHOPPING

Antiques

When you need a slate sink, a clawfoot tub, brass fixtures, or a Palladian window, **Architectural Antiquities** (Indian Point Ln., Harborside, 207/326-4938), on Cape Rosier, is just the ticket—a restorer's delight. Prices are reasonable for what you get, and they'll ship your purchases. Open all year by appointment; ask for directions when you call. Antiques dating from the Federal period through the turn of the 20th century

are the specialties at **Sedgwick Antiques** (Rte. 172, Sedgwick, 207/359-8834).

Used Books

Whimsical signs—Unattended Children Will Be Sold as Slaves; Jackets Please, Gentlemen—adorn the walls of **Wayward Books** (Rte. 15, RFD 26B, Sargentville, 207/359-2397), a bright, open shop camouflaged by an unassuming gray building just north of the suspension bridge to Little Deer Isle. Owned by Sybil Pike, a Library of Congress retiree, Wayward has 15,000 or so "medium-rare" titles in such creative categories as "civil liberties" and "books on books."

Gifts, Crafts, Art Galleries

On Route 175 (Reach Road) in Sedgwick, watch for a small sign for **Mermaid Woolens** (Reach Rd., Sedgwick, 207/359-2747), source of Elizabeth Coakley's wildly colorful handknits—vests, socks, and sweaters. They're pricey but worth every nickel. She also does seascape paintings. Clever woman.

Three varieties of English-style hard cider are specialties at **The Sow's Ear Winery** (Rte. 176 at Herrick Rd., Brooksville, 207/326-4649), a minuscule operation in a funky, gray-shingled building. Winemaker Tom Hoey also produces sulfite-free blueberry, chokecherry, and rhubarb wines; he'll let you sample it all. Ask to see his cellar, where everything happens. No credit cards. The other half of the business, upstairs, is **The Silk Purse,** where weaver Gail Disney creates handwoven rag rugs; she accepts commissions.

ENTERTAINMENT AND EVENTS

◪ Flash in the Pans Community Steel Band Concerts

Every other Monday night 7:30–9 P.M. mid-June to early September, this nearly three-dozen member band (207/374-2172, www.peninsulapan.org) performs for a street dance outside the Buck's Harbor Market. On other nights, they're usually elsewhere on the peninsula. The musicians aren't professionals, but you'd never know it. Admission is usually a small donation to benefit a local cause. It's worth every penny to join the fun.

Eggemoggin Reach Regatta

Wooden boats are big attractions hereabouts, so when a huge fleet sails in for this regatta (usually the first Saturday in August, but the schedule can change), crowds gather. Don't miss the parade of wooden boats. Best locale for watching the regatta itself is on or near the bridge to Deer Isle, or near the Eggemoggin Landing grounds on Little Deer Isle. Contact *WoodenBoat* (207/359-4651) for details.

ACCOMMODATIONS

Cottage Colonies

The two operations in this category feel much like informal family compounds—where you quickly become an adoptee. Don't even think about dropping in, however; successive generations of hosts have catered to successive generations of visitors, and far-in-advance reservations are essential for July and August. Many guests book for the following year before they leave. We're not talking fancy; cottages are old-shoe rustic, of varying sizes and decor. Most of the cottages have cooking facilities, although both colonies offer MAP in July and August. Both also have hiking trails, playgrounds, rowboats, and East Penobscot Bay on the doorstep.

Eggemoggin Reach, which divides the Blue Hill Peninsula from Deer Isle, is prized by skilled sailors.

Jim and Sally Littlefield are the enthusiastic fourth-generation hosts at **Ⓜ Oakland House Seaside Resort** (435 Herrick Rd., Brooksville 04617, 207/359-8521 or 800/359-7352, www.oaklandhouse.com), a sprawling 50-acre complex of 15 wooded and waterfront cottages, as well as Shore Oaks Seaside Inn. Much of this land, now threaded with hiking trails, was part of the original king's grant to Jim's ancestors, way back in 1765. The Homestead, where meals are served, dates from 1767. Jim is the eighth generation on the property; his daughter, Sally, is ninth. Weekly rates for two people, mid-June to Labor Day: $1,268–2,170, plus service charge, MAP; lower rates for children. Thursday is lobster-picnic night, on the beach. Biggest bargains are early May to mid-June and September–October, when you can rent a whole cottage, without meals, for $475–1,375 weekly, plus service charge. Rowboats are free for guests, and the staff organizes boat excursions on request. And wait till you see the gorgeous gardens—enough to warrant two full-time gardeners! Two cottages (Lone Pine and Boathouse) are winterized and available all year; the other cottages are closed in winter. Don't be discouraged by the minimums and the rates; there are lots of last-minute specials.

The fourth generation manages the **Hiram Blake Camp** (220 Weir Cove Rd., Harborside 04642, 207/326-4951, www.hiramblake.com, Memorial Day–late Sept.), but with a difference: the second and third generations still pitch in and help with gardening, lobstering, maintenance, and kibitzing. Thirteen cottages and a duplex line the shore of this 100-acre complex. Don't bother bringing reading matter: the dining room has ingenious ceiling niches lined with countless books. There's a one-week minimum (beginning Sat. or Sun.) July and August, when cottages go for $500–2,400 a week (including breakfast, dinner, and linens). Off-season rates (no meals or linens, but cottages have cooking facilities) are $550–750 a week. Best chances for getting a reservation are in June and September.

B&Bs

A few steps up from the half-mile-long shorefront at the Oakland House cottage colony is **Shore Oaks Seaside Inn** (435 Herrick Rd., Brooksville 04617, 207/359-8521 or 800/359-7352, www.oaklandhouse.com), a handsome green-trimmed stone mansion carefully restored to its Arts and Crafts heritage. Hang out for too long in the common rooms or the veranda rockers and you might never leave; this place is magical. Ten first-, second-, and third-floor rooms (seven with private baths) go for $149–395 MAP (a bargain with gourmet dinners and the weekly lobster feast). Shoulder-season rates (May and late Oct.) are less expensive but still include breakfast and a five-course dinner.

You choose: bed and breakfast or bed and afternoon tea at the inn at **Blue Poppy Garden** (Box 1000, Reach Rd., Rte. 175, Sedgwick 04676, 207/359-2739, 866-332-6664, www.bluepoppygarden.com, $120–150), an antique-filled, 1817 Federal with four guest rooms.

Views from the pier gazebo in front of the Shore Oaks Seaside Inn in Brooksville extend from Eggemoggin Reach to the Camden Hills.

© TOM NANGLE

FOOD

Breakfast, Lunch, and Tea

Competition is stiff for lunchtime seats at the **Morning Moon Café** (junction of Rte. 175 and Naskeag Point Rd., Brooklin, 207/359-2373, 7 A.M.–2 P.M. Tues.–Sat.), mostly because *WoodenBoat* staffers consider it an annex to their offices. "The Moon" is a friendly hangout for coffee, pizza, or great sandwiches and salads—or order it to go.

In North Brooksville, where Route 175/176 crosses the Bagaduce River, stands the **Bagaduce Lunch,** a popular take-out stand (outdoor tables only) open 11 A.M.–8 P.M. daily early May to mid-September. Check the tide calendar and go when the tide is changing; order a clam roll or a hamburger, settle in at a picnic table, and watch the reversing falls. The food is so-so, but the setting is tops.

Afternoon tea under the apple trees—English tea with scones and clotted cream—is the highlight of a visit to the **Blue Poppy Garden** (Reach Rd., Rte. 175, Sedgwick, 207/359-2739, www.bluepoppygarden.com). But there's more—a two-story post-and-beam barn holds a shop with hard-to-resist garden accessories, Portuguese cachepots, cards, a lending library of unusual garden books, and even imported seeds so you can grow your own blue poppies. And two miles of nature trails wind through the premises. Light lunches and afternoon tea are served; call for hours and reservations.

Country (Everything-and-More) Stores

Across the street from the Morning Moon Café, the **Brooklin General Store** (1 Reach Rd., junction of Rte. 175 and Naskeag Point Rd., Brooklin

Blue Hill Peninsula

04616, 207/359-8817, 5:30 A.M.–7 P.M. Mon.–Sat. and 8 A.M.–5 P.M. Sun.), vintage 1872, carries groceries, beer and wine, newspapers, take-out sandwiches, and local chatter.

On Route 175 in Sedgwick, overlooking the Benjamin River, the **Sedgwick Store** (207/359-6689, 7 A.M.–6 P.M. Mon.–Sat. all year) has an even more interesting inventory, including a good supply of gourmet goodies.

Box lunches and boat lunches are specialties at the **Buck's Harbor Market** (Rte. 176, South Brooksville, 207/326-8683, 7 A.M.–8 P.M. Mon.–Sat., 8 A.M.–8 P.M. Sun. all year), a low-key, marginally yuppified general store popular with yachties in summer. With the café here at the market and summertime steel-band street concerts outside, this can be a busy corner.

Casual Dining

Behind the Buck's Harbor Market is the aptly named 🔺 **Café Out Back** (Rte. 176, South Brooksville, 207/326-8683, 5:30–9 P.M. Wed.–Sun.), a quirky, congenial café with indoor and a few outdoor tables. Gourmet pizzas are the specialty, $9–15, but choices ranging from burgers to seafood risotto ($12–26) are offered, too.

Country Inn Dining

Chef Woody is the whiz in the kitchen at 🔺 **Oakland House Seaside Inn** (435 Herrick Rd., Brooksville, 207/359-8521), open to the public by reservation mid-June to mid-Sept. for its daily breakfast buffet, Sunday brunch, Thursday night

shorefront lobster picnic, and superb five-course dinner, with seating beginning at 6 P.M. Entrée range is $14–19. The dining rooms are in the property's original farmstead, which dates from 1867. At dinner, families dine in a separate room from couples, keeping everyone happy.

Almost everything on the menu is local or organic at **The Brooklin Inn** (Rte. 175, Brooklin, 207/359-2777, www.brooklininn.com, 5:30–9 P.M. Tues.–Sun.). The emphasis is on fresh seafood, with the daily changing menu featuring entrées ($18–24) such as wild Alaskan King salmon and local scallops, but less-pricey downhome choices also are available, such as Guinness beef stew or chicken pot pie ($8–10). Upstairs are five simple but comfortable bedrooms ($95 with breakfast) sharing two baths.

Also in Brooklin, at the tip of Flye Point, **The Lookout** restaurant (Flye Point Rd., off Rte. 175, North Brooklin, 207/359-2188, www.acadia.net/lookout/, 5–8:30 P.M. Tues.–Sun.) has a knockout view of Herrick Bay. Dinner is served daily in summer, occasionally off-season. Quality can be inconsistent, but you can't beat the scenery, as long as there's no fog. The Lookout, owned and operated by Flye family descendants for more than 110 years (judging from the look of the place, little has changed in that period), also has eight rustic rooms (with private and shared but all detached baths; $113–135, including breakfast) and seven rustic cottages with kitchens and wood stoves ($866–1,340/week).

Castine

Castine is a gem—a serene New England village with a tumultuous past. It's on the tip of a cape, surrounded by water on three sides, including the entrance to the Penobscot River, which made it a strategic defense point. Once beset by geopolitical squabbles, saluting the flags of three different nations (France, Britain, and Holland), its only crises now are local political skirmishes. This is an unusual community, a National Historic Register enclave that many people never find. The town celebrated its bicentennial in 1996. If you're staying in Blue Hill or even Bar Harbor, spend a day here. Or bunk here and use Castine as a base for exploring here and beyond. Either way, you won't regret it.

Originally known as Fort Pentagoet, Castine received its current name courtesy of Jean-Vincent d'Abbadie, Baron de St.-Castin. A young French nobleman manqué who married a Wabanaki princess named Pidiwamiska, d'Abbadie ran the town in the second half of the 17th century and eventually returned to France.

A century later, in 1779, occupying British troops and their reinforcements scared off potential American seaborne attackers (including Colonel Paul Revere), who turned tail up the Penobscot River and ended up scuttling their more than 40-vessel fleet—a humiliation known as the Penobscot Expedition and still regarded as one of America's worst naval defeats.

During the 19th century, peace and prosperity became the bywords for Castine—with lively commerce in fish and salt—but it all collapsed during the California Gold Rush and the Civil War trade embargo, leaving the town down on its luck.

Today a major presence is Maine Maritime Academy, yet Castine remains the quietest imaginable college town. Students in search of a party school won't find it here; naval engineering is serious business.

What visitors discover is a year-round community with a busy waterfront, an easy-to-conquer layout, a handful of traditional inns and boutiques, wooded trails on the outskirts of town,

© TOM NANGLE

Dozens of historical plaques throughout town bring Castine's turbulent history to life. Pick up a walking map at local businesses.

Blue Hill Peninsula

an astonishing collection of splendid Georgian and Federalist architecture, and water views from nearly every which way you turn.

Of the many historical landmarks scattered around town, one of the most intriguing must be the sign on "Wind Mill Hill," at the junction of Route 166 and State Street:

> On Hatch's Hill there stands a mill. Old Higgins he doth tend it. And every time he grinds a grist, he has to stop and mend it.

In smaller print, just below the rhyme, comes the drama:

> Here two British soldiers were shot for desertion.

Castine indeed has quite a history.

SIGHTS
 Castine Historic Tour

To appreciate Castine fully, you need to arm yourself with the Castine Merchants Association's visitors' brochure/map (all businesses and lodgings in town have copies) and follow the numbers on bike or on foot. With no stops, walking the route takes less than an hour, but you'll want to read dozens of historical plaques, peek into public buildings, shoot some photos, and perhaps even do some shopping.

Highlights of the tour include the late-18th-century **John Perkins House,** moved to Perkins Street from Court Street in 1969 and restored with period furnishings. It's open July and August for guided tours 2–5 P.M. Sunday and Wednesday; admission is $5.

Next door, **The Wilson Museum** (107 Perkins St., 207/326-8545, 2–5 P.M. Tues.–Sun. late May–late Sept., free), founded in 1921, contains an intriguingly eclectic two-story collection of prehistoric artifacts, ship models, dioramas, baskets, tools, and minerals assembled over a lifetime by John Howard Wilson, a geologist/anthropologist who first visited Castine in 1891 (and died in 1936). Among the exhibits are Balinese masks, ancient oil lamps, cuneiform tablets, Zulu artifacts, pre-Inca pottery, and assorted local findings. Don't miss this, even

though it's a bit musty. (The only comparable Maine institutions are the Nylander Museum, in Caribou, and the L. C. Bates Museum, in Hinckley.) Open the same days and hours as the Perkins House, are the **Blacksmith Shop,** where a smith does demonstrations, and the **Hearse House,** containing Castine's 19th-century winter and summer funeral vehicles. Both are free admission. The nonprofit **Castine Scientific Society** (P.O. Box 196, Castine 04421) operates the four-building complex.

At the end of Battle Avenue stands the 19th-century **Dyce's Head Lighthouse,** no longer operating; the keeper's house is owned by the town. Alongside it is a public path (signposted) leading via a wooden staircase to a tiny patch of rocky shoreline and the beacon that has replaced the lighthouse.

© TOM NANGLE

Although no longer operating, 19th-century Dyce's Head Lighthouse remains a popular Castine attraction, and it's a pleasant walk from downtown.

Highest point in town is **Fort George State Park,** site of a 1779 British fortification. Nowadays, little remains except grassy earthworks, but there are interpretive displays and picnic tables.

Main Street, descending toward the water, is a feast for historic-architecture fans. Artist Fitz Hugh Lane and author Mary McCarthy once lived in elegant houses along the elm-lined street (neither building is open to the public). On Court Street between Main and Green stands turn-of-the-20th-century **Emerson Hall,** site of Castine's municipal offices. Since Castine has no official information booth, you may need to duck in here (it's open weekdays) for answers to questions.

Across Court Street, **Witherle Memorial Library,** a handsome early-19th-century building on the site of the 18th-century town jail, looks out on the Town Common. Also facing the Common are the Adams and Abbott Schools, the former still an elementary school. The **Abbott School** (10 A.M.–4 P.M. Tues.–Sat. and noon–4 P.M. Sun. July–Labor Day, reduced schedule spring and fall, free but donation welcome), built in 1859, has been carefully restored for use as a museum/headquarters for the **Castine Historical Society** (P.O. Box 238, Castine 04421, 207/326-4118). A big draw at the volunteer-run museum is the 24-foot-long Bicentennial Quilt, assembled for Castine's 200th anniversary in 1996. The historical society, founded in 1966, organizes lectures, exhibits, and special events (some free) in various places around town.

On the outskirts of town, across the narrow neck between Wadsworth Cove and Hatch's Cove, stretches a rather overgrown canal (signposted British Canal) scooped out by the occupying British during the War of 1812. Effectively severing land access to the town of Castine, the Brits thus raised havoc, collected local revenues for eight months, then departed for Halifax with enough funds to establish Dalhousie College (now Dalhousie University). Wear waterproof boots to walk the canal route; best time to go is at low tide.

If a waterfront picnic sounds appealing, buy the fixings at Bah's Bakehouse and settle in on the grassy earthworks along the harborfront at **Fort Madison,** site of an 1808 garrison (then Fort

The Abbott School is now the headquarters of the Castine Historical Society and its museum.

Porter) near the corner of Perkins and Madockawando Streets. The views from here are fabulous, and it's accessible all year.

Maine Maritime Academy

The state's only merchant-marine college (and one of only seven in the nation), founded in 1941, awards undergraduate and graduate degrees in such areas as marine engineering, ocean studies, and marina management, preparing a student body of about 750 men and women for careers as ship captains, naval architects, and marine engineers. The academy owns a fleet of 90 vessels, including the historic research schooner *Bowdoin,* flagship of Arctic explorer Admiral Donald MacMillan, and the 498-foot training vessel TV *State of Maine,* berthed down the hill at the waterfront. Midshipmen conduct free 30-minute tours of the vessel on weekdays in summer (about mid-July to late August). The schedule is posted at

Blue Hill Peninsula

the dock (usually 8 A.M.–4 P.M.), or call 207/326-4311 to check. Weekday tours of the 50-acre campus can be arranged through the Admissions Office (207/326-2206 or 800/227-8465 outside Maine, www.mainemaritime.edu). Campus highlights include three-story Nutting Memorial Library, in Platz Hall (open daily during the school year, weekdays in summer and during vacations); the Henry A. Scheel Room, a cozy oasis in Leavitt Hall containing memorabilia from late naval architect Henry Scheel and his wife, Jeanne; and the well-stocked bookstore (Curtis Hall, 207/326-9333, 8 A.M.–3 P.M. Mon.–Fri.).

PARKS, PRESERVES, AND RECREATION

Witherle Woods, a 96-acre preserve owned by Maine Coast Heritage Trust and managed by the Conservation Trust of Brooksville, Castine, and Penobscot, is a popular walking area with a maze of numbered trails. The adjacent property is privately owned, so carry a trail map and stick to it. Access is via a shaded path, signposted Hatch Natural Area, from Battle Avenue. Several lodgings keep a supply of maps, or contact (by phone or mail) the **Conservation Trust of Brooksville, Castine, and Penobscot** (P.O. Box 421, Castine 04421, 207/326-9711). The Trust has been protecting the natural resources of Castine, Penobscot, and Brooksville since the early 1980s. Also ask locally about the **Henderson Natural Area** and other preserves, some accessible only by boat.

Golf and Tennis

The **Castine Golf Club** (Battle Ave. and Wadsworth Cove Rd., Castine 04421, 207/326-8844) dates to 1897, when the first tee required a drive from a 30-step-high mound. Redesigned in 1921 by Willie Park Jr., the nine-hole course is open May 15–October 15. Starting times are seldom required, and greens fees are reasonable. The club also has four clay tennis courts. Call to schedule court time.

Swimming

Backshore Beach, a crescent of sand and gravel on Wadsworth Cove Road (turn off Battle Avenue at the Castine Golf Club) is a favorite saltwater swimming spot, with views across the bay to Stockton Springs. Be forewarned, though, that ocean swimming in this part of Maine is not for the timid. Best time to try it is on the incoming tide, after the sun has had time to heat up the mud. At mid- to high tide, it's also the best place to put in a sea kayak. Park along the road.

If a pool sounds more attractive, you can swim in the **Cary W. Bok indoor pool** at Maine Maritime Academy for $4. Call 207/326-4311, ext. 451, for open- and lap-swim times.

Sea Kayaking

Based at Dennett's Wharf is **Castine Kayak Adventures** (15 Sea St., Castine, 207/326-9045, www.castinekayak.com), spearheaded by Maine Guide Karen Francoeur. Known locally as "Kayak Karen," she's particularly adept with beginners, delivering wise advice from beginning to end. All skill levels are accommodated. Three-hour half-day trips are $55; six-hour full-day tours are $105 including lunch. Two-hour sunset tours are $40; the sunrise tour includes breakfast for $45 (offered Wed. morning). Friday nights, there are special two-hour phosphorescence tours, under the stars (weather permitting), for $45 pp. Longer trips are available for $125 per day.

Bicycling

Bicycle rentals are available at Dennett's Wharf (207/326-9045). Rates are $24 full day, $15 half day.

SHOPPING

Antiques and Galleries

Tucked into the back of the 1796 Parson Mason House, one of Castine's oldest residences, **Leila Day Antiques** (53 Main St., 207/326-8786) is a must for anyone in the market for folk art, period furniture, quilts, and unusual contemporary Shard pottery (from Dover-Foxcroft). Access is via a lovely, flower-lined walkway.

McGrath Dunham Gallery (9 Main St., 207/326-9175), a well-lighted, two-story space, shows work by painter Greg Dunham and more than two dozen other artists.

For more artwork, visit the **Adams Gallery** of local oil painters Joshua and Susan Adams (140 Battle Ave., 207/326-8272).

Books

Driving toward Castine on Route 166, watch on your right for a small sign for **Dolphin Books and Prints** (314 Castine Rd, Castine, 207/326-0888), where Pete and Liz Ballou have set up their antiquarian business with approximately 5,000 books as well as framed prints and art.

In downtown Castine, a block up from the waterfront, **The Compass Rose Bookstore and Café** (3 Main St., 207/326-9366 or 800/698-9366) carries an ever-expanding selection of new books, cards, games, and prints chosen by owners Ruth Heffron and John Vernelson. In the back of the shop is a café serving hot and cold drinks (espresso, too), soup, sandwiches, and tasty baked goods.

Gifts and Crafts

Water Witch (Main St., Castine, 207/326-4884) specializes in Indonesian batik and Liberty fabric, clothing, and accessories. Buy off the rack or choose a fabric and a style and Jean de Raat will have it made up flawlessly within a few days. Just down the street, close to the harbor, **Four Flags** (1 Main St., 207/326-8526) carries high-quality Maine and nautical gifts, plus an excellent card selection.

ENTERTAINMENT

Best place for live music is **Dennett's Wharf** (15 Sea St., 207/326-9045). Some performances require a ticket. Also head to **The Reef** (tucked underneath Four Flags facing the parking area and harbor), for pizza and entertainment.

The Trinitarian Church often brings in high-caliber musical entertainment. The Castine Town Band often performs on the common.

ACCOMMODATIONS

Inns

Castine is blessed with four fine traditional inns. This is not the place to come if you require in-room phones, air-conditioning, computer hookups, or fancy bathrooms. Rather, the pace is relaxed and the accommodations reflect the easy elegance of a bygone era.

Nicest of the four is the three-story, Queen Anne–style **⋈ Pentagöet Inn** (26 Main St., P.O. Box 4, Castine 04421, 207/326-8616 or 800/845-1701, www.pentagoet.com, May–late Oct., $99–205). Congenial innkeepers Jack Burke, previously with the foreign service, and Julie Van de Graaf, a pastry chef, took over the century-old inn in 2000 and have given it new life, upgrading rooms and furnishing them with Victorian antiques and adding handsome gardens. Their enthusiasm for the area is contagious. The inn's 16 rooms are spread out between the main house and the adjoining cottage. A hot buffet breakfast and afternoon refreshments are provided. Passports Pub is an adventure. It's chock-full of vintage photos and prints and exotic antiques. Borrow one of the inn's bikes and explore around town. The Main Street location is an easy walk from everything Castine offers, or just sit on the wrap-around porch and take it all in. Dinner here is a treat.

The three-story **Castine Inn** (33 Main St., P.O. Box 41, Castine 04421, 207/326-4365, www.castineinn.com, May–late Oct., $90–225) earns a stellar rating for its stunning semiformal gardens, extremely helpful staff, and mural-lined dining room with award-winning menu. The 15 rooms and four suites are simply but nicely furnished, updated from their 1890s origins, with twin or queen beds, private baths, and good lighting. Lots of interesting artwork is everywhere and there's a very simpatico and unpretentious air, encouraged by enthusiastic innkeepers Amy and Tom Gutow. In the small, English-style pub, hikers, bicyclists, kayakers, and less energetic guests mingle with a loyal local clientele.

Once the summer "cottage" of a Arthur Fuller, a South Boston Yacht Club commodore, **The Manor Inn** (Battle Ave., P.O. Box 873, Castine 04421, 207/326-4861 or 877/626-6746, www.manor-inn.com, $110–230) overlooks town and harbor from five mostly wooded acres elevated above Battle Avenue.

Though the atmosphere is informal, there are lots of elegant architectural touches. Nancy Watson and Tom Ehrman took over in 1998, upgrading beds, linens, and furniture; more renovations are ahead. The 13 second- and third-floor rooms are an eclectic mix—some with canopied beds and fireplaces, all with private baths. A separate guest building has a TV and games as well as Nancy's yoga studio; guests are welcome to join her morning Iyengear classes (Mon., Wed., Fri.; $12 drop-in fee). The trailhead for Witherle Woods is close by. The inn is often the site of weddings and receptions; ask before you book unless you don't mind being the odd man out. Open all year.

Castine's only oceanfront inn is **Castine Harbor Lodge** (147 Perkins St., P.O. Box 215, Castine 04421, 2077/326-4335, www.castinemaine.com, $85–245), an 1893 Edwardian mansion with open, screened, and glassed-in porches positioned to take in the views over Penobscot Bay to the Camden Hills. Most of the 16 rooms have private baths. Rates include a continental buffet breakfast. A separate Honeymoon Cottage ($1,250/week) is right on the water's edge. Also on premises is the Bagaduce Oyster Bar restaurant.

Castine's least-fancy rooms are at the **Village Inn** (P.O. Box 183, Castine 04421, 207/326-9510, $95–120), set back from Main and Water Streets. The rooms (some with shared bath) are above Bah's Bakehouse, but noise doesn't seem to be a huge problem.

Rental Cabins and Cottages

Perched in a field along the edge of Hatch's Cove, with terrific views, are the six two-bedroom, pine-paneled log cabins of **Castine Cottages** (33 Snapp's Way, Rte. 166, P.O. Box 224, Castine 04421, 207/326-8003, www.castinecottages .com) operated by Alan and Diana Snapp. Weekly rate is $625 late June–late September, $500 off-season; when available, cabins are rented nightly for $75–110. Open May–October. You'll need to provide your own sheets and towels. Several Castine Realtors have listings for summer cottage rentals; start with **Castine Realty** (5 Main St., P.O. Box 234, Castine 04421, 207/326-9392, www.castinerealty.com).

FOOD

Casual Dining

On lower Main Street is a tiny sign for **Bah's Bakehouse** (Water St., Castine, 207/326-9510, 7 A.M.–6 P.M. Mon.–Sat., opens at 8 A.M. Sun.), a higgledy-piggledy eatery of three rooms and a deck at the end of an alleyway beneath the Village Inn. Its slogan is "creative flour arrangements," and creative it is. Stop here for morning coffee, cold juices, interesting snacks and salads, homemade soups, wine or beer, and the best sandwiches in town ($2.50–6; eat in or take out). Bah's will pack a picnic basket for you or deliver an order dockside. Open March–December (off-season hours are 7 A.M.–5 P.M. Tues.–Sun.).

Dennett's Wharf (15 Sea St., 207/326-9045, 11 A.M.–9 P.M. May–Columbus Day), next to the Town Dock, is a colorful barn of a place with outside deck and front-row windjammer-watching seats in summer. Kids are welcomed. Best sandwich is grilled crabmeat ($9.95). The crayoned kids' menu includes all the usual favorites, such as mac-'n-cheese and gummy dinosaurs for dessert. Try attaching a dollar bill to the soaring ceiling; countless others have. Service is leisurely; don't dine here if you're in a hurry.

Fine Dining

Jazz music plays softly and dinner is by candlelight at the ■ **Pentagöet** (26 Main St., Castine, 207/326-8616 or 800/845-1701, 5:30–8:30 P.M. Mon.–Sat. May–late Oct.). Choices range from whole grilled lobster to slow-cooked lamb shank. Don't miss the bouillabaisse, if it's available, or the chocolate budino, a scrumptious warm Italian pudding that melts in your mouth. Entrées are in the $18–24 range.

The bilevel dining room at **The Manor Inn** (Battle Ave., Castine, 207/326-4861, 6–8:30 P.M. Mon.–Sat. in summer) overlooks the gardens and lawn. Dinner is served from an extensive menu accented with Asian flavors and Indian curries and other world flavors, accompanied by home-baked breads, and always including vegetarian choices (entrées $16–32); Tuesday night there's an extensive buffet ($25), and on select nights, there's live music. Reservations are essential on Tuesdays and weekends and for the annual July Fourth pig roast. The inn's cozy pub has a smaller and less pricey menu. Open Valentine's Day to late December, but nights vary off-season.

Also worth checking out is **Bagaduce Oyster Bar** at the Castine Harbor Lodge (207/326-4335). Go for hors d'oeuvres and drinks on the extensive porches with views to the Camden Hills. The dining room has a good local reputation, but hours of operation aren't consistent, so it's best to call; reservations are essential. Entrées are in the $20–30 range.

Destination Dining

Chef Tom Gutrow has gained a national reputation for classic and creative fare at the **Castine Inn** (Main St., Castine, 207/326-4365, 6–9 P.M. Wed.–Mon. May–late Oct.), but in 2004 the restaurant closed in August; its future is uncertain. If it does reopen and is still under Gutrow, go, but only if you can afford the $65 fixed price for five courses. Seafood is the specialty. Desserts are superlative. Appetizers and less expensive meals are served in the pub.

INFORMATION AND SERVICES

Information

Castine has no local information office, but all businesses and lodgings in town have copies of the Castine Merchants Association's visitors' brochure/map. For additional information, go to the **Castine Town Office** (Emerson Hall, 67 Court St., Castine, 207/326-4502, www.castine .me.us, 11 A.M.–3 P.M. Mon.–Fri.).

Public Library

Witherle Memorial Library (41 School St., 207/326-4375, 4–8 P.M. Mon., 11 A.M.–5 P.M. Tues.–Fri., and 11 A.M.–2 P.M. Sat.). Also accessible to the public is the **Nutting Memorial Library,** in Platz Hall on the Maine Maritime Academy campus. It's open 8 A.M.–4 P.M. Mon.–Fri. during the summer, longer hours during the school year.

Public Restrooms

Castine has public restrooms on the town dock, at the foot of Main Street.

Deer Isle

"Deer Isle is like Avalon," wrote John Steinbeck in *Travels with Charley* "it must disappear when you are not there." Deer Isle (the name of both the island and its midpoint town) has been romancing authors and artisans for decades, but it's unmistakably real to the quarrymen and fishermen who've been here for centuries. These long timers are a sturdy lot, as even Steinbeck recognized: "I would hate to try to force them to do anything they didn't want to do."

Early-18th-century maps show no name for the island, but by the late 1800s, nearly 100 families lived here, supporting themselves first by farming, then by fishing. In 1789, when Deer Isle was incorporated, 80 local sailing vessels were scouring the Gulf of Maine in pursuit of mackerel and cod, and Deer Isle men were circling the globe as yachting skippers and merchant seamen. At the same time, in the once-quiet village

of Green's Landing (now called Stonington), the shipbuilding and granite industries boomed, spurring development, prosperity, and the kinds of rough hijinks typical of commercial ports the world over.

Green's Landing became the "big city" for an international crowd of quarrymen carving out the terrain on Deer Isle and nearby Crotch Island, source of high-quality granite for Boston's Museum of Fine Arts, the Smithsonian Institution, a humongous fountain for John D. Rockefeller's New York estate, and less showy projects all along the eastern seaboard. The heyday is long past, but the industry did extend into the 20th century (including a contract for the pink granite at President John F. Kennedy's Arlington National Cemetery gravesite). Today, Crotch Island is the site of Maine's only operating island granite quarry.

Measuring about nine miles north to south

Blue Hill Peninsula

To Blue Hill

15

Sargentville

Sedgwick

175

EGGEMOGGIN
LANDING

Billings
Cove

DEER ISLE
INFORMATION
CENTER

Stave
Island

Little

THE INN AT
FERRY LANDING

175

Haven

Deer

Isle

Blastow
Cove

Carney
Island

Causeway
Beach

Eggemoggin

Reach

Benjamin R.

Pickering
Island

REACH
RD

**DEER
ISLE**

North

Deer

15

Isle

Torrey
Pond

DOW RD

Pressey
Cove

Northwest Harbor

Lily
Pond

Conary
Island

Oak
Point

Campbell
Island

Deer Isle
Village

PILGRIM'S INN

Mill
Pond

South

White
Island

Sylvester
Cove

Sunset

Long Cove

Greenlaw Cove

SUNSHINE

Mountainville

Stinson Neck

SALOME
SELLERS
HOUSE

Deer

Southeast
Harbor

Edgar M
Tennis
Preserve

Freese
Island

Sheephead
Island

ISLAND
COUNTRY
CLUB

Sunshine

Benjamin River

Isle

SOUTH DEER ISLE CROSS RD

15

Smalls Cove

Oceanville

HAYSTACK MOUNTAIN
SCHOOL OF CRAFTS

GOOSE COVE RD

15A

OCEANVILLE

GOOSE
COVE LODGE

*Crockett
Cove Woods
Preserve*

AIRPORT RD

*Settlement
Quarry*

Sheep
Island

*Barred Island
Preserve*

Crockett
Cove

Goose Cove

Burnt Cove

Webb Cove

MAIN
ST

Ames
Pond

PRÈS DU PORT

BOYCES MOTEL

Thorofare

Bold Island

Camp
Island

Stonington

THE INN ON THE HARBOR

DEER ISLE GRANITE MUSEUM

Moose
Island

Deer Island

Devil
Island

Saddleback
Island

Crotch
Island

Green
Island

Millet
Island

Bare
Island

Spruce
Island

Ferry to Isle au Haut

(plus another three miles for Little Deer Isle), the island of Deer Isle today has a handful of hamlets (including Sunshine, Sunset, Mountainville, and Oceanville) and two towns—Stonington and Deer Isle—with a population just under 3,000. Road access is via Route 15 on the Blue Hill Peninsula. A huge suspension bridge, built in 1939 over Eggemoggin Reach, links the Sargentville section of Sedgwick with Little Deer Isle; from there, a sinuous, .4-mile causeway connects to the northern tip of Deer Isle.

SIGHTS

Sightseeing on Deer Isle means exploring back roads, browsing the galleries, walking the trails, hanging out on the docks, soaking in the ambience.

Historic Houses and Museums

The 1830 **Salome Sellers House** (Rte. 15A, Sunset Village, 207/348-2897, 1–4 P.M. Wed. and Fri. early July–mid-Sept., free), a repository of local memorabilia, is the headquarters of the **Deer Isle–Stonington Historical Society.** Vol unteer guides love to provide tidbits about various items; seafarers' logs and ship models are particularly intriguing. It's just north of the Island Country Club and across from Eaton's Plumbing.

Close to the Stonington waterfront, the **Deer Isle Granite Museum** (Main St., Stonington, 207/367-6331, 9 A.M.–5 P.M. Memorial Day–Labor Day, free) was established to commemorate the centennial of the quarrying business hereabouts. Best feature of the small museum is a 15-foot-long working model of Crotch Island, center of the industry, as it appeared at the turn of the 20th century. Flatcars roll, boats glide, and derricks move—it all looks very real.

Another downtown-Stonington attraction is a Lilliputian complex known hereabouts as the **"Miniature Village."** Some years ago, the late Everett Knowlton created a dozen and a half replicas of local buildings and displayed them on granite blocks in his yard. Since his death, they've been restored and put on display each summer in town—along with a donation box to support the upkeep. The village is set up on East Main Street (Route 15), across from Bartlett's Supermarket.

A soaring, narrow, pray-as-you-go two-lane bridge is all that connects the Blue Hill Peninsula to Deer Isle.

© TOM NANGLE

© TOM NANGLE

Stonington's boat-filled harbor, with its backdrop of islands, is a shutterbug's delight.

PARKS AND PRESERVES

Foresighted benefactors have managed to set aside precious acreage for respectful public use on Deer Isle. The Nature Conservancy owns two properties, **Crockett Cove Woods Preserve** and **Barred Island Preserve.** For information, contact the Conservancy (14 Maine St., Fort Andross, Brunswick 04011, 207/729-5181). The conscientious steward of other local properties is the **Island Heritage Trust** (3 Main St., at Rte. 15, P.O. Box 42, Deer Isle 04627, 207/348-2455). When the office is open (usually 10:30 A.M.–3 P.M. weekdays July and Aug., 10 A.M.–2 P.M. Tues. and Thurs. off-season), you can pick up notecards, photos, T-shirts, and helpful maps and information on hiking trails and nature preserves. Proceeds benefit the IHT's efforts, including the purchase of 51 acres of the abandoned **Settlement Quarry** on Webb Cove (off Oceanville Rd.) in Stonington.

Settlement Quarry

Here's one of the easiest, shortest hikes (a stroll, really) in the area, leading to an impressive vista. From the parking lot on Oceanville Road (just under a mile off Rte. 15), marked by a carved granite sign, it's about five minutes to the top of the old quarry, where the viewing platform (a.k.a. the "throne room") takes in the panorama—all the way to the Camden Hills on a good day. In early August, wild raspberries are an additional enticement. Three short loop trails lead into the surrounding woods from here. A map is available in the trailhead box.

Shore Acres Preserve and Edgar Tennis Preserve

Inquire locally about these two preserves. The 145-acre Tennis Preserve, in particular, off the Sunshine Road, has very limited parking, so don't try to squeeze in if there isn't room; schedule your visit for another hour or day. When you go, allow at least 90 minutes to enjoy the 1.5-mile yellow-blazed trail. Part of the trail skirts Pickering Cove, with convenient rocky outcrops for a picnic (carry in, carry out, though). The preserve is open sunrise to sunset.

Crockett Cove Woods Preserve
Donated to The Nature Conservancy by benevolent, eco-conscious local artist Emily Muir, 98-acre Crockett Cove Woods Preserve is Deer Isle's natural gem—a coastal fog forest laden with lichens and mosses. Four interlinked trails cover the whole preserve, starting with a short nature trail. Pick up the helpful map/brochure at the registration box. Wear rubberized shoes or boots and respect adjacent private property. The preserve is open sunrise to sunset daily all year. From Deer Isle Village, take Route 15A to Sunset Village. Go 2.5 miles to Whitman Road, then to Fire Lane 88. The local contact phone number is 207/367-2674.

Ames Pond
Ames Pond is neither park nor preserve, but it might as well be. On a back road close to Stonington, it's a mandatory stop in July and August, when the pond wears a blanket of pink and white water lilies. From downtown Stonington, take Indian Point Road east, just under a mile, to the pond. There's no official parking, so if you're shooting photos, pull off the road as far as possible, respecting private property.

Causeway Beach
The most recent addition to the parks and preserves list is the beach along the causeway linking Little Deer Isle to Deer Isle. It's popular for swimming and is also a significant habitat for birds and other wildlife.

RECREATION
The **Deer Isle Walking Trails Group** (R.R. 1, Box 980, Stonington 04681, 207/367-2448) has produced a handy map—*Walking Trails of Deer Isle*—available for $1 at most island lodgings, at the Island Heritage Trust office on Main Street in Deer Isle (207/348-2455), or directly from the trails group. The map shows major and secondary roads, scenic biking and walking paths, birding areas, nature preserves, and boat-launching sites.

GETTING CRAFTY
Internationally famed artisans—sculptors and papermakers, weavers and jewelers, potters and printmakers—become the faculty each summer for the unique **Haystack Mountain School of Crafts** (Sunshine Rd., P.O. Box 518, Deer Isle 04627, 207/348-2306, www.haystack-mtn.org). Chartered in 1950, the school has weekday classes and round-the-clock studio access for the adult students, from beginners to advanced professionals. Portfolio review is required for advanced courses. Two or three evenings a week (8 P.M.), between late June and early August, faculty and visiting artists present slide/lecture programs open to the public. An hour-long Wednesday (1 P.M.) tour of the architecturally and scenically dramatic 40-acre shorefront campus usually includes visits to some of the studios. None of the work is for sale, but various galleries on Deer Isle feature the work of Haystack's artisans. Haystack is seven miles east of Deer Isle Village.

Sporting Outfitters
The biggest operation is **Old Quarry Ocean Adventures** (Stonington, 207/367-8977 or 877/479-8977, mobile 207/266-7778, www.oldquarry.com), with a broad range of outdoor-adventure choices. Bill Baker and Lisa Whittemore's ever expanding enterprise rents canoes, kayaks, sailboats, bikes, moorings, platform tent sites, and cabins. Bicycle rentals are $18 a day or $100 a week. All-day guided tours in single kayaks are $105; tandems are $110. Half-day tours are $55 and $110, respectively. Plenty of other options are available, including sunset tours, gourmet picnic paddles, and lots more. Check the website for details. Rental rates are $55 per day for a single, $65 for a tandem. Half-day rates are $40 and $50, respectively. They'll deliver and pick up anywhere on the island for a fee of $20. If you're bringing your own kayak, you can park your car and launch from here ($5 per boat for launching). Old Quarry is off the Oceanville Road, less than a mile from Route 15, just before you reach the Settlement Quarry preserve. It's well signposted.

Blue Hill Peninsula

A smaller kayaking outfitter is in the village of Sunset—not surprisingly, on the western side of the island. **Granite Island Guide Service** (66 Dunham Point Rd., Deer Isle 04627, 207/348-2668, www.graniteislandguide.com) is owned by Professional Maine Guide Dana Douglass and his wife, Anne. All-day guided trips, including lunch, are $90 adults, $60 children under 12. Half-day trips are $50 adults, $40 children.

Another outfitter is **Finest Kind** (Center District Crossroad, about halfway between Routes 15 and 15A, 207/348-7714). Bicycle rentals are $15 per day or $75 per week. Kayak or canoe rentals are $35 per day solo, $45 per day tandem, including paddles, lifejackets, spray skirts, delivery, and pickup.

With lots of islets and protected coves, **sea kayaking** in the waters around Deer Isle, especially off Stonington, has come up fast in the recreation department.

If you sign up with the **Maine Island Trail Association** (Box C, Rockland 04841, www.mita.org; $45 a year), you'll receive a handy manual that steers you to more than a dozen islands in the Deer Isle archipelago where you can camp, hike, and picnic—eco-sensitively, please. Boat traffic can be a bit heavy at the height of summer, so to best appreciate the tranquillity of this area, try this in September, after the Labor Day holiday. Nights can be cool, but days are likely to be brilliant. (See Accommodations for information on B&Bs that specially cater to sea kayakers.)

As with so many other parts of Maine, the roads on Deer Isle are narrow and winding, and hazardous for **bicycling.**

Swimming

The island's only major freshwater swimming hole is the **Lily Pond,** northeast of Deer Isle Village. Just north of the Shakespeare School, turn into the Deer Run Apartments complex. Park and take the path to the pond, which has a shallow area for small children.

Golf and Tennis

About two miles south of Deer Isle Village, watch for the large sign (on the left) for the **Island Country Club** (Rte. 15A, Sunset, 207/348-2379), a nine-hole public course that's been here since 1928. Starting times are first-come, first-served, and greens fees are low; no credit cards. Open late May to late September. Also at the club are three beautifully maintained tennis courts. Or just commandeer a rocking chair and watch the action from one of the porches. The club's cheeseburgers and salads are among the island's best bargain lunches.

Boat Tours

If you're not up for self-propulsion, from mid-June through early September, the *Miss Lizzie* or the *Mink* departs at 9 A.M. and 2 P.M. daily from the Isle au Haut Boat Company dock in Stonington for a narrated one-hour trip among the islands. Cost is $14 adults, $6 kids. Reservations are advisable, especially in July and August. Parking is available at the pier for $9. The *Miss Lizzie* and the *Mink* are owned by the **Isle au Haut Boat Company** (Seabreeze Ave., Stonington, 207/367-5193, fax 207/367-6503, www.isleauhaut.com), the same company that operates the regular mail boat/passenger-ferry service to offshore Isle au Haut .

Captain Walter Reed's **Guided Island Tours** (207/348-6789, www.guidedislandtours.com) aboard the *Gael* are custom-designed for a maximum of four passengers. Walt is a Registered Maine Guide and professional biologist who also is steward for Mark Island Lighthouse and several uninhabited islands in the area. He provides in-depth perspective and the local scoop. The cost is $37.50 pp for the first hour plus $15 pp for each additional hour. Reservations required; box lunches are available for an additional fee.

SHOPPING

The greatest concentration of shops is in Stonington, where galleries, clothing boutiques, and eclectic shops line Main Street. Galleries are salted throughout Deer Isle and Stonington.

Antiques and Crafts

When you head south, toward Deer Isle Village, you'll come to **Old Deer Isle Parish House**

Antiques (7 Church St., Rte. 15, Deer Isle, 207/348-9964), a funky shop heavy into vintage clothing, antique kitchen utensils, and other collectibles, with an especially nice collection of quilts, rugs, and samplers. No credit cards.

Just a bit south is **Dockside Quilt Gallery** (33 Church St., Deer Isle, 207/348-2531), where Nancy Knowlton and Kelly Pratt stitch beautiful quilts. Also here are Re-Bears, one-of-a-kind teddy bears handcrafted from vintage furs and fabrics. Custom quilts and bears available.

When you get to the bottom of the island, **The Clown** (6 Thurlow's Hill Rd., Stonington, 207/367-6348) awaits. The imaginative owners came up with this combination of art, antiques, and . . . food and wine. Look, it works. Part of the key is the owners' farm in Tuscany, source of extra-virgin olive oil, wines, Deruta pottery, unusual furnishings, and other "necessities." Art openings are also wine tastings—a fine idea.

Art and Craft Galleries

Thanks to the presence and influence of Haystack Mountain School of Crafts, supertalented artists and artisans lurk in every corner of the island. Most are tucked away on back roads, and many have studios open to the public, so watch for roadside signs and pick up a free copy (available in shops and galleries statewide) of the Maine Crafts Association's annual *Maine Guide to Crafts and Culture* (207/780-1807, www.mainecrafts.org). This is just a sampling.

Name a craft and Mary Nyburg probably has an example in her high-ceilinged barn, the **Blue Heron Gallery & Studio** (22 Church St., Deer Isle, 207/348-2940). Formerly a Haystack board member and still an honorary trustee, she provides a retail outlet for the work of the school's internationally renowned faculty—printmakers, blacksmiths, potters, weavers, papermakers, glassworkers, and more. Prices are reasonable.

The **Deer Isle Artists Association** (13 Dow Rd., Deer Isle, 207/348-2330) is headquartered less than a mile northwest of the village. The co-op gallery features two-week exhibits of paintings, prints, drawings, and photos by local pros.

One of the island's premier galleries is Elena Kubler's **The Turtle Gallery** (61 N. Deer Isle

Make no mistake about it, Stonington is a working harbor and locals will capture lobster or tourists, depending upon the season.

© TOM NANGLE

Blue Hill Peninsula

Rd., Rte. 15, Deer Isle, 207/348-9977), in a handsome space formerly known as the Old Centennial House Barn (owned by the late Haystack director Francis Merritt). Group and solo shows of contemporary paintings, prints, and crafts are hung upstairs and down, and there's usually sculpture in the garden. It's just north of Deer Isle Village—across from the Shakespeare School, oldest on the island.

Eastern Bay Gallery (602 Main St., Stonington, 207/367-6368) occupies a bright, airy space at the far end of the main drag. Look for unique jewelry, functional granite objects, knitted hats, pottery, and lovely handwoven chenille pieces.

Here's an interesting juxtaposition—in a pastoral island setting—**William Mor Stoneware and Oriental Rugs** (663 Reach Rd., Deer Isle, 207/348-2822). Bill Mor has been throwing pottery since the 1970s, and you'll see that here, but he also imports natural-dyed Afghan and Tibetan rugs via the nonprofit Cultural Survival organization—stunning work for a worthy cause. Reach Road is a mile south of the Route 15 Little Deer Isle–Deer Isle causeway; the shop is 3.3 miles down the road.

On Route 15, about 500 feet south of Reach Road and almost across from the Holden Homestead, is the compact home of **George Hardy** (207/348-2885), a self-taught folk carver who's been featured in a solo video and turns out incredibly imaginative carved and painted animals. George is here most days. Watch for the Hardy Folk Carving sign, bring your wallet (cash only), and carry home an unusual treasure.

Now for a bit of whimsy. From Route 15 in Deer Isle Village, take the Sunshine Road east 2.9 miles to **Peter Beerits Sculpture** (600 Sunshine Rd., Deer Isle, 800/777-6845). The meadows and woods surrounding the studio teem with whimsical wood and metal sculptures (all for sale). The property is also home to Beerits's other enterprise, **Nervous Nellie's Jams and Jellies,** known for outstandingly creative condiments; sample the hot pepper jelly or blackberry peach conserve or ginger syrup. The promotional brochures are hilarious. Best time to come is May to early October, 9 A.M.–5 P.M., when the

shop operates the ultracasual **Mountainville Café,** serving tea, coffee, and delicious scones—with, of course, Nervous Nellie's products.

Okay, it's not really a gallery, but if you're looking for Maine pottery, weaving, metalwork, pewterware, imported tiles, or walking sticks, go directly to **Harbor Farm** (Rte. 15, Little Deer Isle, 207/348-7755 or 800/342-8003), one of the state's best shops. Based in a mid-19th-century schoolhouse a mile south of the Deer Isle suspension bridge, Lee and Richard McWilliams carry thousands of very unusual, high-quality items. I've had out-of-state friends come here to pick tiles for their kitchen.

ENTERTAINMENT AND EVENTS

Stonington's National Historic Landmark, the 1912 **Opera House** (207/367-2788, www.operahousearts.org), is home to Opera House Arts, which hosts films, plays, lectures, and workshops from Memorial Day to Labor Day.

From early June to late August, on varying weeknights, slide programs, lectures, demonstrations, and concerts start at 8 P.M. at the **Haystack Mountain School of Crafts** in Sunshine (see the sidebar Getting Crafty).

Mid-July brings the **Stonington Lobsterboat Races,** very popular competitions held in the harbor, with lots of possible vantage points. Stonington is one of the major locales in the lobsterboat race circuit.

Island Heritage Trust sponsors a series of walks, talks, and tours from mid-June through mid-September. For information and reservations, call 207/348-2455.

ACCOMMODATIONS
Inns and B&Bs

Pilgrim's Inn (20 Main St., P.O. Box 69, Deer Isle 04627, 207/348-6615, www.pilgrimsinn.com. $129–209) is a beautifully restored Colonial building overlooking the peaceful Mill Pond. The National Historic Register inn began life in 1793 as a boardinghouse named The Ark; be sure to check out the fascinating guestbook, with names dating to 1901. The inn has sloping lawns, bikes for guests, an adjacent gift shop (The Rugosa Rose), and a fine dining room serving dinner to guests and the public by reservation. Open mid-May to mid-October.

Just when you're convinced you're lost, and the paved road has turned to dirt, you arrive at **⋈ Goose Cove Lodge** (Goose Cove Rd., P.O. Box 40, Sunset 04683, 207/348-2508 or 800/728-1963 outside Maine, www.goosecovelodge.com, $185–575), a 20-acre hillside complex of rustic and modern cottages/cabins and main-lodge rooms and suites—all with private baths, most with fireplaces, and many with stunning views of secluded Goose Cove. Request one of the seven older "secluded cabins," with cove-facing decks. Rates vary widely here, and so does the decor; the cost can add up (18 percent service and 7 percent lodging taxes are on top of the quoted rate). All cabins/cottages require a one-week minimum stay (although sometimes there are last-minute opportunities for shorter bookings), and some have a three-person minimum rate July to Labor Day. Rates include breakfast; dinner is additional, but a rate including dinner is planned for 2005. The inn organizes nature walks and astronomy talks and provides maps and descriptions of local trails, including the Nature Conservancy's adjacent Barred Island Preserve. Bikes, kayaks, and games are available for guests. The dining room, open to the public by reservation for dinner, has a reputation well beyond Deer Isle. Children are welcome, and the inn has an extensive free children's program that includes dinner. The inn is open mid-May to mid-October. The lodge is 4.5 miles from Route 15, via Deer Isle Village.

⋈ The Inn on the Harbor (Main St., P.O. Box 69, Stonington 04681, 207/367-2420 or 800/942-2420, www.innontheharbor.com, $115–195) is exactly as its name proclaims. Its expansive deck hangs right over the harbor. Although recently updated, the 1880s complex still has an air of unpretentiousness. Most of the 13 rooms and suites, each named after windjammers, have fantastic harbor views and private or shared decks where you can keep an eye on lobsterboats, small ferries, windjammers, and pleasure craft. (Binoculars are provided.) Rooms on the street can be noisy at night. Rates include a continental buffet breakfast. An espresso bar is open 11 A.M.–4:30 P.M. Nearby are antique, gift, and craft shops; guest moorings are available. Open all year, but call ahead off-season, when rates are lower.

In downtown Stonington, just up the hill from the Inn on the Harbor and convenient for walking to everything (even a small sandy beach a mile away) is **Près du Port** (W. Main St. and Highland Ave., P.O. Box 319, Stonington 04681, 207/367-5007, $110), a bright B&B run by amiable innkeeper Charlotte Casgrain. After many summers at a Deer Isle French summer camp, and a career as a Connecticut French teacher, she's settled here. Two rooms have detached baths, one has a private bath; there are vanity sinks in the rooms. Children are welcome; there's even a toy cupboard to entertain them. No credit cards. Open May–October. When Deer Isle beds are scarce at the height of summer, Charlotte is the best resource for dozens of last-minute overnight rooms in local homes. This location is ideal if you're en route to or returning from Isle au Haut.

Eggemoggin Reach is almost on the doorstep at **The Inn at Ferry Landing** (77 Old Ferry Rd., Deer Isle 04627, 207/348-7760, www.ferrylanding.com, $110–165), overlooking the abandoned Sargentville–Deer Isle ferry wharf. The view is wide open from the inn's "great room," where guests gather to read, play games, talk, and watch passing windjammers. Professional musician Gerald Wheeler has installed two grand pianos in the room; it's a treat when he plays. His wife, Jean, is the hospitable innkeeper, managing three water-view guest rooms and a suite. A harpsichord and a great view are big pluses in the suite. The Mooring, an annex that sleeps five, is rented by the week ($1,300, without breakfast). The inn is open all year except Thanksgiving and Christmas.

Motels

Just after you go over the bridge from Brooksville, immediately on your right and fronting on Eggemoggin Reach is **⋈ Eggemoggin Landing** (204 Little Deer Isle Rd., P.O. Box 126, Little Deer Isle

Blue Hill Peninsula

04650, 207/348-6115, www.acadia.net/eggland, $67–85). Rooms are clean with fabulous views, and rates include a continental breakfast. Sisters Restaurant, a gourmet shop, and a take-out operation are also on the property, as is a small playground, picnic area, dock, and beach (brrrr). Sailing cruises as well as bicycle, sea kayak, and motorboat rentals are available.

Right in downtown Stonington, just across the street from the harbor, is **Boyces Motel** (44 Main St., P.O. Box 94, Stonington, 800/224-2421 or 207/367-2421, www.boycesmotel.com, $60–115). Eleven units, all with TV, phones, and refrigerators; some have kitchens and living rooms, and one has two bedrooms. Boyce's also has a private deck for its guests on the harbor. Ask for rooms well back from Main Street to lessen the noise of locals cruising the street at night. Open year-round.

Seasonal Rentals

For house and cottage rentals by the week, month, or season, contact **Island Vacation Rentals** (P.O. Box 446, Stonington 04681, 207/367-5095, www.deerisleproperties.com). Plan well ahead, as the best properties get snapped up as much as a year in advance. Another rental agency is **Sargent's Rentals** (P.O. Box 115, Stonington 04681, 207/367-5156, www.sargentsrentalsinc.com).

Campgrounds

Deer Isle has only two campgrounds, both owned by **Old Quarry Ocean Adventures** (130 Settlement Rd., Stonington, 207/367-8977, www.oldquarry.com, www.sunshinecampground.com), so plan ahead if you're thinking about camping. **Sunshine Campground** has 22 wooded RV (maximum 40 feet, $26) and tent sites ($22). Facilities include a laundry, firewood, and a small store. Ocean access is available at Old Quarry. Open Memorial Day weekend to mid-October. From Deer Isle Village, the campground is on the Sunshine Road, 5.7 miles east of Route 15. **Old Quarry Ocean Adventures Campground** has both oceanfront and secluded sites for tents; RVs are allowed only in the off-season, although pop-ups are permitted in one site and the parking lot. Platform tent sites are $26–32. Facilities

include swimming pond, hiking trails, laundry, camp store, and kayak launch.

FOOD

Stonington is a dry town, so you'll want to plan for beer or wine with dinner (except for the Pilgrim's Inn, Goose Cove Lodge, and Finest Kind Dining, which have liquor licenses). Burnt Cove Market can fix you up with the regular stuff; buy fine wines at The Clown.

Miscellany

Craving sweets? Head to **Susie Qu's Sweets and Curiosities** (180 Sunset Crossroad, Deer Isle, 207/348-6013, 9 A.M.–3 P.M. Mon.–Sat.) for a fine selection of cookies and pies as well as gifty items.

Best pizza on the island? Head for **Burnt Cove Market** (Rte. 15, Stonington, 207/367-2681, 6 A.M.–8 P.M., to 9 P.M. Fri. and Sat., opens at 9 A.M. Sun.). Besides pizza, you can get fried chicken and sandwiches, plus beer and wine.

Between May and October, every Friday the Congregational Church parking lot in Deer Isle Village is the locale for the **Deer Isle–Stonington Farmers' Market,** selling smoked meats, fresh herbs and flowers, produce, maple syrup, jams and jellies, and more. Hours are 10 A.M.–noon.

Family-Friendly Home Cooking

In July or August, don't show up at **Finest Kind Dining** (70 Center District Crossroad, Deer Isle, 207/348-7714, 5–9 P.M., mid-May–mid-Oct.) without a dinner reservation. This log-cabin family restaurant is no longer a secret. Nothing fancy—just good, homemade all-American food served conscientiously in a come-as-you-are setting. Pizza, pasta, prime rib, seafood. And save room for dessert. Wheelchair access; liquor license. The restaurant, owned by the Perez family, is halfway between Route 15 and Sunset Road (Route 15A).

M Harbor Café (Main St., Stonington 04681, 207/367-5099, 6 A.M.–8 P.M. Mon.–Thurs., to 9 P.M. Fri. and Sat., and to 2 P.M. Sun.) is *the* place to go for breakfast (you can eavesdrop on the local fisherfolk if you're early enough), but it's also reliable for lunch and dinner (especially on Friday nights for the seafood fry, with free seconds). The food is well prepared, and there's a lot more than fried fish on the menu. Try to snag the front window table and watch the world go by.

The **Fisherman's Friend Restaurant** (40 School St., Rte. 15A, Stonington, 207/367-2442, 11 A.M.–8 P.M. daily, to 9 P.M. Fri. and Sat. July and Aug.) gets high marks for respectable food, generous portions, fresh seafood, and outstanding desserts. It's all very casual—pine paneling, booths, and reasonable prices—the Friday night fish fry is $7.50. BYOL. It's open April–October.

Casual Dining

Setting a new tone for dining in downtown Stonington is **Maritime Café** (27 Main St., Stonington, 207/367-2600, 11:30 A.M.–2:30 P.M. and 5:30–8:30 P.M.). Big windows frame the harbor from the dining room, and there's also seating on the harborside deck. The menu emphasis seafood (no surprise), but there are other choices and always a vegetarian selection. Entrées run $17–23. Note: If you bring your own wine, you'll be charged a corkage fee.

Lobster, crab cakes, and even New England pot roast are on the menu at **Sisters Restaurant** (204 Little Deer Isle Rd., P.O. Box 126, Little Deer Isle 04650, 207/348-6115). The owners initially gained fame with their commercial fresh salsa. The informal dining area has views of Eggemoggin Reach on one side, a cove on the other. Entrées are $14–19. Also on the premises is a take-out window where you can get lobster, fried fish, and other such fare.

When the weather's perfect, and you want seafood that's a bit different, in a fabulous setting, **Cockatu** (Carter's Seafood, 24 Carter Ln., off Oceanville Rd., Stonington, 207/367-0900, noon–8 P.M. July and Aug.) delivers. Fresh seafood, right out of the fish store, is cooked to order with some interesting preparations available ($13–22). It's takeout by definition: order inside then grab an outside table with serene views over idyllic Webb Cove and by the cockatoo, from which the operation gets its name. You won't find a finer place or

better price for lobster, either. Do save room for the homemade but fancy desserts. BYOL.

Creativity defines the menu at **Lily's Café** (450 Airport Rd. at Rte. 15, Stonington, 207/367-5936, 7 A.M.–4 P.M. Mon., Tues., and Fri., to 8 P.M. Wed. and Thurs.), in a cute house at the corner of the Airport Road just over two miles from downtown. It's all very casual; order at the counter and find a table. (Some of the tables have fun windowpane shadowboxes.) Eat here or assemble a *haut gourmet* picnic: veggie and meat sandwiches, Mediterranean salads, cheeses, and homemade soups and breads. BYOL. Alas, it's closed weekends.

Fine Dining

At the **Pilgrim's Inn** (Main St., Sunset Rd., Deer Isle Village, 207/348-6615), dinner is a scheduled affair, elegantly casual, in the restored barn. At 6 P.M., delicious hors d'oeuvres are served in the common room; at 6:30 P.M., seating for dinner begins (entrées $18–26). Chef Jonathan Chase has a long-standing reputation for creative fare using local ingredients, many from the area's gardens. Reservations are required. This is a grown-up kind of place, so don't bring children unless they qualify as angelic. Open mid-May to mid-October.

Running head-to-head with the Pilgrim's Inn in the culinary department is **Goose Cove Lodge** (Goose Cove Rd., Sunset, 207/348-2508, Tues.–Sun. by reservation), where creative four-course dinners are served to guests and the public in the attractive main lodge restaurant, called The Point. The view is gorgeous. Each night there's also a special children's menu (part of the children's program); entertainment follows dinner three nights a week. Call well ahead for holiday and weekend reservations; Goose Cove may be remote, but it's no secret. Open mid-May to mid-October.

Lobster-in-the-Rough

New owners at **Eaton's Lobster Pool** (Blastow's Cove, Little Deer Isle, 207/348-2383, 4:30–9 P.M. daily mid-June to mid-Sept., Fri.–Sun. in spring and fall) have gussied up the place a bit, including adding beer and wine service. You'll find more interesting food and faster service at other island restaurants, but you'd be hard put to find a better view than here on Blastow's Cove—but you'll pay for it. Dramatic sunsets can even subdue the usual din in the rustic dining room. Reservations are advisable, especially on weekends. Look for signs across from the chamber of commerce information booth.

INFORMATION AND SERVICES

Information

The **Deer Isle–Stonington Chamber of Commerce** (P.O. Box 459, Stonington 04681, 207/348-6124, www.deerislemaine.com) has a summer information booth on a grassy triangle on Route 15 in Little Deer Isle, a quarter of a mile after crossing the bridge from Sargentville (Sedgwick). Staffed by volunteers, the office has a rather erratic schedule, even during the summer: allegedly 10 A.M.–4 P.M. weekdays and 11 A.M.–5 P.M. Sunday.

Public Library

Across from the Pilgrim's Inn is the **Chase Emerson Memorial Library** (Main St., Deer Isle Village, 207/348-2899, 11 A.M.–3 P.M. Mon. and Wed., 9 A.M.–noon Sat.). Those hours complement those of the **Stonington Public Library** (Main St., Stonington, 207/367-5926, 12:30–4:30 P.M. Tues. and Fri., 10 A.M.–noon Sat.).

Public Restrooms

Public restrooms are at the Atlantic Avenue Hardware pier and at the Stonington Town Hall, Main Street, and at the Chase Emerson Library in Deer Isle Village.

Isle au Haut

Eight miles off Stonington lies 4,700-acre Isle au Haut, roughly half of which belongs to Acadia National Park. Pronounced variously as "I'll-a-HO" or "I'LL-a-ho," the island has nearly 20 miles of hiking trails, excellent birding, a tiny village, and one rustic, romantic, and pricey inn.

About 60 souls call 5,800-acre Isle au Haut home year-round, most of them eking out a living from the sea. Each summer, the population temporarily swells with day-trippers, campers, and cottagers—then settles back in fall to the measured pace of life on an offshore island.

Samuel de Champlain, threading his way through this archipelago in 1605 and noting the island's prominent central ridge, came up with the name of Isle au Haut—High Island. Appropriately, the tallest peak (543 feet) is now named Mount Champlain.

More recent fame has come to the island thanks to island-based author Linda Greenlaw, of *Perfect Storm* fame, who wrote *The Lobster Chronicles.* Although that book piqued interest, Isle au Haut remains uncrowded and well off the beaten tourist track.

Most of the southern half of the six-mile-long island belongs to Acadia National Park, thanks to the wealthy summer visitors who began arriving in the 1880s. It was their heirs who, in the 1940s, donated valuable acreage to the federal government. Today, this offshore division of the national park has a well-managed 20-mile network of trails, a few lean-tos, several miles of unpaved road, and summertime passenger-ferry service to the park entrance.

In the island's northern half are the private residences of fisherfolk and summer folk, a minuscule village (including a market and post office), a five-mile paved road, and a lighthouse inn. The only vehicles on the island are owned by residents.

If spending the night on Isle au Haut sounds appealing (it is), you'll need to plan well ahead; it's no place for spur-of-the-moment sleepovers. (Even spontaneous day trips aren't always possible.)

◪ ACADIA NATIONAL PARK

Mention Acadia National Park and most people think of Bar Harbor and Mount Desert Island, where more than three million visitors arrive each year. The Isle au Haut section of the park sees maybe 5,000 visitors a year—partly because only 48 people a day (not counting campers) are allowed to land here. But the remoteness of the island and the scarcity of beds and campsites also contribute to the low count.

Near the town landing, where the year-round mail boat docks, is the **Park Ranger Station,** where you can pick up trail maps and park information—and use the island's only public facilities (outhouses).

A loop road circles the whole island; an unpaved section goes through the park, connecting with the paved nonpark section. Walking is easy. Beyond the road, none of the park's 20 miles of trails could be labeled "easy"; the footing is rocky, rooty, and often squishy. But the trails *are* well marked, and the views—of islets, distant hills, and ocean—maximize the effort.

The most used park trail is the four- to five-mile (one-way) **Duck Harbor Trail,** connecting the town landing with Duck Harbor. Figure about two hours each way. (You can use this route or follow the road to get to the campground when the summer ferry ends its Duck Harbor run.) Toughest trail is probably **Duck Harbor Mountain,** about 1.2 miles (one-way) that'll take you about three hours round-trip. For terrific shoreline scenery, take the **Western Head** and **Cliff Trails,** at the island's southwestern corner. If the tide is out (and *only* if it's out), you can walk across the tidal flats to the quaintly named Western Ear for views back toward the island. Western Ear is private, so don't linger. The **Goat Trail** adds another four miles (round-trip) of moderate hiking east of the Cliff Trail; views are fabulous and birding is good, but you'll need to decide whether there's time to catch the return mail boat.

The best part about staying overnight on Isle au Haut is that you'll have so much more than seven hours to enjoy this idyllic island.

RECREATION

Hiking on national park trails is the major recreation on Isle au Haut, and even in the densest fog, you'll see valiant hikers going for it. **Biking** is a bit iffier, limited to the 12 or so miles of paved and unpaved roads. If you're staying at The Keeper's House, bicycles are handy around the village and for going swimming. Mountain bikes are not allowed on the park's hiking trails, and rangers try to discourage park visitors from bringing them to the island. The mail boat carries bikes only to the town landing, not to the park's Duck Harbor Landing.

For **freshwater swimming,** head for Long Pond, a skinny, 1.5-mile-long swimming hole running north-south on the east side of the island. You can bike over there, clockwise along the road, almost five miles, from the town landing. Or bum a ride from an island resident. If you're only here for the day, though, there's not enough time to do this *and* get in any hiking. Opt for the hiking.

ACCOMMODATIONS AND FOOD

There are no restaurants on Isle au Haut, so if you're coming for a day trip, bring sufficient food and water. If you're staying overnight, accommodations provide meals.

The most exotic and priciest overnight option is **The Keeper's House** (P.O. Box 26, Lighthouse Point, Isle au Haut 04645, off-island 207/367-2261, $300–375), Maine's only lightstation inn. Attached to Robinson's Point Light (automated) and within night sight of three other lighthouses, the five-room inn gets booked up months ahead. Judi Burke, daughter of a Cape Cod lightkeeper, bought the 1907 National Historic Register building with her husband, Jeff, in 1986. They're avid recyclers and environmentalists. The top-floor Garret Room has the only private bath. The three other rooms in the main building share two baths. Best view is from The Keeper's Room, overlooking the light tower and Isle au Haut Thorofare. Detached from the main house is the rustic Oil House, with a solar shower and private outhouse. Guests relax outdoors or gather in the small living room. Rates include breakfast, lunch, and candlelight dinners; no red meat is served. BYOL and pack light. Added to the rate is a 15 percent service charge and 7 percent lodging tax; ouch! Single-speed bikes are available free for guests. If you're going hiking or biking, the Burkes will pack you a

Blue Hill Peninsula

Stay at The Keeper's House on Isle au Haut, and the island's lighthouse is out your front door.

lunch. No electricity, no phones, no smoking, no credit cards, no pets, no stress. Nirvana. Open mid-May–October.

Camping

You'll need to get your bid in early to reserve one of the five six-person lean-tos at **Duck Harbor Campground,** open May 15–October 15. Before April 1, contact the park for a reservation request form: Acadia National Park (P.O. Box 177, Bar Harbor 04609, 207/288-3338, www.nps.gov/acad). Anytime from April 1 on *(not before, or they'll send it back to you),* return the completed form, along with a check for $25, covering camping for up to six people for a maximum of five nights May 15–June 15, three nights June 15–September 15, and five nights again September 15–October 15. Competition is stiff in the height of summer, so list alternate dates. The park refunds the check if there's no space; otherwise, it'll send your "special-use permit" (*DO NOT* forget to bring it along). There's no additional camping fee.

Unless you don't mind backpacking nearly five miles to reach the campground, try to plan your visit between mid-June and Labor Day, when the mail boat makes a stop in Duck Harbor. It's wise to call the Isle au Haut Company for the current ferry schedule before choosing dates for a lean-to reservation.

Trash policy is carry-in/carry-out, so pack a trash bag or two with your gear. Also bring a container for carting water from the campground pump, since it's .3 mile from the lean-tos. It's a longish walk to the general store for food—when you could be off hiking the island's trails—so bring enough to cover your stay.

GETTING THERE

Unless you have your own vessel, the only access to Isle au Haut's town landing is via the private boat owned by the **Isle au Haut Boat Company** (Seabreeze Ave., P.O. Box 709, Stonington 04681, 207/367-5193, fax 207/367-6503, www.isleauhaut.com), which generally operates four daily trips Monday–Saturday and two on Sunday between mid-June and Labor Day. Other months, there are two or three trips Monday–Saturday. Best advice is to request a copy of the current schedule, covering dates, variables, fares, and extras.

April to mid-October round-trips are $32 adults, $16 kids under 12 (two bags per adult, one bag per child). Round-trip surcharges: bikes ($16), kayaks/canoes ($30 minimum), pets ($8). Weather seldom affects the schedule, but be aware that ultraheavy seas could cancel a trip.

From mid-June to Labor Day, Monday–Saturday, there is twice-daily ferry service from Stonington to Duck Harbor, at the edge of Isle au Haut's Acadia National Park campground. For a day trip, the schedule allows you seven hours on the island. No boats or bikes are allowed on this route, and no dogs are allowed in the campground. A ranger boards the boat at the town landing and goes along to Duck Harbor to answer questions and distribute maps. Before mid-June and after Labor Day, and on Sundays in the peak season, you'll be off-loaded at the Isle au Haut town landing, about five miles from Duck Harbor. The six-mile passage from Stonington to the Isle au Haut town landing takes 45 minutes; the trip to Duck Harbor tacks on 15 minutes more.

Ferries depart from the **Isle au Haut Boat Company Dock** (Seabreeze Ave., off E. Main St. in downtown Stonington). Parking ($9 outside, $11 indoors, per day) is available next to the ferry landing. Arrive at least an hour early to get all this settled so you don't miss the boat. Better yet, spend the night on Deer Isle before heading to Isle au Haut.

Acadia Region

Summer folk have been visiting Mount Desert Island (MDI) for millennia. The earliest Native Americans discovered fabulous fishing and clamming, good hunting and camping, and invigorating salt air here; today's arrivals find variations on the same theme: thousands of lodgings and campsites, hundreds of restaurant seats, dozens of shops, plus 40,000 acres of Acadia National Park.

It's no coincidence that artists were a large part of the 19th-century vanguard here: the dramatic landscape, with both bare and wooded mountains descending to the sea, still inspires everyone who sees it. Once the word got out, painterly images began confirming the reports,

and the surge began. Even today, no saltwater locale on the entire eastern seaboard can compete with the variety of scenery on Mount Desert Island.

Those pioneering artists brilliantly portrayed this area, adding romantic touches to landscapes that really need no enhancement. From the 1,530-foot summit of Cadillac Mountain, preferably at an off hour, you'll sense the grandeur of it all—the slopes careening toward the bay and the handful of islands below looking like the last footholds between Bar Harbor and Bordeaux.

French explorer Samuel de Champlain apparently gets credit for naming it l'Ile des Monts

©TOM NANGLE

Must-Sees

Look for **M** to find the sights and activities you can't miss and **M** for the best dining and lodging.

M Park Loop Road: If you do nothing else on Mount Desert, drive this magnificent road that takes in many of Acadia National Park's highlights (page 304).

M Carriage Roads: Whether you walk, bike, or ride in a horse-drawn carriage, do make it a point to see Mr. Rockefeller's roads and bridges (page 305).

M Jordan Pond House: For more than a century, it's been afternoon tea and popovers on the

Duck Brook Bridge in Acadia National Park

lawn of the Jordan Pond House. Do make reservations for the afternoon pick-me-up, perhaps for after walking or biking the many carriage roads that lead here (page 308).

M Abbe Museum: The downtown Abbe Museum and its seasonal museum at Sieur de Monts Springs are fascinating places to while away a few hours and learn about Maine's Native American heritage (page 311).

M Dive-In Theater Boat Cruise: Got kids? Don't miss this tour, where Diver Ed brings the undersea world aboard (page 316).

M Somes Sound: It's worth the journey to the quiet side of the island to see the only fjord on the East Coast (page 327).

M Asticou and Thuya Gardens: Magical and enchanting these two peaceful gardens. While Zen-like Asticou is best seen in spring, Thuya delivers color through summer and also has hiking paths (page 328).

M Wendell Gilley Museum: Gilley's intricately carved birds, from miniature shorebirds to life-size birds of prey, are a marvel to behold (page 332).

M Schoodic Section of Acadia National Park: Remote and raw best describe the crashing surf against slabs of pink granite at the tip of the Schoodic peninsula. If your plans don't extend beyond Mount Desert, you can take a ferry from Bar Harbor and the free Explorer bus to get here (page 343).

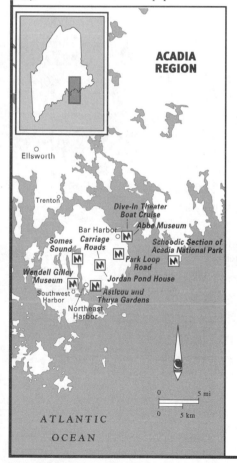

ACADIA REGION

Ellsworth

Trenton

Dive-In Theater Boat Cruise

Abbe Museum

Bar Harbor

Somes Sound

Carriage Roads

Schoodic Section of Acadia National Park

Park Loop Road

Wendell Gilley Museum

Jordan Pond House

Southwest Harbor

Asticou and Thuya Gardens

Northeast Harbor

0   5 mi

0   5 km

ATLANTIC OCEAN

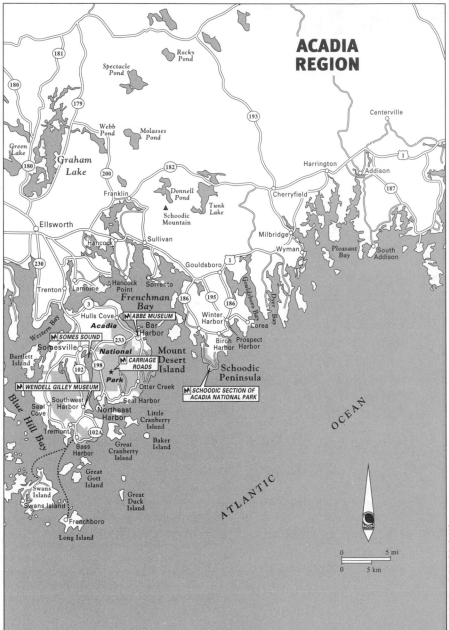

ACADIA
REGION

Rocky
Pond

Spectacle
Pond

Centerville

Webb
Pond

Molasses
Pond

Green
Lake

Graham
Lake

Harrington

Addison

Franklin

Donnell
Pond

Cherryfield

Schoodic
Mountain

Tunk
Lake

Ellsworth

Milbridge

Hancock

Sullivan

Wyman

Pleasant
Bay

South
Addison

Gouldsboro

Hancock
Point

Sorrento

Trenton

Lamoine

Frenchman
Bay

Winter
Harbor

Corea

Hulls Cove

ABBE MUSEUM

Bar
Harbor

Birch
Harbor

Prospect
Harbor

Acadia

SOMES SOUND

Somesville

National

Mount
Desert
Island

Schoodic
Peninsula

Bartlett
Island

CARRIAGE
ROADS

Park

SCHOODIC SECTION OF
ACADIA NATIONAL PARK

WENDELL GILLEY MUSEUM

Otter Creek

OCEAN

Seal Harbor

Seal
Cove

Southwest
Harbor

Northeast
Harbor

Little
Cranberry
Island

Tremont

Blue Hill Bay

Bass
Harbor

Great
Cranberry
Island

Baker
Island

Great
Gott
Island

ATLANTIC

Swans
Island

Great
Duck
Island

Swans Island

Frenchboro

Long Island

MOON

0   5 mi

0   5 km

© AVALON TRAVEL PUBLISHING, INC.

Déserts (pronounced Mount de-SERT), "island of bare mountains," when he sailed by in 1604. The island is anything but deserted today. Even as you approach the island, via the shire town of Ellsworth and especially in Trenton, you'll run the gauntlet of a minor-league Disneyland, with water slides, bumper cars, and enough high-cholesterol eateries to stun the surgeon general. Don't panic. Acadia National Park lies ahead. Even on the most crowded days, if you venture more than a few steps into the park, you'll find you have it nearly to yourself. I've hiked popular and easy Great Head on the weekend of July 4 and met fewer than a dozen others along the way.

An essential key to understanding this special region is its islands—each, like people, with a distinct personality. Some are linked to the mainland by causeways or bridges, others are reachable only by ferry. Mount Desert Island heads almost anyone's list, but it's so eminently accessible that it almost doesn't qualify as an "island."

As you drive or bike around Mount Desert— vaguely shaped like a lobster claw and indented by Somes Sound (the only fjord on the United States' east coast)—you'll cross and re-cross the national-park boundaries, reminders that Acadia National Park, covering a third of the island, is indeed the major presence here. It affects traffic, indoor and outdoor pursuits, and, in a way, even the climate.

The other major presence is Bar Harbor, largest and best known of the island's communities. It's the source of just about anything you could want (if not need), from T-shirts to tacos, books to bike rentals. The contrast with Acadia is astonishing, as the park struggles to maintain its image and character.

Bar Harbor shares the island with Southwest Harbor, Tremont, and a number of small villages: Bass Harbor, Bernard, Northeast Harbor, Seal Harbor, Otter Creek, Somesville, and Hall Quarry. From Bass, Northeast, and Southwest Harbors, private and state ferries shuttle bike and foot traffic to offshore Swans Island, Frenchboro (Long Island), and the Cranberry Isles (and cars to Swans Island).

On the peaceful eastern fringe of Hancock County, at the tip of the Schoodic Peninsula, a stunning pocket of Acadia National Park sees only a fraction of the visitors who descend on the main part of the park. And towns lining the eastern shore of Frenchman Bay have some of the best views of all: front-row seats facing the peaks of Mount Desert Island. It's no wonder many artists and artisans make their homes here; for the inspiring scenery, no doubt.

PLANNING YOUR TIME

So much to do, so little time. That's the lament of most visitors. While you can circumnavigate Mount Desert Island in a day, hitting the highlights along the **Park Loop** with just enough time to oohhh and aahhh at each, to appreciate Acadia, you need time to hike the trails, ride the **carriage roads,** get afloat on a whale-watching cruise or a sea kayak, visit museums, and explore an offshore island or two. A week or longer is best, but you can get a taste of Acadia in 3–4 days.

Plan on devoting a full day to the park, including allowing about three hours to drive the Park Loop. You'll want to stop for tea and popovers at **Jordan Pond House.** Finish the day with a sunset carriage ride

Spend one day in and around Bar Harbor, perhaps taking a sail or whale-watching tour or going out with **Diver Ed** in the morning, visiting the **Abbe Museum** in the afternoon, and spending the late afternoon and early evening browsing the shops.

Spend another day exploring Northeast Harbor and Southwest Harbor, allowing the better part of a day to visit the **Wendell Gilley Museum** and **Thuya** and **Asticou** gardens, drive along the edge of **Somes Sound,** and prowl around the shops and galleries in both towns. If you want to visit an offshore island, visit only one of these two towns and set off from there, allowing a half day.

You'll need yet another day to explore the **Schoodic section of Acadian National Park.** While you can take the ferry from Bar Harbor over for the day and use the Island Explorer buses to loop through the park and Winter Harbor, you'll need a car and more time to visit the numerous galleries in this region, and if you're a fan of fine craft, they're well worth it.

Getting There and Around

The closest major airport is Bangor International, in Bangor, 50 miles away.

The **Hancock County/Bar Harbor Airport** (Rte. 3, Bar Harbor Rd., Trenton 04605, 207/667-7171, www.bhbairport.com), 12 miles from downtown Bar Harbor, is centrally located for anyone headed for Mount Desert Island. **USAirways/Colgan Air** (800/428-4322, www.colganair.com), operates daily commuter-plane service from Boston to Bar Harbor Airport, with a stop in Rockland (Knox County Municipal Airport). Flight time is about 80 minutes. The airline will also arrange other connections beyond Boston. Hertz, Budget, and Enterprise have rental-car offices at the Bar Harbor Airport; in summer, be sure to reserve a car well in advance. From late June through Columbus Day, the Island Explorer provides bus service between Hancock County/Bar Harbor Airport and several locations on Mount Desert Island. Island destinations include village centers and Acadia National Park. By car, Bar Harbor is 268 miles from Boston, but a good chunk of that mileage consists of two-lane roads. Don't count on averaging 60 mph, especially in midsummer.

Vermont Transit (800/522-8737, www.vermonttransit.com) operates one round-trip daily between Bar Harbor and Bangor, via Ellsworth, and connecting with Portland, Boston, and New York City.

West Bus Service (800/596-2823 or 207/546-2823, www.westbusservice.com) provides daily service between Bangor and Calais, with a scheduled stop in Ellsworth and flag stops in Hancock, Sullivan, and Gouldsboro.

Downeast Transportation (207/667-5596, www.state.me.us/mdot/opt/transit/brochures/downeast.htm) provides intra- and inter-town service throughout the region, with a schedule that varies by the day. It's best to check the website, then call with questions.

Bar Harbor is the starting point for the summertime car-and-passenger ferry to **Yarmouth, Nova Scotia,** which shaves more than 600 miles off the driving route. From late May through mid-October, the high-speed 900-passenger catamaran called *The Cat,* owned by Bay Ferries (888/249-7245 or 207/288-3395, www.catferry.com),

zips to Yarmouth in 165 minutes, departing Bar Harbor at 8 A.M. daily. (Yarmouth is on Atlantic time.) From late June to early September, there's also a 4 P.M. run (except Wed.). Adult one-way fare is $55, senior $50, youth 11–17 $35, child 3–10 $25. Family fare (two adults and two children) is $255 in summer. Vehicle fare varies with length. In peak season, it's approximately $110 to $170 one-way, with discounts for round-trip. A bicycle is $10. A round-trip day cruise is $59 adult, $50 senior, $25 youth, $20 child. All fares are subject to $3 pp security fee. No pets are allowed in the passenger areas; special kennels are available for pets on a first-come, first-served basis. Vehicle reservations are wise. U.S. citizens need a photo ID; foreign visitors need a passport and any required visas. From July to mid-October, the **Yarmouth County Tourism Association** (507/288-9432 or 902/742-5355) staffs an information office at the ferry terminal (121 Eden St., Rte. 3, Bar Harbor 04609).

Instead of working yourself into a tizzy in traffic or wasting precious hours searching for a parking spot, leave your car at your accommodation. The best thing that ever happened to Mount Desert Island, traffic-wise, was the 1999 establishment of the *free* **Island Explorer** bus network, which operates from late June through mid-October and uses clean, propane-powered buses. Routes cover all but the westernmost side of the island as well as Winter Harbor and the Schoodic section of the park; the schedules are available at all information centers, most lodgings, and many shops and restaurants. Or check www.exploreacadia.com. Although there are scheduled stops, the bus drivers are very amenable to stopping almost anywhere they think it's safe. They also carry bikes. The propane-powered buses connect with the Swans Island ferry, the Cranberry Isles mail boat, the Winter Harbor ferry, and the Nova Scotia ferry. The downtown route (number 2) begins at 6:55 A.M. and continues frequently until 11 P.M. Other routes begin at 6:45, 7:30, 8:30, and 9 A.M. It's amazingly well organized, and expansion is planned.

The **MDI Water Taxi** (207/244-7312), a converted lobsterboat homeported in Northeast Harbor, provides on-demand trips anywhere you'd like to go, mid-May to Thanksgiving. Reservations are essential.

The **Bar Harbor Ferry** (207/288-2984, www.barharborferry.com, round-trip $24/adult, $15/child, $5/bike), a passenger-only service, operates between Bar Harbor and Winter Harbor, making it easy for visitors to move back and forth without driving. The ferry departs Bar Harbor every two hours, beginning at 8 A.M., hourly in peak season 8 A.M.–6 P.M., and departs Winter Harbor every two hours, hourly in peak season, 7 A.M.–5 P.M. The free **Island Explorer** bus meets the ferry, late June to mid-October on either end.

Ellsworth

Twenty miles east of Bucksport on Route 1, Ellsworth—Hancock County's shire town—unfortunately has earned a reputation as the summertime bottleneck to Bar Harbor. In fact, there's much more here, including handsome architectural remnants of the city's 19th-century lumbering heyday (which began shortly after its incorporation in 1800).

These days, Ellsworth is the region's shopping mecca. Antique shops and small stores line Main Street, Route 1, in the downtown section; supermarkets, strip malls, and big-box stores line Routes 1 and 3 between Ellsworth and Trenton. Amidst all this roadside clutter, there are a few gems worth visiting.

SIGHTS
The Black House
Very little has changed at the **Woodlawn Museum**, the Colonel Black House (W. Main St./Surry Rd., Rte. 172, Ellsworth, 207/667-8671, www.woodlawnmuseum.com, 10 A.M.–5 P.M. Tues.–Sat. and 1–4 P.M. Sun. June–Sept., 1–4 P.M. Tues.–Sun. May and Oct., $7.50 adults, $3 children 5–12) since George Nixon Black donated it to the town in 1928. Completed in 1828, the Georgian house is a marvel of preservation, one of Maine's best, filled with Black family antiques and artifacts. Enthusiastic docents lead hour-long tours, beginning on the hour, to point out the circular staircase, rare books and artifacts, canopied beds, a barrel organ, and lots more. Even kids appreciate all the unusual stuff. Afterward, plan to picnic on the manicured grounds, then explore two sleigh-filled barns, the Memorial Garden, and the two miles of mostly level trails in the woods up beyond the house. Restrooms are next to the parking area. On several Wednesday afternoons in July and August, there are elegant teas in the garden (or in the carriage house if it's raining). China, silver, linens, special-blend tea, sandwiches, pastries, and live music—for $12 a person. Call for reservations. The grounds are accessible all year. In winter, there's cross-country skiing on the trails. On Route 172, a quarter mile southwest of Route 1, watch for the small sign and turn into the winding uphill driveway.

For the Birds
En route to Bar Harbor, watch carefully on the right for the sign that marks **Birdsacre** (Rte. 3, Bar Harbor Rd., Ellsworth, 207/667-8460), a 185-acre urban sanctuary. Wander the trails in this peaceful preserve—spotting wildflowers, birds, and well-labeled shrubs and trees—and you'll have trouble believing you're surrounded by prime tourist territory. The sanctuary is open all year, sunrise to sunset. At the sanctuary entrance is the 1850 **Stanwood Homestead Museum**, with period furnishings and wildlife exhibits. Once owned by noted ornithologist Cordelia Stanwood, the volunteer-operated museum is open for tours by chance or appointment, mid-May to mid-October. To be sure, call ahead for an appointment. Admission is free to the preserve and the homestead, but donations are greatly appreciated. Birdsacre is also a wildlife rehabilitation center, so expect to see all kinds of winged creatures, especially hawks and owls, in various stages of rescue. Some will be returned to the wild, while others remain here for educational purposes. Stop by the Nature Center for even more exhibits.

Acadia Region

THE TRENTON GAUNTLET

Unless you're arriving by boat, you can't get to Mount Desert Island without first going through Trenton, straddling Route 3 from Ellsworth southward. Big-box stores, restaurants, motels, amusements, and gift shops line the congested six-mile strip, and some are worth at least a genuflect. If you're traveling with children, count on being begged to stop.

Here's a selection of family favorites.

Seacoast Fun Park (Bar Harbor Rd., Rte. 3, Trenton, 207/667-3573, www.seacoastfunparks .com) has water slides, minigolf, and go-karts as well as an indoor paintball arena, 32-foot climbing wall, and more. A Max Pass ($22 pp) covers all-day water slides and one ride; a Multi Pass ($18 adults, $16 kids under 4'10") covers all-day golf and two rides. Other packages are available, or pay separate fees for individual activities.

Acadia Zoo (446 Bar Harbor Rd., Rte. 3, Trenton, 207/667-3244, www.acadiazoo.org, $6 adults, $5 seniors and kids 3–12), a nonprofit educational facility, has more than 100 exotic and not-so-exotic creatures—reindeer, bison, wolves, moose, and more. Enter the barn and—voilà—you're in a simulated rainforest populated with monkeys, Amazon fishes, and tropical birds and reptiles. Shows featuring the zoo's bears, moose, big cats, primates, and wolves are scheduled throughout the day.

The Great Maine Lumberjack Show (Rte. 3, 207/667-0067, www.mainelumberjack.com, 7 P.M. mid-June to late Aug., $7.75 adult, $5.75 kids) is a 75-minute "Olympics of the Forest" hosted by "Timber" Tina Scheer, who's been competing around the world since she was seven. Watch 14 events, including axe throwing, cross-cut sawing, log rolling, speed climbing, and more. Some are open to participation. (Kids can learn log-rolling by appointment.) Performances are held rain or shine. Seating is under a roof, but dress for the weather if it's inclement. The ticket office opens at 6 P.M.

Scenic Flights (Bar Harbor Rd., Rte. 3, Trenton, 207/667-7627), provides low-level flightseeing services in the Mount Desert Island region. Flights range 22–40 minutes and begin at $45 per person, with a two-passenger minimum. The flights are based at Hancock County/Bar Harbor Airport, just north of Mount Desert Island and 12 miles

north of downtown Bar Harbor. Flights are first-come, first-served; the wait is seldom longer than 20 minutes. Planes operate daily, weather permitting, mid-May–October (fall foliage flights are fabulous); winter flights can be arranged by appointment.

A sister business, **Island Soaring** (Bar Harbor Rd., Rte. 3, Trenton, 207/667-7627, www.island soaring.com), lets you soar in silence, with daily

Soar in silence above Mt. Desert Island with Island Soaring, based at Bar Harbor Airport in Trenton.

glider flights based out of Bar Harbor Airport. The one- or two-passenger gliders are towed to at least a 2,500 altitude, than released. An FAA-certified pilot guides the glider. Rates begin at $119 for two, $89 for one, for a 20-minute flight. Best time to fly is between noon and 3 P.M., as there's usually more thermal activity then.

Route 3 (Bar Harbor Road) is lined with eateries, including several lobster "pounds" that deserve a stop. One of the best-known and longest-running (since 1956) is **Trenton Bridge Lobster Pound** (Rte. 3, Bar Harbor Rd., Trenton, 207/667-2977, 11 A.M.–7:30 P.M. Mon.–Sat. Memorial Day–Columbus Day), on the right, next to the bridge leading to Mount Desert Island. Watch for the "smoke signals"—steam billowing from the huge vats; the lobster couldn't be much fresher.

Before or after visiting Mount Desert Island, if you're headed farther Down East—to Lamoine, the eastern side of Hancock County, and beyond—there's a good shortcut from Trenton. About five miles south of Ellsworth on Route 3, just north of the Acadia Zoo, turn east onto Route 204.

© TOM NANGLE

One Ringy-Dingy

What was life like before cell phones or touchtone dialing? Find out at **The Telephone Museum** (166 Wimkumpaugh Rd., Ellsworth, 207/667-9491, www.ellsworth.org/ringring, 1–4 P.M. Thurs.–Sun. July.–Sept., $4 adult, $2 kids), a hands-on museum with the largest collection of old-fashioned switching systems in the East, including many from Maine. Place a call to see how these old systems work. To find the museum, head 10 miles north on Route 1A (toward Bangor), then go left on Winkumpaugh Road for 1 mile.

SHOPPING

Antiques and Books

You're unlikely to meet a single soul who has left the **Big Chicken Barn Books and Antiques** (Rte. 1, 1768 Bucksport Rd., Ellsworth, 207/667-7308) without buying *something*. You'll find every kind of collectible on the vast first floor, courtesy of more than four dozen dealers. Climb the stairs for books, magazines, old music, and more. With 21,000 square feet, this place is addictive. Free coffee, hassle-free browsing. The Big Chicken is 11 miles east of Bucksport, 8.5 miles west of Ellsworth.

The 40-plus-dealer **Old Creamery Antique Mall** (207/667-0522) has two shops: the original, 6,000-square-foot shop (13 Hancock St.) and a smaller shop just around the corner (163 Main St., Rte. 1).

Eclectic Shops

Don't miss **Rooster Brother** (29 Main St., Rte. 1, Ellsworth, 207/667-8675 or 800/866-0054), for gourmet cookware, cards, and books on the main floor; coffee, tea, candy, cheeses, a huge array of exotic condiments, fresh breads, and other gourmet items on the lower level; and discounted merchandise on the third floor. You can easily pick up all the fixings for a fancy picnic here. The shop is in a handsome old riverside building on busy Route 1. Access to the store's parking lot can be tricky at times because of traffic patterns, so be cautious and patient.

It's hard to categorize **J & B Atlantic Co.** (142 Main St., Rte. 1, 207/667-2082). It takes up a good portion of the block, with room after room filled with furniture, home accessories, gifts, books, and antiques.

John Edwards Market (158 Main St., Ellsworth, 207/667-9377) is a two-fold find. Upstairs is a natural foods store. Downstairs is the **Wine Cellar Gallery,** a terrific space showcasing Maine artists throughout the year.

Sporting Goods and Toys

For an extensive sporting-gear inventory, plus advice on outdoors activities, stop in at **Cadillac Mountain Sports** (34 High St., Rte. 1, Ellsworth, 207/667-7819).

If there are kids on your shopping list, pay a visit to the **Toymaker Gift Shop** (Rte. 1A, Ellsworth, 207/667-3714), run by a guy who happens to look a lot like Santa Claus. All sorts of wooden toys, many made in Maine, as well as other wooden ware are inside. It's seven miles north of the intersection with Route 3.

Discount Shopping

You can certainly find bargains at the **L.L. Bean Factory Store** (150 High St., Rte. 1, Ellsworth, 207/667-7753), but this is an outlet, so scrutinize the goods for flaws and blemishes before buying. Across the road is **Reny's Department Store** (Ellsworth Shopping Center, High St., Rte. 1, Ellsworth, 207/667-5166), a Maine-based discount operation with a you-never-know-what-you'll-find philosophy. Trust me, you'll find something here.

ENTERTAINMENT

The carefully restored Art Deco **Grand Auditorium of Hancock County** (100 Main St., Ellsworth, 207/667-9500) is the year-round site of films, concerts, plays, and art exhibits. Most films are at 7:30 P.M. Call for schedule.

First-run films, usually showing twice a night, plus bargain matinees in midsummer, are on the docket at **Hoyts Cinemas Maine Coast Mall** (225 High St., Rte. 1, Ellsworth, 207/667-3251).

A summer highlight is the **Ellsworth Concert Band** concert series, held Wednesday evenings in July and August in the plaza outside Ellsworth

City Hall (an imposing building just north of Main St.). If it rains, it's held inside City Hall. Practice begins at 6:30 P.M., concerts start at 8 P.M., and the 50-member community band even welcomes visitors with talent and instruments. Just show up at practice time. The repertoire is mostly marches and show music; a prize goes to the person who correctly identifies a mystery tune.

FOOD

Breakfast, Lunch, and Miscellany

Order breakfast anytime at **The Riverside Café** (151 Main St., Ellsworth, 207/667-7220, 6 A.M.–3 P.M. Mon.–Fri., 7 A.M.–3 P.M. Sat., and 7 A.M.–2 P.M. Sun.). Juices are fresh (if a bit pricey), buckwheat pancakes are outstanding, but try the veggie Benedict, with spinach and tomato. Lunch menu includes homemade soups, salads, sandwiches, grilled sandwiches, and high-cal desserts; skip the fried-seafood platters. Sunday brunches are legendary. And the café's name? It used to be down the street, overlooking the Union River.

On the Main Street spur heading east from Ellsworth (also called Washington Junction Road), **Larry's Bakery** (241 Main St., Ellsworth, 207/667-2557, 6 A.M.–5 P.M. Mon.–Sat.) may look unassuming, but *everyone* goes there for bread, rolls, pies, and Saturday night's baked beans. No preservatives are used. No credit cards.

Go to **Frankie's Café & Good Stuff** (40 High St., Rte. 1, in the Cadillac Mountain Sports building, 207/667-7701, 8 A.M.–5:30 P.M. Mon.–Fri.), for excellent Mediterranean/vegetarian specialties ($5–6)—veggie-rice pie, *spanakopita,* brie pasta pie, sesame-butter-topped bagels. Pâté and meat sandwiches are available. Everything's very casual. There's only a handful of tables, so order food to go if it's crowded (which it often is).

Ice cream doesn't get much finer than that sold at **Morton's Ice Cream** (13 School St., Ellsworth, 207/667-1146, 11:30 A.M.–5:30 P.M. Tues.–Fri.), a tiny shop with a deservedly giant reputation for homemade Italian gelato, sorbet, and ice cream.

The **Ellsworth Farmers' Market** gets under way behind 245 High Street, next to Larry's Pastry, June to late October, Monday and Thursday 2–5:30 P.M. and Saturday 9:30 A.M.–12:30 P.M.

Ethnic Fare

The Mex (191 Main St., Ellsworth, 207/667-4494, 11 A.M.–9 P.M. daily, to 10 P.M. Sat. and Sun.) has been a popular local eatery since 1979. The menu is punnily entertaining ("Juan-derful Beginnings"), service is good, and you won't go hungry. Lots of vegetarian choices. Entrées are $10–16. Take home a bottle of the fiery hot sauce.

Relatively new on the scene and earning rave reviews is chef Richard Hanson's **Cleonice Mediterranean Bistro** (112 Main St., Ellsworth, 207/664-7554, 11:30 A.M.–9 P.M. Tues.–Sat.), named for his mother. Gleaming woodwork and brass lighting fixtures combine for a golden glow in the long dining room, lined with wooden booths on one side, a 32-foot wooden bar, dating from 1938, on the other. The fare is outstanding, especially the tapas and meze selections (most around $5). Dinner entrée range is $18–22. Do treat yourself to a carafe of the Tunisian spiced lemonade, made with lemon, rose blossoms, and spices ($7).

For well-prepared, classic Italian, from spaghetti alla marinara to scallops carbonara, and calzones to pizzas, seek out **Turiglio's Ristorante Italiana** (59 Franklin St., just off Main St., 5 P.M.–close Tues.–Sun.); most entrées are in the $8–14 range.

Lobster

If you simply can't wait to get on the island for a lobster feed, stop at **Trenton Bridge Lobster Pound** (Rte. 3, Bar Harbor Rd., Trenton, 207/667-2977, 11 A.M.–7:30 P.M. Mon.–Sat. Memorial Day–Columbus Day), on the right, just before the bridge leading to Mount Desert Island. Watch for the "smoke signals"—steam billowing from the huge vats; the lobster couldn't be much fresher.

INFORMATION AND SERVICES

Information

It can be hard to spot the **Ellsworth Area Chamber of Commerce** (163 High St., P.O. Box 267, Ellsworth 04605, 207/667-5584, www.ellsworth chamber.org) amid the malls and fast-food places lining High Street (Route 1). Watch for a small gray building topped by an Information Center sign (on the right, close to the road, when heading toward Bar Harbor, just before Shaw's Plaza). Open daily during July and August, Monday–Saturday in late June and early September, weekdays the rest of the year.

Hospitals

Maine Coast Memorial Hospital (50 Union St., Ellsworth, 207/664-5311), the largest hospital in the area, has 24-hour emergency-room service. Healthcare Express (207/664-5341), at the hospital, handles minor problems daily between noon and 8 P.M.

Local Library

Don't miss a chance to visit one of the state's loveliest libraries, the **Ellsworth Public Library** (46 State St., Ellsworth, 207/667-6363). The National Historic Register Federalist building was donated to the city in 1897 by George Nixon Black, grandson of the builder of the Woodlawn Museum. Services include photocopies, computer and Internet access, lectures, art exhibits, and a popular paperback exchange (take one and leave one). Open 9 A.M.–5 P.M. Monday, Tuesday, and Friday, to 8 P.M. Wednesday and Thursday, to 2 P.M. Saturday.

Newspapers

The respected *Ellsworth American* (207/667-2576), published weekly, has been around since the mid-19th century. The *Ellsworth Weekly,* a newcomer, appears every Thursday (207/667-5514). In summer and fall, the *Ellsworth American* publishes *Out & About in Downeast Maine,* a very helpful free monthly vacation supplement in tabloid format.

Getting There and Around

Vermont Transit (800/522-8737, www.vermonttransit.com) operates one round-trip daily between Bar Harbor and Bangor, via Ellsworth, and connecting with Portland, Boston, and New York City.

West Bus Service (800/596-2823 or 207/546-2823, www.westbusservice.com) provides daily service between Bangor and Calais, with a scheduled stop in Ellsworth and flag stops in Hancock, Sullivan, and Gouldsboro.

Downeast Transportation (207/667-5596, www.state.me.us/mdot/opt/transit/brochures/downeast.htm) provides intra-and inter-town service throughout the region, with a schedule that varies by the day. It's best to check the website, then call with questions.

Acadia National Park

Note: Please see front color map for Mount Desert Island/Acadia National Park.

America's first national park east of the Mississippi River, and the only national park in the northeastern United States, Acadia National Park covers more than 40,000 acres on Mount Desert Island, the neighboring Schoodic Peninsula, and several islands close by and farther offshore. Within the boundaries of this splendid space are mountains, lakes, ponds, trails, fabulous vistas, and several campgrounds. Each year, more than three million visitors bike, hike, and drive into and through the park. Yet even at the height of summer, when the whole world seems to have arrived here, it's possible to find peaceful niches and less-trodden paths.

The easiest way to get around the park is on the bicycle rack-equipped, *free* **Island Explorer** bus network. Pick up a schedule at any info center or ask in local shops and restaurants. It's also posted on www.exploreacadia.com.

HISTORY

Thanks to the drive and determination of a handful of astute environmentalists, Acadia National Park became reality on January 19, 1929, after previous incarnations as Sieur de Monts National Monument (1916) and Lafayette National Park (1919). Inspired and prodded by dedicated conservationist George B. Dorr, benevolent summer and year-round citizens donated land and campaigned for federal recognition of the park. Starting as the Hancock County Trustees of Public

ACADIA NATIONAL PARK HIGHLIGHTS

The highlights listed here are all within the park territory on Mount Desert Island. The park also occupies territory on the Schoodic Peninsula and Isle au Haut, and on several islands in the bay. Many of the locations mentioned are accessible from various parts of the island via the very convenient Island Explorer bus. Be sure to take advantage of this cost-free, hassle-free service, operating on many routes around the island from late June to Labor Day.

Cadillac Mountain: Acadia's prime feature is the tallest point on the eastern seaboard, allegedly where the sun's first rays land. You can drive, bike, or hike to the 1,530-foot summit for head-swiveling vistas, plus a gift shop and restrooms. Be sure to walk the paved, .3-mile Summit Trail loop for the full effect.

Carriage Roads: On the eastern side of Mount Desert Island, 57 miles of meandering, crushed-stone paths, crossing 17 handsome stone bridges, welcome walkers, bikers, horseback riders, snowshoers, and cross-country skiers.

Hiking Trails: Besides the carriage roads, the park has more than 120 miles of easy, moderate, and rugged trails just for hikers.

Naturalist Programs: Park rangers present lectures and lead one- to three-hour walks and hikes throughout the summer season. Most are free, some require reservations; many are specially geared to children and families. For reservations, call 207/288-5262. Park rangers also accompany several natural and cultural history cruises, all requiring reservations and fees.

Park Loop Road: If you have only a few hours for exploring Acadia, the best capsule experience is the paved, 20-mile Park Loop Road, followed clockwise. The road to the Cadillac Mountain summit adds another seven miles, round-trip, to this total. One of the Island Explorer bus routes covers a large section of this loop. Among the sights on the loop: Sand Beach, Thunder Hole (best visited when the surf is wild), Otter Cliffs (a giant headland), Bubble Rock (a precarious-looking glacial leftover), and Eagle Lake.

Bass Harbor Head Light: This cliffside lighthouse within park boundaries at the southern tip of Mount Desert Island is a prime photo-op site.

Reservations, the group acquired land parcel by parcel, eventually turning it over to federal jurisdiction. Corporate giant John D. Rockefeller Jr., owner of a sprawling summer estate on Mount Desert Island, was responsible for securing nearly a third of the park's prime acreage and for building the unique 57-mile carriage-road system (44 miles of carriage roads belong to the park; another 13 miles are privately owned but open to the public). In 1935, his contribution was valued at $4 million. Even today, the park continues to expand as philanthropic individuals donate more land (including island acreage) to benefit future generations.

SIGHTS

Park Loop Road

The best way to fully appreciate Acadia is to hike the trails, bike the carriage roads, canoe and swim the ponds, and camp overnight. But if your time is limited, the 20-mile Park Loop Road, a National Scenic Byway, covers scenic highlights, including access to the summit of Cadillac Mountain. (Going to the summit and back adds another seven miles.) A drive-it-yourself tour CD or tape ($13) is available at the Thompson Island visitor center and the park's visitor center. Start at the parking lot below the Hulls Cove visitor center and follow the signs pointing in a clockwise direction; part of the loop is one-way. Traffic gets heavy at midday in midsummer, so aim for an early morning start. Maximum speed is 35 mph, but be alert for gawkers and photographers stopping without warning. Along the route are lots of trailheads, scenic overlooks, Sand Beach, Thunder Hole, Otter Cliffs, Jordan Pond House, and Eagle Lake, plus the Cadillac summit. North of Sand Beach is the park's entrance station. The park admission fee is $20 per vehicle (valid for a week), or $40 for an annual pass (80 percent of the fee stays in the park). To drive up Cadillac without doing the rest of the Park Loop Road, take the Cadillac Mountain access road off Route 233, west of Bar Harbor. It's 3.5 miles to the top.

The road is also open to bicyclists (as are the carriage roads, unlike the hiking trails, where bikes are banned). While the carriage roads are more scenic (and don't permit cars), the Park Loop Road provides a workout and a sightseeing opportunity for mountain bikers. (But don't do this in the middle of the day; get an early start or go late in the day to minimize breathing car and RV exhaust fumes.)

Carriage Roads

In 1913, John D. Rockefeller Jr. began laying out what eventually became a 57-mile carriage-road system, overseeing the project through the 1940s. Motorized vehicles have never been allowed on these lovely graded byways, making them real escapes from the auto world. Devoted now to multiple uses, the "Rockefeller roads" see hikers, bikers, baby strollers, horse-drawn carriages, even wheelchairs. Busiest times are 10 A.M.–2 P.M.

Pick up a free copy of the carriage-road map at any of the centers selling park passes. Fortunately, a $6 million restoration campaign, undertaken during the 1990s, has done a remarkable job of upgrading surfaces, opening overgrown panoramas, and returning the roads to their original 16-foot width.

The most crowded carriage roads are those closest to the visitor center—the Witch Hole Pond Loop, Duck Brook, and Eagle Lake. Avoid these, opting instead for roads west of Jordan Pond. Or go early in the morning or late in the day. Better still, go off-season, when you can enjoy the fall foliage (late Sept./early Oct.) or winter's cross-country skiing.

If you need a bicycle to explore the carriage roads, see the *Bar Harbor and Vicinity* and *Southwest Harbor and Vicinity* sections for rental information. Be forewarned that hikers are allowed on the carriage roads that spill over onto private property south of the Jordan Pond House, but these areas are off-limits to bicyclists. The no-biking areas are signaled with Green Rock Company markers. The carriage-

FRIENDS OF ACADIA

One of the park's greatest assets today is an energetic membership organization called Friends of Acadia (FOA), founded in 1986 to preserve and protect the park for resource-sensitive tourism and myriad recreational uses. You can join FOA and support the cause for $35 a year (43 Cottage St., P.O. Box 45, Bar Harbor 04609, 207/288-3340 or 800/625-0321, www.friends ofacadia.org), or just lend a hand while you're here. FOA organizes volunteer work parties for Acadia trail and carriage-road maintenance—call the recorded information line (207/288-3934) for the work locations; tools and training are provided. This is a terrific way to give something back to the park, and the camaraderie is contagious. Be sure to take your own water, lunch, and bug repellent. Dress in layers.

If you happen to be in the area on the first Saturday in November, call the office to register for the annual fall cleanup, which requires several hundred volunteers. Bring water and gloves; there's a free barbecue at midday for everyone who participates.

Even if you don't have time to join a work party, be a conscientious trailkeeper as you hike, and carry a trash bag.

road map clearly indicates the biking/no-biking areas. *Bicyclists must be especially speed-sensitive on the carriage roads, keeping an eye out for hikers, horseback riders, small children, and the hearing impaired.*

To recapture the early carriage-roads era, take one of the horse-drawn open-carriage tours run by **Carriages in the Park,** based at Wildwood Stables (Park Loop Rd., P.O. Box 241, Seal Harbor 04675, 207/276-3622, www.acadia.net/wild wood), a mile south of the Jordan Pond House. Six one- and two-hour trips start daily at 9:30 A.M. mid-June to Columbus Day. Reservations are not required, but they're encouraged, especially in midsummer. Best outing is the two-hour Sunset at the Summit to the top of Day Mountain. Cost is $22 adults, $9 children 6–12, $6 ages 2–5. Other routes are $16–18 per adult, $8–9 children, $4.50–6 little kids.

RECREATION

Hikes

If you're spending more than a day on Mount Desert Island, plan to buy a copy of *A Walk in the Park: Acadia's Hiking Guide,* by Tom St. Germain (see Suggested Reading in the Know Coastal Maine chapter), which details more than 60 hikes, including some outside the park. Remember that pets are allowed on park trails, but only on leashes no longer than six feet. Four of the Island Explorer bus routes are particularly useful for hikers, alleviating the problems of backtracking and car-jammed parking lots. Here's a handful of favorite Acadia hikes, from easy to rugged.

Jordan Pond Nature Trail: Start at the Jordan Pond parking area. This is an easy, one-mile, handicapped-accessible, wooded loop trail; pick up a brochure. Include Jordan Pond House (for tea and popovers) in your schedule.

Ship Harbor Nature Trail: Start at the Ship Harbor parking area, on Route 102A between Bass Harbor and Seawall Campground, in the southwestern corner of the island. The easy, 1.3-mile loop trail leads to the shore; pick up a brochure at the trailhead. Ship Harbor is particularly popular among birders seeking warblers, and you just might spot an eagle while you picnic on the rocks. An even easier trail, with its parking area just east of the Ship Harbor parking area, is **Wonderland.** It's 1.4 miles round-trip. Across Route 102A from Wonderland is **Seawall Bog,** attractive primarily to birders. Be sure to stay on the trails (worn but not marked); the peat underfoot is especially fragile.

Great Head Trail: This moderately easy, 1.4-mile loop trail starts at the eastern end of Sand Beach, off the Park Loop Road. Park in the Sand Beach parking area and cross the beach to the trailhead. Or take Schooner Head Road from downtown Bar Harbor and park in the small area where the road dead-ends. There are actually two trail loops here, both of which have enough elevation to provide terrific views.

Beech Mountain: A moderate hike, Beech Mountain's summit has an abandoned fire tower, from which you can look out toward Long Pond and the Blue Hill Peninsula. A knob near the top is a prime viewing site for the migration of hawks (and other raptors) in September. Round-trip on the wooded route is about 1.2 miles, although a couple of side trails can extend it. You'll have less competition here, in a quieter part of the park. Take Route 102 south from Somesville, heading toward Pretty Marsh. Turn left onto Beech Hill Road and follow it to the parking area at the end.

Beehive Trail and **Precipice Trail:** These two are the park's toughest routes, with sheer faces and iron ladders; Precipice often is closed (usually mid-Apr. into late July) to protect nesting peregrine falcons. If challenges are your thing and these trails are open (check beforehand at the visitor center), go ahead. But a fine alternative in the difficult category is the **Beachcroft Trail** on Huguenot Head. Also called the Beachcroft Path, the trail is best known for its 1,500 beautifully engineered granite steps. Round-trip is about 2.2 miles, or you can continue a loop at the top, taking in the Bear Brook Trail on Champlain Mountain, for about 4.4 miles. The parking area is just north of Route 3, near Sieur de Monts Spring, and just west of the Park Loop Road, near the Jackson Laboratory.

If you would prefer to hike with a guide, the Registered Maine Guides of **On the Rocks Acadia Hiking Adventures** (104 Rte. 3, Hulls Cove, Bar Harbor, 207/288-8032, www.ontherocks.com, $29) will take you on an easy four-hour morning or afternoon hike or sunset hike. Shuttle transportation to the hiking site, drinks, snacks, and the guide are included.

Rock Climbing

The park's only approved rock-climbing areas are Otter Cliffs and the south wall of Champlain Mountain. Sadly, rope friction and overuse have led to receding vegetation on Otter Cliffs. Registration boxes exist at both locations. Unless you're a pro, the best advice is to contact an outfitter in Bar Harbor and sign on for a half-day climbing experience, including professional lessons and at least one rappel. From mid-May to October, **Acadia Mountain Guides Climbing School** (198 Main St., Bar Harbor, 207/288-8186 or 888/232-9559, off-season 207/866-7562) offers all levels of

© TOM NANGLE

A relatively easy hike, Great Head rewards hikers with panoramic ocean views.

instruction and guided climbs for individuals and families in Acadia as well as in Camden, Clifton, and Baxter State Park. All gear is provided. Costs vary widely, depending on site, number of climbers, and session length.

Swimming

Sand Beach, next to the Park Loop Road and near the park entrance station, is the park's only sandy beach on salt water. Lifeguards are on duty during the summer, and even then, the biggest threat can be hypothermia. The water is terminally glacial, and even though kids seem not to notice, they can become chilled quickly. The best solution is to walk to the far end of the beach, where a warmer, shallow stream meets the ocean. On a hot August day, arrive early; the parking lot fills up. Bring a picnic.

A less-crowded saltwater beach, not in the park, is at the head of the appealing harbor in chic Seal Harbor, a few miles east of Northeast Harbor.

Don't assume you can swim in any freshwater pond or lake you encounter. Six island locations—Upper and Lower Hadlock Ponds, Bubble and Jordan Ponds, Eagle Lake, and the southern half of Long Pond—are drinking-water reservoirs where swimming and windsurfing are banned (but boating is allowed). Don't let your dog swim in these ponds, either.

The most popular freshwater swimming site, staffed with a lifeguard and inevitably crowded on hot days, is **Echo Lake,** south of Somesville on Route 102. If you have a canoe, kayak, or rowboat, you can reach swimming holes in **Round, Seal Cove,** or **Somes Pond** (all on the western side of Mount Desert). The eastern shore of **Hodgdon Pond** (also on the western side of the island) is accessible by car (via Hodgdon Road and Long Pond Fire Road). **Lake Wood** (at the northern end of Mount Desert) has a small beach and auto access. To get to Lake Wood from Route 3, head west on Crooked Road to unpaved Park Road. Turn left and continue to the parking area, which will be crowded on a hot day, so arrive early.

CAMPING

The only accommodations within Acadia National Park are two campgrounds, **Seawall** and **Blackwoods,** neither of which has RV hookups.

In addition, the park operates a handful of lean-to campsites at its Duck Harbor location on Isle au Haut (see the Isle au Haut section in the Blue Hill Peninsula chapter). Commercial campgrounds and a variety of other lodgings are all over Mount Desert Island.

Both Acadia National Park campgrounds have seasonal restrooms (no showers) and dumping stations. Both also have amphitheaters, where park rangers present free, hour-long evening programs (usually at 9 P.M.) during the summer on a variety of natural- and cultural-history topics. Noncampers are also welcome at these events.

With more than 300 campsites, **Blackwoods Campground** (just off Rte. 3, five miles south of Bar Harbor) is open all year. Reservations are required only May–October (800/365-2267; have your credit card handy). Cost is $20 per site per night. Camping is $10 per night in November and April, free December–March. Off-season facilities include pit toilets, fire rings, and a hand-operated water pump.

No reservations are required or accepted at **Seawall Campground** (on Rte. 102A, four miles south of Southwest Harbor), but you'll need to arrive as early as 8 A.M. in midsummer to secure one of the 200 or so sites. Seawall is open Memorial Day weekend through September. Cost is $20 per night for drive-up sites and $14 per night for walk-in sites.

JORDAN POND HOUSE

The only full-service restaurant within the park is the Jordan Pond House (Park Loop Rd., 207/276-3316, 11:30 A.M.–8 P.M. mid-May–late Oct., to 9 P.M. July and Aug.), a modern facility in a spectacular waterside setting. Jordan Pond House began life as a rustic 19th-century teahouse; wonderful old photos still line the walls of the current incarnation, which went up after a disastrous fire in 1979. Afternoon tea is still a tradition, with tea, popovers, and extraordinary strawberry jam, served on the lawn daily 11:30 A.M.–5:30 P.M. in summer, weather permitting. Not exactly a bargain at $7, but it's worth it. However, Jordan Pond is far from a secret, so expect to wait for seats at the height of summer. (You cannot make lunch or tea reservations, but you *can* call ahead to put your name on the waiting list for seats.) Jordan Pond House is on the Island Explorer's Route 5. *A health note:* Perhaps because of all the sweet drinks and jam served outdoors, patrons at the lawn tables sometimes find themselves pestered by bees. They don't usually sting unless you pester them back, but if you're hyperallergic to bee stings, or are with anyone who is, be alert.

INFORMATION AND RESOURCES

National Park Visitor Center

The modern **Hulls Cove Visitor Center** (Rte. 3, 207/288-3338, Hulls Cove, 8 A.M.–4:30 P.M., mid-April through Oct., to 6 P.M. July and Aug.) is eight miles southeast of the causeway to the island. Here you can rendezvous with pals, make reservations for natural- and cultural-history programs, watch a short park presentation, rent or buy cassette guides, admire the view of Frenchman Bay, and use the restrooms. Pick up a copy of the summertime *Beaver Log*, a tabloid listing the schedule of park activities, plus tide calendars and the entire schedule for the marvelous free **Island Explorer** shuttle bus (see Getting There and Around). If you didn't purchase one at the Thompson Island information center, buy a park pass while you're here, or buy one in the information building next to the Village Green in downtown Bar Harbor. From November to April, information is available at **Acadia National Park Headquarters** (Rte. 233, about 3.5 miles west of downtown Bar Harbor, 8 A.M.–4:30 P.M. except Thanksgiving, Christmas, and New Year's Day).

The best independent resource for all the communities of Mount Desert Island is the **Mount Desert Island Regional Information Center** (Rte. 3, Thompson Island, 207/288-3411, 9 A.M.–6 P.M. mid-May through June and Sept. and Oct., 9 A.M.–8 P.M. July and Aug.), a joint project of four chambers of commerce and the National Park Service. Information is here on the park and its campground vacancies, and you can purchase park passes (but be sure to stop also at the Acadia National Park Visitor Center). The modern building, on bridge-linked Thompson Island in Mount Desert Narrows, has restrooms, pay phones, scads of brochures and maps, and particularly congenial staffers, including park rangers, who will help you find a bed or campsite, pick a trail, and plan your visit. Across the road is an attractive picnic spot overlooking the Narrows.

It pays to do some advance planning to help narrow your choices for within the park. To plan for a park visit, contact Information, Acadia National Park (P.O. Box 177, Bar Harbor, ME 04609, 207/288-3338, www.nps.gov/acad). Be sure to request a park map, a carriage-road map, a hiking-trail list, and camping information. The park also publishes an access guide, detailing wheelchair accessibility of information centers, campgrounds, shops, cruises, museums, and trails. Other flyers worth requesting cover geology, plants, birds, mammals, and the park's history.

A for-profit operation that sounds as if it's connected to Acadia National Park but isn't, the **Acadia Information Center** (Rte. 3, Bar Harbor Rd., Trenton, 207/667-8550 or 800/358-8550, www.acadiainfo.com, 10 A.M.–8 P.M. mid-May–mid-Oct.) is the first information center you'll encounter on your way to the island. Clean restrooms and racks of brochures and maps make

it worth stopping. It's on the right, only 1,000 feet before the bridge to Thompson Island.

(See Suggested Reading under Acadia National Park/Mount Desert Island for a selection of books that will prove very helpful if you're spending any amount of time in the national park.)

Hospitals

Maine Coast Memorial Hospital (50 Union St., Ellsworth, 207/664-5311), the largest hospital in the area, has 24-hour emergency-room service. Healthcare Express (207/664-5341), at the hospital, handles minor problems daily between noon and 8 P.M.

Mount Desert Island's only full-service hospital is **Mount Desert Island Hospital** (10 Wayman Ln., Bar Harbor, 207/288-5081), with a 24-hour emergency room.

If you have an emergency while in the park, call 911 or 207/288-3891. The nearest hospital is in Bar Harbor. The nearest major medical center is in Bangor, via a congested route that can take well over an hour at the height of summer. Best advice for averting emergencies: be cautious and sensible in everything you undertake in the park. Don't hike alone or go off the trails—people are seriously injured or killed falling from the cliffs nearly every year.

Bar Harbor and Vicinity

In 1996, Bar Harbor celebrated the bicentennial of its founding (as Eden). In the late 19th century and well into the 20th, the town grew to become one of the East Coast's fanciest summer watering holes.

In those days, steamboats arrived from points south, large and small resort hotels sprang up, and exclusive mansions (quaintly dubbed "cottages") were the venues of parties thrown by resident Drexels, DuPonts, Vanderbilts, and prominent academics, journalists, and lawyers. The "rusticators" came for the season, with huge entourages of servants, children, pets, and horses. The area's renown was such that by the 1890s, even the staffs of the British, Austrian, and Ottoman embassies retreated here from summers in Washington, D.C.

The establishment of the national park, in 1919, and the arrival of the motorcar changed the character of Bar Harbor and Mount Desert Island; two world wars and the Great Depression took an additional toll in myriad ways, but the coup de grâce for Bar Harbor's era of elegance came in 1947.

Nothing in the history of Bar Harbor and Mount Desert Island stands out like the Great Fire of 1947, a wind-whipped conflagration that devastated more than 17,000 acres on the eastern half of the island and leveled gorgeous mansions, humble homes, and more trees than anyone could ever count. Only three people died, but property damage was estimated at $2 million. Whole books have been written about the October

Acadia Region

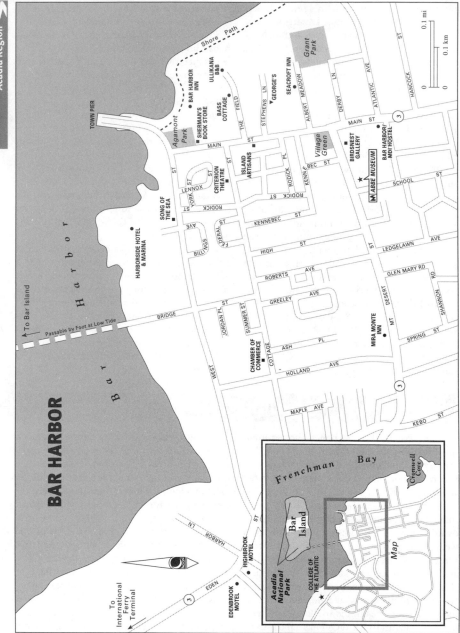

BAR HARBOR

Harbor

Bay

To Bar Island

Passable by Foot at Low Tide

TOWN PIER

To International Ferry Terminal

Shore Path

Grant Park

SEACROFT INN

ULIKANA B&B

BAR HARBOR INN

SHERMAN'S BOOK STORE

BASS COTTAGE

GEORGE'S

Agamont Park

MAIN ST

THE FIELD ST

STEPHENS LN

ALBERT MEADOW

DERBY LN

MAIN ST

ATLANTIC AVE

HANCOCK ST

Village Green

BIRDSNEST GALLERY

BAR HARBOR/ MDI HOSTEL

ABBE MUSEUM

SCHOOL ST

LENNOX ST

YORK ST

CRITERION THEATRE

ISLAND ARTISANS

RODICK PL

KENNEBEC ST

RODICK ST

KENNEBEC ST

SONG OF THE SEA

RODICK ST

FEDERAL ST

KENNEBEC ST

HIGH ST

LEDGELAWN AVE

HARBORSIDE HOTEL & MARINA

AVE

BILLINGS

ROBERTS AVE

GLEN MARY RD

RD

DESERT ST

SHANNON ST

BRIDGE

JORDAN PL

SUMMER ST

GREELEY AVE

MIRA MONTE INN

MT

SPRING ST

WEST ST

CHAMBER OF COMMERCE

ASH PL

COTTAGE ST

HOLLAND AVE

MAPLE AVE

KEBO ST

HIGHBROOK MOTEL

ST

HARBOR LN

EDEN

EDENBROOK MOTEL

Frenchman Bay

Cromwell Cove

Bar Island

Acadia National Park

COLLEGE OF THE ATLANTIC

Map

0.1 mi
0.1 km
0

© AVALON TRAVEL PUBLISHING, INC.

inferno; fascinating scrapbooks in Bar Harbor's Jesup Memorial Library dramatically relate the gripping details of the story. Even though some of the elegant cottages have survived, the fire altered life here forever.

Land in Bar Harbor in mid-July and you'll find it tough to believe that the year-round population is only about 4,530. Bar Harbor is liveliest (in both positive and negative senses) in July and August, but the season keeps stretching, especially as cruise ships extend the season on both ends. Many clued-in travelers try to take advantage of September's prime weather, relative quiet, and spectacular foliage, although even September activity has stepped up in recent years. In the dead of winter, the town is close to moribund, kept alive by devoted year-rounders; the students and faculty of the College of the Atlantic, a unique four-year liberal-arts college geared to environmental studies; and the staff of the internationally recognized Jackson Laboratory for Mammalian Research.

If you're traveling with children, Bar Harbor can be a very convenient base of operations, comprising a smallish downtown area where kids can walk around, play in the parks, hang out at the waterfront, buy ice cream, and hit the movies. It's also a source for sporting-gear rentals and the starting point for boat, bus, kayaking, and walking tours. Staying downtown can be a real plus, but the high cost of even ordinary lodging is a minus—especially for families. Bar Harbor Chamber of Commerce staffers are particularly adept at rounding up rooms, but don't abuse their helpfulness; contact them early and plan well ahead for a height-of-summer holiday.

SIGHTS

Acadia National Park comes right up to the edge of town, providing enough sights and activities to fill weeks, but the Bar Harbor area has attractions of its own.

St. Saviour's Episcopal Church

St. Saviour's (41 Mt. Desert St., Bar Harbor, 207/288-4215, 7 A.M. to dusk), close to downtown Bar Harbor, boasts Maine's largest collection of Tiffany stained-glass windows. Ten originals are

Bar Harbor is very much a working harbor, filled with lobster and excursion boats as well as dinghies.

here; an 11th was stolen in 1988 and replaced by a locally made window. Of the 32 non-Tiffany windows, the most intriguing is a memorial to Clarence Little, founder of the Jackson Laboratory and a descendant of Paul Revere. Images in the window include the laboratory, DNA, and mice. In July and August, volunteers regularly conduct free tours of the Victorian-era church (completed in 1878); call for the schedule or make an appointment for an off-season tour. The church is open for self-guided tours (8 A.M.–8 P.M.)—pick up a brochure in the back. If you're intrigued by old cemeteries, spend time wandering the 18th-century town graveyard next to the church.

Abbe Museum

The fabulous Abbe Museum is a superb place to introduce children (and adults) to prehistoric and historic Native American tools, crafts, and other cultural artifacts, with an emphasis on

Maine's Micmac, Maliseet, Passamaquoddy, and Penobscot tribes. Everything about this privately funded museum, established in 1927, is tasteful. It has two campuses. The new main campus (26 Mt. Desert St., Bar Harbor, 207/288-3519, www.abbemuseum.org, 9 A.M.–5 P.M. Feb.–Dec.—call ahead off-season as hours may change, $6 adults, $2 ages 6–15), incorporating the former YMCA, is home to more than 50,000 objects spanning nearly 12,000 years. Museum-sponsored events include craft workshops, hands-on children's programs, archaeological field schools, and the **Native American Festival** (held at the College of the Atlantic usually the first Saturday in July).

Admission to the in-town Abbe also includes admission to the museum's original site in the park, about 2.3 miles south of Bar Harbor, at Sieur de Monts Spring, where Route 3 meets the Park Loop Road (9 A.M.–4 P.M. mid-May–mid-Oct.). Admission to only Sieur de Monts Spring Abbe is $2 adults, $1 children 6–15.

While you're at the summertime Abbe Museum, take the time to wander the paths in the adjacent **Wild Gardens of Acadia,** a three-quarter-acre microcosm of more than 400 plant species native to Mount Desert Island. Twelve separate display areas, carefully maintained and labeled by the Bar Harbor Garden Club, represent native plant habitats; pick up the map/brochure that explains each.

Oceanarium

At the northern edge of Mount Desert Island, 8.5 miles northwest of downtown Bar Harbor, is this understated but fascinating spot, also called the Maine Lobster Museum and Hatchery (1351 Rte. 3, Bar Harbor, 207/288-5005, 9 A.M.–5 P.M. Mon.–Sat. mid-May to mid-Oct.), one of the island's two related oceanariums. As with its sister site (in Southwest Harbor), this low-tech, high-interest operation awes the kids, and it's pretty darn interesting for adults, too. David and Audrey Mills have been at it since 1972 and are determined to educate visitors while showing them a good time. At this facility, visitors on tour view thousands of tiny lobster hatchlings, enjoy a museum, and meander along a salt marsh walk, where you can

check out tidal creatures and vegetation. There's also a touch tank, which might be moved back to the Southwest Harbor facility. All tours begin on the hour and half hour. Allow 2–3 hours to see everything. Bring a lunch to enjoy in the picnic area. Tickets are $10 adults, $6 children 4–12. This gets rather pricey for a family, but combination tickets, covering both sites, are available.

College of the Atlantic

A museum, a gallery, and a pleasant campus for walking are reasons to visit the college (105 Eden St., Rte. 3, Bar Harbor, 207/288-5395, www.coamuseum.org), which specializes in human ecology, or humans' interrelationship with the environment. In a handsome renovated building, the **George B. Dorr Natural History Museum** (207/288-5015) showcases regional birds and mammals in realistic dioramas made by COA students. Biggest attraction for children is the please-touch philosophy, allowing kids to feel fur, skulls, and even whale baleen. Tickets are $3.50 adults, $1.50 teenagers, and $1 children (3–12). The museum is open 10 A.M.–5 P.M. Monday–Saturday mid-June to Labor Day. Call for off-season hours.

Across the way is the **Ethel H. Blum Gallery,** a small space that hosts some intriguing exhibits (10 A.M.–4 P.M. Tues.–Sat. in summer, 9 A.M.–5 P.M. Mon.–Fri. during the academic year).

Also on campus is a **Beatrix Farrand Garden,** which is undergoing restoration, and below that an ill-maintained **shorefront nature path.** The garden, designed in 1928, contained more than 50 varieties of roses and was the prototype for the rose garden at Dumbarton Oakes, in Washington, D.C. Both are known for Farrand's use of garden rooms, such as the terraces in this garden. If you choose to take the shore path, be extremely careful and don't let little ones get ahead. There are cliff sections, some without guard rails, others where the rails are rotted.

Whale Museum

College of the Atlantic reopened the **Bar Harbor Whale Museum** (52 West St., Bar Harbor, www.coa.edu/alliedwhale, noon–8 P.M. in June, 9 A.M.–9 P.M. in July and Aug., 10 A.M.–8 P.M. in

Sept. and Oct.) in collaboration with Acadian Whale Adventures. Features include a life-sized model of a prehistoric walking whale, a pilot whale skeleton, seals, marine birds, a 22-foot-long minke porpoise, and exhibits on whales. There's also a mesmerizing video of whales in their habitat. Admission is free, but donations support marine mammal research and conservation. While here, ask about COA's **Adopt A Finback Whale** program. Biologists from Allied Whale, at the college, have identified more than 1,000 finbacks. Your $30–50 contribution supports research and nets you a color photo of your whale, a brief history of it, and a book, as well as an adoption certificate and newsletter subscription.

Local History

The Bar Harbor Historical Society (33 Ledgelawn Ave., Bar Harbor 04609, 207/288-0000, 1–4 P.M. Mon.–Sat. mid-June to mid-Oct., free) has fascinating displays, stereopticon images, and a scrapbook about the 1947 fire that devastated the island. The photographs alone are worth the visit. In winter, it's open by appointment.

Hulls Cove Tool Barn and Davistown Museum Sculpture Garden

Part shop, part nature center, part art gallery, the Hulls Cove Tool Barn and Sculpture Garden (Breakneck Rd., behind Hulls Cove General Store, Hulls Cove, 207/288-5126, 9 A.M.–5 P.M. daily June–Labor Day, Thurs.–Sun. Labor Day–Columbus Day, Sat. and Sun. in winter, www.jonesport-wood.com) is just one of creative Skip Brack's enterprises. Inside the barn is an extensive selection of old tools, with an emphasis on woodworking hand tools. Paths lace through perennial gardens, woods, and fields at the Davistown Museum Sculpture Garden, which surrounds the barn and continues across the street. Throughout the garden are sculptures by noted Maine artists and found-object creations by Brack.

Research Laboratories

Some of the world's top scientists work year-round or come to Bar Harbor in summer to work at two renowned scientific laboratories.

World renowned in genetic research, **The Jack-** son Laboratory for Mammalian Research (610 Main St., Rte. 3, Bar Harbor, 207/288-6000, www.jacksonlaboratory.org) breeds special mice used to study cancer, diabetes, muscular dystrophy, and other diseases—with considerable success. More than two million mice are shipped out of here each year. The free, hour-long "summer visitor program," held on most Wednesdays from late June to early September, begins at 3 P.M. in the lab's auditorium and includes a lively audiovisual program explaining the lab's impressive work, one of the staff scientists describing his or her work, and a Q&A session. To check on the topic, or for other information, call 207/288-6051. The lab is 1.5 miles south of downtown Bar Harbor.

No less impressive is the **Mount Desert Island Biological Laboratory** (Old Bar Harbor Rd., Salisbury Cove, 207/288-3605, www.mdibl.org), one of the few scientific research institutions in the world dedicated to studying marine animals to learn more about human health and environmental health and the only comprehensive effort in the country to sequence genomes. Public tours are offered Wednesdays at 10:30 A.M. and 1:30 P.M. from late June through late August, beginning at Maren Auditorium. The program begins with a presentation by a laboratory scientist about the lab's history and research, and a short video. Then a naturalist talks about animal life in Frenchman Bay and how it pertains to the lab's research. It includes a hands-on presentation at the touch tank, filled with marine animals from Frenchman Bay, a visit to a 15-foot glass tank with other marine creatures, and a stroll through the visitor center, where there are smaller tanks. The tour takes about an hour. To avoid crowds, go on a nice day. The lab also presents an evening lecture series. Most are serious scientific talks, but there's also usually one children's program. The lab is six miles north of Bar Harbor off Route 3.

Bar Harbor and Park Tours

The veteran of the Bar Harbor–based bus tours is **Acadia National Park Tours** (tickets at Testa's Restaurant, Bayside Landing, 53 Main St., Bar Harbor, 207/288-3327), operating May–October. A 2.5-hour, naturalist-led tour of Bar Harbor and Acadia departs at 10 A.M. and 2 P.M. daily from downtown Bar Harbor (look for the green-and-white bus across from Testa's). Reservations are wise in midsummer and during fall-foliage season (late Sept. and early Oct.); pick up reserved tickets 30 minutes before departure. Cost is $20 adults, $10 children under 13.

If you have a time crunch, **Oli's Trolley** (1 West St., Bar Harbor, 208/288-9899, www.acadia islandtours.com) operates a one-hour trolley-bus tour five times daily (between 10 A.M. and 6 P.M.) in July and August, including Bar Harbor mansion drive-bys and the Cadillac summit. Dress warmly; it's an open-air trolley. Cost is $15 adults, $10 children under 12.

For private tours of the park and other parts of the island, contact Michael Good at **Down East Nature Tours** (Knox Rd., Town Hill, Bar Harbor, 207/288-8128). A biologist with a special interest in birds, he'll take neophyte birders on a four-hour tour they won't forget; tours happen 8 A.M.–noon or 1–5 P.M. and cost about $60 pp including transportation from your lodging. Shorter tours are available; call for details. What better place to begin a life list than Acadia National Park? Bring your own binoculars, but Michael supplies a spotting scope.

Take a 75-minute walking tour of downtown Bar Harbor with **A Step Back in Time**, based at Acadia Bike and Canoe (48 Cottage St., Bar Harbor, 207/288-9605). The costumed guide leads you up one street and down the other, all the while staying in Victorian character and sharing the secrets of the rich and famous (and often outrageous) of the 19th century. Sounds kitschy, but it's most entertaining, primarily for adults. The tours occur daily at 4 P.M. mid-June through September, although that schedule may change when cruise boats are in port. Additional tours are added from time to time. Reservations aren't required, but they're wise. Cost is $12 per person.

RECREATION

Although Acadia steals the limelight for much of the island's recreation, Bar Harbor has its own pursuits—plus several outfitters for anyone headed to the park.

Visitors to Bar Harbor have been strolling along the town's Shore Path since the late 19th century. It's an easy walk, with great views of the harbor, Porcupine Islands, and several handsome mansions.

Walks

A real treat is a stroll along downtown Bar Harbor's **Shore Path,** a well-trodden, granite-edged byway built around 1880. Along the craggy shoreline are granite-and-wood benches, town-owned **Grant Park** (great for picnics), birch trees, and several handsome mansions that escaped the 1947 fire. Offshore are the four Porcupine Islands. The path is open 6:30 A.M.–dusk, and leashed pets are okay. Allow about 30 minutes for the mile loop, beginning next to the town pier and the Bar Harbor Inn and returning via Wayman Lane. There's also access to the path next to the Balance Rock Inn.

Check local newspapers or the Bar Harbor Chamber of Commerce visitor booklet for the times of low tide, then walk across the gravel bar (wear hiking boots or rubberized shoes) to wooded **Bar Island** (formerly Rodick's Island) from the foot of Bridge Street in downtown Bar Harbor. Shell heaps recorded on the eastern end of the island indicate that Native Americans enjoyed this turf in the distant past. You'll have the most time to explore the island during new-moon or full-moon low tides, but no more than two to four hours—about two hours before and two hours after low tide. Be sure to wear a watch so you don't get trapped (for up to 10 hours). The foot of Bridge Street is also an excellent kayak launching site.

About a mile from downtown, along Main Street (Route 3), is **Compass Harbor**, a section of the park where you can stroll through woods to the water's edge and explore the overgrown ruins of park cofounder George Dorr's home.

Bear right at the fork just after the Thompson Island information center on Route 102/198 to reach **Indian Point/Blagden Preserve**, a lovely preserve owned by The Nature Conservancy. Five trails wind through forested, 110-acre Indian Point/Blagden Preserve, a rectangular Nature Conservancy parcel with island, hill, and bay vistas. Seal-watching and birding are popular—harbor seals on offshore rocks and woodpeckers (plus 130 other species) in blowdown areas. To spot the seals, plan your hike around low tide, when they'll be sprawled on the rocks close to shore. Wear rubberized shoes. Bring binoculars or use the telescope installed here for the purpose. To keep from disturbing the seals, watch quietly and avoid jerky movements. Park near the preserve entrance and follow the Big Woods Trail, running the length of the preserve. A second parking area is farther in, but then you'll miss much of the preserve. When you reach the second parking area, just past an old field, bear left along the Shore Trail to see the seals. Register at the caretakers' house (just beyond the first parking lot, where you can pick up bird and flora checklists), and respect private property on either side of the preserve. Open dawn–6 P.M. daily all year. From the junction of Routes 3 and 102/198, continue 1.8 miles to Indian Point Road and turn right. Go 1.7 miles to a fork and turn right. Watch for the preserve entrance on the right, marked by a Nature Conservancy oak leaf.

Golf

Duffers first teed off in 1891 at **Kebo Valley Golf Club** (100 Eagle Lake Rd., Rte. 233, Bar Harbor, 207/288-5000, May–Oct.), Maine's oldest club.

The 17th hole is legendary; it took President William Howard Taft 27 tries to sink the ball in 1911. Kebo is very popular, with a gorgeous setting, an attractive clubhouse, and decent food service, so tee times are essential; greens fees are the highest on the island.

Bike Rentals

With all the great biking options, including 44 miles of carriage roads and some of the best roadside bike routes in Maine, you'll want to bring a bike or rent one here. Two firms are based in downtown Bar Harbor, and both handle repairs and rentals. Expect to pay $18–20 per day for a rental bike. **Acadia Bike & Canoe** (48 Cottage St., Bar Harbor, 207/288-9605 or 800/526-8615) opens daily at 8 A.M. in spring, summer, and fall. Down the street is the **Bar Harbor Bicycle Shop** (141 Cottage St., Bar Harbor 04609, 207/288-3886, 9 A.M.–6 P.M.).

© TOM NANGLE

You don't need to bring your bicycle. Bar Harbor has a number of well-stocked shops catering to cyclists.

Rock and Ice Climbing

Eager to scale those cliffs? **Acadia Mountain Guides Climbing School** (198 Main St., Bar Harbor, 207/288-8186 or 888/232-9559, www.acadiamountainguides.com) offers instruction and guiding. Rates are $190 for one, $250 for two, for a full day; $100 for one, $160 for two, half day. A half-day family fun climb is $179; full day is $289 for up to four. Weekly sunset climbs are $49.

 Dive-In Theater Boat Cruise

You don't have to go diving in these frigid waters; others will do it for you. When the kids are clamoring to touch slimy sea cucumbers and starfish at various touch tanks in the area, they're likely to be primed for **Diver Ed's** Dive-In Theater Boat Cruise (55 West St., Bar Harbor, 207/288-3483, www.divered.com), operating from the Harborside

© TOM NANGLE

A catamaran is a fast and stable boat, ideal for whale-watching cruises that venture far offshore. If you go, bring lots of extra clothing, as it can be downright cold out at sea.

Hotel Marina. Former Bar Harbor harbormaster Ed Monat heads the crew aboard the 46-passenger *Seal,* which goes a mile or two offshore and sends down two professional divers (including Ed) with video cameras. You stay on deck, all warm and dry, and watch the action on a TV screen. There's communication back and forth, so the kids can ask questions as the divers pick up urchins, starfish, crabs, lobsters, and other sea life. The divers bring up a bag of touchable specimens when they surface—another chance to pet some slimy creatures. Great concept, and it's a big hit. The 2.5-hour trips depart three times daily Monday–Saturday. Cost is $30 adults, $25 seniors, $20 children ages 5–12, $5 younger than 5; usually twice weekly there's a park ranger or naturalist on board, and those trips cost an additional $3.50.

Whale-Watching Excursions

Whale-watching boats go as much as 20 miles offshore, so no matter what the weather in Bar Harbor, dress warmly and bring more clothing than you think you'll need.

Whale-watching, puffin-watching, and combo excursions are offered by **Bar Harbor Whale Watch Company** (1 West St., Bar Harbor, 207/288-2386 or 800/942-5374, BarHarborWhales.com), sailing from the town pier (1 West St.) in downtown Bar Harbor. The company operates under various names, including Acadian Whale Watcher, and has a number of boats. Most trips are accompanied by a naturalist (often from Allied Whale at the College of the Atlantic), who regales passengers with all sorts of interesting trivia about the whales, porpoises, seabirds, and other marinelife spotted along the way. In season, some trips go out as far as the puffin colony on Petit Manan light. Trips depart daily from late May through late October, but with so many options, it's impossible to list the schedule, so call. Tickets are $39–43 adults, $25 children 6–14, $8 children under six. Note: Trips often go longer than the 2.5–3 hours advertised. Don't plan anything else too tightly around the trip. Either before or afterward, be sure to visit the Whale Museum.

Sailboat Cruises

Captain Steve Pagels, under the umbrella of

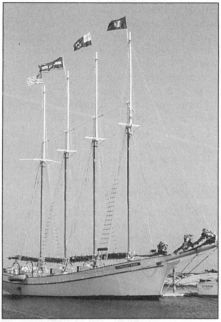

The 151-foot, steel-hulled, four-masted windjammer *Margaret Todd* sails daily from the Bar Harbor Inn pier.

© TOM NANGLE

Downeast Windjammer Cruises (207/288-4585 or 207/288-2373, www.downeastwindjammer .com), offers two-hour day sails on the 151-foot steel-hulled *Margaret Todd,* a gorgeous four-masted schooner. Trips depart daily at 10 A.M. and 2 and 6:30 P.M. mid-May to mid-October (weather permitting), from the Bar Harbor Inn pier, just east of the town pier in downtown Bar Harbor. Buy tickets either at the pier or at 27 Main Street; plan to arrive at least a half hour early. Cost is $29.50 adult, $19.50 ages 11 and younger, $27.50 senior.

Sea Kayaking

Sea kayaking is wildly popular along the Maine coast, and Bar Harbor has become a major kayaking destination. No experience is necessary to join tours operated by any of the firms in Bar Harbor. Half-day ($47), full-day ($69; bring your own lunch), and multiday sea-kayak tours

are on the schedule organized by **Coastal Kayaking Tours** (48 Cottage St., Bar Harbor, 207/288-9605 or 800/526-8615, www.acadia fun.com). Best option for beginners is the 2.5-hour harbor tour, beginning at 9 A.M. ($36). By prearrangement, special half-day family tours, departing at 1:30 P.M., can handle kids eight and over ($47). A 2.5-hour sunset cruise begins around 5 P.M. (depending on season), at $36, and a three-day inn-to-inn tour is $599. Other kayak trips are offered mid-May through September. All trips are weather-dependent, and reservations are essential. Rental canoes ($30), ruddered kayaks ($45 solo, $55 tandem), and open cockpits ($25 single, $335 double) are available.

Lobster Cruises

When you're ready to learn The Truth about lobsters, sign up for a cruise aboard Captain John Nicolai's *Lulu,* a traditional Maine lobsterboat. Operating daily May–September, *Lulu* departs from the Harborside Hotel and Marina, in Bar Harbor (55 West St., 207/963-2341 or 866/235-2341, www.lululobsterboat .com), about 8 A.M., doing four or five two-hour trips each day. Captain Nicolai provides an entertaining commentary on anything and everything, but especially about lobsters and lobstering. He hauls a lobster trap and explains intimate details of the hapless critter. (Lobstering is banned on Sunday June–August; the cruises operate, but there's no hauling that day.) Reservations are required; six passengers max. Cost is $25 adults, $22 seniors, $15 children under 12. No credit cards. Free parking in the hotel's lot.

SHOPPING

Bar Harbor's boutiques are indisputably visitor-oriented; many shut down for the winter, even removing or covering their signs and blanketing the windows. Shop-till-you-droppers will be happy here only between Memorial Day weekend and Columbus Day. (Remember, too, that Bar Harbor isn't MDI's only shopping area.)

Acadia Region

Galleries and Crafts

Birdsnest Gallery (12 Mt. Desert St., Bar Harbor, 207/288-4054) has a well-earned reputation for a fine selection of paintings, sculpture, and prints. Prices match the quality.

Downtown Bar Harbor's best craft gallery is **Island Artisans** (99 Main St., Bar Harbor, 207/288-4214). More than 50 Maine artists are represented here, and the quality is outstanding. Don't miss it. You'll find basketwork, handmade paper, wood carvings, blown glass, jewelry, weaving, metalwork, ceramics, and more. (Island Artisans has a summertime branch at 119 Main St. in Northeast Harbor.)

Colorful, creative, and fun describes the works displayed at **Leapin Lizard Gallery** (227 Main St., Bar Harbor, 207/288-2227). Inside—and outdoors in the sculpture garden—is a bit of everything: paintings, sculpture, ceramics, garden art, and jewelry.

More than 100 contemporary American artists are represented by **Eclipse Gallery** (12 Mount Desert St., Bar Harbor, 207/288-9048), which specializes in handblown glass and complementary works.

Books

Toys, cards, and newspapers blend in with the new-book inventory at **Sherman's Book Store** (56 Main St., Bar Harbor, 207/288-3161). Even some fusty clutter is here, but it's all user-friendly. Sherman's is just the place to pick up maps and trail guides for fine days and puzzles for foggy days.

Souvenir Gifts and Crafts

Souvenir shops are *everywhere* on Mount Desert Island, so why single out the Acadia Shops? If you need Maine-made mementos for Uncle Harry and Aunt Mary, if the kids need trinkets for friends back home, the Acadia Corporation has several shops in downtown Bar Harbor that can cover it all. Price range is broad, quality is fairly high, and clerks are especially friendly at **The Acadia Shop** (85 Main St., Bar Harbor, 207/288-5600). Another branch, **Acadia Outdoors** (45 Main St., Bar Harbor, 207/288-2422), features sportswear and outdoor accessories.

Musical Instruments

Most vacationers don't expect to shop for musical instruments, but everyone with an affinity for folkloric music gravitates toward **Song of the Sea** (47 West St., Bar Harbor 207/288-5653), a unique, jam-packed harborfront shop where you can find guitars, banjos, harmonicas, and tin whistles—but also such esoterica as hammered dulcimers, bagpipes, and psalteries. Ed and Anne Damm are extremely knowledgeable and helpful, even to the point of playing instruments over the phone for call-in orders.

ENTERTAINMENT

At the height of the summer season, plenty of live entertainment varies from pub music to films to classical concerts.

The **Bar Harbor Town Band** performs free Monday and Thursday evenings (8 P.M.) July to mid-August on the Village Green (Main St. and Mount Desert St., Bar Harbor).

Above Rupununi's restaurant, **Carmen Verandah** (119 Main St., Bar Harbor, 207/288-2766) is the weekend place to be and be seen. Everything gets rolling about 9:30 P.M.—blues, rock, salsa, funk, zydeco, ska, reggae, you-name-it—and there's lots of space for dancing. Other nights, there's a DJ. Darts and pool round out the picture. Open all year.

You never know quite what's going to happen at **Improv Acadia** (15 Cottage St., Bar Harbor, 207/288-2503, $12). Every show is different, as actors use audience suggestions to create spots. Shows are staged two or three times a night, mid-June to mid-October, with the first show being kid-friendly.

The **Bar Harbor Music Festival,** a summer tradition since 1967, emphasizes up-and-coming musical talent in a series of classical, jazz, and pops concerts, usually Fridays and Sundays, at various island locations early July to early August. Advance tickets are $20 adult, $12 student, and can be purchased at the festival office building (59 Cottage). Reservations are wise (207/288-5744 in July and August, 212/222-1026 off-season). In even-numbered years, the **Mount Desert Garden Club Tour** presents a rare chance to visit some of Maine's most spectacular private gardens the second or third Saturday in July (confirm the date with the Bar Harbor Chamber of Commerce).

Movies

In 2001, new owners assumed the reins of the beautifully refurbished National Historic Landmark **Criterion Theater** (35 Cottage St., Bar Harbor 04609, 207/288-3441 for films or 207/288-5829 for concerts, www.criteriontheater.com), built in 1932. Now, in addition to screening films, the Criterion puts on concerts, plays, and other special events. Adults soak up the nostalgia of this Art Deco classic with nearly 900 seats; kids just call it "awesome." Beer, wine, and creative appetizers and sandwiches ($9) are now available, and the theater is open all year.

You can enjoy pizza with your picture show at **Reel Pizza Cinerama** (33 Kennebec Pl., Bar Harbor, film 207/288-3811, food 207/288-3828). Two screenings nightly; all seats $5. Doors

open at 4:30 P.M.; it's best to get there early for the best seats.

EVENTS

Bar Harbor is home to numerous special events. Here's just a sampling. For more, call 207/288-5103, or visit www.barharbormaine.com.

In late May, the annual **Warblers & Wildflowers Festival** attracts birders and nature lovers. Events include morning birdsong walks, garden tours, art, lectures, and other events.

In late June **Legacy of the Arts** is a weeklong celebration of music, art, theater, dance, and history.

The **Fourth of July** is always a big deal in Bar Harbor, celebrated with a blueberry-pancake breakfast (6 A.M.), a parade (10 A.M.), a seafood festival (11 A.M. on), a band concert, and fireworks. A highlight is the Lobster Race, a crustacean competition drawing contestants such as Lobzilla and Larry the Lobster in a four-lane saltwater tank on the Village Green.

The Maine Indian Basket Maker's Association, along with the Abbe Museum and College of the Atlantic, sponsors the annual Native American Festival on the college campus in early July, where members of Maine's four tribes share their culture and heritage and sell their collectible baskets and other art and craft work.

© TOM NANGLE

And Independence Day celebrations in the island's smaller villages evoke a bygone era.

The Abbe Museum, the College of the Atlantic, and the Maine Indian Basketmakers Alliance sponsor the annual **Native American Festival**, 10 A.M.–4 P.M. the first Saturday in July, featuring baskets, beadwork, and other handicrafts for sale, and Indian drumming and dancing. Free admission; held at College of the Atlantic, Bar Harbor.

The **Arcady Music Festival** (207/288-2141 or 207/288-3151, www.arcady.org) presents evening concerts late July through August at various locations. Bar Harbor concerts usually are Thursday at 8 P.M. in the Holy Redeemer Church. The array of music is broad, from ragtime to classical.

The **Directions Craft Show** fills the second or third weekend of August with extraordinary displays and sales of crafts by members of Directions. You'll find it at Mount Desert Island High School (Rte. 233, Eagle Lake Rd.). Hours are Friday 5–9 P.M., Saturday and Sunday 10 A.M.–5 P.M.

ACCOMMODATIONS

Bar Harbor alone has thousands of beds in hotels, motels, inns, B&Bs, and cottages, not to mention campsites—and the rest of the island adds to the total. Nonetheless, lodgings can be scarce at the height of summer (particularly the first two weeks in August), which happens to coincide with an outrageous peak period for room rates. Off-season, there's plenty of choice, even after the seasonal places shut down, and rates are always lower, often dramatically so.

Hotels

One of the town's best-known, most-visible, and best-situated hotels is the **Bar Harbor Inn** (Newport Dr., P.O. Box 7, Bar Harbor 04609, 207/288-3351 or 800/248-3351, www.barharbor inn.com, $199–369), a sprawling complex on eight acres overlooking the harbor and Bar Island. The 153 rooms and suites vary considerably in style, from traditional inn to motel, in three different buildings. Continental breakfast is in-

cluded, and special packages, with meals and activities, are available—an advantage if you have children. The kids also will appreciate the heated outdoor pool. Rooms in the Oceanfront Lodge are good choices, with reasonable rates and terrific views. The Main Inn rooms have seen the most recent upgrades. Service is attentive. Open April–November.

Newest and fanciest hotel in town is **Harborside Hotel & Marina** (55 West St., Bar Harbor 04609, 207/288-5033 or 800/238-5033, www.theharborsidehotel.com, $179–279), fronting on the water in downtown Bar Harbor. Almost all of the 185 rooms and suites have a water view and semiprivate balconies; some have whirlpool tubs; deluxe rooms have marble baths, and some have large outdoor hot tubs. Deluxe studios have 1–3 bedrooms, and penthouse suites have full kitchens. Rates include a continental breakfast buffet. An adjacent spa is expected to open in 2005 in the beautifully restored Bar Harbor Club. Future plans include a restaurant open only to guests and members, saltwater and freshwater pools, tennis courts, and other amenities. Open mid-May–October.

Motels

At the opposite end of the budgetary scale is the **Edenbrook Motel** (96 Eden St., Rte. 3, Bar Harbor 04609, 207/288-4975, www.acadia .net/edenbrook, $70–95), with an excellent location 1.5 miles from Acadia's main entrance, 1 mile from downtown, and 500 yards from the ferry servicing Canada. Four tiers of buildings are built on a hillside; those on the second floor in the highest building have balconies with panoramic ocean views. The 47 rooms are basic motel style but spacious, and all have phones, TV, and in-room coffee. Open late May–late October.

A little fancier and right next door is the **Highbrook Motel** (94 Eden St., Rte. 3, Bar Harbor 04609, 207/288-3591 or 800/338-9688, www.highbrookmotel.com, $78–138), with 26 rooms in two hillside buildings. Each room has air-conditioning, TV, telephone, and a coffeemaker, and most have refrigerators. Nicest rooms are in the quiet back building. Coffee, tea, and breakfast pastry are available in the morning. Open late May–late October.

Inns and B&Bs

Few innkeepers have mastered the art of hospitality as well as Roy Kasindorf and Helene Harton, owners of the ◫ **Ullikana Bed & Breakfast** (16 The Field, Bar Harbor 04609, 207/288-9552, www.ullikana.com, $160–295), a Victorian Tudor house close to Bar Harbor's Shore Path. They genuinely enjoy their guests. Helene's a whiz in the kitchen; after one of her multi-course breakfasts, usually served on the waterview patio, you won't be needing lunch. She's also a decorating genius, blending antiques and modern art, vibrant color with soothing hues, folk art and fine art, with a result like a finely tuned orchestra. Roy excels at helping guests select just the right hike, bike route, or other activity. Afternoon refreshments provide a time for guests to gather and share experiences. Ten comfortable rooms all have private baths; many have working fireplaces, and some have private terraces with water views. Helene and Roy also own The Yellow House, next door, with six lovely rooms decorated in old Bar Harbor style and a huge living room filled with antique wicker. Both are open late May–October.

New owners have completely renovated the **Bass Cottage** (14 The Field, Box 242, Bar Harbor 04609, 207/288-1234 or 866/782-9224, www.basscottage.com, $225–340). Corporate refugees Teri and Jeff Anderholm purchased the 1885 26-room cottage in 2003 and spent a year gutting it, salvaging the best of the old, and blending in new to turn it into a stylish 10-room inn. Guest rooms are soothingly decorated with cream and pastel-colored walls and have phones and TV with DVD (a DVD library is available); many rooms have fireplaces and whirlpool tubs. The spacious and elegant public rooms flow from one to another. Teri puts her culinary degree to use preparing baked goods, fruits, and savory and sweet entrées for breakfast and evening refreshments. A guest pantry is stocked with tea, coffee, and snacks. Open May into November.

Energetic Marian Burns, a former math/science teacher and former president of the Maine Innkeepers Association, is the reason everything runs smoothly at **Mira Monte Inn** (69 Mount Desert St., Bar Harbor 04609, 207/288-4263 or 800/553-5109, $165–245), close (but not too close) to downtown. Born and raised here, and an avid gardener, Marian's a terrific resource for island exploring. Try to capture her during wine and cheese (5–7 P.M.), and ask about her experience during the 1947 Bar Harbor fire. And don't miss her collection of antique Bar Harbor hotel photos. The 13 Victorian-style rooms have air-conditioning, cable TV, and either a balcony or fireplace, and some have whirlpool tubs; two efficiency suites and one fully equipped apartment-style unit in a separate building are ideal for families. Early and late in the season, Marian organizes special-rate theme weekends. Rates include an extensive hot-and-cold breakfast buffet. Open early May to early November (the two suites are open all year). Marian also owns the nearby **Atlantean**, an elegant Tudor-style inn ($170–285). Each of the eight spacious rooms has air-conditioning, TV, phone, and CD player; some have whirlpool tubs and fireplaces.

Much less pricey and a find for families is the **Seacroft Inn** (18 Albert Meadow, Bar Harbor 04069, 207/288-4669 or 800/824-9694, www.seacroftinn.com, $99–129), well situated just off Main Street and near the Shore Path. All rooms in Bunny and Dave Brown's white, multigabled cottage have phones, TV, refrigerator, and microwave, and a breakfast basket is delivered to your room each morning (subtract $5 from the rate if you don't want it). Some rooms can be joined as family suites. There's also an apartment, available by the week for $1,550. Open year-round, but no breakfast or housekeeping in winter.

Outside of town in a serene location with fabulous views of Frenchman Bay is Jack and Jeani Ochtera's ◫ **The Bay Ledge Inn & Spa** (150 Sand Point Rd., Bar Harbor 04069, 207/288-4204 summer or 207/875-3262 winter, www.innatbayledge.com, $160–375), an oasis of calm tucked under towering pines and atop an 80-foot cliff. Terraced decks descend to a pool and hot tub and on to the lawn, which stretches to the cliff's edge. Stairs descend to a private stone beach below. It's an elegant, casual retreat.

Almost all guest rooms have water views. Beds are topped with down comforters and feather beds, some rooms have whirlpool tubs, and second-floor rooms have private decks. A sauna and steam shower are available. Open May–October. Also available are cottages ($160–175), which lack the view but have use of the inn's facilities. Newest addition is the adjacent Summer House at Bay Ledge, a shingled two-bedroom, two-bath cottage with a deck 25 feet from the edge of Frenchman Bay. It's available for weekly rental late May–October ($1,400–3,000).

Hostel

The **Bar Harbor/Mount Desert Island Hostel** (321 Main St., P.O. Box 32, Bar Harbor 04609, 207/288-5587, www.barharborhostel.com, $21 HI members, $25 nonmembers and students) reopened in 2004 in its own beautifully renovated building on the edge of town. Inside are dorms for men and women, a family room, and a well-equipped kitchen; outside is an organic garden, where you can help yourself to the produce. Reservations (best by mail) are essential, as this is a popular location. Open April–October.

Campgrounds

Near the Thompson Island information center are two well-sited campgrounds, both large and well maintained and both on an Island Explorer bus route. Next to the causeway, and 10 miles northwest of Bar Harbor, **Bar Harbor KOA** (136 County Rd., Bar Harbor 04609, 207/288-3520 or 888/562-5605, www.barharborkoa.com, $21–41, mid-May to mid-Oct.), previously known as Barcadia, occupies 32 acres with 2,500 feet of shorefront. Many of the 200 open, grassy, and wooded tent and RV sites have terrific views. Facilities include coin showers and laundry, playground, beach, game areas, on-site sea kayak and canoe rental and tour outfitter, and a small shop. Pets are allowed. Open mid-May to mid-October.

Mt. Desert Narrows Camping Resort (1219 Rte. 3, Bar Harbor 04609, 207/288-4782, www.narrowscamping.com, $30–80/site varying with location and hookups, May–late Oct.), 1.5 miles east of the causeway, has a fantastic view over Thomas Bay and the Narrows. The 40-acre campground has 239 wooded and open tent and RV sites, heated pool, convenience store, canoe and kayak rentals, volleyball and basketball courts, playground, coin laundry, free movie nights and hay rides, and live entertainment mid-June to Labor Day. Pets are allowed.

Seasonal Rentals

Maine Island Properties (P.O. Box 1025, Mount Desert 04609, 207/244-4348, www.maineisland properties.com) lists about 100 cottages available by the week or month. In high season (June to Labor Day), rates begin at around $1,000 a week.

FOOD

You won't go hungry in Bar Harbor, and you won't find chain fast-food places. The summer tourism trade and the College of the Atlantic students have created a demand for pizzerias, vegetarian bistros, brewpubs, and a handful of creative restaurants. But of course almost every restaurant has some variant of lobster. And even if you're using Bar Harbor as a base of operations, don't miss opportunities to explore restaurants elsewhere on the island.

The island's best collection of good, inexpensive eateries, most open year-round, is along Rodick Street, from Reel Pizza down to Rosalie's, which actually fronts on Cottage Street. You'll find a good ethnic mix here, from Mexican to Thai to Italian; not a lobster in sight.

Miscellany

Only a masochist could bypass **Ben and Bill's Chocolate Emporium** (66 Main St., Bar Harbor, 207/288-3281 or 800/806-3281), a long-running taste-treat-cum-experience in downtown Bar Harbor. The homemade candies and more than 50 ice cream flavors (including a dubious lobster flavor, $35 a bucket to go) are nothing short of outrageous; the whole place smells like the inside of a chocolate truffle. The shop, a cousin of three Massachusetts ice cream parlors, is open March–December, daily 9 A.M.–10 P.M. in spring and fall, 9 A.M.–midnight in summer.

J.H. Butterfield Co. (152 Main St., Bar Har-

Acadia Region

Even if you don't try lobster ice cream, do stop in at Ben and Bill's in downtown Bar Harbor for one of its other fabulous homemade ice creams or chocolates.

bor, 207/288-3386) is a fine place to pick up fixings for a fancy picnic.

Probably the least-expensive lunch or ice cream option in town is the **West End Drug Co.** (105 Main St., Bar Harbor, 207/288-3318), where you can get grilled cheese sandwiches and other old-fashioned white bread basics as well as frappes and sundaes at the fountain.

Bar Harbor has a super natural foods store, the **Alternative Community Market** (16 Mount Desert St., Bar Harbor, 207/288-8225), where you can purchase sandwiches. There's limited seating indoors and on the deck.

Between Mother's Day and late October, **Eden Farmers' Market** operates out of the YMCA parking lot off Lower Main Street in Bar Harbor each Sunday, 10 A.M.–1 P.M.

Pizza, Sandwiches, and Baked Goods

An unscientific but reliable local survey gives the best-pizza ribbon to **Rosalie's Pizza & Italian Restaurant** (46 Cottage St., Bar Harbor, 207/288-5666), where the Wurlitzer jukebox churns out tunes from the 1950s. This family-owned standard gets high marks for consistency with

its homemade pizza (in four sizes or by the slice), calzones, and subs—lots of vegetarian options. Beer and wine are available. Rosalie's opens daily at 11 A.M., all year.

Combine a pizza with a first-run or art flick at **Reel Pizza Cinerama** (33 Kennebec Pl., Bar Harbor, film 207/288-3811, food 207/288-3828), where you order your pizza, grab an easy chair, and watch for your number to come up on the bingo board. Screenings usually begin at 6 and 8:30 or 9 P.M. Pizzas ($12–20) have cinematic names—Zorba the Greek, The Godfather, Manchurian Candidate. Then there's the Mussel Beach Party—broccoli, tomatoes, goat cheese, and smoked mussels. You get the idea. Reel Pizza opens daily at 4:30 P.M. and has occasional Saturday matinees; closed Monday in winter. Be sure to arrive early; the best chairs go quickly.

Efficient, friendly, cafeteria-style service makes **EPI Sub and Pizza Shop** (8 Cottage St., Bar Harbor, 207/288-5853, 10 A.M.–8 P.M., to 9 P.M. July and Aug.) an excellent choice for picnics or a quick break from sightseeing. The dozen-plus sub-sandwich choices at EPI's (short for epicurean) are bargains (try the Cadillac). If the weather closes in, there are always the pinball machines in the back room. No credit cards. Closed Sunday in November, December, and from February to mid-May.

Soups, salads, sandwiches, and smoothies fill the menu at **Nature's Way Café** (15 Cottage St., Bar Harbor, 207/288-4100, opens 7 A.M.), making it a good place to pick up a healthful breakfast or lunch. There's also PB&J for the kids.

For a light, inexpensive breakfast or lunch, you can't go wrong at 🖫 **Morning Glory Bakery** (39 Rodick St., Bar Harbor, 207/288-3041, 7 A.M.–4 P.M. Mon.–Fri., 8 A.M.–1 P.M. Sat.). Espresso and other fancy coffees, fresh-squeezed juices, smoothies, fresh-baked goodies ($1–2), and sandwiches ($5) are all made from scratch. Planning a day in the park? Call ahead for a boxed lunch ($7), with sandwich, drink, and choice of two: chips, fruit, salad of the day, or cookie.

Brewpubs and Microbreweries

Bar Harbor's longest-lived brewpub is the **Lompoc Café** (36 Rodick St., Bar Harbor, 207/288-9392, 11:30 A.M.–9 P.M. late April–mid-Dec.), serving creative lunches and dinners daily ($8–19). How about a lobster and avocado quesadilla? After 9 P.M., there's just beer and thin-crust pizza until about 1 A.M. The congenial café has a beer garden, a bocce court, and open mic night Thursdays and live entertainment (blues, bluegrass, and jazz) Fridays and Saturdays May–October.

Lompoc's signature Bar Harbor Real Ale and five or six others are brewed by the **Atlantic Brewing Company** (15 Knox Rd., Town Hill, in the upper section of the island, 207/288-2337 or 800/475-5417). Free brewery tours, including tasting, are given daily at 2, 3, and 4 P.M. Memorial Day to Columbus Day. In summer, the brewery also operates a tavern/café serving sandwiches, burgers, and deli plates, 11:30 A.M.–5 P.M. Every Saturday **MainelyMeat Bar-B-Q** sets up an all-you-can-eat barbecue at noon for $12. It's extremely popular, so go early to avoid disappointment.

Bar Harbor Brewing Company & Soda Works (135 Otter Creek Rd., Rte. 3, Bar Harbor, 207/288-4592), begun in 1990 by Tod and Suzi Foster as a mom-and-pop operation, remains a small, friendly, hands-on enterprise producing five kinds of beer and ale in a basement microbrewery. Start off at the log-cabin tasting room/gift shop, where kids can sample Old Fashioned Bar Harbor Root Beer. Free tours begin every 20 minutes between 3:30 and 5 P.M. Tuesday–Friday late June–August. The brewery is 4.5 miles south of downtown Bar Harbor.

Casual Family-Friendly Dining

Once a Victorian boarding house and later a 1920s speakeasy, **Galyn's Galley** (17 Main St., Bar Harbor, 207/288-9706, 11:30 A.M.–2:30 P.M. and 4–10 P.M., March–Nov.) has been a popular eatery since 1986. Lots of plants, modern decor, reliable service, a great downtown location, and several indoor and outdoor dining areas contribute to the loyal clientele. The cuisine is consistently good if not outstandingly creative (dinner entrées $15–18). Reservations advisable in midsummer.

Just down the street from Galyn's, **Rupununi** (119 Main St., Bar Harbor, 207/288-2886) gets its name from a river in Guyana—the inspiration of owner Mike Boland, a College of the Atlantic grad. Billed as "an American bar and grill," Rupununi draws a lively, fun crowd for great burgers (even ostrich burgers, $7), veggie and meat dinner entrées ($10–20), some Caribbean and Mediterranean touches, and about two dozen beers on draft. The daily poacher's special usually means buffalo or venison. On Sunday, jazz is part of the mix; on Friday nights, acoustic guitar. Open daily 11–1 A.M. Upstairs is **Carmen Verandah** (see Entertainment). Also part of the ever-expanding Rupununi empire is **Joe's Smoke Shop,** an upscale cigar bar next door.

Set back from the road behind the Leapin Lizard Gallery's sculpture garden is the very popular **McKay's Public House** (231 Main St., Bar Harbor, 207/288-2002, 11:30 A.M.–3 P.M. and 5–10 P.M.), a comfortable pub with seating indoors in small dining rooms or at the bar or outdoors, in the garden. Classic pub fare includes shepherd's pie with lamb, fish and chips, and bangers and mash, ($10). Reubens and burgers are $7–8. At dinner, fancier entrées, like coconut-encrusted red snapper, are also available, most in the $16–20 range.

Fifties memorabilia and old toys fill **Route 66 Restaurant** (21 Cottage St., Bar Harbor, 207/288-3708, 7 A.M.–8 P.M. or so), a fun restaurant that's a real hit with kids (check out the train running around just below the ceiling). Nothing fancy here, but a wide-ranging menu that includes sandwiches, burgers, pizza, steak, chicken, seafood, and kids' choices. Dinner choices run around $8–18, breakfast $3–7, lunch $7–12.

Eclectic Fare

Around the corner from Rupununi, in a funky side-street building with higgledy-piggledy decor (well, maroon paint, a wall lined with books, and a refrigerator door loaded with poetry magnets) is a not-very-well-kept secret, **M Café This Way** (14 Mt. Desert St., Bar Harbor, 207/288-4483). Launched by a trio of enthusiastic partners, the café has been a hit since it opened in 1997. This might be the only place in town that doesn't serve lobster. But it *does* serve such eclectic items as artichokes stuffed with trout and crab cakes with tequila-lime sauce ($9). The breakfast menu is a genuine wake-up call; try Green Eggs and Sam ($6). Dinner entrées are in the $14–23 range; the wine list is very selective and the desserts are outstanding. In summer and fall, Café This Way serves breakfast (7–11 A.M. Mon.–Sat. and 8 A.M.–1 P.M. Sun.) and dinner (5:30–9 P.M. daily). In winter and spring, alas, it's open only for breakfast and lunch (Wed.–Sun. 8 A.M.–2 P.M.).

After establishing a solid reputation for breakfast and lunch, **2 Cats** (130 Cottage St., Bar Harbor, 207/288-2808 or 800/355-2828, 7 A.M.–1 P.M. daily and 5 P.M.–close Wed.–Sun.) began serving dinner in 2004 to equally rave reviews. Fun, funky, and fresh best describe both the restaurant and the food. Dinner choices run $14–22. Dine inside or on the patio. Three upstairs rooms are $145–175, with breakfast, of course.

Ethnic and Vegetarian Fare

For Thai food, **Siam Orchard** (30 Rodick St., Bar Harbor, 207/288-9669, 11 A.M.–3 P.M. daily, no lunch Sun.) gets the local's nod. House specials run $9–12, curries and noodle dishes, such as pad Thai, run $5–7 at lunch, $8–12 at dinner. Plenty of choices for vegetarians. Beer and wine only. Open all year.

Sharing the same building is **Gringo's** (30 Rodick St., Bar Harbor, 207/288-2326, 11 A.M.–10 P.M.), a Mexican hole-in-the-wall specializing in take-out burritos, wraps, hand-made salsas, and smoothies, with almost everything less than $7. For a real kick, don't miss the jalapeño brownies.

There's a good chance **M Eden** (28 West St., Bar Harbor, 207/288-4422, 5–9:30ish P.M.) could make a vegetarian out of even the most die-hard meat lover. This small restaurant (reservations highly recommended) is dedicated to using organic ingredients from area farms and preparing vegan entrées such as soy seitan piccata with lemon caper vinaigrette, sautéed greens, and sage-mashed potatoes; Thai noodle bowl with green curry coconut broth, spring vegetables, fresh tofu, and rice noodles; and bento box with grilled tofu, seasoned edamame, baby bok choy, sesame seaweed salad, umeboshi nori roll, and citrus ponzu. Too green? How about rigatoni pasta with crimini mushrooms, sun-dried tomatoes, and sautéed rainbow chard in a garlic wine sauce. Entrées run $12.50–16.

M Havana (318 Main St., Bar Harbor, 207/288-2822, www.havanamaine.com, 5:30–10 P.M. May–late Oct., Wed.–Sat. the rest of the year) promises "American fine dining with Latin flair," and it delivers. The innovative cuisine, bright orange walls and white table-cloths, and a jazz duo providing the background have made it a hit. Hot choices include fusion—grilled Chilean swordfish, pasta with Bahian coconut sauce, Jamaican jerk lamb, tuna with Asian mushroom salsa. Entrée range is $16–35; for $5.50, you get a glass of *mojito*, the Cuban national drink. Save room for the chocolate truffle torte or the pumpkin cheesecake with a bourbon glaze. Reservations essential on weekends.

Fine Dining

One of Bar Harbor's fine longtime reliables, **George's** (7 Stephens Ln., Bar Harbor 04609, 207/288-4505, www.georgesbarharbor.com, 5:30–10 P.M. late May–Oct.), occupies three attractively laid-out rooms in a restored home on a downtown side street. Specialties are wild game, seafood, Greek-inspired lamb, and outrageous desserts. Appetizers ($10 and $12) are seafood- and Mediterranean-oriented. Entrées are $25; prix-fixe menus are $37 and $40. Reservations are essential in July and August. There's terrace dining when weather permits. The restaurant is behind the First National Bank, where there's free evening parking.

It seems almost every year, something (name, menu, style) changes at **Thrumcap** (123 Cottage St., Bar Harbor, 207/288-3884, 5:30–9:30 P.M. Mon.–Sat.), but it always wins top marks for both food and atmosphere. Most recently it's been offering a four-course, prix-fixe dinner for $39. Usually about 20 wines are available by the glass for $7–10.

The view's the thing at the Bar Harbor Inn's **Reading Room Restaurant** (Newport Dr., Bar Harbor, 207/288-3351, www.barharborinn.com); request a window seat. Once the stuffy Bar Harbor Reading Room, a gentlemen's club, the dining room still has a sweeping curve of windows overlooking Bar Island and Frenchman Bay. Dinner entrées, emphasizing meat and seafood, are commendably creative ($19–30); the wine list is good, desserts are so-so. Soft music plays in the background. Despite the elegant setting, dress is informal, and there's a children's menu. The Sunday brunch buffet ($23 adults, $11.50 kids, 11:30 A.M.–2:30 P.M.) is extremely popular; in good weather, it's also served on the terrace. Reservations are essential. Breakfast (mid-Apr.–Oct.) is 7–10:30 A.M., lunch (on the terrace, weather permitting) begins at 11:30 A.M., dinner is 5:30–9:30 P.M.

Five miles south of Bar Harbor is the nondescript **Burning Tree** (Rte. 3, Otter Creek, 207/288-9331, 5–10 P.M. Wed.–Mon. late June–early Oct., plus Tuesday in Aug.), which is anything but nondescript inside. Bright and airy, with about 16 tables in three areas, it's one of Mount Desert Island's best restaurants, serving a casually chic crowd. Reservations are essential in summer. Specialties are imaginative seafood entrées—such as curry pecan flounder, cioppino, Maryland (yes!) crab cakes—and vegetarian dishes made from organic produce. Scallop kebabs have *lots* of scallops, the specialty crab cakes are 90 percent crabmeat, and edible flowers garnish the entrées ($16–23). The homemade breads and desserts are delicious. At the height of summer, service can be a bit rushed and the kitchen runs out of popular entrées. Solution: Plan to eat early; it's worth it.

INFORMATION AND SERVICES

Information

The **Bar Harbor Chamber of Commerce** (93 Cottage St., P.O. Box 158, Bar Harbor 04609, 207/288-5103 or 888/540-9990, www.BarHarborMaine.com), close to the downtown action, has an especially helpful staff accustomed to a steady stream of summer traffic. The office is open 8 A.M.–5 P.M. daily in summer, 8 A.M.–4:30 P.M. weekdays off-season. The only drawback is a certain myopia: there's little information here on other parts of the island, so you'll need to remedy that by stopping at one of the information centers near the bridge from the mainland. If you've managed to bestir yourself early enough to catch sunrise on the Cadillac summit, stop in at the chamber of commerce office and request an official membership card for the **Cadillac Mountain Sunrise Club** (they'll take your word for it).

Hospitals

Maine Coast Memorial Hospital (50 Union St., Ellsworth, 207/664-5311), the largest hospital in the area, has 24-hour emergency-room service. Healthcare Express (207/664-5341), at the hospital, handles minor problems daily between noon and 8 P.M.

Mount Desert Island's only full-service hospital is **Mount Desert Island Hospital** (10 Wayman Ln., Bar Harbor, 207/288-5081), with a 24-hour emergency room.

Local Library

Jesup Memorial Library (34 Mount Desert St., Bar Harbor, 207/288-4245) is open all year (10 A.M.–5 P.M. Tues.–Sat., to 7 P.M. Wed.).

Public Restrooms

Downtown Bar Harbor has public restrooms at the town pier, in the municipal parking lot near the Village Green, and on the School Street side of the athletic field, where there is RV parking. Restrooms are also at the Mount Desert Island Hospital and the International Ferry Terminal.

Parking

RVs are not allowed to park near the town pier; designated RV parking is alongside the athletic field, Lower Main and Park Streets, about eight blocks from the center of town.

Northeast Harbor and Vicinity

Some sort of Northeast Harbor bush telegraph must have been operating in the Philadelphia area in the late 19th century, because Main Liners from the City of Brotherly Love have been summering in and around this village since then. Sure, they also show up in other parts of Maine, but it's hard not to notice the preponderance of Pennsylvania license plates surrounding Northeast Harbor's elegant "cottages" from mid-July to mid-August. (In the last decade, the Pennsylvania plates have been joined by growing numbers from the District of Columbia, New York, and Texas.)

Actually, even though Northeast Harbor is a well-known name with special cachet, it isn't even an official township; it's a zip-coded village within the town of Mount Desert.

The small downtown area's attractive boutiques and eateries cater to a casually posh clientele, while the well-protected harbor attracts a tony crowd of yachties. For their convenience, a palm-sized annual directory, *The Redbook*, discreetly lists owners' summer residences and winter addresses—but no phone numbers. The directory also includes listings for the village of Seal Harbor—an even more exclusive village a few miles east of Northeast Harbor where style maven Martha Stewart bought a palatial estate in 1997, to the chagrin of long-timers.

© TOM NANGLE

The best views of sailboats in Somes Sound, the only fjord on the United States' east coast, are from Sargent Drive in Northeast Harbor, or from aboard an excursion boat.

SIGHTS

Somes Sound

As you head toward Northeast Harbor on Route 198 from the northern end of Mount Desert Island, you'll begin seeing cliff-lined Somes Sound on your right. This glacier-sculpted fjord juts five miles into the interior of Mount Desert Island from its mouth, between Northeast and Southwest Harbors. Watch for the right-hand turn for Sargent Drive (no RVs allowed) and follow the lovely,

© TOM NANGLE

Yachts fill picturesque Northeast Harbor, a tony port that's also the departure point for some cruises to offshore islands.

granite-lined route along the east side of the sound. Halfway along, a marker explains the geology of this natural fjord, the only one on the eastern seaboard. There aren't many pullouts en route, and traffic can be fairly steady in midsummer, but don't miss it. An ideal way to appreciate Somes Sound is from the water—sign up for an excursion out of Northeast or Southwest Harbor.

Asticou and Thuya Gardens

If you have the slightest interest in gardens (even if you don't, for that matter), allow time for Northeast Harbor's two marvelous public gardens. Information about both is available from the local chamber of commerce. If gardens are extra-high on your priority list, inquire locally about visiting the private Rockefeller garden, accessible on a very limited basis.

Maine's best spring showcase is the **Asticou Azalea Garden,** a 2.3-acre pocket where about 70 varieties of azaleas, rhododendrons, and laurels—many from the classic Reef Point garden of famed landscape designer Beatrix Farrand—burst into bloom. When Charles K. Savage, beloved former innkeeper of the Asticou Inn, learned that

the Reef Point garden was being undone in 1956, he went into high gear to find funding and managed to rescue the azaleas and provide them with the gorgeous setting they have today, across the road and around the corner from the inn. Oriental serenity is the key—with a Japanese sand garden, stone lanterns, granite outcrops, pink-gravel paths, and a tranquil pond—so try to visit early in the season, and early in the morning, to savor the effect. The garden is on Route 198, at the northern edge of Northeast Harbor, immediately north of the junction with Peabody Drive (Route 3). Watch for a tiny sign on the right, marking access to the parking area. Although Asticou is open daily, all year, prime time for azaleas is mid-May to mid-June.

Behind a carved wooden gate on a forested hillside not far from Asticou lies an enchanted garden also designed by Charles K. Savage, and inspired by Beatrix Farrand. Special features of **Thuya Garden** are perennial borders, sculpted shrubbery, and Oriental touches. On a misty summer day, when few visitors appear, the colors are brilliant. Adjacent to the garden is **Thuya Lodge** (207/276-5130), former summer cottage of Joseph

Curtis, donor of this awesome municipal park. The lodge, with an extensive botanical library and quiet rooms for reading, is open Monday–Saturday 10 A.M.–4:30 P.M. and noon–4:30 P.M. Sunday late June to Labor Day. The garden is open daily 7 A.M.–7 P.M. A collection box next to the front gate requests a small donation. To reach Thuya, continue on Route 3 beyond Asticou Azalea Garden and watch for the Asticou Terraces parking area (no RVs, two-hour limit) on the right. Cross the road and climb the Asticou Terraces Trail (.4 mile) to the garden. Or drive .2 mile beyond the Route 3 parking area, watching for a minuscule Thuya Garden sign on the left. Go half a mile up the driveway to the parking area.

After you've visited Thuya Garden, go outside the back gate, where you'll see a sign for the Eliot Mountain Trail, a 1.4-mile moderately difficult round-trip (lots of exposed roots). Near the summit, Northeast Harbor spreads out before you. If you're here in August, sample the wild blueberries. Eliot Mountain is not an Acadia National

If you have even the slightest interest in gardens, Northeast Harbor's Thuya Garden is worth visiting. Exit out the back gate to climb Eliot Mountain Trail, with fabulous views over Northeast Harbor.

© TOM NANGLE

Park trail, and much of it is on private land, so stay on the path and be respectful of private property.

Petite Plaisance

On Northeast Harbor's quiet South Shore Road, Petite Plaisance is a museum commemorating noted Belgian-born author and college professor Marguerite Yourcenar (pen name of Marguerite de Crayencour), first woman elected to the prestigious Académie Française. From the early 1950s to 1987, Petite Plaisance was her home, and it's hard to believe she's no longer here; her intriguing possessions and presence fill the two-story house. Free, hour-long tours of the first floor are given in French or English, depending on visitors' preferences. French-speaking visitors often make pilgrimages here. The house is open daily June 15–August 31. No children under 12 are allowed. Call 207/276-3940 at least a day ahead, between 9 A.M. and 4 P.M., for an appointment and directions, or write: Petite Plaisance Trust, P.O. Box 403, Northeast Harbor 04662. Yourcenar devotees should request directions to Brookside Cemetery in Somesville, seven miles away, where she is buried.

Great Harbor Maritime Museum

Annual exhibits focusing on the maritime heritage of the Mount Desert Island area are held in the small, eclectic Great Harbor Maritime Museum (125 Main St., Northeast Harbor, 207/276-5262, 10 A.M.–5 P.M. Tues.–Sun. late June to Labor Day, plus weekends in Sept. and Oct., $3), housed in the old village fire station and municipal building. ("Great Harbor" refers to the Somes Sound area—Northeast, Southwest, and Seal Harbors, as well as the Cranberry Isles.) Yachting, coastal trade, and fishing receive special emphasis. Special programs and exhibits are held during the summer.

RECREATION

Bicycling

The cramped **Northeast Harbor Bike Shop** (118 Main St., Northeast Harbor, 207/276-5480) rents bikes for $18 full day, $14 half day, or $75 for the week.

Boating Excursions

Northeast Harbor is the starting point for most of the boats headed for the **Cranberry Isles.** The vessels depart from the commercial floats at the end of the concrete Municipal Pier on Sea Street. (See Cranberry Isles.)

Captain Rob Liebow's 75-foot *Sea Princess* (207/276-5352, www.barharborcruises.com) carries visitors as well as an Acadia National Park naturalist on a 2.5-hour morning trip around the mouth of Somes Sound and out to Little Cranberry Island (Islesford) for a 50-minute stopover. The boat leaves Northeast Harbor daily at 9:45 A.M. mid-May to mid-October. Cost is $18 adults, $12 children under 12, free for children under four. An afternoon trip, departing at 1 P.M. on the same route, spends less time on Islesford but also visits Southwest Harbor. Tickets are the same price as for the morning trip. The *Sea Princess* also does a scenic 1.5-hour Somes Sound cruise, departing daily at 3:45 P.M., late June to early September. Cost is $15 adults, $10 children under 12. The same months, a three-hour sunset/dinner cruise departs at 5:30 P.M. for the Islesford Dock Restaurant on Little Cranberry (Islesford). Cost is $15 adults, $10 children (not including dinner). Reservations are advisable for all trips, although even that provides no guarantee, since the cruises require a rather hefty 15-passenger minimum.

SHOPPING

Upscale shops, galleries—don't miss **Shaw Jewelry**—and boutiques, with clothing, crafts, housewares, quilts, antiques, and antiquarian books, line both sides of Main Street, making for intriguing browsing and expensive buying.

ACCOMMODATIONS

If money's no object and a haute ambience appeals, spring for the **N Asticou Inn** (Rte. 3, Northeast Harbor 04662, 207/276-3344 or 800/258-3373). Built in 1883 and refurbished periodically, the classic inn has 27 rooms and 23 suites, plus several modern cottages. Facilities include clay tennis courts, outdoor pool, and access to the Northeast Harbor

Golf Club. The elegant, mural-lined dining room has fabulous views of the harbor. Jackets and ties are advised for dinner. The inn is open mid-May to late October. July and August rates are $302–362, MAP, $225–285 without meals. Try to plan a late-May or early-June visit; you're practically on top of the Asticou Azalea Garden, and Thuya Garden is a short walk away.

Less pricey and far less formal, **The Maison Suisse Inn** (144 Main St., Northeast Harbor 04662, 207/276-5223 or 800/624-7668, www.maisonsuisse.com, $145–285) is a lovely shingle-style inn set off the street behind a rustic garden. Ten rooms are in the main inn, another five in the guest cottage behind it. All have private baths, oversized beds, TV, and phone; some have a fireplace. Breakfast is provided at a restaurant across the street.

The casual elegance of a bygone era still exists at **Grey Rock Inn** (Rte. 3/198, Northeast Harbor, 207/276-9360 summer, 207/244-4437 winter, www.greyrockinn.com, $185–375, mid-May–late Oct.), an antique-filled mansion with to-die-for views over Northeast Harbor to the outer islands. Guest rooms are comfortable and large; many have fireplaces. Common rooms, most with fireplaces, flow from one to another. Trails lace the property's seven acres, which are bordered by Acadia National Park on two sides. Head out for a hike, perhaps to the summit of Noumbega Mountain, or stroll down the street to downtown Northeast Harbor. Rates include a full breakfast. Note: The owners can be eccentric.

FOOD

Miscellany

In the **Pine Tree Market** (121 Main St., Northeast Harbor, 207/276-3335, 7 A.M.–7 P.M. Mon.–Sat., 8 A.M.–6 P.M. Sun.) you'll find gourmet goodies, a huge wine selection, resident butcher, fresh fish, deli, and homemade breads and pastries.

Pop into **Full Belli Deli** (Sea St., Northeast Harbor, 207/276-4299, 8 A.M.–4 P.M. Mon.–Sat., to 2 P.M. Sun.) for soups, fat sandwiches, and breakfast fare.

From June well into October, the **Northeast**

Harbor Farmers' Market is set up each Thursday, 9 A.M.–noon, in the parking lot of Wallace Moving and Storage on Millbrook Road (the continuation of Sargent Drive). Look for cheeses, cider, maple syrup, breads and cookies, berries, and vegetables.

Casual Dining

Real local color and crab cakes ($15.95) and crab sandwiches are *the best* at the **Docksider** (14 Sea St., Northeast Harbor, 207/276-3965, 11 A.M.–9 P.M., summer only), a low-key, family-friendly, unassuming, hole-in-the-wall place inevitably jammed with devoted locals and summer folk. Just up the hill from the chamber office, the Docksider has an outside deck, plus a couple of veteran (since forever) waitresses, no view, and a reputation far and wide. At $21.95, the shore dinner (chowder, clams, boiled lobster, potato or salad) is one of the best bargains in the state. Wine and beer only. If you're smitten, buy one of the T-shirts, featuring an upright lobster announcing, "Frankly, I don't give a clam." Note: Early-bird specials and a 10 percent discount 4:30–6 P.M.

Expect to wait in line for a table at **⚓ 151 Main St.** (151 Main St., Northeast Harbor, 207/276-9898, opens at 5 P.M. Tues.–Sat.) because no reservations are accepted. The setting is unpretentious, the food sophisticated, with choices ranging from thin-crust pizzas to gussied-up meatloaf to Thai curry shrimps. Entrées run $6–14 for small plates, $10–22 for large plates, $9–13 for pizzas, and $8–16 pasta dishes.

Tucked in a shady corner of a parking lot behind Shaw's Jewelry is a gem. **⚓ La Matta Cena** (5 Old Firehouse Ln., Northeast Harbor, 207/276-3305, noon–4 P.M. and 5:30–9:30 P.M.) serves "spirited Tuscan cuisine" in a rustic garden setting warmed by heat lamps (there are also tables inside). The Mediterranean-inspired food is fabulous; much is sourced locally, and pastas and gelato are made on the premises. Most entrées run $18–24.

Fine Dining

The elegant, mural-lined dining room at the **As-**ticou Inn (Rte. 3, 207/276-3344 or 800/258-3373) is open to the public for Sunday brunch (11:30 A.M.–2:30 P.M.) and dinner (6–10 P.M., entrées $26–33) by reservation. Jackets and ties are advised for dinner. Lunch is also open to the public, served 11:30 A.M.–5 P.M.; reservations aren't needed.

INFORMATION AND SERVICES

Information

The harborfront Chamber Information Bureau (also called the Yachtsmen's Building) of the **Mount Desert Chamber of Commerce** (18 Harbor Rd., P.O. Box 675, Northeast Harbor 04662, 207/276-5040, 8 A.M.–5 P.M. mid-June to mid-Oct.) covers the villages of Somesville, Northeast Harbor, Seal Harbor, Otter Creek, Pretty Marsh, Hall Quarry, and Beech Hill. The extremely cordial staff can provide information on Northeast Harbor's gardens, museums, and trails, in addition to food and lodging. They even rent tennis rackets (reserve court time here, too). Coin-operated ($1.50, quarters only) hot showers, designed primarily but not exclusively for the boating crowd, are available here round the clock. You can even rent a hair dryer. The coffee and tea are free. Request a free copy of the annual *Mt. Desert Chamber of Commerce Village/Island Guide & Northeast Harbor Port Directory.*

Hospitals

Maine Coast Memorial Hospital (50 Union St., Ellsworth, 207/664-5311), the largest hospital in the area, has 24-hour emergency-room service. Healthcare Express (207/664-5341), at the hospital, handles minor problems daily between noon and 8 P.M.

Mount Desert Island's only full-service hospital is **Mount Desert Island Hospital** (10 Wayman Ln., Bar Harbor, 207/288-5081), with a 24-hour emergency room.

Public Restrooms

Restrooms are at the end of the building housing the Great Harbor Maritime Museum, in the town office on Sea Street, and at the harbor.

Southwest Harbor and Vicinity

From Town Hill drive south toward Somesville and then on to Southwest Harbor, which considers itself the hub of Mount Desert Island's quiet side. In fact, in summer, Southwest Harbor's tiny downtown district is probably the busiest spot on the whole western side of the island (west of Somes Sound), but that's not saying a great deal. It has the feel of a settled community, a year-round flavor that Bar Harbor sometimes lacks. And it competes with the best in the scenery department. The Southwest Harbor area deserves the nod as a very convenient base for exploring Acadia National Park, the island's less-crowded villages, and offshore Swans Island.

© TOM NANGLE

A gently arching footbridge is just one of the reasons to visit Somesville's historic district.

Officially, the town of Southwest Harbor includes only the villages of Manset and Seawall, but nearby is lovely Somesville as well as Tremont, which includes the villages of Bernard and Bass Harbor. Also within striking distance is Seal Cove.

Be sure to drive or bike around the smaller villages, especially Somesville, Bass Harbor, and Bernard. Views are fabulous, the pace is slow, and you'll feel you've stumbled upon "the real Maine." The Somesville Historic District, with its distinctive arched white footbridge, is especially appealing, but traffic gets congested here along Route 102, so rather than just rubbernecking, plan to stop and walk around.

A broad swath of Acadia National Park cuts right through the center of this side of the island, and many of its hiking trails are far less congested than elsewhere in the park.

SIGHTS
Ⓜ Wendell Gilley Museum
In the center of Southwest Harbor, the Gilley Museum (Herrick Rd., corner of Rte. 102, Southwest Harbor, 207/244-7555, www.wendell gilleymuseum.org, 10 A.M.–4 P.M. Tues.–Sun. June–Oct., to 5 P.M. in July and Aug., Fri.–Sun. in May, Nov., and Dec., $5 adults, $2 kids 5–12) was established in 1981 to display the life work of local woodcarver Wendell Gilley (1904–1983). The modern, energy-efficient museum houses more than 200 of his astonishingly realistic bird specimens. Special summer exhibits feature other wildlife artists. Many days, a local artist gives woodcarving demonstrations, and the gift shop carries an ornithological potpourri—books to binoculars to carving tools. Kids over eight appreciate this more than younger ones.

Southwest Harbor Oceanarium
Touching a sea cucumber or a starfish may not be every adult's idea of fun, but kids sure enjoy

the hands-on experience at the Oceanarium (Clark Point Rd., Southwest Harbor, 207/244-7330), sister-site to the Bar Harbor Oceanarium. A knowledgeable naturalist introduces creatures from a watery touch tank during a tour of the oceanarium. Twenty other exhibits line the walls of this intriguing, low-tech museum next to the Coast Guard station. Note: This site didn't open in 2004 but was expected to reopen in 2005, rates and hours to be determined. Combo tickets with the Bar Harbor site are the best deal.

The Seal Cove Auto Museum

On the westernmost side of the island, a nondescript blue building camouflages The Seal Cove Auto Museum (Pretty Marsh Rd., Rte. 102, Seal Cove, 207/244-9242, www.sealcove automuseum.org, 10 A.M.–5 P.M. daily June–late Sept., $5 adults, $2 kids under 12), a fantastic collection of more than 100 antique autos and several dozen antique motorcycles—many from the turn of the 20th century. It's easy for kids of any age to spend an hour here, reminiscing and/or fantasizing. The museum is about six miles southwest of Somesville. Or, if you're coming from Southwest Harbor, take Seal Cove Road (partly unpaved) west to Route 102 and go north about 1.5 miles.

Bass Harbor Head Light

At the southern end of Mount Desert's western "claw," follow Route 102A to the turnoff toward Bass Harbor Head. Drive or bike to the end of Lighthouse Road, walk down a steep wooden stairway, and look up and to the right. Voilà! Bass Harbor Head Light—its red glow automated since 1974—stands sentinel at the eastern entrance to Blue Hill Bay. Built in 1858, the 26-foot tower and lightkeeper's house are privately owned, but the dramatic setting is a photographer's dream. Winter access to the parking lot may be limited, but otherwise the area is open all year. Not far from the light (east along Route 102A) are the trailheads for the easy Ship Harbor and Wonderland nature trails, part of Acadia National Park (see Recreation under Acadia National Park).

RECREATION

Acadia National Park is the recreational focus throughout Mount Desert Island; on the island's western side, the main nonpark recreational activities are bike-, boat-, and picnic-related.

At the Southwest Harbor/Tremont Chamber of Commerce office, or at any of the area's stores, lodgings, and restaurants, pick up a free copy of the *Trail Map/Hiking Guide,* a very handy foldout map showing more than 20 hikes on the west side of Mount Desert Island. Trail descriptions include distance, time required, and skill levels (easy to strenuous).

Picnic spots are everywhere on this side of the island, but an Acadia National Park site that many people miss is the **Pretty Marsh Picnic Area,** overlooking Pretty Marsh Harbor. Dense woods shelter grills and tables, and you can walk down to the shoreline and even launch a sea kayak. Kids love this place, but be prepared with insect repellent. The picnic area is just west of Route 102, on the westernmost side of Mount Desert Island.

Bicycle Rentals

Southwest Cycle (Main St., Southwest Harbor, 207/244-5856 or 800/649-5856) rents bikes by the day and week and is open all year (June–Sept., hours are 8:30 A.M.–5:30 P.M. Mon.–Sat. and 10 A.M.–4 P.M. Sun.). The staff at Southwest Cycle will fix you up with maps and lots of good advice for three loops (10–30 miles) on the western side of Mount Desert. Rentals are $19. The shop also rents every imaginable accessory, from baby seats to jogging strollers.

Canoeing/Kayaking

Across the road from Long Pond, the largest lake on Mount Desert Island, **National Park Canoe and Kayak Rental** (145 Pretty Marsh Rd., Rte. 102, Mount Desert, 207/244-5854 or 877/378-6907, www.acadia.net/canoe) makes canoeing or kayaking a snap. Just rent the boat, carry it across to Pond's End, and launch it. Be sure to pack a picnic. Half-day rate (8:30 A.M.–12:30 P.M. or 1–5 P.M.) for a canoe is $25, full-day rate is $37, weekly rate is $135; solo kayak is $24 half day, $35 full day, $135 per week; tandem kayak is $25 half day, $48 full day, $180 per week. A do-it-yourself sunset canoe or kayak tour (from 5 P.M. to sunset) is $15 pp. Reservations are advisable, and essential in July and August. Open mid-May to mid-October.

If you've brought your own canoe (or kayak), launch it here at Pond's End and head off. It's four miles to the southern end of the lake. If the wind kicks up, skirt the shore; if it *really* kicks up from the north, don't paddle too far down the lake, as you'll have a devil of a time getting back.

You can swim at Pond's End, and in the upper half of the lake, but swimming is banned in the lower half, as it's used for drinking water. Almost the entire west side of Long Pond is national park property, so plan to picnic and swim along there; tuck into the sheltered area west of Southern Neck, a crooked finger of land that points northward from the western shore. Stay clear of private property on the east side of the lake.

For guided sea kayak trips, call **Maine State Kayak** (254 Maine St., Southwest Harbor, 207/244-9500 or 877/481-9500, www.maine statekayak.com), which offers paddles in Pretty Marsh, Blue Hill Bay, Somes Sound, and occasionally Cranberry Island, depending upon winds, visibility, and tides. Half-day trips, 8:30 A.M.– 12:30 P.M., 10 A.M.–2 P.M., and 2–6 P.M., cost $46 pp in July and August, $42 late May through June and September, and usually include island or beach breaks and the best opportunities for wildlife sightings. Rates include shuttle transportation, paddling equipment, and a guide.

Golf

Play a quick nine at the **Causeway Club** (Fernald Point Rd., 207/244-3780), which edges the ocean. Be forewarned: It's more challenging than it looks.

Sailing and Power Boat Rentals and Lessons

Mansell Boat Rental Co. (Shore Rd., Manset, next to Hinckley, 207/244-5625, www.mansell boatrentals.com) rents sail and power boats by the day or week. A keel day sailor is $180 per day. A 13.6 Boston Whaler is $175 per day. Also avail-

able are sailing lessons: $195 for a three-hour sail lesson cruise for two, which includes rigging and unrigging the boat; $75 per hour for private lessons, minimum two hours.

Island Tours

Cruise around Somes Sound, the Cranberry Isles, and Baker's Island aboard the *Elizabeth T* with **Great Harbor Cruises** (207/466-5200 cell or 207/244-9160, www.greatharbortours.com). Tours vary by day and cost $15–25 for adults, $15–20 for kids under 16. Options include a lunch cruise to Cranberry island, a Baker Island tour, and a Somes Sound to Northeast Harbor cruise. The boat departs from the dock at Southwest Boat, near the end of Clark Point Road.

High praise goes to **Island Cruises** (Little Island Marine, Shore Rd., Bass Harbor, 207/244-5785) for its daily, narrated lunch cruise to Frenchboro, $25 adult, $15 kids 11 and younger. Buy lunch on the island or bring a picnic, take a walking tour, and visit the island museum. On the return trip, the captain will demonstrate hauling lobster traps. In the afternoon, a nature cruise is offered around the outer islands of Blue Hill Bay. Cost is $20 adult, $15 kids 11 and younger.

Astronomy

Find out what's hidden in the night sky. Lessons, viewings, and classes, as well as telescope rentals, are available at **Island Astronomy** (Steamboat Wharf Rd., Bernard, 207/244-9477, www.island astro.com). An introductory 90-minute daytime telescope workshop is $20 adult, $10 child. Ninety-minute daytime workshops are $10 adult, $5 kids. Presentations are $5 adult, free kids. Telescope rentals begin at $7 per day plus a $28 setup fee. A good selection of binoculars and telescopes are available for purchase, if you get hooked. The shop's on the water near Thurston's—look for the lighthouse-shaped building; call for hours.

SHOPPING

The best shopping locales on this side of the island are Southwest Harbor and the villages of Somesville and Bernard. Mind you, there aren't *lots* of shops, but the small selection is interesting.

Crafts and Gifts

In the middle of Southwest Harbor's small shopping area is Jess Morehouse's **Sand Castle Ocean and Nature Store** (360 Main St., Southwest Harbor, 207/244-4118), a delightful shop with a huge range of handcrafted items, most with a marine theme. Representing the work of several dozen artisans, the shop has windchimes, jewelry, ceramics, ship models, and lots of other surprises.

Local artisans show and sell their works at **Flying Mountain Artisans** (28 Main St., Rte. 102, Southwest Harbor, 207/244-0404). Lots of creative goods here, from quilts to blown glass.

Antiques

Stop in at **E. L. Higgins** (Bernard Rd., Bernard, 207/244-3983). In two onetime classrooms in an 1890s schoolhouse, Edward Higgins has the state's best collection of antique wicker furniture, about 400 pieces at any given time.

Books, Charts, and Music

The two-story **Port in a Storm Bookstore** (Main St., Rte. 102, Somesville, 207/244-4114 or 800/694-4114) is totally seductive, guaranteed to lighten your wallet. High ceilings, comfortable chairs, whimsical floor sculptures, open space, and Somes Cove views all contribute to the ambience. Inventory is not huge, but it's well selected—especially nature and children's books—and the staff is very knowledgeable. Especially in summer, noted authors often appear to lecture or sign their books.

Set off Main Street and facing the new town green is a wonderful little book shop, **Rue Cottage** (360 Main St., Southwest Harbor, 207/244-5542), which invites visitors to call it the "Luddite Bookstore." It sells an intriguing mix of old and new books, making it a delight for browsers.

Southwest Harbor is the home of one of the nation's premier boatbuilders, **The Hinckley Company** (130 Shore Rd., Southwest Harbor, 207/244-5531), a name of stellar repute since the 1930s. There are no tours of the Hinckley complex, but most yachters can't resist the urge to look in at the yard. Plus you can stop in at the **Hinckley Ship'Store** (207/244-7100 or 800/

446-2553) and pick up books, charts, and all sorts of Hinckley-logo gear.

Mainely A Cappella (11 Seal Cove Rd., Southwest Harbor, 800/827-2936) is the largest source of a cappella music in the world, with more than 2,500 titles. Available are CDs, sheet music, songbooks, instructional materials, and more.

ENTERTAINMENT

Life Is a Cabaret

It's not too far to drive from Southwest Harbor to Bar Harbor for evening dinner and entertainment, but Southwest has a cabaret theater that even draws customers in the reverse direction for fabulous entertainment and so-so food: **The Deck House Restaurant and Cabaret Theater** (Great Harbor Marina, Rte. 102, Southwest Harbor, 207/244-5044, www.thedeckhouse.com). Try to arrive for dinner by 6:30 P.M. to enjoy the spectacular harbor view and order your meal (entrées are $22; appetizers and salads are à la carte). The cathedral-ceilinged dining room holds 140, and the table is yours for the evening for $7.50 pp (reservations are essential in midsummer). About 8:15 P.M., the young waitstaff, chameleonlike, unveils its other talents—singing, dancing, even storytelling and puppetry. After hearing the dozen or so numbers, you won't be surprised to learn that many Deck House staff have moved on to Broadway and beyond. The Deck House is open mid-June to mid-September.

Repertory Theater

Since the early 1970s, the **Acadia Repertory Theatre** (Rte. 102, Somesville, 207/244-7260, www.acadiarep.com, $20 adults, $15 students, $10 kids under 16) has been providing first-rate professional thespian repertory on the stage of Somesville's antique Masonic Hall. Classic plays by Wilde, Goldsmith, even Molière have been staples, as has the annual Agatha Christie mystery. Performances run late June to late August, Tuesday–Sunday at 8:15 P.M., with 2 P.M. matinees on the last Sunday of each play. Special children's plays occur Wednesday and Saturday at 10:30 A.M. Tickets for children's theater programs are $7 adults, $5 kids.

EVENTS

In 2005, Southwest Harbor is celebrating its centennial with lectures, tours, concerts, parades, fireworks, shows, and other special events from February through November, with most scheduled June through September.

In early October, Smuggler's Den Campground on Route 102 in Southwest Harbor is home to the annual **Octoberfest and Food Festival** (207/244-9264 or 800/423-9264, www.acadiachamber.com), a one-day celebration with crafts, food, games, music, and about two dozen Maine microbrewers presenting about 80 different brews.

ACCOMMODATIONS

As the Asticou Inn is to Northeast Harbor, so is the Claremont to Southwest Harbor. On the other end of the lodging scale, there are several commercial campgrounds in this part of the island, plus an Acadia National Park campground.

Inn

When you're ready to splurge, **The Claremont** (22 Claremont Rd., Southwest Harbor 04679, 207/244-5036 or 800/244-5036, www.theclaremonthotel.com) may well be your choice, but you'll have to plan a year ahead to land a room in July or August. Most popular time is the first week in August, during the annual Claremont Croquet Classic. This yellow-clapboard grande dame, dominating a six-acre hilltop overlooking Somes Sound, caters to honeymooners, yuppies, and gentrified folk. Dating from 1884, the main building has 26 rooms (with bath and phones), most of them recently refurbished. Other accommodations are in the six-room Phillips House, one-suite Clark House, and new Cole Cottage, with two rooms and one efficiency. Rooms in these buildings are $229–245 MAP, mid-July to Labor Day, plus a hefty 15 percent service and Maine sales tax. (Rooms without water views can be rented at a B&B rate, $175) Also on the premises are 14 cottages ($185–250, mid-June to mid-Sept.); they can go as high as $2,300 a week in midsummer. The hotel and

dining room are open early June to mid-October; cottages are open late May to mid-October.

The Claremont Dining Room, with a view from every table, serves breakfast and dinner (jackets and ties requested for dinner). Dining-room reservations are wise in midsummer. In July and August, informal lunches and cocktails are served in the shorefront Boat House.

B&Bs

The only amenity not provided at the tasteful Victorian **Inn at Southwest** (371 Main St., Rte. 102, Box 593, Southwest Harbor 04679, 207/244-3835, www.inatsouthwest.com, $110–185) is a TV, but no one misses it. Guests gather for games, reading, conversation, and afternoon tea in a huge living room with fireplace and comfortable couches. Built in 1884 as the Freeman Cottage, the elegant building has 13 dormers and a wraparound veranda. Nine second- and third-floor guest rooms—named for Maine lighthouses and full of character—are fitted out with wicker furniture, ceiling fans, down comforters, and lots more. All have private baths (some are detached). Open May through October.

Across the lane **The Kingsleigh Inn 1904** (373 Main St., P.O. Box 1426, Southwest Harbor 04679, 207/244-5302, www.kingsleighinn.com, $130–160) is a very attractive Queen Anne manse with eight well-thought-out rooms (private baths) on three floors. If you're sensitive to street noise, request a back-facing (harbor-view) room, although air-conditioners muffle the sound in summer. There's a separate guest phone, and afternoon tea comes with delicious baked treats. The huge turret suite, with fireplace, TV, telescope, large bathroom, and lots of comfortable wicker furniture, is $175–260, depending on the season.

On a quiet side street is the **⚑ Lindenwood Inn** (118 Clark Point Rd., Box 1328, Southwest Harbor 04679, 207/244-5335 or 800/307-5335, www.lindenwoodinn.com, $105–275), where the linden-blossom fragrance can be intoxicating in summer. Jim King, the Australian owner, has imaginatively decorated the inn's 15 rooms and poolside bungalow with artifacts from everywhere. After hiking Acadia's trails, the heated pool and hot tub are especially welcome, and after that, perhaps the inn's full bar, serving guests only. Open all year.

Originally part of the Island House, **N Harbour Cottage Inn** (9 Dirigo Rd., Box 258, Southwest Harbor 04679, 207/244-5738 or 888/843-3022, www.harbourcottageinn.com) has evolved into a lovely B&B with eight rooms ($110–159) and three suites ($135–250). Most rooms have whirlpool baths or steam-sauna showers, some have fireplaces, and all have telephones, TV, and computer ports. Rates include a full breakfast and use of beach bicycles. Box lunches are available, and the inn stocks a nice selection of wine and beer. Also part of Harbour Cottage is **Pier One,** which offers five weekly waterfront suites ($1,260–1,575), including a studio cottage, all with kitchens, TV, and phone. Guests have private use of 150-foot pier, and they can dock or launch canoes or kayaks or other small boats from right outside their doors.

Peter and Bethany Nickum Tague provide a quiet, restorative retreat at **The Yellow Aster** (53 Clark Point Rd., Box 1513, Southwest Harbor 04679, 207/244-4422 or 800/724-7228, www.yellowaster.com, $115). Breakfast features natural and organic foods, whole grain breads, and fresh produce. You can arrange for a massage therapist to ease out the kinks after a day exploring the park (ask about packages that include two nights' lodging, a sea kayak tour, and a massage). There's even an in-house gallery featuring the works of local artisans.

Next door is **Central House Inn** (51 Clark Point Rd., P.O. Box 503, Southwest Harbor 04079, 207/244-0100 or 877/205-0289, www.centralhouseinn.com, $145–175), which owner Terry Prebble has meticulously remodeled (lots of sherbet colors—lemon and lime exterior, raspberry living room) and great art throughout. Three guest rooms in subdued shades have gas fireplaces, air-conditioning, and hidden cable TV/DVD. The bathrooms have huge tiled showers with three shower heads; one room also has a whirlpool tub. On the third floor a new 750-square-foot loft apartment will be available by the week.

In Manset, with jaw-dropping views down Somes Sound, is **The Moorings** (Shore Rd., Box 744, Southwest Harbor 04679, 207/244-5523 or 207/244-3210 or 800/596-5523, www.mooringsinn.com), owned and operated by the King family for more than 40 years. The oceanfront complex is part B&B, part motel, and part cottage rental. Ten rooms in the Main House are named after locally built sailing vessels. Rates ($65–120) include juice, coffee, and doughnuts. The Lighthouse View Wing ($105) has motel-style rooms with refrigerator, microwave, waterfront decks, and incredible views (spend the afternoon counting the Hinckley yachts). Also on the property are cottage units, a combination of rooms and efficiencies ($104–150). One mile distant is Eagle Watch Cottage, with two bedrooms and harbor views, and King's Mark, a garden-style apartment, with two bedrooms ($150 each per night).

In 2004, Ann and Charlie Bradford sold the family home that had housed their long-time B&B and reopened a petite version of the **Island House** (36 Freeman Ridge., P.O. Box 1006, Southwest Harbor 04679, 207/244-5180, www.islandhousebb.com, $110) in their new custom home, built atop a ridge in a quiet neighborhood. They've downsized the guest space to just two rooms, plus a guest living and dining room, all on one level, but Anne's warm hospitality and delicious full breakfasts are the same. Also available is a separate carriage-house apartment ($150). Open all year. From June through September, the Bradfords also rent Wood-Sea, a comfortable two-bedroom summer cottage, near Bass Harbor Head Light, about five miles from Southwest Harbor; call for rates.

Sleep Aboard

For something completely different, consider chartering a private B&B trip aboard a Friendship sloop with **Downeast Friendship Sloop Charters** (Box 1533, Southwest Harbor 04679, 207/266-5210, www.downeastfriendshisloop.com, $300). You'll sail from Great Harbor Marina, in Southwest Harbor, to a quiet cove, where you'll be treated to a lobster dinner with wine before retiring to your private cabin, trimmed in mahogany and teak. Sorry, no en suite bathroom, but there is a private marine head on board.

Wake to the scent of fresh coffee, and accompany that with a huge breakfast: blueberry pancakes, blueberry muffins, bagels, fruits, and juices. You'll be back at the marina by 9 A.M., where hot showers are available.

Campgrounds

A smallish, low-key campground in an outstanding setting, **Somes Sound View Campground** (86 Hall Quarry Rd., Mount Desert 04660, 207/244-3890 or off-season 207/244-7452) has 60 tight tent and RV (maximum 28 feet) sites on a hillside, with some on the ocean's edge. Facilities include hot showers (if you're camping on the lowest levels, it's a good hike up to the bath house); nearest store is two miles. Sites are $25–40 in July and August, less early and late in the season. No credit cards. Open late May to mid-October. The campground is two miles south and east of Somesville and a mile east of Route 102.

Just outside of town, on a quiet road cutting through the woods, is **White Birches Campground** (195 Seal Cove Rd., Southwest Harbor, 207/244-3797 or 888/716-0727, www.maine camper.com), with sites in a field and in the woods ($23 tent, $27 RV, $50–65 camping cabin). Facilities include a heated outdoor pool.

On the eastern edge of Somesville, just off Route 198 at the head of Somes Sound, the **M Mount Desert Campground** (516 Somes Sound Dr., Rte. 198, Somesville, Mount Desert 04660, 207/244-3710, www.mountdesertcamp ground.com) is especially centrally located for visiting Bar Harbor, Acadia, and the whole western side of Mount Desert Island. The campground has 152 wooded tent sites, about 45 on the water, spread out on 58 acres. Reservations are advisable for this popular and low-key campground, which gets high marks for maintenance, noise control, and convenient tent platforms. Another plus is The Gathering Place, where campers can relax, play games, and purchase coffee and fresh-baked treats or ice cream. Rates are $28–39 a night ($39 for the waterfront sites). Electrical hookups are available for $1 per night. No pets July–Labor Day. No trailers over 20 feet. Kayak and canoe rentals are available. Open mid-June to mid-September.

FOOD

Pizza Plus

Some of the island's most creative sandwiches and pizza toppings emerge from **Little Notch Pizzeria** (340 Main St., Southwest Harbor, 207/244-3357, 11 A.M.–8 P.M. Mon.–Sat. May to Oct., 11 A.M.– 7 P.M. weekdays Nov.–April), next to the library in Southwest Harbor's downtown. How about a broccoli, sausage, and black-olive pizza? Freshly baked breads, outrageous desserts, a couple of dinner entrées, and homemade soups, stews, and chowders make the Little Notch a winner.

Eclectic

By day, **Eat-a-Pita** (326 Main St., Southwest Harbor, 207/244-4344, 8 A.M.–9 P.M.) is a casual, order-at-the-counter restaurant, serving breakfast and lunch. At night, it morphs into **Café 2**, a tad more formal with full service. Sit inside or on the pleasant streetside patio. Dinner entrées are in the $12–22 range.

Seafood with a View

Super-fresh seafood, a renowned baked lobster-seafood casserole, and a great location on the water have made **Seafood Ketch** a real hit (McMullin Ave., Bass Harbor, 207/244-7463, 11 A.M.–9 P.M. late May–late Oct.). Try to snag one of the tables on the patio overlooking the harbor. Kids' menu. Most entrées run $17–20, but sandwiches and lighter fare are available.

Ethnic Accents

The **M Seaweed Café** (146 Seawall Rd., Rte. 102A, Southwest Harbor, 207/244-0572, 5:30–9:30 P.M. Tues.–Sat. in summer, weekends in winter) used to be a secret but no longer is. Reservations are essential at this recently expanded place, tucked away on the "back side" of Southwest Harbor. Chef/owner Bill Morrison, a veteran of Aspen and the personal-chef business, uses organic and natural ingredients and fresh local seafood in his menu, which includes a fine array of sushi choices ($8–14 for a full roll). Entrée range is $17–19, and noodle dishes are $9–17. For a starter, try the outstanding mussels in sake with Thai curry, cilantro, and lime.

In 2004, **XYZ Restaurant** (80 Seawall Rd., Rte. 102A, Manset, 207/244-5221, 5:30–9 P.M.) moved to this new location, at the end of a dirt driveway rising slowly to a crest—look for the faux cacti in the parking lot. With seating inside and on the porch, this popular spot continues to deliver the flavors of interior Mexico: Xalapa, Yucatan, and Zacatecas (hence XYZ). The margaritas are terrific.

Locals know you can count on **DeMuro's Top of the Hill** (Rte. 102, Southwest Harbor, 207-244-0033, 4:30 P.M.–close) for a really good meal at a very fair price. Dine in the country-style, pine dining room or on the weatherized patio. The Italian-influenced menu (try the excellent veal Italiano) has something in all price ranges ($9–18), but the real steal is the Lobster Paloozah special for $18.95, including a cup of clam chowder, steamed mussels, a boiled lobster, pasta or potato, and vegetable.

Upscale Casual

Gold walls, artwork, wood floors, and a giant hearth set the tone for **Red Sky** (14 Clark Point Rd., 207/244-0476, 5:30–10 P.M.), which opened in 2003 and quickly gained a loyal following. The creative fare (entrées $17–28) might include lobster risotto, pumpkin ravioli, or maple-glazed baby-back ribs. A huge fireplace dominates the dining room, and there also are chairs at the bar.

Fine Dining

The Claremont Dining Room (22 Claremont Rd., 207/244-5036 or 800/244-5036), with a view from every table, is open to the public for breakfast and dinner (jackets and ties requested for dinner). Dining-room reservations are wise in midsummer. In July and August, informal lunches and cocktails are served in the shorefront Boat House, also open to the public.

Lobster-in-the-Rough

M **Thurston's Lobster Pound** (Steamboat Wharf Rd., Bernard, 207/244-7600, 11 A.M.–8 P.M. early and late in the season, to 8:30 P.M. in July and Aug., Memorial Day–Columbus Day) wins the award for the island's best lobster pound, with a screened dining room that practically sits in the water. It also has chowders, sandwiches, and terrific desserts. Beer and wine are available. Be sure

to read the directions at the entry and order before you find a table on one of two levels.

Much more rustic—almost extremely so—is **The Captain's Galley at Beals' Lobster Pier** (182 Clark Point Rd., 207/244-7178 or 207/244-3202, 9 A.M.–8 P.M., closes at 5 P.M. after Labor Day), where you eat on covered picnic tables on the working dock. In addition to lobster, steamers, and fresh fish, you'll find chowders, steamers, ice cream, and baked desserts. It's at the end of the road, adjacent to the Coast Guard Base.

INFORMATION AND SERVICES

Information

At the corner of Route 103 and Seal Cove Road, in the Southwest Harbor Shoppes minimall, **Southwest Harbor/Tremont Chamber of Commerce** (Main St., P.O. Box 1143, Southwest Harbor 04679, 207/244-9264 or 800/423-9264, fax 207/244-4185, www.acadia.net/swhtrcoc) is open 9 A.M.–noon and 1–5 P.M. Monday–Friday, 9 A.M.–3 P.M. Saturday, and 10 A.M.–2 P.M. Sunday.

Hospitals

Maine Coast Memorial Hospital (50 Union St., Ellsworth, 207/664-5311), the largest hospital in the area, has 24-hour emergency-room service. Healthcare Express (207/664-5341), at the hospital, handles minor problems daily between noon and 8 P.M.

Mount Desert Island's only full-service hospital is **Mount Desert Island Hospital** (10 Wayman Ln., Bar Harbor, 207/288-5081), with a 24-hour emergency room.

Local Library

The **Southwest Harbor Public Library** (338 Main St., Southwest Harbor, 207/244-7065, 9 A.M.–5 P.M. Mon.–Fri., to 8 P.M. Wed., and 9 A.M.–noon Sat.) recently renovated to double its size.

Public Restrooms

In downtown Southwest Harbor, public restrooms are at the southern end of the parking lot behind the Main Street park and near the fire station. Across Main Street, Harbor House also has a restroom, as does the Swans Island ferry terminal in Bass Harbor.

Islands Near Mount Desert

The most popular island day-trip destinations from Mount Desert Island are the Cranberry Isles and Swans Island. Most commercial and mail boats for the Cranberries depart from Northeast Harbor, although one line originates in Southwest Harbor (both carry bikes but no cars); state car ferries for Swans Island depart from Bass Harbor, south of Southwest Harbor.

CRANBERRY ISLES

The Cranberry Isles, south of Northeast and Seal Harbors, comprise Great Cranberry, Little Cranberry (called Islesford), Sutton, Baker, and Bear Islands. Islesford and Baker include property belonging to Acadia National Park. Bring a bike and explore the narrow, mostly level roads on the two largest islands (Great Cranberry and Islesford), but *remember to respect private property.* Unless you've asked permission, *do not* cut across private land to reach the shore.

Lobstering and other fishing industries are the commercial mainstay, boosted in summer by the various visitor-related pursuits. Artists and writers come for a week, a month, or longer; day-trippers spend time on Great Cranberry and Islesford.

Largest of the islands is **Great Cranberry,** with a general store, a small historical museum, and a gift shop, but not much else except pretty views.

The second-largest island is **Little Cranberry,** locally known as Islesford. It's easy to spend the better part of a day here exploring. Begin at **The Islesford Historical Museum,** operated by the National Park Service (207/288-3338, 10 A.M.–noon and 12:30–4:30 P.M. Mon.–Sat. and 10:45 A.M.–noon and 12:30–4:30 P.M. Sun., mid-June to Labor Day, free). The exhibits focus on local history, much of it maritime, so displays include ship models, household goods, fishing gear, and other memorabilia. Also on Islesford are public restrooms (across from the museum), a handful of shops, and a general store. For lunch, bring a picnic or head to **The**

Islesford Dock (207/244-7494, 11 A.M.–3 P.M. and 5–9 P.M. Tues.–Sun. late June–Labor Day), where prices are moderate, the food is home-cooked, and the views across to Acadia's mountains are incredible. If you want to spend the night, reserve ahead at the **Braided Rugs Inn** (Box 15, Islesford 04646, 207/244-5943, $70), with three shared-bath rooms.

Getting to the Cranberries

Decades-old, family-run **Beal & Bunker,** departing from the Municipal Pier (Northeast Harbor, 207/244-3575), provides year-round mail boat/passenger service to the Cranberries from Northeast Harbor. The ferries don't carry cars, but you can take a bike. Or just plan to explore on foot. The summer season, with more frequent trips, runs mid-June through Labor Day. The first boat departs Northeast Harbor's Municipal Pier Monday–Saturday at 7:30 A.M., first Sunday boat is 10 A.M.; the last boat for Northeast Harbor leaves Islesford at 6:30 P.M. and (Great) Cranberry at 6:45 P.M. The boats do a bit of to-ing and fro-ing on the three-island route (including Sutton in summer), so be patient as they make the circuit. It's a people-watching treat. If you just did a round-trip and stayed aboard, the loop would take about 1.5 hours. Round-trip tickets (covering the whole loop, including intraisland if you want to visit both Great Cranberry and Islesford) are $14 adults, $7 kids under 12 (free for kids under three). Bicycles are $5 round-trip.

Cranberry Cove Ferry (Upper Town Dock, Clark Point Rd., Southwest Harbor, 207/244-5882) operates a summertime ferry service to the Cranberries mid-June through Labor Day. First departure from Southwest Harbor is 7 A.M.; last departure is 6 P.M. from Islesford, 6:20 P.M. from (Great) Cranberry. Later departures may be available in July and August. Round-trip fares are $16 adults, $10 children. Bicycles are $5 round-trip. Off-season, call to check on the schedule.

FRENCHBORO (LONG ISLAND)

S ince Maine has more Long Islands than anyone cares to count, most of them have other labels for easy distinction. Here's a case in point—a Long Island known universally just as Frenchboro, the name of its harbor village. With a year-round population hovering around 50, Frenchboro has had ferry service only since 1960. Since then, the island has acquired phone service, electricity, and satellite TV, but don't expect to notice much of that when you get there. It's a very quiet place where islanders live as islanders always have—making a living from the sea and proud of it. In 1999, when more than half the island (914 acres, including 5.5 miles of shorefront) went up for sale by a private owner, an incredible fund-raising effort collected nearly $3 million, allowing purchase of the land in January 2000 by the Maine Coast Heritage Trust. Some of the funding has been put toward restoration of the village's church and one-room schoolhouse; islanders and visitors still have full access to all the acreage, but interested developers will have to look elsewhere.

Frenchboro is the subject of *Hauling by Hand,* a fascinating, well-researched "biography" published in 1999 by eighth-generation islander Dean Lunt, now a journalist in Portland. (See Suggested Reading in the Know chapter.) For helpful information on visiting Frenchboro, visit his website, www.islandportpress.com/frenchboro.

A good way to get a sense of the place is to take the 3.5-hour lunch cruise run by Eric and Kim Strauss of **Island Cruises** (Little Island Marine, Shore Rd., Bass Harbor, 207/244-5785, www.acadiainfo.com). The 41-passenger *R. L. Gott* departs daily during the summer at 11 A.M. The trip allows enough time for a walking tour and lunch before returning through the sprinkling of islands along the 8.3-mile route. Cost is $25 adults, $15 children 11 and younger. Be sure to reserve, and double-check if the weather looks iffy. Most of the trip is in sheltered water, but rough seas can put the kibosh on it. Island Cruises also does an afternoon nature cruise among the islands. You'll find the Island Cruises dock by following signs to the Swans Island Ferry and turning off at the sign shortly before the ferry dock.

For an even longer stay on Frenchboro, plan to take the *R. L. Gott* during her weekly run for the Maine State Ferry Service. Each Friday, from early April to late October, the *Gott* departs Bass Harbor at 8 A.M., arriving in Frenchboro at 9 A.M. The return trip to Bass Harbor is at 6 P.M., allowing nine hours on the island. Round-trip cost is $12 adults, $5.25 children. Take a picnic with you, or stop at **Lunt's Dockside Deli** (207/334-2922), open only in July and August. The island has a network of maintained trails through the woods and along the shore, easy and not-so-easy; some can be squishy and some are along bouldery beachfront. (You'll get a sketchy map on the boat.) In the center of the island is a beaver pond. The **Frenchboro Historical Society** (noon–5 P.M. Memorial Day–Labor Day), just up from the dock, has interesting old tools and other local artifacts.

Overnight accommodations are available at the **Harbor House Inn** (207/334-2973 or 207/334-2991, May–late Sept.).

Captain John Dwelley (207/244-5724) operates a water-taxi service to the Cranberries. His six-passenger *Delight* makes the run from Northeast, Southwest, or Seal Harbor for $40 a trip in the daytime, $45 5–8 P.M., and $50 8–11 P.M. or 6–8 A.M.

SWANS ISLAND

Six miles off Mount Desert Island lies scenic, 6,000-acre Swans Island (pop. about 450), named after Colonel James Swan, who bought it and

two dozen other islands as an investment in 1786. As with the Cranberries, fishing—especially lobstering—is the year-round way of life here; summer sees the arrival of artists, writers, and other seasonal visitors.

With plenty of relatively level terrain (but narrow roads), and a not-impossible amount of real estate to cover, Swans is ideal for a bicycling day trip. The island has no campsites, no public restrooms, a tiny motel and a tiny B&B. Visitors who want to spend more than a day tend to rent cottages by the week.

© TOM NANGLE

Sand Beach is one of the highlights along Acadia National Park's Park Loop. It's extremely popular on warm summer days, but even then the water is shockingly cold.

If you can be flexible, wait for a clear day, then catch the first ferry (7:30 A.M.) from Bass Harbor. At the ferry office, request a Swans Island map (and take advantage of the restroom). Keep an eye on your watch so you don't miss the last ferry (4:30 P.M.) back to Bass Harbor.

Pack a picnic or plan to stop for picnic fixings at the **General Store** in Minturn, one of the island's three villages, on the east side of Burnt Coat Harbor. Then pedal around to the west side of the harbor and down the peninsula to **Hockamock Head Light** (officially, Burnt Coat Harbor

Light). From the ferry landing, Hockamock Head is about five miles, but it's not difficult.

The distinctive square lighthouse, built in 1872 and now automated, sits on a rocky promontory overlooking Burnt Coat Harbor, Harbor Island, lobsterboat traffic, and crashing surf. The keeper's house is unoccupied; the grounds are great for picnics.

If it's hot, ask for directions to one of two prime island swimming spots **Fine Sand Beach** (saltwater) or **Quarry Pond** (freshwater). Fine Sand Beach is on the west side of Toothacher Cove; you'll have to navigate a short stretch of unpaved road to get there, but it's worth the trouble. Be prepared for chilly water, however. Quarry Pond is in Minturn, not far from the post office.

Getting to Swans Island

Swans Island is a six-mile, 40-minute trip on the car ferry *Captain Henry Lee*. Between mid-April and late October, the ferry makes five or six round-trips a day, the first from Bass Harbor at 7:30 A.M. (Sun. 9 A.M.) and the last from Swans Island at 4:30 P.M. Other months, the first and last runs are the same, but there are only four or five trips. For more information, contact **Maine State Ferry Service** (800/491-4883 for daily recorded info, www.state.me.us/mdot/opt/ferry/maine-ferry-service.php). Round-trip fares are $12 adults, $5.25 children 5–11. Bikes are $11.50 round-trip per adult, $5.75 per child. Round-trip ticket for vehicle and driver is $34.50 May through October. Reservations are accepted only for vehicles (be in line at least 15 minutes before departure).

To reach the Bass Harbor ferry terminal on Mount Desert Island, follow the distinctive blue signs, marked Swans Island Ferry, along Routes 102 and 102A.

Eastern Hancock County

Sneak around to the eastern side of Frenchman Bay, and you'll see this region from a whole new perspective. One hour from Acadia National Park's visitor center, you'll find Acadia's mountains silhouetted against the sunset, the surf slamming onto Schoodic Point, the peace of a calmer lifestyle. Although far fewer than the millions who visit the Mount Desert section of the park come here, it is being discovered, in part due to a passenger ferry service linking Bar Harbor to Winter Harbor and the addition of the free Explorer buses, which circulate through the town and park.

If you're coming from Trenton—the funnel to Mount Desert—duck east via Route 204 toward Lamoine and its state park. From Ellsworth, follow Route 1 toward Hancock, Sullivan, Sorrento, Gouldsboro, and Winter Harbor.

The biggest attractions in Eastern Hancock County are the spectacular vignettes and vistas—of offshore lighthouses, distant mountains, close-in islands, and unchanged villages. Check out each finger of land: Lamoine, Hancock Point, Sorrento, and Winter Harbor's Grindstone Neck.

Winter Harbor, on the Gouldsboro Peninsula, is known best as the gateway to the Schoodic Peninsula, Acadia National Park's only mainland acreage. It shares the area with an old-money, low-profile, Philadelphia-linked summer colony on exclusive Grindstone Neck. Loop around the Schoodic Peninsula (on a National Scenic Byway).

Then circle the Gouldsboro Peninsula and detour to Corea. Gouldsboro—including the not-to-be-missed villages of Birch Harbor, Corea, and Prospect Harbor—earned its own minor fame from Louise Dickinson Rich's 1958 book *The Peninsula,* a tribute to her summers on Corea's Cranberry Point—"a place that has stood still in time." Since 1958, change has crept into Corea, but not so's you'd notice. It's still the same quintessential lobster-fishing community, perfect for photo ops.

Another option is to head inland and follow

Route 182, a designated Maine Scenic Highway, from Hancock to Cherryfield.

Besides the jaw-dropping scenery, the calling cards for the region are the outdoor recreation opportunities and, believe it or not, shopping. You can easily do your gift shopping for the year at the dozens of artists' and artisans' studios tucked throughout this region.

M SCHOODIC SECTION OF ACADIA NATIONAL PARK

Slightly more than 2,000 of Acadia National Park's acres are on the mainland, and they're all here on the **Schoodic Peninsula** (www.acadia schoodic.org). Along the six-mile one-way (counterclockwise) road that loops through the park there are picnic spots, a few hiking trailheads, an offshore lighthouse, and scenic turnouts. There's no camping in the park, but Ocean Wood Campground (see Accommodations), on the Schoodic Peninsula, is convenient and beautiful. The world-class scenery, free admission, and the general lack of congestion make Schoodic the preferred Acadia destination of many a savvy visitor. If you want to help preserve the environment, consider getting around on the free **Island Explorer** buses, which allow you to get off and on at will. *Note:* When you see a viewpoint you like, stop; it's a long way around to return.

To reach the park boundary from Route 1 in Gouldsboro, take Route 186 south to Winter Harbor. Continue through town, heading east, then turn right and continue to the park-entrance sign, just before the bridge over Mosquito Harbor.

Just after the bridge, the first landmark is **Frazer Point Picnic Area,** with lovely vistas, picnic tables, and handicapped-accessible restrooms. Other spots are fine for picnics, but this is the only official one. If you've brought bikes, leave your car here and do a counterclockwise 12.2-mile loop through the park and back to your car via Birch Harbor and Route 186. It's a fine day trip.

GALLERY HOPPING

Art and artisan studios and galleries are numerous, and it's easy to while away a day browsing and buying. Begin by picking up copies of the *Artist Studio Tour Map*, which details and provides directions to about a dozen galleries in Franklin, Sullivan, and Hancock, and the *Schoodic Peninsula* brochure, which notes galleries and shops on the peninsula. Both are widely available and free. Here's a sampling of some favorites.

Begin by taking Eastside Road, just before the Hancock-Sullivan Bridge, and drive 1.5 miles south to the Wray family's **Gull Rock Pottery** (325 Eastside Rd., Hancock, 207/422-3990). You'll find wheel-thrown, hand-painted, dishwasher-safe pottery decorated with blue-and-white Japanese-style motifs.

Cross the Hancock-Sullivan Bridge, then take your first left off Route 1 onto Taunton Drive to find the next three galleries. Drawing from her experiences as an oil painter and from her life in Japan, Peg McAloon creates masterful one-of-a-kind quilts at **Wildfire Run Quilt Boutique** (Taunton Dr., Sullivan, 207/422-3935).

Nearby **Lunaform** (Cedar Ln., West Sullivan, 207/422-0923) is in a class by itself. First there's the setting—the beautifully landscaped grounds surrounding an abandoned granite quarry. Then there's the realization that many of the wonderfully aesthetic garden ornaments created here look like hand-turned *pottery*, when in fact they're hand turned, but made of steel-reinforced concrete. Off Route 1, take the first right onto Track Road; after a half mile, go left onto Cedar Lane.

Bet you can't keep from smiling at the whimsical animal sculptures and fun furniture of talented sculptor/painter Philip Barter. His work is the cornerstone of the eclectic **Barter Family Gallery** (Shore Rd., Sullivan, 207/422-3190). But there's more: Barter's wife and seven children have put their considerable skills to work producing hooked and braided rugs, jewelry, and other craft items. The gallery is 2.5 miles off Route 1.

Return to Route 1, then head north on Route 200 to find the next two galleries. Artist Paul Breeden, best known for the remarkable illustrations, calligraphy, and maps he's done for *National Geo-*

graphic, Time-Life Books, and other national and international publications, displays and sells his paintings at the **Spring Woods Gallery and Willowbrook Garden** (40A Willowbrook Ln., Sullivan, 207/422-3007). Also filling the handsome modern gallery space are paintings by Ann Breeden, metal sculptures and silk scarves by the talented Breeden offspring, and Pueblo artifacts from the American Southwest. Be sure to allow time to meander through the garden.

Overlooking Hog Bay, 3.6 miles north of Route 1, Charles and Susanne Grosjean have been the key players at **Hog Bay Pottery** (245 Hog Bay Rd., Route 200, Franklin, 207/565-2282), since 1974. Inside the casual, laid-back showroom are Charles's functional, nature-themed pottery and Susanne's stunning handwoven rugs.

More galleries dot the Schoodic Peninsula. To find these three, loop down to Winter Harbor then back up on Route 186. Since 1985, Rod Lee's **Lee Art Glass Studio** (293 Main St., Winter Harbor, 207/963-7004) has created fused-glass tableware by taking two pieces off window glass and firing them on terra cotta or bisque molds at 1,500 degrees. What makes the end result so appealing are the colors and the patterns—crocheted doilies or stencils—impressed into the glass. The almost-magical results are beautiful, delicate-looking, yet functional.

Jody Miller's **Sea Myst Gallery and Gardens** (150 Corea Rd., Rte. 195, Prospect Harbor, 207/963-7667) is just .7 mile off Route 186. Jody's modern light-filled home gallery is filled with fine crafts, and the gardens are filled with statuary.

Visiting the **U.S. Bells Foundry & Watering Cove Pottery** (56 West Bay Rd., Rte. 186, Prospect Harbor 04669, 207/963-7184) is a treat for the ears, as browsers try out the many varieties of cast-bronze bells made in the adjacent foundry by Richard Fisher. If you're lucky, he may have time to explain the process—particularly intriguing for children, and a distraction from their instinctive urge to test every bell in the shop. The store also carries wood-fired stoneware and porcelain by Liza Fisher, as well as a selection of American crafts, including quilts.

From the picnic area, the **Park Loop Road** becomes one-way. Go about 2.5 miles and watch for a narrow, unpaved road on the left, leading a mile up to the open ledges on 440-foot Schoodic Head. (Don't confuse it with Schoodic Mountain, which is well north of here.) For exercise, hike up, although you'll need to keep an eye out for cars.

Another stop best planned from the picnic area is Raven's Head, a Thunder Hole-type cliff with sheer drops to the churning surf below (no fences, so not a good place for little ones) and fabulous views. To find this unmarked sight, pull over at the third pullout on the left after the picnic area, then cross the road and follow the short path. Be extremely careful here and stay well away from the cliff's edge.

Continue on the Park Loop Road, and hang a right onto a short, two-way spur to **Schoodic Point.** Just before it is a small info center, staffed by volunteers and park rangers, located on the site of a former top-secret U.S. Navy base that became part of the park in 2002. Plans call for the campus to eventually become the Schoodic Education & Research Center if funding ever becomes a reality. Occasional lectures and programs are held here.

Just beyond the info center is the point where the parking lot, amazingly, seldom fills up. Check local newspapers for the time of high tide and try to arrive here then; the word *awesome* is overused, but it sure fits Schoodic Point's surf performance on the rugged pink granite. *Caution:* If you've brought children, keep them well back from the water; a rogue wave can sweep them off the rocks all too easily. It *has* happened. Picnics are great here (make sure you bring a litter bag), and so are the tidepools at mid- to low tide. Birding is spectacular during spring and fall migrations.

Return to the Park Loop Road and go about a mile to the Blueberry Hill parking area. Across the road is the trailhead to the 180-foot-high **Anvil** headland, and then on up to Schoodic Head. Allow 2–3 hours for the clockwise Schoodic Head–Anvil loop back to your car. From Blueberry Hill, continue another two miles to the park exit, just before Birch Harbor.

RECREATION

Donnell Pond Public Reserved Land

More than 14,000 acres have been preserved for public access in Donnell Pond Public Reserved Land (Maine Bureau of Parks and Lands, 207/827-1818, www.state.me.us/doc/parks), a huge mountain-and-lake area north and east of Sullivan. Developers had their eyes on this gorgeous real estate in the 1980s, but preservationists fortunately rallied to the cause. Route 182, an official Scenic Highway, cuts right through the Donnell Pond preserve.

Major water bodies here are **Donnell Pond** (big enough by most gauges to be called a lake) and **Tunk** and **Spring River Lakes;** all are accessible for boats (even, alas, powerboats). Tunk Lake has a few campsites in its southwestern corner. The eastern and southern shores of Donnell Pond have primitive, first-come, first-served sites (no charge), which are snapped up quickly on midsummer weekends. Schoodic Beach, the prime swimming area, is in the southeastern corner of Donnell Pond.

By boat, trailheads at Schoodic Beach and Black Beach provide access to **Caribou, Black,** and **Schoodic Mountains,** with connector trails. None are easy but it's great hiking—and there's a tower on 1,069-foot Schoodic. The Caribou–Black Mountain Loop, clockwise, is about a seven-mile round-trip from the Black Beach boat-access trailhead.

To reach the boat-launching area for Donnell Pond from Route 1 in Sullivan, take Route 200 north to Route 182. Turn right and go about 1.5 miles to a right turn just before Swan Brook. Turn and go not quite two miles to the put-in; the road is poor in spots but adequate for a regular vehicle. The Narrows, where you'll put in, is lined with summer cottages ("camps" in the Maine vernacular); keep paddling eastward to the more open part of the lake.

To reach the vehicle-access trailhead for Schoodic Mountain from Route 1 in East Sullivan, drive just over four miles northeast on Route 183 (Lake Road). Cross the Maine Central Railroad tracks and turn left onto an unpaved road (marked as a Jeep track on the

Acadia Region

USGS map). Continue to the parking area and trailhead. Follow the Schoodic Mountain Loop clockwise, heading westward first. To make a day of it, pack a picnic and take a swimsuit (and don't forget a camera and binoculars for the summit views). On a brilliantly clear day, you'll see Baxter State Park's Katahdin, the peaks of Acadia National Park, and the ocean beyond. For such rewards, this is a popular hike, so don't expect to be alone on summer and fall weekends.

Still within the preserve boundaries, but farther east, you can put in a canoe at the northern end of Long Pond and paddle southward into adjoining Round Pond. In early August, Round Mountain, rising a few hundred feet from Long Pond's eastern shore, is a great spot for gathering blueberries and huckleberries. The put-in for Long Pond is on the south side of Route 182 (park well off the road), about two miles east of Tunk Lake.

George Dallas Dixon Memorial

A pleasant shore path begins and ends at the Dixon Memorial Rock and leads along the water's edge and rises through the woods and by cottages on eastern Grindstone Neck. The views are fabulous. To find it, take Beach Street to Club House Lane, proceed across the four-way intersection, then go left on Steamboat Lane, following it to the oval at the end.

Golf

Play a nine-hole round at the **Grindstone Neck Golf Course** (Grindstone Ave., Winter Harbor, 207/963-7760, early June–Sept.), just for the dynamite scenery and for a glimpse of this exclusive, late-19th-century summer enclave. Established in 1895, the public course attracts a tony crowd; 150-yard markers are cute little birdhouses. Tee times usually aren't needed, but call to make sure.

Bike, Canoe, and Sea Kayak Outfitters and Tours

Jody Miller purchased **Moose Look Guide Service** (150 Corea Rd., Rte. 195, Prospect Harbor, 207/963-7223) and moved it to her Sea Myst Gallery and Gardens home shop. Bikes ($16), canoes ($30), and freshwater and sea kayaks ($30–50) are rented on a 24-hour basis. She plans to also offer guided tours at sunrise and sunset.

Antonio Blasi, a Registered Maine Sea Kayak and Recreational Guide, leads guided tours of Frenchman or Taunton Bay and hiking and camping expeditions through **Hancock Point Kayak Tours** (58 Point Rd., Hancock, 207/422-6854, antren@verizon.net). A three-hour paddle, including all equipment, safety and paddling demonstrations, and usually an island break, is $45. You have a choice of single or double kayak. Minimum age is 10 for a double, 12 for a single. Overnight kayak camping trips are $150 per person. A day hike is $35 per person. Other choices are available.

Atlantic Kayak Tours Inc. (Rte. 1, Sullivan, 208/422-3213) offers half- and full-day tours ($43 and $65) on six bays: Taunton, Egypt, Frenchman, Hog, Flanders, and Skillings. Tours are limited to six tandem kayaks. Expect to see plenty of seabirds, perhaps eagles, owls, and hawks, seals, and maybe even a porpoise. On full-day tours, a lobster dinner may be ordered in advance for an additional fee.

The Maine Department of Transportation has mapped and provides info on area bicycle routes. These include the Schoodic Peninsula, with 13- and 29-mile loops, and Downeast Route/East Coast Greenway Trail, a 140-mile trail stretching from Ellsworth to Calais. PDF maps with tour details are available on www.exploremaine.org /bike/bt_downeast.html, or you can request hard copies by calling 207/624-3250.

Scenic Boat Tours

Robertson Sea Tours & Adventures (207/546-3883 or 207/461-7439, www.robertsonseatours .com, May 15–Oct. 1) offers a puffin cruise to Petit Manan and a scenic island cruise from Bunker's Wharf aboard the *Mairi Leigh,* a classic Maine lobsterboat. The Petit Manan Puffin Cruise (Wed.–Sat.) lasts two hours and is $50 for adults, $40 for kids 12 and younger. The island cruise (Wed.–Sat., $40 for adults, $30 for kids) lasts two hours and cruises the shoreline and islands of the eastern Schoodic peninsula.

SHOPPING

Antiques

Browsers, dreamers, and collectors are welcome at **Art & Old Things** (70 Taunton Dr., Sullivan, 207/422-3551), a one-stop antiques and collectibles shop, art gallery, and sculpture garden that's just plain fun to visit. The eclectic gallery features the work of Joe Martell and other regional artists; the shop is filled with antiques, junktiques, and shabby chic furniture, decorative items, home accents, and architectural pieces; the garden is accented with granite and marble sculptures and unique functional artwork. The shop is just 500 yards off Route 1, just beyond Gazebo Park.

Food and Wine

German and Italian presses, Portuguese corks, and Maine fruit all go into the creation of Bob and Kathe Bartlett's award-winning dinner and dessert wines: apple, pear, blueberry, raspberry, blackberry, strawberry, and loganberry. Founded in 1982, **Bartlett Maine Estate Winery** (Chicken Mill Pond Rd., R.R. 1, Box 598, Gouldsboro 04607, 207/546-2408, 10 A.M.–5 P.M. Mon.–Sat. Memorial Day to Columbus Day, or by appointment off-season) produces more than 20,000 gallons annually in a handsome wood-and-stone building designed by the Bartletts. No tours, but you're welcome to sample the wines, and you can buy single bottles and gift packages. Bartlett's is a half mile south of Route 1 in Gouldsboro.

This area boasts not one, but two excellent smokehouses. **Sullivan Harbor Smokehouse** (Rte. 1, Sullivan, 207/422-3735 or 800/422-4014) and **Grindstone Neck of Maine** (311 Newman St., Rte. 186, just north of downtown Winter Harbor, 207/963-7347, or 866/831-8734). Both sell smoked salmon and other goodies, such as spreads.

Cindy and Bill Thayer's enthusiasm is contagious as they explain their prolific 133-acre certified-organic farm—home to hairy Scotch Highland cattle, turkeys, sheep, pigs, chickens, and border collies. At **Darthia Farm** (W. Bay Rd., Rte. 186, Gouldsboro 04607, 207/963-

7771, 207/963-2770, or 800/285-6234), kids love feeding the pigs and riding on the hay wagon; parents can check out Hattie's Shed for Cindy's outstanding ikat weavings and work by half a dozen other craftspeople. The Farm Store sells fresh produce as well a herbal salves and vinegars and other products. Tours and horse-drawn wagon rides occur each Tuesday and Thursday at 2 P.M. Cost is $2 pp. The farm is 1.7 miles south of Route 1.

Chickadee Creek Stillroom (Rte. 186, West Gouldsboro, 207/963-7283 or 800/969-4372) is the Toys "R" Us of herb fanciers. Jeanie and Fred Cook seem to have thought of everything—potpourri, teas, wreaths, fresh herbs for cooking. The barn/shop is 1.7 miles south of Route 1. Request a copy of the mail-order catalog.

ENTERTAINMENT AND EVENTS

The **Pierre Monteux School for Conductors and Orchestra Musicians** (Rte. 1, Hancock, 207/422-3931), a prestigious summer program founded in 1943, has achieved international renown for training dozens of national and international classical musicians. It presents two well-attended concert series starting in late June and running through July. The Wednesday series (7:30 P.M., $7) features chamber music; the Sunday concerts (5 P.M., $12 adults, $5 students) feature symphonies. An annual children's concert usually is held on a Monday (1 P.M.) in early to mid-July. In early August, **The Harald Saeverud String Quartet Program** (207/963-2102 or 207/454-0333, www.saeverud.com) presents another series (Wed. at 7:30 P.M. and Sun. at 5 P.M., $15 adult, $5 student). All concerts are held in the school's Forest Studio.

The energetic **Schoodic Arts for All** (207/963-2569, www.schoodicarts.org), a volunteer organization, presents events year-round, including concerts, art classes, coffeehouses, and workshops, many of which are held at historic Hammond Hall, in downtown Winter Harbor. The organization is best known for the Schoodic Arts Festival, in early August, two weeks jam-packed with daily workshops and nightly performances, for

Oceanside Meadows Innstitute is the centerpiece of a 200-acre property, with walking trails, a real sand beach, and an active environmental program.

all ages. Call for a schedule, and register early for any program that you don't want to miss.

The **Oceanside Meadows Innstitute for Arts and Sciences** (207/963-5557, www.oceaninn .com) presents a series of Thursday night events from late June to late September, with a break during the Schoodic Arts Festival. The wide-ranging calendar includes lectures and concerts as well as art shows. Some are free, others are $10 in advance or $12 at the door.

Winter Harbor's summer highlight is the annual **Lobster Festival,** second Saturday in August. The gala day-long event includes a parade, live entertainment, games, and more crustaceans than you could ever consume.

ACCOMMODATIONS
Country Inns

Buffered from the highway by a tall hedge, **Le Domaine** (Rte. 1, HC 77, Box 496, Hancock 04640, 207/422-3395 or 800/554-8498, www .ledomaine.com) has gained a five-star reputation for its restaurant, founded by the mother of present owner/chef Nicole Purslow in 1946—

long before fine dining had cachet here. But that's only part of the story. Above the restaurant is a charming, five-room, country-French inn, newly updated in the spring of 2000. The 80-acre inn property, nine miles east of Ellsworth, is virtual Provence, an oasis transplanted magically to Maine. On the garden-view balconies, or on the lawn out back, you're oblivious to the traffic whizzing by. Better yet, follow the lovely wooded trail to a quiet pond. Three guest rooms ($285, MAP, $200 B&B) and two suites ($370, MAP, $285 B&B) all are named after locales in Provence. Continental breakfast, usually including croissants, can be served in your room or in the dining room. Alert the inn if you'll be arriving after 5:30 P.M., when the staff has to focus on dinner. The ultra-French restaurant is open to the public Tuesday–Sunday 6–9 P.M. Reservations are essential, especially in July and August. Le Domaine's season is early June through November.

Follow Hancock Point Road 4.8 miles south of Route 1 to the three-story, gray-blue **Crocker House Country Inn** (Hancock Point Rd., HC 77, Box 171, Hancock 04640, 207/422-6806),

Rich and Liz Malaby's antidote to Bar Harbor's summer traffic. Built as a summer hotel in 1884, the inn underwent rehabbing a century later, but it retains a decidedly old-fashioned air. Eleven rooms (private baths) are $110–155. Breakfast is included. Nearby are clay tennis courts, quiet walking routes past Hancock Point's elegant seaside "cottages," and a unique octagonal public library. The Malabys will pack picnic lunches (extra charge) for day trips to Campobello Island, Acadia, or Lamoine State Park. If you're arriving by boat, request a mooring. Two dining rooms are open to the public for dinner and Sunday brunch; reservations are essential. The inn is open daily May through October, then weekends in November and December.

B&Bs

About 12 miles east of Ellsworth is the **Ṁ Island View Inn** (12 Miramar Ave., Sullivan 04664, 207/422-3031, www.maineus.com/islandview, $95–135, late May–mid-Oct.); its name is the height of understatement. Out front are the peaks of Mount Desert, a remarkable panorama. Four of the seven rooms (all private baths and decks) capture the view from this updated 1889 summer home run by Evelyn Joost and her daughter Sarah. The inn evokes the easy elegance of days gone by. The Island View has a private beach, but the water is terminally chilly. Experienced sailors can rent the inn's Rhodes 18 sloop, ($45 half day, $74 for the day). Guests have free use of a canoe, a paddleboat, and a dinghy.

Sorrento is such a low-key place that lots of people don't realize it has a B&B, an ultracasual homestay-style one at that, **Bass Cove Farm Bed & Breakfast** (312 Eastside Rd., Rte. 185, Sorrento 04677, 207/422-3564, www.basscovefarm .com, $55–90) was opened in 1992 by spinner/weaver/gardener/editor Mary Ann Solet and her husband, Michael Tansey, a group-home supervisor whose résumé also includes the Harry S. Truman Manure Pitchoff Championship at the annual Common Ground Country Fair. The 1840s-era farmhouse uses solar-heated water; the cleaning is done with nontoxic products. Mary Ann can rattle off dozens of ideas for exploring the area, particularly in the craft department, and she raids her extensive vegetable garden daily to produce a hearty, healthful breakfast. Guest rooms have quilt-covered beds and other homey touches—some share baths. A one-bedroom apartment on the second floor rents for $350–375 a week.

Aptly named, **The Sunset House Bed & Breakfast** (Rte. 186, West Gouldsboro 04607, 207/963-7156 or 800/233-7156, www.sunset housebnb.com, $79–99, May–late Oct.) overlooks the setting sun off to the west and water from more than one direction. Most of the seven rooms (four with private baths) in Carl and Kathy Johnson's charming three-story very Victorian home have water views. Jones Pond, Gouldsboro's freshwater swimming hole, borders the property; bring a canoe and launch it here—but not before launching into award-winning chef Carl's generous breakfast. In winter, you can go ice-skating and cross-country skiing. Sunset House is a quarter mile south of Route 1, on a nerve-defying curve in the village of West Gouldsboro.

Overlooking the Gouldsboro Peninsula's only sandy saltwater beach, **Ṁ Oceanside Meadows Innstitute** (Rte. 195, Corea Rd., P.O. Box 90, Prospect Harbor 04669, 207/963-5557, www .oceaninn.com, $128–198, May–late Oct.) is a jewel of a place on 200 acres with fabulous gardens, wildlife habitat, and walking trails. The elegant 1860s Captain's House has seven attractive rooms, and the 1820 Shaw farmhouse next door has another seven. Breakfast is an impressive four-course event, staged by the energetic husband-and-wife team of Sonja Sundaram and Ben Walter, who seem to have thought of everything—hot drinks available all day, a guest fridge, beach toys, even detailed guides to the property's trails and habitats (great for entertaining kids). As if all that weren't enough, Sonja and Ben have totally restored the 1820 timber-frame barn out back—creating the **Oceanside Meadows Innstitute for the Arts and Sciences.** Local art hangs on the walls, and from June into September, the 125-seat barn has a full schedule of classical concerts and lectures on natural history, Native American traditions, and more, usually on Thursday nights. The inn's website is also a phenomenal resource on area activities. Oceanside Meadows is six miles off Route 1.

Watch lobsterboats unload their catch at the dock opposite **Elsa's Inn on the Harbor** (179 Main St., Prospect Harbor 04669, 207/963-7571, www.elsasinn.com, $105–155). Jeffrey and Cynthia Alley, their daughter, Megan, and her husband, Glenn, and grandson Andrew have turned Jeff's mother Elsa's home into a warm and welcoming inn. The Alley family roots in the area go back more than 10 generations, so you're guaranteed to receive solid information on where to go and what to do. Every room has an ocean view, and Megan, an experienced innkeeper whose career included positions at Ritz Carlton and luxury boutique hotels, pampers guests with luxurious linens, down duvets, terry robes, evening turndown service, afternoon refreshments, and a hearty hot breakfast. After a day exploring, settle into a rocker on the veranda and gaze out to Prospect Harbor Light.

Off the beaten path is Bob Travers and Barry Canner's **Black Duck Inn on Corea Harbor** (Crowley Island Rd., P.O. Box 39, Corea 04624, 207/963-2689 www.blackduck.com, $104–130, May.–mid-Oct.), literally the end of the line on the Gouldsboro Peninsula. Set on 12 acres in this timeless fishing village, the B&B has four handsomely decorated rooms and plenty of common space. Across the way, perched on the harbor's edge, are two little seasonal cottages, one rented by the day (three-night minimum) and one by the week. The inn and Corea are geared to wanderers, readers, and anyone seeking serenity (who isn't?). Rocky outcrops dot the property and a nature trail meanders to a mill pond; in early August, the blueberries are ready. If the fog socks in, the large parlor has comfortable chairs and loads of books.

Something of a categorical anomaly, **The Bluff House Inn** (Rte. 186, P.O. Box 249, Gouldsboro 04607, 207/963-7805, www .bluffinn.com, $95–130) is part motel, part hotel, part B&B—a seemingly successful mix in a contemporary building overlooking Frenchman Bay on the west side of the Gouldsboro

Peninsula. Verandas wrap around the first and second floors, so bring binoculars for osprey and bald eagle sightings. The eight second-floor rooms are decorated "country" fashion, with quilts on the very comfortable beds. (In hot weather, request a corner room.) Breakfast is generous continental, including excellent baked goodies. In summer, walk the steep path to the shore; in winter, you can cross-country ski on the owner's 400 acres across the road. Open all year.

Motel and Cottages

The rustic **Pines** (17 Main St., Rte. 186, Winter Harbor, 207/963-2296, www.ayuh.net, $55–70) comprises a mix of motel-style rooms and efficiencies and small cabins. The overall property could use some attention, but the rooms are clean, and the location at the entrance to the Schoodic Loop road is primo, especially for those wanting to bicycle. Owner Marshall Rust runs a very laid-back operation: prospective guests are welcome to tour open rooms, choose one, and cross it off on a door sign that promises he'll catch up with you later; those with reservations are told how to find their room. Marshall's wife, Almeda, runs a day-care center out of their home, and if there's room and your child adjusts easily to new situations, you might be able to take advantage of it.

Also rustic are **Albee's Cottages** (Rte. 186, Prospect Harbor, 207/963-2336 or 800/963-2336, www.theshorehouse.com, $69–106/night or $455–715/week, May–mid-Oct.), a cluster of 10 white cottages, decorated with braided rugs and quilts. Nothing fancy here but the waterfront location. You can also arrange with Larry, the property manager, for a lobster dinner on the premises.

Sullivan Harbor Farm (Rte. 1, P.O. Box 96, Sullivan 04664, 207/422-3735 or 800/422-4014, www.sullivanharborfarm.com, $885–1,450/week), perhaps best known for its superb smoked salmon, also has three cottages on its property with views of Frenchman Bay. Owners Joel Frantzman and Leslie Harlow enthusiastically share their area knowledge and have a canoe and kayak available for guests' use.

Campgrounds

In July and August, when every single campsite on Mount Desert Island is booked solid, those in the know go eight miles southeast of Ellsworth to the wooded, no-frills campground at 55-acre **Lamoine State Park** (Rte. 184, Lamoine 04605, 207/667-4778, mid-May–mid-Oct.). Park facilities include a pebble beach and picnic area with a spectacular view, a boat-launch ramp, fishing pier, and a children's play area. Day-use admission is $3 adults, $1 children 5–11. Camping (62 sites) is $20 per site per night for nonresidents; two-night minimum. No hookups. To guarantee a site in July and August, using MasterCard or Visa, call 207/287-3824 or visit www.campwithme.com; reservation fee is $2 per site per night. The park is accessible off-season for daytime activities.

On a wooded finger of land projecting eastward from the Schoodic Peninsula, ◪ **Ocean Wood Campground** (P.O. Box 111, Birch Harbor 04613, 207/963-7194, early May–late Oct.) gets kudos for eco-sensitivity, noise control, and 17 fantastic wilderness sites, most on the ocean. Don't expect frills; nature provides the entertainment. The 70 campsites (some with hookups) are $22–33, depending on location and services. Pets (leashed) are allowed at regular sites, but not at the wilderness ones. No credit cards; free hot showers. The campground is a terrific base for exploring the Schoodic section of Acadia National Park.

FOOD

Make a point to attend one of the many **public suppers** held throughout the summer in this area and so many other rural corners of Maine. Typically benefiting a worthy cause, these usually feature beans or spaghetti and the serendipity of plain potluck. Everyone saves room for the homemade pies.

Miscellany

Once a true, old-fashioned country store with a classic traditional soda fountain and penny candy, **J.M. Gerrish Provisions** (352 Main St., Winter Harbor 04693, 207/963-2727, 8 A.M.–5 P.M.),

known as Gerrish's Store, has changed since coming under the same ownership of nearby Mama's Boy Bistro. It's now an upscale specialty foods store and deli. You can still get ice cream, but the penny candy selection is tiny (and a far cry from a penny). Fresh-baked goodies, such as scones and muffins, and fancy coffees are available all day long; soups, salads, and fancy sandwiches ($4–6) are served 11 A.M.–3 P.M.

Pick up veggies, meats, eggs, cheeses, and handcrafted fiber products as well as jams, preserves, and baked goods at the **Winter Harbor Farmers' Market** (Mama's Boy Bistro parking lot, corner Newman St. and Rte. 186, Winter Harbor, 9 A.M.–noon Tues., late June–early Sept.).

Pizza with a View

In "downtown" Prospect Harbor is the best picnic solution in the area. The **Downeast Deli** (corner Routes 186 and 195, Prospect Harbor 04669, 207/963-2700, 10 A.M.–8 P.M. Sun.–Thurs., to 9 P.M. Fri. and Sat.) will fix you right up with dozens of sandwich choices: hot or cold hoagies, hot dogs and burgers, reubens, deli-style sandwiches, and really good pizza with a wide array of mix and match choices (try a New York White topped with smoked salmon). The desserts are homemade. Service is swift. Take it with you or head upstairs and grab a window table and enjoy the harbor views.

Family Fare

Don't be put off by the lobster "sculpture" outside **Ruth & Wimpy's Kitchen** (792 Rte. 1, Hancock 04640, 207/422-3723, 11 A.M.–9 P.M. Apr.–Dec.); you'll probably see a crowd as well. This family-fare standby serves hefty sandwiches, about two dozen lobster dishes, pizza, pasta, and steak. Prices begin at $2.25 for a cheeseburger and climb to $24.95 for a twin-tail lobster dinner. Antique license plates and collections of miniature cars and trucks accent the interior. It's five miles east of Ellsworth, close to the Hancock Point turnoff.

Family fare, from fried food to pizza, is on the menu at **Old Post Office Restaurant & Take Out** (679 S. Gouldsboro Rd., Gouldsboro,

207/963-7280, 11 A.M.–8 P.M.). It's a good place to pick up a picnic lunch if you're on your way down the peninsula and heading for the park. You can dine inside or on the deck.

Best place for grub and gossip in Winter Harbor is **Chase's Restaurant** (193 Main St., Winter Harbor 04693, 207/963-7171, 6 A.M.–9 P.M.), a seasoned, no-frills booth-and-counter operation that turns out first-rate fish chowder, fries, and onion rings, a surprising vegetarian lasagna, and downright cheap breakfasts. No credit cards.

Casual Dining

Make it a point to find **M Bunkers Wharf** (260 E. Schoodic Dr., Birch Harbor, 207/963-2244, 11:30 A.M.–10 P.M. Mon.–Sat., brunch 10 A.M.–3 P.M. Sun.). The dining room overlooks a working wharf, and there's a big stone fireplace to ward off the chill on inclement days. Crisp white linens and fresh flowers add a formal touch in the dining room, yet the feeling is unpretentious. You can also dine in the pub or on the patio that's practically in the harbor. Dinner entrées are $17 and up.

Chipper's (Rte. 1, Hancock, 207/422-8238, 5–9 P.M.) is a reliable choice for good food. The wide-ranging menu includes rack of lamb, but the emphasis is on seafood; the crab cakes get rave reviews. Entrées are in the $15–25 range.

You can't miss **Mama's Boy Bistro** (10 Main St., Winter Harbor, 207/963-2365, 5 A.M.–9 P.M. Tues.–Sun.), which dominates the waterfront and, depending on your point of view, is either a charming New England-style building or a New York-influenced monstrosity. Whatever. The à la carte menu emphasizes local fresh and organic foods. The food earns rave reviews, although some complain that the portions are too small for the prices. The lounge/bar is a nice place to relax, if a bit pricey. The dining area centers around a huge open kitchen, and it is often noisy. Entrées run $19–28; a five-course Bistro Tasting menu is $55, pair it with wine for an additional $30. Open mid-May–mid-October.

The ultra-French restaurant **Le Domaine** (Rte. 1, Hancock, 207/422-3395, www.ledomaine.com)

has gained a five-star reputation. It has a 5,000-bottle wine cellar and lovely Provençal decor. It's open to the public Tuesday–Sunday 6 P.M.–9 P.M. Reservations are essential, especially in July and August. The tab may dent your budget (entrées $22–30), but stack that up against plane fare to France. Le Domaine's season is early June through November.

Crocker House Country Inn (Hancock Point Rd., Hancock, 207/422-6806) has two dining rooms open to the public for dinner (daily 5:30–9 P.M.; entrées $22–30) and Sunday brunch (11 A.M.–2 P.M. Memorial Day through Labor Day); reservations are essential. The inn is open daily May–October, then weekends in November and December.

Lobster-in-the-Rough

Thank goodness the Frenchman Bay Conservancy purchased the land overlooking Frenchman Bay's only reversing falls, and thank goodness the conservancy leases the site to **M Tidal Falls Lobster Pound** (off Eastside Rd., Hancock, 207/422-6457, 5–9 P.M. daily and noon–9 P.M. Thurs.–Sun. June 21–Labor Day). Come for the lobster (market price), but landlubbers will find New York sirloin ($16.95) and kids can order hot dogs ($2.50). Order at the window, then grab a picnic table either on the lawn or in the screen house. Eastside Road is just south of the Hancock-Sullivan bridge; follow it one mile and look for a sign on your left. Follow the gravel road to the end.

INFORMATION

Information

For Schoodic information, contact the **Schoodic Peninsula Chamber of Commerce** (P.O. Box 381, Winter Harbor 04693, 207/963-7658 or 800/231-3008 outside Maine, www.acadia-schoodic.org, and request its handy map/brochure, revised annually.

Hospitals

Maine Coast Memorial Hospital (50 Union St., Ellsworth, 207/664-5311), the largest hospital in the area, has 24-hour emergency-room service. Healthcare Express (207/664-5341), at the hospital, handles minor problems daily between noon and 8 P.M.

Local Libraries

The **Dorcas Library** (Rte. 186, Prospect Harbor, 207/963-4027) is open 4–8 P.M. Monday, 1:30–4 P.M. and 6–8 P.M. Wednesday, 1:30–4 P.M. Saturday. In July and August, the library also is open 10 A.M.–noon.

The **Winter Harbor Public Library** (18 Chapel Ln, Winter Harbor, 207/963-7556) is open 1:30–4 P.M. Wednesday, Friday, and Saturday, also 6–8 P.M. Wednesday.

The Down East Coast

"Down East," people say, is the direction the wind blows—the prevailing southwest wind that powered 19th-century sailing vessels along this rugged coastline. But to be truly Down East, in the minds of most Mainers, you have to be physically here, in Washington County—a stunning landscape of waterways, forests, blueberry barrens, rocky shoreline dotted with islands and lighthouses, and independent, pocket-size communities, many still dependent upon fishing or lobstering for their economies.

At one time, *most* of the Maine coast used to be as underdeveloped as this part of it. You can set your clock back a generation or two while you're here; you'll find no giant malls and only a couple of fast-food joints. While there are a handful of restaurants offering fine dining, for the most part, your choices are limited to family-style restaurants specializing in home cooking with an emphasis on fresh (usually fried) seafood and lobster rolls. Nor will you find grand resorts or even not-so-grand hotels. Motels, tourist cabins, and small inns and B&Bs dot the region. The upside is, prices, too, are a generation removed. If you're

© TOM NANGLE

Must-Sees

M Petit Manan National Wildlife Refuge: More than 300 birds have been sighted at Petit Manan Point, but even if you're not a birder, come for the hiking and, in August, the blueberries (page 358).

M Great Wass Island Preserve: The finest natural treasure in this part of Maine is the Great Wass Archipelago, partly owned by The Nature Conservancy, with opportunities for hiking and birding (page 363).

West Quoddy Head State Park.

© TOM NANGLE

N

The Down East Coast

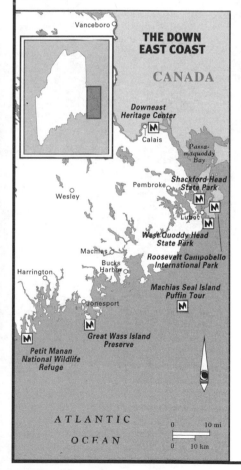

M Machias Seal Island Puffin Tour: Take the boat from Jonesport to Machias Seal Island, home to Atlantic puffins (the clowns of the sea), as well as razorbill auks, Arctic terns, and common murres. Another puffin-sighting excursion boat leaves from Cutler (pages 365 and 371).

M West Quoddy Head State Park: The candy-striped lighthouse is a Maine coast icon, and even a short hike along the paths edging the cliffs reaps big rewards (page 376).

M Roosevelt Campobello International Park: Make it an international vacation by venturing over to this New Brunswick park, home to the Roosevelt Cottage and miles of hiking trails, and jointly managed by the United States and Canada (page 380).

M Shackford Head State Park: The reward for hiking the easy Shackford Head Trail is a panoramic view over Cobscook Bay, from Eastport to Campobello (page 386).

M Downeast Heritage Center: Put your visit Down East into perspective in one stop at this engaging museum that explores the people, history, economy, and environment of Washington County (page 392).

The Down East Coast

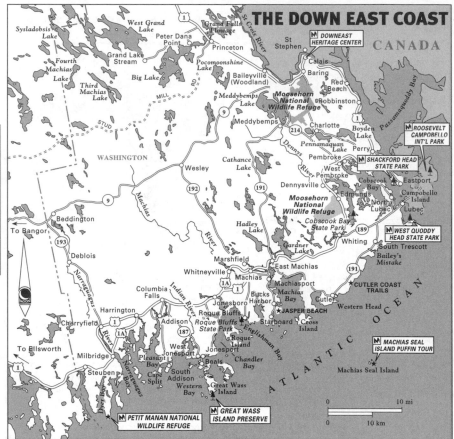

searching for the Maine of your memories or your imagination, this is it.

When eastern Hancock County flows into western Washington County, you're on the Down East Coast (also called the Sunrise Coast). From Steuben eastward to Jonesport, Machias, and Lubec—then "around the corner" to Eastport and Calais—Washington County is twice the size of Rhode Island, covers 2,528 square miles, has about 35,000 residents, and stakes a claim as the first U.S. real estate to see the morning sun. The region also includes handfuls of offshore islands—some accessible by ferry, charter boat, or private vessel. (Some, with sensitive bird-nest-

ing sites, are off-limits during the summer.) At the uppermost point of the coast, and conveniently linked to Lubec by a bridge, New Brunswick's Campobello Island is a popular day-trip destination—the locale of Franklin D. Roosevelt's summer retreat. Other attractions in this area include festivals, concert series, art and antique galleries, lighthouses, two Native American reservations, and the great outdoors for hiking, biking, birding, sea kayaking, whale-watching, camping, swimming, and fishing.

One of the Down East Coast's millennial buzzwords has been eco-tourism, and local conservation organizations and chambers of commerce have targeted and welcomed visitors willing to be careful of the fragile ecosystems here—visitors who will contribute to the economy while respecting the natural resources and leaving them untrammeled, visitors who don't cross the fine line between light use and overuse. Low-impact tourism is essential for this area. However, outfitters and canoe, kayak, and bicycle rental outlets are few and far between.

One natural phenomenon no visitor can affect is the tide—the inexorable ebb and flow, predictably in and predictably out. If you're not used to it, even the six- to 10-foot tidal ranges of southern Maine may surprise you. But along this coastline, the tides are astonishing—as much as 28 feet of difference in water level within six hours. Old-timers tell stories of big money lost betting on horses racing the fast-moving tides.

Another surprise to visitors may be how early the sun rises—and sets—on the "sunrise coast." Keep in mind that if you cross into Canada in either Lubec or Calais, you enter Atlantic time, and you'll need to set your clock ahead one hour.

Yet another distinctive natural feature of Washington County is its blueberry barrens (fields). Depending on the time of year, the fields will be black (torched by growers to jumpstart the crop), blue (ready for harvest), or maroon (fall foliage, fabulous for photography). In early summer, a million rented bees set to work pollinating the blossoms. By August, when a blue haze forms over the knee-high shrubs, bent-over bodies use old-fashioned wooden rakes to harvest the ripe berries. It's backbreaking work, but the employment lines usually form quickly when newspaper ads announce the advent of the annual harvest.

One bit of advice you might not receive from the tourism people is that warm clothing is essential in this corner of Maine. It may be nicknamed the Sunrise Coast, but it also gets plenty of fog, rain, and cool temperatures. Temperatures tend to be warmer, and the fog diminishes, as you head toward the inland parts of the county, but you can *never* count on that. Mother Nature is an accomplished curveball pitcher, and el Niño and la Niña periodically provide an assist.

PLANNING YOUR TIME

Down East Maine is not for those in a hurry. Traffic ambles along. Towns are few and far between. Nature is the biggest calling card here, and to appreciate it, you'll need time to hike, bike, canoe, sea kayak, or take an excursion boat. Although Route 1 follows the coast in general, it's often miles from the water. You'll want to ramble down the peninsulas to explore the seaside villages, see lighthouses, or hike in parks and preserves. You'll likely need at least three days, ideally five days or longer.

Avid bird-watchers should allow the better part of a day at any of the top birding sites: **Petit Manan, Great Wass Island, Moosehorn National Wildlife Refuge,** or the puffin colony at **Machias Seal Island.** Lighthouse fans and coastal moseyers need about three days to edge the coastline to see places such as **West Quoddy Head State Park,** home of the candy-striped lighthouse. Nature-loving hikers will want to spend at least a half day at West Quoddy Head ambling along the coastal trails, visiting the peat bog, and watching for whales. Another hike with big rewards is Eastport's **Shackford Head,** which provides panoramic views over Cobscook Bay to Campobello and beyond.

History and architecture buffs should plan two days to visit sites in Columbia Falls, Machias/Machiasport, and on **Campobello Island.** And it's worth it to visit Calais if for no other reason than to spend a few hours in the **Downeast Heritage Center.** Although it comes at the end of the road, so to speak, it puts the region's culture, heritage, economy, and peoples in perspective.

If walking and hiking are on your Washington County agenda—and they should be—be sure to send for a copy of *Cobscook Trails*, published by the Quoddy Regional Land Trust (Rte. 1, P.O. Box 49, Whiting 04691, 207/733-5509, qrlt@maineline.net). Many of the parks and preserves described in this section are included in the QRLT booklet.

The Maine Department of Transportation has mapped and provides info on area bicycle routes. These include Washington County Downeast, a

94-mile route with numerous shorter possibilities; Passamaquoddy Bay, with 27-, 38-, and 50-mile loops; and Downeast Route/East Coast Greenway Trail, a 140-mile trail stretching from Ellsworth to Calais. PDF maps with tour details are available on www.exploremaine.org, or you can request hard copies by calling 207/624-3250.

Of course, if you want to settle in and adjust to the rhythm of the tide and slower pace of life, it's best to rent a shorefront cottage and spend a week. No matter where you stay, you can explore all of the Down East Coast with day trips, although that may mean a few early mornings to get it all in.

The nearest major airport is Bangor International Airport. While a bus does service Route 1 from Bangor to Calais, truly, you need a car to explore this region. Driving from Bangor, you have two choices. Take Route 1A south to Ellsworth, where it connects with Route 1 north, then follow it up the coast. (That's the way this chapter is organized.) The other choice is to beeline for Calais via "The Airline," a 98-mile section of Maine Route 9 connecting Bangor and Calais (or, to be exact, the towns of Eddington and Baring); it's this area's major inland artery, a recently rebuilt two-lane highway used by a colorful array of commuters, visitors, sportspeople, and logging-truck drivers. Mostly it's a convenient shortcut, and sometimes not even that, since there's just a smattering of restaurants, shops, and lodgings along the way. The road, built for postal stagecoaches in the mid-19th century, trims nearly 60 miles off the trip between Calais and Bangor compared to the longer coastal Route 1. Hazards in bygone days were bad weather, wolves, and marauding bandits; today, they are bad weather, moose, and go-for-broke fuel and lumber trucks. Once in Calais, head south on Route 1.

Western Washington County

The pace begins to slow a bit by the time you've left Hancock County and entered western Washington County, the beginning of the Down East Coast. In this little pocket are the towns of Steuben, Milbridge, Cherryfield, and Harrington.

Life can be tough here nowadays, where once great wooden ships slid down the ways and brought prosperity and trade to shippers, builders, and barons of the timber industry. Cherryfield's stunning houses are evidence enough. The barons now control the blueberry fields, covering much of the inland area of western Washington County and annually shipping millions of pounds of blueberries out of headquarters in Milbridge (pop. 1,330) and Cherryfield (pop. 1,200). The big names here are Jasper Wyman & Sons and Cherryfield Foods.

Milbridge straddles Route 1 and the Narraguagus River (nar-ra-GWAY-gus, a Native American name meaning "above the boggy place"), once the state's premier source of Atlantic salmon. Cherryfield is at the tidal limit of the Narraguagus. Even though Route 1A trims maybe three miles off the trip from Milbridge to Harrington (pop. 900), resist the urge to take it. Take Route 1 from Milbridge to Cherryfield—the Narraguagus Highway—and then continue to Harrington. You just shouldn't miss Cherryfield.

SIGHTS

Petit Manan National Wildlife Refuge

Occupying a 2,166-acre peninsula in Steuben with 10 miles of rocky shoreline (and three offshore islands), outstandingly scenic Petit Manan National Wildlife Refuge (Pigeon Hill Rd., Steuben, mailing address P.O. Box 279, Milbridge 04658, 207/546-2124), sees only about 15,000 visitors a year, most of those likely birders, as more than 250 different birds have been sighted here. The moderately easy, four-mile round-trip Birch Point Trail and easy, 1.5-mile round-trip Hollingsworth Trail provide splendid views and opportunities to spot wildlife along the shore and in the fields, forests, and marshland. The Hollingsworth Trail, leading you to the shoreline, is the best. This is foggy territory,

© TOM NANGLE

On a clear day, you can see the towering lighthouse on Petit Manan Island from the shoreline.

but on clear days, you can see the 123-foot light-house on Petit Manan Island, 2.5 miles offshore. From Route 1, on the east side of Steuben, take Pigeon Hill Road. Six miles down is the first parking lot, for the Birch Point Trail; another half mile takes you to the parking area for the Hollingsworth Trail; space is limited. If you arrive in August, help yourself to blueberries. The refuge is open daily all year, sunrise to sunset; cross-country skiing is permitted in winter.

Local History

A group of energetic residents worked tirelessly to establish the **Milbridge Historical Society Museum** (S. Main St., Milbridge 04658, 207/546-4471, 1–4 P.M. Sat. and Sun. June and Sept., and Tues. July and Aug., donations accepted). Displays in the large exhibit room focus on Milbridge's essential role in the shipbuilding trade, but kids will enjoy such oddities as an amputation knife used by a local doctor and a re-created country kitchen.

Scenic Fall-Foliage Routes

In fall—roughly early September to early October in this part of Maine—the post-har-vest blueberry fields take on brilliant scarlet hues, then maroon. They're gorgeous. The best barren-viewing road is **Route 193** between Cherryfield and Beddington, via Deblois, the link between Routes 1 and 9—a 21-mile stretch of granite outcrops, pine windscreens, and fiery-red fields.

Also in fall, consider taking a lovely alternate route from Hancock County into western Washington County. A few miles east of Ellsworth, **Route 182** veers northeast off Route 1 to Franklin and on to Cherryfield, a 25-mile stretch of sparkling ponds, brilliant colors, and no civilization. Schoodic Mountain, Donnell Pond, and Tunk Lake are just three of the natural treasures along the way. As you enter Washington County and land in Cherryfield, you're brought gently back to civilization by a whole town full of architectural treasures.

Cherryfield Historic District

Imagine a little town this far Down East having a 75-acre National Register Historic District with 52 architecturally significant buildings. If architecture appeals, don't miss Cherryfield. The **Cherryfield-Narraguagus Historical Society** (P.O. Box 96, Cherryfield 04622) has produced a free brochure/map, *Guide to the Cherryfield Historic District,* which you can obtain in advance or pick up once you get here. Architectural styles included on the route are Greek Revival, Italianate, Queen Anne, Colonial Revival, Second Empire, Federal, and Gothic Revival—dating from 1803 to 1940, with most being late 19th century.

Boating Excursion

Robertson Sea Tours & Adventures (Milbridge Marina, Fickett's Point Rd., 207/546-3883 or 207/461-7439, www.robbertsonseatours.com, May 15–Oct. 1) offers a puffin cruise to Petit Manan and a scenic island cruise from Milbridge aboard the ***Mairi Leigh,*** a classic Maine lobster-boat. The Petit Manan Puffin Cruise lasts three hours and is $50 for adults, $40 for kids 12 and younger. The island cruise ($40 for adults, $30 for kids) lasts two hours plus, passes seven islands, and highlights the region's aquaculture industry.

SHOPPING

Artisans' studios dot the region. **Arthur Smith** (Rogers Point Rd., Steuben, 207/546-3462) is the real thing when it comes to chainsaw carvings. He's an extremely talented artist who looks at a piece of wood and sees an animal in it. His carvings of great blue herons, eagles, wolves, porcupines, flamingoes, and other creatures are incredibly detailed, and his wife, Marie, paints them in lifelike colors. Don't expect a fancy studio; much of the work can be viewed roadside.

Also in Steuben, but on the other end of the spectrum, is **Ray Carbone** (460 Pigeon Hill Rd., Steuben, 207/546-2170), whose masterful wood, stone, and bronze sculptures and fine furniture are definitely worth stopping to see, if not buy.

ENTERTAINMENT

The only cinema in western Washington County is the updated, air-conditioned **Milbridge Theatre** (Main St., Rte. 1, Milbridge 207/546-2038, www.maineexchange.com), a classic movie house that's been here since 1937. First-run films, with a good sound system, go on at 7:30 P.M.; all seats are $4.50. It's open daily Memorial Day weekend through October; weekends in April, November, and December; closed January–March. Occasionally there are Saturday or Sunday matinees at 2 P.M.

The Humboldt Field Research Institute sponsors weekly **Eagle Hill Summer Lectures** (59 Eagle Hill Rd., Steuben, 207/546-2821, www.eaglehill.us, 7:30 P.M. Thurs., early July to late Aug., free) presented by guest lecturers and scholars on wide-ranging topics, from ant-like litter beetles and forensic microscopy to coastal geography and lighthouses. The institute also is offering occasional Saturday evening presentations with dinner for $15. To find the institute, take Dyer Bay Road off Route 1, bearing left at the fork to Mogador Road for a total of 3.6 miles; turn left at a gravel pit on Schooner Point road, then right on Eagle Hill Road.

Check locally for the concert schedule of the

Cherryfield Band, an impressive community group with about three dozen enthusiastic members. They're in demand from May to December, but best of all are their concerts, usually Tuesday evenings, in the lovely downtown bandstand, overlooking the Narraguagus River.

FESTIVALS AND EVENTS

The biggest event in this end of Washington County, and even beyond, is the **Milbridge Anniversary Celebration,** the last weekend in July, drawing hundreds of visitors. The Saturday-afternoon highlight is the codfish relay race—hilarious enough to have been featured in *Sports Illustrated* and on national television. The four-member teams, clad in slickers and hip boots, *really do* hand off a greased cod instead of the usual baton. Race rules specify that runners must be "reasonably sober" and not carry the codfish between their teeth or legs. Also on the schedule are blueberry pancake breakfasts, a fun parade, kids' games, auction, dance, beano and cribbage tournaments, craft booths, and a lobsterbake.

ACCOMMODATIONS

B&Bs and Motels

One of Cherryfield's 52 Historic Register buildings, the 1803 **Ricker House** (Park St., P.O. Box 256, Cherryfield 04622, 207/546-2780, mid-May–Nov., $65) borders the Narraguagus River and makes a superb base for exploring inland and Down East Maine. Jean and Bill Conway keep coming up with unending lists of things to do—*after* a huge breakfast, maybe a loll on the lovely sunporch, then a stroll to the river, where there's a canoe. Three second-floor bedrooms share a bath; two have a view of the river. Bicycles are available for guests; tennis courts are across the street. No credit cards.

Billy and Jackie Majors' strikingly modern **Guagus River Inn** (295B Kansas Rd., Milbridge, 207/546-9737, www.guagusriverinn.com, $70–150) is passive solar design. Plenty of space to spread out here in a huge recreation room with exercise equipment, an indoor lap pool, living room, deck, and rolling lawns down to the river. Rates include a full breakfast.

Many of the 28 rooms at **The Red Barn Motel** (5 North Main St., Milbridge, 207/546-7721, hleighton@maineline.net, $65) overlook the Narraguagus River. All have air-conditioning and TV. Pets are welcome. All meals are available at the adjacent restaurant.

Campgrounds

Since 1958, the Ayers family has opened its property on Joy Cove to campers. **Mainayr Campground** (321 Village Rd., Steuben, 207/542-2690, www.maineayr.com, Memorial Day–Columbus Day) has 35 tenting and RV sites, which go for $18.25. Utility connections and waterfront sites are higher. Also on the premises are a playground, laundry, beach for tidal swimming, camp store, and fresh lobsters.

Bill and Mary Martin's **Bayview Campground** (39 Ficketts Point Rd, Milbridge, 207/546-2946) is a private spot on Narraguagus Bay. Twenty RV and tent sites ($17–20) are spread out on 20 acres bordered by water and woods. A boat launch is 800 feet from the campground, and there's a small saltwater beach on-site. Free hot showers.

Covering seven acres on the tidal Harrington River, small, low-key **Sunset Point Campground,** (Marshville Rd., Harrington 04643, 207/483-4412, www.sunsetpointcampground.com, May 15–Oct. 15) has 30 open sites ($12–15 for a tent site; $20–24 for an RV site), a playground, and saltwater swimming. Lobster usually is available, either live or cooked, for around $7 per pound. Leashed pets are allowed. From Route 1, east of Harrington, take the road toward Marshville for 2.8 miles; the campground is on the right.

FOOD

Casual Dining

Trust me on this. Ignore the exterior and venture into **ℕ Country Charm** (336 Village Rd., Steuben 04680, 207/546-3763, 6 A.M.–8 P.M. Tues.–Sun., until 2 P.M. Mon.). The fried fish is fabulously fresh, crispy, light, and cheap, even by local standards. You easily can get out of here for less than $10 pp, far less if you're on a tight

budget. The original dining room has, well, country charm (sit here if you want to listen in on the local gossip); the newer ones (added when a real kitchen replaced the original blue trailer) are purely functional. Don't be shy about arriving early for breakfast; coffee's on by 5:30 A.M., even though the kitchen doesn't open until 6. Hungry? Order the Charm Special: two eggs, bacon, sausages, pancakes, toast, and coffee all for a whopping $4.50; omelets begin at $2.25.

Even less fancy is **Port Side Snack Bar** (Rte. 1, Steuben, 207/546-7676, 10 A.M.–8 P.M.). Fried seafood, burgers, chowders, pizza, and subs; everything's made from scratch.

In the heart of Milbridge is the aptly named **Red Barn Restaurant** (5 N. Main St., Milbridge, 207/546-7721, 7 A.M.–9 P.M., opens at 8 A.M. on Sun.), a locally popular spot for breakfast, lunch, and dinner, featuring ample portions of award-winning down-home clam chowder, lobster stew, fried seafood, and steaks at wallet-friendly prices. Open all year, the restaurant is set back a bit from Main Street and easiest to reach from Bridge Street (just off Route 1).

Farmers' Market

You can easily pick up enough goodies for a picnic lunch or to stock a cottage kitchen at the **Milbridge Farmers Market** (Milbridge Market parking lot, Main St., Milbridge, 9 A.M.–noon Sat. early June–mid-Oct.). Choose from fresh baked goods, goat cheese, organic veggies and meats, eggs, and other goodies. Go early for the best selection.

INFORMATION

Several communities in western Washington County have banded together to form the **Downeast Coastal Chamber of Commerce** (P.O. Box 331, Harrington 04643, 207/483-2131, www.downeastcoastalchamber.org). Addison, Cherryfield, Columbia Falls, Deblois, Harrington, Jonesport/Beals, Milbridge, Steuben, and a few others are included. The **Washington County Promotions Board** (P.O. Box 605, Machias 04654, 800/377-9748) can also help with general information.

Jonesport/Beals Area

Between western Washington County and the Machias Bay area is the molar-shaped Jonesport Peninsula, reached from the west via the attractive little town of Columbia Falls, bordering Route 1. Rounding the peninsula are the picturesque towns of Addison, Jonesport, and Beals Island, and less scenic Jonesboro. First settled around 1762, Columbia Falls (pop. about 550) still has a handful of houses dating from the late 18th century, but its best-known structure is the early-19th-century Ruggles House.

On the banks of the Pleasant River, just south of Columbia Falls, Addison (pop. 1,150) once had four huge shipyards cranking out wooden cargo vessels that circled the world. Since that 19th-century heyday, little seems to have changed, and the town today may be best known as the haunt of painter John Marin, who first came to Maine in 1914.

Jonesport and Beals Island, with a combined population of about 2,185, are traditional hard-working fishing communities—old-fashioned, friendly, and photogenic. Beals, connected to Jonesport via an arched bridge over Moosabec Reach, is named for Manwarren Beal Jr. and his wife, Lydia, who arrived around 1773 and quickly threw themselves into the Revolutionary War effort. But that's not all they did—the current phone book covering Jonesport and Beals Island lists dozens of Beal descendants (as well as dozens of Alleys and Carvers, other early names).

Even more memorable than Manwarren Beal was his six-foot, seven-inch descendent Barnabas, dubbed "Tall Barney" for obvious reasons. The larger-than-life fellow became the stuff of legend all along the Maine coast—and a popular Jonesport restaurant preserves his name.

Also legendary here is the lobsterboat design known as the Jonesport hull. People from away won't recognize its distinctive shape, but count on the fishing pros to know it. The harbor here is jam-packed with Jonesport lobsterboats, and

© TOM NANGLE

Lobsterboats crowd the scenic harbor in Jonesport, a traditional fishing village.

PUFFINS

The chickadee is the Maine state bird, and the bald eagle is our national emblem, but probably the best-loved bird along the Maine coast is the Atlantic puffin *(Fratercula arctica)*, a member of the auk (Alcidae) family. Photographs show an imposing-looking creature with a quizzical mien; amazingly, this larger-than-life seabird is only about 12 inches long. Black-backed and white-chested, the puffin has bright orange legs, "clown-makeup" eyes, and a distinctive, rather outlandish red-and-yellow beak. Its diet is fish and shellfish.

Almost nonexistent in this part of the world as recently as the 1970s, the puffin (or "sea parrot") has recovered dramatically thanks to the unstinting efforts of Cornell University ornithologist Stephen Kress and his Project Puffin. Starting with an orphan colony (of two) on remote Matinicus Rock, Kress painstakingly transferred nearly a thousand puffin chicks (also known fondly as "pufflings") from Newfoundland and used artificial nests and decoys to entice the birds to adapt to and reproduce on Eastern Egg Rock in Muscongus Bay.

In 1981, thanks to the assistance and persistence of hundreds of interns and volunteers, and despite the predations of great black-backed gulls, puffins finally were fledged on Eastern Egg, and the rest, as they say, is history. Within 20 years, more than three dozen puffin couples were nesting on Eastern Egg Rock, and still more had established nests on other islands in the area. Kress's methods have received international attention, and his proven techniques have been used to reintroduce bird populations in remote parts of the globe. In 2001, *Down East* magazine singled out Kress to receive its prestigious annual Environmental Award.

How and Where to See Puffins

Puffin-watching, like whale-watching, involves heading offshore, so be prepared with warm clothing, rubber-soled shoes, a hat, sunscreen, binoculars, and, if you're motion-sensitive, appropriate medication.

Although the Maine Audubon Society undertakes evening excursions from New Harbor to Eastern Egg Rock two or three times a summer, and Hardy Boat Cruises has puffin-watching trips from New Harbor daily between early June and mid-August, there are daily up-close-and-personal opportunities for puffin-watching along the Down East Coast—specifically, on Machias Seal Island, aboard boats departing from Cutler and Jonesport. Weather permitting, you'll be allowed to disembark on the 20-acre island.

Naturalist and skilled skipper Andy Patterson begins his puffin tours from Cutler in mid-May, departing each morning (about 7 A.M.) aboard the 40-footer *Barbara Frost.* The season wraps up in late August. Cost is $60 a person. Contact **Bold Coast Charters** (207/259-4484).

Captain John Norton—son of Barna Norton, the veteran of puffin-watching trips—departs from the waterfront in Jonesport at about 7 A.M. daily, late May–August. Cost is $60. Contact **Norton of Jonesport** (888/551-4895 or 207/497-5933).

Adopt-a-Puffin Program

Stephen Kress's Project Puffin has devised a clever way to enlist supporters via the Adopt-a-Puffin program. For a $100 donation, you'll receive a certificate of adoption, vital statistics on your adoptee, annual updates, and a T-shirt. Email adoption requests to orders@projectpuffin.org.

The Down East Coast

---

souped-up versions are consistent winners in the summertime lobsterboat-race series.

SIGHTS

◪ Great Wass Island Preserve

Allow a whole day to explore 1,579-acre Great Wass Island, an extraordinary preserve even when it's drenched in fog—a not-infrequent event.

Owned by The Nature Conservancy (Fort Andross, 14 Maine St., Brunswick 04011, 207/729-5181), the preserve is at the tip of Jonesport's peninsula. The easiest hiking routes are the wooded, two-mile Little Cape Point and 1.5-mile Mud Hole trails—retrace your path for each. (Making a loop by connecting the two along the rocky shoreline adds considerably to the time and difficulty, but do it if you have the time; allow

© TOM NANGLES

The 1818 Ruggles House in Columbia Falls is famous for its intricately carved moldings, Palladian window, and flying staircase.

about six hours and wear waterproof footwear.) Expect to see beach-head iris (like blue flag) and orchids, jack pine, a peat bog, seals, pink granite, pitcher plants, lots of warblers, and maybe some grouse. Carry water and a picnic; wear bug repellent. No camping, fires, or pets; no toilet facilities. Daytime access only. To reach the preserve from Route 1, take Route 187 to Jonesport (12 miles), then cross the arched bridge to Beals Island. Continue across Beals to the Great Wass causeway (locally called "the Flying Place"), then go three miles on Black Duck Cove Road to the parking area (on the left). Watch for the Nature Conservancy oak-leaf symbol. At the parking area, pick up a trail map and a bird checklist.

Also owned by The Nature Conservancy is 21-acre **Mistake Island,** accessible only by boat. Low and shrubby, Mistake has a Coast Guard–built boardwalk from the landing at the northwest corner to **Moose Peak Light,** standing 72 feet above the water at the eastern end of the island. The only negative on this lovely island is rubble left behind when the government leveled the keeper's house.

Ruggles House

Behind a picket fence on a quiet street in Columbia Falls stands the remarkable Ruggles House (Main St., P.O. Box 99, Columbia Falls 04623, 207/483-4637, www.ruggleshouse.com, 9:30 A.M.–4:30 P.M. Mon.–Sat., 11 A.M.–4:30 P.M. Sun. June–Oct. 15, $5 adults, $2 children). Built in 1818 for Judge Thomas Ruggles—lumber baron, militia captain, even postmaster—the tiny house on a grand scale boasts a famous flying (unsupported) staircase, intricately carved moldings, Palladian window, and unusual period furnishings. Rescued in the mid-20th century and maintained by the Ruggles House Society, this gem has become a magnet for savvy preservationists. A quarter mile east of Route 1, it's open for hour-long guided tours.

At the house, pick up a copy of the Columbia Falls **walking-tour brochure,** which details the intriguing history of other houses in this hamlet.

Maine Central Model Railroad

Here's Nirvana for model-train enthusiasts. Harold ("Buz") Beal and his wife, Helen, have created a fantastic model railroad layout—the Maine Central Model Railroad—covering about 900 square feet in a building next to their house. It features 4,000 trees, 396 train cars, 3,000 feet of track, 11 bridges and trestles, 200 switches. . . . The trains wind through towns modeled on real Maine places. Look for Stephen King's house in Bangor. Buz Beal, a 26-year Coast Guard veteran, figures railroading is in his blood; his grandfather was a Canadian Pacific engineer. Visitors are welcome any day of the year, but it's best to call ahead (207/497-2255) to be sure someone's home. On Route 187, about four miles northeast of downtown Jonesport, watch for the Church Enterprises sign on the right, then take the next left to the Beals' house. A railroad crossing sign marks the driveway. (Route 187 makes a loop through the peninsula; the Beals are on the easternmost side of the loop—7.7 miles south of Route 1.) There's no charge, but donations are welcomed. Buzz will usually run at least one train for visitors, but it takes three people to operate the full model. That usually occurs on Sunday evenings.

BOATING EXCURSIONS

M Machias Seal Island Puffin Tour

A great-grandson of legendary local "Tall Barney" Beal, Captain Barna Norton began offering puffin-watching trips to Machias Seal Island (MSI) in 1940 in a 33-foot boat incautiously named *If.* Now his son, Captain John, has taken over the helm of **Norton of Jonesport** (8 Sea St., Jonesport, 207/497-5933 or 888/551-4895, www.machiassealisland.com, $60). He captains *Chief,* heading 20 miles offshore to an island claimed by both the United States and Canada—a colorful saga. To preserve the fragile nesting sites of Atlantic puffins and arctic terns, access to the 15-acre island is restricted. Passengers are off-loaded into small boats, but sea swells sometimes prevent landing. (The captain supplies wristbands to queasy passengers.) The trip is *not* appropriate for small children or unsteady adults. The boat departs Jonesport around 7 A.M. and returns around noon. Wear

waterproof hiking boots, take a hat, and pack some munchies.

Island Cruise

Operating as **Coastal Cruises** (Kelley Point Rd., R.R. 1, Box 1360, Jonesport, 207/497-3064), Captain Laura Fish does daily (weather permitting) three-hour Moosabec Reach cruises in her 23-foot powerboat *Aaron Thomas.* Among the sights are Great Wass Island and Mistake Island. Cost is $40 adults, $25 children under 18; six-person maximum. Reservations are required. Trips depart from Jonesport and operate May to mid-October.

SHOPPING

Gifts and Crafts

Flower-design majolica pottery and whimsical terra-cotta items are specialties at **Columbia Falls Pottery** (150 Main St., P.O. Box 235, Columbia Falls 04623, 207/483-4075 or 800/235-2512, fax 207/483-2905), an appealing shop in a rehabbed country store next to the Ruggles House. Veteran potter April Adams keeps the inventory fresh, and the company does a hefty mail-order business. A newly renovated, two-bedroom apartment is available for rental upstairs either as one unit by the week for $700 or, when available, by the room, for $120–150 per night.

Crandon House Gallery (141 Main St., Columbia Falls, 207/483-3871), across the street from the Ruggles House, has a small but well-chosen selection of fine art and crafts.

In downtown Jonesport, **Church's True Value** (Main St., Rte. 187, Jonesport 04649, 207/497-2778) carries all the usual hardware items, plus gifts, souvenirs, and sportswear. Helpful owners John and Sharon Church can also answer any question about the area and solve most any problem.

FESTIVALS AND EVENTS

The biggest annual event hereabouts is the wingding Jonesport **Fourth of July** celebration, with several days of special activities, including barbecues, beauty pageant, kids' games, fireworks, and the famed **Jonesport Lobsterboat Races** in Moosabec Reach.

The mid-August **Machias Wild Blueberry Festival,** in neighboring Machias, is an easy jaunt from the Jonesport/Beals area.

ACCOMMODATIONS

B&Bs

At **M Pleasant Bay Bed & Breakfast and Llama Keep** (338 West Side Rd., P.O. Box 222, Addison, 207/483-4490, www.pleasantbay.com, $50–125), Joan and Lee Yeaton manage to pamper more than 40 llamas and a herd of red deer as well as their two-legged guests. Three miles of trails wind through the 110 acres, and a canoe is available for guests. Three lovely rooms (private and shared baths) and one suite, with microwave and refrigerator, all have water views. Rates include a delicious breakfast. Arrange in advance for a llama walk. Open all year. The farm borders Pleasant Bay, 3.9 miles southwest of Route 1.

Ireland meets Alaska on the outskirts of Columbia Falls, where Jack and Maureen Murphy opened **The Dream Catcher** (Rte. 1, P.O. Box 157, Columbia Falls 04623, 207/483-0937, http://home.midmaine.com/~catcher, $80) in an 1885 house and filled it with Alaskan and Irish artifacts and plenty of quilts. The Irish part is obvious; the Alaskan comes from their years working there as nurses. Three rooms, each with private bath, are named County Limerick, County Cork, and New York. County Cork has a four-poster and a fireplace; New York can become a two-bedroom suite. Guests have the use of two parlors, one with a TV. Breakfast is breathtaking—even including dessert; forget about lunch. Open all year. Even though the house is on Route 1, it's elevated and buffered a bit from the road; there's a peaceful deck out back. The B&B sign is very small; watch carefully for it.

The fanciest digs in Jonesport are at **M Harbor House on Sawyer Cove** (P.O. Box 468, Sawyer Sq., Jonesport 04649, 207/497-5417, www.harborhs.com, $110), hospitably run by Maureen and Gene Hart—she an ex-nurse, he an ex-engineer. Two very comfortable and spacious second-floor suites (private baths)—named Beach Rose and Lupine and decorated accordingly—have incredible views of Moosabec Reach. Binoculars are provided so you can watch the action, including passengers embarking on the Norton puffin trip. The Harts operate an antique shop, selling what they call "curiosities," on the first floor of this fascinating old building, once Jonesport's telegraph office. Harbor House is open all year.

The **Loft on Cranberry Cove** (56 Kelley Point Rd., Jonesport, 207/497-2139, ddhiggi@hotmail.com, $125) is a nicely decorated and well appointed apartment, with fireplace, harbor views, and a balcony overlooking a private beach. It's located above a garage. Proprietor Dorothy Higgins provisions the apartment with all sorts of goodies, from fresh eggs to wine and cheese. Pets are welcome. Rates decrease with length of stay.

Seasonal Rentals

Close to the best sandy beach on the peninsula, the **Church Family Cottages** (49 Sandy River Beach Rd., Jonesport, 207/497-2829, www.oceancottagesmaine.com), managed by Keith Church, are three rustic, well-maintained cottages available by the week. Best view is from Sandpiper, which sleeps six and rents for $1,000 a week; the others (Linnet and Lemon Drop) are $700 a week. Bring your own sheets and towels. Open May–October. The cottages are seven miles south of Route 1 and four miles northeast of downtown Jonesport. Keith also manages a fourth cottage, Harbor View ($700 a week), an eccentric little place with a spectacular panoramic view, on Main Street in downtown Jonesport.

FOOD

Miscellany

Craving carbs? Head for Lois Hubbard's home bakery, called **The Farm** (1561 Mason's Bay Rd., Rte. 187, R.R. 1, Box 3115, Jonesport, 207/497-5949). In addition to specialty breads, Lois produces 15 flavors of whoopie pies, including blueberry. The bakery, 3.3 miles south of the Jonesboro end of Route 1, is open all year.

If you need a break from the fried fish that dominates most menus in this part of Maine, seek out **Emporium Natural Foods** (56 Sawyer Sq., Jonesport, 207/497-5634, 11:30 A.M.–1 P.M.) for lunch. This bigger-than-it-first-appears market, tucked under The Jonesport Emporium, serves take-out lunch, with sandwiches, salads, homemade organic soup, and chowder. All orders are custom made using organic breads, vegetables, and condiments. No indoor seating.

Home Cooking

For local color, start at **Tall Barney's** (52 Main St., Rte. 187, Jonesport, 207/497-2403, 4 A.M.–8 P.M. Mon.–Sat., 6 A.M.–8 P.M. Sun.), where you'll find homemade baked beans and chowders, pizza, and more—and you won't break the bank. Sit back and watch the servers chat up the lobstermen regulars camped out at the big center table, known locally as the Liars' Table. Join them, if you dare. No credit cards. The restaurant is just before the bridge to Beals Island; watch for the statue of Barney.

INFORMATION AND SERVICES

Information

In downtown Jonesport, the best source of local information is **Church's True Value** (Main St., Rte. 187, Jonesport 04649, 207/497-2778, open every day but Sun.). Another reliable source is Maureen Hart at **Antiques on the Harbor** (on Sawyer Cove, 207/497-5417).

Several communities in western Washington County have banded together to form the **Downeast Coastal Chamber of Commerce** (P.O. Box 331, Harrington 04643, 207/483-2131, www.downeastcoastalchamber.org). Addison, Cherryfield, Columbia Falls, Deblois, Harrington, Jonesport/Beals, Milbridge, Steuben, and a few others are included. The **Washington County Promotions Board** (P.O. Box 605, Machias 04654, 800/377-9748) can also help with general information.

The **Machias Bay Area Chamber of Commerce** (12 E. Main St., Machias 04654, 207/255-4402, www.machiaschamber.org) handles inquires for the Machias area as well as Jonesport (10 A.M.–3 P.M. Mon.–Fri.). It stocks brochures, maps, and information on area hiking trails.

Public Restrooms

You'll find restrooms at the Citgo station at the Four Corners Shopping Center, Route 1 in Columbia, midway between Harrington and Columbia Falls. This minimall also has an ATM, supermarket (picnic fare available), drugstore, sportswear shop, and department store. In Jonesport, there's a port-o-let at the marina.

Getting There

West Bus Service (800/596-2823) operates one trip a day in each direction between Bangor (connecting with Greyhound and Concord Trailways buses and Bangor International Airport) and Calais, via Ellsworth, with a scheduled stop in Perry. Flag stops are available en route, including Jonesboro, Columbia, Milbridge, Whiting, Dennysville, and Pembroke.

Machias Bay Area

The only negative thing about Machias (muh-CHY-us; pop. 2,675) is its Micmac Indian name, meaning "bad little falls" (even though that's accurate—the midtown waterfall here *is* treacherous). A contagious local esprit pervades this shire town of Washington County, thanks to antique homes, a splendid river-valley setting, Revolutionary War monuments, and a small but busy university campus.

If you regard crowds as fun, an ideal time to land here is during the renowned annual Machias Wild Blueberry Festival, third weekend in August, when harvesting is under way in Washington County's blueberry fields and you can stuff your face with blueberry-everything—muffins, jam, pancakes, ice cream, pies. You can also collect blueberry-logo napkins, T-shirts, magnets, pottery, and jewelry. The menu at the local McDonald's even lists blueberry pancakes and sundaes that weekend. Other summer draws include a chamber-music series, art shows, and semiprofessional theater performances. Within a few miles are day-trips galore—options for hiking, biking, golfing, swimming, and sea kayaking.

Also included within the Machias sphere are the towns of Roque Bluffs, Jonesboro, Whitneyville, Marshfield, East Machias, and Machiasport. Just to the east, between Machias and Lubec, are the towns of Whiting and Cutler.

HISTORICAL SIGHTS

History is a big deal in this area, and since Machias was the first settled Maine town east of the Penobscot River, lots of enthusiastic amateur historians have helped rescue homes and sites dating from as far back as the Revolutionary War.

English settlers, uprooted from communities farther west on the Maine coast, put down permanent roots here in 1763, harvesting timber to ensure their survival. Stirrings of revolutionary discontent surfaced even at this remote outpost, and when British loyalists in Boston began usurping some of the valuable harvest, Machias

patriots plotted revenge. By 1775, when the armed British schooner *Margaretta* arrived as a cargo escort, local residents aboard the sloop *Unity*, in a real David-and-Goliath episode, chased and captured the *Margaretta*. On June 12, 1775, two months after the famed Battles of Lexington and Concord (and five days before the Battle of Bunker Hill), Machias Bay was the site of what author James Fenimore Cooper called "The Lexington of the Sea"—the first naval battle of the American Revolution. The name of patriot leader Jeremiah O'Brien today appears throughout Machias—on a school, a street, a cemetery, and a state park.

Museums

One-hour guided tours vividly convey the atmosphere of the 1770 **Burnham Tavern** (Main St., Rte. 192, Machias, 207/255-4432 during open hours or 207/255-8898, 9 A.M.–5 P.M. Mon.–Fri. mid-June–Sept., and by appointment off-season, $5 adults, $.25 for kids under 12), where upstart local patriots met in 1775 to plot revolution against the British. Job and Mary Burnham's tavern/home next served as an infirmary for casualties from the Revolution's first naval battle, just offshore. Lots of fascinating history lies in this National Historic Site maintained by the Daughters of the American Revolution. Hanging outside is a sign reading, "Drink for the thirsty, food for the hungry, lodging for the weary, and good keeping for horses, by Job Burnham." If you're here in early August, you can join in the museum's annual **lawn party,** including lunch, tours, and handicraft sales.

Headquarters for the Machiasport Historical Society and one of the area's three oldest residences, the 1810 **Gates House** (344 Port Rd., Machiasport, 207/255-8461, 12:30–4:30 P.M. Tues.–Sat. July and Aug., donation appreciated) was snatched from ruin and restored in 1966. The National Historic Register building overlooking Machias Bay contains fascinating period furnishings and artifacts, many related to the

TWO SCENIC ROUTES

The drives described below can also be bike routes (easy to moderately difficult), but be forewarned that the roads are narrow and shoulderless, so caution is essential. Heed biking etiquette.

Route 191, the Cutler Road

Never mind that Route 191, between East Machias and West Lubec, is one of Maine's most stunning coastal drives—you can still follow the entire 27-mile stretch and meet only a handful of cars. **East Machias** even has its own historic district, with architectural gems dating from the late 18th century along High and Water Streets. Farther along Route 191, you'll find fishing wharves, low moorlands, a hamlet or two, and islands popping over the horizon. The only peculiarly jarring note is the 26-tower forest of North Cutler's Naval Computer and Telecommunications Station, nearly a thousand feet high—monitoring global communications—but you'll see this only briefly. (At night, the skyscraping red lights are really eerie, especially if you're offshore aboard a boat.) Off Route 191 are minor roads and hiking trails worth exploring, especially the coastal trails. About three miles south of the Route 191 terminus, you can also check out **Bailey's Mistake**, a hamlet with a black-sand (volcanic) beach. And the name? Allegedly it stems from one Captain Bailey who, misplotting his course and thinking he was in Lubec, drove his vessel ashore here one night in the late 19th century. Unwilling to face the consequences of his lapse, he and his crew off-loaded their cargo of lumber and built themselves dwellings. Whether true or not, it makes a great saga. Even though it's in the town of **Trescott,** and the hamlet is really South Trescott, everyone knows this section as Bailey's Mistake.

Route 92, Starboard Peninsula

Pack a picnic and set out on Route 92 (beginning at Elm Street in downtown Machias) down the 10-mile length of the Starboard Peninsula to a stunning spot known as the Point of Maine. Along the way are the villages of Larrabee, Bucks Harbor, and Starboard, all part of the town of Machiasport. In Bucks Harbor is the turnoff (a short detour to the right) to **Yoho Head,** a controversial upscale development overlooking Little Kennebec Bay.

South of the Yoho Head turnoff is the sign for **Jasper Beach**. From the Jasper Beach sign, continue 1.4 miles to two red buildings (the old Starboard School House and the volunteer fire department). Turn left onto a dirt road and continue to a sign reading Driveway. Go around the right side of a shed and park on the beach. (Keep track of the tide level, though.) You're at **Point of Maine,** a quintessential Down East panorama of sea and islands. On a clear day, you can see offshore **Libby Island Light,** the focus of Philmore Wass's entertaining narrative *Lighthouse in My Life.*

lumbering and shipbuilding era. The museum is four miles southeast of Route 1. Limited parking on a hazardous curve.

Centre Street Congregational Church

Machias's most distinctive landmark is the steeple of the 1836 Gothic Revival Centre Street Congregational Church (7 Center St., Machias, 207/255-6665, www.centrestreetchurch.org), paradoxically situated on *Center* Street. The community-oriented parishioners spearhead the annual Maine Wild Blueberry Festival, and the church is the site of the July and August Machias Bay Chamber Concerts.

O'Brien Cemetery

Old-cemetery buffs will want to stop at O'Brien Cemetery, resting place of the town's earliest settlers. It's next to Bad Little Falls Park, close to downtown, off Route 92 toward Machiasport. A big plus here is the view, especially in autumn, of blueberry barrens, the waterfall, and the bay.

Fort O'Brien State Memorial

The American Revolution's first naval battle was fought just offshore from Fort O'Brien in June 1775. Now a State Historic Site, the fort was built and rebuilt several times—originally to guard Machias during the Revolutionary War.

Only Civil War–era earthworks now remain, plus well-maintained lawns overlooking the Machias River. Take Route 92 from Machias about five miles toward Machiasport; the parking area is on the left.

UNIVERSITY OF MAINE AT MACHIAS

Founded in 1909 as Washington State Normal School, University of Maine at Machias (9 O'Brien Ave., Machias 04654, 207/255-1200, www.umm.maine.edu) is now part of the state university system. During the summer, the **UMM Art Galleries** (Powers Hall, 1–4 P.M. Mon.–Fri., or by appointment) feature works from the university's expanding permanent collection of Maine painters—including John Marin, William Zorach, Lyonel Feininger, and Reuben Tam. Rotating exhibits occur throughout the school year.

UMM's **Center for Lifelong Learning** has a state-of-the-art fitness center, six-lane heated pool, and the George Simpson Murdock Bookstore, which stocks more than textbooks. The pool and fitness room are open to the public daily; call for schedule. A one-day pass is $6; a three-day pass is $15. Summer bookstore hours are 8:30 A.M.–4 P.M. For additional information, call 207/255-1403.

Also open to the public is **Merrill Library** (207/255-1284, 8 A.M.–4:30 P.M. Mon.–Fri. in summer).

RECREATION

Parks and Preserves

Just as dedicated as the historical preservationists are the hikers, birders, and other eco-sensitive outdoors enthusiasts who've helped preserve thousands of acres in this part of Maine for public access and appreciation.

At **Bad Little Falls Park,** alongside the Machias River, stop to catch the view from the footbridge overlooking the roiling falls (especially in spring). Bring a picnic and enjoy this midtown oasis tucked between Routes 1 and 92.

Thanks to a handful of foresighted year-round and summer residents, spectacular, crescent-shaped **Jaspar Beach**—piled high with ocean-polished jasper and other rocks—has been preserved by the town of Machiasport. No sand here, just stones, in intriguing shapes and colors. Resist the urge to fill your pockets with souvenirs, maybe settling for just a single special rock. Parking is limited; no facilities. From Route 1 in downtown Machias, take Route 92 (Machias Rd.) 9.5 miles southeast, past the village of Bucks Harbor. Watch for a large sign on your left. The beach is on Howard's Cove, .2 mile off the road, and accessible all year.

Southwest of Machias, six miles south of Route 1, is the 275-acre **Roque Bluffs State Park** (Roque Bluffs Rd., Roque Bluffs 04648, 207/255-3475). Saltwater swimming this far north is for the young and brave, but this park also has a 60-acre freshwater pond warm and shallow enough for toddlers and the old and timid. Facilities include primitive changing rooms, outhouses, a play area, and picnic tables (no food or lifeguards). Views go on forever from the wide-open, mile-long sweep of sand beach. Admission is $2 adults, $1 children 5–11. The fee box relies on the honor system. The park is open daily May 15–September 15, but the beach is accessible all year.

On Route 191, about 4.5 miles northeast of the center of Cutler, watch for the parking area (on the right) for the **Cutler Coast Public Preserve,** a 12,000-acre preserve with nearly a dozen miles of beautifully engineered hiking trails on the seaward side of Route 191. Allow 5–6 hours to do the shorter, 5.8-mile **Black Point Brook Loop,** providing an easy start for about 1.5 miles before getting to the Coastal Trail, a stretch of moderately rugged hiking southward along dramatic, tree-fringed shoreline cliffs. Then head back via the Black Point Brook cutoff and connect with the Inland Trail to return to your car (or bicycle). Bring binoculars and plenty of film; the views from this wild coastline are fabulous. Also bring insect repellent—inland boggy stretches are buggy. Carry a picnic and commandeer a granite ledge overlooking the surf. Precipitous cliffs and narrow stretches can make the shoreline section of this trail perilous for small children or insecure adults, so use extreme caution and common sense. There are no facilities in the preserve. If you're here in August, you can stock up on blueberries and even some wild raspberries. Another option, the 9.8-mile **Fairy Head Loop,** starts the same way as the Black Point Brook Loop but continues southward along the coast, leading to three primitive campsites (stoves only, no fires), available on a first-come, first-served basis. There's no way to reserve these, so you take your chances. Unless you have gazelle genes, the longer loop almost demands an overnight. Information on the preserve, including a helpful map, is available from the **Maine Bureau of Parks and Lands** (22 State House Station, Augusta 04333, 207/287-3821, www.state.me.us/doc/parks).

Golf

With lovely water views, and tidal inlets serving as obstacles, the nine-hole **Great Cove Golf Course** (387 Great Cove Rd., off Roque Bluffs Rd., Jonesboro, 207/434-7200) is a good challenge. Reasonable greens fees, carts, and a snack bar; you can also rent clubs. From Jonesboro (Route 1), go 3.5 miles east and south on Roque Bluffs Road. Open May–October.

You can play a quick nine at **Barren View Golf Course** (Rte. 1, Jonesboro, 207-434-6531, www.barrenview.com). A pro shop, snack bar, carts, and club rentals are available.

Canoeing, Sea Kayaking, and Biking

If you've brought your own sea kayak, there are public launching ramps in Bucks Harbor (east of the main Machias Road) and at Roque Bluffs State Park. You can also put in at Sanborn Cove, beyond the O'Brien School on Route 92, about five miles south of Machias, where there's a small parking area. Before setting out, be sure to check the tide calendar and plan your strategy so you don't have to slog through acres of muck when you return.

Sunrise Canoe and Kayak (.02 mile off Rte. 1 on an unnamed road, behind Joyce's Lobster House, Machias, 207/255-3375, www.sunrise canoeandkayak.com) rents canoes and kayaks

for $20 per day, sit-on-top kayaks for $15 per day, and offers sea kayak excursions, $48 half day, $65 full day. Sunrise also rents bikes for $15 per day.

The spectacular **Machias River,** one of Maine's most technically demanding canoeing rivers, is a dynamite trip mid-May to mid-June, but no beginner should attempt it. Best advice is to sign on with an outfitter/guide. The run lasts 4–6 days, the latter if you start from Fifth Machias Lake. Expect to see such wildlife as osprey, eagles, ducks, loons, moose, deer, beaver, and snapping turtles. Be aware, though, that the Machias is probably the buggiest river in the state, and blackflies will form a welcoming party. Bring khaki duds; the bugs are attracted to colors. The major portage is at Upper Holmes Falls; trying to run the half-mile-long rips would buy you a ticket to the morgue. **Sunrise Expeditions** (4 Union Plaza, Ste. 2, Bangor, 800/748-3730 or 207/942-9300, www.sunrise-exp.com) offers fully outfitted trips for $895–1,250.

Machias Seal Island Puffin Tour

Andy Patterson, the skipper of the 40-footer *Barbara Frost,* operates the **Bold Coast Charter Company** (P.O. Box 364, Cutler 04626, 207/259-4484, www.boldcoast.com), homeported in Cutler Harbor. Andy provides knowledgeable narration, answers questions in depth, and shares his considerable enthusiasm for this pristine corner of Maine. He's best known for his five-hour **puffin-sighting trips** to Machias Seal Island (mid-May through Aug., departing between 7 and 8 A.M.). All trips are dependent on weather and tide conditions, and reservations are required. Cost is $60 a person (but don't bring small children or unsteady adults). No credit cards. Daily access to the island is restricted, and swells can roll in, so passengers occasionally cannot disembark, but the curious puffins often surround the boat, providing plenty of photo opportunities. No matter what the air temperature on the mainland, be sure to dress warmly and wear sturdy shoes. The *Barbara Frost*'s wharf is on Cutler Harbor, just off Route 191. Look for the Little River Lobster Company sign; you'll depart from the boat-launching ramp.

SHOPPING

Influenced by traditional Japanese designs, Connie Harter-Bagley markets her dramatic ceramics at **Connie's Clay of Fundy** (Rte. 1, Box 345, East Machias, 207/255-4574, www.clayoffundy .com), on the East Machias River. If she's at the wheel, you can also watch her work. The shop, four miles east of downtown Machias, is open all year, usually 9 A.M.–6 P.M. daily.

ENTERTAINMENT, FESTIVALS, AND EVENTS

The University of Maine at Machias is the cultural focus in this area, particularly during the school year. **Stage Front: The Arts Downeast** puts on an annual series of concerts, plays, recitals, and other events in the Performing Arts Center at the University of Maine at Machias. The summer series, once a month, usually features classical and pops concerts, including at least one performance by the energetic Steuben-based Opera Maine organization. Contact UMM (207/255-1384) for schedule information.

Tuesday-evening **Machias Bay Chamber Concerts** occur early July to mid-August at 7:30 P.M. at the Centre Street Congregational Church. Concerts are accompanied by art exhibits. Tickets are $12 for adults, $5 for students, and free for kids ages 12 and younger. For a current schedule, call 207/255-3849.

The **Machias Wild Blueberry Festival** (www.machiasblueberry.com) is the summer highlight, running Friday–Sunday the third weekend in August, featuring a pancake breakfast, road races, concerts, a craft show, a baked-bean supper, an homegrown musical, and more. The blueberry motif is everywhere. It's organized by Centre Street Congregational Church, in downtown Machias.

ACCOMMODATIONS

Inns

Victoriana rules at the **Riverside Inn** (Rte. 1, P.O. Box 373, East Machias, 207/255-4134, www.riversideinn-maine.com, $95–130), a meticulously restored early-19th-century sea captain's home. Relax on the deck overlooking the East

© TOM NANGLE

The wild blueberry baking contest is big business during the annual Machias Wild Maine Blueberry Festival in August. Be sure to pick up one of the cookbooks filled with winning recipes from previous years.

Machias River and you'll forget you're a few steps from a busy highway. Sit in the lovely terraced perennial gardens and you'll feel the same way. Two rooms and two suites all have private baths. Reservations are essential at the popular dining room.

Oooh, here's a find. The lovely ◪ **Tide Run Inn** (Destiny Bay Rd., Cutler, 207/259-3800, www.tiderun.com, $125) adds a new dimension to the salty fishing community of Cutler. It opened in 2004 in a restored 1873 farmhouse overlooking Destiny Bay and with views to Little River Lighthouse. Three upstairs guest rooms each have TV, private bath (one's detached), and comfy furnishings, complete with cozy featherbeds. The inn's restaurant is quickly gaining renown.

B&Bs and Guesthouses

Six months of renovation preceded the opening of the 1850s **Captain Cates House B&B** (Rte. 92, Machiasport, 207/255-8812, www.captain cates.com $95), about four miles south of Machias. Kay and Lise Duckworth have loaded their comfortable house with interesting antiques and delved into the family history of Captain J. W. Cates, who sailed the world and bought this house in 1865. Six rooms share three baths. Five rooms have views of the Machias River across the street. (The third-floor Starboard room has an awkward mid-room chimney.) Breakfast is served in the formal dining room. A modern addition in back has a lovely summertime puzzle/sitting room opening onto a patio. No credit cards. Open all year.

The second generation now operates **Micmac Farm Guesthouses** (Rte. 92, Machiasport 04655, 207/255-3008, www.micmacfarm.com, May–late Oct., $85/night, $525/week). Stay in one of Anthony and Bonnie Dunn's three comfortable, well-equipped cottages, and you'll find yourself relaxing on the deck overlooking the tidal Machias River and watching for seabirds, seals, and eagles. No breakfast is provided, but each wood-paneled cottage has a kitchenette and dining area. Pets and children are welcome. There's also a river-view room in the restored 18th-century Gardner House, with

a private bath with whirlpool tub. Guests have use of the farmhouse, including a library. A light breakfast is provided for Gardner House guests. Micmac Farm, 2.5 miles south of Machias, is a lovely oasis.

Motels

The second generation now runs **The Bluebird Motel** (Rte. 1, Machias, 207/255-3332, $60–64), a clean, upgraded 1950s-style motel. Forty pine-paneled rooms have cable TV, phones, air-conditioning, and large baths. The motel is set back from Route 1 enough to keep down noise, but request a room in the rear section if you're a light sleeper. The motel, a mile south of downtown, has wheelchair-accessible rooms. Pets are allowed in some units. Open all year.

The best feature of the two-story **Machias Motor Inn** (26 E. Main St., Rte. 1, Machias, 207/255-4861, $70–92) is its location overlooking the tidal Machias River; sliding doors open onto decks-with-a-view. Twenty-eight guest rooms and six efficiencies have extra-long beds, plus cable TV, air-conditioning, and phones with data ports. Next door is Helen's Restaurant—famed for seasonal fruit pies and an all-you-can-eat weekend breakfast buffet. Pets ($5 fee) are welcome at the motel. The motel is within easy walking distance to downtown, perfect if you're here for the Blueberry Festival. Open all year.

For inexpensive digs, you can't beat the ◪ **Blueberry Patch** (Rte. 1, Jonesboro, 207/434-5411, $45–58), a clean and bright motel and tourist cabins, with three efficiency units. Nothing fancy here, but all rooms have satellite TV, air-conditioning, and phones, and there's even a pool and small playground. If you're taller than six feet, choose a motel room rather than a cabin (cabin bathrooms are tiny). Rates include coffee and muffins in the morning; the Whitehouse Restaurant, next door, is open for breakfast, lunch, and dinner.

FOOD

Watch the local papers for listings of **public suppers, spaghetti suppers,** or **baked bean suppers,** a terrific way to sample the culinary talents of

◪ **The Down East Coast**

local cooks. Most begin at 5 P.M., and it's wise to arrive early to get near the head of the line. The suppers often benefit needy individuals or struggling nonprofits—always worth supporting—and where else can you eat nonstop for under $10?

Breakfast, Lunch, and Miscellany

Guess who's the brains behind **Grandma's Kitchen** (Rte. 1, HC 74, Box 20, East Machias, 207/259-3656)? It's a clever fellow named Austin-Willis Wood, who works night and day to make jams, ice cream, brownies, single-portion dinner entrées—even cake mixes, so you can claim you've done it yourself. Using great old secret recipes (that's the Grandma part), he produces cranberry/orange relish, fudge, blueberry syrup, and more. Several hundred pies go out the door between Thanksgiving and Christmas. Grandma's Pantry occupies a renovated farm building on the left side just after you leave East Machias.

Craving something healthful? You can pick up breads and muffins as well as sandwiches and soups at **Whole Life Organic Market** (80 Main St., Machias, 207/255-8855, 9 A.M.–6 P.M. Mon.–Sat., 10 A.M.–4 P.M. Sun.). There's a small but pleasant seating area, too. Open year-round.

Another source for fresh, healthful foods is the **Machias Valley Farmers' Market** (8 A.M.– noon Sat., and often Wed. and Fri., May–Oct.). It's held on "The Dike," a low causeway next to the Machias River. It's usually a good source for blueberries in late July and August.

Family Dining

The second generation is in the kitchen at **Joyce's Lobster House** (Rte. 1, Machias, 207/255-0719, 4–8 P.M. Mon.–Sat., 11:30 A.M.–8 P.M. Sun.). Of course there's lobster and fried seafood, but Joyce's daughter Debbie and her partner, Peter Rossi, have added a nice selection of Italian specialties. Entrées are in the $10–15 range, but you can get out of here for much less with the sandwich menu.

Family-owned, and very popular all day long, is **The Blue Bird Ranch** (3 E. Main St., Rte. 1, Machias, 207/255-3351, 6 A.M.–8:30 P.M.), named for the Prout family's other enterprise, Blue Bird Ranch Trucking Company. Service is

efficient, food is hearty, portions are ample in the three dining rooms.

Casual Dining

Machias lucked out when Susan Ferro, owner, artist, and chef—she claims she got her start garnishing mud pies as a kid—opened the **M Artist's Café** (3 Hill St., Machias, 207/255-8900, 11 A.M.–2 P.M. Mon.–Fri. and 5–8 P.M. Mon.–Sat.) in a small house across from the university. The dining rooms are decorated with paintings by Ferro and other local artists. Luncheon sandwiches—named The Impressionist, Garden of Eden, The Rococo, etc.—are always a reasonably priced adventure ($5–7). Dinner entrées, which change frequently and usually include a vegetarian option, are $14–18. Beer and wine are available. Be sure to reserve for dinner, especially on weekends.

Reservations are essential at the popular dining room at **Riverside Inn** (Rte. 1, East Machias, 207/255-4134). The pricey, wide-ranging dinner menu (served 5–8 P.M. Tues.–Sun.) has a bit of everything, with an emphasis on seafood.

The restaurant at **Tide Run Inn** (Destiny Bay Rd., Cutler, 207/259-3800, 11:30 A.M.–2 P.M. and 5–8 P.M. Tues.–Sat.) is quickly gaining renown as a dining destination. Ask for a table on the porch if the weather's good. The emphasis is on fresh local and organic products, especially seafood. Entrées run $8–11 at lunch, $10–20 at dinner.

INFORMATION AND SERVICES
Information

Several communities in western Washington County have banded together to form the **Downeast Coastal Chamber of Commerce** (P.O. Box 331, Harrington 04643, 207/483-2131, www.downeastcoastalchamber.org). Addison, Cherryfield, Columbia Falls, Deblois, Harrington, Jonesport/Beals, Milbridge, Steuben, and a few others are included. The **Washington County Promotions Board** (P.O. Box 605, Machias 04654, 800/377-9748) can also help with general information.

The **Machias Bay Area Chamber of Commerce** (12 E. Main St., Machias 04654, 207/255-

4402, www.machiaschamber.org) handles inquires for the Machias area as well as Jonesport (10 A.M.–3 P.M. Mon.–Fri.). It stocks brochures, maps, and information on area hiking trails.

Hospitals
Down East Community Hospital (Upper Court St., Rte. 1Λ, Machias, 207/255-3356) has a 24-hour emergency room.

Libraries
Summer hours at the handsome stone **Porter Memorial Library** (52 Court St., Machias,

207/255-3933), built in 1892, are 11 A.M.–5 P.M. Tuesday and Friday, 11 A.M.–4 P.M. Saturday, and 11 A.M.–8 P.M. Wednesday.

Getting There
West Bus Service (800/596-2823) operates one trip a day in each direction between Bangor (connecting with Greyhound and Concord Trailways buses and Bangor International Airport) and Calais, via Ellsworth, with a scheduled stop in Perry. Flag stops are available en route, including Jonesboro, Columbia, Milbridge, Whiting, Dennysville, and Pembroke.

Lubec and Vicinity

Literally the beginning of America—at the nation's easternmost point—Lubec (pop. 1,730) can serve as a base for exploring New Brunswick's Campobello Island, the Cutler coastline, and territory to the west. With a couple of appealing B&Bs and more than 90 miles of meandering waterfront, Lubec conveys the aura of realness: a

hardscrabble fishing community that extends a welcome to visitors.

Settled in 1780 and originally part of Eastport, Lubec was split off in 1811 and named for the German port of Lübeck (for convoluted reasons still not totally clear). The town's most famous resident was Hopley Yeaton, first captain in

Lubec Landmarks is working to preserve the McCurdy Smokehouse, the last operating herring-smoking operation in the country.

the U.S. Revenue-Marine (now the U.S. Coast Guard), who retired here in 1809.

Along the main drag (Water Street), a number of shuttered buildings reflect the town's roller-coaster history. Once the world's sardine capital, Lubec no longer has a packing plant, but aquaculture has come to the forefront, and new businesses are slowly arriving.

SIGHTS

Mulholland Market and McCurdy Smokehouse

Lubec Landmarks (207/733-2068) is working to preserve these two local landmarks. The smokehouse complex, the last operating herring-smoking operation in the country, can be seen on the water side of Water Street. Plans call for it eventually to be open to the public. Mulholland Market (Water St., noon–4:30 Tues.–Sun., donation requested) is the organization's headquarters. Inside are displays about the smokehouses and exhibits of local art.

Lubec Historical Society

The society's small museum in the Old Columbian Store (Main St., 207/733-4696, 9 A.M.–3 P.M. Mon., Wed., and Fri., free) doubles as a visitor information center. Among the historical and genealogical displays is a working model of the machine used in the infamous Gold from Seawater swindle of 1898. Volunteers will gladly fill you in on that or you can pick up a brochure. While here, also pick up the *Lubec Historic Walking Tour* brochure, which highlights about a dozen historical sites in downtown Lubec. The museum is on the left as you're entering town, just beyond Uncle Kippy's restaurant.

WEST QUODDY HEAD STATE PARK

Beachcombing, hiking, picnicking, and an up-close look at Maine's only red-and-white-striped lighthouse are the big draws at 480-acre Quoddy Head State Park (West Quoddy Head Rd., Lubec, 207/733-0911, 9 A.M.–sunset May

THE QUODDY LOOP

It's easy to make it a two-nation vacation and avoid backtracking along Route 1 by looping through Canada. In July and August, East Coast Ferries (Deer Island, New Brunswick, 877/747-2159 or 506/747-2159, www.eastcoastferries.nb.ca) operates funky, bargelike car ferries between Eastport and Deer Island, and then on to Campobello Island—and vice versa. The ferry schedule is in Atlantic time, so adjust for the one-hour time distance when planning, since Eastport is on Eastern time and the two Canadian islands are on Atlantic time. Campobello departures are on the hour, beginning at 9 A.M. Atlantic time (8 A.M. EDT). Eastport departures are on the half hour, beginning at 9:30 A.M. Atlantic time (8:30 A.M. EDT). Check the schedule carefully to avoid missing the last boat back to Eastport. (If you take a car, you can drive back to Eastport from Campobello via Lubec. It's 1.5 miles by water and almost 50 miles by road.) The ferry landing in Eastport is just off Water Street, .3 mile north of Washington Street, next to the Eastport Chowder House Restaurant. Fees, in Canadian funds, for car and driver, are $14 for Deer Island/Campobello, $11 for Deer Island/Eastport (no credit cards); passengers without cars are $3 on each. It all seems very informal, and the trip is an adventure, but remember that you're crossing the Canadian border. United States citizens need valid identification (such as a driver's license); non-U.S. citizens need a passport; most non-Europeans also need a Canadian visa.

15–Oct. 15, $2 adults, $1 kids), the easternmost point of U.S. land. Begin with a visit to the Visitor Center (Keeper's House, 207/733-2180, www.westquoddy.com, 10 A.M.–4 P.M. daily late May–mid-Oct., free), operated by the enthusiastic West Quoddy Head Light Keepers Association, a volunteer group. Inside are exhibits on lighthouse memorabilia, local flora and fauna, and area heritage; a gallery displaying local works; and a staffed information desk.

West Quoddy Head Light, towering 83 feet above mean high water, was built in 1808. (Its counterpart, East Quoddy Head Light, is on

© TOM NANGLE

Candy-striped West Quoddy Head Light is an icon on the Down East Coast. A visitors center and museum are located at its base.

New Brunswick's Campobello Island.) Views from the lighthouse grounds are fabulous, and whale sightings are common in summer. The lighthouse tower is open annually for one day in June, during Lighthouse Week, and other times when the Coast Guard is on site.

The cliffs of Canada's Grand Manan Island are visible from the park's grounds. A 1.75-mile, moderately difficult trail follows the 90-foot cliffs to Carrying Place Cove, and an easy, mile-long boardwalk winds through a unique moss and heath bog designated as a National Natural Landmark. The park opens daily at 9 A.M. mid-May to mid-October. Be forewarned that the park gate is locked at sunset. In winter, the park is accessible for snowshoeing. From Route 189 on the outskirts of Lubec, take South Lubec Road (well signposted) to West Quoddy Head Road. Turn left and continue to the parking area.

RECREATION

Tag along with Lubec's **Pathfinders Walking Group** (207/733-4984 or 207/733-4813)—enthusiastic area residents who go exploring every week, year-round, usually meeting Sundays at 2 P.M. for a two-hour ramble. Nonmembers are welcome, there's no fee, and you'll see a Lubec (and more) that most visitors never encounter.

Yet another place to appreciate nature and to walk is **Cottage Garden** (943 N. Lubec Rd., Lubec, 207/733-2902, dawn–dusk), a lovely oasis developed by Gretchen and Alan Mead. You can wander through the herb, streamside, alpine, rhododendron, and perennial gardens. The Meads' newest addition is the **Shoreline Nature Center,** with exhibits, films, and guides to nature trails. There's no charge for wandering, but you'll probably be tempted by the small print, craft, and gift shop on the premises. Artists are welcome to set up their easels here.

SHOPPING

Nearly 20 area fiber artisans sell their wares at **Water Street Fiberarts Studio** (67 Water St., 207/733-4869). The small shop is chock-full of handmade items such as sweaters, mittens, socks, herbal soap, scarves, children's clothing, hats, slippers, and even black-fly houses.

Lighthouse buffs should stop at **West Quoddy Gifts** (Quoddy Head Rd., one mile before the lighthouse, 207/733-2457). It's stocked with souvenirs and gifty items, many with a lighthouse theme.

ENTERTAINMENT

Contra dances, with the Black Sox String Band, a fun, talented local group, are held on the second Tuesday of the month, beginning at 7:30 P.M., at the Lubec Grange, on the corner of Route 189 and the North Lubec Road. Contras, waltzes, polkas, two-step, and other dances are all taught. Suggested donation is $5. Call Alan Furth (207/733-2154).

Classical music is the focus (for the most part)

The Down East Coast

at **SummerKeys** (207/733-22316 or 973/316-6220 off-season, www.summerkeys.com), a music camp for adults; no prior experience required for the week-long programs in piano, voice, oboe, flute, clarinet, guitar, violin, and cello. Free concerts by visiting artists, faculty, and students are held Wednesday evenings at 7:30 P.M., from late June through early September, in the Congregational Christian Church on Church Street.

During summer, weekly concerts are held at the town bandstand on Main Street.

An ambitious, grassroots group has launched **Cobscook Community Learning Center** (Timber Cove Rd., Trescott, 207/733-2154, www.the cclc.org). In spring 2004, it began constructing a timber-frame building that will house CCLC's year-round programs, an open pottery studio, and multi-use classrooms. Plans call for the eventual construction of four additional buildings, an amphitheater, outdoor dance floor, hiking and walking trails, and more on the center's 60-acre campus. The center's mission is "to enrich the lives of local community members through grassroots collaboration, using the arts, the rich social fabric, and the natural surroundings as the medium." Festivals, adult education, indigenous education, sustainable and value-added eco-ventures, youth programs, and more are planned. Already in progress is the annual **Cobscook Gathering,** a one-week educational program in August that blends arts, environment, and leadership courses. Do call to see what's on the schedule.

ACCOMMODATIONS

Many visitors use Lubec as a base for day trips to Campobello Island, so it's essential to reserve rooms ahead at the height of summer. Several lodgings are also available on Campobello.

B&Bs

Built in 1860 by a British sea captain, **Peacock House Bed and Breakfast** (27 Summer St., Lubec, 207/733-2403 or 888/305-0036, www.peacockhouse.com, $85–125) has long been one of Lubec's most prestigious residences. Among the notables who have stayed here are Donald MacMillan, the famous Arctic explorer,

and U.S. senators Margaret Chase Smith and Edmund Muskie. Three rooms and four suites. Suites have TV and sitting area; one has a gas fireplace and a refrigerator. One room is wheelchair-accessible.

Unusual antiques fill the guest and sitting rooms of the 19th-century **M Home Port Inn** (45 Main St., Lubec 04652, 207/733-2077 or 800/457-2077, www.homeportinn.com, May–Oct., $85–99), ensconced on a Lubec hilltop. Each of the seven rooms has a private bath, although some are detached. Rates include a generous continental breakfast.

Piano students at SummerKeys often practice on the living room piano at **BayViews** (6 Monument St., Lubec, 207/733-2181, May–Oct., $50–80), providing impromptu concerts for other guests. The 1824 Victorian house sits on two acres edging Johnson Bay. It's a relaxed B&B, filled with eclectic antiques, art, and books. (Owner Kathryn Rubeor has a master's in English literature.) It's an easy walk to town, if you can tear yourself away from the back deck or lawn chairs or hammock. Breakfast is a bountiful continental, with fresh fruit and juice, home-baked bread, and homemade granola and toppings. One huge suite perfect for a family and one twin room, with a piano, have private baths; two doubles and one single share a bath. A five-bedroom, three-bath waterfront house also is available for $1,100 per week.

Motel

If you're traveling with small children, the **Eastland Motel** (County Rd., Rte. 189, R.R. 1, Box 6915, Lubec, 207/733-5501, www.eastlandmotel.com, $52–62) is Lubec's best bet. Four miles southwest of town, near the Lubec Municipal Airport (used infrequently), the motel has 20 clean rooms with cable TV and air-conditioning. Request one of the 12 rooms in the newer section. Free morning coffee. The motel is open all year.

Rental House

The farmhouse on the Bell family's 200-year-old saltwater farm, **Tide Mill Farms** (40 Tide Mill Rd., Edmunds, two miles north of Rte. 189, 207/733-2110, www.tidemillfarm.com) is available for weekly rental. Ocean views are available from throughout the century-old farmhouse, which has five bedrooms and 1.5 baths. Amenities include a TV/VCR, washer/dryer, and gas grill. Linens are provided. Original settler Robert Bell built a tidal grist mill here, and one of the stones still lies on the point. Explore the farm's 1,600 acres, including six miles of shorefront as well as forest and mountain trails. Watch for eagles, seals, and loons. The property is home to the organic farm of the same name, and you'll see farm animals and operations.

Campground

The 80-acre **South Bay Campground** (591 County Rd./Rte. 189, R.R. 1, Box 6565, Lubec, 207/733-1037 or 877/733-1037, southbay@midmaine.com, mid-May–mid-Oct.), has 74 RV and tent sites, a third on the shore of beautiful South Bay. Eight private island sites (accessible on foot at low tide) are also available. Noise regulations are strictly enforced. Facilities include a game room and a pool. Leashed pets are allowed. Open mid-May to mid-October, the campground is about seven miles from Route 1.

FOOD

Miscellany

You can't go wrong with a stop at **Bold Coast Smokehouse** (224 County Rd./Rte. 189, 207/733-88912 or 888/733-0807, www.boldcoastsmokehouse.com). Vinny and Holly Gartmayer are masters of the smoking process, creating delectable hot and cold smoked salmon, smoked fish spreads, smoked salmon sticks (great for picnics), and other goodies. Pick up the catalog; you'll definitely want to order more when you return home.

Oh, my! **Seaside Chocolate** (72 Water St., 207/733-2575 or 800/282-7220, www.seasidechocolate.com) gives meaning to the term sinfully delicious. Partners Monica Elliott and Eugene Greenlaw create sumptuous handmade gourmet chocolates in their second-story shop. Visitors can watch the process and sample chocolates before purchasing (Smart move: You're guaranteed to buy after you taste.) Among the chocolates

are scrumptious bonbons, blueberry wine and raspberry wine truffles, peanut butter cups made with homemade peanut butter, and other mouthwatering treats.

Stave off a midday hunger attack with home-baked goodies from **Mindy's Bakery** (272 County Rd./Rte. 189, 207/733-2002). Depending on the baker's whim, the kitchen shop might include breads, cookies, brownies, muffins, cakes, or pies. Also selling home-baked goods, but with an organic twist, is **Sun Porch Industries** (99 Johnson St.), a tiny natural and organic food store.

Just before the bridge to Campobello is **Not so Famous Phil's,** a homemade ice cream parlor with indoor and outdoor seating. Ice cream, sorbet, and crepes are available in sizes including big, not-so-big, and not-so-not-so-big.

Area farms and producers sell their goods at the **Whiting Corner Farmers' Market** (junction Rte. 1 and Rte. 189, Whiting, 9 A.M.–noon Sat.) and the **Lubec Farmers' Market** (Quoddy Dolphin, 10 A.M.–2 P.M. Sun.).

The **Atlantic House Coffee Shop** (52 Water St., Lubec, 207/733-0906, 7 A.M.–9 P.M. May–Oct.) is one of the brightest spots on a rather forlorn street. Breakfast pastries, tasty sandwiches, great desserts, and decent coffee—load up before you head out for a hike. Give yourself time, though; service can be slow.

Family Dining

Both of these restaurants are always for sale, but don't let that deter you, as they're also about the only spots for a not-fancy meal. Still, you might ask locally about which is better, as that seems to change with the season, if not by the week.

Depending on your source, **Uncle Kippy's** (County Rd., Rte. 189, Lubec, 207/733-2400, 11 A.M.–8 P.M. daily), gets high and higher marks in Lubec for wholesome cooking. A sign out front announces, Stop in or we'll both starve. Steak and seafood are specialties—at unfancy prices—and the pizza is the area's best.

No matter where you sit in **Phinney's Seaview** (County Rd., Rte. 189, Lubec, 207/733-0941), you've got a view of the water. If weather permits, settle on the deck with a beer or one of the seafood specialties. In summer, you can pick up fresh fish and lobsters at the adjacent fish market. Open 6:30 A.M.–9 P.M. daily late May through September, 7 A.M.–8 P.M. Friday–Tuesday the rest of the year. Occasionally closed in January.

Fine Dining

The finest dining in the area is at the ⋈ **Home Port Inn** (45 Main St., Lubec, 207/733-2077 or 800/457-2077, 5–8 P.M. May–Oct., $85–99). Reservations are advisable for this very popular restaurant—a sunken dining room with tables for 30. Specialty is seafood; creative entrées run $12–23.

INFORMATION AND SERVICES

Information

The **Cobscook Bay Area Chamber of Commerce** (P.O. Box 42, Whiting, www.cobscookbay .com) covers the Cobscook Bay region, including Lubec.

In Whiting, **The Puffin Pines,** a country gift store with visitor information, is an easy stop on Route 1. Other local sources for brochures and advice are the **Eastland Motel** (County Rd., Rte. 189), the **Old Columbian Store** (Main St., Lubec, 207/733-4696, 9 A.M.–3 P.M. Mon., Wed., and Fri.) and the **Visitor Center** (West Quoddy Head Light, 207/733-2180, www.westquoddy.com, 10 A.M.–4 P.M. daily late May–mid-Oct.).

Hospitals

The **Regional Medical Center at Lubec** (43 South Lubec Rd., Lubec, 207/733-5541, 8 A.M.–5 P.M. Mon.–Fri.) can handle minor medical and dental emergencies; a doctor is on call for emergencies around the clock.

Libraries

The **Lubec Memorial Library** (corner Water St. and School St., Lubec, 207/733-2491, 10 A.M.–4 P.M. Mon., Tues., and Fri., 10 A.M.–8 P.M. Wed., and 10 A.M.–2 P.M. Sat.) has a public restroom.

Getting There

West Bus Service (800/596-2823) operates one trip a day in each direction between Bangor (connecting with Greyhound and Concord Trailways buses and Bangor International Airport) and Calais, via Ellsworth, with a scheduled stop in Perry. Flag stops are available en route, including Jonesboro, Columbia, Milbridge, Whiting, Dennysville, and Pembroke.

Campobello Island

⋈ ROOSEVELT CAMPOBELLO INTERNATIONAL PARK

Just over the Franklin D. Roosevelt Memorial Bridge from Lubec lies 10-mile-long Campobello Island, in Canada's New Brunswick province. Since 1964, 2,800 acres of the island have been under joint U.S. and Canadian jurisdiction as Roosevelt Campobello International Park, commemorating U.S. President Franklin D. Roosevelt. FDR summered here as a youth, and it was here that he contracted infantile paralysis (polio) in 1921. The park, covering most of the island's southern end, has well-maintained trails, picnic sites, and dramatic vistas, but its center-piece is the imposing Roosevelt Cottage, a mile northeast of the bridge.

Roosevelt Cottage and Visitor Centre

Little seems to have changed in the 34-room red-shingled Roosevelt "Cottage" overlooking Passamaquoddy Bay since President Roosevelt last visited in 1939. The grounds are beautifully landscaped, and the many family mementos—especially those in the late president's den—bring history alive. It all feels very personal, far less stuffy than most presidential memorials.

Stop first at the park's Visitor Centre, where you can pick up brochures (including a trail map), use the restrooms, and see a short video setting the stage for the cottage visit. Then walk across to the house/museum (10 A.M.–6 P.M. Atlantic daylight time—9 A.M.–5 P.M. EDT—last tour at 5:45 P.M., mid-May to mid-Oct., free). Complimentary outside walking tours of the estate and on-site presentations on local ecology are given, weather and staff permitting. For more information, contact **Executive Secretary, Roosevelt Campobello International Park** (P.O. Box 129, Lubec 04652, or 459 Rte. 774, Welshpool, Campobello, NB, Canada E5E 1A4, 506/752-2922 seasonal, www.fdr.net).

The Park by Car

If time is short, or you're unable to hike, at least take some of the park's driving routes—**Cranberry Point Drive,** 5.4 miles round-trip from the Visitor Centre; **Liberty Point Drive,** 12.4 miles round-trip, via Glensevern Road, from the Visitor Centre; and **Fox Hill Drive,** a 2.2-mile link between the other two main routes. Even with the car, you'll have access to beaches, picnic sites, spruce and fir forests, and great views of lighthouses, islands, and the Bay of Fundy.

Just west of the main access road from the bridge is the **Mulholland Point Picnic Area,** where you can spread out your lunch next to the distinctive red-capped lighthouse overlooking Lubec Narrows.

Hiking and Picnicking

Within the international park are 8.5 miles of walking/hiking trails, varying from dead easy to moderately difficult. Easiest is the 1.4-mile (round-trip) walk from the Visitor Centre to **Friar's Head Picnic Area,** named for its distinctive promontory jutting into the bay. For the best angle, climb up to the observation deck on the "head." Grills and tables are here for picnickers.

The most difficult—and most dramatic—trail is a 1.9-mile stretch from **Liberty Point to Raccoon Beach,** along the southeastern shore of the island. Precipitous cliffs can make parts of this trail chancy for small children or insecure adults, so use caution. Liberty Point is incredibly rugged, but observation platforms make it easy to see the tortured rocks and wide-open Bay of Fundy. At broad Raccoon Beach, you can walk the sands,

have a picnic, or watch for whales, porpoises, and osprey. To avoid returning via the same route, park at Liberty Point and walk back along Liberty Point Drive from Raccoon Beach. If you're traveling with nonhikers, arrange for them to meet you with a vehicle at Con Robinson's Point.

You can also walk the park's perimeter, including just over six miles of shoreline, but only if you're in good shape, have waterproof hiking boots, and can spend an entire day on the trails. Before attempting this, however, inquire at the Visitor Centre about trail conditions and tide levels.

CAMPOBELLO BEYOND THE INTERNATIONAL PARK

Take a day or two and explore Campobello beyond the park; overnighters have several lodging and food options. You can also continue by ferry from here to New Brunswick's Deer Island.

Herring Cove Provincial Park

New Brunswick's provincial government does a conscientious job of running Herring Cove Provincial Park (506/752-2396 or 800/561-0123), with picnic areas, 91 campsites (506/752-7010), a four-mile trail system, a mile-long sandy beach, freshwater Glensevern Lake, and the nine-hole championship-level **Herring Cove Golf Course** (506/752-2467). The park is open early June–September.

East Quoddy Head Light

Consult the tide calendar before planning your assault on East Quoddy Head Light (also known as Head Harbour Light), at Campobello's northernmost tip. It's on an islet accessible only at low tide. The distinctive white light tower bears a huge red cross. (You're likely to pass near it on whale-watching trips out of Eastport.) From the Roosevelt cottage, follow Route 774 through the village of Wilson's Beach and continue on an unpaved road to the parking area. A stern Canadian Coast Guard warning sign tells the story:

Extreme Hazard. Beach exposed only at low tide. Incoming tide rises 5 feet per hour and may leave you stranded for 8 hours. Wading or swimming are extremely dangerous due to swift currents and cold water. Proceed at your own risk.

So there. It's definitely worth the effort for the bay and island views from the lighthouse grounds, often including whales and eagles. Allow about an hour before and after dead low tide (be sure your watch coincides with the Atlantic-time tide calendar).

ACCOMMODATIONS AND FOOD

In midsummer, if you'd like to overnight on the island, be sure to reserve lodgings well in advance; Campobello is a popular destination. Nearest backup beds are in Lubec, and those fill up, too.

M The Owen House (11 Welshpool St., Welshpool, Campobello Island, NB, Canada, 506/752-2977, www.owenhouse.ca, mid-May–mid-Oct., CAN$112–297) is the island's best address, an elegant early-19th-century inn on 10 acres overlooking Passamaquoddy Bay and Eastport in the distance. Eight guest rooms (private and shared baths). Just north of the inn is the Deer Island ferry landing.

The Lupine Lodge (610 Rte. 774, Welshpool, Campobello Island, NB, Canada E5E 1A5, 506/752-2555, www.lupinelodge.com, early June–mid-Oct., CAN$50–105), an updated summer estate of Roosevelt kin, is only a quarter mile from the Roosevelt cottage. Bay views from the 11-acre grounds are terrific. The 11 rooms in two buildings have private baths (some have fireplaces). The adjacent restaurant serves breakfast, lunch, and dinner; special arrangements can be made for tea.

Don't expect culinary creativity on Campobello, but you won't starve—at least during the summer season. Best choice is **Family Fisheries** (1977 Rte. 774, Wilson's Beach, 506/752-2470, 10 A.M.–9 P.M.), a seafood restaurant and fish market toward the northern end of the island.

INFORMATION AND SERVICES

Information

For information on Campobello Island, contact **Campobello Island Tourism Association** (506/752-7010, www.campobello.com).

To visit Campobello, you'll have to pass Customs checkpoints on the U.S. and Canada ends of the Franklin D. Roosevelt Memorial Bridge (Lubec, U.S., Customs 207/733-4331; Campobello, Canada, Customs 506/752-2091, fax 506/752-1080).

Be aware that crossing this short little bridge takes an hour, because there's a one-hour time difference between Lubec and Campobello. Lubec (like the rest of Maine) is on eastern standard time; Campobello, like the rest of Canada's Maritime Provinces, is on Atlantic time, an hour later. As soon as you reach the island, set your clock ahead an hour.

There is no need to convert U.S. currency to Canadian for use on Campobello; U.S. dollars are accepted everywhere on the island, but prices tend to be quoted in Canadian dollars.

Just after Canadian Customs waves you through from Lubec, stop at the **Tourist Information Centre** (506/752-2997), on your right. The staff can fix you up with trail maps of the international park and New Brunswick propaganda, then steer you toward the Roosevelt property.

Eastport and Vicinity

When you leave Whiting and continue north on Route 1 around Cobscook Bay, it's hard to believe that life could slow down any more than it already has, but it does. The landscape's raw beauty is occasionally punctuated by farmhouses or a convenience store, but little else.

Edmunds Township's claims to fame are its splendid public lands—Cobscook Bay State Park and a unit of Moosehorn National Wildlife Refuge. Just past the state park, loop along the scenic shoreline before returning to Route 1.

Pembroke, once part of adjoining Dennysville, claims Reversing Falls Park, where you can watch (and hear) ebbing and flowing tides draining and filling Cobscook Bay.

A statue of a giant fisherman is a souvenir from a reality TV series filmed in Eastport.

If time allows a short scenic detour, especially in fall, turn left (northwest) on Route 214 and drive 10 miles to quaintly named Meddybemps, allegedly a Passamaquoddy word meaning "plenty of alewives [herring]." Views over Meddybemps Lake, on the north side of the road, are spectacular, and you can launch a canoe or kayak into the lake here, less than a mile beyond the junction with Route 191 (take the dead-end unpaved road toward the water).

Backtracking to Route 1, heading east from Pembroke, you'll come to Perry, best known for the Sipayik (Pleasant Point) Indian Reservation, a Passamaquoddy settlement, two miles east of Route 1, that's been here since 1822. Drop down Route 191, which cuts through the reservation's heart. If there's time, stop at the small Waponahki Museum. Or plan a visit around the reservation's August Indian Days celebration.

The city (yes, it's officially a city) of Eastport (pop. 1,900) is on Moose Island, connected by causeway to the mainland at Sipayik (Pleasant Point). Views are terrific on both sides, especially at sunset, as you hopscotch from one blob of land to another and finally reach this minicity, where the sardine industry was introduced as long ago as 1875. Five sardine canneries once operated here, employing hundreds of local residents who snipped the heads off herring and stuffed them into cans—one of those esoteric skills not easily translatable to other tasks. In the 1990s, the focus was on fish farming. In the new century, entrepreneurs and artisans seem to be leading the way.

Settled in 1772, Eastport has had its ups and downs, mostly mirroring the fishing industry. It's currently on an upswing, as people "from away" have arrived to soak up the vibe of a small town with a heavy Down East accent. A big push came in 2001, when the Fox Network reality-TV series "Murder in Small Town X" was filmed here; the city morphed into the village of Sunrise, Maine, and local residents eagerly filled in as extras. The huge waterfront statue of a fisherman is a remnant of the filming.

Although there are still too many closed shops

TIDES

Nowhere in Maine is the adage "Time and tide wait for no man" more true than along the Washington County coastline. The nation's most extreme tidal ranges occur in this area, so the hundreds of miles of tidal shore frontage between Steuben and Calais provide countless opportunities for observing tidal phenomena. Every six hours or so, the tide begins either ebbing or flowing. The farther Down East you go, the higher (and lower) the tides. Although tides in Canada's Bay of Fundy are far higher, the highest tides in New England occur along the St. Croix River, at Calais.

Tides govern coastal life—particularly Down East, where average tidal ranges may be 10 to 20 feet and extremes approach 28 feet. Everyone is a slave to the tide calendar, which coastal-community newspapers diligently publish. Boats tie up with extra-long lines; clammers and wormdiggers schedule their days by the tides; hikers have to plan for shoreline exploring; and kayakers need to plan their routes to avoid getting stuck in the muck.

Tides, as we all learned in elementary school, are lunar phenomena, created by the gravitational pull of the moon; the tidal range depends on the lunar phase. Tides are most extreme at new and full moons—when the sun, moon, and earth are all aligned. These are spring tides, supposedly because the water springs upward (the term has nothing to do with the season). And tides are smallest during the moon's first and third quarters—when the sun, earth, and moon have a right-angle configuration. These are neap tides ("neap" comes from an Old English word meaning "scanty"). Other lunar/solar phenomena, such as the equinoxes and solstices, can also affect tidal ranges.

The best time for shoreline exploration is on a new-moon or full-moon day, when low tide exposes mussels, sea urchins, sea cucumbers, starfish, periwinkles, hermit crabs, rockweed, and assorted nonbiodegradable trash. Rubber boots or waterproof, treaded shoes are essential on the wet, slippery terrain.

Caution is also essential in tidal areas. Unless you've carefully plotted tide times and heights, don't park a car or bike or boat trailer on a beach; make sure your sea kayak is lashed securely to a tree or bollard; don't take a long nap on shoreline granite; and don't cross a low-tide land spit without an eye on your watch.

A perhaps apocryphal but almost believable story goes that one flatlander stormed up to a ranger at Cobscook Bay State Park one bright summer morning and demanded indignantly to know why they had had the nerve to drain the water from her shorefront campsite during the night. When it comes to tides . . . you have to go with the flow.

and neglected buildings downtown, that's beginning to change as artists and artisans and entrepreneurs renovate them into studios and shops.

Until 1811, the town also included Lubec, which is about 2.5 miles across the water in a boat, but 40-something miles in a car. A ferry now shuttles passengers back and forth for Lubec's SummerKeys concerts, and locals hold out hope that a regular schedule will be established.

SIGHTS

Historic Walking Tour

The best way to appreciate Eastport's history is to pick up and follow the route in *A Walking Guide to Eastport,* available at many local points. The handy map/brochure spotlights the city's 18th-, 19th-, and early-20th-century homes, businesses, and monuments, many now on the National Register of Historic Places. Among the highlights are historic homes converted to B&Bs, two museums, and a large chunk of downtown Water Street, with many handsome brick buildings erected after a disastrous fire swept through in 1886.

Raye's Mustard Mill Museum

How often do you have a chance to watch mustard being made in a turn-of-the-20th-century mustard mill? Drive by **J. W. Raye & Co.** (83 Washington St., Rte. 190, Eastport, 207/853-4451 or 800/853-1903, www.rayesmustard.com,

© TOM NANGLE

The Down East Coast

At Raye's Mustard Mill Museum in Eastport, you can take a short tour highlighting the 100-plus-year-old process and then taste samples and purchase your favorite.

9 A.M.–5 P.M.), at the edge of Eastport, and stop in for a free 15-minute tour, offered at 10 A.M., 11 A.M., 2 P.M., and 3 P.M. daily. You'll get to see the granite millstones, the mustard seeds being winnowed, and enormous vats of future mustard. Tours are on-demand weekdays, by appointment weekends. Raye's sells mustard under its own label and produces it for major customers under their labels. The shop stocks all of Raye's mustard varieties (samples available), other Maine-made food, and gift items, and it also has a small cafe, where you can purchase sandwiches and salads. A proper tea a is served midafternoon.

The Tides Institute and Museum of Art

One of the most promising additions to Eastport's downtown is The Tides Institute (43 Water St., 207/853-4047, www.tidesinstitute.com, 10 A.M. to 5 P.M. Tues.–Sun., to 8 P.M. on the first Mon. of the month, closed Tues. and Sun. in winter, free), in a former bank that it's restoring. The institute's impressive goals are to build significant cultural collections and to produce new culturally important works employing printmaking, letterpress, photography, bookmaking,

oral history, and other media. For its collection, the institute is focusing on works by artists and photographers associated with the Passamaquoddy region. Already, it has significant works by artists such as John Marin and photographers such as Lewis Hine and a nice selection of baskets by Native Americans. These and others are displayed in rotating shows that also highlight contemporary area artists. The Research and Reference Library has more than 4,000 volumes. The institute also offers workshops by visiting artists in printmaking and other topics. These are open to the public by advance reservations. Definitely stop in for a visit.

Passamaquoddy Indian Reservation

Baskets, tools, beadwork, a birch-bark canoe, and photo-lined walls are all part of the **Waponahki Museum** (Rte. 190, Perry, 207/853-4001), on Sipayik (Pleasant Point Reservation). The small collection is dedicated to preserving the history and culture of Maine's Passamaquoddy Indians. The museum has spurred revival of the Passamaquoddy language, now being taught and written. The most interesting time to visit is in August, during

Sipayik's annual **Indian Ceremonial Days.** The museum—two miles east of Route 1 and seven miles north of Eastport—is open all year (8–11 A.M. and 11:30 A.M.–2 P.M. Mon.–Fri.), but the schedule can be erratic, so call ahead to be sure. Admission is free, but donations are welcomed.

Ask at the museum or locally about basket-makers who might sell from their homes. The fancy and work baskets are treasures, constantly escalating in price. It's a real treat to be able to purchase one from the maker.

"Woodie" Tours

Eastport has a generous helping of eccentricity and individuality—which is just fine by most people here—and Jim Blankman fits in perfectly. Jim gives tours in his 1947 "woodie" bus. Remember those? This one was used as a commuter for sardine-factory workers. Calling his business (and business is a loose term, as he doesn't even advertise) **Island Tours** (37 Washington St., Eastport 04631, 207/853-4831), Jim drives his group to a water-view spot, spreads out a lavish picnic, allows time for the feast, and then does a little tour around the area. All this takes about three hours, starting around noon. (He'll also do sunset tours.) Cost is $20 adults, $10 children; four people minimum, 11 maximum. Reservations are required, at least a day ahead (call in the evening). Do it. The tour without lunch takes about 90 minutes and just isn't the same, but if you must, it's $5 a person. When he's not doing the tours, look for Jim down near the breakwater in a shop on Water Street displaying the products of his fine carpentry skills—street luges, "woodie" trailers, musical instruments, and even coffins (made to order).

PARKS AND PRESERVES

One section of **Moosehorn National Wildlife Refuge** adjoins Cobscook Bay State Park, but the headquarters and major recreational tracts are near Calais.

Shackford Head State Park

Ninety-acre Shackford Head (off Deep Cove Rd., Eastport, free) is on a peninsula that juts into Cobscook Bay. It has five miles of wooded trails;

the easiest and best is one-mile round-trip Shackford Head, rising gently to a 175-foot-high headland with wide-open views of Eastport and, depending on weather, Campobello Island, Lubec, Pembroke, and even Grand Manan. The trail's continuation onto the steeper Ship Point Trail adds another half-mile. The trailhead and parking area are just east of the Washington County Community College Marine Technology Center, at the southern end of town. This state preserve is particularly good for families. Use bug repellent and carry binoculars and a camera. There's a toilet near the parking area, but no other facilities. Pick up a map/brochure here. A memorial with plaques details the history of five Civil War ships that were decommissioned and burned on Cony Beach between 1901 and 1920 by the U.S. government. Eastport's huge tides allowed the ships to be brought in and beached, then taken apart as the tide receded. Fourteen Eastport men served on four of the ships.

Cobscook Bay State Park

A 3.5-mile network of nature trails, picnic spots, great birding and berry-picking, hot showers, a boat launch, and wooded shorefront campsites make 888-acre Cobscook Bay State Park (Rte. 1, Edmunds Township, 207/726-4412) one of Maine's most spectacular state parks. It's even entertaining just to watch the 24-foot tides surging in and out of this area at five or so feet an hour; there's no swimming because of the undertow. Reserve well ahead to get a place on the shore. To guarantee a site in July and August, using MasterCard or Visa, call 207/287-3824 or visit www.campwithme.com; reservation fee is $2 per site per night, two-night minimum. The park is open daily mid-May to mid-October; trails are groomed in winter for cross-country skiing, and one section goes right along the shore. Summer day-use fees are $3 adults, $1 children 5–11; children under five are free. Nonresident camping fees are $19 per site per night; fees for Maine residents are $14.

Reversing Falls Park

There's plenty of room for adults to relax and kids to play at the 140-acre Reversing Falls Park, in West Pembroke—plus shorefront ledges and a front-row seat overlooking a fascinating tidal phenomenon. Pack a picnic, then check newspapers or information offices for the tide times, so you can watch the saltwater surging through a 300-yard-wide passage at about 25 knots, creating a whirlpool and churning "falls." The park is at Mahar Point in West Pembroke, 7.2 miles south of Route 1. Coming from the south (Dennysville), leave Route 1 in West Pembroke when you see the Triangle Grocery Store. Turn right and go .3 mile to Leighton Point Road, where you'll see a sign saying Shore Access 5.5 miles. Turn right and go 3.8 miles, past gorgeous meadows, low shrubs, and views of Cobscook Bay. Turn right at a very tiny Reversing Falls sign, posted high on a telephone pole. Go about 1.5 miles to the end, then turn left onto a gravel road and continue two miles to the park.

Gleason Cove

This quiet park and boat-launch site is a delightful place to walk along the shorefront or to grab a table and spread out a picnic, while drinking in the dreamy views over fishing weirs and islands in Passamaquoddy Bay. It's now threatened with a liquefied natural gas port, so it may not be around in this form much longer. To get here, take Shore Road (opposite the New Friendly Restaurant), then take a right on Gleason Cove Road. No facilities.

RECREATION

Golf

Downeast Adventure Golf (Rte. 1, Perry, 207/731-9595, $6 adults, $5 kids 5–11) is an 18-hole championship miniature golf course on 2.5 acres, with night lights. Also on site is a practice green.

Whale-Watching and Scenic Cruises

Eastporter Butch Harris gave the waterfront a shot in the arm when he purchased the sleek *Sylvinia Beal,* a historic, 84-foot schooner built in 1911. His company, **Eastport Windjammers**, offers a number of options to sail. The three-hour whale-watching cruise departs daily at

1:30 P.M. and heads out into the prime whale-feeding grounds of Passamaquoddy Bay—passing the Old Sow whirlpool (largest tidal whirlpool in the Northern Hemisphere), salmon aquaculture pens, and Campobello Island. En route, you'll see bald eagles, porpoises, possibly puffins and osprey, and more. Best months are July and August, when sightings are frequent, but Butch is a skilled spotter, so if they're there, he'll find them. The cost is $35 for adults, $18 for children 12 and younger. A two-hour sunset cruise departs the Eastport Pier at 7 P.M. and costs $25 for adults, $15 for children.

Deep-Sea Fishing

Eastport Windjammers (104 Water St. at the head of the breakwater, 207/853-2500 or 207/853-4303 before 10 A.M. and 6–8 P.M., www.eastportwindjammers.com) also offers a four-hour fishing trip on the *Quoddy Dam,* with all equipment provided. No license is required for recreational saltwater fishing. Bring a cooler or fish container if you want to keep your catch. The trip costs $25 for adults and $15 for children. It leaves from the Eastport Breakwater at 8 A.M.

Sea Kayaking, Canoeing, and Hiking

Explore the region by sea kayak with **Cobscook Hikes & Paddles** (207/726-4776 summer, 207/454-2130 winter, ftorek@midmaine.com), which services the area between Whiting and Calais. Registered Maine Guides Stephen and Tessa Ftorek lead three-hour ocean or lake paddles, designed to meet your interests and ability, for $50 pp. Two-hour sunrise or sunset paddles are $40. On Friday nights, you can watch luminescent organisms sparkle in the water on a two-hour Phosphorescent Paddle, for $40. The Ftoreks also offer guided full-day ($80) and half-day ($40) hikes.

Quoss Boats (Rte. 1, Perry, 207/731-9595) rents lake kayaks for $40 per day, including paddle, life jacket, and portage. Renters must be swimmers, older than 21, and provide a major credit card for deposit. A half-day rental, when available, is $27. Kayaks are only for lake and estuary paddling, and introductory lessons are available. You can take them to one of the many pretty lakes on the inland side of Route 1.

SHOPPING
Art, Crafts, and Antiques

Eastport has long been a magnet for artists and craftspeople yearning to work in a supportive environment, but the influx has increased in recent years. Proof of this is **The Eastport Gallery** (52 Water St., Eastport, 207/853-4166, www .eastportgallery.com, mid-June–Sept.), a cooperative whose works in varied media line the walls of a downtown building. The gallery also sponsors the annual **Paint Eastport Day,** usually held the second Saturday in September, when anyone is invited to paint a local scene; a reception and "wet paint" auction follow.

New on Eastport's art scene is **The Commons** (51 Water St. 207/853-4123), a waterfront building that's been beautifully renovated by a gaggle of energetic women with local ties into a fabulous gallery displaying works by 40 area artists and artisans. A common space is used for classes and presentations.

In the same building as the Eastport Arts Center, **Earth Forms** (5 Dana St., Eastport, 207/853-2430) features potter Donald Sutherland's intriguing (and sometimes whimsical) wheel-thrown work—self-described as "functional, nonfunctional, and dysfunctional" pottery. You can often see him at work on his wheel. It's tough to walk out without buying one of these special pieces.

Next door to Earth Forms is **Rose Garden Antiques and Design** (9 Dana St., 207/853-9598), an eclectic collection of antiques, collectibles, and art. Owners Linda and Al Salleroli are renovating the building and have included an indoor garden, working artist studios, a coffee shop, and space for independent vendors as well as public restrooms. A gallery with rotating shows is planned.

Woodworker Roland LaVallee's gallery **Crow Tracks** (11 Water St., 207/853-2336) is filled with his intricate carvings of birds and local fauna. The tiny garden entryway just doubles the pleasure of a visit.

It's a delight to wander through the sculpted mermaids, angels, goddesses, flora, and fauna in the garden at **Ostrander** (83 Clark St., corner of Brewster St., Eastport, 207/853-4342). Inside are more sculptures, paintings, and garden art by Elizabeth Ostrander.

Do pick up a copy of the *Tucked Away in Downeast Maine Artisan's Studio Tour* brochure, which describes and provides hours and directions to many artists and artisans in the area. These include the **Red Wagon Quilt & Craft Shop** (430 Rte. 1, Pembroke, 207/726-4043), which sells a large assortment of quilts by area artisans; **Salt Meadow Gallery & Studio** (Hersey Rd., Pembroke, 207/726-5153), in a log cabin chockfull of hand-painted floorcloths, hand-printed woodcuts, pottery, quilts, furniture, wearable art, and more; **Done Roving Farm & Carding Mill** (20 Charlotte Rd., Charlotte, 207/454-8148), where fiber artist Paula Farra creates and sells handspun yarns and felts in a variety of fibers; **Daylily Weaving & Dyeworks** (103 Shore Rd., Perry, 207/952-0224), with graceful, colorful, wearable art; and **Moose Island Quilting** (45 Gin Cove Rd., Perry, 207/853-2506), quilt artist Dana Bard's home studio (and while you're in the neighborhood, visit her neighbor, megaltented quilt artist Susan Plachy).

Hand-Sewn Shoes

Shoemaking was once a major industry in Maine, but today only a couple of places still sew shoes by hand. One of them is **Quoddy Trail Moccasin Co.** (1041 U.S. Rte. 1, Perry, 207/853-2488, www.quoddytrail.com). The company was started by Harry Smith Shorey and is now run by his descendant, Kevin Shorey, and his wife, Kirsten. Overruns and seconds are sold at discounted prices at the Shoreys' store, the **Quoddy Wigwam** (Rte. 1 & Shore Rd., 207/853-4812), where you can also see a huge stuffed moose and purchase Native American baskets and souvenirs. Call or ask at the store to arrange a tour of the low-key factory to see where the leather is cut and how it's sewn into moccasins, boat shoes, slippers, and other models, or to arrange for a custom pair ($70 and up; the best-selling model retails for $140) to be made.

Gifts and a Whole Lot More

Describing **45th Parallel: The Store** (Rte. 1, Perry, 207/853-9500) is a tough assignment. You really have to *go there* and see for yourself. The aesthetic displays are worth the trip to this eclectic emporium. Housed in a one-story log building two miles (in the Calais direction) from the junction of Routes 190 and 1, the 45th Parallel is part antique shop, part gift shop, part global marketplace—and entirely seductive. Tiny white lights glimmer here and there, antique architectural remnants hang from the ceiling, and every little niche holds yet another fascinating treasure. It's open daily May through October, then weekends in November and December.

Do stop in, if only for a few minutes, at **S.W. Wadsworth & Son** (42 Water St., 207/853-4343), the oldest ship chandlery in the country and the oldest retail business in Maine. In addition to hardware and marine gear, you'll find nautical gifts and souvenirs.

ENTERTAINMENT

The **Eastport Arts Center** (Water St. and Dana St., Eastport, 207/853-2358) is an umbrella organization for local arts groups, with headquarters and performing space in a former Masonic hall. You can pick up a brochure with a complete schedule, which usually includes concerts, films, puppet shows, an Elderhostel program, and other cultural events. Also based here is **SummerArts** (207/853-6179, www.summerarts.com), a five-week series of classes and workshops.

Stage East, an enthusiastic local theater group, mounts regular productions at the center, with performances scheduled Thursday, Friday, and Saturday at 7 P.M. and Sunday at 3 P.M. For tickets ($8), call the box office at The Motel East (207/853-4747).

The center works with Butch Harrison to provide a ferry to the free **SummerKeys** concerts, held Wednesday nights from late June to early September in Lubec. Transportation is aboard the *Quoddy Dam,* departing Eastport at 6:30 P.M. and returning around 9:30 P.M. Ferry tickets are $12 in advance, $15 for walk ons if space is available;

purchase them at the *Sylvina Beal* ticket office on Water Street or call 207/853-2500.

For **live music,** find out what's happening any Saturday night at La Sardina Loca (28 Water St., Eastport, 207/853-2739).

FESTIVALS AND EVENTS

For a small community, Eastport manages to pull together and put on plenty of successful events during the year.

Eastport's annual four-day **Fourth of July—Old Home Week** extravaganza includes a parade, pancake breakfasts, barbecues, a flea market, an auction, races, live entertainment, and fireworks. This is one of Maine's best July Fourth celebrations and attracts a crowd of more than 10,000. Lodgings are booked months in advance, so plan ahead.

Indian Ceremonial Days, a three-day Native American celebration, includes children's games, canoe races, craft demos, talking circles, fireworks, and traditional food and dancing at Sipayik, the Pleasant Point Reservation, in Perry, the second weekend in August.

The **Eastport Salmon Festival** celebrates the area's aquaculture industry. If you like salmon, you'll *love* this event, which combines a salmon barbecue, craft booths, live entertainment, and boat trips at the Eastport breakwater 11 A.M.–4 P.M. the Sunday after Labor Day.

ACCOMMODATIONS

Lodgings in Eastport can fill up in summer, and since it's literally the end of the road, it's wise to reserve ahead. Fortunately, choices include a good selection of B&Bs, plus a fine motel, so it's a great place to spend the night.

B&Bs

In 1833, renowned artist John James Audubon stayed at the elegant **Weston House** (26 Boynton St., Eastport, 207/853-2907 or 800/853-2907, www.westonhouse-maine.com, $70–85), so one of the three second-floor guest rooms bears his name—and walls lined with Audubon bird prints. All rooms share 2.5 baths, but don't let that dissuade you from staying at this lovely home. Jett and John Peterson's family antiques and interesting art and crafts fill the beautifully decorated house on a quiet side street two blocks above the waterfront. Breakfast is outstanding (Jett is Eastport's favorite caterer), complete with candelabra and classical music. Outside are croquet and badminton facilities, plus lovely gardens with a gazebo, chairs, and table. Tea and sherry are available in the afternoon. With advance notice, Jett will prepare a private dinner and serve it in the formal dining room, a smart and delicious choice given Eastport's limited restaurants.

The comfortably furnished **Milliken House Bed & Breakfast** (29 Washington St., Eastport, 207/853-2955 or 888/507-9370, www.eastport-inn.com, $75–85) is a good choice for families, but be forewarned that you'll have to carry your luggage up at least one, and perhaps two, tall flights of stairs. Hosts Bill and Mary Williams welcome children and pets. Breakfasts are huge and served family style in the very-Victorian dining room. Five rooms and one suite all have private baths. Call ahead if you're coming in winter.

At the 1775 **Todd House** (1 Capen Ave., Eastport, 207/853-2328, $60–95), Eastport native Ruth McInnis converts guests willingly into instant history buffs. The National Historic Register Cape-style house, built during the Revolutionary War on Todd's Head, has character, from the book, basket, and arrowhead collections to the beautiful quilts. Six first- and second-floor rooms (two with private baths, some with water views) are nicely furnished. A generous continental breakfast is served in the lovely common room. It's a 10-minute walk into town. Guests can grill dinner in the backyard fireplace. Well-behaved pets and children are welcome.

Motel

Here's a motel with the spirit of a B&B. Enthusiastic about their adopted community, host Owen Lawlor and manager Deb Moore at **M The Motel East** (23A Water St., Eastport, 207/853-4747, www.eastportme.info, $90–110) provide all kinds of advice and guarantee you'll enjoy the area. Got a problem or question? Owen or Deb can solve it or answer it. Guests at the modern, three-story

hostelry have front-row seats on Passamaquoddy Bay, overlooking Campobello Island, and you can walk to everything downtown. Six good-sized rooms and eight efficiency suites have phones and cable TV. Request a balcony room. Free coffee in the lobby. Open all year. The separate Friar Roads Cottage is available for $150 a day.

Apartments

On the second floor of **The Commons** (51 Water St., 207/853-4123, www.thecommonseastport.com), a newly renovated downtown building on the waterfront, are two nicely appointed apartments, with decks and spectacular harbor views. Tide Watcher sleeps seven, has two baths, and rents for $850 per week; Water's Edge sleeps six, has one bath, and rents for $800. Both have well-equipped kitchens and comfy living rooms.

Campground

On the outskirts of town is the quiet, well-maintained, waterfront **Seaview Campground** (16 Norwood Rd., Eastport, 207/853-4471, info @eastportmaine.com), just off Route 190, 70 tent and RV open and semiwooded sites, nine cabins, and a four-unit motel. Shorefront sites on Harrington Cove have great views, but they're snapped up quickly. Cabins have excellent vistas. The camp store, open 7 A.M.–10 P.M., sells lobster live or cooked for around $7–8 a pound. There's also a recreation hall, dock, laundry, and a restaurant (open 7 A.M.–8 P.M.) serving breakfast, lunch, and dinner. Leashed pets are allowed only at RV and tent sites. Tent sites are $13–18, RV sites are $20–35, depending upon location and season. One- to three-bedroom cabins are $75–110 per day or $400–650 a week; motel rooms are $65–85 a day. Open mid-May to mid-October.

FOOD

The restaurant scene in Eastport is always in flux, with many places seeming to change hands every year or so. Even the long-time standbys were for sale when I visited, so it's a good idea to ask locals for updated info and reviews.

Breakfast, Lunch, and Miscellany

One of Eastport's dining secrets is **The Blue Iris** (31 Water St., Eastport, 207/853-2440, 6:30 A.M.– 2 P.M.), which shares space with a floral shop. Well-spaced indoor tables and outdoor ones on a bilevel deck all have water views. Breakfast is served all day; lunch is available beginning at 11 A.M. With the exception of lobster and crabmeat rolls or clubs, a chicken Caesar, and perhaps daily specials, nothing on the menu is more than $5. It's all good, and service is cheerful.

The best pizza in Eastport comes from **Frank's Pizzaria and Deli** (34 Water St., Eastport, 207/853-2709, 11 A.M.–8 P.M. Mon.–Sat.), where you can also get subs, wraps, burgers, salads, chicken, and even pasta. There are only a dozen seats, so grab your stuff and eat it elsewhere. No credit cards.

When you're wandering around the Eastport breakwater, you'll notice the line at **Rosie's Hot Dog** (municipal pier, Eastport, no phone, Mon.–Sat. at 11 A.M., Sun. at noon), a veteran take-out stand open only in summer. Rosie's tube steaks are the best around.

The **Sunrise County Farmers' Market** sets up its tables next to Raye's Mustard Mill (Washington St., Eastport, 11 A.M.–2 P.M. Thurs. between late June and Oct.).

Casual Dining

A popular roadside eatery with a well-deserved reputation, the aptly named **New Friendly Restaurant** (1014 Rte. 1, Perry, 207/853-6610, 11 A.M.–8 P.M. Mon.–Fri.) lays on home-cooked offerings for "dinnah" (a Maine-ism meaning lunch), specializing in steak and seafood. Don't be surprised to find it crowded. Liquor license, air-conditioning.

A downtown-Eastport institution since 1924, the **Wa-Co Diner and Dining Room** (47 Water St., 207/853-4046, 6 A.M.–9 P.M.), pronounced WHACK-o (short for Washington County or, the story goes, for Nelson Watts and Ralph Colwell), is a must-do local-color stop. Nancy Bishop, a native Eastporter, returned after 35 years and spruced up the place in 1997, changing the image a bit with a bright dining room and bay-view deck added to the diner-style booths

and counter—but the service remains friendly and the food inexpensive (although a few fancier entrées top out at $25) and filling. You can order from both menus in the dining room, but only the diner menu in the counter and booths. No credit cards.

And there's another funky place almost across the street. How many restaurants keep Christmas lights going year-round—on an upside-down Christmas tree? How many places have umbrella tables *inside*? In downtown Eastport, **La Sardina Loca** (28 Water St., 207/853-2739, 4 P.M. to closing Wed.–Sun.), which translates as "the crazy sardine," bills itself as the easternmost Mexican restaurant in the United States. It's not the most authentic Tex-Mex (no sangria or guacamole), but it's okay—and the place will keep you entertained (some nights with live music). Menu prices run $6–14. The schedule can be unpredictable, so call ahead or take your chances.

Time your meal right, and you can watch the Deer Isle ferry arrive and depart or view the windjammer *Sylvinia Beal* sail by from the bilevel **Eastport Chowder House** (167 Water St., 207/853-4700, 11 A.M.–9 P.M.). Seafood, natch, is the specialty, with entrées in the $10–14 range. Although the food and service were both good when I visited (I could have done without the blaring technorock music), this restaurant has had several incarnations—ask locally for its current reputation, or take your chances. The bar/lounge, below, has deck seating and closes later.

Very casual and inexpensive is **The Happy Crab** (35 Water St., 207/853-9900, 11 A.M.– 8 P.M. Mon.–Sat., 2–8 P.M. Sun.), a grill and sports bar with weekday blue plate specials and a Friday night fish fry for $7.95, with free seconds. Pizza and finger food are usually available after 8 P.M., until the bar closes.

INFORMATION AND SERVICES

Information

The volunteer-run **Eastport Area Chamber of Commerce** (office at Motel East, 23A Water St., 207/853-4644, www.eastport.net) produces *The*

Eastport Area Business Guide, a useful directory/map of places to sleep, eat, shop, and play. Websites with information on Eastport abound: www.eastportme.info, www.eastportforpride.org (owned by an organization determined to preserve and spruce up downtown Eastport), www.eastportme.com (the official city site), and www.cobscookbay.com.

Brochures are available at the **Quoddy Maritime Museum and Visitor Center** (70 Water St., 10 A.M.–6 P.M. June–Sept.), along with other brochures. In the museum section of the center is a huge model of the failed 1936 Passamaquoddy Tidal Power Project (an idea whose time hadn't come when it was proposed).

Hospitals

The **Regional Medical Center at Lubec** (43 South Lubec Rd., Lubec, 207/733-5541, 8 A.M.–5 P.M. Mon.–Fri.) can handle minor medical and dental emergencies; a doctor is on call for emergencies around the clock.

Libraries

The handsome stone **Peavey Memorial Library,** built in 1893, is named after the inventor of the Peavey grain elevator (26 Water St., Eastport, 207/853-4021, noon–8 P.M. Mon., noon–5 P.M. Tues. and Thurs., 10 A.M.–5 P.M. Wed. and Fri., and 10 A.M.–3 P.M. Sat.).

Public Restrooms

Restrooms are available at the library and Rose Garden Antiques and Design; in summer, there are portable toilets on Eastport's breakwater.

Getting There

West Bus Service (800/596-2823) operates one trip a day in each direction between Bangor (connecting with Greyhound and Concord Trailways buses and Bangor International Airport) and Calais, via Ellsworth, with a scheduled stop in Perry. Flag stops are available en route, including Jonesboro, Columbia, Milbridge, Whiting, Dennysville, and Pembroke.

Calais and Vicinity

Calais (CAL-us) is as far as you'll get on the coast of Maine; from here on, you're headed inland.

Europeans showed up in this area as early as 1604, when French adventurers established an ill-fated colony on St. Croix Island in the St. Croix River—16 whole years before the Pilgrims even thought about Massachusetts. After a winter-long debacle, all became relatively quiet until 1779, when the first permanent settler arrived.

The most interesting time to show up in Calais (pop. 3,890) is during the nine-day International Festival, the first or second week in August, when the city and neighboring St. Stephen, New Brunswick, go all out with dances, concerts, races, barbecues, and fireworks—reinforcing the transborder cooperation that has long benefited both communities. Currently there are two ways to cross the border: a downtown bridge that's due to be replaced and a quieter, smaller crossing in Mill Town, a few miles north, off Route 1.

Southeast of Calais is tiny Robbinston, a booming shipbuilding community in the 19th century but today little more than a 500-person blip on the map. Highlights nowadays are a wonderful chocolate shop and the Calais-Robbinston "milestones."

SIGHTS
⚅ Downeast Heritage Center

The $6.5 million Downeast Heritage Center (39 Union St., Calais, 207/454-7878 or 877/454-2500, www.downeastheritage.org, 8 A.M.–6 P.M. July–Sept., 9 A.M.–5 P.M. the rest of the year, $6 adult, $4 ages 62 and older, $3 ages 6–12, $20 per family) opened in the renovated Calais Train Station in May 2004, with three permanent, interactive exhibits highlighting more than 12,000 years of regional history. It's a must-visit for anyone, as it explains the region's shipbuilding, forestry, blueberrying, and fishing heritage; Passamaquoddy culture; and the St. Croix settlement. The center also has video presentations, performances, and cultural demonstrations in its

GRAND LAKE STREAM

For a tiny community of about 200 year-rounders, Grand Lake Stream has a well-deserved, larger-than-life reputation. It's the center of a vast area of rivers and lakes, ponds and streams—a recreational paradise. It's the literal town at the end of the world, remote in every sense of the word.

The famous stream is a narrow, three-mile neck of prime scenic and sportfishing water connecting West Grand Lake and Big Lake. A dam spans the bottom of West Grand, and just downstream is a state-run salmon hatchery. Since the mid-19th century, the stream and its lakes have been drawing fishing fans to trout and landlocked-salmon spawning grounds, and fourth and fifth generations now return here each year.

Fly-fishers arrive in May and June for landlocked salmon and smallmouth bass (the stream itself is fly-fishing only); families show up in July and August for canoeing, birding, swimming, fishing, and hiking; hunters arrive in late October for game birds and deer; and snowmobilers, snowshoers, and cross-country skiers descend as the snow piles up.

Canoe-building has contributed to the area's mystique. The distinctive Grand Lake canoe (or "Grand Laker"), a lightweight, square-sterned, motorized 20-footer, was developed in the 1920s specifically for sportfishing in these waters. In the off-season, several villagers still hunker down in their workshops and turn out these stable cedar beauties. (Interested? Call Bill Shamel, 207/796-8199.)

If you're in Grand Lake Stream only for the day, head for the public landing and bear right after the intersection with the Pine Tree Store, where you'll find a parking area, a dock, a portable toilet, and a boat launch. You can also walk the path on the western shore of the stream.

The region has the greatest concentration of Registered Maine Guides in the state, which gives you an indication of the fishing, hunting, and canoeing opportunities here. Truly the best way to experience Grand Lake Stream is with a member of the **Grand Lake Stream Guides Association** (mail@grandlakestreamguides.com, www.grandlakestreamguides.com). The website lists members and specialties. You can arrange for one of these skilled guides to lead you on a fishing expedition, wildlife or photographic safari, or canoeing trip for a half day or longer.

A great time to visit the village is the last full weekend in July, for the annual **Grand Lake Stream Folk Art Festival** (207/796-8199, 10 A.M.–5 P.M. Sat. and Sun., $5 one day, $8 both days), held on the town's grassy ballfield. Tents shelter approximately 50 top-notch, juried artisans. Nonstop bluegrass and folk music is another attraction. There's an exhibit highlighting the region's canoe-building tradition and another displaying antique and contemporary quilts. Breakfast, lunch, and snacks are available. Complementing the festival are lakeside barbecues by the guides, usually lobster on Friday evening, chicken on Saturday evening, with tickets available at the Pine Tree Store, across from the festival grounds. A contra dance takes place Saturday night, and a music jam, open to anyone, takes place Sunday morning. Leashed pets are welcome on festival grounds.

The volunteer-run **Grand Lake Stream Chamber of Commerce** (P.O. Box 124, Grand Lake Stream 04637, www.grandlakestream.com) produces a brochure listing accommodations, shops, and services. The **Pine Tree Store** (Water St., P.O. Box 129, Grand Lake Stream 04637, 207/796-5027, pinetreestore@earthlink.net) is also a good source of local information, and it sells pizza, sandwiches, and general store merchandise.

To get to Grand Lake Stream, head north on Route 1 from Calais through Princeton. About two miles north of Princeton, turn left (west) onto Grand Lake Stream Road (also called Princeton Road). Continue about 10 miles to the village.

© TOM NANGLE

Every July, the sleepy fishing town of Grand Lake Stream comes alive for a high-end Folk Arts Festival that includes displays and demonstrations by skilled artisans, nonstop music and food, and exhibits highlighting the town's quilt-making and canoe-building heritage.

theater. Programs include a rotating schedule of presentations on artists, birding, basketmaking, battles and forts, touch-tank demonstrations, and other topics.

The center offers a daily 2.5- to 3-hour **boat tour** that cruises down the St. Croix river and around St. Croix island, site of the first French settlement in the Northeast. Along the way, guides discuss the region's history and heritage, point out wildlife such as seals, eagles and ospreys, and even pull a lobster trap. The cost is $35 per adult, $22 for kids 6–12. Reservations are required by 12:30 P.M.; the boat leaves from the Calais town pier, behind the library, at 12:45 P.M., although that may vary with weather and tide.

Walking Tour

Pick up a copy of the *Walking Tour Guide to Calais Residential Historic District* at the Maine Visitor Information Center, on the waterfront. The guide, produced by the St. Croix Historical Society, briefly covers the town's history and maps and describes the architecture and early

owners of 23 historic houses, four of which are listed on the National Register of Historic Places.

St. Croix Island

Unless you have your own boat, you can't get over to 6.5-acre St. Croix Island, an International Historic Site under joint U.S. and Canadian jurisdiction (Rte. 1, Red Beach Cove, eight miles south of Calais, www.nps/sacr, free).

The island is the site of the pioneering colony established by French explorers Samuel de Champlain and Pierre du Gua (Sieur de Monts) in 1604. Doomed by disease, mosquitoes, lack of food, and a grueling winter, 35 settlers died; in spring, the emaciated survivors abandoned their effort and moved on to Nova Scotia. In 1969, archaeologists found graves of 23 victims, but the only monument on the island is a commemorative plaque dating from 1904.

The current in the St. Croix River is strong, and tidal ranges can be as high as 28 feet, so neophyte boaters shouldn't even attempt a crossing, but local residents often picnic and swim off the island's sandy beach on the southern end. For a better understanding of the historic colony, visit the Downeast Heritage Center. The attractive 16-acre roadside rest area on Route 1 at **Red Beach Cove** was greatly improved for the 400th anniversary of the settlement in 2004. A short heritage trail, with bronze statues depicting various key persons or cultures in the development of the colony, ends on the point with views of the island. Also here are picnic tables, restrooms, a gravel beach, and a boat launch. It's a great place to stop for a picnic.

Whitlock Mill Lighthouse

From the lovely Pikewoods Rest Area, beside Route 1, about four miles southeast of Calais, there's a prime view of 32-foot-high Whitlock Mill Lighthouse, on the southern shore of the St. Croix River. Built in 1892, the green flashing light is accessible only over private land, so check it out from this vantage point. Besides, you can also have a picnic break here.

Calais-Robbinston Milestones

A quirky little local feature, the Calais-Robbinston milestones are a dozen red-granite chunks marking each of the 12 miles between Robbinston and Calais. Presaging today's highway mileage markers, late-19th-century entrepreneur and journalist James S. Pike had the stones installed on the north side of Route 1 to keep track of the distance while training his pacing horses.

RECREATION

Parks and Preserves

More than 50 miles of trails and gravel roads wind through the 17,257-acre Baring Unit of the **Moosehorn National Wildlife Refuge** (Charlotte Rd., Baring, 207/454-7161, http://moosehorn.fws.gov/, sunrise–sunset daily, free), on the outskirts of Calais. Start with the 1.2-mile **nature trail** near the refuge headquarters, and get ready for major-league wildlife-watching: 35 mammal and 220 bird species have been spotted in the refuge's fields, forests, ponds, and marshes. Wear waterproof shoes and insect repellent. In August, help yourself to wild blueberries. During November deer-hunting season,

either avoid the refuge Monday–Saturday or wear a hunter-orange hat and vest. Trails are accessible by snowshoes, snowmobile, or cross-country skis in winter. To reach refuge headquarters, take Route 1 north from downtown Calais about three miles. Turn left onto the Charlotte Road and go 2.4 miles to the headquarters sign. The office is open 7:30 A.M.–4 P.M. Monday–Friday all year (except major national holidays); you can pick up free trail maps, bird checklists, and other informative brochures. If you want to help support the conservation of wildlife in eastern Maine and educational programs, you can join Friends of Moosehorn National Wildlife Refuge (R.R. 1, Box 202, Ste. 12, Baring 04694). A check for a mere $10 will do the trick.

By the way, if you don't have time to walk the trails, watch for the elevated man-made nesting platforms—avian high-rises for bald eagles—outside of Calais alongside Route 1 north (near the junction with the Charlotte Road). Depending on the season, you may spot a nesting pair or even a fledgling. The chicks (usually twins but occasionally triplets) hatch around mid-May and try their wings by early August. A 400-square-foot observation deck across Route 1 is the best place for eagle-watching.

Continuing on the Charlotte Road past the Moosehorn refuge headquarters, you'll come to **Round Lake** (locally called Round Pond), a lovely spot where you can picnic, swim, or put in a kayak or canoe. Across the road, with a great lake view, is the interesting old Round Pond Cemetery, dating from the early 19th century. (Why do graveyards always have the best views?) Just after the cemetery, a left turn puts you on Pennamaquam Lake Road (or Charlotte Road) toward Perry; a right turn takes you to Route 214, near Pembroke.

About six miles south of Calais, watch for signs pointing to **Devil's Head,** and take the dirt road on the river side. The 315-acre site has a mile of frontage on the St. Croix River estuary and views to St. Croix Island. It was acquired by a consortium of conservation-minded organizations as a nature-based tourist initiative. A road, with two parking areas, descends to the shoreline, and there are pit toilets and a marked hiking trail, approximately 1.5 miles looping from the road, leading to the highest point of coastal land north of Cadillac Mountain. According to locals, the headland was originally called d'Orville Head, but it morphed into Devil's Head.

Golf

At the nine-hole **St. Croix Country Club** (River Rd., Rte. 1, Calais 04619, 207/454-8875, late April–late Oct.), the toughest and most scenic hole is the seventh, one of five holes on the river side of Route 1. Starting times usually aren't needed for the course, on the southeastern outskirts of Calais.

Bicycling

If you've brought your own bike, shoulders are wide enough along most of Route 1 in this area for comfortable cycling. Figure on 26–28 miles each way between Eastport and Calais, perhaps a bit much for a one-day round-trip. If you're staying in Robbinston, figure on a 25-mile round-trip to pedal to Calais and cross over to St. Stephen. Robbinston is also a good base for biking to Eastport—about 30 miles round-trip, slightly longer if you take the more scenic **Shore Road,** east of and parallel to Route 1, between Perry and North Perry.

SHOPPING

If you stop in at **Katie's on the Cove** (Rte. 1, Mill Cove, Robbinston, 207/454-3297 or 800/494-5283, 10 A.M.–5 P.M. Tues.–Sat., late May–mid-Oct.), do it at your own risk. Chocoholics may need a restraining order. Joseph and Lea Sullivan's family operation, begun in 1982, has become a great success story. They now produce about four dozen varieties of homemade fudge, truffles, caramels, peanut brittle, even marzipan. Quality and prices are high. The candies are available in Washington County gift shops and elsewhere in Maine (including Maine Black Bear Paws at L.L. Bean), and the Sullivans do mail orders, but the aroma alone is worth a trip to the source. The shop, 12 miles southeast of Calais and about 15 miles west of Eastport, is no place for unruly or demanding kids—space is limited and the candy is pricey.

ENTERTAINMENT AND FESTIVALS

First-run films show at the three-screen **State Cinemas** (79 Main St., Calais, 207/454-8830, $5.75). Sunday matinees are usually at 1:30 P.M.

The **Brewer House** (Rte. 1, Robbinston, 12 miles south of Calais, 207/454-0333, $10 suggested donation) sponsors a chamber music festival in August. The concerts features faculty members of the Harald Saeverud String Quartet Program of the Pierre Monteux School, in Hancock. Director Trond Saeverud resides in Robbinston.

Calais, Maine, and St. Stephen, New Brunswick, collaborate the first or second week of August for the nine-day **International Festival** of dinners, concerts, dances, a craft fair, ball games, and cross-border parade and road race. Newspapers carry schedules (just be sure to note which events are on eastern time and which are on Atlantic time).

ACCOMMODATIONS

B&Bs

The classic, Greek Revival-style **M Brewer House** (Rte. 1, P.O. Box 88, Robbinston 04671, 207/454-0333, www.brewerhousebnb.com, $95–155) commands a knoll opposite the boat launch in Robbinston. Built by Captain John N. Marks in 1828, the house is distinguished by columns both in front and back, French nine-over-nine windows with carved Grecian moldings, Ionic pilasters, marble fireplaces, silver doorknobs, and an elliptical staircase—obviously the good captain was successful. The house also served as a stop on the Underground Railroad. The four guest rooms are furnished with antiques; some have ocean views, and some have shared baths. There's also a two-bedroom apartment, where pets are welcome. A full breakfast is served. The B&B has an artsy feel, as the J.B. Siem Gallery is on the property, and chamber concerts featuring violinist Trond Saeverud are presented here. The innkeepers speak English, German, Danish, Norwegian, Swedish, and a little Japanese.

Motels and Cottages

The gingerbread-trimmed **Redclyffe Shore Motel & Dining Room** (Rte. 1, Robbinston 04671, 207/454-3270, www.redclyffeshoremotorinn .com, $62–73) sits on a bluff above the St. Croix River as it widens into Passamaquoddy Bay. The 16 motel units have cable TV, phones, and sunset-facing river views. Redclyffe is locally popular for its greenhouse-style dining room, with ocean views, serving moderately priced entrées ($12–22) daily 5–9 P.M. Dinner reservations are a good idea in July and August, especially during the International Festival. It's 12 miles south of Calais. The motel is open mid-May through October; the restaurant is open mid-May through December.

About 5.5 miles southeast of Calais, family-run **M Heslin's Motel and Cottages** (Rte. 1, Calais 04619, 207/454-3762, www.mainerec.com/ heslins.html, May–late Oct.) has motel rooms ($62–70), cabins ($49–80), and rustic house-keeping cottages ($70–125/night, $420–750/week) on 60 acres alongside the St. Croix River. Some cottages are oceanfront. All units are heated and have TV; motel rooms have air-conditioning and phones; the more expensive cottages have kitchens. A big plus is a heated swimming pool. In the motel's informal river-view restaurant, steaks and fresh seafood ($12–20) are the specialties, served daily 5–9 P.M. Small portions are available for kids and seniors. The cocktail lounge draws a loyal local clientele.

Campgrounds

High enough for a great view of the St. Croix River, **Hilltop Campground** (371 Ridge Rd., R.R. 1, Box 298, Robbinston 04671, 207/454-3985, mid-May–mid-Oct.) has 84 tent and RV sites on 100 wooded and open acres, plus a pool, a trout pond, a small store, and laundry facilities. Sites are $15–22 a night.

FOOD

Miscellany

If you're near downtown Calais, order picnic sandwiches to go at **Border Town Subz** (311 Main St., Calais, 207/454-8562, 10 A.M.–9 P.M. Mon.–Fri. and 11 A.M.–6 P.M. Sat.), a reliable local favorite. There are lots of choices, including vegetarian, and three sandwich lengths. It's open all year but closes at 6 P.M. weekdays and at 3 P.M. Saturday September–May.

Another choice for picnic fixings, cottage staples, and other goodies is the **Sunrise County Farmers' Market** (11 A.M.–3 P.M. Tues. late June–Oct.). Look for it across from the information center on Union Street.

Casual Dining

White Christmas lights brighten the ceiling of **M Bernardini's** (257 Main St., Calais, 207/454-2237, 11 A.M.–8 P.M. Mon.–Sat.), a very popular downtown restaurant that has earned its repute with always-reliable Tuscany-inspired Italian cuisine, augmented by a few surprises, such as a crabmeat-stuffed avocado special that's a real winner; entrées are $10–14. The pleasant dining room is accented by wood-work salvaged from a local church. Save room for the tiramisu.

Calais' other restaurant is on a side street, off Route 1, just north of the center of town. **The Chandler House** (20 Chandler St., Calais, 207/454-7922, 4–11 P.M. Tues.–Sun.) serves the usuals and is known for its prime rib.

INFORMATION AND SERVICES

Information

On the banks of the St. Croix River, near the Ferry Point Bridge just off Route 1 (Main Street) in downtown Calais, is an especially convenient and attractive **Maine Visitor Information Center** (7 Union St., Calais, 207/454-2211), with clean restrooms and scads of brochures, including those produced by the **St. Croix Valley Chamber of Commerce** (207/454-2308 or 888/422-3112, www.visitcalais.com). The information center is open 9 A.M.–5 P.M. daily all year (and some evening hours in summer).

Hospitals

Calais Regional Hospital (50 Franklin St., Calais, 207/454-7521) is Washington County's largest hospital and has round-the-clock emergency care.

The Down East Coast

Libraries

Next door to the information center is the imposing stone **Calais Free Library** (9 Union St., Calais, 207/454-2758, noon–8 P.M. Mon. and Tues., 9 A.M.–5 P.M. Wed. and Fri., and 9 A.M.–6 P.M. Thurs.).

Public Restrooms

Restrooms are available at the Maine Visitor Information Center (7 Union St., Calais) and the St. Croix International Heritage Site (in Red Beach). The headquarters of the Moosehorn National Wildlife Refuge has portable toilets

Getting There

The nearest major airport is Bangor International Airport.

West Bus Service (800/596-2823) operates one trip a day in each direction between Bangor (connecting with Greyhound and Concord Trailways buses and Bangor International Airport) and Calais, via Ellsworth, with a scheduled stop in Perry. Flag stops are available en route, including Jonesboro, Columbia, Milbridge, Whiting, Dennysville, and Pembroke.

Crossing into Canada

If you plan to cross into Canada, you'll have to pass Customs checkpoints on both the Calais (U.S., 207/454-3621) and St. Stephen (Canada, 506/466-2363) ends of the bridges.

Pay attention to your watch, too—Calais is on eastern time, St. Stephen (as well as the rest of Canada's Maritime Provinces) is on Atlantic time.

Know
Coastal Maine

The Land

IN THE BEGINNING . . .

Maine is an outdoor classroom for Geology 101, a living lesson in what the glaciers did and how they did it. Geologically, Maine is something of a youngster; the oldest rocks, found in the Chain of Ponds area in the western part of the state, are only 1.6 billion years old—more than two billion years younger than the world's oldest rocks.

But most significant is the great ice sheet that began to spread over Maine about 25,000 years ago, during the late Wisconsin Ice Age. As it moved southward from Canada, this continental glacier scraped, gouged, pulverized, and depressed the bedrock in its path. On it continued, charging up the north faces of mountains, clipping off their tops, and moving southward, leaving behind jagged cliffs on the mountains' southern faces and odd deposits of stone and clay. By about 21,000 years ago, glacial ice extended well over the Gulf of Maine, perhaps as far as the Georges Bank fishing grounds.

But all that began to change with meltdown, beginning about 18,000 years ago. As the glacier melted and receded, ocean water moved in, covering much of the coastal plain and working its way inland up the rivers. By 11,000 years ago, glaciation had pulled back from all but a few minor corners at the top of Maine, revealing the south coast's beaches and the unusual geologic traits—eskers and erratics, kettleholes and moraines, even a fjord—that make the rest of the state such a fascinating natural laboratory.

Today's Landscape

Three distinct looks make up the contemporary Maine coastal landscape. (Inland—beyond the scope of this book—are even more distinct biomes: serious woodlands and mountains as well as lakes and ponds and rolling fields.)

© TOM NANGLE

Sand Beach is one of the highlights along Acadia National Park's Park Loop.

ESTUARIES AND MUDFLATS

Maine's estuaries, where fresh and salt water meet, are ecosystems of outstanding biological importance. South of Cape Elizabeth, where the Maine coast is low and sandy, estuaries harbor large salt marshes of spartina grasses that can tolerate the frequent variations in salinity as runoff and tides fluctuate. Producing an estimated four times more plant material than an equivalent area of wheat, these spartina marshes provide abundant nutrients and shelter for a host of marine organisms that ultimately account for as much as 60 percent of the value of the state's commercial fisheries.

a fishing Great Blue Heron

The tidal range along the Maine coast varies 9–26 vertical feet, southwest to northeast. Where the tide inundates sheltered estuaries for more than a few hours at a time, spartina grasses cannot take hold, and mudflats dominate. Although it may look like a barren wasteland at low tide, a mudflat is also a highly productive environment, and home to abundant marinelife. Several species of tiny primitive worms called nematodes can inhabit the mud in densities of 2,000 or more per square inch. Larger worm species are also very common. One, the bloodworm, grows up to a foot in length and is harvested in quantity for use as sportfishing bait.

More highly savored among the mudflat residents is the soft-shelled clam, famous for its outstanding flavor and an essential ingredient of an authentic Maine lobsterbake. But because clams are suspension feeders—filtering phytoplankton through their long siphon, or "neck"—they can accumulate pollutants that cause illness, including hepatitis. Many Maine mudflats are closed to clam harvesting because of leaking septic systems, so it's best to check with the state's Department of Marine Resources or the local municipal office before digging a mess of clams yourself.

For birds—and birders—salt marshes and mudflats are an unparalleled attraction. Long-legged wading birds such as glossy ibis, snowy egret, little blue heron, great blue heron, tricolored heron, green heron, and black-crowned night heron frequent the marshes in great numbers throughout the summer, hunting the shallow waters for mummichogs and other small salt-marsh fish, crustaceans, and invertebrates. From mid-May to early June, and then again from mid-July until mid-September, migrating shorebirds pass through Maine to and from their subarctic breeding grounds. On a good day, a discerning birder can find 17 or more species of shorebirds probing the mudflats and marshes with pointed bills in search of their preferred foods. In turn, the large flocks of shorebirds don't escape the notice of their own predators—merlins and peregrine falcons dash in to catch a meal.

(Contributed by William P. Hancock, Maine Audubon)

Know Coastal Maine

© TOM NANGLE

Know Coastal Maine

THE ROCKY SHORELINE AND THE MARINE ENVIRONMENT

On Maine's more exposed rocky shores—the dominant shoreline from Cape Elizabeth all the way Down East to Lubec—where currents and waves keep mud and sand from accumulating, the plant and animal communities are entirely different from those in the inland aquatic areas. The most important requirement for life in this impenetrable, rockbound environment is probably the ability to hang on tight. Barnacles, the calcium-armored crustaceans that attach themselves to the rocks immediately below the high-tide line, have developed a fascinating battery of adaptations to survive not only pounding waves but also prolonged exposure to air, solar heat, and extreme winter cold. Glued in place, however, they cannot escape being eaten by dog whelks, the predatory snails that also inhabit this intertidal zone. Whelks are larger and more elongate than the more numerous and ubiquitous periwinkle, accidentally transplanted from Europe in the mid-19th century.

Also hanging onto these rocks, but at a lower level, are the brown algae—seaweeds. Like a marine forest, the four species of rockweed provide shelter for a wide variety of life beneath their fronds. A world of discovery awaits those who make the effort to go out onto the rocks at low tide and look under the clumps of seaweed and into the tidepools they shelter. Venture into these chilly waters with mask, fins, and wetsuit and still another world opens for natural history exploration. Beds of blue mussels, sea urchins, sea stars, and sea cucumbers dot the bottom close to shore. In crevices between and beneath the rocks lurk rock crabs and lobsters. Now a symbol of the Maine coast and the delicious seafood it provides, the lobster was once considered "poor man's food"—so plentiful that it was spread on fields as fertilizer. Although lobsters are far less common than they once were, they are one of Maine's most closely monitored species, and their population continues to support a large and thriving commercial fishing industry.

Sadly, the same cannot be said for most of Maine's other commercially harvested marine fish. When Europeans first came to these shores four centuries ago, cod, haddock, halibut, hake, flounder, herring, and tuna were abundant. No longer. Overharvested, their seabed habitat torn up by relentless dragging, these groundfish have all but disappeared. It will be decades before these species can recover—and then only if effective regulations can be put in place soon.

The familiar doglike face of the harbor seal, often seen peering alertly from the surface just offshore, provides a reminder that wildlife populations are resilient—if given a chance. A century ago, there was a bounty on harbor seals because it was thought they ate too many lobsters and fish. Needless to say, neither fish nor lobsters increased when the seals all but disappeared. With the bounty's repeal and the advent of legal protection, Maine's harbor seal population has bounced back to an estimated 15,000–20,000. Scores of them can regularly be seen basking on offshore ledges, drying their tan, brown, black, silver, or reddish coats in the sun. Though it's tempting to approach for a closer look, avoid bringing a boat too near these haulout ledges, as it causes the seals to flush into the water and imposes an unnecessary stress on the pups, which already face a first-year mortality rate of 30 percent.

Positive changes in our relationships with wildlife are even more apparent with the return of birds to the Maine coast. Watching the numerous herring gulls and great black-backed gulls soaring on a fresh ocean breeze today, it's hard to imagine that a century ago, egg collecting had so reduced their numbers that they were a rare sight. In 1903, there were just three pairs of common eiders left in Maine; today, 25,000 pairs nest along the coast. With creative help from dedicated researchers using sound recordings, decoys, and prepared burrows, Atlantic puffins are recolonizing historic offshore nesting islands. Osprey and bald eagles, almost free of the lingering vestiges of DDT and other pesticides, now range the length of the coast and up Maine's major rivers.

(Contributed by William P. Hancock, Maine Audubon)

Along the **Southern Coast,** from Kittery to Portland, are fine-sand beaches, marshlands, and only the occasional rocky headland. The **Mid-Coast** and **Penobscot Bay,** from Portland to the Penobscot River, feature one finger of rocky land after another, all jutting into the Gulf of Maine and all incredibly scenic. **Acadia** and the **Down East Coast,** from the Penobscot River to Eastport and including fantastic Acadia National Park, has many similarities to the Mid-Coast (gorgeous rocky peninsulas, offshore islands, granite everywhere), but, except on Mount Desert Island, takes on a different look and feel by virtue of its slower pace, higher tides, and quieter villages.

GEOGRAPHY

Bounded by the Gulf of Maine (Atlantic Ocean), the St. Croix River, New Brunswick Province, the St. John River, Québec Province, and the state of New Hampshire (and the only state in the Union bordered by only one other state), Maine is the largest of the six New England states, roughly equivalent in size to the five others combined—offering plenty of space to hike, bike, camp, sail, swim, or just hang out. The state—and the coastline—extends from 43°05′ to 47°28′ north latitude, and 66°56′ to 80°50′ west longitude. (Technically, Maine dips even farther southeast to take in five islands in the offshore Isles of Shoals archipelago.) It's all stitched together by 22,574 miles of highways and 3,561 bridges.

Maine's more than 5,000 rivers and streams provide nearly half of the watershed for the Gulf of Maine. The major rivers are the Penobscot (350 miles), the St. John (211 miles), the Androscoggin (175 miles), the Kennebec (150 miles), the Saco (104 miles), and the St. Croix (75 miles). The St. John and its tributaries flow northeast; all the others flow more or less south or southeast.

CLIMATE

Whoever invented the state's oldest cliché—"If you don't like the weather, wait a minute"—must have spent at least several minutes in Maine.

The good news, though, is that if the weather is lousy, it's bound to change before too long. And when it does, it's intoxicating. Brilliant, cloud-free Maine weather has lured many a visitor to put down roots, buy a retirement home, or at least invest in a summer retreat.

The serendipity of it all necessitates two caveats: *Always pack warmer clothing than you think you'll need.* And *never arrive without a sweater or jacket—even at the height of summer.*

The National Weather Service assigns Maine's coastline a climatological category distinct from climatic types found in the interior.

The **coastal** category, which includes Portland, runs from Kittery northeast to Eastport and about 20 miles inland. Here, the ocean moderates the climate, making coastal winters warmer and summers cooler than in the interior (relatively speaking, of course). From early June through August, the Portland area—fairly typical of coastal weather—may have 3–8 days of temperatures over 90°F, 25–40 days over 80°, 14–24 days of fog, and 5–10 inches of rain. Normal annual precipitation for the Portland area is 44 inches of rain and 71 inches of snow (the snow total is misleading, though, since intermittent thaws clear away much of the base).

The Seasons

Maine has four distinct seasons: summer, fall, winter, and mud. Lovers of spring need to look elsewhere in March, the lowest month on the popularity scale with its mud-caked vehicles, soggy everything, irritable temperaments, tank-trap roads, and often the worst snowstorm of the year.

Summer can be idyllic—with moderate temperatures, clear air, and wispy breezes—but it can also close in with fog, rain, and chills. Prevailing winds are from the southwest. Officially, summer runs from June 20 or 21 to September 20 or 21, but June, July, and August is more like it, with temperatures in the Portland area averaging 70°F during the day and in the 50s at night. The normal growing season is 148 days.

A poll of Mainers might well show autumn as

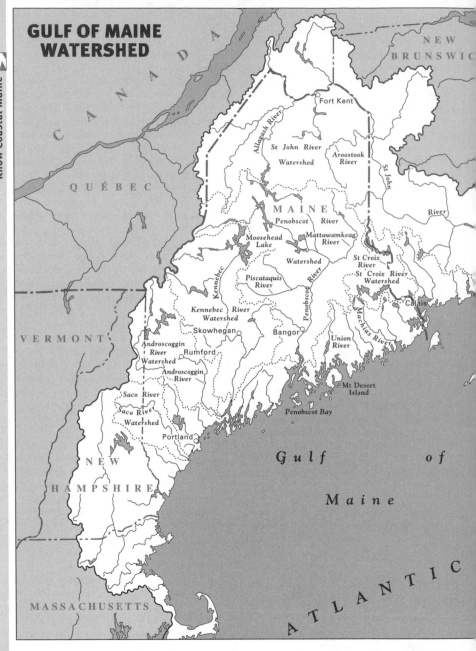

GULF OF MAINE
WATERSHED

CANADA

NEW
BRUNSWIC

QUÉBEC

Fort Kent

Allagash River

St John River
Watershed

Aroostook
River

St John

MAINE

Penobscot River

River

Moosehead
Lake

Mattawamkeag
River

Kennebec

Watershed

Piscataquis
River

Penobscot River

St Croix
River

St Croix River
Watershed

Calais

Kennebec River
Watershed

Skowhegan

Bangor

Union
River

Machias River

VERMONT

Androscoggin
River
Watershed

Rumford

Androscoggin
River

Mt Desert
Island

Saco River

Saco River
Watershed

Portland

Penobscot Bay

Gulf   of

NEW

HAMPSHIRE

Maine

MASSACHUSETTS

ATLANTIC

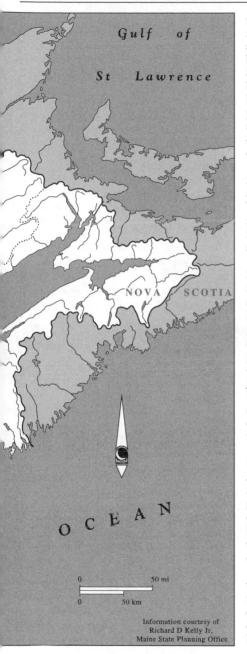

Gulf of

St Lawrence

NOVA SCOTIA

OCEAN

MOON

| 0 | | 50 mi |
| 0 | | 50 km |

Information courtesy of
Richard D Kelly Jr,
Maine State Planning Office

the favorite season—days are still warmish, nights are cool, winds are optimum for sailors, and the foliage is brilliant. Fall colors usually begin appearing far to the north about mid-September, reaching their peak in that region by the end of the month. The last of the color begins in late September in the southernmost part of the state and fades by mid-October. Early autumn, however, is also the height of hurricane season, the only potential flaw this time of year.

Winter, officially December 20 or 21 to March 20 or 21, means deep snow and cold inland and an unpredictable potpourri along the coastline. When the cold and snow hit the coast, it's time for cross-country skiing, ice fishing, snowshoeing, ice-skating, ice-climbing, and winter trekking and camping.

Spring, officially March 20 or 21 to June 20 or 21, is the frequent butt of jokes. It's an ill-defined season that arrives much too late and departs all too quickly. Ice floes dot inland lakes and ponds until "ice-out" (the departure of winter ice from ponds, lakes, rivers, and streams), in early to mid-May; spring planting can't occur until well into May; lilacs explode in late May and disappear by mid-June. And just when you finally can enjoy being outside, blackflies stretch their wings and satisfy their hunger pangs. Along the coast, onshore breezes often keep the pesky creatures to a minimum.

Northeasters and Hurricanes

A northeaster is a counterclockwise, swirling storm that brings wild winds out of—you guessed it—the northeast. These storms can occur any time of year, whenever the conditions brew them up. Depending on the season, the winds are accompanied by rain, sleet, snow, or all of them together.

Hurricane season officially runs June–November but is most prevalent late August–September. Some years, the Maine coast remains out of harm's way; other years, head-on hurricanes and even glancing blows have eroded beaches, flooded roads, splintered boats, downed trees, knocked out power, and inflicted major residential and commercial damage. Winds—the greatest culprit—average 74–90 mph. A **hurricane watch** is announced on radio and TV about 36 hours beforehand, followed by a **hurricane warning,** indicating that the storm is imminent. Find shelter, away from plate-glass windows, and wait it out. If especially high winds are predicted, make every effort to secure yourself, your vehicle, and your possessions. Resist the urge to head for the shore to watch the show; rogue waves, combined with ultrahigh tides, have been known to sweep away unwary onlookers.

Sea Smoke and Fog

Sea smoke and fog, two atmospheric phenomena resulting from opposing conditions, are only distantly related. But both can radically affect visibility and therefore be hazardous. In winter, when the ocean is at least 40°F warmer than the air, billowy sea smoke rises from the water, creating great photo ops for camera buffs but especially dangerous conditions for mariners.

In any season, when the ocean (or lake or land) is colder than the air, fog sets in, creating perilous conditions for drivers, mariners, and pilots. Romantics, however, see it otherwise, reveling in the womblike ambience and the muffled moans of foghorns. Between April and October, Portland averages about 31 days with heavy fog, when visibility may be a quarter mile or less.

Storm Warnings

The National Weather Service's official daytime signal system for wind velocity consists of a series of flags representing specific wind speeds and sea conditions. Beachgoers and anyone planning to venture out in a kayak, canoe, sailboat, or powerboat should heed these signals. The flags are posted on all public beaches, and warnings are announced on TV and radio weather broadcasts, as well as on cable TV's Weather Channel and the NOAA broadcast network.

History

Prehistoric Mainers: The Paleoindians

As the great continental glacier receded northwestward out of Maine about 11,000 years ago, some prehistoric grapevine must have alerted small bands of hunter-gatherers—fur-clad Paleoindians—to the scrub sprouting in the tundra, burgeoning mammal populations, and the ocean's bountiful food supply. Because come they did—at first seasonally, then year-round. Anyone who thinks tourism is a recent Maine phenomenon need only explore the shoreline in Damariscotta, Boothbay Harbor, and Bar Harbor, where heaps of cast-off oyster shells and clamshells document the migration of early Native Americans from woodlands to waterfront. "The shore" has been a summertime magnet for millennia.

Archaeological evidence from the Archaic period in Maine—roughly 8000–1000 B.C.—is fairly scant, but paleontologists have unearthed stone tools and weapons and small campsites attesting to a nomadic lifestyle supported by fishing and hunting (with fishing becoming more extensive as time went on). Toward the end of the tradition, during the late Archaic period, emerged a rather anomalous Indian culture known officially as the Moorehead phase but informally called the Red Paint People; the name is due to their curious trait of using a distinctive red ocher (pulverized hematite) in burials. Dark red puddles and stone artifacts have led excavators to burial pits as far north as the St. John River. Just as mysteriously as they had arrived, the Red Paint People disappeared abruptly and inexplicably around 1800 B.C.

Following them almost immediately—and almost as suddenly—hunter-gatherers of the Susquehanna Tradition arrived from well to the south, moved across Maine's interior as far as the St. John River, and remained until about 1600 B.C., when they, too, enigmatically vanished. Excavations have turned up relatively so-phisticated stone tools and evidence that they cremated their dead. It was nearly 1,000 years before a major new cultural phase appeared.

The next great leap forward was marked by the advent of pottery making, introduced about 700 B.C. The Ceramic period stretched to the 16th century, and cone-shaped pots (initially stamped, later incised with coiled-rope motifs) survived until the introduction of metals from Europe. Houses of sorts—seasonal wigwam-style dwellings for fishermen and their families—appeared along the coast and on offshore islands.

The Europeans Arrive

The identity of the first Europeans to set foot in Maine is a matter of debate. Historians dispute the romantically popular notion that Norse explorers checked out this part of the New World as early as A.D. 1000. Even an 11th-century Norse coin found in 1961 in Brooklin (on the Blue Hill Peninsula) probably was carried there from farther north.

Not until the late 15th century, the onset of the great Age of Discovery, did credible reports of the New World (including what's now Maine) filter back to Europe's courts and universities. Thanks to innovations in naval architecture, shipbuilding, and navigation, astonishingly courageous fellows crossed the Atlantic in search of rumored treasure and new routes for reaching it.

John Cabot, sailing from England aboard the ship *Mathew,* may have been the first European to reach Maine, in 1498, but historians have never confirmed a landing site. No question remains, however, about the account of Giovanni da Verrazzano, an Italian explorer commanding *La Dauphine* under the French flag, who reached the Maine coast in May 1524, probably at the tip of the Phippsburg Peninsula. Encountering less-than-friendly Native Americans, Verrazzano did a minimum of business and sailed onward. His brother's map of the site labels it "The Land of Bad People." Esteban Gomez and John Rut followed in Verrazzano's wake, but nothing came of their exploits.

Nearly half a century passed before the Maine coast turned up again on European explorers' itineraries. This time, interest was fueled by reports of a Brigadoon-like area called Norumbega (or Oranbega, as one map had it), a myth that arose, gathered steam, and took on a life of its own in the decades following Verrazzano's voyage.

By the early 17th century, when Europeans began arriving in more than twos and threes and getting serious about colonization, Native American agriculture was already under way at the mouths of the Saco and Kennebec Rivers, the cod fishery was thriving on offshore islands, Indians far to the north were hot to trade furs for European goodies, and the birch-bark canoe was the transport of choice on inland waterways.

In mid-May 1602, Bartholomew Gosnold, en route to a settlement off Cape Cod aboard the *Concord,* landed along Maine's southern coast. The following year, merchant trader Martin Pring and his boats *Speedwell* and *Discoverer* explored farther Down East, backtracked to Cape Cod, and returned to England with tales that inflamed curiosity and enough sassafras to satisfy royal appetites. Pring produced a detailed survey of the Maine coast from Kittery to Bucksport, including offshore islands.

On May 18, 1605, George Waymouth, skippering the *Archangel,* reached Monhegan Island, 11 miles off the Maine coast, and moored for the night in Monhegan Harbor (still treacherous even today, exposed to the weather from the southwest and northeast and subject to meteorological beatings and heaving swells. Yachting guides urge sailors not to expect to anchor, moor, or tie up there). The next day, Waymouth crossed the bay and scouted the mainland. He took five Indians hostage and sailed up the St. George River, near present-day Thomaston. As maritime historian Roger Duncan has put it,

The Plimoth Pilgrims were little boys in short pants when George Waymouth was exploring this coastline.

Waymouth returned to England and awarded his hostages to officials Sir John Popham and Sir Ferdinando Gorges, who, their curiosity piqued, quickly agreed to subsidize the colonization effort.

In 1607, the *Gift of God* and the *Mary and John* sailed for the New World carrying two of Waymouth's captives. After returning them to their native Pemaquid area, Captains George Popham and Raleigh Gilbert continued westward, establishing a colony (St. George or Fort George) at the tip of the Phippsburg Peninsula in mid-August 1607 and exploring the shoreline between Portland and Pemaquid. Frigid weather, untimely deaths (including Popham's), and a storehouse fire doomed what's called the Popham Colony, but not before the hundred or so settlers built the 30-ton pinnace *Virginia,* the New World's first such vessel. When Gilbert received word of an inheritance waiting in England, he and the remaining colonists returned to the Old World.

In 1614, swashbuckling Captain John Smith, exploring from the Penobscot River westward to Cape Cod, reached Monhegan Island nine years after Waymouth's visit. Smith's meticulous map of the region was the first to use the "New England" appellation, and the 1616 publication of his *Description of New-England* became the catalyst for permanent settlements.

The French and the English Square Off

English dominance of exploration west of the Penobscot River in the early 17th century coincided roughly with French activity east of the river.

In 1604, French nobleman Pierre du Gua, Sieur de Monts, set out with cartographer Samuel de Champlain to map the coastline, first reaching Nova Scotia's Bay of Fundy and then sailing up the St. Croix River. In midriver, just west of present-day Calais, a crew planted gardens and erected buildings on today's St. Croix Island while de Monts and Champlain went off exploring. The two men reached the island Champlain named *l'Isle des Monts Deserts* and present-day Bangor before returning to face the winter with their ill-fated compatriots. Scurvy, lack of fuel and water, and a ferocious winter wiped out nearly half of the 79 men. In spring 1605, de Monts, Champlain, and other survivors headed southwest, exploring the coastline all the way to Cape Cod before heading northeast again and settling permanently at Nova Scotia's Port Royal (now Annapolis Royal).

Eight years later, French Jesuit missionaries en route to the Kennebec River ended up on Mount Desert Island and, with a band of French laymen, set about establishing the St. Sauveur settlement. But leadership squabbles led to building delays, and English marauder Samuel Argall—assigned to reclaim English territory—arrived to find them easy prey. The colony was leveled, the settlers were set adrift in small boats, the priests were carted off to Virginia, and Argall moved on to destroy Port Royal.

By the 1620s, more than four dozen English fishing vessels were combing New England waters in search of cod, and year-round fishing depots had sprung up along the coast between Pemaquid and Portland. At the same time, English trappers and dealers began usurping the Indians' fur trade—a valuable income source.

The Massachusetts Bay Colony was established in 1630, and England's Council of New England, headed by Sir Ferdinando Gorges, began making vast land grants throughout Maine, giving rise to permanent coastal settlements, many dependent on agriculture. Among the earliest communities were Kittery, York, Wells, Saco, Scarborough, Falmouth, and Pemaquid—places where they tilled the acidic soil, fished the waters, eked out a barely-above-subsistence living, coped with predators and endless winters, bartered goods and services, and set up local governments and courts.

By the late 17th century, as these communities expanded, so did their requirements and responsibilities. Roads and bridges were built, preachers and teachers were hired, and militias were organized to deal with internecine and Indian skirmishes.

Even though England yearned to control the entire Maine coastline, her turf, realistically, was primarily south and west of the Penobscot River. The French had expanded from their Canadian colony of Acadia, for the most part north and east of the Penobscot. Unlike the absentee bosses who controlled the English territory, French merchants actually showed up, forming good relationships with the Indians and cornering the market in fishing, lumbering, and fur trading. And French Jesuit priests converted many a Native American to Catholicism. Intermittently, overlapping Anglo-French land claims sparked locally messy conflicts.

In the mid-17th century, the strategic heart of French administration and activity in Maine was Fort Pentagoet, a sturdy stone outpost built in 1635 in what is now Castine. From here, the French controlled coastal trade between the St. George River and Mount Desert Island and well up the Penobscot River. In 1654, England captured and occupied the fort and much of French Acadia, but, thanks to the 1667 Treaty of Breda, title returned to the French in 1670, and Pentagoet briefly became Acadia's capital.

A short but nasty Dutch foray against Acadia in 1674 resulted in Pentagoet's destruction ("level'd with ye ground," by one account) and the raising of a third national flag over Castine.

The Indian Wars (1675–1760)

Caught in the middle of 17th- and 18th-century Anglo-French disputes throughout Maine were the Wabanaki (People of the Dawn), the collective name for the state's major Native American tribal groups, all of whom spoke Algonquian languages. Modern ethnographers label these groups the Micmacs, Maliseets, Passamaquoddies, and Penobscots.

In the early 17th century, exposure to European diseases took its toll, wiping out three-quarters of the Wabanaki in the years 1616–1619. Opportunistic English and French traders quickly moved into the breach, and the Indians struggled to survive and regroup.

But regroup they did. Less than three generations later, a series of six Indian wars began, lasting nearly a century and pitting the Wabanaki most often against the English but occasionally against other Wabanaki. The conflicts, largely provoked by Anglo-French tensions in Europe, were King Philip's War (1675–1678), King William's War (1688–1699), Queen Anne's War (1703–1713), Dummer's War (1721–1726), King George's War

(1744–1748), and the French and Indian War (1754–1760). Not until a get-together in 1762 at Fort Pownall (now Stockton Springs) did peace effectively return to the region—just in time for the heating up of the revolutionary movement.

Comes the Revolution

Near the end of the last Indian War, just beyond Maine's eastern border, a watershed event led to more than a century of cultural and political fallout. During the so-called Acadian Dispersal, in 1755, the English expelled from Nova Scotia 10,000 French-speaking Acadians who refused to pledge allegiance to the British Crown. Scattered as far south as Louisiana and west toward New Brunswick and Québec, the Acadians lost farms, homes, and possessions in this *grand dérangement.* Not until 1785 was land allocated for resettlement of Acadians along both sides of the Upper St. John River, where thousands of their descendants remain today. Henry Wadsworth Longfellow's epic poem *Evangeline* dramatically relates the sorry Acadian saga.

In the District of Maine, on the other hand, with relative peace following a century of intermittent warfare, settlement again exploded, particularly in the southernmost counties. The 1764 census tallied Maine's population at just under 25,000; a decade later, the number had doubled. New towns emerged almost overnight, often heavily subsidized by wealthy investors from the parent Massachusetts Bay Colony. With almost 4,000 residents, the largest town in the district was Falmouth (later renamed Portland).

In 1770, 27 Maine towns became eligible, based on population, to send representatives to the Massachusetts General Court, the colony's legislative body. But only six coastal towns could actually afford to send anyone, sowing seeds of resentment among settlers who were thus saddled with taxes without representation. Sporadic mob action accompanied unrest in southern Maine, but the flashpoint occurred in the Boston area.

On April 18, 1775, Paul Revere set out on America's most famous horseback ride—from Lexington to Concord, Massachusetts—to announce the onset of what became the American

Revolution. Most of the Revolution's action occurred south of Maine, but not all of it.

In June, the Down East outpost of Machias was the site of the war's first naval engagement. The well-armed but unsuspecting British vessel HMS *Margaretta* sailed into the bay and was besieged by local residents angry about a Machias merchant's sweetheart deal with the British. Before celebrating their David-and-Goliath victory, the rebels captured the *Margaretta,* killed her captain, then captured two more British ships sent to the rescue.

In the fall of 1775, Colonel Benedict Arnold—better known to history as a notorious turncoat—assembled 1,100 sturdy men for a flawed and futile "March on Québec" to dislodge the English. From Newburyport, Massachusetts, they sailed to the mouth of the Kennebec River, near Bath, and then headed inland with the tide. In Pittston, six miles south of Augusta and close to the head of navigation, they transferred to a fleet of 220 locally made bateaux and laid over three nights at Fort Western in Augusta. Then they set off, poling, paddling, and portaging their way upriver. Skowhegan, Norridgewock, and Chain of Ponds were among the landmarks along the grueling route. The men endured cold, hunger, swamps, disease, dense underbrush, and the loss of nearly 600 of their comrades before reaching Québec in late 1775. In the Kennebec River Valley, Arnold Trail historical signposts today mark highlights (or, more aptly, lowlights) of the expedition.

Four years later, another futile attempt to dislodge the British, this time in the District of Maine, resulted in America's worst naval defeat until World War II—a little-publicized debacle called the Penobscot Expedition. On August 14, 1779, as more than 40 American warships and transports carrying more than 2,000 Massachusetts men blockaded Castine to flush out a relatively small enclave of leftover Brits, a seven-vessel Royal Navy fleet appeared. Despite their own greater numbers, about 30 of the American ships turned tail up the Penobscot River. The captains torched their vessels, exploding the ammunition and leaving the survivors to walk in disgrace to

Augusta or even Boston. Each side took close to a hundred casualties, three commanders—including Paul Revere—were court-martialed, and Massachusetts was about $7 million poorer.

The American Revolution officially came to a close on September 3, 1783, with the signing of the Treaty of Paris between the United States and Great Britain. The U.S.-Canada border was set at the St. Croix River, but, in a massive oversight, boundary lines were left unresolved for thousands of square miles in the northern District of Maine.

Trade Troubles and the War of 1812

In 1807, President Thomas Jefferson imposed the Embargo Act, banning trade with foreign entities—specifically, France and Britain. With thousands of miles of coastline and harbor villages dependent on trade for revenue and basic necessities, Maine reeled. By the time the act was repealed, under President James Madison in 1809, France and Britain were almost unscathed, but the bottom had dropped out of New England's economy.

An active smuggling operation based in Eastport kept Mainers from utter despair, but the economy still had continued its downslide. In 1812, the fledgling United States declared war on Great Britain, again disrupting coastal trade. In the fall of 1814, the situation reached its nadir when the British invaded the Maine coast and occupied all the shoreline between the St. Croix and Penobscot Rivers. Later that same year, the Treaty of Ghent finally halted the squabble, forced the British to withdraw from Maine, and allowed the locals to get on with economic recovery.

Statehood

In October 1819, Mainers held a constitutional convention at the First Parish Church on Congress Street in Portland. (Known affectionately as "Old Jerusalem," the church was later replaced by the present-day structure.) The convention crafted a constitution modeled on that of Massachusetts, with two notable differences: Maine would have no official church (Massachusetts had the Puritans' Congregational Church), and Maine would place no religious requirements or restrictions on its gubernatorial candidates. When votes came in from 241 Maine towns, only nine voted against ratification.

For Maine, March 15, 1820, was one of those good news/bad news days: after 35 years of separatist agitation, the District of Maine broke from Massachusetts (signing the separation allegedly, and disputedly, at the Jameson Tavern in Freeport) and became the 23rd state in the Union. However, the Missouri Compromise, enacted by Congress only 12 days earlier to balance admission of slave and free states, mandated that the slave state of Missouri be admitted on the same day. Maine had abolished slavery in 1788, and there was deep resentment over the linkage.

Portland became the new state's capital (albeit only briefly; it switched to Augusta in 1832), and William King, one of statehood's most outspoken advocates, became the first governor.

Trouble in the North Country

Without an official boundary established on Maine's far northern frontier, turf battles were always simmering just under the surface. Timber was the sticking point—everyone wanted the vast wooded acreage. Finally, in early 1839, militia reinforcements descended on the disputed area, heating up what has come to be known as the Aroostook War, a border confrontation with no battles and no casualties (except a farmer who was shot by friendly militia). It's a blip in the historical timeline, but remnants of fortifications in Houlton, Fort Fairfield, and Fort Kent keep the story alive today. By March 1839, a truce was negotiated, and the 1842 Webster-Ashburton Treaty established the border once and for all.

Maine in the Civil War

In the 1860s, with the state's population slightly more than 600,000, more than 70,000 Mainers suited up and went off to fight in the Civil War—the greatest per capita show of force of any northern state. About 18,000 of them died in the conflict. Thirty-one Mainers were Union Army generals, the best known being Joshua L.

Chamberlain, a Bowdoin College professor, who commanded the Twentieth Maine regiment and later became president of the college and governor of Maine.

During the war, young battlefield artist Winslow Homer, who later settled in Prouts Neck, south of Portland, created wartime sketches regularly for such publications as *Harper's Weekly*. In Washington, Maine Senator Hannibal Hamlin was elected vice president under Abraham Lincoln in 1860 (he was removed from the ticket in favor of Andrew Johnson when Lincoln came up for reelection in 1864).

Maine Comes into Its Own

After the Civil War, Maine's influence in Republican-dominated Washington far outweighed the size of its population. In the late 1880s, Mainers held the federal offices of acting vice president, Speaker of the House, secretary of state, Senate majority leader, Supreme Court justice, and several important committee chairmanships. Best known of the notables were James G. Blaine (journalist, presidential aspirant, and secretary of state) and Portland native Thomas Brackett Reed, presidential aspirant and Speaker of the House.

In Maine itself, traditional industries fell into decline after the Civil War, dealing the economy a body blow. Steel ships began replacing Maine's wooden clippers, refrigeration techniques made the block-ice industry obsolete, concrete threatened the granite-quarrying trade, and the output from Southern textile mills began to supplant that from Maine's mills.

Despite Maine's economic difficulties, however, wealthy urbanites began turning their sights toward the state, accumulating land (including islands) and building enormous summer "cottages" for their families, servants, and hangers-on. Bar Harbor was a prime example of the elegant summer colonies that sprang up, but others include Grindstone Neck (Winter Harbor), Prouts Neck (Scarborough), and Dark Harbor (on Islesboro in Penobscot Bay). Vacationers who preferred fancy hotel-type digs reserved rooms for the summer at such sprawling complexes as Kineo House (on

Moosehead Lake), Poland Spring House (west of Portland), or the Samoset Hotel (in Rockland). Built of wood and catering to long-term visitors, these and many others all eventually succumbed to altered vacation patterns and the ravages of fire.

As the 19th century spilled into the 20th, the state broadened its appeal beyond the well-to-do who had snared prime turf in the Victorian era. It launched an active promotion of Maine as "The Nation's Playground," successfully spurring an influx of visitors from all economic levels. By steamboat, train, and soon by car, people came to enjoy the ocean beaches, the woods, the mountains, the lakes, and the quaintness of it all. (Not that these features didn't really exist, but the state's aggressive public relations campaign at the turn of the 20th century stacks up against anything Madison Avenue puts out today.) The only major hiatus in the tourism explosion in the century's first two decades was 1914–1918, when 35,062 Mainers joined many thousands of other Americans in going off to the European front to fight in World War I. Two years after the war

ended, in 1920 (the centennial of its statehood), Maine women were the first in the nation to troop to the polls after ratification of the Nineteenth Amendment granted universal suffrage.

Maine was slow to feel the repercussions of the Great Depression, but eventually they came, with bank failures all over the state. Federally subsidized programs, such as the Civilian Conservation Corps (CCC) and the Works Progress Administration (WPA), left lasting legacies in Maine.

Politically, the state has contributed notables on both sides of the aisle. In 1954, Maine elected as its governor Edmund S. Muskie, only the fifth Democrat in the job since 1854. In 1958, Muskie ran for and won a seat in the Senate, and in 1980 he became secretary of state under President Jimmy Carter. Muskie died in 1996.

Elected in 1980, Waterville's George J. Mitchell made a respected name for himself as a Democratic senator and Senate majority leader before retiring in 1996, when Maine became only the second state in the union to have two women senators (Olympia Snowe and Susan

Lobstering remains a vital part of Maine's coastal economy, increasing in importance as you head north.

Collins, both Republicans). After his 1996 re-election, President Bill Clinton appointed Mitchell's distinguished congressional colleague and three-term senator, Republican William Cohen of Bangor, as secretary of defense, a position he held through the rest of the Clinton administration. Mitchell spent considerable time during the Clinton years as the U.S. mediator for Northern Ireland's "troubles" and subsequently headed an international fact-finding team in the Middle East. Both Mitchell and Cohen have retired to the private sector, but no one will be surprised to see them on the national stage again.

Government

State Government

Politics in Maine isn't quite as variable and unpredictable as the weather, but pundits are almost as wary as weather forecasters about making predictions. Despite a long tradition of Republicanism dating from the late 19th century, Maine's voters and politicians have a national reputation for being independent-minded—electing Democrats, Republicans, or independents more for their character than their political persuasions.

Four of the most notable recent examples are Margaret Chase Smith, Edmund S. Muskie, George J. Mitchell, and William Cohen—two Republicans and two Democrats, all Maine natives. Republican Senator Margaret Chase Smith proved her flintiness when she spoke out against McCarthyism in the 1950s. Ed Muskie, the first prominent Democrat to come out of Maine, won every race he entered except an aborted bid for the presidency in 1972. George Mitchell, as mentioned under History, has gained a stellar reputation, as has William Cohen. In a manifestation of Maine's strong tradition of bipartisanship, Mitchell and Cohen worked together closely on many issues to benefit the state and the nation (they even wrote a book together).

In the 1970s, Maine elected an independent governor, James Longley, whose memory is still respected (Longley's son was later elected to Congress as a Republican, and his daughter to the state senate as a Democrat). In 1994, Maine voted in another independent, Angus King, a relatively young veteran of careers in business, broadcasting, and law. The governor serves a term of four years, limited to two terms.

The state's Supreme Judicial Court has a chief justice and six associate justices.

Maine is ruled by a bicameral, biennial citizen legislature comprising 151 members in the House of Representatives and 35 members in the state senate, including a relatively high percentage of women and a fairly high proportion of retirees. Members of both houses serve two-year terms. Along with the governor, they meet at the State House in Augusta to pass legislation and administer an annual state budget of around $2 billion. In 1993, voters passed a statewide term-limits referendum restricting legislators to four terms.

Whereas nearly two dozen Maine cities are ruled by city councils, about 450 smaller towns and plantations retain the traditional form of rule: annual town meetings. Town meetings generally are held in March, when newspaper pages bulge with reports containing classic quotes from citizens exercising their rights to vote and vent. A few examples: "I believe in the pursuit of happiness until that pursuit infringes on the happiness of others"; "I don't know of anyone's dog running loose except my own, and I've arrested her several times"; and "Don't listen to him; he's from New Jersey."

Nonresidents are welcome to attend town meetings. Although, of course, you can't vote, a town meeting is a great way to experience true local government. Refreshments are usually available—typically, proceeds benefit some local cause—and sometimes there's even a potluck lunch or supper. The meeting provides the live entertainment.

ECONOMY

When the subject of the economy comes up, you'll often hear reference to the "two Maines," as if a line bisected the state in half, east to west. There's much truth to the image. Southern Maine is prosperous with good jobs (although never enough), lots of small businesses, and a highly competitive real estate market. Northern Maine struggles along, suffering from its immensity and lack of infrastructure as much as its low population density.

The coast follows that same pattern. The Southern Coast reaps the benefit of its proximity to Boston. Not only is it a favorite weekend getaway for Boston-area residents, it's increasingly becoming part of Boston's suburbs as more and more people move there and commute to the city. Tourism thrives here seasonally. Retail is strong, thanks to Kittery. And traditional maritime-related businesses continue, although real estate pressures have contributed to their weakening, as fisherfolk struggle to hold on to wharves and to live near where they work.

Portland is the state's largest city and has a strong economy, supported by tourism and maritime-related businesses. Years ago, Portland made the wise decision to preserve its waterfront for maritime use, so it's still very much a working waterfront. Not surprisingly, Freeport's economy

is retail based. Brunswick, Bath, and the surrounding towns are supported by the three Bs: Bowdoin College, Brunswick Naval Air Station, and Bath Iron Works.

Mid-Coast and Penobscot Bay and increasingly the Blue Hill Peninsula have strong maritime-related businesses, including lobstering, fishing, clamming, worm-digging, and their support services. Also driving this region is a vital creative economy of artists and artisans, boat builders and cabinet makers, and entrepreneurial professionals, such as architects and designers. Small businesses, technology-based companies, and telemarketing provide employment, as does tourism. These three regions are also extremely popular with retirees, who often take up second careers or are active in the local community as mentors and volunteers.

The farther Down East you travel, the harder it is to eke out a living. In Washington County, many folks cobble together some semblance of year-round employment wreath making, fishing, clamming, guiding, logging, blueberry raking, and whatever else is available. Tribal officials in this region are currently hoping to bring a liquefied natural gas port to Perry, increasing prospects for tribal members, but strong opposition exists. As one local official told me: "Everyone complains that there are no jobs, but whenever an opportunity comes along, no one wants to risk changing the lifestyle." And that's a conundrum that's bound to continue for at least the foreseeable future.

The People

Mainers are an independent lot, many exhibiting the classic Yankee characteristics of dry humor, thrift, and ingenuity. Those who can trace their roots back at least a generation or two in the state and have lived here through the duration can call themselves natives; everyone else, no matter how long they've lived here, is "from away."

Mainers react to outsiders depending upon how those outsiders treat them. Treat a Mainer with a condescending attitude, and you'll receive a cold shoulder at best. Treat a Mainer with respect, and you'll be welcome, perhaps even invited in to share a mug of coffee. Mainers are wary of outsiders, and often with good reason. Many outsiders move to Maine because they fall in love with its independence and rural simplicity, then they demand that the farmer stop spreading that stinky manure on his farmlands, or they insist that the town initiate garbage pickup, or they build a glass-and-timber mcmansion in the midst of white clapboard historical homes.

In most of Maine, money doesn't impress folks. Truth is, that lobsterman in the old truck and the well-worn work clothes might be sitting on a small fortune. Or living on it. Perhaps nothing has caused more troubles between natives and newcomers than the rapidly increasing value of land and the taxes that go with that. For many visitors, Maine real estate is a bargain they can't resist.

If you want real insight into Maine character, listen to a CD or watch a video by one Maine master humorist, Tim Sample. As he often says, "wait a minute, it'll sneak up on you."

Maine's population didn't top the one million mark until 1970. Thirty years later, according to the 2000 census, the state had 1,274,923 residents. Along the coast, Cumberland County, comprising the Greater Portland area, has the highest head count.

Despite the longstanding presence of several substantial ethnic groups, plus four Native American tribes (about 1 percent of the population), diversity is a relatively recent phenomenon in Maine, and the population is about 95 percent Caucasian. A steady influx of refugees, beginning after the Vietnam War, forced the state to address diversity issues, and it continues to do so today.

Natives and "People from Away"

People who weren't born in Maine aren't natives. Even people who *were* may experience close scrutiny of their credentials. In Maine, there are natives and *natives*. Every day, the obituary pages describe Mainers who have barely left the houses in which they were born—even in which their grandparents were born. We're talking roots!

Along with this kind of heritage comes a whole vocabulary all its own—lingo distinctive to Maine or at least New England. (For help in translation, see the Glossary.)

Part of the "native" picture is the matter of "native" produce. Hand-lettered signs sprout everywhere during the summer advertising Native corn, Native peas, even—believe it or not—Native ice. In Maine, homegrown is well grown.

"People from away," on the other hand, are those whose families haven't lived here year-round for a generation or more. But people from away (also called flatlanders) exist all over Maine, and they have come to stay, putting down roots of their own and altering the way the state is run, looks, and *will* look. Senators Snowe and Collins are natives, but Governor King came from away, as did most of his cabinet members. You'll find other flatlanders as teachers, corporate executives, artists, retirees, writers, town selectmen, and even lobsterers.

In the 19th century, arriving flatlanders were mostly "rusticators" or "summer complaints"—summer residents who lived well, often in enclaves, and never set foot in the state off season. They did, however, pay property taxes, contribute to causes, and provide employment for local residents. Another 19th-century wave of people from away came from the bottom of the economic ladder: Irish escaping the potato famine and French-Canadians fleeing poverty in Québec.

Both groups experienced subtle and overt anti-Catholicism but rather quickly assimilated into the mainstream, taking jobs in mills and factories and becoming staunch American patriots.

The late 1960s and early 1970s brought bunches of "back-to-the-landers," who scorned plumbing and electricity and adopted retro ways of life. Although a few pockets of diehards still exist, most have changed with the times and adopted contemporary mores (and conveniences).

Today, technocrats arrive from away with computers, faxes, cell phones, and other high-tech gear and "commute" via the Internet and modern electronics. Maine has played a national leadership role in telecommunications reform—thanks to the university system's early push for installation of state-of-the-art fiber optics.

Native Americans

In Maine, the *real* natives are the Wabanaki (People of the Dawn)—the Micmac, Maliseet, Penobscot, and Passamaquoddy tribes of the eastern woodlands. Many live in or near three reservations, near the headquarters for their tribal governors. The Passamaquoddies are at Pleasant Point, in Perry, near Eastport, and at Indian Township, in Princeton, near Calais. The Penobscots are based on Indian Island, in Old Town, near Bangor. Other Native American population clusters—known as "off-reservation Indians"—are the Aroostook Band of Micmacs, based in Presque Isle, and the Houlton Band of Maliseets, in Littleton, near Houlton.

In 1965, Maine became the first state to establish a Department of Indian Affairs, but just five years later the Passamaquoddy and Penobscot tribes initiated a 10-year-long land-claims case involving 12.5 million Maine acres (about two-thirds of the state) weaseled from the Indians by Massachusetts in 1794. In late 1980, a landmark

© TOM NANGLE

Robert Henri founded a summer artists' colony on Monhegan in 1903, which attracted such luminaries as Rockwell Kent, Edward Hopper, George Bellows, Randall Davy, and later Reuben Tam, William Kienbusch, and the Wyeths. Monhegan's active artist colony remains a key reason to visit the island.

agreement, signed by President Jimmy Carter, awarded the tribes $80.6 million in reparations. Despite this, the tribes still struggle to provide jobs on the reservations and to increase the overall standard of living. A 2003 referendum to allow the tribes to build a casino was defeated. The latest attempt to increase jobs and money is a controversial plan to bring a liquified natural gas port to tribal lands in Perry.

One of the true success stories of the tribes is the revival of traditional arts as businesses. The Maine Indian Basketmakers Alliance has an active apprenticeship program, and two renowned basketmakers—Clara Keezer and the late Mary Gabriel—have achieved National Heritage Fellowships. Several well-attended annual summer festivals—in Bar Harbor and Perry—highlight Indian traditions and heighten awareness of Native American culture. Basketmaking, canoe-building, and traditional dancing are all parts of the scene. The splendid Abbe Museum in Bar Harbor features Indian artifacts, interactive displays, historic photographs, and special programs. Gift shops have begun adding Native American jewelry and baskets to their inventories.

Acadians and Franco-Americans

Within about three decades of their 1755 expulsion from Nova Scotia in *le grand dérangement,* Acadians had established new communities and new lives in northern Maine's St. John Valley. Gradually, they explored farther into central and southern coastal Maine and west into New Hampshire. The Acadian diaspora has profoundly influenced Maine and its culture, and it continues to do so today. Along the coast, French is spoken on the streets of Biddeford, where there's an annual Franco-American festival and an extensive Franco-American research collection.

African Americans

Although Maine's African-American population is small, the state has had an African-American community since the 17th century; by the 1764 census, there were 322 slaves and free blacks in the District of Maine. Segregation remained the rule, however, so in the 19th century, blacks established their own parish, the Abyssinian Church, in Portland. Efforts are under way to restore the long-closed church as an African-American cultural center and gathering place for Greater Portland's black community. For researchers delving into "Maine's black experience," the University of Southern Maine, in Portland, houses the African-American Archive of Maine, a significant collection of historic books, letters, and artifacts donated by Gerald Talbot, the first African American to serve in the Maine legislature.

Finns

Finns came to Maine in several 19th-century waves, primarily to work the granite quarries on the coast and on offshore islands and the slate quarries in Monson, near Greenville. Finnish families clustered near the quarries in St. George and on Vinalhaven and Hurricane Islands—all with landscapes similar to those of their homeland. Today, names such as Laukka, Lehtinen, Hamalainen, and Harjula are interspersed among the Yankee names in the Mid-Coast region.

Russians, Ukrainians, and Byelorussians

Arriving after World War II, Slavic immigrants established a unique community in Richmond, just inland from Bath. Only a tiny nucleus remains today, along with an onion-domed church, but a stroll through the local cemetery hints at the extent of the original colony.

The Newest Arrivals: Refugees from War

War has been the impetus for the more recent arrival of Asians, Africans, Central Americans, and Eastern Europeans. Most have settled in the Portland area, making that city the state's center of diversity. Vietnamese and Cambodians began settling in Maine in the mid-1970s. A handful of Afghanis who fled the Soviet-Afghan conflict also ended up in Portland. Somalis, Ethiopians, and Sudanese fled their war-torn countries in the early to mid-1990s, and Bosnians and Kosovars arrived in the last half of the 1990s. With every new conflict comes a new stream of immigrants—world citizens are becoming Mainers, and Mainers are becoming world citizens.

Culture

Every creative soul longs for inspiration and motivation to jump-start a painting or a poem, a statue or a novel. Maine has exerted a powerful lunarlike gravitational pull on creative types. The craggy shoreline, dense forests, and visually rich beauty—infused with hidebound Yankee traditions and an often harsh existence—have inspired artists and writers to create work of national and international repute.

Beginning around the mid-19th century, when people from away descended on Maine for their summer getaways, little pockets of creative energy flourished (largely but not exclusively along the coast), and art and literature reaped the benefits. These weren't Maine's first artists or earliest writers, but they represented a turning point, a stepped-up pace of artistic and literary activity.

FINE ART

In 1850, in a watershed moment for Maine landscape painting, Hudson River School artist par excellence Frederic Edwin Church (1826–1900) vacationed on Mount Desert Island. Influenced by the luminist tradition of such contemporaries as Fitz Hugh Lane (1804–1865), who summered in nearby Castine, Church accurately but romantically depicted the dramatic tableaux of Maine's coast and woodlands that even today attract slews of admirers.

By the 1880s, however, impressionism had become the style du jour and was being practiced by a coterie of artists who collected around Charles Herbert Woodbury (1864–1940) in Ogunquit. His program made Ogunquit the best-known summer art school in New England. After Hamilton Easter Field established another art school in town, modernism soon asserted itself. Among the artists who took up summertime Ogunquit residence was Walt Kuhn

(1877–1949), a key organizer of New York's 1913 landmark Armory Show of modern art.

Meanwhile, a bit farther south, impressionist Childe Hassam (1859–1935), part of writer Celia Thaxter's circle, produced several hundred works on Maine's remote Appledore Island, in the Isles of Shoals off Kittery, and illustrated Thaxter's *An Island Garden.*

Another artistic summer colony found its niche in 1903, when Robert Henri (born Robert Henry Cozad; 1865–1929), charismatic leader of the Ashcan School of realist/modernists, visited Monhegan Island, about 11 miles offshore. Artists who followed him there included Rockwell Kent (1882–1971), Edward Hopper (1882–1967), George Bellows (1882–1925), and Randall Davey (1887–1964). Among the many other artists associated with Monhegan images are William Kienbusch (1914–1980), Reuben Tam (1916–1991), and printmakers Leo Meissner (1895–1977) and Stow Wengenroth (1906–1978).

But colonies were of scant interest to other notables, who chose to derive their inspiration from Maine's stark natural beauty and work mostly in their own orbits. Among these are genre painter Eastman Johnson (1824–1906); romantic realist Winslow Homer (1836–1910), who lived in Maine for 27 years and whose studio in Prouts Neck (Scarborough) still overlooks the surf-tossed scenery he so often depicted; pointillist watercolorist Maurice Prendergast (1858–1924); John Marin (1870–1953), a cubist who painted Down East subjects, mostly around Deer Isle and Addison (Cape Split); Lewiston native Marsden Hartley (1877–1943), who first showed his abstractionist work in New York in 1909 and later worked in Berlin; Fairfield Porter (1907–1975), whose family summered on Great Spruce Head Island, in East Penobscot Bay; Andrew Wyeth (born 1917), whose reputation as a romantic realist in the late 20th century surpassed that of his illustrator father, N. C. Wyeth (1882–1945).

On a parallel track was sculptor Louise Nevelson (1899–1988), raised in a poor Russian-immigrant family in Rockland and far better known outside her home state for her monumental wood sculptures slathered in black or gold. Two other noted sculptors with Maine connections were William Zorach and Gaston Lachaise, both of whom lived in Georgetown, near Bath.

Today, Maine has no major community known exclusively for its summer art colony. Sure, there are artistic clusters here and there, united by the urge for creative networking and moral support—especially when threatened with reduced government subsidy. Among these artistic pockets, all close to the ocean, are the Kennebunks, Portland, Monhegan Island, Rockland, Blue Hill, Deer Isle, Gouldsboro, and Eastport.

Year-round or seasonal Maine residents with national (and international) reputations include Lincolnville's Neil Welliver and Alex Katz, North Haven's Eric Hopkins, Deer Isle's Karl Schrag, Tenants Harbor's Jamie Wyeth (third generation of the famous family), Kennebunk's Edward Betts, and Cushing's Lois Dodd and Alan Magee.

The two best collections of Maine art are at the **Portland Museum of Art** (7 Congress Sq., Portland 04101, 207/775-6148) and **The Farnsworth Art Museum** (352 Main St., Rockland 04841, 207/596-6457). The Farnsworth, in fact, focuses only on Maine art, primarily from the 20th century. In 1996, both museums saw their already-impressive holdings greatly enhanced when philanthropic collector Elizabeth Noyce bequeathed her comprehensive Maine collection to them. The Farnsworth is the home of the Wyeth Center, featuring the works of three generations of Wyeths.

The **Ogunquit Museum of American Art,** appropriately, also has a very respectable Maine collection (in a spectacular setting). Other Maine paintings, not always on exhibit, are at the Bowdoin College Museum of Art, in Brunswick.

CRAFTS

Any survey of Maine art, however brief, must include the significant role of crafts in the state's artistic tradition. As with painters, sculptors, and writers, craftspeople have gravitated to Maine—most notably since the establishment in 1950 of the **Haystack Mountain School of Crafts** (Sunshine Road, P.O. Box 518, Deer Isle 04627, 207/348-2306, fax 207/348-2307, www.haystack-mtn.org). Started in the Belfast area, the school put down roots on Deer Isle in 1960. Each summer, internationally famed artisans—sculptors, glassmakers, weavers, jewelers, potters, papermakers, and printmakers—become the faculty for the unique school, which has weekday classes and 24-hour studio access for adult students on its handsome 40-acre campus.

Portland is the headquarters for the **Maine Crafts Association** (15 Walton St., Portland 04103, 207/780-1807, www.mainecrafts.org), which has nearly 150 members and produces a very useful annual directory of artisans and exhibits.

DOWN EAST LITERATURE

Maine's first big-name writer was probably the early 17th-century French explorer Samuel de Champlain (1570–1635), who scouted the Maine coast, established a colony in 1604 near present-day Calais, and lived to describe in detail his experiences. Several decades after Champlain's forays, English naturalist John Josselyn visited Scarborough and in the 1670s published the first two books accurately describing Maine's flora and fauna (aptly describing, for example, black flies as "not only a pesterment but a plague to the country").

Today, Maine's best-known author lives not on the coast but just inland in Bangor—Stephen King (born 1947), wizard of the weird. Many of his dozens of horror novels and stories are set in Maine, and several have been filmed for the big screen here. King and his wife, Tabitha, also an author, are avid fans of both education and team sports and have generously distributed their largesse among schools and teams in their hometown as well as other parts of the state.

Chroniclers of the Great Outdoors

John Josselyn was perhaps the first practitioner of Maine's strong naturalist tradition in American letters, but the Pine Tree State's rugged scenic beauty and largely unspoiled environment have given rise to many ecologically and environmentally concerned writers.

The 20th century saw the arrival in Maine of crusader Rachel Carson (1907–1964), whose 1962 wake-up call, *Silent Spring,* was based partly on Maine observations and research. The Rachel Carson National Wildlife Refuge, headquartered in Wells and comprising 10 chunks of environmentally sensitive coastal real estate, covers nearly 3,500 acres between Kittery Point and the Mid-Coast region.

The tiny town of Nobleboro, near Damariscotta, drew nature writer Henry Beston (1888–1968), author of, among other things, *The Outermost House* (about Cape Cod); his *Northern Farm* lyrically chronicles a year in Maine. Beston's wife, Elizabeth Coatsworth (1893–1986), wrote more than 90 books—including *Chimney Farm,* about their life in Nobleboro.

Fannie Hardy Eckstorm (1865–1946), born in Brewer to Maine's most prosperous fur trader, graduated from Smith College and became a noted expert on Maine (and specifically Native American) folklore. Among her extensive writings, *Indian Place-Names of the Penobscot Valley and the Maine Coast,* published in 1941, remains a sine qua non for researchers.

The out-of-doors and inner spirits shaped Cape Rosier adoptees Helen and Scott Nearing, whose 1954 *Living the Good Life* became the bible of Maine's back-to-the-landers.

Classic Writings on the State

Historical novels, such as *Arundel,* were the specialty of Kennebunk native Kenneth Roberts (1885–1957), but Roberts also wrote *Trending into Maine,* a potpourri of Maine observations and experiences (the original edition was illustrated by N. C.

Wyeth). Kennebunkport's Booth Tarkington (1869–1946), author of the *Penrod* novels and *The Magnificent Ambersons,* described 1920s Kennebunkport in *Mary's Neck,* published in 1932.

A little subgenre of sociological literary classics comprises astute observations (mostly by women) of daily life in various parts of the state. Some are fiction, some nonfiction, some barely disguised romans à clef. Probably the best-known chronicler of such observations is Sarah Orne Jewett (1849–1909), author of *The Country of the Pointed Firs,* a fictional 1896 account of "Dunnet's Landing" (actually Tenants Harbor); her ties, however, were in the South Berwick area, where she spent most of her life. Also in South Berwick, Gladys Hasty Carroll (1904–1999) scrutinized everyday life in her hamlet, Dunnybrook, in *As the Earth Turns* (a title later "borrowed" and tweaked by a soap-opera producer). Lura Beam (1887–1978) focused on her childhood in the Washington County village of Marshfield in *A Maine Hamlet,* published in 1957, while Louise Dickinson Rich (1903–1972) entertainingly described her coastal Corea experiences in *The Peninsula,* after first having chronicled her rugged wilderness existence in *We Took to the Woods.* Ruth Moore (1903–1989), born on Gott's Island, near Acadia National Park, published her first book at the age of 40. Her tales, recently brought back into print, have earned her a whole new, appreciative audience. Elisabeth Ogilvie (born 1917) came to Maine in 1944 and lived for many years on remote Ragged Island, transformed into "Bennett's Island" in her fascinating "tide trilogy": *High Tide at Noon, Storm Tide,* and *The Ebbing Tide.* Ben Ames Williams (1887–1953), the token male in this roundup of perceptive observers, in 1940 produced *Come Spring,* an epic tale of hardy pioneers founding the town of Union, just inland from Rockland.

Seldom recognized for her Maine connection, antislavery crusader Harriet Beecher Stowe (1811–1896) lived in Brunswick in the mid-19th century, where she wrote *The Pearl of Orr's Island,* a folkloric novel about a tiny nearby fishing community.

Mary Ellen Chase was a Maine native, born in Blue Hill in 1887. She became an English professor at Smith College in 1926 and wrote about 30 books, including some about the Bible as literature. She died in 1973.

Two books do a creditable job of excerpting literature from throughout Maine—something of a daunting task. The most comprehensive is *Maine Speaks: An Anthology of Maine Literature,* published in 1989 by the Maine Writers and Publishers Alliance. *The Quotable Moose: A Contemporary Maine Reader,* edited by Wesley McNair and published in 1994 by the University Press of New England, focuses on 20th-century authors.

A World of Her Own

For Marguerite Yourcenar (1903–1987), Maine provided solitude and inspiration for subjects ranging far beyond the state's borders. Yourcenar was a longtime Northeast Harbor resident and the first woman elected to the prestigious Académie Française. Her house, now a shrine to her work, is open to the public by appointment in summer.

Essayists, Critics, and Humorists Native and Transplanted

Maine's best-known essayist is and was E. B. White (1899–1985), who bought a farm in tiny Brooklin in 1933 and continued writing for *The New Yorker. One Man's Meat,* published in 1944, is one of the best collections of his wry, perceptive writings. His legions of admirers also include two generations raised on his classic children's stories *Stuart Little, Charlotte's Web,* and *The Trumpet of the Swan.*

Writer and critic Doris Grumbach, who settled in Sargentville, not far from Brooklin but far from her New York ties, wrote two particularly wise works from the perspective of a Maine transplant: *Fifty Days of Solitude* and *Coming into the End Zone.*

Maine's best contemporary exemplar of humorous writing is the late John Gould, whose life in rural Friendship has provided grist for many a tale. Gould's hilarious columns in the *Christian Science Monitor* and his steady book output have made him the icon of Maine humor.

Pine Tree Poets

Born in Portland, Henry Wadsworth Longfellow (1807–1882) is Maine's most famous poet; his marine themes clearly stem from his seashore childhood (in "My Lost Youth," he wistfully rhapsodized, "Often I think of the beautiful town/That is seated by the sea").

Widely recognized in her own era, poet Celia Thaxter (1835–1994) held court on Appledore Island in the Isles of Shoals, welcoming artists, authors, and musicians to her summer salon. Today, she's best known for *An Island Garden,* published in 1894 and detailing her attempts at horticultural TLC in a hostile environment.

Edna St. Vincent Millay (1892–1950) had connections to Camden, Rockland, and Union and described a stunning Camden panorama in "Renascence."

Whitehead Island, near Rockland, was the birthplace of Wilbert Snow (1883–1977), who went on to become president of Connecticut's Wesleyan University. His 1968 memoir, *Codline's Child,* makes fascinating reading.

A longtime resident of York, May Sarton (1912–1995) approached cult status as a guru of feminist poetry and prose—and as an articulate analyst of death and dying during her terminal illness.

Among respected Maine poets today are Philip Booth (born 1925), a resident of Castine; William Carpenter (born 1940), of Stockton Springs; and Appleton's Kate Barnes (born 1932), named Maine's Poet Laureate from 1996 to 1999. Although she comes by her acclaim legitimately, Barnes is also genetically disposed, being the daughter of writers Henry Beston and Elizabeth Coatsworth.

Maine Lit for Little Ones

Besides E. B. White's children's classics, *Stuart Little, Charlotte's Web,* and *The Trumpet of the Swan,* America's kids were also weaned on books written and illustrated by Maine island summer resident Robert McCloskey (1914–2003), notably *Time of Wonder, One Morning in Maine,* and *Blueberries for Sal.* Neck-and-neck in popularity is prolific Walpole illustrator-writer

Barbara Cooney (1917–1999), whose award-winning titles included *Miss Rumphius, Island Boy,* and *Hattie and the Wild Waves.* Cooney produced more than 100 books, and it seems as if everyone has a different favorite.

Maine can also lay partial claim to Kate Douglas Wiggin (1856–1923), author of the eternally popular *Rebecca of Sunnybrook Farm;* she spent summers at Quillcote, in Hollis, just west of Portland.

Getting There

Maine has two major airports, two major bus networks, a toll highway, limited Amtrak service, and some ad hoc local transportation systems that fill in the gaps.

BY AIR

Coastal Maine's major airline gateway is **Portland International Jetport** (PWM, 207/774-7301, www.portlandjetport.org), although visitors headed farther northeast sometimes prefer **Bangor International Airport** (BGR, 207/947-0384, www.flybangor.com). The "international" in their names is a bit misleading. Charter flights from Europe often stop at Bangor for refueling and customs clearance, and sometimes bad weather also diverts flights there. Boston's Logan Airport is the nearest airport with direct flights from Europe and other worldwide destinations.

You'll undoubtedly want to fly into Bangor if you're going to Bar Harbor and Acadia National Park or the Down East coastal counties of Washington and Hancock. But Portland is the more logical airport choice if you're visiting southern Maine—the beaches, Portland, or the coastal towns up to Damariscotta. If your destination is the Camden/Rockport area, which is equidistant between the two airports, your choice is a toss-up. Being on the coast, the Portland airport is more subject to fog shutdowns than Bangor, but many Bangor flights originate (or stop) in Boston, where fog delays can afflict Logan Airport even more.

An increasingly popular choice for bargain hunters is **Southwest Airlines** (800/435-9792), which operates economical flights into Manchester, New Hampshire. Ground transportation is available between Manchester and the Portland Jetport

via **Mermaid Transportation** (800/696-2463, www.gomermaid.com); call for reservations.

All the airlines increase their flight frequency during the summer to accommodate stepped-up demand.

Airlines serving both Portland and Bangor are **American** (800/433-7300), **Continental** (800/523-3273), **Delta** (800/221-1212), **Northwest** (800/225-2525), and **US Airways** (800/428-4322). Also serving Portland is **Independence Air** (800/359-3594).

Portland Jetport Facilities

Portland's amenities include a newsstand/gift shop, coffee shop, restaurant/lounge, restrooms, large waiting area, ATM, and plenty of coin- and card-operated telephones. Avis, Budget, Hertz, and National car-rental agencies have offices in the terminal; nearby Alamo runs a continuous shuttle. There's a business center in the gate area with Internet access. Visitor information is dispensed from a desk (not always staffed, unfortunately) between the gates and the baggage-claim area. No need to rush out to grab your luggage, though—Portland has one of the slowest baggage-claim operations in the country. Plan to stop at the restrooms, browse through the gift shop, and pick up tourism information after you arrive—and even then you may still have to wait for your luggage. Complaints to management elicit the response that Portland is the terminus of many airline routes, and the airline companies (who provide the baggage handlers and unloading equipment) give low priority to locations that don't require fast turnaround. As a result, carry-on luggage is a plus here. Baggage-handling offices surround the luggage carousels. Airlines are responsible for luggage, so if you have a problem, contact a representative from your airline. If you have an emergency, contact the airport manager (207/773-8462).

Ground Transportation: Free **Explorer** (207/774-9891 or 800/377-4457, www.portland explorer.org) buses link all Portland transportation hubs—the airport, Portland Transportation Center, Vermont Transit terminal, Scotia Prince Ferry, and Casco Bay Lines—with hotels on the route. Portland's **Metro** bus line (207/774-0351) provides scheduled service throughout the city. **Taxis** are available outside baggage claim.

If you're planning to arrive in Portland and head directly up the coast anywhere between the airport and Camden, call ahead to **Mid-Coast Limousine** (800/937-2424 or 207/236-2424) and schedule a pickup. You might be lucky and find one of its limos at the airport, but it operates by reservation, so don't take the chance.

Bangor Airport Facilities

Bangor's airport has scaled-down versions of Portland's facilities but all the necessary amenities: Avis, Budget, Hertz, and National rental cars (with Enterprise and Thrifty nearby); newsstand/gift shop; and waiting area with restrooms and phones. Baggage claim tends to be more efficient than Portland's. If you need help, contact the airport manager (207/947-0384).

Ground Transportation: Bangor Area Transportation (BAT) (www.bgrme.org) buses connect the airport to downtown Bangor. Buses run Monday–Saturday. **West's Coastal Connection** leaves directly from the airport twice each afternoon for Calais, with stops in Ellsworth, Gouldsboro, Machias, and Perry. Flag stops on request in Hancock, Sullivan, Milbridge, Columbia Falls, Jonesboro, Whiting, Dennysville, and Pembroke. **Taxis** are available outside baggage claim.

Regional Airports

Airports accessible via US Airways/Business Express from Boston are **Hancock County Airport** (207/667-7329, www.bhbairport.com) near Bar Harbor and **Knox County Regional Airport** (207/594-4131, http://knoxcounty.mid-coast.com) at Owls Head, near Rockland and Camden. Colgan Air is the local affiliate of US Airways Express at these two airports. Hancock County Airport has rental-car offices for Budget and Hertz and is also serviced by the Island Explorer bus from late June through Columbus Day. Knox County has a Budget car-rental desk.

Boston Logan Airport

If you fly into Boston (BOS), you easily can get to Maine via rental car (all major companies serve the airport, but it's not pleasant to navigate Logan in a rental car) or Concord Trailways bus (the easiest and least-expensive option). You'll need to connect to North Station to take Amtrak's Downeaster train. Another option is **Mermaid Transportation** (800/696-2463, www.gomermaid.com), which operates the best van service between Boston and Portland. Pickup and dropoff, by reservation only, are at Portland Jetport and Logan Airport.

BY CAR

The major highway access to coastal Maine from the south is the **Maine Turnpike,** which links with I-95 at the New Hampshire border. Other busy access points are **Route 1,** also from New Hampshire; **Route 302,** from North Conway, New Hampshire, entering Maine at Fryeburg; **Route 2,** from Gorham, New Hampshire, to Bethel, and a couple of crossing points from New Brunswick into Washington County in northeastern Maine.

BY BUS

Concord Trailways (800/639-3317, www.concordtrailways.com) departs downtown Boston (South Station Transportation Center) and Logan Airport for Portland about 10 times daily, making pickups at all Logan airline terminals (lower level). The Portland bus terminal is the Portland Transportation Center, Thompson Point Road, just west of I-295. The fare is $23 one-way, $37 round-trip. If you're headed for downtown Portland from the bus terminal, board the Metro city bus at the terminal and show your Concord Trailways bus ticket to receive a free trip.

Three daily nonexpress buses continue from

Portland along the coast as far as Searsport, then head inland to the Trailways terminal in Bangor. In Bangor, once-a-day connections are available to the coastal communities of Ellsworth, Machias, and Calais.

BY RAIL

Amtrak's Downeaster (800/872-7245, www.thedowneaster.com, $21 one-way) makes four daily round-trip runs between Boston's North Station and Portland's Transportation Center, with stops in Wells, Saco, and seasonally in Old Orchard Beach (May–Oct.). The Wells Regional Transportation Center is staffed for information, has restrooms, an ATM, and a climate-controlled waiting area. There's seasonal trolley service to the beach. Taxis on-site. The Saco station is near downtown and on the Tri-Town Shuttlebus route; taxis are available on-site. The Old Orchard Beach station is adjacent to the chamber of commerce and steps from the beach. It's serviced by the Tri-Town Shuttlebus service and a seasonal trolley; taxis are on-site. Call or check the website for discounted fares and special rates for children and seniors. From the station, Portland's Metro municipal bus service will take you gratis to downtown Portland; just show your Amtrak ticket stub.

Getting Around

By Bus

Ground transportation exists in Maine, but it's far from adequate. For instance, only two long-distance bus companies cover the state, and only one covers coastal Maine. No smoking is allowed on buses.

Concord Trailways (800/639-3317) has the most extensive bus network, with routes designed to assist students, island ferry passengers, and day-trippers. Buses from Boston's Logan Airport stop in downtown Portland and follow a mostly coastal route through Brunswick, Bath, Wiscasset, Damariscotta, Waldoboro, Rockland, Camden, Belfast, and Searsport, ending in Bangor, and then follow the same route in reverse. (During the school year, the route also includes Bowdoin College in Brunswick and the University of Maine campus in Orono.)

Once-a-day buses to and from Calais coordinate with the Bangor bus schedules. The Calais line, stopping in Ellsworth, Gouldsboro, Machias, and Perry (near Eastport), is operated by **West's Bus Service,** in Steuben (800/596-2823 or 207/546-2823). Flag stops along the route are permitted; see the regional chapters for information.

Portland and South Portland have **city bus service,** with some wheelchair-accessible vehicles. A number of smaller communities have established **local shuttle vans** or **trolley-buses,** but most of the latter are seasonal. Trolley-buses operate (for a fee) in Ogunquit, Wells, the Kennebunks, Portland, Bath, and Boothbay. Mount Desert Island and the Gouldsboro Peninsula have the **Island Explorer,** an excellent free summer (from late June) bus service.

By Car

No matter how much time and resourcefulness you summon, you'll never really be able to appreciate coastal Maine without a car. Down every little peninsula jutting into the Atlantic lies a picturesque village or park or ocean view. Even I-95, the state's major artery, boasts scenic vistas that bring photographers to a screeching halt. (Of course, a radar-equipped cop can deliver the same result for any driver.)

Note that the interstate can be a bit confusing to motorists; it's important to consult a map and pay close attention to the green directional signs to avoid heading off in the wrong direction. Between York and Augusta, I-95 is the same as the Maine Turnpike. I-295 splits from I-95 in Portland and heads up the coast to Brunswick, before veering inland and rejoining I-95 in Gardiner. Service areas are infrequent on the turnpike and interstate and are not on both sides of the highway, so stop when you see one; don't wait for the next one. All exit numbers along I-95 reflect distance in miles from the border. Exits on I-295 reflect distance from where it splits from I-95 just south of Portland at Exit 44.

If your destination is the Mid-Coast, take I-295 to Brunswick, then pick up Route 1 north. If it's Penobscot Bay, consider taking I-95 (you'll save time by splitting off and looping around on I-295) to Augusta, then taking Route 17 to Rockland or Route 3 to Belfast. If your destination is the Blue Hill Peninsula or above, stay on I-95 to Bangor, then take Route 1A to the coast. If it's Calais, stay on I-95 to Bangor, then take Route 9 to Route 1 south to Calais.

Maximum speed on I-95 and the Maine Turnpike is 65 mph—55 mph on some stretches. In snow, sleet, or dense fog, the limit drops to 45 mph; only rarely does the highway close. On other highways, the speed limit is usually 55 mph in rural areas and posted in built-up areas. Note that the Maine Turnpike is a toll highway.

Two lanes wide from Kittery in the south to Fort Kent at the top, U.S. Route 1 is the state's most congested road, particularly in July and August. Mileage distances can be extremely deceptive, since it will take you much longer than anticipated to get from point A to point B. If you ask anyone about distances, chances are good that you'll receive an answer in hours rather than miles. Plan accordingly. If you're trying to make time, it's best to take the Maine Turnpike or I-95; if you want to see Maine, take U.S. 1 and lots of little offshoots.

That said, bear in mind that the Maine Turnpike itself becomes megacongested on summer weekends, and especially summer *holiday* weekends. More than 300,000 vehicles use the turnpike on Memorial Day, Fourth of July, and Labor Day weekends. Worst times on the turnpike are Friday 4–8 P.M. (northbound), Saturday 11 A.M.– 2 P.M. (southbound; most weekly cottage rentals run from Saturday noon to Saturday noon), and Sunday 3–7 P.M. (southbound). On three-day holiday weekends, avoid heading southbound on Monday between 3 and 7 P.M.

Rental cars are available at the Portland, Bangor, and most smaller airports. All the major chains are represented—Alamo, Avis, Budget, Hertz, National, Thrifty, even Rent-A-Wreck. If you're planning to arrive on a July or August weekend, or a summer holiday weekend, call well ahead for a reservation or you may be out of luck.

Almost all **gas stations** in Maine are self-serve (pumps are marked Self; at those marked Full, an attendant will pump the gas for you), and many now allow you to pay at the pump with a credit card. (Many also have ATMs, but you'll usually have to pay a bank surcharge.) Note: Irving stations have extremely clean restrooms and usually have a good selection of teas and coffees in addition to fast foods.

Important Driving Regulations: Seat belts are mandatory in Maine. Maine allows **right turns at red lights,** after you stop and check for oncoming traffic. In rare cases, you'll see a No Turn on Red sign—in which case, heed it. *Never* pass a **stopped school bus** in either direction. Wait until the bus's red lights have stopped flashing and all children are well off the road. Maine law also requires drivers to turn on their car's **headlights** any time the windshield wipers are operating.

Roadside Assistance: Since Maine is enslaved to the automobile, it's not a bad idea for vacationers to carry membership in AAA in case of breakdowns, flat tires, and other car crises. Contact your nearest AAA office or AAA Northern New England (425 Marginal Way, Portland 04101, 207/780-6800 or 800/482-7497, www.aaanne.com). The emergency road service number is 800/222-4357.

For real-time information on road conditions, weather, construction, and major delays, dial 511 in Maine, 866/282-7578 from out of state, or visit www.511maine.gov. Information is available in both English and French.

Hitchhiking

Even though Maine's public transportation network is woefully inadequate, and the crime rate is one of the lowest in the nation, it's still risky to hitchhike or pick up hitchhikers.

THE LOBSTER EXPERIENCE

No Maine visit can be considered complete without the "real Maine" experience of a "lobsta dinnah" at a lobster wharf/pound/shack. Keep an eye on the weather, pick a sunny day, and head out.

If you spot a lobster place with Restaurant in its name and no outside dining, keep going. What you're looking for is the genuine article. You want to eat outdoors, at a wooden picnic table, with a knockout view of boats and the sea. Whatever place you choose, the drill is much the same, and the "dinners" are served anytime from noon on (some places close as early as 7 P.M.). First of all, dress very casually so you can manhandle the lobster without messing up your good clothes. If you want beer or wine, call ahead and ask if the place serves it; you may need to bring your own, since many such operations don't have beer/wine licenses, much less liquor licenses. In the evening, carry some insect repellent, in case mosquitoes crash the party. (Many places light citronella candles or dispense Skin-So-Soft to keep the bugs at bay.)

A basic one-pound lobster and go-withs (cole slaw or potato salad, potato chips, perhaps corn-on-the-cob, and butter or fake butter for dipping) should run $15 or less. Depending on your hunger, though, you may want to indulge in a shore dinner (lobster, steamed clams, potato chips, and maybe cole slaw or corn), for which you may have to part

© TOM NANGLE

You won't find a better lobster pound on Mount Desert Island than Thurston's, in Bernard.

with $15–22. Don't skip dessert; many lobster pounds are known for their homemade pies.

It's not unusual, either, to see lobster-wharf devotees carting picnic baskets with hors d'oeuvres, salads, and baguettes. I've even seen candles and champagne. Creativity abounds, but don't stray too far from the main attraction—the crustaceans.

Typically, you'll need to survey a chalkboard or whiteboard menu and step up to a window to order. You'll either give the person your name or get a number. A few places have staff to take your order or deliver your meal, but usually you head back to the window when your name or number is called. Don your plastic lobster bib and begin the attack. If you're a neophyte, watch a pro at a nearby table. Some pounds have "how-to" info printed on paper placemats. If you're really worried (you needn't be), contact the Maine Lobster Promotion Council (382 Harlow St., Bangor 04401, www.mainelobsterpromotion.com). It publishes a brochure with detailed instructions. Don't worry about doing it "wrong"; you'll eventually get what you came for, and it'll be an experience to remember.

For the ultimate lobster feeding frenzy, plan to be in Rockland the first weekend in August, when volunteers at the annual Maine Lobster Festival stoke up the world's largest lobster cooker and serve thousands of pounds of lobsters nonstop to more than 50,000 enthusiastic diners.

Here (in alphabetical order) are 22 great places to experience lobster. All are described in more detail in the regional chapters.

Bernard (Mount Desert Island): Thurston's Lobster Pound (207/244-7600)

East Boothbay: Lobsterman's Wharf, (207/633-3443)

Cape Elizabeth (near Portland): The Lobster Shack (207/799-1677)

Castine: Dennett's Wharf (207/326-9045)

Damariscotta/Pemaquid Peninsula: Broad Cove Marine Services, Medomak (207/529-5186); Shaw's Fish and Lobster Wharf, New Harbor (207/677-2200); Pemaquid Fishermen's Co-op, Pemaquid Harbor (207/677-2801); Muscongus Bay Lobster, Round Pond (207/529-5528); Round Pond Lobster Co-Op, Round Pond (207/529-5725); South Bristol Fishermen's Co-op, South Bristol (207/644-8224)

East Belfast: Young's Lobster Pound (207/338-1160)

Georgetown (near Bath): Five Islands Lobster Company (207/371-2990)

Kittery Point: Chauncey Creek Lobster Pier (207/439-1030)

Lincolnville Beach: The Lobster Pound (207/789-5550)

Little Deer Isle: Eaton's Lobster Pool (207/348-2383)

Ogunquit (Perkins Cove): Barnacle Billy's Lobster Pound (207/646-5575)

Portland: Portland Lobster Company (207/775-2112)

Small Point (near Bath): The Lobster House (207/389-1596)

South Freeport: Harraseeket Lunch & Lobster Co. (207/865-4888)

South Thomaston (near Rockland): Waterman's Beach Lobster (207/596-7819)

Southport (near Boothbay Harbor): Robinson's Wharf (207/633-3830)

Spruce Head (near Rockland): Miller's Lobster Company (207/594-7406)

Tenants Harbor (near Thomaston): Cod End (207/372-6782)

Trenton (near Bar Harbor): Trenton Bridge Lobster Pound (207/667-2977)

MAINE FOOD SPECIALTIES

Everyone knows Maine is *the* place for lobster, but there are quite a few other foods that you should sample before you leave.

For a few weeks in May, right around Mother's Day (the second Sunday in May), a wonderful delicacy starts sprouting along Maine woodland streams: **fiddleheads,** the still-furled tops of the ostrich fern *(Matteuccia struthiopteris).* Tasting vaguely like asparagus, fiddleheads have been on May menus ever since Native Americans taught the colonists to forage for the tasty vegetable. Don't go fiddleheading unless you're with a pro, though; the lookalikes are best left to the woods critters. If you find them on a restaurant menu, indulge.

As with fiddleheads, we owe thanks to Native Americans for introducing us to **maple syrup,** one of Maine's major agricultural exports. The annual crop averages 110,000 gallons. The syrup comes in four different colors/flavors (from light amber to extra dark amber), and inspectors strictly monitor syrup quality. The best syrup comes from the sugar or rock maple, *Acer saccharum.* On Maine Maple Sunday (usually the fourth Sunday in March), several dozen syrup producers open their rustic sugarhouses to the public for "sugaring-off" parties—to celebrate the sap harvest and share the final phase in the production process. Woodsmoke billows from the sugarhouse chimney while everyone inside gathers around huge kettles used to boil down the watery sap. (A single gallon of syrup starts with 30–40 gallons of sap.) Finally, it's time to sample the syrup every which way—on pancakes and waffles, in tea, on ice cream, in puddings, in muffins, even just drizzled over snow. Most producers also have containers of syrup for sale. For a list of participating sugarhouses, contact the Maine Department of Agriculture (207/287-3491, www.getrealmaine.com).

The best place for Maine maple syrup is atop pancakes made with **Maine wild blueberries.** Packed with antioxidants and all kinds of good-for-you stuff, these flavorful berries are prized by bakers because they retain their form and flavor when cooked. Much smaller than the cultivated versions, wild blueberries are also raked, not picked. Although most of the Down East barren barons harvest their crops for the lucrative wholesale market, a few growers let you pick your own blueberries in mid-August. Contact the Wild Blueberry Commission (207/581-1475) or the state Department of Agriculture (207/287-3491) for locations, recipes, and other wild-blueberry information, or log on to the website of the Wild Blueberry Association of North America, headquartered in Bar Harbor: www.wildblueberries.com.

The best place to simply *appreciate* blueberries is Machias, site of the renowned annual Wild Blueberry Festival, held the third weekend in August. While harvesting is under way in the surrounding fields, you can stuff your face with blueberry-everything—muffins, jam, pancakes, ice cream, pies. Plus you can collect blueberry-logo napkins, T-shirts, fridge magnets, pottery, and jewelry.

Another don't miss while in Maine is **Maine-made ice cream.** Skip the overpriced Ben & Jerry's outlets. Locally made ice cream is fresher and better, and often comes in an astounding range of flavors. The big name in the state is Gifford's, with regional companies being Shain's and Round Top. All beat the out-of-state competition by a longshot. Even better are some of the one-of-a-kind dairy bars and farm stands. Good bets are Brown's, in York; The Gothic, in Belfast; and Ben & Bill's, in Bar Harbor.

Finally, whenever you get a chance, shop at a farmers' market. Their biggest asset is serendipity—you never know what you'll find. Everything is locally grown and often organic. Herbs, unusual vegetables, seedlings, baked goods, meat, free-range chicken, goat cheese, herb vinegars, berries, exotic condiments, smoked salmon, maple syrup, honey, and jams are just a few of the possibilities. For a list of all the markets (including those in inland areas), contact the Maine Department of Agriculture.

Tips for Travelers

VISAS AND OFFICIALDOM

Since 9/11, security has been excruciatingly tight for foreign visitors. It's crucial to plan well ahead, pack diligently, and have all necessary paperwork. It's also wise to make two sets of copies of all paperwork, one to carry separately on your trip and another left with a trusted friend or relative at home.

Citizens from 27 countries can enter the United States for tourism or business for 90 days or fewer without obtaining a visa. These are Andorra, Australia, Austria, Belgium, Brunei, Denmark, Finland, France, Germany, Iceland, Ireland, Italy, Japan, Liechtenstein, Luxembourg, Monaco, the Netherlands, New Zealand, Norway, Portugal, San Marino, Singapore, Slovenia, Spain, Sweden, Switzerland, and the United Kingdom. Travelers on the program must have return tickets and machine-readable passports that are valid for six months beyond intended visit dates. For details, see www.travel.state.gov/visa. Note that according to the site, a visa does not guarantee entry into the United States. A visa allows a foreign citizen to travel to the U.S. port-of-entry, and the Department of Homeland Security U.S. immigration inspector authorizes or denies admission to the country.

Most Canadian citizens need no visa, but do need valid identification that establishes both identity and citizenship to enter the United States through Maine or any other crossover point. Documents that are acceptable for identifying citizenship are birth certificate, citizenship certificate, and passport. Photo identification may be required. Duty-free limits for Canadians returning home are CAN$50 after a 24-hour stay, CAN$200 after 48 hours, and CAN$750 after seven days (not counting departure day).

There is no limit on the amount of money or traveler's checks a nonresident may bring into the United States. If the amount exceeds $10,000, however, it's necessary to fill out an official report form.

No fruit, vegetables, or plant materials can be taken across the border in either direction.

SMOKING

Maine now has laws banning smoking in restaurants, bars, and lounges as well as enclosed areas of public places, such as shopping malls. Only a handful of B&Bs and country inns permit smoking, and more and more motels, hotels, and resorts are limiting the number of rooms where smoking is permitted. Many accommodations have instituted high fines for anyone who smokes in a nonsmoking room.

ACCOMMODATIONS, FOOD, AND ALCOHOL

Accommodations

For all accommodation listings, rates are quoted for peak season, which is usually July and August but may extend through foliage (mid-October). Rates drop, often dramatically, in the shoulder and off-season at accommodations that remain open. Especially during peak season, many accommodations require a two- or three-night minimum.

For the best rates, be sure to check Internet specials and to ask about packages. Many accommodations also provide discounts for members of travel clubs such as AAA, to seniors and the military, and other such groups. Unless otherwise noted, accommodations have private baths.

Food

Days and hours of operation listed for places serving food are for peak season. These do change often, sometimes even within a season, and it's not uncommon for a restaurant to close early on a quiet night. To avoid disappointment, call before making a special trip.

Alcohol

As in the rest of the country, Maine's minimum drinking age is 21 years—and bar owners, bartenders, and serving staff can be held legally accountable for serving underage imbibers. Owners and employees also may be held liable for accidents caused by *legal* drinkers. Stiff anti-drunken

Know Coastal Maine

driving efforts in Maine (including random road-blocks, license revocation or suspension, hefty fines, and jail terms) have reduced but by no means halted the fatalities. If your blood alcohol level is .08 percent or higher, you are legally considered to be operating under the influence.

TIME ZONE

All of Maine is in the eastern time zone—same as New York; Washington, D.C.; Philadelphia; and Orlando, Florida. Eastern standard time (EST) runs from the last Sunday in October to the first Sunday in April; eastern daylight time (EDT), one hour later, prevails otherwise. Surprising to many first-time visitors is how early the sun rises in the morning and how early it sets at night in midsummer.

If your itinerary also includes Canada, remember that the provinces of New Brunswick and Nova Scotia are on Atlantic time—one hour later than eastern.

Health and Safety

There's too much to do in Maine, and too much to see, to spend even a few hours laid low by illness or mishap. Be sensible—get enough sleep, wear sunscreen and appropriate clothing, know your limits and don't take foolhardy risks, heed weather and warning signs, carry water and snacks while hiking, don't overindulge in food or alcohol, always tell someone where you're going, and watch your step. If you're traveling with children, quadruple your caution.

Lyme Disease

A bacterial infection that causes severe arthritis-like symptoms, Lyme disease (named after the Connecticut town where it was first identified, in 1975) has been documented in Maine since 1986. Health officials monitor the situation carefully and issue cautionary warnings during prime tick season—mid-May into August. Atlanta's Centers for Disease Control and Prevention (www.cdc.gov) has cited the wooded, marshy areas of Maine's southernmost counties, York and Cumberland, as the highest-risk areas. From there northward along the coast to Mount Desert Island, the risk is considered low to moderate.

Lyme disease is spread by bites from tiny deer ticks (not the larger dog ticks; they don't carry it), which feed on the blood of deer, mice, songbirds, and humans. Symptoms include joint pain, extreme fatigue, chills, a stiff neck, headache, and a distinctive ring-like rash. Except for the rash, which occurs in about 80 percent of victims, the symp-toms mimic those of other ailments, such as the flu, so the disease is hard to diagnose. The rash, which expands gradually and usually is not painful, may appear from three days to a month after a bite. If left untreated, Lyme disease eventually can cause heart and neurological problems and debilitating arthritis. Preventive measures are essential. If you suspect you've been exposed, seek medical assistance.

Best advice is to take precautions: wear a long-sleeved shirt and long pants, and tuck the pant legs into your socks. Light-colored clothing makes the ticks easier to spot. Buy tick repellent at a supermarket or convenience store and use it liberally on your legs. Spray it around your cuffs and beltline. While you're hiking, try to keep to the center of trails, away from long grasses. After any hike, check for ticks—especially behind the knees and in the armpits, navel, and groin. Monitor children carefully. If you find a tick or suspect you have been bitten, head for the nearest hospital emergency room. If you spot a tick on you (or anyone else), remove it with tweezers and save it for analysis. Not all deer ticks are infected.

Rabies

Incidents of rabies—a life-threatening, nerve-attacking disease for which there is no cure unless treated immediately—have increased dramatically in Maine since 1994. No human has ever survived a case of rabies, and the disease is horrible, so *do not* approach, or let any child approach, any of the animals known to transmit it: raccoons, skunks, squirrels, bats, and foxes. Domestic dogs are required to have biennial rabies inoculations, thus providing a front line of defense for humans. If you're bitten by any animal, especially one acting suspiciously, head for the nearest hospital emergency room. For statewide information about rabies, contact the Maine Disease Control Administration in Augusta (207/287-3591).

Allergies (in the Land of Bees and Lobster)

If your medical history includes extreme allergies to shellfish or bee stings, you know the risks of eating a lobster or wandering around a wildflower meadow. However, if you come from a landlocked area and are new to crustaceans, you might not be aware of the potential hazard. Statistics indicate that less than 2 percent of adults have a severe shellfish allergy, but for those victims, the reaction can set in quickly. Immediate treatment is needed to keep the airways open. If you have a history of severe allergic reactions to *anything*, be prepared when you come to the Maine coast dreaming of lobster feasts. Ask your doctor for a prescription for EpiPen (epinephrine), a preloaded, single-use syringe containing .3 milligrams of the drug—enough to tide you over until you can get to a hospital.

Seasickness

Samuel Butler, the 19th-century author of *Erewhon*, wrote, "How holy people look when they are sea-sick." And he wasn't kidding. Seasickness conjures visions of the pearly gates and an overwhelming urge for instant salvation. Fortunately, even though the ailment seems to last forever, it's only temporary—depending on where you are, what remedies you have, and how your system responds. If you're planning to do any boating in Maine—particularly sailing—you'll want to be prepared. (Being prepared in fact may keep you from succumbing, since fear of seasickness just about guarantees you'll get it.)

Seasickness allegedly stems from an inner-ear imbalance caused by boat motion, but researchers have had difficulty explaining why some people on a vessel become violently ill and others have no problem at all.

To prevent seasickness, try to stay in good shape. Get enough sleep and food, and keep your clothing warm and dry (not easy, of course, on a heeling sailboat). Some veteran sailors swear by salted crackers, sips of water, and bites of fresh ginger. If you start feeling queasy, keep your eyes on the horizon and stay as far away as possible from odors from the engine, the galley, the head, and other seasick passengers. If you become seasick, keep sipping water to prevent dehydration.

Dramamine, Marezine, and Bonine, taken several hours before a boat trip, have long been the preventives of choice. They do cause drowsiness, but anyone who's been seasick will tell you he'd rather be drowsy. Another popular preventive is the scopolamine patch (available by prescription under the trademark Transderm Scop; not advised for pregnant women, the elderly, or children), which gradually releases medication into the bloodstream for up to three days. Discuss the minor side effects with the physician who gives you the prescription, and read directions and cautions carefully before using.

And some people swear by the pressure bracelet, which operates somewhat on the principle of acupressure, telling your brain to ignore the fact that you're not on terra firma. Great success has been reported with these prophylactics in the last decade. Before embarking, especially if the weather is at all iffy, go ahead and put on a patch or a bracelet. Any such preventive measure also improves your mental attitude, relieving anxiety.

Sunstroke

Since Maine lies between 43° and 48° north latitude, sunstroke is not a major problem, but don't push your luck by spending an entire day frying on the beach in southern coastal Maine. Not only do you risk sunstroke and dehydration, but you're also asking for skin cancer down the road. Early in the season, slather yourself, and especially children, with plenty of PABA-free sunblock. (PABA can cause skin rashes and eruptions, even on people not abnormally sensitive.) Depending on your skin tone, use sun protection factor (SPF) 15 or higher. If you're in the water a long time, slather on some more. Start with 15–30 minutes of solar exposure and increase gradually each day. If you don't get it right, watch for symptoms of sunstroke: fever, profuse sweating, headache, nausea or vomiting, extreme thirst, and sometimes hallucinations. To treat someone with sunstroke, find a breezy spot and place a cold, wet cloth on the victim's forehead. Change the cloth frequently so it stays cold. Offer lots of liquids—strong tea or coffee, fruit juice, water, soft drinks (no alcohol).

Hypothermia and Frostbite

Wind and weather can shift dramatically in Maine, especially at higher elevations, creating prime conditions for contracting hypothermia and frostbite. At risk are hikers, swimmers, canoeists, kayakers, sailors, skiers, even cyclists.

When body temperature plummets below the normal 97° to 98.6°F, hypothermia is likely to set in. Symptoms include disorientation, a flagging pulse rate, prolonged shivering, swelling of the face, and cool skin. Quick action is essential to prevent shock and keep body temperature from dropping into the 80s, where cardiac arrest can occur. Emergency treatment begins with removal of as much wet clothing as possible without causing further exposure. Wrap the victim in anything dry—blankets, sleeping bag, clothing, towels, even large plastic trash bags—to keep body heat from escaping. Be sure the neck and head are covered. Or practice the buddy system—climb into a sleeping bag with the victim and provide skin contact. Do not rub the skin, apply hot water, or elevate the legs. If he or she is conscious, offer high-sugar snacks and nonalcoholic hot drinks (but, again, no alcohol; it dilates blood vessels and disrupts the warming process). As quickly as possible, transport the victim to a hospital emergency room.

When extremities begin turning blue or gray, with red blotches, frostbite may be setting in. As with hypothermia, add warmth slowly but do not rub frostbitten skin. Offer snacks and warm, nonalcoholic liquids.

Even during the height of summer, be on the alert for mild hypothermia when children stay in the ocean too long. Bouncing in and out of the water, kids become preoccupied, refuse to admit they are cold, and fall prey to wind chill.

To prevent hypothermia and frostbite, dress in layers and remove or add them as needed. Wool, waterproof nylon (such as Gore-Tex), and synthetic fleece (such as Polartec) are the best fabrics for repelling dampness. Polyester fleece lining wicks excess moisture away from your body. If you plan to buy a down jacket, be sure it has a waterproof shell; down will just suck up the moisture from snow and rain. Especially in winter, always cover your head, since body heat escapes quickly through the head; a ski mask will protect ears and nose. Wear wool- or fleece-lined gloves and wool socks.

Special Considerations during Hunting Season

During Maine's fall hunting season (October to Thanksgiving weekend)—and especially during the November deer season—walk or hike only in wooded areas marked No Hunting, No Trespassing, or Posted. And even if an area *is* closed to hunters, don't decide to explore the woods during deer or moose season without wearing a "hunter orange" (read: eye-popping fluorescent) jacket or vest. If you take your dog along, be sure it, too, wears an orange vest. Deer hunters are required to wear two items of orange clothing—a hat and usually a vest. Orange gear is available in sporting-goods stores, hardware stores, and some supermarkets and convenience stores. Hunting is illegal on Sundays.

During hunting season, moose and deer are on the move and made understandably skittish by the hunters invading their turf. Moose are primarily found inland, but deer are everywhere, and even the occasional moose strays into coastal Maine. At night, particularly in wooded areas, these huge creatures often end up alongside or in the roads, so ratchet up your defensive-driving skills. Reduce your normal speed, use high beams when there's no oncoming traffic, and remain extra-alert. In a moose vs. car encounter, no one

THE MAINE ISLAND TRAIL

In the early 1980s, a "trail" of coastal Maine islands was only the germ of an idea. By the end of the millennium, the Maine Island Trail Association (MITA) counted nearly 4,000 members dedicated to conscientious (i.e., low- or no-impact) recreational use of about 100 public and private islands along 325 miles of Maine coastline between Portland and Machias.

Access to the trail is by private boat only, and the best choice is a sea kayak, to navigate shallow or rock-strewn coves. Sea-kayak rentals are available in many towns along the coast, and several outfitters offer island tours. Best source of information is the Maine Association of Sea Kayaking Guides and Instructors (MASKGI), whose members agree to adhere to the "leave no trace" philosophy.

The trail's publicly owned islands are open to anyone; the private islands are restricted to MITA members, who pay $45 a year for the privilege (and, I should add, the responsibility). With the fee comes the *MITA Guidebook*, providing directions to and information for each of the islands. With membership comes the expectation of care and concern. "Low impact" means different things to different people, so MITA experienced acute growing pains when enthusiasm began leading to "tent sprawl."

To cope with and reverse the overuse, MITA has created an "adopt-an-island program," in which volunteers become stewards for specific islands and keep track of their use and condition. MITA members are urged to pick up trash, use tent platforms where they exist, and continue elsewhere if an island has reached its assigned capacity (stipulated on a shoreline sign and/or in the guidebook).

A superb complement to the *MITA Guidebook* is a copy of *Hot Showers!* by Lee Bumsted, a former MITA staff member (see Suggested Reading). Recognizing the need for alternating island camping and warm beds, she has almost singlehandedly alleviated island stress and strain. Some of the B&Bs and inns listed in her guide give discounts to MITA members.

Membership information is available from Maine Island Trail Association (P.O. Box C, Rockland 04841, 207/596-6456, www.mita.org).

---

wins, and human fatalities are common. An encounter between a deer and a car may be less dangerous to humans (although the deer usually dies), but some damage is inevitable.

Information and Services

MONEY

Currency

Since Maine's Down East coast borders Canada, don't be surprised to see a few Canadian coins mixed in with American ones when you receive change from a purchase. In such cases, Canadian and U.S. quarters are equivalent, although the exchange rate is in fact drastically different. Most services (including banks) will accept a handful of Canadian coins at par, but you'll occasionally spot No Canadian Currency signs.

If you need to exchange foreign currency—other than Canadian dollars—do it at or near border crossings or in Portland. In small communities, such transactions are more complicated; you may end up spending more time and money than necessary.

Banks and Automated Teller Machines

Typical banking hours are 9 A.M.–3 P.M. weekdays, occasionally with later hours on Friday. Drive-up windows at many banks tend to open as much as an hour earlier and stay open an hour or so after lobbies close. Some banks also maintain Saturday morning hours. But as long as you have an automated teller machine (ATM) or debit card or a credit card, you can go anywhere in coastal Maine at any time and withdraw money from your personal checking, savings, or credit-card account.

Credit Cards and Traveler's Checks

Bank credit cards have become so preferred and so prevalent that it's nearly impossible to rent a car or check into a hotel without one (the alternative is payment in advance or a hefty cash deposit). MasterCard and Visa are most widely accepted in Maine, and Discover and American Express are the next most popular; Carte Blanche, Diners Club, and EnRoute (Canadian) lag far behind. Be aware, however, that small restaurants (including lobster pounds), shops, and B&Bs off the beaten track might not accept credit cards or nonlocal personal checks; you may need to settle your account with cash or traveler's checks.

Taxes

Maine charges a 5 percent sales tax on items such as gifts, snacks, books, clothing, and video rentals, and a 7 percent tax on all bar, restaurant, and lodging bills. Bear in mind, especially when making reservations by phone, that restaurants and lodgings usually do *not* include the 7 percent tax when quoting their prices. A whopping 10 percent tax is added to car-rental rates.

Tipping

The longtime restaurant tipping standard—15 percent of the total bill—still prevails in most of Maine. One exception is Portland, where a big-city 20 percent rate isn't unusual in the upscale restaurants. Of course, the restaurant tip always should depend on the quality of the service. If you've ever worked in a restaurant, you know how much tips are appreciated—but they need to be earned. Don't penalize a waitperson for the kitchen's mistakes or incompetence, but do reduce the tip if the service is sloppy. If for any reason you don't tip, do let a host or hostess know the reason, so you're not just considered chintzy.

Taxi drivers expect a 15 percent tip; airport porters expect at least $1 per bag, depending on the difficulty of the job. If a porter simply unloads a suitcase from a car, $.50 is plenty; if he has to escort you to a ticket counter—and especially if he arranges for speedier service—a dollar per bag is appropriate.

Usual tip for housekeeping services in accommodations is $1–2 per person, per night, depending upon the level of service. It's not necessary to tip at B&Bs, if the owners do the housekeeping.

Some accommodations add a 10- to 15-percent service fee onto rates.

TOURISM INFORMATION AND MAPS

Maine Tourism Association

The **Maine Tourism Association** (325 Water St., Hallowell 04347, 207/623-0363, www.mainetourism.com) publishes the free, annual magazine-style guidebook *Maine Invites You,* which details sights throughout the state and provides listings of chambers of commerce and other info helpful for travelers. Call, write, or visit the website to request a copy and a state map.

State Visitor Information Centers

The Maine Tourism Association operates state visitor information centers in Calais, Fryeburg (May–October), Hampden, Houlton, Kittery, and Yarmouth. These are excellent places to visit to stock up on brochures, pick up a map, ask advice, and utilize restrooms.

Maine Online

The Maine Office of Tourism has established an award-winning website, www.visitmaine.com. You'll find chamber of commerce addresses, articles, photos, information on lodgings, and access to a variety of Maine tourism businesses. But hundreds of other Maine pages are also up and running, so surf away. You can use the website to request a free state map and copy of *Maine Invites You.* The state's toll-free **information hotline** is 888/MAINE-45 (888/624-6345).

Local Chambers of Commerce and Tourism Offices

Tourism is Maine's second-largest source of revenue, so almost every community of any size has some kind of information office, varying from York's mansionlike quarters to tiny log cabins. Information on these is listed in the destination chapters.

Maps

Peek in any Mainer's car, and you're likely to see a copy of *The Maine Atlas and Gazetteer,* published by DeLorme Mapping Company, in Yarmouth. Despite an oversize format inconvenient for hiking and kayaking, this 96-page paperbound book just about guarantees that you won't get lost (and if you're good at map reading, it can get you out of a lot of traffic jams). Scaled at one-half inch to the mile, it's meticulously compiled from aerial photographs, satellite images, U.S. Geological Survey maps, GPS readings, and timber-company maps, and it is revised annually. It details back roads and dirt roads and shows elevation, boat ramps, public lands, campgrounds and picnic areas, and trailheads. DeLorme products are available nationwide in book and map stores, but you can also order direct (800/452-5931, www.delorme.com). The atlas is $19.95 and shipping is $4 (Maine residents need to add 5 percent sales tax).

The **Maine Tourism Association** also publishes a free state map, but is in no way as detailed as DeLorme's map book.

COMMUNICATIONS AND MEDIA

Postal and Shipping Services

Post offices in Maine cities and towns are open six days a week, Mon.–Sat., usually 8 A.M.–5 P.M.,

although Saturday service in small communities typically is 8 A.M.–noon.

Cities and large towns have strategically placed Express Mail, UPS (800/742-5877), and Federal Express (800/463-3339) boxes. Other national/international delivery services available in Maine are Airborne Express (800/247-2676) and DHL (800/225-5345). Ask locally about businesses that provide packing and shipping services.

If you expect to receive mail while visiting Maine, have your correspondents address it to you c/o General Delivery in the town or city where you expect to be and mark it "Hold for arrival on [your estimated arrival date]." Be sure to give them that post office's correct zip code (every post office has a national zip code directory; overseas residents can check with the nearest U.S. embassy or consulate, or log on to www.usps.com).

Area Code

Maine still has only one telephone area code, **207.** To call long distance in-state and out-of-state, dial 1 plus the area code before the number. For directory assistance, dial 411.

Toll-Free Calling

Any number with an area code of 800, 888, 877, 866, 855, 844, 833, or 822 is toll-free.

Internet Access

Internet access is widely available at libraries and coffeehouses. Most hotels and many inns and B&Bs also offer Internet access; many provide data ports or WIFI.

Glossary

To help you translate some of the lingo off the beaten track (e.g., country stores and county fairs, farmstands and flea markets), here's a sampling of local terms and expressions, followed by a list of place-names that have difficult or unusual pronunciations.

alewives—herring

ayuh—yes

barrens—as in "blueberry barrens"; fields where wild blueberries grow

beamy—wide (as in a boat or a person)

beans—shorthand for the traditional Saturday-night meal, which always includes baked beans

blowdown—a forest area leveled by wind

blowing a gale—very windy

camp—a vacation house (small or large), usually on fresh water and/or in the woods

chance—serendipity or luck (as in "open by appointment or by chance")

chicken dressing—chicken manure

chowder (pronounced "chowdah")—soup made with lobster, clams, or fish, or a combination thereof; lobster version sometimes called lobster stew

chowderhead—mischief- or troublemakers, usually interchangeable with idiot

coneheads—tourists (because of their presumed penchant for ice cream)

cottage—a vacation house (anything from a bungalow to a mansion), usually on salt water

culch (also cultch)—"stuff"; the contents of attics, basements, and some flea markets

cull—a discount lobster, usually minus a claw

cunnin'—cute (usually describing a baby or small child)

dinner (pronounced "dinnah")—the noon meal

dinner pail—lunchbox

dite—a very small amount

dooryard—the yard near a house's main entrance

downcellar—in the basement

Down East—with the prevailing wind; the old coastal sailing route from Boston to Nova Scotia

dry-ki—driftwood, usually remnants from the logging industry

ell—a residential structural section that links a house and a barn; formerly a popular location for the "summer kitchen," to spare the house from woodstove heat

exercised—upset; angry

fiddleheads—unopened ostrich-fern fronds, a spring delicacy

finest kind—top quality; good news; an expression of general approval; also, a term of appreciation

flatlander—a person not from Maine, often but not exclusively someone from the Midwest

floatplane—a small plane equipped with pontoons for landing on water; the same aircraft often becomes a skiplane in winter

flowage—a water body created by damming, usually beaver handiwork (also called "beaver flowage")

frappe—a thick drink containing milk, ice cream, and flavored syrup, as opposed to a milk shake, which does not include ice cream (but beware: a frappe offered in other parts of the United States is an ice-cream sundae topped with whipped cream!)

from away—not native to Maine

galamander—a wheeled contraption formerly used to transport quarry granite to building sites or to boats for onward shipment

gore—a sliver of land left over from inaccurate boundary surveys. Maine has several gores; Hibberts Gore, for instance, has a population of one.

got done—quit a job; was let go

harbormaster—local official who monitors water traffic and assigns moorings; often a very political job

hardshell—lobster that hasn't molted yet (more scarce, thus more pricey in summer)

hod—wooden "basket" used for carrying clams

ice-out—the departure of winter ice from ponds, lakes, rivers, and streams; many communities have ice-out contests, awarding prizes for guessing the exact time of ice-out, in April or May

Italian—long soft bread roll sliced on top and filled with peppers, onions, tomatoes, sliced meat, black olives, and sprinkled with olive oil, salt, and pepper; veggie versions available

jimmies—chocolate sprinkles, like those on an ice cream cone

lobster car—a large floating crate for storing lobsters

Maine Guide—a member of the Maine Professional Guides Association, trained and tested for outdoor and survival skills; also called Registered Maine Guide

market price—restaurant menu term for "the going rate," usually referring to the price of lobster or clams

molt—what a lobster does when it sheds its shell for a larger one; the act of molting is called ecdysis (as a stripper is an ecdysiast)

money tree—a collection device for a monetary gift

mud season—mid-March to mid-April, when back roads and unpaved driveways become virtual tank traps

nasty neat—extremely meticulous

near—stingy

notional—stubborn, determined

off island—the mainland, to an islander

place—another word for a house (as in "Herb Pendleton's place")

pot—trap, as in "lobster pot"

public landing—see "town landing"

rake—hand tool used for harvesting blueberries

rusticator—a summer visitor, particularly in bygone days

scooch (or scootch)—to squat; to move sideways

sea smoke—heavy mist rising off the water when the air temperature suddenly becomes much colder than the ocean temperature

select—a lobster with claws intact

Selectmen—the elected men and women who handle local affairs in small communities; the First Selectman chairs meetings. In some towns, "people from away" have tried to propose substituting a gender-neutral term, but in most cases the effort has failed.

shedder—a lobster with a new (soft) shell; generally occurs in July and August (more common then, thus less expensive than hardshells)

shire town—county seat

shore dinner—the works: chowder, clams, lobster, and sometimes corn-on-the-cob, too; usually the most expensive item on a menu

short—a small, illegal-size lobster

slumgullion—tasteless food; a mess

snapper—an undersize, illegal lobster

soda—cola, root beer, etc. (often referred to as "pop" in other parts of the country)

softshell—see "shedder"

some—very (as in "some hot")

spleeny—overly sensitive

steamers—clams (before or after they are steamed)

sternman—a lobsterman's helper (male or female)

summer complaint—a tourist

supper (pronounced "suppah")—evening meal, eaten by Mainers around 5 or 6 P.M. (as opposed to flatlanders and summer people, who eat dinner between 7 and 9 P.M.)

tad—slightly; a little bit

thick-o'-fog—zero-visibility fog

to home—at home

tomalley—a lobster's green insides; considered a delicacy by some

town landing—shore access; often a park or a parking lot, next to a wharf or boat-launch ramp

upattic—in the attic

Whoopie! Pie—the trademarked name for a high-fat, calorie-laden, cakelike snack that only kids and dentists could love

wicked cold!—frigid

wicked good!—excellent

williwaws—uncomfortable feeling

ADVENTURES IN LEARNING

A surprising number of educational programs geared to adults operate along the Maine coast. Whether you want to improve your foreign language skills, learn to take photographs, work on crafting furniture, learn to sail, or practice outdoor survival, there's a course for you. Here's a sampling.

In 1974, enterprising entrepreneurs Pat and Patsy Hennin jumped on the do-it-yourself bandwagon and established the **Shelter Institute** to train neophytes in energy-efficient home design and construction techniques. Since then, thousands of students have taken courses here, and enthusiastic alumni (and their building projects) span the globe. Students range in age from late teens to early 80s. A one-week post-and-beam course, for instance, is $750 per person. Courses take place on the school's 68-acre campus in Woolwich, five miles north of Bath (873 Route 1, Woolwich 04579, 207/442-7938, fax 207/442-7939, www.shelterinstitute.com). Visitors are welcome any time, and anyone who appreciates fine woodworking tools *has* to visit the institute's Woodbutcher Tools retail shop and bookstore, open Monday–Saturday.

Watershed Center for the Ceramic Arts (19 Brick Hill Rd., Newcastle 04553, 207/882-6075, www.watershedcenterceramicarts.org), a nationally known summer residency retreat for ceramic artists, offers fall and winter community pottery courses for adults, children, and families. No experience is necessary for off-season programs. Some courses go on the road via Watershed's unique "Mudmobile," which clocks about 10,000 miles a year. The center also organizes therapeutic workshops for AIDS patients, at-risk juveniles, and senior citizens. Call or write for course information. (Although the address is Newcastle, Watershed is just north of the Route 27 turnoff from Route 1 to Boothbay Harbor.)

Word-of-mouth seems to be the best marketing tool for **The Carpenter's Boatshop** (440 Old County Rd., Pemaquid 04558, 207/677-3768). Founded in 1979 by Bobby Ives, an engaging Congregational minister, and his wife, Ruth, the boatshop accepts interested applicants of any denomination to join a community dedicated to both spirituality and boatbuilding. This is no laid-back, contemplative religious retreat; serious boatbuilding supports the community. Sessions run from mid-September to mid-June, and there's no tuition. Room and board are provided. The diverse group of 6–8 students all become part of the boatbuilding crew, working at least 40 hours a week in the huge shingled barn/boatshop. Each student builds a 9.5-foot Monhegan skiff, contributes to the construction of three types of stock wooden boats, helps with all the daily chores, and spends Saturday morning doing valuable community service on the Pemaquid Peninsula. During daily prayer gatherings, students can participate or use the time for reading or other reflective pursuits. Marine author Peter Spectre, an admitted skeptic, admiringly describes this unique program: "Just consider what all these people have done for themselves and the community."

Part of the international Outward Bound network, **Hurricane Island Outward Bound** School (75 Mechanic St., P.O. Box 429, Rockland 04841, 207/594-5548 or 800/341-1744, www.hurricaneisland.org) was founded in 1964 as a maritime adjunct to the national wilderness survival program. Maine sea courses take place on offshore Hurricane Island, a former granite-quarrying site; land-based courses are held around Newry, in western Maine's mountains. An extensive course catalog is available.

Begun in 1986 to provide language classes for adults, **Penobscot School** (28 Gay St., Rockland 04841, 207/594-1084, www.languagelearning.org) has become a multicultural clearinghouse with ties around the globe. In fall, winter, and spring, the school offers day and evening courses in nearly a dozen languages, sponsors ethnic dinners and festivals, organizes language-immersion weekends, and puts on international study programs in local schools. From July to September, international students (ages 18–65) arrive at the school for intensive three-week English-language courses. So many alumni have talked up the summer program that every opening has a waiting list. On summer weekdays, visitors are often invited for lunch at the school to interact with students practicing their English. Call for information.

Bay Island Sailing School (117 Tillson Ave., Rockland 04841, 207/596-7550 or 800/421-2492, www.sailme.com) is an American Sailing Association–approved summer program that has weekday, weekend, and live-aboard learn-to-sail classes—and special courses for teenagers and women. Contact the school for details.

Students come from all over the world to the prestigious **Maine Photographic Workshops** (P.O. Box 200, Rockport 04856, 207/236-8581, www.meworkshops.com), where international photo luminaries teach one- and two-week courses, summer and fall, to neophytes and professionals. A degree-granting program, called Rockport College, continues during the winter. Courses are fairly pricey; evening slide lectures are open to the public.

Alumni of the one-, two-, and 12-week workshops at the **Center for Furniture Craftsmanship** (25 Mill St., Rockport 04856, 207/594-5611, www.woodschool.org), established in 1993, can't say enough about their experiences. Courses are for various skill levels, from beginner to pro. The center can help arrange for lodging and meals. Open all year.

Based at Belfast's former Crosby Middle School, the **National Theatre Workshop of the Handicapped** (96 Church St., P.O. Box 1138, Belfast 04915, 207/338-6894, www.ntwh.org) is a phenomenal organization founded in 1977 and introduced to Belfast in 1998. Jesuit Brother Rick Curry, disabled since birth, established NTWH in New York City's Soho district to provide jobs in the performing and fine arts for people with disabilities. Author of *The Secrets of Jesuit Breadmaking*, as well as countless articles on drama and disabilities, Brother Curry oversees art and drama workshops and productions in Belfast for 50 residential students from May to October.

CAN YOU GET THERE FROM HERE?

Countless names for Maine cities, towns, villages, rivers, lakes, and streams have Native American origins; some are variations on French; and a few have German derivations. Below are some pronunciations to give you a leg up when requesting directions along the Maine coast.

Arundel—ih-RUN-d'l
Bangor—BANG-gore
Bremen—BREE-m'n
Calais—CAL-us
Castine—kass-TEEN
Damariscotta—dam-uh-riss-COTT-uh
Harraseeket—hare-uh-SEEK-it
Isle au Haut—i'll-a-HO, I'LL-a-ho (subject to plenty of dispute, depending on whether or not you live in the vicinity)

Katahdin—kuh-TA-din
Lubec—loo-BECK
Machias—muh-CHIGH-us
Matinicus—muh-TIN-i-cuss
Medomak—muh-DOM-ick
Megunticook—muh-GUN-tuh-cook
Monhegan—mun-HE-gun
Mount Desert—mount duh-ZERT
Narraguagus—nare-uh-GWAY-gus
Naskeag—NASS-keg
Passagassawakeag—puh-sag-gus-uh-WAH-keg
Passamaquoddy—pass-uh-muh-QUAD-dee
Pemaquid—PEM-a-kwid
Saco—SOCK-oh
Schoodic—SKOO-dick
Steuben—stew-BEN
Topsham—TOPS-'m
Wiscasset—wiss-CASS-it
Woolwich—WOOL-itch

Suggested Reading

DESCRIPTIONS AND TRAVEL

Batignani, K. W. *Maine's Coastal Cemeteries: A Historic Tour.* Camden, ME: Down East Books, 2004. A guide to 35 cemeteries with intriguing histories, unusual epitaphs, and notable carvings.

Bumsted, L. *Hot Showers! Maine Coast Lodgings for Kayakers and Sailors.* 2nd ed. Brunswick, ME: Audenreed Press, 2000. Excellent, well-researched resource for anyone cruising the shoreline and yearning for alternatives to a sleeping bag.

Calhoun, C. C. *Maine.* 3rd ed. New York: Fodor's Travel Publications, Compass American Guides, 2000. Entertaining, literate prose; outstanding photography.

Curtis, W. *Maine: Off the Beaten Path.* 5th ed. Old Saybrook, CT: Globe Pequot Press, 2003. Intro-

duction to offbeat and unexpected locales; a good supplementary guide for would-be explorers.

Dwelley, M. J. *Spring Wildflowers of New England.* 2nd ed. Camden, ME: Down East Books, 2000. Back in print after several years, this beautifully illustrated gem is an essential guide for exploring spring woodlands.

Edwardsen, E. *Longstreet Highroad Guide to the Maine Coast.* Atlanta: Longstreet Press, 1999. Attractively presented general guide, with especially helpful natural-history information.

Hancock, T. *The Gardens of Maine.* Farmington, ME: Heritage Publishing, 1997. Parks, public gardens, and significant landscaping throughout the state. Biggest emphasis is on southern Maine.

Karlin, L., and R. Sawyer-Fay. *Gardens Maine Style.* Camden, ME: Down East Books, 2001.

A beautiful book depicting and describing private and some public gardens.

The Maine Atlas and Gazetteer. Yarmouth, ME: DeLorme, updated annually. You'll be hard put to get lost if you're carrying this essential volume with 70 full-page (oversize format) topographical maps with GPS grids.

Morrison, P. M. *The Guide to Maine Golf Courses.* Camden, ME: Down East Books, 2000. Useful, descriptive information about Maine golf courses built prior to publication.

Pierson, E. C., J. E. Pierson, and P. D. Vickery. *A Birder's Guide to Maine.* Camden, ME: Down East Books. An expanded version of *A Birder's Guide to the Coast of Maine.* No ornithologist, novice or expert, should explore Maine without this valuable guide.

Taft, H., J. Taft, and C. Rindlaub. *A Cruising Guide to the Maine Coast.* 4th ed. Peaks Island: Diamond Pass Publishing. Don't even consider cruising the coast without this volume.

LITERATURE, ART, AND PHOTOGRAPHY

Curtis, J., W. Curtis, and F. Lieberman. *Monhegan: The Artists' Island.* Camden, ME: Down East Books, 1995.

Maine Speaks: An Anthology of Maine Literature. Brunswick, ME: Maine Writers and Publishers Alliance, 1989.

McNair, W., ed. *The Maine Poets: An Anthology of Verse.* Camden, ME: Down East Books, 2003. McNair's selection of best works by Maine's finest poets.

Middleton, D., and B. Morrison *The Photographers Guide to the Maine Coast.* Woodstock, VT: Countryman Press, 2004. Find out where

to go, how to get there, when to go, and how to take perfect photos.

Spectre, P. H. *Passage in Time.* New York: W. W. Norton, 1991. A noted marine writer cruises the coast aboard traditional windjammers; gorgeous photos complement the colorful text.

Van Riper, F. *Down East Maine: A World Apart.* Camden, ME: Down East Books, 1998. Maine's Washington County, captured with incredible insight and compassion by a master photographer and insightful wordsmith.

LOBSTERS AND LIGHTHOUSES

Caldwell, W., *Lighthouses of Maine.* Camden, ME: Down East Books, 1986. A historical tour of Maine's lighthouses, with the emphasis on history, legends, and lore.

Corson, T. *The Secret Life of Lobsters.* New York: HarperCollins, 2004. Everything you wanted—or perhaps didn't want—to know about lobster.

Hartnett, R., and P. D. Bachelder *Maine Lighthouse Map & Guide.* Hartnett House Map Publishing, 2000. An illustrated map and guide providing directions on how to locate all Maine beacons as well as brief histories.

Thompson, C. *Maine Lighthouses: A Pictorial Guide.* 3rd ed. Mount Desert, ME: CatNap Publications, 2001. What they look like, how to find them, and a bit of background detail.

HISTORY

Duncan, R. F., E. G. Barlow, K. Bray, and C. Hanks. *Coastal Maine: A Maritime History.* Countrymen Press, 2002. Updated version of the classic work.

Isaacson, D., ed. *Maine: A Guide "Down East."*

2nd ed. Maine League of Historical Societies and Museums, 1970. Revised version of the Depression-era WPA guidebook. Still interesting for background reading.

Judd, R. W., E. A. Churchill, and J. W. Eastman, eds. *Maine: The Pine Tree State from Prehistory to the Present.* Orono: University of Maine Press, 1995. The best available Maine history, with excellent historical maps.

Paine, L. P. *Down East: A Maritime History of Maine.* Gardiner, ME: Tilbury House, 2000. A noted maritime historian provides an enlightening introduction to the state's seafaring tradition.

MEMOIRS

Dawson, L. B. *Saltwater Farm.* Westford: Impatiens Press, 1993. Witty, charming stories of growing up on the Cushing peninsula.

Greenlaw, L. *The Lobster Chronicles: Life on a Very Small Island.* New York: Hyperion, 2002. Swordfishing boat captain Linda Greenlaw's account of returning to life on Isle au Haut after weathering *The Perfect Storm.*

Lunt, D. L. *Hauling by Hand: The Life and Times of a Maine Island.* Frenchboro, ME: Islandport Press, 1999. A sensitive history of Frenchboro (a.k.a. Long Island), eight miles offshore, written by an eighth-generation islander, now a journalist.

Peavey, E. *Maine & Me: 10 Years of Down East Adventures.* Camden, ME: 2004. A collection of essays and articles by a writer for *Down East* magazine.

Wass, P. B. *Lighthouse in My Life: The Story of a Maine Lightkeeper's Family.* Camden, ME: Down East Books, 1987. Offshore adventures, growing up on Libby Island, near Machias.

NATURAL HISTORY

Bennett, D. *Maine's Natural Heritage: Rare Species and Unique Natural Features.* Camden, ME: Down East Books, 1988.

Conkling, P. W. *Islands in Time: A Natural and Cultural History of the Islands of the Gulf of Maine.* 2nd ed. Camden, ME: Down East Books, and Rockland, ME: Island Institute, 1999. A thoughtful overview by the president of Maine's Island Institute.

Kendall, D. L. *Glaciers & Granite: A Guide to Maine's Landscape and Geology.* Unity, ME: North Country Press, 1993. Explains why Maine looks the way it does.

RECREATION

Bicycling

Stone, H. *25 Bicycle Tours in Maine: Coastal and Inland Rides from Kittery to Caribou.* 3rd ed. Woodstock, VT: Countryman Press/Backcountry Guides, 1998.

Hiking and Walking

AMC Maine Mountain Guide. 9th ed. Boston: Appalachian Mountain Club Books, 2005. The definitive statewide resource for going vertical. In a handy small format. (AMC has eliminated Acadia National Park and expanded its separate guide on Acadia's peaks.)

Cobscook Trails: A Guide to Walking Opportunities around Cobscook Bay and the Bold Coast. 2nd ed. Whiting: Quoddy Regional Land Trust, 2000. Essential handbook for exploring this part of the Down East Coast. Excellent maps.

Collins, J., and J. E. McCarthy. *Nature Walks in Southern Maine.* Boston: Appalachian Mountain Club Books. Easy walks, mostly horizontal, and good natural-history commentary. Maps are primitive but do the job.

Gibson, J. *50 Hikes in Coastal and Southern Maine.* 3rd ed. Woodstock, VT: Countryman Press/Backcountry Guides, 2001. Well-researched, detailed resource by a veteran hiker.

Roberts, P. *On the Trail in Lincoln County.* Newcastle/Damariscotta, ME: Lincoln County Publishing, 2003. A great guide to more than 60 walks in preserves from Wiscasset through Waldoboro, with detailed directions to trailheads.

Seymour, T. *Hiking Maine.* 2nd ed. Helena, MT: Falcon Press, 2002. Helpful—especially for less-well-known hikes in the Mid-Coast region. Not as comprehensive, statewide, as the Gibson hiking guide or the *AMC Maine Mountain Guide.*

Paddling

AMC River Guide: Maine. 3rd ed. Boston: Appalachian Mountain Club Books, 2002. Detailed guide to canoeing or kayaking Maine's large and small rivers.

The Maine Island Trail: Stewardship Handbook and Guidebook. Rockland, ME: Maine Island Trail Association, updated annually. Available only with MITA membership (annual dues $45), providing access to dozens of islands along the watery trail.

Miller, D. *Kayaking the Maine Coast: A Paddler's Guide to Day Trips from Kittery to Cobscook.* Woodstock, VT: Countryman Press/Backcountry Guides, 2000. A well-researched volume by a veteran kayaker. With her book and a copy of *Hot Showers!,* you're all set.

Wilson, A., and J. Hayes. *Quiet Water Canoe Guide, Maine: Best Paddling Lakes and Ponds for All Ages.* 2nd ed. Boston: Appalachian Mountain Club Books, 2005. Comprehensive handbook, with helpful maps, for inland paddling.

ACADIA NATIONAL PARK/ MOUNT DESERT ISLE

Abrell, D. *A Pocket Guide to the Carriage Roads of Acadia National Park.* 2nd ed. Camden, ME: Down East Books, 1995.

Brandes, K. M., *Moon Handbooks Acadia National Park.* Emeryville, CA: Avalon Travel Publishing, 2004. A comprehensive guidebook with detailed information on the park and the region surrounding it.

Brechlin, E. D. *A Pocket Guide to Paddling the Waters of Mount Desert Island.* Camden, ME: Down East Books, 1996.

Gillmore, R. *Great Walks of Acadia National Park & Mount Desert Island.* rev. ed. Goffstown, NH: Great Walks, 1994.

Helfrich, G. W., and G. O'Neil. *Lost Bar Harbor.* Camden, ME: Down East Books, 1982. Fascinating collection of historic photographs of classic, late-19-century "cottages," many obliterated by Bar Harbor's Great Fire of 1947.

Minutolo, A. *A Pocket Guide to Biking on Mount Desert Island.* Camden, ME: Down East Books, 1996.

Monkman, J., and M. Monkman, *Discover Acadia National Park: A Guide to the Best Hiking, Biking, and Paddling.* Boston: Appalachian Mountain Club Books, 2000. A comprehensive guide to well-chosen hikes, bike trips, and paddling routes, accompanied by an excellent pull-out map.

Roberts, A. R. *Mr. Rockefeller's Roads.* Camden, ME: Down East Books, 1990. The story behind Acadia's scenic carriage roads, written by the granddaughter of John D. Rockefeller (who created them).

St. Germain, T. A., Jr. *A Walk in the Park: Acadia's*

Hiking Guide. 10th ed. Bar Harbor: Park-man Publications, 2004. The best Acadia National Park hiking guide, in a handy Michelin-type vertical format. Part of the proceeds go to Friends of Acadia's Acadia Trails Forever campaign.

Internet Resources

GENERAL INFORMATION

State of Maine
www.maine.gov

Everything you wanted to know about Maine and then some, with links to all government departments and Maine-related sites. Among other information on this site is info on accessible arts and recreation.

Maine Office of Tourism
www.visitmaine.com

The biggest and most useful of all Maine-related tourism sites, with sections for where to visit, where to stay, things to do, trip planning, packages, calendar of events, and search capabilities. Also lodging specials and a comprehensive calendar of events.

Maine Tourism Association
www.mainetourism.com

Find lodging, camping, restaurants, attractions, services, and more as well as links for weather, foliage, transportation planning, and chambers of commerce.

Maine Information
www.maine.info

A privately operated site with a mother lode of links handy for vacation planners.

Portland Papers
www.mainetoday.com

Home site for Maine's largest newspaper has current news and extensive information on travel, outdoor activities, entertainment, and sports.

Maine Emergency Management Association
www.state.me.us/mema/weather/weather.htm

Five-day weather forecasts broken down by 32 zones.

Island Institute
www.islandinstitute.org

The institute serves as a clearinghouse/advocate for Maine's islands; the website provides links to the major year-round islands.

TRANSPORTATION

Maine Department of Transportation
www.exploremaine.org

Explore Maine is an invaluable site for trip planning, with information on and links to airports, rail service, bus service, automobile travel, and ferries, as well as links to other key travel-planning sites.

Maine Department of Transportation
www.511maine.gov

Site provides real-time information about major delays, accidents, road construction, and weather conditions. You can get the same info and more by dialing 511 in-state.

Portland Maine Transportation Page
www.transportme.com

Provides information on all modes of transit to, from, and within Portland. You can connect to bus, train, and airport information, including schedules.

PARKS AND RECREATION

Department of Conservation, Maine Bureau of Parks and Lands
www.maine.gov/doc/parks

Information on state parks, public reserved lands, and state historic sites, details on facilities such as camp sites, picnic areas, and boat launches. Make state campground reservations online.

Acadia National Park
www.nps.gov/acad
Information on all sections of Acadia National Park. Make ANP campground reservations online.

Maine Audubon
www.maineaudubon.org
Information about Maine Audubon's eco-sensitive headquarters in Falmouth and all of the organization's environmental centers statewide. Activity and program schedules are included.

The Nature Conservancy
www.nature.org/wherewework/northamerica/states/maine/
Information about Maine preserves, field trips, and events.

Maine Land Trust Network
www.mltn.org
Maine has dozens of land trusts statewide managing lands that provide opportunities for hiking, walking, canoeing, kayaking, and other such activities.

Healthy Maine Walks
www.healthymainewalks.com
Lists places for walking statewide.

Maine Island Trail Association
www.mita.org
Information about the association and its activities along with membership details.

Maine Professional Guides Association
www.maineguides.org
Find licensed and Registered Maine Guides for sporting adventures, including sea kayaking, hunting, fishing, and recreation such as canoeing trips and wildlife safaris.

Maine Association of Sea Kayaking Guides & Instructors
www.maineseakayakguides.com
Information and links to about two dozen members who meet state requirements to lead commercial trips.

Bicycle Coalition of Maine
www.bikemaine.org
Tons of information for bicyclists including routes, shops, events, organized rides, and much more.

Golf Maine
www.golfme.com
Lists member courses, stay-and-play packages, and golf links statewide.

Maine Birding
www.mainebirding.net
A must-visit site for anyone interested in learning more about birding in Maine, includes news, checklists, events, forums, trips, and more.

Maine Windjammer Association
www.sailmainecoast.com
Thirteen windjammer schooners homeported in Rockland, Camden, and Rockport belong to this umbrella organization; links to the websites of all the vessels for online and phone information and reservations.

ARTS AND ENTERTAINMENT

Music
www.mainemusic.org
Comprehensive site covering almost everything having to do with music in the state, from performances and festivals to musicians, composers, and instrument makers.

Maine Fiber Arts
www.mainefiberarts.org
Everything you wanted to know about fiber artists, farms producing fiber, fiber-related events and festivals, fiber-arts teachers, fiber-arts exhibitions and more. Fiber arts include rugs, sculpture, sewing, basketry, quilting, weaving, spinning, beadwork, etc.

Maine Archives and Museums
www.mainemuseums.org
Information on and links to museums, archives, historical societies, and historic sites in Maine.

Maine Art Museum Trail
www.maineartmuseums.org
Information on art museums with significant collections statewide, including Ogunquit Museum of Art (Ogunquit); Portland Museum of Art (Portland); Bowdoin College Museum of Art (Brunswick); and The Farnsworth Art Museum (Rockland).

Maine Maritime Heritage Trail
www.maritimemaine.org
Information about and links to maritime museums, boatbuilding schools, lighthouses, historic homes, fishing, naval history, forts, historic sites, and much more.

SHOPPING

Maine Antiques Dealers Association
www.maineantiques.org
Lists member dealers statewide by location and specialty and provides information on upcoming antiques events.

Maine Antiquarian Booksellers Association
www.mainebooksellers.org
Lists independent shops that specialize in used, antiquarian, and rare books.

ACCOMMODATIONS

Maine Innkeepers Association
www.maineinns.com
Lodging search for member motels, hotels, inns, and B&Bs statewide and lodging specials.

Maine Campground Owners Association
www.campmaine.com
Find private campgrounds statewide.

FOOD AND DRINK

Maine Restaurant Association
www.mainerestaurant.com
Statewide trade organization site provides searchable listings of member restaurants by name or location.

Maine Department of Agriculture
www.getrealmaine.com
Information on all things agricultural, including fairs, farmers' markets, farm vacations, places to buy Maine foods, berry- and apple-picking sites, and more.

Maine Brewers' Guild
www.drinkmainebeer.com
Find breweries and brewpubs statewide.

Maine Lobster Promotion Council
www.mainelobsterpromo.com
All lobster, all the time, with links for ordering Maine lobster and organizing your own lobsterbake, plus recipes for preparing lobster in more ways than you ever thought possible.

Wild Blueberry Association of North America
www.wildblueberries.com
Information on blueberries as well as numerous recipes.

Index

Art Centers, Festivals, and Museums

Lighthouses

Lobster Pounds (Eateries)

Acknowledgments

For Tom, and for my parents, who made the wise decision to move to Maine when I was a child.

Although I've lived in Maine since childhood (yes, I will always be a "from away"), and have traveled the coast extensively for both work and pleasure, every time I revisit a place, I find something new or changed, sometimes subtly, other times dramatically. Restaurants open and close. Outfitters change their offerings. B&Bs are sold. New trails are cut. Museums expand. Hotels renovate. And on it goes. Which all goes to say, I couldn't have done this without the help of many people, who served as additional eyes and ears.

I'll start with Kathleen Brandes, who wrote the first edition of this book and whose friendship I valued and whose work and dedication I respected long before I began working on this edition. My appreciation for her extensive research, her ability to capture a place or a person with a quick turn of phrase, and her dead-on accuracy has no bounds. I'm also thankful for her encouraging words throughout the process.

Big thank yous, too, to those who sat down with me and shared local info, sheltered me along the way, fed me, helped with arrangements, verified information, called me with updates, or simply encouraged me: Barbara and Tim Rogers, Bill and Cathy Shamel, Jett Peterson, Kathryn Rubecor, Maureen Hart, Ben and Sonja Walter-Sundaram, Roy Kasindorf and Helene Harton, Anne Bradford, Stephanie Sea- cord, Mary and Don Hartley, Jack Burke and Julie Van de Graaf, Traci Klepper, Linda Briggs Hause, Marti Mayne, Molly Sholes, Phil Cross-

man, Paul and Sharon Mrozinsky, Bob Smith, Steve and Merci Normand, Chip Gray, Marcie Parker, Linda Fish, Barbara Whitten, Barbara Hathaway, Anita Taggersell, Jean Ginn Marvin, Patricia and Ken Mason, Gary Dominguez, Greg Burke, Nat and Lynn Bowditch, Barbara and Tim Rogers, and especially Charlene Williams and Rose Whitehorse of Nancy Marshall Communications. I couldn't have done this without all your help and support.

More thank yous are due to the folks at Moon Handbooks who shepherded me through the process: Bill Newlin, Rebecca Browning, Amy Scott, Deb Dutcher, and especially my editors, Kevin McLain and Kay Elliott. Also thank you to the many other behind-the-scenes Moon staffers who worked on this book, and more thanks to those who are promoting it, especially Michelle de Grasse and Matt Kaye.

I save my biggest thanks for my husband, Tom, who drove me everywhere and didn't complain (too much) when I made him backtrack two or three times along the same stretch of road, while seeking an elusive address; who waited patiently while I visited practically every restaurant, inn, and B&B along the coast; who let me order for him in restaurants; who tackled research projects; and who supported me in every way possible throughout the entire process, all while shooting photographs for the book. I couldn't have done it without him.

And to you, dear reader, thank you for using this book to plan your visit to Coastal Maine.

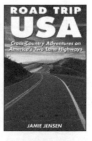

Jordan Pond House – popovers
Acadia Park loop
— Cadillac Mountain

Bar Harbor dinner
Ogunquit lobster form p.48
Ogunquit → dinner → Waterman's Beach
Marginal Way lobster?
Kennebunkport → Camden Garden tour →

Mount Battie   Camden

Monhegan   → York Nubble Light Ho

U.S.~Metric Conversion

1 inch = 2.54 centimeters (cm)
1 foot = .304 meters (m)
1 yard = 0.914 meters
1 mile = 1.6093 kilometers (km)
1 km = .6214 miles
1 fathom = 1.8288 m
1 chain = 20.1168 m
1 furlong = 201.168 m
1 acre = .4047 hectares
1 sq km = 100 hectares
1 sq mile = 2.59 square km
1 ounce = 28.35 grams
1 pound = .4536 kilograms
1 short ton = .90718 metric ton
1 short ton = 2000 pounds
1 long ton = 1.016 metric tons
1 long ton = 2240 pounds
1 metric ton = 1000 kilograms
1 quart = .94635 liters
1 US gallon = 3.7854 liters
1 Imperial gallon = 4.5459 liters
1 nautical mile = 1.852 km

To compute Celsius temperatures, subtract 32 from Fahrenheit and divide by 1.8. To go the other way, multiply Celsius by 1.8 and add 32.

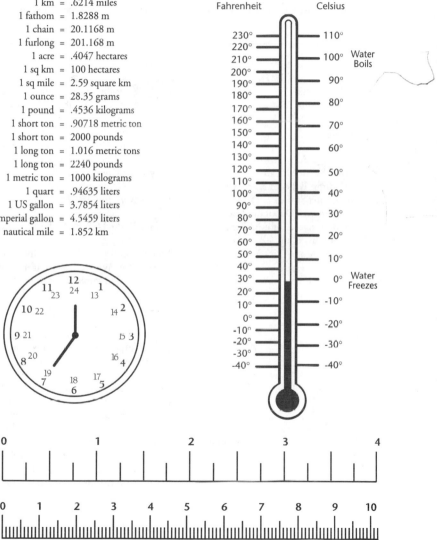

Keeping Current

Although we strive to produce the most up-to-date guidebook humanly possible, change is unavoidable. Between the time this book goes to print and the moment you read it, a handful of the businesses noted in these pages will undoubtedly change prices, move, or even close their doors forever. Other worthy attractions will open for the first time. If you have a favorite gem you'd like to see included in the next edition, or see anything that needs updating, clarification, or correction, please drop us a line. Send your comments via email to atpfeedback@avalonpub.com, or use the address below.

Moon Handbooks Coastal Maine
Avalon Travel Publishing
1400 65th Street, Suite 250
Emeryville, CA 94608, USA
www.moon.com

Editors: Kay Elliott, Amy Scott
Series Manager: Kevin McLain
Acquisitions Editor: Rebecca K. Browning
Copy Editor: Deana Shields
Graphics Coordinator: Deborah Dutcher
Production Coordinator: Tabitha Lahr
Cover Designer: Kari Gim
Interior Designer: Amber Pirker
Map Editor: Kevin Anglin
Cartographers: Kat Kalamaras, Sheryle Veverka
Indexer: Deana Shields

ISBN: 1-56691-630-5
ISSN: 1538-5051

Printing History
1st Edition—2002
2nd Edition—May 2005
5 4 3 2 1

Text © 2005 by Hilary Nangle.
Maps © 2005 by Avalon Travel Publishing, Inc.
All rights reserved.

Avalon Travel Publishing is an Imprint of Avalon Publishing Group, Inc.

Some photos and illustrations are used by permission and are the property of the original copyright owners.

Front cover photo: © Tom Nangle

Printed in the USA by Malloy